WORLD REPORT
2022
EVENTS OF 2021

HUMAN
RIGHTS
WATCH

Cover photo: A protester released from prison after three weeks of detention is reunited with her mother in Yangon, Myanmar, March 24, 2021. The three-finger salute, adapted from "The Hunger Games," is a widely used sign of civil disobedience.

© 2021 The New York Times/Redux.

Cover and book design by Rafael Jiménez

www.hrw.org

Human Rights Watch defends the rights of people worldwide.

We scrupulously investigate abuses, expose facts widely, and pressure those with power to respect rights and secure justice.

Human Rights Watch is an independent, international organization that works as part of a vibrant movement to uphold human dignity and advance the cause of human rights for all.

Human Rights Watch began in 1978 with the founding of its Europe and Central Asia division (then known as Helsinki Watch). Today it also includes divisions covering Africa, the Americas, Asia, Europe and Central Asia, the Middle East and North Africa, and the United States. There are thematic divisions or programs on arms; business and human rights; children's rights; crisis and conflict; disability rights; the environment and human rights; international justice; lesbian, gay, bisexual, and transgender rights; refugee rights; and women's rights.

The organization maintains offices in Amman, Amsterdam, Beirut, Berlin, Bishkek, Brussels, Chicago, Geneva, Goma, Hong Kong, Johannesburg, Kiev, Kinshasa, London, Los Angeles, Miami, Moscow, Nairobi, New York, Paris, San Francisco, São Paulo, Seoul, Silicon Valley, Stockholm, Sydney, Tokyo, Toronto, Tunis, Washington DC, and Zurich, and field presences in more than 50 other locations globally.

Human Rights Watch is an independent, nongovernmental organization, supported by contributions from private individuals and foundations worldwide. It accepts no government funds, directly or indirectly.

Table of Contents

This annual World Report is dedicated to the memory of our beloved colleague Dewa Mavhinga, Southern Africa director at Human Rights Watch, who died on December 4, aged 42. Dewa was a respected and principled human rights researcher, a fearless advocate and an indefatigable champion for human rights victims across Southern Africa. Colleagues and partners remember him for his unwavering dedication and depth of knowledge, but most of all for his warmth, generosity and unfailing kindness.

With Autocrats on the Defensive, Can Democrats Rise to the Occasion?

By Kenneth Roth, *Executive Director*

The conventional wisdom these days is that autocracy is ascendent, democracy on the decline. That view gains currency from the intensifying crackdown on opposition voices in China, Russia, Belarus, Myanmar, Turkey, Thailand, Egypt, Uganda, Sri Lanka, Bangladesh, Venezuela, and Nicaragua. It finds support in military takeovers in Myanmar, Sudan, Mali, and Guinea, and undemocratic transfers of power in Tunisia and Chad. And it gains sustenance from the emergence of leaders with autocratic tendencies in once- or still-established democracies such as Hungary, Poland, Brazil, El Salvador, India, the Philippines, and, until a year ago, the United States.

But the superficial appeal of the rise-of-autocracy thesis belies a more complex reality—and a bleaker future for autocrats. As people see that unaccountable rulers inevitably prioritize their own interests over the public's, the popular demand for rights-respecting democracy often remains strong. In country after country, large numbers of people have recently taken to the streets, even at the risk of being arrested or shot. There are few rallies for autocratic rule.

In some countries ruled by autocrats that retain at least a semblance of democratic elections, opposition political parties have begun to paper over their policy differences to build alliances in pursuit of their common interest in ousting the autocrat. And as autocrats can no longer rely on subtly manipulated elections to preserve power, a growing number are resorting to overt electoral charades that guarantee their desired result but confer none of the legitimacy sought from holding an election.

Yet, autocrats are enjoying their moment in the sun in part because of the failings of democratic leaders. Democracy may be the least bad form of governance, as Winston Churchill observed, because the electorate can vote the government out, but today's democratic leaders are not meeting the challenges before them. Whether it is the climate crisis, the Covid-19 pandemic, poverty and inequality, racial injustice, or the threats from modern technology, these leaders are often too mired in partisan battles and short-term preoccupations to address these

1

problems effectively. Some populist politicians try to divert attention with racist, sexist, xenophobic or homophobic appeals, leaving real solutions elusive.

If democracies are to prevail in the global contest with autocracy, their leaders must do more than spotlight the autocrats' inevitable shortcomings. They need to make a stronger, positive case for democratic rule. That means doing a better job of meeting national and global challenges—of making sure that democracy delivers on its promised dividends. It means standing up for democratic institutions such as independent courts, free media, robust legislatures, and vibrant civil societies even when that brings unwelcome scrutiny or challenges to executive policies. And it demands elevating public discourse rather than stoking our worst sentiments, acting on democratic principles rather than merely voicing them, unifying us before looming threats rather than dividing us in the quest for another do-nothing term in office.

Most of the world today looks to democratic leaders to solve our biggest problems. The Chinese and Russian leaders did not even bother showing up at the climate summit in Glasgow. But if democratic officials continue to fail us, if they are unable to summon the visionary leadership that this demanding era requires, they risk fueling the frustration and despair that are fertile ground for the autocrats.

The Perils of Unaccountable Autocrats

The first goal of most autocrats is to chip away at the checks and balances on their authority. Democracy worthy of its name requires not only periodic elections but also free public debate, a healthy civil society, competitive political parties, and an independent judiciary capable of defending individual rights and holding officials to the rule of law. As if autocrats all read from the same playbook, they inevitably attack these restraints on their power—independent journalists, activists, judges, politicians, and human rights defenders. The importance of these checks and balances was visible in the United States where they impeded President Donald Trump's attempt to steal the 2020 election, and in Brazil where they are already working to impede President Jair Bolsonaro's threat to do the same in the election scheduled for 2022.

A lack of democratic process leaves autocrats unaccountable to the public. That makes them more likely to serve their own political interests—and those of their cronies or military supporters. Autocrats claim to deliver better results than democrats, but they usually deliver mainly for themselves.

The Covid-19 pandemic spotlighted this self-serving tendency. Many autocratic leaders downplayed the pandemic, turned their backs on scientific evidence, spread false information, and failed to take basic steps to protect the health and lives of the public. Their motives ranged from populist pandering to evading criticism for not having done enough to prevent the virus from spreading or to buoy social-protection systems. As infections and deaths surged, some of those leaders threatened, silenced, or even imprisoned the healthcare workers, journalists and others who reported, protested, or criticized their failed response—causing a lack of public debate that tended to breed distrust and make matters even worse.

Variations of this scenario played out in Egypt, India, Hungary, Greece, Tajikistan, Brazil, Mexico, Nicaragua, Venezuela, Tanzania under the late President John Magufuli, and the United States under Trump. Some autocrats used the pandemic as a pretext to halt demonstrations against their rule, while at times allowing rallies in their favor, as in Uganda, Russia, Thailand, Cambodia, and Cuba.

Even in China, where the government's vast lockdowns limited Covid-19's spread, the official cover-up of human-to-human transmission in Wuhan during the critical first three weeks of January 2020 while millions fled or passed through the city helped the virus go global. To this day, Beijing refuses to cooperate with an independent investigation into the origins of the virus.

Autocrats also frequently devote government resources to self-serving projects rather than public needs. In Hungary, for example, Prime Minister Viktor Orban has spent European Union subsidies on football stadiums, which he used to pay off cronies, while leaving hospitals in a decrepit state. In Egypt, President Abdel Fattah al-Sisi allowed healthcare facilities to languish while the army and its vast business enterprises flourished, and he pursued such grandiose projects as building a new administrative capital to the east of Cairo. As Russia's economy declined, the Kremlin increased spending on the military and the police.

Autocrats' ability to act more quickly, unencumbered by the checks and balances of democracy, can paradoxically be their undoing. The free debate of democratic rule can slow decision-making, but it also ensures that diverse views are heard. Autocrats tend to suppress opposing views, leading to such ill-considered decisions as the move by Turkey's President Recep Tayyip Erdoğan to lower interest rates in the face of spiraling inflation. Sri Lanka's former president, Mahinda Rajapaksa, built a port with Chinese loans and rushed through construction, leading to economic losses so great that Beijing gained control of the port for 99 years. India's economic growth has yet to recover fully from the abrupt decision of Prime Minister Narendra Modi's government to eliminate high-value currency notes—an effort to contain corruption that hurt the most marginalized people who rely primarily on cash for subsistence.

As Chinese President Xi Jinping consolidates his individual power, he needs to address the challenges of a slowing economy, a debt crisis, a housing bubble, a shrinking workforce as the population ages, and troubling inequality—without free debate about solutions by the country's citizens. Similar one-man rule previously led to the Chinese Communist Party's disastrous Cultural Revolution and Great Leap Forward, which killed millions of people. Yet instead of encouraging public discussion of how to manage today's problems, Xi is overseeing crimes against humanity in Xinjiang, bending the legal system to his will, purging political allies, and extending the surveillance state into every nook and cranny of the country. Such unchallenged decision-making is a recipe for disastrous mistakes.

The Popular Embrace of Democracy

Even when intrusive surveillance and severe repression ultimately curtail demonstrations, the large numbers of people who joined them showed the public's desire for democracy. Repression may yield resignation, but that should not be confused with support. Few people want the oppression, corruption, and mismanagement of autocratic rule.

Many autocrats thought they had learned to manipulate voters through managed elections. They would allow periodic balloting, but only after, by their calculation, tilting the playing field sufficiently to prevail. They would censor the media, limit civil-society organizations, disqualify opponents, and selectively confer state benefits. Some would demonize disfavored groups— immigrants and asylum seekers, lesbian, gay, bisexual and transgender (LGBT) people, racial or religious minorities, women who demand their rights—to divert attention from their inability or unwillingness to deliver actual results. This manipulation was often enough to declare "victory" but not so blatant as to deprive the exercise of all legitimacy.

As the corruption and mismanagement of autocratic rule became undeniable, though, some voters became less susceptible to the autocrats' election-management techniques. In certain countries where some degree of political pluralism was still tolerated, broad coalitions of political parties have begun to form, spanning the political spectrum. Such alliances reflect growing awareness that partisan differences pale in comparison to a common interest in removing a corrupt or autocratic ruler.

In the Czech Republic, such a coalition defeated Prime Minister Andrej Babiš at the ballot box. In Israel, a broad coalition ended the long-time rule of Prime Minister Benjamin Netanyahu. Similar alliances of opposition parties have formed ahead of forthcoming elections against Orban in Hungary and Erdoğan in Turkey. A comparable tendency within the US Democratic Party contributed to the selection of Joe Biden to contest the 2020 election against Trump.

Electoral Charades

In these circumstances, managed elections have become less effective, forcing autocrats to resort to increasingly stark forms of electoral manipulation. For Russian parliamentary elections, the authorities disqualified virtually every viable opposition candidate, banned protests, and silenced critical journalists and activists. Russian authorities imprisoned the leading opposition figure, Alexei Navalny (after nearly killing him with a nerve agent), designated his organizations as "extremist," and hindered efforts by his team to organize a "smart voting" strategy to select the least objectionable remaining opponent of the ruling party.

In Hong Kong, where an informal primary system among pro-democracy candidates threatened an embarrassing defeat for pro-Beijing candidates, the Chinese government ripped up the one-country-two-systems arrangement, imposed a draconian "national security" law that effectively ended the territory's political freedoms, and allowed only "patriots" (meaning pro-Beijing candidates) to run for office. The Bangladeshi government of Prime Minister Sheikh Hasina jailed, forcibly disappeared, and executed members of the political opposition, and deployed security forces to intimidate voters and candidates.

In Nicaragua, President Daniel Ortega imprisoned all leading opponents and dozens of government critics and revoked the legal status of the main opposition parties. Belarusian President Alexander Lukashenko did the same with his main opponents but did not count on the enormous electoral appeal of Sviatlana Tsikhanouskaya, who replaced her husband as a candidate and may have won the stolen election before having to flee the country.

In Uganda, President Yoweri Museveni, facing a young, charismatic, and popular opponent, banned his rallies, and security forces shot his supporters. Iran's ruling clerics disqualified all but hardliners from competing in presidential elections. Uzbekistan's leadership refused to register any opposition parties, ensuring that there would be no genuine challenge to President Shavkat Mirziyoyev's continued rule. The Cambodian and Thai governments dissolved popular opposition parties and forced opposition politicians into exile or prison.

What is left after such blatant undermining of elections is no longer managed democracy but "zombie democracy"—the walking dead of democracy, a charade that has no pretense of a free and fair contest. These autocrats have moved from manipulated co-option to rule by repression and fear. Some cite this unabashed oppression as evidence of rising autocratic power, but in fact it often represents the opposite—an act of desperation by dictatorial leaders who know they have lost any prospect of popular support. They apparently hope their pretense will be less provocative than overt rejection of democracy, but the cost is the loss of any legitimacy that they hoped to secure from the veneer of an electoral exercise.

Beijing's Quest for International Approval

The Chinese government offers a variation on this theme. On the mainland, it has never countenanced elections. The constitution imposes the dictatorship of the Chinese Communist Party, and in recent years the government increasingly has asserted the alleged superiority of its system over the messiness of democracy. Yet the government goes to great lengths to avoid testing that proposition.

In international forums such as the United Nations Human Rights Council, Chinese officials trumpet as a sufficient measure of human rights the growth of its gross domestic product. Predictably, they fight any effort to assess their record on civil and political rights, such as their detention of one million Uyghur and other Turkic Muslims in Xinjiang to force them to abandon their religion, culture, and language. But they also reject any criticism of their economic and social policies that flags unequal rights or discrimination.

To avoid such scrutiny, Beijing deploys a range of carrots and sticks in its foreign relations. The carrots include the one-trillion-dollar Belt and Road Initiative, ostensibly an infrastructure development program that promotes a Beijing-led "common destiny" but one so opaque that it lends itself to corrupt leaders siphoning off funds while leaving their people stuck with unsustainable debts. The sticks were evident in the economic retaliation that Beijing imposed on Australia for having the audacity to seek an independent inquiry into the origins of Covid-19, or Beijing's threat to withhold Covid vaccines from Ukraine unless its government withdrew from a joint governmental statement at the UN Human Rights Council criticizing persecution in Xinjiang. Whether by cutting off countries or companies from access to the Chinese market or threatening members of the Chinese diaspora or their families back home, Beijing now routinely extends its censorship efforts to critics abroad.

Beijing especially does not want to subject itself to the unfettered scrutiny of people across China, which is why it censors (and often detains) domestic critics. When the one territory under its control that was free to express itself—Hong Kong—demonstrated through mass protests its opposition to Communist Party rule, Beijing crushed those freedoms. Similar fear of a domestic verdict on their rule can be seen in other dictatorial and monarchial governments that have never risked even "managed" elections, such as Cuba, Vietnam, North Korea, Turkmenistan, Eswatini, Saudi Arabia, and the United Arab Emirates.

Power at Any Price

In the ultimate logic of autocratic rule, some autocrats are so determined to cling to power that they are willing to risk humanitarian catastrophe. Syria's President Bashar al-Assad epitomizes this callous calculation, having gone so far as to bomb (with Russian help) hospitals, schools, markets, and apartment buildings in areas held by the armed opposition, leaving parts of the country devastated and depopulated. Venezuela's Nicolas Maduro has similarly presided over the ruination of his country—hyperinflation, a destroyed economy, and millions of people fleeing.

Myanmar's junta and the Taliban in Afghanistan seem to display a similar disregard for public welfare, as did the Ethiopian government in pursuing a conflict that began in the Tigray region and the Sudanese military even though it has now made a pretense of return to sharing the government with those seeking democracy. Hoped-for bailouts from opponents of democracy— China, Russia, Saudi Arabia, or the United Arab Emirates—rarely suffice to salvage the autocrat from such me-over-the people destruction.

In short, the autocrats' alleged rise is more qualified than often assumed. Whether they face people in the streets seeking democracy, broad political coalitions that resist their attacks on democracy, or the difficulty of controlling elections when people see through their self-serving rule, autocrats are often running scared. The hoopla about the rise of autocrats aside, theirs is not an enviable position.

Democracies Falling Short

Yet democracies today hardly have a stellar record in addressing societal ills. It is widely understood that, ultimately, democracies rise or fall by the power of their example, but too often that example has been disappointing. Today's democratic leaders are not rising to the challenges facing the world.

Yes, democracies are messy by their nature. The division of power inevitably slows its exercise, but that is the price of avoiding tyranny—a concern that especially permeates the US system of government. However, democracies these days are failing in ways that transcend the inherent limitations of democratic checks and balances. That disappointing performance comes even though the pluralism of democracies—their free media, vibrant civil societies, and independent legislatures and courts—often exerts pressure on governments to address serious problems.

The climate crisis poses a dire threat, yet democratic leaders are only nibbling at the problem, seemingly incapable of overcoming national perspectives and vested interests to take the major steps needed. Democracies responded to the pandemic by developing highly effective mRNA vaccines with remarkable speed, but they have failed to ensure that the people of lower-income countries share this life-saving invention, resulting in countless needless deaths and increasing the likelihood of variants circumventing the vaccines.

Some democratic governments took steps to mitigate the economic consequences of the lockdowns used to protect people's health and curb the spread of Covid-19 but have yet to tackle the broader and persistent problem of widespread poverty and inequality or to build adequate systems of social protection for the next inevitable economic disruption. Democracies regularly debate the threats posed by technology—the dissemination of hatred and disinformation by social-media platforms, the large-scale invasion of our privacy as an economic model, the intrusiveness of new surveillance tools, the biases of artificial intelligence—but have taken only baby steps to address them.

Yes, these problems are large, but as the climate debate shows, the bigger the problem, the more evident it is that every government has a responsibility to contribute to the solution. That recognition provides an opportunity for greater accountability, but many democratic leaders still hope to get by with soft commitments to which no one will hold them. Their caution is hardly a recipe for effectiveness.

These democracies fare no better when acting outside their borders. When they should be consistently backing democrats over autocrats, they frequently descend to the compromises of realpolitik, in which bolstering autocratic "friends"—to curtail migration, fight terrorism, or protect supposed "stability"—takes precedence over the principled defense of democracy. Egypt's Sisi and Uganda's Museveni have been prominent beneficiaries of this misguided logic.

Similar rationalization—in this case, countering the Chinese government—lies behind the general silence among democratic leaders that has greeted Modi's increasingly autocratic rule in India. The United States, the European Union, the United Kingdom, Canada, and Australia sought to strengthen ties with India on security, technology, and trade with only vague mentions of "shared democratic values" and no willingness to hold the Modi government to account for the repression of civil society and the failure to protect religious minorities from attacks.

Biden's Mixed Signals

In contrast to Trump's embrace of friendly autocrats when he was US president, Biden took office promising a foreign policy that would be guided by human rights. But he continued to sell arms to Egypt, Saudi Arabia, the United Arab Emirates, and Israel despite their persistent repression. In the face of an autocratic trend in Central America, Biden mainly addressed the issue in traditional rival Nicaragua while elsewhere prioritizing efforts to curtail migration rather than autocracy. A preoccupation with migration also led Biden to tread softly with Mexican President Andrés Manuel López Obrador despite his attacks on the media and judiciary and his Covid denialism.

During key summits, Biden seemed to lose his voice when it came to public denunciation of serious human rights violations. The US State Department has issued occasional protests about repression in certain countries, and in extreme cases the Biden administration introduced targeted sanctions on some officials responsible, but the influential voice of the president was often missing. After meeting with China's Xi, Russia's Vladimir Putin, and Turkey's Erdoğan, Biden noted that they had discussed "human rights" but offered few specifics about what was said or what consequences might ensue if repression continued. The people of those countries—the primary agents of change, who could have used a boost in these difficult times—were left uncertain about the backing they had received.

Biden's embrace of international institutions has also been selective, even if it was a considerable improvement over Trump's attacks on them. Under Biden, the US government successfully ran for a seat on the UN Human Rights Council which Trump had abandoned, rejoined the World Health Organization after Trump moved to quit it, and re-committed to the global fight against climate change after Trump disparaged it.

In addition, Biden lifted Trump's sanctions against the International Criminal Court prosecutor. But he maintained the US government's opposition to the prosecutor investigating US torture in Afghanistan or Israeli war crimes and crimes against humanity in the Occupied Palestinian Territory, even though both Afghanistan and Palestine have conferred jurisdiction to the court for crimes committed on their soil, and neither the US nor the Israeli government has conscientiously prosecuted these crimes.

European Selectivity

Other Western leaders displayed similar weakness in their defense of democracy. Former German Chancellor Angela Merkel's government helped to orchestrate global condemnation of the Chinese government's crimes against humanity in Xinjiang. But while holding the European Union presidency, Germany helped to promote an EU investment deal with China despite Beijing's use of Uyghur forced labor. Rather than conditioning the deal on ending the forced labor, or even adopting the International Labour Organization treaty banning it, Merkel settled for Beijing promising to think about perhaps one day joining the treaty. It took the European Parliament to reject that abandonment of principle.

The government of French President Emmanuel Macron also helped to coordinate broad condemnation of Beijing's conduct in Xinjiang but was blind to the abysmal rights situation in Egypt. Egyptians under Sisi are living through the worst repression in the country's modern history, yet the French government continues to sell it arms, and Macron even gave Sisi La Légion d'honneur, France's highest award. Similarly, Macron announced an enormous arms sale to the United Arab Emirates despite its military's involvement in the countless unlawful attacks against civilians in Yemen, and he became the first Western leader to meet with the Saudi crown prince, Mohammed bin Salman, since the 2018 murder of the independent journalist Jamal Khashoggi. In addition, the French government failed to address the operations of the French energy giant Total in Myanmar despite revenue from its operations funding the junta's crimes against humanity.

The European Union still has not acted on its new power to condition large-scale subsidies to Hungary and Poland on their autocratic leaders' respect for democracy, human rights, and the rule of law. It has not even taken the step of finding those governments in "serious breach" of the values of the EU treaty after the scrutiny procedure for both countries was initiated under the EU's Article 7 because of their attacks on democratic rule. As the Polish government closed its border to asylum seekers passing through Belarus, fears rose that its actions would become the EU's latest excuse to ignore the government's moves to undermine an independent judiciary and attack the rights of women and LGBT people. Without a course correction, the EU risks being diminished from a club of democracies to a mere trading bloc.

More broadly, the requirement of unanimity in matters of European Union foreign policy was increasingly abused by a few member states to mute and undermine a swift, principled, and firm collective EU response to crackdowns on democracy and human rights. However, in a positive move, a majority of EU members has decided to act together as "like-minded" states. Josep Borrell, the EU's high representative for foreign affairs, has also shown a willingness to represent established EU positions on his own authority without the signoff of all EU members.

Global Inconsistency

Outside of the West, governments have taken at least some action for democracy against overt military coups—the Association of Southeast Asian Nations (ASEAN) in the case of Myanmar, the African Union with regard to Sudan, Guinea, and Mali.

But they have shown no comparable interest in addressing endemic rights abuses by longstanding autocratic leaders, such as those ruling in Vietnam, Cambodia, and Thailand in Asia or Rwanda, Uganda, and Egypt in Africa. The Organization of American States has stood up against the dictatorships of Maduro in Venezuela and Ortega in Nicaragua but still gives a pass to the autocratic tendencies of Bolsonaro in Brazil and President Nayib Bukele in El Salvador. Sri Lanka faced little pressure to respect rights as the Rajapaksa brothers returned to office despite their history of presiding over war crimes.

In the Middle East, authoritarian governments, especially Saudi Arabia and the United Arab Emirates, provided financial and other support to prop up Sisi's repressive rule in Egypt, applauded President Kais Saied's power grab in Tunisia, and continued to back Bahrain's zero tolerance for dissent. Iran continued to back Syria's Assad despite the crimes against humanity that he oversaw in putting down the rebellion against his rule. The UAE, Turkey, Russia, and Egypt all armed abusive actors in Libya.

Meanwhile, the Russian government promoted far-right politicians in Western democracies with the hope of discrediting those democracies and hence alleviating pressure on the Kremlin to respect the desire of Russians for greater democracy.

UN Disappointment

UN Secretary-General António Guterres showed slightly more willingness in the past year to criticize specific governments for their human rights violations rather than resort to general exhortations to respect rights that no particular government feels any pressure to heed. Yet Guterres mentioned mainly weak governments that were already pariahs, such as Myanmar's junta after the military coup. Even after he secured a second term and no longer needed to worry about China's veto of his aspirations, Guterres refused to publicly condemn the Chinese government's crimes against humanity in Xinjiang.

The UN high commissioner for human rights, Michelle Bachelet, allowed her inability to gain unfettered access to Xinjiang—access that Beijing has not granted after years of negotiation and probably never will—to become an excuse to delay publication of a report on Xinjiang for more than three years, using the remote monitoring on which Human Rights Watch and many others rely. In early December, her spokesperson said he hoped the assessment would be issued in the weeks to come. Pressure will then mount on the members of the UN Human Rights Council to address the Chinese government's crimes against humanity.

The Need to Rise to the Occasion

The outcome of the high-stakes battle between autocracy and democracy remains uncertain. Due to the tendency of unaccountable governments to deliver poorly for their people, the autocrats are on the defensive as popular protests mount, broad pro-democracy political coalitions emerge, and mere managed elections, as opposed to electoral charades, prove unreliable.

Yet despite democracy's broad appeal, its fate depends in large part on the actions of democratic leaders. Will they address the major challenges before us, elevate rather than debase public debate, and act consistently, both at home and abroad, with the democratic and human rights principles they claim to defend? Being the least bad system of governance may not be enough if public despair at democratic leaders' failure to meet today's challenges leads to public indifference about democracy. The defense of human rights requires not only curbing autocratic repression, but also improving democratic leadership.

HUMAN
RIGHTS
WATCH

"Years Don't Wait for Them"

Increased Inequality in Children's Right to Education
Due to the Covid-19 Pandemic

WORLD REPORT
2022

COUNTRIES

HUMAN
RIGHTS
WATCH

"No Forgiveness for People Like You"
Executions and Enforced Disappearances under the Taliban in Afghanistan

Afghanistan

After the Taliban takeover of the country in August, the protracted Afghanistan conflict abruptly gave way to an accelerating human rights and humanitarian crisis. The Taliban immediately rolled back women's rights advances and media freedom—among the foremost achievements of the post-2001 reconstruction effort. Most secondary schools for girls were closed, and women were prohibited from working in most government jobs and many other areas. The Taliban beat and detained journalists; many media outlets closed or drastically scaled back their reporting, partly because many journalists had fled the country. The new Taliban cabinet included no women and no ministers from outside the Taliban's own ranks.

In many cities, the Taliban searched for, threatened, and sometimes detained or executed former members of the Afghan National Security Forces (ANSF), officials of the former government, or their family members.

As the Taliban entered Kabul on August 15, thousands of people tried to flee the country, but chaos and violence at the airport impeded the evacuation of many at-risk Afghans.

The Taliban victory propelled Afghanistan from humanitarian crisis to catastrophe, with millions of Afghans facing severe food insecurity due to lost income, cash shortages, and rising food costs.

In the six months before the takeover, fighting between government forces and the Taliban caused a sharp rise in civilian casualties from improvised explosive devices (IEDs), mortars, and airstrikes. The Islamic State of Khorasan Province (the Afghan branch of the Islamic State, known as ISKP) carried out attacks on schools and mosques, many targeting minority Hazara Shia.

Unlawful Killings, Enforced Disappearances, Violations of Laws of War

The United Nations reported that Taliban forces were responsible for nearly 40 percent of civilian deaths and injuries in the first six months of 2021, although many incidents were unclaimed. Women and children comprised nearly half of

17

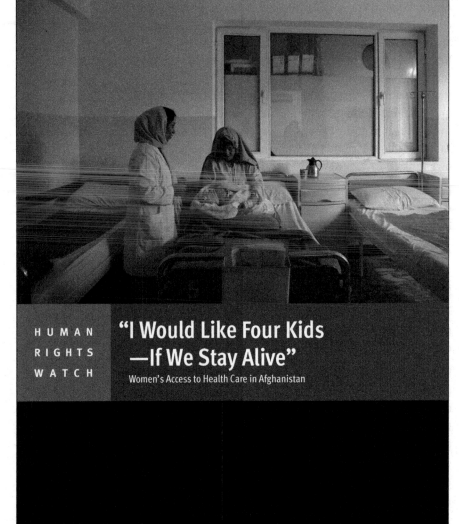

HUMAN
RIGHTS
WATCH

"I Would Like Four Kids —If We Stay Alive"
Women's Access to Health Care in Afghanistan

all civilian casualties. Attacks by the ISKP included assassinations and a number of deadly bombings.

Many attacks targeted Afghanistan's Hazara Shia community. On May 8, three explosions at the Sayed al-Shuhada school in Kabul killed at least 85 civilians, including 42 girls and 28 women, and injured over 200—the vast majority from the Hazara community. The attack was unclaimed but occurred in a predominantly Hazara neighborhood that ISKP had repeatedly targeted. On October 8, a suicide bombing during Friday prayer at a Shia mosque in Kunduz killed at least 72 people and injured over 140; the ISKP claimed responsibility. On March 4, gunmen fatally shot seven Hazara laborers at a plastics factory in Jalalabad.

Taliban forces in several provinces carried out retaliatory killings of at least dozens of former officials and security force personnel. After the Taliban took control of Malistan, Ghazni, in mid-July, they killed at least 19 security force personnel in their custody, along with a number of civilians. Advancing Taliban forces killed at least 44 former security force members in Kandahar after the Taliban captured Spin Boldak in July. All had surrendered to the Taliban. There were credible reports of detentions and killings in other provinces as well as Kabul.

Both the Taliban and ISKP carried out targeted killings of civilians, including government employees, journalists, and religious leaders. On January 17, 2021, unidentified gunmen fatally shot two women judges who worked for Afghanistan's high court and wounded their driver. ISKP claimed responsibility for killing nine polio vaccinators in Nangarhar between March and June. On June 9, gunmen killed 10 humanitarian deminers in Baghlan; ISKP claimed responsibility. In August, an ISKP suicide bombing at Kabul's airport killed 170 civilians, including many Afghans trying to flee the country.

Taliban forces also forcibly evicted people from their homes in a number of provinces including Daykundi, Uruzgan, Kunduz, and Kandahar, in apparent retaliation for the residents' perceived support for the former government. In the largest of these expulsions, in September, hundreds of Hazara families from the Gizab district of Uruzgan province and neighboring districts of Daykundi province were forced to abandon their homes and flee.

Both the Taliban and Afghan government security forces were responsible for killing and injuring civilians in indiscriminate mortar and rocket attacks, and civilian casualties from the former government forces' airstrikes more than doubled in the first half of 2021 compared with the same period in 2020. In one incident, on January 10, an airstrike in Nimroz killed 18 civilians, including seven girls, six women, and four boys; two civilian men were injured.

On August 15, as the Taliban entered Kabul, a strike force unit from the former government's National Directorate of Security captured and executed 12 former prisoners who had just been released, according to witnesses.

On August 29, the US launched a drone strike on a car it claimed was filled with explosives headed for Kabul's airport. The car was actually driven by an NGO employee scheduled for evacuation to the US. Two weeks later the US Defense Department admitted the strike had been a "tragic mistake," killing 10 civilians, including seven children.

Women's and Girls' Rights

In the weeks after the Taliban takeover, Taliban authorities announced a steady stream of policies and regulations rolling back women's and girls' rights. These included measures severely curtailing access to employment and education and restricting the right to peaceful assembly. The Taliban also searched out high-profile women and denied them freedom of movement outside their homes.

The Taliban have said they support education for girls and women, but on September 18 they ordered secondary schools to reopen only for boys. Some secondary schools for girls subsequently reopened in a few provinces, but as of October the vast majority remained shut. On August 29, the acting minister of higher education announced that girls and women could participate in higher education but could not study with boys and men. A lack of female teachers, especially in higher education, likely means this policy will lead to de facto denial of access to education for many girls and women.

Women who had taught boys in classes above sixth grade or men in mixed classes at university have been dismissed in some areas because teaching males is no longer allowed. In many parts of Afghanistan, Taliban officials have banned or restricted female humanitarian workers—a move that could likely worsen access to health care and humanitarian aid. The Taliban have also dismissed almost all female government employees. In September, the Taliban's

Ministry of Rural Development ordered only men to return to their jobs, saying women's return to work was "postponed" until it prepared a "mechanism for how they will work." When women have been allowed to return to work, they have faced requirements for gender segregation in their workplaces.

In September, the Taliban eliminated the Ministry for Women's Affairs and repurposed its building as the Ministry for the Propagation of Virtue and Prevention of Vice, an institution mandated to enforce rules on citizens' behavior, including how women dress, and when or whether women can move outside the home unaccompanied by a male relative. The shelters that had been established for women fleeing violence have been closed, and some the women who lived in them have been transferred to women's prisons.

Freedom of Media, Speech, and Assembly

The Afghan media came under growing threat since the beginning of the year, principally from the Taliban. The ISKP also carried out a number of deadly attacks on journalists.

On December 21, 2020, Rahmatullah Nekzad, head of the Ghazni journalists' union, was fatally shot as he walked from his home to a local mosque. Although the Taliban denied responsibility, Nekzad had previously received threats from local Taliban commanders.

The ISKP took responsibility for killing Malala Maiwand, a TV presenter for Enikass News in Jalalabad, along with her driver, Tahar Khan, on December 10, 2020. In two separate attacks in Jalalabad on March 2, 2021, gunmen fatally shot three women who worked at Enikass News dubbing foreign language news reports.

After the Taliban takeover, nearly 70 percent of all Afghan media outlets closed, and others were operating under threat and self-censoring. In September, the Taliban authorities imposed wide-ranging restrictions on media and free speech that included prohibitions on "insulting national figures" and reports that could have a "negative impact on the public's attitude." On September 7, Taliban security forces detained two journalists from the Etilaat-e Roz media outlet and severely beat them in custody before releasing them. The reporters had been covering protests by women in Kabul. The Taliban detained at least 32 journalists after taking power in Kabul.

Beginning on September 2, Afghan women carried out demonstrations in several cities to protest against Taliban policies violating women's rights. In Herat, Taliban fighters lashed protesters and fired weapons indiscriminately to disperse the crowd, killing two men and wounding at least eight more. The Taliban subsequently banned protests that did not have prior approval from the Justice Ministry in Kabul. Some protests nevertheless continued.

On July 6, the former Afghan government announced it was unlawful to broadcast news "against the national interest." On July 26, four journalists were arrested by the former government's intelligence agency after they returned from Spin Boldak, Kandahar, where they had been investigating the Taliban's takeover of the district. They were not released until after Kandahar fell to the Taliban on August 13.

International Justice and Investigations into Abuses

On September 27, the prosecutor for the International Criminal Court filed an application before the court's judges seeking authorization to resume an investigation in Afghanistan following the collapse of the former Afghan government. Prosecutor Karim Khan stated, however, that his investigation would focus only on crimes allegedly committed by the Taliban and the Islamic State and deprioritize other aspects of the investigation, namely alleged crimes committed by the forces of the former Afghan government and US military and CIA personnel.

On August 24, the UN Human Rights Council held a special session, requested jointly by Afghanistan and the Organisation of Islamic Cooperation (OIC), but the negotiations—led by Pakistan as OIC coordinator—failed to create any new monitoring mechanism. At its next regular session, the UN Human Rights Council adopted on October 7 a European Union-led resolution establishing a special rapporteur on Afghanistan, supported by experts, including on "fact-finding, forensics, and the rights of women and girls."

In June, Afghan witnesses testified by video link in the defamation trial against Australian newspapers brought by former Australian SAS officer Ben Roberts-Smith. In 2018, *The Age, Sydney Morning Herald,* and *Canberra Times* had published accounts of alleged killings of civilians and other abuses by SAS units, and by Roberts-Smith himself. Those abuses are being examined by Australian investigators.

Key International Actors

On April 14, US President Joe Biden announced a full US troop withdrawal from Afghanistan. The expedited withdrawal did not include plans for evacuating many Afghans who had worked for the US and NATO forces or for programs sponsored by donor countries.

Canada, the EU, United Kingdom, United States, and other countries evacuated several hundred thousand Afghans who had worked directly with those governments, their military forces, or organizations they supported. Thousands more Afghans remained at risk—including human rights defenders, women's rights activists, journalists, and lesbian, gay, bisexual, and transgender people—with no way of exiting the country safely. Although EU members evacuated some Afghans, as of November, none had made commitments to take in more refugees. Member states pledged one billion euros in humanitarian aid.

After the Taliban takeover, the New York Federal Reserve cut off the Afghanistan Central Bank's access to its US dollar assets. The International Monetary Fund prevented Afghanistan from accessing funding including Special Drawing Rights. In August, donors stopped payments from the World Bank-administered Afghanistan Reconstruction Trust Fund, previously used to pay civil servants' salaries, accelerating Afghanistan's economic collapse.

In September, the UN Security Council authorized a six-month renewal of the UN Assistance Mission in Afghanistan (UNAMA). The future of the mission, which among other things is mandated to promote the rights of Afghan women and girls and to monitor, investigate, and report on alleged human rights abuses, is uncertain. UN Secretary-General António Guterres is expected to make recommendations to the council in early 2022 on UNAMA's future.

As of November, the Taliban government had not been formally recognized by any other country. In September, the EU set five benchmarks for engagement with the Taliban government, among them, respect for human rights, in particular those of women and girls, and establishing an inclusive and representative government.

At the G20 meeting on September 23, China's Foreign Minister Wang Yi called for an end to all economic sanctions on Afghanistan, said that China expected the Taliban government to eventually become more inclusive, and called on the Taliban to "resolutely" fight international terrorism.

As of November 1, Russia, Turkey, and Iran stated they would not acknowledge a Taliban-led government until they formed an "inclusive" administration. Russia invited Taliban representatives to international talks on Afghanistan in Moscow on October 20.

While Pakistan stopped short of recognizing the Taliban government, it called for greater international engagement with the Taliban, while also urging them to create a more "inclusive" government.

Throughout the year, the deteriorating situation in Afghanistan was repeatedly addressed by UN special procedures, treaty bodies, and the UN High Commissioner for Human Rights.

Algeria

After a wide crackdown in 2020 on the "Hirak," a pro-reform protest movement that pushed President Abdelaziz Bouteflika to resign in April 2019, Algerian authorities widened the scope of the repression in 2021 to include Islamists and activists for the autonomy of the Kabylie region. Scores of protesters, politicians, human rights defenders, and journalists were arrested and prosecuted, some sentenced to years in prison, often on speech-related charges, while political parties were shut down. More than 230 individuals were being held in prison because of their peaceful speech or activism as of November, according to a group monitoring arrests. The government labelled a loosely defined pro-autonomy movement in the Kabylie region and an Islamist group as "terrorist organizations," and arrested several individuals, including human rights activists and a lawyer, under the accusation of being connected to those groups.

Political Rights and Freedom of Association

The months preceding the legislative elections held on June 12 saw a marked increase in arrests and prosecutions for speech offenses in Algeria.

Up until the election, in an apparent attempt to disrupt the weekly Hirak demonstrations, security forces habitually rounded up large numbers of protesters, releasing most by the end of the day without bringing them to trial.

On May 18, the High Security Council, an official body headed by President Abdelmadjid Tebboune, labelled two political movements, the Islamist opposition group Rachad and the Movement for the Self-Determination of the Kabylie region (MAK) as "terrorist organizations."

The MAK, created in 2001, describes itself as a movement seeking autonomy from Algiers as a prelude to founding an independent state in Kabylie "through peaceful means" and denies any involvement in violent activities. Rachad, an Islamist opposition party, was founded in 2007 and claims to "rely on non-violence and peacefulness in any political or social change."

On June 8, after he dissolved parliament and called new elections, President Tebboune amended the penal code by presidential decree, expanding Algeria's

already overbroad definition of terrorism to include "any act targeting state security, national unity, or the stability and normal functioning of institutions that
aims to ... work toward or incite, by any means whatsoever, gaining power or
changing the system of governance by non-constitutional means," or "undermine the integrity of the national territory or incite [others] to do so, by any
means whatsoever." Among other concerns, the law could be used to target non-
violent protesters and political opposition groups seeking changes to the government.

On April 23, police arrested university scholar and human rights defender Kad-
dour Chouicha, and the journalists and human rights activists Jamila Loukil
(Chouicha's wife) and Said Boudour, in Oran. A tribunal in that city later charged
them with "conspiring against State security, inciting citizens to take up arms
against authorities, propaganda of foreign origin or inspiration likely to harm national interest, and enlistment in a terrorist organization." Amnesty International
dismissed the charges as "trumped up."

According to an account by Frontline Defenders, as Chouicha and Boudour left
the court on April 28, police rearrested them and questioned them about their
human rights work and their alleged involvement with Islamist groups, "which
they categorically denied." As time of writing, Chouicha, Boudour, and Loukil
were provisionally free and awaiting trial.

On April 4, police arrested Mohamed Tadjadit and Malik Riahi in Algiers, then
Tarek Debaghi, Soheib Debaghi, and Noureddine Khimoud the next day in Batna,
500 kilometers from Algiers. The five men, all Hirak members, were arrested in
connection to a YouTube video posted on April 3, in which some of them appeared to console a boy who said he was 15 years old and had just been sexually
molested by police agents after they arrested him during a protest. A prosecutor
in Algiers said the allegation of sexual molestation of the boy was unfounded,
and later accused the five protesters of "forming a criminal association, spreading false news, drug possession, broadcasting images that can harm a minor,
and incitement of a minor to debauchery." The five men were still in pretrial detention at time of writing. Tadjadid, also known as "the poet of the Hirak" for his
recitation of his own protest poems before crowds of protesters, had been in and
out of prison since the beginning of the protests.

In May, the Ministry of Interior petitioned courts to "suspend" two small political
parties, the Union for Change and Progress (UCP) and the Socialist Workers Party

(PST,) on the grounds that they had not completed their legal registration requirements. The same month, the ministry also petitioned to dissolve the Youth Action Rally (RAJ), a civil society organization whose president, Abdelouahab Fersaoui, had spent seven months in prison between October 2019 and May 2020 for "harming the integrity of the national territory" after he criticized government policies on Facebook. The petition said that RAJ had engaged in activities "different from those it was created for," including "suspicious activities with foreigners" and activities "of a political nature for the purpose of creating chaos and disturbing the public order." The tribunal ordered RAJ dissolved on October 13.

On June 30, Fethi Ghares, the leader of Democratic and Social Movement (MDS) opposition party, was arrested in Algiers. A prosecutor charged him with "insulting the president of the republic" and "disseminating information that could harm national interest and undermine public order." An investigative judge remanded him in custody pending investigation, for "insulting President Tebboune." He remained in pretrial detention at time of writing.

On August 24, Karima Nait Sid, the co-president of the World Amazigh Congress, an association promoting the rights of the Amazigh ethnic group, was detained incommunicado in an unknown location for three days, according to Frontline Defenders. She resurfaced on September 1 before a prosecutor in Algiers, who charged her with "undermining state security and belonging to a terrorist organization," apparently in reference to MAK. She was detained in a prison in Tipaza awaiting trial at time of writing.

On August 25, Slimane Bouhafs, an Amazigh activist and Christian convert who spent two years in prison between 2016 and 2018 for "offending the prophet of Islam" and was registered as a refugee with the United Nations in Tunisia in 2020, went missing from his home in Tunis. His whereabouts were unknown until September 1, when he appeared in a court in Algiers. A relative of Bouhafs told Human Rights Watch that witnesses who lived in the same building in Tunis saw three unidentified men carrying a seemingly unconscious Bouhafs out of the building and into a waiting car. Kader Houali, Bouhafs' lawyer, said his client had been charged on six counts, including endangering the security of the state, call to public disturbance, and terrorism offenses. At time of writing, Bouhafs remained in detention awaiting trial.

On September 14, the police arrested journalist and prominent Hirak figure Fodil Boumala. Two days later, an investigative judge in Algiers opened an investigation into accusations of "disseminating false statements published on Boumala's Facebook account and undermining national unity," according to his lawyer. Boumala remained in pretrial detention at time of writing. He had been arrested twice and spent more than five months in prison since Hirak protests began in 2019.

The National Committee for the Liberation of Detainees, a group tracking political detainees, in November listed 231 persons, including Hirak protesters, human rights defenders, journalists, politicians and civil society activists as behind bars for expressing dissent.

Freedom of Speech

On April 22, a court in Algiers sentenced religion scholar Saïd Djabelkhir to three years in prison for "offending the Prophet of Islam" and "denigrating the dogma or precepts of Islam," after private citizens complained about his critical writings on Islam.

On May 14, the police arrested Radio M journalist Kenza Khatto and kept her in detention for five days. On June 1, she appeared under provisional release before a judge in Algiers who sentenced her to three months of suspended prison for "participation in an unarmed gathering" and "dissemination of news that could undermine national unity" for no apparent motive other than her coverage of the Hirak protests.

On May 18, Radio M's director Ihsane El Kadi was placed under judicial control for "undermining national unity" and "publications that harm the national interest," after publishing an article criticizing the labelling of Rachad and MAK as terrorist groups. The judicial supervision of El Kadi involved several restrictions, including the obligation to report a police station weekly, the confiscation of his passport, and requiring the permission of local authorities for him to leave the governorate of Algiers.

On June 13, the Ministry of Communication withdrew the accreditation of the French TV France 24, citing unspecified "breaches of ethics" and the channel's "manifestly hostile agenda against Algeria." Two weeks later, authorities withdrew the accreditation of Saudi TV channel Al-Arabiya under unspecified accusations of "propagating misinformation and practicing media manipulation." Unaccredited foreign TV channels are not allowed to cover press conferences, film in the street, set up live broadcasts, or conduct much of their routine activities. Most of foreign TV channels operating in Algeria work in a legal limbo most of the time due to the delays in obtaining one-year accreditations. According to the local branch of Reporters Without Borders, most foreign channels as of October 1, 2021, had not been accredited yet for 2021.

On June 26, authorities arrested former MP Nordine Ait Hamouda in Bejaia, then transferred him to Algiers the next day and remanded him in custody pending investigation for "insulting symbols of the state," and "attacking a former President of the Republic." The charges pertain to comments Ait Hamouda made on the privately-owned local Al Hayat TV channel a few days earlier calling historic figures including Emir Abdelkader and Houari Boumediene "traitors." For the same reason, the Ministry of Communication ordered on June 23 a one-week suspension of Al Hayat TV. Ait Hamouda was granted provisional release on August 23 after two months in El Harrach prison in Algiers. His trial is still pending.

On August 12, journalist Rabah Kareche, the correspondent of the newspaper *Liberté* in the southern city of Tamanrasset, was sentenced to one year in prison, including eight months suspended, for "undermining national security, national unity and public order via the deliberate dissemination of false information." Kareche had been in pretrial detention since April 18. The day before his arrest, policemen had interrogated him in a police station in Tamanasset about his coverage of a local protest against revisions in district boundaries. Kareche was released on October 19.

On September 13, authorities arrested Mohamed Mouloudj, and later charged him with "spreading false news, harming national unity and belonging to a terrorist group," the latter charge in reference to the MAK movement. After an investigative judge in Algiers questioned Mouloudj on his contacts with MAK founder Ferhat Mehenni, Mouloudj answered that the contacts were part of his journalistic work. The judge placed him in pretrial detention, where he remained at the time of writing.

Judicial Independence

On May 30, the High Council of Magistracy (HCM), an official body presided by the president of the Republic, dismissed judge Sadedine Merzoug, spokesperson of the Free Magistrates Club, an un-recognized independent organization founded in 2016. The reason the HCM provided for firing Merzoug was that he "violated his obligation of confidentiality" by posting multiple pro-Hirak statements on Facebook. The French daily Le Monde wrote that Merzoug's explicit support of the Hirak earned him been five disciplinary sanctions since the Hirak started in 2019.

Migrants, Asylum Seekers, and Refugees

Algerian authorities continued collective expulsions to Niger and Mali of thousands of migrants, including hundreds of children, often without individual screenings or due process. Migrants reported cases of violence, theft of their belongings, arbitrary detention, detention of children with adults, poor treatment in detention, and other mistreatment by Algerian authorities during arrests, detention, and expulsions to land borders. Between January and July, Algerian authorities expelled 13,602 people to Niger, including 8,858 Nigeriens, according to the UN refugee agency (UNHCR); as of October, Alarm Phone Sahara in Niger reported that over 18,000 people had been expelled.

Authorities forcibly repatriated most Nigeriens in truck convoys per a 2014 bilateral oral agreement, while they left others of over 20 nationalities, mostly Sub-Saharan Africans, in the desert at the Niger border. Those expelled included at least 51 asylum seekers or other "persons of concern" to UNHCR, in violation of the principle of non-refoulement under international refugee law.

Though a party to the African and UN refugee conventions, Algeria continued to lack a national asylum law and protection framework. Refugees and asylum seekers had free access to public education and primary healthcare, but administrative barriers hindered their access to school and work. According to UNHCR, the government said it would include refugees in its national Covid-19 vaccination plan, and vaccinations for Sahrawi refugees began in May 2021.

Women's Rights

Article 326 of the penal code, a colonial-era relic, allows a person who abducts a minor to escape prosecution if he marries his victim.

Algeria's Family Code allows men to have a unilateral divorce without explanation but requires women to apply to courts for a divorce on specified grounds.

Feminicides Algerie reported that some 38 women and girls were killed in 2021, including 33 reported to have been killed by their husbands, former husbands, fathers, brothers, sons or another family member. Although, a 2015 law made assault on a spouse punishable by up to 20 years in prison and a life sentence for injuries resulting in death, the law does not set out any further measures to prevent abuse or adequately protect survivors, such as protection orders.

The penal code does not explicitly criminalize corporal punishment of children; surveys have found more than 85 percent experience violent discipline in the home.

Sexual Orientation and Gender Identity

Same-sex relations are punishable under article 338 of the penal code by up to two years in prison and adultery is punishable under article 339 of the penal code with one to two years imprisonment. Restrictions on freedom of association also pose obstacles to the work of lesbian, gay, bisexual and transgender (LGBT) groups.

According to a global survey on "state-sanctioned homophobia", published in 2017, an Algerian law that prohibits the registration of organizations whose aims are inconsistent with "public morals," and which prescribes criminal penalties for members of unregistered organizations, poses risks to LGBT groups, as well as to human rights organizations that otherwise might support them.

Angola

The human rights situation in Angola achieved one key improvement in 2021 with the entry into force of the new penal code. The code decriminalizes same-sex conduct, protects the rights of children in conflict with the law, criminalizes genital mutilation and sexual harassment, and expands the circumstances under which abortion is legally permitted. However, the government has made little progress on broader human rights issues. State security forces were implicated in serious human rights abuses, including summary executions, excessive use of force against peaceful protesters, and arbitrary detentions. Authorities also used draconian media laws to limit the work of journalists. Cases of sexual abuse of children continued to increase. Several provinces in southern Angola faced the worst drought in 40 years, causing over 1.3 million people to face hunger, with many crossing the border into Namibia in search of food.

Humanitarian Crisis in the Southern Region

Southern Angola faced the worst drought since 1981, which severely affected access to food in three provinces. The World Food Program (WFP) said that more than 1.3 million people in Cunene, Huila, and Namibe provinces faced severe hunger. Of those, 114,000 were children under the age of 5, who were suffering or likely to suffer from acute malnutrition. In March, the Namibian press reported that hundreds of Angolans fleeing the drought had crossed the border into Namibia in search of food.

In July, a local nongovernmental organization (NGO), the Association Building Communities (Associação Construindo Comunidades, ACC), called the situation "catastrophic," and urged the Angolan government to declare a state of emergency in the region. During a September visit of the Angolan President Joao Lourenço to the region, the governor of Cunene, Gerdina Didalelwa, said that the drought had caused a movement of people "never seen before," with 4,000 people displaced within Cunene province and 2,000 to Namibia. In September, the Angolan government set up a task force largely made up of officials from government institutions to distribute humanitarian aid to victims of the drought.

Abuses by State Security Forces

Angolan state security forces continued to be implicated in serious human rights abuses, including summary executions, excessive use of force against peaceful protesters, and arbitrary detentions throughout 2021.

On January 30, police killed at least 10 protesters, when they indiscriminately fired at people who had peacefully gathered to demand better public services, such as water and electricity supply, in the diamond-rich town of Cafunfu, in Lunda Norte province. Following the violence, graphic video footage shared on social media showed uniformed Angolan police officers and soldiers walking among the dead and injured on a road, kicking and beating detainees. The Angolan police chief, Paulo de Almeida, initially rejected calls for an independent investigation into alleged excessive use of force against protesters, but the police department laterannounced that two senior officers implicated in the violence had been dismissed. They were implicated in the mishandling of corpses and the mistreatment of detained protesters, including kicking and beatings.

In February, the Angolan NGO Mosaiko accused police of intimidating activists and religious missionaries in Lunda Norte, after officers prevented priests and Mosaiko activists from leaving their homes.

Security forces continued to use force to prevent peaceful protests. On November 11, 2020, Angola's Independence Day, the police used live bullets, teargas, and dogs to disperse a peaceful anti-government protest, killing one protester in Luanda. In April, police used bullets and teargas to disperse a group of students who took to the streets in Luanda, the Angolan capital, to protest the increase of school fees. In August, police used dogs and batons to disperse a group of about 20 people who tried to protest in front of the parliament building in Luanda.

Children's Rights

Authorities struggled to protect the rights of children, as cases of sexual abuse of children continued to increase. In June, the National Children's Institute, INAC, revealed that over 4,000 children below age 14 had been sexually abused since June 2020. INAC said most of the victims were girls from Luanda, who were sexually abused by neighbors and family friends. Local children rights' activists said official government numbers reflected only reported cases of sexual abuse. In many cases, abusers offer money to the family of the victim to convince it not to report such abuses or to close a criminal case.

In September, the Ministry of Social Action, Family and Women's Promotion disclosed the existence of a child prostitution network in the fishing village of Cahota, in Benguela province, allegedly controlled by Chinese migrants. Media reports had alleged that dozens of girls, some as young as 13, had become pregnant, and at least 17 girls had borne children to Chinese men, after being sexually abused. As of October, authorities had arrested at least one man in connection with the case, and police investigations were still ongoing. The government did not publicly disclose what type of assistance, if any, it had provided to the victims.

Before the Covid-19 pandemic, 18 percent of Angolan children were out of primary school. After the pandemic's start in 2020, schools were closed for 195 days, and partially open to certain ages or in certain areas, for 106 days, affecting 8.7 million children. In 2021, schools were partially closed in January and February, but open for the remainder of the year.

Freedom of Media

Authorities continued to use draconian media laws to repress and harass journalists. In June, journalists Coque Mukuta and Escrivão José were charged with criminal defamation after two ruling party officials filed separate complaints about articles they published. The Committee to Protect Journalists, CPJ, reported at least six other cases of criminal defamation complaints against journalists in Angola since March.

Millions of Angolans across the country are still denied access to free, diverse, and impartial information, as Angola remained the only southern African country without community radio stations.

Authorities reduced the number of private television stations in April, when the Ministry of Telecommunications, Information Technologies and Social Communication announced the suspension of the licenses of three television channels, resulting in the loss of hundreds of jobs. The ministry said the media companies were operating under provisional registrations and would remain suspended until the regularization of their status. In August, Secretary of State for Social Communication Nuno Caldas Albina said that the media companies would not be allowed to resume any time soon, despite at least two of them having submitted the required documentation.

Sexual Orientation and Gender Identity

In a positive step, Angola's new penal code, which came into force on February 10, no longer criminalizes consensual same-sex conduct. Parliament had passed the new legislation in January 2019 to replace the obsolete penal code of 1886, but the president did not sign it into law until November 2020.

The new penal code removed the contentious provisions that punished people who "habitually indulge in the practice of vices against nature," which targeted the lesbian, gay, bisexual and transgender community, and limited their access to employment, health care, and education. The new law prohibits violence and discrimination on the basis of sexual orientation among other things, including for employment, with a punishment of up to two years' imprisonment.

Key International Actors

Angola continued its efforts in conflict resolution and peace building across central Africa, playing leading roles in the Economic Community of Central African States, ECCAS, and the International Conference on the Great Lakes Region, ICGLR.

On July 27, Angola's parliament approved the deployment of 20 officers and a transport aircraft to Mozambique as part of the Southern African Development Community (SADC) mission in support of Mozambique's military operations against armed Islamist groups in its northern Cabo Delgardo province.

In September, following a meeting with Angolan President João Lourenço, United States National Security Adviser Jake Sullivan reaffirmed his support in resuming the US- Angola Strategic Dialogue as the centerpiece of bilateral engagement between the countries.

In his address at the 76th session of the United Nations General Assembly in September, President Lourenço pushed for universal and open access to Covid-

19 vaccines to "allow for wider production and equitable distribution on a global scale." He also called on the international community to take "appropriate and sufficient action" to discourage military coups in Africa, as was recently experienced in Mali and Guinea.

Argentina

Longstanding human rights problems in Argentina include police abuse, poor prison conditions, and endemic violence against women. In December 2020, Congress passed a landmark bill to legalize abortion up to the fourteenth week of pregnancy, ending a nearly century-old exception model that put the life and health of women at risk. However, implementation remains a challenge.

Some government-promoted proposed legal reforms to the justice system and the Attorney General's Office pose a risk to their independence. Delays in appointing permanent judges, likewise, undermine the justice system. Impunity for the 1994 bombing of the AMIA Jewish center in Buenos Aires continues to be a concern.

A legislative election in November, which the opposition won, has modified the Senate's composition, making it harder for the government coalition to pass laws without a meaningful debate.

Confronting Past Abuses

Pardons and amnesty laws shielding officials implicated in the 1976-1983 dictatorship's crimes were annulled by the Supreme Court and federal judges in the early 2000s. As of June 2021, the Attorney General's Office reported 3,493 people charged, 1,030 convicted, and 159 acquitted. Of 631 investigations into crimes against humanity, judges had issued rulings in 256.

As of August 2021, 130 people illegally taken from their parents as children during the dictatorship had been identified and many had been reunited with their families, according to the Abuelas de Plaza de Mayo, a human rights group.

The large number of victims, suspects, and cases of alleged crimes of the dictatorship makes it difficult for prosecutors and judges to bring those responsible to justice.

The fate of Jorge Julio López, a torture victim who disappeared in 2006—a day before he was due to attend the trial of one of his torturers—remains unknown.

Prison Conditions and Abuses by Security Forces

The National Penitentiary Office reported 176 alleged cases of torture or ill-treatment in federal prisons in 2020 and 77 from January through June 2021. The Attorney General's Office reported 16 violent deaths of people detained in federal prisons in 2020.

Almost half of the 11,290 detainees in federal prisons have not been convicted of a crime but are awaiting trial, the government reports. Hundreds of people were conditionally released by judicial decisions in 2020 to prevent the spread of the virus that causes Covid-19, but no meaningful reform has been undertaken to address pretrial detention.

In February 2021, the National Penitentiary Office reported that 58 detainees had died in federal prisons in 2020—the highest figure in the last 10 years—17 reportedly from Covid-19. Between January and June 2021, the National Penitentiary Office reported 16 deaths.

Security forces occasionally employ excessive force. In 2020, the Ombudsperson's Office reported 297 cases of violence by security officers.

The Ombudsperson's Office reported abuses by security forces enforcing the lockdown established to prevent the spread of Covid-19. Prosecutors continued to investigate the killing and possible enforced disappearance of Facundo Astudillo Castro and Luis Espinosa, two young men who went missing in the context of the national lockdown in 2020 and were later found dead.

Authorities in Argentina's northern province of Formosa employed abusive and unsanitary measures to prevent the spread of the novel coronavirus, including holding people in "isolation" and "quarantine" centers in circumstances that amounted to arbitrary detention. Authorities limited journalists' ability to report on the situation, allegedly used excessive force against people who protested the Covid-19 regulations, and arrested and brought criminal charges against some.

Freedom of Expression

In February, a federal judge opened a criminal investigation against a former director and deputy director of Argentina's Federal Intelligence Agency for leading a conspiracy for the illegal surveillance of journalists, union members, and politicians under the administration of former President Mauricio Macri.

High level authorities, including President Alberto Fernández, have used hostile rhetoric against independent journalists, accusing them of spreading "fake news" when reporting on issues of public interest, such as irregularities in the distribution of Covid-19 vaccines.

A 2016 law created a national agency to ensure public access to government information and protect personal data. From 2017 to August 2021, individuals had filed 20,660 information requests. Authorities responded to most within a month, the legal deadline. As of August 2021, citizens had filed 1,220 appeals, in most cases after authorities had failed to respond by the deadline.

Some provinces and municipalities lack freedom of information laws, undermining transparency.

Judicial Independence

The Fernández administration has been attempting to overhaul the country's judiciary.

A "council of experts" appointed by President Fernández in August 2020 to propose reforms to the Magistrate's Council, the Supreme Court, and the Attorney General's Office presented its report in December 2020. Recommendations included modifying the Magistrate's Council's structure and establishing a term limit for the attorney general, currently a lifetime appointment. Some of the 11 experts on the council had ties to officials under investigation, including the lawyer of Vice President Cristina Fernández de Kirchner, whose position grants her immunity from arrest on multiple corruption charges.

In September 2020, the Senate passed a government-promoted bill creating dozens of new criminal courts to be staffed by temporary judges (pending appointment of tenured judges). Previously, delays in appointing tenured judges often left temporary judges in place for years. The Supreme Court ruled in 2015 that this undermined judicial independence. As of September 2021, 239 federal and national judgeships remained vacant.

In November 2020, the Senate passed another government-promoted bill reducing the legislative majority needed to appoint an attorney general and establishing a term limit, in line with the council's recommendation.

The House of Representatives had not discussed either bill at time of writing.

The Ombudsperson's Office

The Ombudsperson's Office, which is structurally independent from the executive and has powers to document and investigate acts by the national government, remains vacant. The office has not operated normally since 2013, when the mandate of the then-deputy ombudsperson expired. Congress has failed to appoint an ombudsperson since 2009. The office's performance and ability to protect rights has been limited.

Impunity for the AMIA Bombing

Twenty-seven years after the bombing of the Argentine Israelite Mutual Association (AMIA) in Buenos Aires that killed 85 people and injured more than 300, court battles continue and no one has been convicted. Argentine prosecutors have alleged it was carried out by Iranian suspects.

In January 2015, Alberto Nisman, the investigating prosecutor at that time, was found dead with a gunshot wound to the head and a pistol beside him; he had accused then-President Cristina Fernández de Kirchner of covering up Iran's role in the attack. In June 2018, an appeals court said Nisman's death appeared to be a murder. As of September 2021, no one had been convicted in connection with his death.

In March 2018, an appeals court upheld a decision ordering pretrial detention for now-Vice President Fernández de Kirchner for allegedly conspiring with Iranian officials to undermine the bombing investigation during her presidency. In December 2019, a federal court overturned the order. During a public hearing in July 2021, Fernández de Kirchner accused the courts of "legal persecution." In October, a federal court dismissed the case against Fernández de Kirchner and officials in her government, finding that Fernández de Kirchner's alleged conduct did not constitute a crime.

In February 2019, a court acquitted former President Carlos Menem of interference in the initial investigation into the bombing but convicted a former head of intelligence and a judge. An appeal of the judge's conviction remained pending as of September 2021.

Indigenous Rights

Indigenous people face obstacles accessing justice, land, education, health care, and basic services. Argentina has repeatedly failed to implement laws protecting Indigenous peoples' right under international law to free, prior, and informed consent to government and business decisions that may affect their rights. Debates on a national law on Indigenous communal ownership of traditional lands, which the Argentine Constitution protects, are continually postponed.

Children's Rights

At least 357,000 children—and up to 694,000—discontinued their schooling during 2020 in Argentina, UNICEF reported. Due to Covid-19 related restrictions, most schools were closed between March and December 2020 and for shorter periods in some parts of the country in 2021, when a gradual return to classes took place. The impact was greatest on low-income families, UNICEF said, and around 20 percent of those who dropped out in 2020 were still without schooling in May 2021.

Women's and Girls' Rights

In December 2020, Argentina's Congress passed a landmark bill to legalize abortion up to the 14th week of pregnancy. The law also allows termination of pregnancies after that term in cases of rape or when the life or health of the pregnant person is at risk. However, there are reports of obstacles to access legal abortion, including lack of access to information about the law, improper use of conscientious objection by healthcare professionals, and undue delays. Women with disabilities who are under court orders specifically restricting their legal capacity in connection with the exercise of their reproductive rights, or who have been declared legally incompetent, are required to have assistance from their legal representative or relative to consent to abortions, which creates obstacles for their exercise of this right.

Also in December, Congress approved a separate law to provide support to pregnant people and their children for the first 1,000 days of the child's life.

Despite a 2009 law detailing comprehensive measures to prevent and prosecute violence against women, their unpunished killing remains a serious concern. The latest available data from the National Registry of Femicides, administered by the Supreme Court, reported 251 femicides—the murder of women based on their gender—and only four convictions, in 2020.

Sexual Orientation and Gender Identity

In 2010, Argentina became the first Latin American country to legalize same-sex marriage.

In 2012, Argentina passed a Gender Identity Law allowing anyone to change their gender and name on identity cards and birth certificates through a simple administrative procedure.

In July 2021, President Fernández recognized non-binary identities, enabling citizens and non-national residents to choose a third gender category, "X" (neither male or female), on identity cards and passports. Argentina is the first country in Latin America to establish such a category.

Key International Actors and Foreign Policy

In 2018, the International Monetary Fund (IMF) and the Macri administration agreed on a US$57 billion loan. At time of writing, the Fernández administration was re-negotiating the IMF loan amid a deep economic crisis that predates the pandemic and was deepened by it. The crisis has severely impacted people living in poverty, who according to government statistics amount to 40 percent of the population.

As a member of the United Nations Human Rights Council, Argentina has supported UN scrutiny of rights violations in Belarus, Ethiopia, Eritrea, Nicaragua, and Venezuela. In October 2021, Argentina was re-elected for the 2022-2024 term.

However, Argentina's foreign policy towards Venezuela and Nicaragua has been inconsistent. It abstained from an Organization of American States (OAS) resolution rejecting Venezuela's December 2020 elections, which are widely considered to have been fraudulent. It also abstained, in June and October 2021, from OAS resolutions condemning arrests of Nicaraguan presidential opposition candidates and critics. Argentina and Mexico, which also abstained in both opportunities, issued a statement justifying their June decision under the principle of non-intervention in the internal affairs of states.

In November 2021, Argentina voted in favor of an OAS resolution that condemned Nicaraguan presidential elections saying the elections "were not free, fair or transparent, and lack democratic legitimacy."

In 2021, Argentina withdrew from the Lima Group, a coalition of governments monitoring Venezuela's poor human rights record, and from a 2018 request to the Prosecutor's Office of the International Criminal Court—made together with Canada, Colombia, Chile, Paraguay, and Peru—for an investigation into possible crimes against humanity committed in Venezuela.

While Argentina rightfully condemned repression against protesters by the Colombian police, it failed to criticize abuses against demonstrators in Cuba.

Argentina hosted a virtual summit on climate change in September 2021 with representatives from Latin American and Caribbean countries, the US special envoy on climate change, and the UN secretary-general.

In September 2020, two Argentine girls were killed in neighboring Paraguay during an operation by members of a military-led elite unit against Paraguay's main guerrilla group. Serious deficiencies and irregularities marred Paraguay's investigation, and in October 2021, Argentina and Paraguay agreed to establish an expert international forensic team to work on the case.

In June 2020 and September 2021, Argentina informed the UN secretary-general that it was temporarily derogating some of its obligations under the International Covenant on Civil and Political Rights to address the Covid-19 pandemic.

Armenia

The 2020 truce ending the six-week war between Armenia and Azerbaijan in and around Nagorno-Karabakh largely held, but periodic skirmishes made for a fragile situation on the post-war front lines.

The political crisis following the defeat of ethnic Armenian forces was largely defused in the June snap election, which resulted in a decisive victory for the ruling party and reconfirmation of Nikol Pacinian as prime minister. International observers found the polls genuinely competitive and in line with international standards.

Domestic violence, discrimination against people with disabilities, barriers to effective pain treatment and palliative care, and violence and discrimination based on sexual orientation and gender identity persisted. Striving to fight rising incidents of hate speech, authorities introduced regulations which may undermine freedom of speech.

Aftermath of Nagorno-Karabakh Conflict

Ethnic Armenian prisoners continued to be detained and prosecuted by Azerbaijan. In September 2021, the Armenian Ombudsman's Office stated that at least 41 prisoners of war (POWs) and 4 civilian detainees remain in Azerbaijani custody. Numerous Armenian POWs were subjected to cruel and degrading treatment and torture by Azerbaijani forces either when they were captured, during their transfer, or while in custody at various detention facilities. (See Azerbaijan chapter). In 2021, nearly 100 Armenian POWs and civilian detainees were returned by Azerbaijan.

The fighting compounded the loss of education due to Covid-19-related school closures. According to official data, at least 71 schools were damaged or destroyed on the Armenian side and 54 on the Azerbaijani side.

Ongoing incidents of military hostilities threaten the safety and livelihoods of civilians residing in villages in Nagorno-Karabakh and along the Armenia-Azerbaijan border, mostly on the Armenian side. Russian peacekeepers reported the October 9 killing of a civilian in Martakert (Aghdara) district, while he was farming, due to gunfire from the Azerbaijani side. With no independent human rights monitoring in Nagorno-Karabakh, there is no mechanism to address problems arising from cross-border shootings and other insecurities.

In August, the Azerbaijani prosecutor-general's office said that since the cease-fire, 23 Azerbaijani civilians were killed and 36 were injured by anti-personnel and anti-vehicle mines laid in areas over which Azerbaijan re-established control. Among them were two Azerbaijani journalists and a local official, who were killed on June 4. Landmine contamination in all of the seven regained regions around Nagorno-Karabakh is reported to be extensive and widespread. In July, Armenia handed over landmine maps, detailing the location of around 92,000 anti-vehicle and anti-personnel mines in Fizuli and Zangelan regions; Azerbaijan handed over 15 captured Armenian soldiers in exchange for the maps. Neither Armenia nor Azerbaijan have ratified the international treaty prohibiting antipersonnel landmines.

A report by International Partnership for Human Rights, an independent group, on international humanitarian law violations during the Nagorno-Karabakh war, found "prima facie evidence of two extrajudicial executions of wounded Azerbaijani combatants by Armenian/Nagorno-Karabakh soldiers." It also documented the ill-treatment, including torture, of seven Azerbaijani POWs by these forces. (See Azerbaijan chapter for allegations of executions of Armenian troops by Azerbaijan forces).

Human Rights Watch is not aware of any investigations by Armenian authorities into alleged war crimes committed by Armenian forces during the war.

Accountability for Law Enforcement Abuse and Torture in Custody

Torture and ill-treatment in custody remains a problem and it is often perpetrated with impunity. Even when criminal investigations are launched in response to allegations of torture, they are rarely effective.

According to Helsinki Citizen's Assembly Vanadzor (HCAV), a local non-governmental organization, criminal investigations are mostly closed on the basis of findings that no crime was committed or suspended for the lack of a suspect. The group reported that no one has been convicted for torture since 2015, when torture became a specific offense. In all instances in which officials were held accountable for acts of physical abuse, they were convicted for general "abuse of office" offenses.

Freedom of Speech and Protection of Human Rights Defenders

The recent war and political crises triggered heated public debates, which often included inflammatory speech by members of parliament and other public officials that was at times directed against human rights defenders and activists. The government undertook several attempts, including by introducing legislative amendments, to tackle the spread of hateful and degrading speech.

During the first six months of 2021, the Committee to Protect Freedom of Expression, a local media advocacy group, documented 15 cases, with 17 victims, of physical violence against journalists perpetrated by both public officials and private individuals.

During a parliamentary session on August 11, the speaker of parliament forbade journalists from filming a quarrel between pro-government and opposition parliamentarians. Special forces ordered journalists to stop filming, and then ordered them out of their gallery in parliament.

Authorities pursued spurious criminal incitement charges against Sashik Sultanyan, the chairperson of a nongovernmental group, Yezidi Center for Human Rights. The charges stem from an interview Sultanyan gave to the website Yezidinews.am, where he alleged discrimination of Yezidi minorities in Armenia. The National Security Service, which brought the charges, wrongly characterized as "incitement" Sultanyan's interview, which was protected speech. The court review was pending at time of writing.

Disability Rights

In 2021, authorities continued to establish inclusive education across the country. In April, the government approved a plan to establish inclusive education in preschools, which contained 16 action steps to be completed by 2023. Nevertheless, many children with disabilities remain segregated in orphanages, special schools, or at home with little or no education.

There are 473 children with disabilities living in five state orphanages, 463 of whom live in three orphanages for children with disabilities. The government has not announced comprehensive plans to relocate children with disabilities to birth or foster families or transform these three institutions into community-based service providers, but rather the government and donors continue to invest in them. An unknown number of children with disabilities also continue to live in six private orphanages, with minimal government oversight.

Children with disabilities also frequently remain in institutions indefinitely when they become adults, stripped of their legal capacity and right to independent living. Adults with psychosocial or intellectual disabilities can be deprived of legal capacity, or the right to make decisions, and Armenia lacks supported decision-making mechanisms.

In May, parliament adopted the Law on the Rights of Persons with Disabilities, which includes guarantees of accessibility, independent living, and access to justice, and bans disability-based discrimination. The new law, however, does not create a dedicated body to oversee the law's implementation.

Violence against Women and Children

Domestic violence remains a persistent problem. Domestic violence cases are largely underreported. According to official data, during the first six months of 2021, authorities investigated 326 criminal domestic violence complaints. Of the 326, charges were brought against 145 persons, and in 90 of those the husband was identified as the alleged perpetrator.

The 2017 family violence law requires police to urgently intervene "when there is a reasonable assumption of an immediate threat of repetition or the continuation of violence" in the family. But in practice, law enforcement bodies lack awareness and training on protection mechanisms included in the law, such as protection orders, and do not adequately apply or enforce them.

There are only two domestic violence shelters, both in the capital, Yerevan, run by nongovernmental organizations, each with a capacity for five women and their children. This is far below the Council of Europe standard of one shelter space per 10,000 people. Armenia also lacks a general hot-line service for survivors of domestic violence.

Armenia signed the Council of Europe Convention on Preventing and Combating Violence against Women and Domestic Violence (Istanbul Convention) in 2018, but the ratification process remained stalled.

Sexual Orientation and Gender Identity (SOGI)

Lesbian, gay, bisexual, and transgender (LGBT) people in Armenia continue to face harassment, discrimination, and violence. The criminal code does not recognize animus due to sexual orientation or gender identity as aggravating criminal circumstances in hate crimes.

Fear of discrimination and possible humiliation due to public disclosure of their sexual orientation or gender identity prevent many LGBT people from reporting crimes against them, even when these are clearly motivated by anti-LGBT bias. But even when reported, investigations into such crimes are often inconclusive or ineffective.

PINK Armenia, an LGBT rights group, documented 12 incidents of physical attacks based on sexual orientation or gender identity from January through August 2021, and eight cases of threats and calls for physical and psychological violence. In 13 cases, violence and threat of violence was committed by a family member.

Victims of four attacks filed complaints with the police, who dismissed three of them claiming no crime had been committed. PINK Armenia has no information about the fourth. Police issued warnings in two of the three cases in which the violence was committed by a family member, but did not issue any restraining measures.

During the pre-election period, politicians used homophobia to advance their campaigns by smearing LGBT people as a threat to the family, national identity, and national security. Some opposition forces accused civil society organizations of destroying national values and spreading LGBT "propaganda."

Armenia does not have comprehensive anti-discrimination legislation.

Key International Actors

The Minsk Group of the Organization for Security and Co-operation in Europe, co-chaired by the United States, France, and Russia, re-engaged on Nagorno-Karabakh negotiations. During 2021, the co-chairs issued several statements on the aftermath of the war, reiterating their willingness to visit the region and calling on the parties to return all POWs and other detainees; exchange "all data necessary to conduct effective demining of conflict regions" and lift "restrictions on access to Nagorno-Karabakh, including for representatives of international humanitarian organizations"; preserve and protect religious and cultural heritage; and foster "direct contacts and co-operation between conflict-affected communities." After a long hiatus, the Minsk Group co-chairs met in New York during the UN General Assembly.

The European Union also called on the parties to refrain from military actions and called on Azerbaijan to release all prisoners of war and detainees.

A November 2021 memorandum by Council of Europe Commissioner for Human Rights Dunja Mijatović recommended, among other things, to "ensure free and unhindered access of humanitarian assistance and international human rights missions to all areas affected by the conflict."

A September resolution by the Parliamentary Assembly of the Council of Europe called on Azerbaijani authorities to free all remaining prisoners and urged Armenian authorities to release all mine maps. It also called on the sides to ensure accountability for the crimes committed during the war.

In their August joint statement, the UN special rapporteurs on minority issues, on the situation of human rights defenders, and on the promotion and protection of the right to freedom of expression called on Armenia to drop charges against Sashik Sultanyan.

In its May report, the European Committee for the Prevention of Torture and Inhuman or Degrading Treatment criticized de facto detention of people with disabilities who remain in psychiatric facilities involuntarily due to the absence of appropriate community-based services. The committee urged the government to prioritize these services and de-institutionalization.

The European Committee of Social Rights' January conclusions criticized Armenia's insufficient access to housing and public transportation for people with disabilities; failure to ban employment discrimination on grounds of sexual orientation; and the lack of an explicit statutory guarantee of equal pay for women and men for equal work.

In March, the EU-Armenia Comprehensive and Enhanced Partnership Agreement, which includes provisions on strengthening democracy, the rule of law and human rights, entered into force.

Also in March, US Secretary of State Antony Blinken stressed the importance of the rule of law and democratic institutions in a call with Prime Minister Pashinyan.

Australia

Australia is a vibrant multicultural democracy with a strong record of protecting civil and political rights, but serious human rights issues remain. The Australian government's failure to address the significant overrepresentation of First Nations people in the criminal justice system and cruel treatment of asylum seekers tarnishes the country's global standing.

As the Covid-19 pandemic continued, there was a lack of equitable vaccine access for at-risk communities in 2021, including First Nations people and prisoners in New South Wales. Australia is one of a handful of countries that has severely restricted free movement internationally to respond to the pandemic. Until November 2021, Australia banned its citizens from traveling abroad unless they meet strict criteria and limited the return of citizens through strict arrival caps.

Asylum Seekers and Refugees

2021 marked eight years since the Australia government reintroduced offshore processing of asylum seekers who arrive by boat. Approximately 230 refugees and asylum seekers remained in Papua New Guinea and Nauru at time of writing, with more than 900 refugees admitted to the United States under an Australia-US resettlement deal. Australia announced it will end its offshore agreement with Papua New Guinea at the end of 2021, transferring people who remain there to Nauru or giving them the option to remain in PNG with a promise of a "permanent migration pathway."

More than 80 refugees and asylum seekers transferred to Australia from Papua New Guinea and Nauru for medical or other reasons remain in detention. Australia has rejected offers by New Zealand to take some of the refugees. At least 12 refugees and asylum seekers have died in Australia's offshore processing system since 2013, 6 of them suicides.

Some of the refugees and asylum seekers transferred from Papua New Guinea and Nauru to Australia have been detained in hotel rooms, where access to sunlight, space to exercise, and fresh air is limited. A Kurdish refugee who spent more than 14 months detained in a Melbourne hotel room sued the Australian government, arguing its use of hotels for immigration detention is unlawful. In October, more than 20 asylum seekers contracted Covid-19 while in hotel detention.

An ethnic Tamil asylum seeker couple from Sri Lanka and their two Australian-born children spent two years in immigration detention on Christmas Island. In June, their 3-year-old daughter was airlifted to a hospital in Perth after she fell seriously ill and medical facilities on the island were inadequate. Following the medical emergency, the government allowed the family to remain in Australia temporarily, but has denied the family's application for permanent visas.

Following the Taliban takeover of Afghanistan in August, Australian Prime Minister Scott Morrison rejected calls to allow at least 4,200 Afghans in Australia on temporary visas to be given a pathway to permanent residency. The government earmarked 3,000 humanitarian visas in 2021 for Afghans. The government evacuated 3,500 people from Afghanistan to Australia after the Taliban took over Kabul. 3,000 of these evacuees were Afghan nationals with Australian visas. At time of writing, more than 200 Australian citizens or visa holders remain stranded in Afghanistan after failed attempts to evacuate them.

Indigenous Rights

Indigenous Australians are significantly overrepresented in the criminal justice system, with Aboriginal and Torres Strait Islander people comprising 30 percent of Australia's adult prison population, but just 3 percent of the national population.

At least 11 Indigenous people died in custody in Australia in 2021.

A coronial inquest into the death of a 36-year-old Aboriginal man in a New South Wales prison after he had an asthma attack, found there was a "confused, unreasonably delayed, and uncoordinated" medical response by prison staff. In March, a prison officer faced court on charges of manslaughter over the shooting death of an Aboriginal prisoner who was handcuffed and shackled at the time.

In March, the state of Victoria announced the creation of a truth and justice commission to investigate two centuries of violence, abuse, and discrimination against Australia's First Nations people, modelled on the South African Truth and Reconciliation Commission.

Children's Rights

Indigenous children are 17 times more likely to be incarcerated than non-Indigenous children.

Approximately 500 children under the age of 14 were imprisoned in the past year across Australia. In January 2021, Australia disregarded calls by 31 UN member states who recommended the government raise the age of criminal responsibility from 10 years old to the internationally recommended minimum of 14 years.

New punitive bail laws for children introduced in the Northern Territory led to an increase in the number of children in detention, the majority of them Indigenous. Similar laws introduced in Queensland created, contrary to international human rights law, a presumption against bail for children charged with crimes such as assault, attempted robbery, unauthorised use of a motor vehicle where the child is a driver, and dangerous driving.

Covid-19

Australia has restricted the rights of its own citizens to enter and leave their own country.

Strict arrival quotas due to limited quarantine facilities left more than 43,000 Australian citizens stranded abroad.

From March 2020 to November 2021, Australia banned its citizens from leaving the country as a public health measure during the Covid-19 pandemic, unless they met strict criteria. In August 2021, the ban was expanded to include Australians who normally live abroad. This punitive approach to travel left tens of thousands of Australian families separated from their loved ones.

After a spike in Covid-19 cases in India in May, the Australian government announced a temporary measure of banning Australians who had been in India from entering Australia. Those who disobeyed could face fines of up to AU$66,000 (US$56,000) or five years in prison. No bans on citizens were put in place following similar spikes in 2020 in the US and UK.

Strict and inflexible domestic travel restrictions inside Australia left families separated and others unable to return home, with individuals refused permission to travel across state borders for compassionate reasons or medical treatment, despite willingness to abide by quarantine restrictions.

In July 2021, Australia had one of the lowest vaccination rates among high-income countries, due to a shortage in vaccine supply and a botched rollout of its national vaccination program.

Although the Australian federal government designated Aboriginal and Torres Strait Islander adults as a priority group for vaccinations in January 2021, vaccination rates for Indigenous communities lagged behind the rate of the total population in most parts of Australia.

In New South Wales, Covid-19 spread quickly inside prisons among prisoners who had not yet been offered the chance to be vaccinated. The state government failed to ensure equitable vaccine access for prisoners, with prisoner vaccination rates lagging well behind the general population.

Freedom of Expression

Human Rights Watch research found that Australian universities are failing to protect the academic freedom of students from China and of academics who criticize the Chinese Communist Party, leaving them vulnerable to harassment and intimidation by Chinese government supporters. Chinese pro-democracy students in Australia alter their behavior and self-censor to avoid threats and harassment from fellow classmates and being "reported on" by them to authorities back home.

A new regulation was introduced into parliament in August that would make it easier to deregister nongovernmental organizations if they promote protests in which minor offenses occur.

Disability Rights

The Royal Commission into Violence, Abuse, Neglect and Exploitation of People with a Disability continued its hearings in 2021, focusing on a range of issues including the experiences of First Nation children with disability in out-of-home care, and concerns that the Covid-19 vaccine rollout for people with disabilities has been too slow.

HUMAN
RIGHTS
WATCH

"They Don't Understand the Fear We Have"

How China's Long Reach of Repression Undermines
Academic Freedom at Australia's Universities

Western Australia's prisons remain damaging and at times deadly for people with disabilities. A Human Rights Watch analysis of deaths in those prisons from 2010-2020 found that about 60 percent of adult prisoners who died had a disability. Due to limited resources, mental health services in prisons are inadequate.

Rights of Older People

The Royal Commission into Aged Care Quality and Safety released its final report in March 2021, calling for fundamental reform of the aged care system, including increased accountability for violations in aged care facilities, minimum staffing requirements, and greater access to home and community support services for older people.

The Covid-19 pandemic has highlighted systemic understaffing and gaps in regulation. Many aged care facilities use dangerous drugs, often without informed consent, to control the behavior of older people with dementia. The government has not banned the practice and has not conducted sufficient monitoring of facilities' compliance with existing regulations.

Terrorism and Counterterrorism

The Australian government has failed to repatriate nationals arbitrarily detained by Kurdish-led authorities in northeast Syria as Islamic State suspects and family members. At time of writing, approximately 80 Australians including 47 children and 20 women remained held in harsh conditions in locked camps and prisons. The government helped bring home eight children from northeast Syria in 2019.

A bill to create new police powers to conduct online surveillance of criminal suspects and take over their accounts was passed by parliament in August, despite the legislation failing to implement safeguards recommended by a parliamentary committee.

Climate Change Policy and Impacts

Australia is among the top 20 emitters and one of the world's biggest per capita emitters of the greenhouse gases responsible for the climate crisis, and the resulting toll on human rights around the globe.

The third largest exporter of fossil fuels globally, Australia's fossil fuel companies also benefit from significant tax breaks, with fossil fuel subsidies increasing 48 percent since the Paris agreement in 2015.

In 2015, the government pledged to reduce emissions by 26 to 28 percent by 2030 compared to 2005 levels. In October, just days before the COP26 Climate conference in Glasgow, Australia announced it had set a target for net zero carbon emissions by 2050. However, it does not include a commitment to end fossil fuels and did not reveal how it would achieve this target.

The government has continued to actively support the expansion of fossil fuel industries at the expense of renewables, approving several new coal mines including one requiring public financing.

In a major ruling in a case brought on behalf of survivors from the devastating 2019-20 bushfires, in August a court in New South Wales ordered the state's Environmental Protection Authority to take concrete and specific steps to safeguard against climate change.

In September, the Western Australia state government announced an end to the logging of native forests in an effort to preserve carbon sinks.

Foreign Policy

In August, the Australian government announced an intention to strengthen its targeted sanctions regime on human rights grounds, but no legislation has been introduced and the scope of the sanctions remains unclear.

Unlike the UK, US, Canada, and the EU, the Australian government has not imposed targeted sanctions on senior military leaders in Myanmar responsible for the February coup and ensuing rights violations.

Australia joined statements condemning the Chinese governments violations in Xinjiang, Hong Kong, and Tibet at the UN Human Rights Council in June, and on Xinjiang at the UN General Assembly in October.

In August, the Senate passed a bill banning the importation of goods made by forced labor, after concerns over human rights abuses in Xinjiang. However, the government voted against the bill in the Senate.

In September, Australia publicly announced that it would back the Indian and South African proposal for a waiver of the TRIPS agreement, the World Trade Organization's intellectual property rules for Covid-19 vaccines and other health products to enable quicker and fairer access for low-income countries.

Australia pledged AU$100 million (US$74 million) in humanitarian assistance to Afghanistan following the Taliban takeover of the country. No action was taken to compensate victims of alleged war crimes by Australian SAS forces as documented in the Brereton report, which found credible information of 23 incidents of unlawful killing, which killed 39 people.

Australia has not endorsed the Safe Schools Declaration, an intergovernmental pledge now supported by 112 countries to protect education in times of conflict.

Azerbaijan

The 2020 truce ending the six-week war between Armenia and Azerbaijan in and around Nagorno-Karabakh largely held, but periodic skirmishes made for a fragile situation on the post-war front lines.

The ceasefire enabled the start of reconstruction in areas where Azerbaijan re-established control. In areas under the control of de-facto Nagorno Karabakh authorities, ethnic Armenians face risk of injury or captivity when they travel, tend to livestock, or engage in farming near the front lines. These and other issues, including Nagorno-Karabakh's long-term status, perpetuated tensions and pointed to the need for greater international involvement.

In March, the government released, under a presidential pardon, nearly 40 opposition activists, religious believers, journalists, human rights defenders, and other perceived critics imprisoned on politically motivated charges. But dozens of others remained wrongfully imprisoned, while authorities targeted critics and other dissenting voices.

In the period since the war's start, tensions between the government and political opposition declined. However, the government remained hostile to dissenting voices. Restrictive laws continued to prevent nongovernmental organizations (NGOs) from operating independently. Reports of torture and ill-treatment persisted throughout the year.

Nagorno Karabakh: Landmines, Prisoners of War (POWs)

In August, the Prosecutor General's Office said that since the ceasefire, 23 Azerbaijani civilians were killed and 36 were injured by anti-personnel and anti-vehicle mines laid in areas that had previously been under Armenian forces' control. Among them were two Azerbaijani journalists and a local official, who were killed on June 4. Landmine contamination in all of the seven regained regions around Nagorno Karabakh is reported to be extensive (See Armenia chapter). Neither Azerbaijan nor Armenia has ratified the international treaty prohibiting anti-personnel landmines.

The fighting compounded the loss of education due to Covid-19-related school closures. According to official data, at least 71 schools were damaged or destroyed on the Armenian side and 54 on the Azerbaijani side. Despite the severe damage to schools during the conflict, Azerbaijan had yet to endorse the Safe Schools Declaration, an international agreement to protect education during armed conflict signed by 112 countries.

Azerbaijani forces subjected numerous Armenian POWs to physical abuse and acts of humiliation. Human Rights Watch also documented torture and other abuse by Azerbaijani forces against Armenian civilians, including against older people, as well as a case of extrajudicial execution in early 2021. Allegations of at least a dozen other extrajudicial executions of Armenian troops and civilians in 2020 and early 2021 also came to light. (See Armenia chapter for allegations of torture and executions of Azerbaijani troops by Armenian/Nagorno-Karabakh forces).

In 2021, Azerbaijan returned more than 100 Armenian POWs and civilian detainees. In September, the Armenian ombudsman's office stated that at least 41 POWs and four civilian captives remained in Azerbaijani custody; the exact number remaining in custody is unclear. The Azerbaijani government refuses to acknowledge any of these detainees as POWs.

Although Azerbaijani authorities consistently claimed that all remaining Armenian soldiers in custody were terrorism suspects, they dropped terrorism charges during the trials against several dozen and convicted them for illegal border crossing and weapons possession. Many were among the 30 whom Azerbaijan released in June and July in exchange for landmine maps.

Azerbaijani courts have also sentenced at least six ethnic Armenians, some of whom are reportedly civilians, on a variety of other charges. The charges include terrorism, espionage, and, in two cases, torturing Azerbaijani citizens during the Karabakh war of the 1990s.

In December 2020, several international media outlets reported that Azerbaijani authorities arrested four servicemen for desecrating the bodies of dead Armenian soldiers and vandalizing gravestones at Armenian cemeteries. At time of writing, they remained in pretrial detention, and no other Azerbaijani forces have been held accountable for crimes during the war.

Prosecuting Political Opposition

In January, Popular Front Party of Azerbaijan (APFP) member Niyameddin Ahmedov faced new, dubious charges of incitement and trafficking in banned items. Ahmedov has been in custody since his May 2020 arrest on financing terrorism charges, which stem from allegations that he received funds from an exiled government critic to destabilize the country and assassinate political figures. Police allegedly beat Ahmedov in custody in an attempt to coerce him to falsely testify against an APFP leader. Ahmedov denies all charges. In October, a court sentenced him to 13 years in prison.

In April, a court sentenced Said Mamedzade Bakuvi, an APFP activist, to three-and-a-half years in prison on bogus hooliganism charges, but in June substituted the penalty with a suspended sentence and released him.

In June, courts handed 12 APFP members, including five party leaders – Fuad Gahramanli, Mammad Ibrahim, Bakhtiyar Imanov, Asif Yusifli and Ayaz Maharramli on suspended sentences ranging from two to four years, on spurious public order violations and other charges related to a pro-war protest a year earlier.

In February, Mehdi Ibrahimov, son of the APFP deputy chairman, received a 15-month suspended sentence on bogus charges of spreading Covid-19.

In March, President Ilham Aliyev pardoned APFP member Mahammad Imanli, who had been sentenced in December 2020 to one year in prison on false criminal charges of spreading Covid-19.

Also in March, police arrested Lachin Valiyev, an opposition activist, on bogus drugs-related charges and allegedly coerced him to give incriminating statements against the APFP leadership. Valiyev confessed the drug charges under apparent duress. He remained in pretrial custody at time of writing.

Other APFP members serving prison sentences on bogus charges handed down in previous years include Alizamin Salayev, Saleh Rustamov, Agil Maharramov, and Pasha Umudov.

In July, an appeals court replaced the house arrest of Tofig Yagublu, a leading politician of the opposition Musavat party, with a 30-month conditional sentence. Yagublu had been under house arrest due to health complications arising from his hunger strike to protest his unjust 2020 conviction on bogus hooliganism charges, for which he had been sentenced to four years and three months in prison.

In May, the Azerbaijani Bar Association, which is seen as closely tied to the government, reinstated lawyers Shahla Humbatova and Irada Javadova, who had been disbarred in previous years in apparent retaliation for their work on politically sensitive cases.

Freedom of Expression

In March, a court sentenced blogger Elchin Hasanzade and activist Ibrahim Salamov to eight months in prison on defamation charges, for corruption and other allegations they made against the head of Mingechevir city's housing and maintenance department. They were released in November.

In February, an appeals court upheld a lower court's spurious high treason verdict against journalist Polad Aslanov, for which he continues to serve a 16-year prison sentence.

In July, a report by the Organized Crime and Corruption Reporting Project (OCCRP) alleged Azerbaijan has been spying on over a thousand independent activists and journalists, using Pegasus surveillance software that gave the government access to their phones. Investigative journalist Khadija Ismayilova and blogger Mehman Huseynov were among those reportedly targeted.

Gender-Based Violence

Gender-based violence remained pervasive but underreported. Serious gaps continued in the official response including lack of protection and recourse for survivors.

Restrictions related to Covid-19 additionally led to a surge in domestic violence, and shelter managers said they saw increases in the numbers of women seeking shelter. Womens' rights activists reported police failure to register or respond to reports of domestic violence, and significant barriers to accessing the few available shelters.

In what appears to be a growing crisis of murders of women by their partners or relatives, victims were often unable to escape abuse due to lack of shelter space and inadequate police response. In July alone, journalists reported that five women were murdered by their partners. In August, Azerbaijan's General Prosecutor's Office released data showing that in the first half of 2021, 33 women in the country had been killed; women's rights researchers said that most were killed by their husbands, partners, or family members. The prosecutor's office publicly encouraged women to use a government hotline to report violence.

On March 8, Baku police briefly detained activists to prevent them from holding an International Women's Day march to protest gender-based violence and to call on the government to ratify the Council of Europe's Convention on the Prevention of Violence against Women and Domestic Violence.

Torture and Ill-Treatment in Detention

Authorities typically dismissed complaints of torture and other ill-treatment in custody, and the practice continued with impunity. Ill-treatment is rampant in police custody, allegedly to coerce confessions, while denying detainees access to family, independent lawyers, or independent medical care.

Throughout 2021, details emerged supporting allegations that in 2017, military and security officials tortured detainees to extract confessions and other testimony on treason charges. Most of the arrests took place in Tatar region, against military personnel. The World Organization Against Torture (OMCT), stated that at least 78 were detained, and 25 sentenced to between 12 and 20 years in prison, in closed trials, "with multiple cases of torture." At least five of the detainees died within days of their arrest in May 2020.

In August, a court sentenced Yunis Safarov, accused of an attempt on the life of the Ganja city mayor, to life imprisonment. Courts sentenced nine other defendants in this case to prison terms from 18 to 20 years. Safarov and all the defendants testified in court that police had beat them repeatedly to elicit confessions and testimony. No effective investigations followed the allegations.

Key International Actors

In February, a group of United Nations human rights special procedures mandate holders called on Armenia and Azerbaijan to investigate "allegations of serious human rights violations committed during the [Nagorno-Karabakh] conflict and its aftermath in order to hold perpetrators to account and provide redress to the victims." The UN human rights experts called for the release of prisoners of war (POWs) captured in the conflict and for the return of bodies to families for burial.

In May, the European Parliament adopted a resolution calling on Azerbaijan to unconditionally release Armenian POWs and ensure their access to lawyers, doctors and human rights defenders. It also urged Azerbaijan to cooperate with the European Court of Human Rights (ECtHR) in investigating reports about inhuman treatment of POWs.

In April, Council of Europe Human Rights Commissioner, Dunja Mijatovic, expressed concern at "dehumanising scenes, including wax mannequins depicting dead and dying Armenians soldiers" that are included in displays at the Trophy Park, dedicated to Azerbaijan's victory in the Nagorno-Karbakh war. Mijatovic said "I consider such images highly disturbing and humiliating." In October, Azerbaijan removed the displays of wax mannequins and the helmets of soldiers seized during the war.

A September resolution by the Parliamentary Assembly of the Council of Europe (PACE) called on Azerbaijani authorities to free all remaining captives and urged Armenian authorities to release all mine maps. It also called on the sides to ensure accountability for the crimes committed during the war.

In March, the US government welcomed the presidential pardon, and called on the government to release everyone "considered to have been incarcerated for exercising their fundamental freedoms." Also in March, US Secretary of State Anthony Blinken called for reinstatement of Humbatova to the Bar Association.

In May, following its human rights dialogue with Azerbaijan, the European Union welcomed the reinstatement of Humbatova and Javadova and highlighted the importance of accountability for violations of international humanitarian law. The EU repeatedly called for Azerbaijan to release all "prisoners and detainees" captured in the Nagorno-Karabakh conflict.

In June, the PACE rapporteur on political prisoners in Azerbaijan said the problem of political prisoners in Azerbaijan, as described in its January 2020 resolution, "has been neither duly recognized nor adequately addressed by the authorities, let alone resolved."

In a separate statement, the PACE Legal Affairs Committee expressed "particular disappointment" at the failure by the Azerbaijani delegation to the Assembly to co-operate with the rapporteur on political prisoners as well as the Azerbaijani authorities' continuing failure to implement fully European Court judgments.

In August, reacting to the spike in killings of women by their families in July, the British Embassy in Azerbaijan expressed concern over the killing of Azerbaijani women, and called on the Azerbaijani government to sign the Istanbul Convention.

Bahrain

Bahraini activists commemorated the 10th anniversary of the 2011 uprising in Bahrain amid continuing heavy repression. Since 2017, Bahraini authorities have banned all independent media in the country and dissolved all significant opposition groups. Authorities failed to hold officials accountable for torture and ill-treatment. Oversight mechanisms are not independent of the government.

Three detainees died in Bahraini prisons in 2021 amid allegations of medical negligence. Health and hygiene conditions in Bahrain's overcrowded prisons remain serious, leading to two major Covid-19 outbreaks. Prison authorities violently suppressed a peaceful sit-in at the Jau Prison, and security forces summoned for interrogation and arrested individuals who participated in protests calling for the release of their family members from detention.

There are 26 individuals currently on death row, all at imminent risk of execution. The government has put six people to death since it ended a moratorium on executions in 2017, most recently in 2019.

Bahrain continued to deny access to independent rights monitors and the United Nations special procedures, including the special rapporteur on torture.

Freedom of Expression, Association, and Peaceful Assembly

Bahrain further restricted online content by amending the Press Law to require that news and broadcasting sites register and obtain Ministry of Information Affairs approval, and to ban electronic media from publishing content that conflicts with "national interest" or the constitution.

Between June 2020 and May 2021, at least 58 people were arrested, detained, or prosecuted for their online activities, Freedom House reported.

In July 2021, it was reported that Bahrain, already believed to be a customer of the NSO Group's Pegasus spyware had entered phone numbers of potential targets into a database, which was leaked. In August 2021, Citizen Lab reported that the iPhones of nine Bahraini activists were successfully hacked with NSO Group's Pegasus spyware between June 2020 and February 2021. NSO Group has repeatedly denied the news reports.

Thirteen prominent dissidents have been serving lengthy prison terms since their arrest in 2011 for their roles in pro-democracy demonstrations. They include Abdulhadi al-Khawaja, a founder of the Bahrain Center for Human Rights, as well as Hassan Mushaima and Abduljalil al-Singace, leaders of the opposition group Al Haq; all are serving life terms.

Al-Singace began a hunger strike on July 8 to protest inhumane prison conditions and to demand that a book that he wrote in prison, and which prison authorities confiscated, be returned to his family. Between July and September, al-Singace lost nearly 20 kilograms and is suffering from pre-existing medical conditions, his family says, for which he has not received adequate treatment.

Shaikh Ali Salman, leader of Al-Wifaq, Bahrain's largest but now forcibly dissolved opposition political society, is also serving a life term after the Court of Cassation upheld his sentence in January 2019 on trumped up charges of allegedly spying for Qatar.

In June 2020, authorities released from prison prominent human rights defender Nabeel Rajab to serve the rest of his 5-year sentence for speech offenses under the 2017 alternative sentencing law.

No independent media have operated in Bahrain since the Information Affairs Ministry suspended *Al Wasat*, the country's only independent newspaper, in 2017. Foreign journalists rarely have access to Bahrain, and Human Rights Watch and other rights groups are routinely denied access.

Death Penalty

The Bahrain Institute for Rights and Democracy (BIRD) and Reprieve found that since the 2011 uprising, 51 people have been sentenced to death. Of those, 26 individuals are currently on death row, all at imminent risk of execution, having exhausted all legal remedies. In July 2020, the Court of Cassation upheld the death sentences of Mohamed Ramadan and Hussein Ali Moosa, despite unfair trials and credible evidence that their convictions were based on confessions coerced under torture.

According to BIRD and Reprieve, of the 51 people sentenced to death since 2011, at least 31 were convicted under Bahrain's overbroad terrorism law, and of those, 20 alleged torture.

Bahrain has executed six men since it ended a moratorium in 2017 on use of the death penalty.

Security Forces and Prisons

At least three prisoners died during 2021, allegedly from the lack of adequate medical care.

On April 6, the Police Media Center announced that Abbas Malallah died of a heart attack, but Malallah's family claimed that during his 10 years in prison he had been suffering from chronic illnesses, and other prisoners told Bahraini rights groups that the Jau prison authorities did not respond to Malallah's pleas for medical attention before he lost consciousness.

Malallah's death prompted protests in Bahrain, including an April 17 sit-in in Jau Prison protesting the prison authorities' medical negligence, particularly during the Covid-19 pandemic. According to a Bahraini human rights activist, the authorities summoned at least 10 protesters for interrogation on April 6, and detained family members of several prominent political prisoners. The UN high commissioner for human rights expressed concern that security forces used "unnecessary and disproportionate force" to dismantle the peaceful sit-in at the prison on April 17 and reportedly held many prisoners incommunicado.

In an apparent response to the Covid-19 pandemic, the Public Prosecution announced on April 8 the release of 73 detainees under the alternative sentencing law. A Covid-19 outbreak at Jau Prison, which is notoriously crowded, led to the death of Husein Barakat on June 9. Bahrain's Interior Ministry has not released accurate information on the number of infections, but rights groups said scores of detainees had contracted Covid-19 and that detainees were not provided with personal protective equipment, adequate medical care, or the ability to communicate with their families.

On July 25, Hasan Abdulnabi, who suffered from sickle cell disease, died amid allegations that he was denied adequate medical treatment at the Dry Dock Detention Center.

Authorities have failed to credibly investigate and prosecute officials and police officers who allegedly committed serious violations, including torture, since the 2011 protests.

Children's Rights

Police beat children arrested in protest-related cases in early February 2021, in the lead up to the 10th anniversary of the uprising in Bahrain, and threatened them with rape and electric shocks. Prosecutors and judges, who refused to allow the children's parents or lawyers to be present during their interrogations and ordered their detention, enabled the abuses. A government report denied that security forces beat, insulted, or threatened to rape the boys.

In a positive development, on February 14, King Hamad bin Isa Al Khalifa approved Law No. 4/2021 on Child Restorative Justice and Protection from Abuse, which raises the age of criminal responsibility from 7 to 15, defines a child as anyone under 18, and provides for special child courts and separate detention facilities for children.

Bahrain did not implement the UN Committee on the Rights of the Child's 2019 recommendation "to explicitly prohibit the use of corporal punishment in all settings"; the Children's Act of 2012 does not address corporal punishment.

Arbitrary Citizenship Revocations

In 2019, King Hamad reinstated the citizenship of 551 individuals and courts restored the nationality of another 147 individuals. Bahrain amended its citizenship revocation laws in 2019, restricting the power to strip nationality to the cabinet. The king and the judiciary no longer have the power to unilaterally strip Bahrainis of their citizenship for national security or terrorism crimes. Citizenship revocations since 2012 had been handed down by the courts, or by royal decree, or by order of the Interior Ministry. Almost 300 persons whom the authorities had stripped of their citizenship in recent years remained without Bahraini nationality, rendering most of them stateless.

Migrant Workers

Abuses against migrant workers, especially migrant domestic workers, worsened during the Covid-19 pandemic. In 2020, the authorities paid the salaries of 100,000 citizens working in the private sector between April and June but did not provide similar benefits to migrant workers who comprise most of Bahrain's workforce. Migrant workers reported facing dismissal, reduced or unpaid wages, and evictions from their accommodation.

In 2017, Bahrain introduced a unified standard contract for domestic workers which requires detailing the nature of the job, rest hours, and days off. But the standard contract does not limit working hours, set out the minimum wage or specify what rest days workers are entitled to.

Bahrain included irregular migrants in its Covid-19 vaccination program.

Women's Rights, Gender Identity, and Sexual Orientation

Bahraini family laws discriminate against women's right to divorce and inherit. Article 353 of the penal code exempts perpetrators of rape from prosecution if they marry their victims. Bahrain's parliament proposed to repeal that article in 2016, but the cabinet rejected the proposal. Article 334 of the penal code reduces the penalties for perpetrators of so-called honor crimes.

In August, women launched a campaign with the Arabic hashtag "Citizenship is My Right and My Children's" to demand the right to transmit Bahraini nationality to their children on an equal basis to men.

Bahrain's penal code criminalizes adultery and sexual relations outside marriage, a violation of the right to privacy which disproportionately harms women and migrant women. Women who are pregnant outside marriage, as well as women who report rape, can find themselves prosecuted for consensual extramarital sex. Although no law explicitly criminalizes same-sex relations, authorities have used vague penal code provisions against "indecency" and "immorality" to target sexual and gender minorities.

In December 2018, Bahrain amended its labor law to ban discrimination based on sex, origin, language or creed, and sexual harassment in the workplace, but the law does not refer to sexual orientation, gender identity, disability, or age.

Key International Actors

Bahrain has not responded to visit requests by the UN special rapporteur on human rights defenders sent in 2012 and 2015. Bahrain has also not responded to visit requests in recent years by the UN special rapporteurs on torture, freedom of expression and freedom of assembly.

Bahrain continued to participate in Yemen military operations as part of the Saudi Arabia-led coalition, which is responsible for serious laws of war violations.

The US maintains a major naval base in Bahrain. The State Department reported in June that the US had active arms sales cases with Bahrain worth more than US$6 billion under the Foreign Military Sales (FMS) program. The United States thanked Bahrain for helping evacuate Afghans after the Taliban took over the country. In August, the Bahraini government allowed evacuation flights from Afghanistan to land at its airport.

On March 24, 22 human rights groups and unions and 57 British members of parliament urged Formula One to conduct an independent inquiry into allegations of human rights abuses associated with the Bahrain Grand Prix, which Bahrain has hosted since 2004.

In March, the European Parliament adopted a resolution deploring Bahrain's human rights abuses and urging the EU to take a more resolute approach, which is yet to materialize. In April, on the 60th birthday of dual Bahraini-EU jailed human rights defender Abdulhadi al-Khawaja, the EU special representative for human rights reiterated a call for his release.

Bangladesh

The ruling Awami League government made clear in 2021 it has no intention of addressing a pattern of grave abuses, including extrajudicial killings, torture, and enforced disappearances by its security forces. Authorities cracked down on critics, journalists, and even children who criticized the government or dared to question its response to the Covid-19 pandemic.

In September, Mohib Ullah, 46, a leader among the nearly one million Rohingya refugees in Bangladesh documenting the Myanmar military's crimes against the Rohingya and advocating for the refugees' rights in international forums, was shot and killed by unidentified gunmen in Kutupalong camp in Cox's Bazar. He had faced death threats in recent years for his work. In the month following, Bangladesh authorities failed to ensure security in the camps and another seven refugees were murdered in an attack on an Islamic seminary in the camp.

In October, the government signed a Memorandum of Understanding with UNHCR to begin operations on Bhasan Char island, where Bangladesh authorities had already relocated almost 20,000 refugees in violation of its commitments to wait for a technical assessment of habitability, safety, sustainability, and protection needs.

From May to August, Bangladesh saw its most deadly wave of Covid-19 infections to date. Hospitals were overwhelmed and health care workers reported a lack of adequate medical equipment.

In October, four people died when police reportedly opened fire to contain a mob, and at least three more people died amid a spate of sectarian violence targeting Bangladesh's Hindu minority. More than 100 are reported injured.

Disappearances and Extrajudicial Killings

Bangladesh security forces continue to commit enforced disappearances and extrajudicial killings with impunity.

In August, after Human Rights Watch released a report documenting enforced disappearances by Bangladesh security forces under the Awami League-led government from 2009 to 2020, the government denied the findings. Officials also

HUMAN
RIGHTS
WATCH

"Where No Sun Can Enter"
A Decade of Enforced Disappearances in Bangladesh

denied allegations made during a briefing held by the Tom Lantos Human Rights Commission of the United States House of Representatives. Relatives of some of those forcibly disappeared said that police refused to accept any complaint that included allegations against law enforcement and that some families faced threats and harassment.

Torture

In February, writer Mushtaq Ahmed died in prison after being held in pretrial detention for nine months for posting criticism of the government's response to the Covid-19 pandemic on Facebook. Ahmed Kabir Kishore, a cartoonist held on similar grounds, filed a legal claim alleging he was tortured and described the torture Mushtaq had also faced in custody.

Law enforcement and intelligence agencies in Bangladesh, as well as police and soldiers seconded into the Rapid Action Battalion (RAB), are credibly accused of torture and ill-treatment of detainees and suspects. Despite insisting that it complies with international law, the government has failed to act on concrete recommendations from the UN Committee Against Torture to prevent and address torture.

Freedom of Expression and Association

Human rights defenders continue to be targeted with surveillance, politically motivated charges, and arbitrary detention.

Authorities use the Digital Security Act (DSA) to harass and indefinitely detain journalists, activists, and others critical of the government, resulting in a chilling effect on expression of dissent. In March, UN High Commissioner for Human Rights Michelle Bachelet called for an overhaul of the DSA. Instead, the Law Ministry approved a proposal to expand the number of special tribunals specifically for these types of cyber "crimes."

At least 80 journalists were reportedly attacked, injured, or killed while performing their jobs in 2021, as of September. Those who expose government corruption or express dissent are particularly at risk. In May, authorities arrested journalist Rozina Islam following her reporting on malpractices in response to the Covid-19 pandemic. At least 17 journalists, a majority of them photographers, were injured covering protests over the visit by Indian Prime Minister Narendra Modi in March. During these protests, there were also reports that Facebook and Facebook Messenger services were restricted in Bangladesh.

Authorities have resorted to targeting the family members in Bangladesh of critical activists and journalists who are living abroad. With widespread repression of the media, journalists in Bangladesh have taken to self-censoring at unprecedented levels.

In May, nine organizations wrote to Michelle Bachelet, the UN High Commissioner for Human Rights, raising concerns over continuing attacks on the media, including arbitrary arrests, torture, and extrajudicial killings.

Covid-19

Bangladesh reported over 1 million new confirmed cases of Covid-19 and more than 20,000 deaths from January through October 2021. Just over 12 percent of the population was fully vaccinated at time of writing.

Overburdened hospitals and a scarcity of much-needed intensive care facilities have exacerbated existing disparities in access to healthcare. As of October, nearly 10,000 healthcare workers also had tested positive for the virus that causes Covid-19, according to the Bangladesh Medical Association.

At time of writing, schools had been closed for more than 450 days since the pandemic's start in 2020. Over 1.6 million students were affected, with many facing barriers to accessing remote education, including lack of internet access, lack of electricity, and needing to work to support their families. A BRAC survey found that more than half of students surveyed were not following government-televised classes. Girls in particular faced barriers to staying in school, and non-governmental organizations reported a concerning rise in child marriage.

Women and Girls' Rights

According to Bangladeshi human rights organization Ain o Salish Kendra, over 200 women were reportedly murdered by their husband or husband's family in 2021. Promises by the Bangladesh government to take sexual and gender-based violence seriously rang hollow, as women and girls faced pervasive sexual violence while the government again stalled on passing a sexual harassment law or making amendments to the discriminatory rape law.

The Bangladesh Policewomen Network launched a strategic plan for 2021-2023 to improve gender equality in the police force.

Sexual Orientation and Gender Identity

Same-sex conduct is criminalized in Bangladesh. In August, 6 men were finally convicted for the brutal murder of prominent Bangladeshi gay rights activists Xulhaz Mannan and Mahbub Rabbi Tonoy in 2016. Yet, five years after the murder, lesbian, gay, bisexual, and transgender people and advocates continued to face violence and threats of violence without adequate protection from the police.

To encourage employment, the authorities announced in June that companies where transgender people make up at least 10 percent of the workforce would be given tax breaks. Many who identify as Hijra, Kothi, or transgender in Bangladesh are facing economic devastation amid the pandemic.

Labor Rights

In July, 52 workers, most of them women and children as young as 12, died after a massive fire broke out at a factory in Rupganj, Narayanganj District. Labor activists said that police subsequently harassed workers and relatives of the deceased who gathered to protest, and alleged that police fired rubber bullets and tear gas amid clashes with the protesters.

In August, international retailers, trade unions, and factory owners signed a new agreement to replace the Bangladesh Accord on Fire and Building Safety.

Refugees

The Bangladesh government has expressed increasing frustration with shouldering the prolonged humanitarian crisis, particularly as the February coup in Myanmar made the prospect of a safe and dignified return for the refugees ever more distant.

HUMAN
RIGHTS
WATCH

"An Island Jail in the
Middle of the Sea"

Bangladesh's Relocation of Rohingya Refugees to Bhasan Char

Instead of working with the UN to shore up resources and improve conditions in the refugee camps, the government relocated nearly 20,000 Rohingya refugees to remote Bhasan Char island. Refugees on the island face inadequate healthcare, lack of education, and barriers to freedom of movement. While the authorities have said relocation to the island is voluntary, a Human Rights Watch report found that many refugees were transferred without full, informed consent and prevented from returning to the mainland or being reunited with their families in Cox's Bazar.

Hundreds have attempted to flee the island, and many have died at sea. Others, caught trying to escape, have been arrested and held without charge for long periods, and some were beaten up by security forces.

The main refugee settlement in Cox's Bazar is severely overcrowded, with risks of communicable diseases, fires, monsoons, and lack of prevention efforts and services for survivors of domestic and sexual violence. Refugees faced tightened restrictions on their rights to information, movement, and livelihood. Education in camp "learning centers" has been halted since March 2020 due to Covid-19 lockdowns.

Bangladesh authorities have prohibited the construction of stronger shelters in the camps capable of withstanding not just the annual monsoon, but also frequent dry-season fires. In March, barbed wire fencing trapped thousands of refugees while a massive fire spread through the camps. The number of fires has been increasing at a disturbing rate—in just the first four months of 2021 there were 84 incidents in the camps, more than in all of 2020.

Climate Change Policies and Actions

Bangladesh is among the countries most vulnerable to the impacts of climate change, despite having contributed little to the greenhouse gas emissions causing rising temperatures. Due to climate change, cyclones will become more intense and frequent, posing a growing threat to tens of millions of people living along the country's low-lying coastline, many of whom could face food insecurity due to reduced agricultural productivity and mass displacement due to rising sea levels.

During 2021, the government announced a scaling back of plans to build coal-fired power plants and the cancellation of numerous proposed projects. However, construction continues on several plants, which, when operational, will not only emit greenhouse gases but also toxic pollutants that impact the health of local populations. The plant under construction at Rampal poses a serious threat to the Sundarbans, the world's largest mangrove forest, a UNESCO world heritage site where rich biodiversity supports the livelihood of hundreds of thousands of people and provides a critical buffer against the impacts of sea level rise and extreme weather.

Key International Actors

In August, the Guernica 37 Chambers law offices made a formal submission to the British Foreign, Commonwealth and Development Office recommending sanctions for 15 current and former senior RAB officers for alleged involvement in human rights abuses and corrupt practices under the Global Human Rights Sanctions Regulations 2020.

In March 2021, UN High Commissioner Bachelet affirmed that "[al]legations of torture and ill-treatment by the Rapid Action Battalion have been a long-standing concern."

Human Rights Watch addressed a letter to Commonwealth Secretary-General Baroness Patricia Scotland calling for her to publicly clarify comments she made praising Prime Minister Sheikh Hasina just days after the death of a dissident writer, Mushtaq Ahmed, in custody.

In February, 13 diplomats expressed grave concern about Ahmed's death and called for "a swift, transparent, and independent inquiry." The government responded by telling the media to "stop giving publicity to this sort of nuisance."

In February, the Bangladesh chief of army staff, Gen. Aziz Ahmed, met with US military officials and high-level UN officials amid the release of a disturbing investigation by Al Jazeera alleging involvement of members of the general's family in abuses by Bangladeshi security forces as well as the commission of grave human rights abuses by military units under his command.

The Al Jazeera investigation documented that the government had illegally purchased highly invasive spyware from Israel. The military reacted to the evidence by saying that the equipment was for an "army contingent due to be deployed in the UN peacekeeping mission." The UN denied that it was deploying such equipment with Bangladeshi contingents in peacekeeping operations and called on Bangladeshi authorities to investigate the claims of corruption.

In August, Israeli digital intelligence agency Cellebrite announced that it would stop selling technology to Bangladesh following reports that it was being used by RAB.

Since 2017, serious shortcomings in Bangladesh's human and labor rights record have jeopardized the trade preferences unilaterally granted by the EU through its Everything But Arms (EBA) scheme.

In September, the US announced it would contribute nearly $180 million in additional humanitarian assistance for Rohingya refugees, Bangladeshi host communities, and the people of Myanmar in response to the Rohingya refugee crisis. The UN's Rohingya Humanitarian Crisis Joint Response Plan for 2021 had about a third of the funding it needed as of August 31.

Belarus

Mass peaceful protests, which had erupted across Belarus in response to President Aliaksandr Lukashenko's manipulation of the August 2020 presidential vote, largely wound down by the end of 2020 due to the government's relentless and vicious crackdown. The authorities, however, escalated smear campaigns and prosecutions against political and civic activists, independent journalists and human rights defenders on trumped up, politically motivated charges. In July, Lukashenko announced a "purge" of civil society, and the authorities went on a rampage shutting down dozens of independent mass media outlets and human rights groups, including the most prominent ones in the country.

At time of writing, at least 862 people were behind bars on politically motivated charges. Some of them faced beatings, threats, ill-treatment, and inhumane detention conditions. The authorities disbarred close to thirty lawyers for representing victims in politically motivated prosecutions and protesting human rights abuses.

Governmental Crackdown on Peaceful Protests

When dispersing peaceful protests, the authorities, including plain-clothes law enforcement officers, resorted to excessive use of force. Police arbitrarily detained people for wearing or exhibiting the white-red-white stripe pattern associated with the protest movement, at times using brutal force, and charged them with violating rules on public gatherings even if they were detained during raids on apartment buildings.

According to Human Rights Center "Viasna," at least 8,712 people were detained in connection with the protests between November 2020 and October 2021 and many of them experienced ill-treatment and/or inhuman detention conditions. Courts sentenced more than half of them to administrative fines and short-term sentences; at least 850 faced criminal charges.

In November 2020, activist Raman Bandarenka died after a vicious beating, allegedly by plain clothed police officers or their proxies. The authorities claimed the police had found him on the street, drunk and already beaten. There has been no effective investigation into his death.

In March, authorities toughened administrative sanctions for violating rules on public gatherings. In June, a set of amendments on the law on mass gatherings entered into force, banning all protests without official permission. Later that month authorities introduced criminal liability for joining at least two unauthorized protests over a year and toughened sanctions for calls for participation in unsanctioned protests and broadly defined extremist crimes.

In August, the governmental Belarusian Investigative Committee completed their preliminary inquiry into the allegations of torture and other ill-treatment of peaceful protesters by law enforcement officers in August 2020 and stated that they found no grounds for launching criminal investigations into the 4,644 claims filed by or on behalf of the alleged victims.

Freedom of Expression and Attacks on Journalists

The Belarusian Association of Journalists (BAJ) documented 184 cases of arbitrary detention, fines, use of excessive force against and administrative arrests of journalists between January and mid-November 2021. At time of writing, 26 journalists were behind bars on bogus criminal charges, another two media workers were under house arrest and one sentenced to 18 months of restriction of liberty without imprisonment.

In May, Belarusian authorities forced down a Ryanair flight on false pretenses of a terrorist threat and detained Raman Pratasevich, former chief-editor of a leading opposition Telegram channel Nexta, which Belarusian authorities had banned as "extremist," and his girlfriend Sofya Sapega, a Russian national. In the weeks following their arrest, governmental broadcasters ran interviews with Pratasevich purportedly confessing, evidently under duress, to organizing mass riots and naming his supposed associates. At time of writing, Pratasevich was under house arrest on charges of "organizing mass riots," "organizing activities violating public order," and "inciting hatred." Sapega was also under house arrest on charges of "organizing mass riots" and "inciting hatred."

During the year, courts sentenced four journalists—Katsiaryna Andreyeva (Bakhvalava), Daria Chultsova, Katsiaryna Barysevich and Siarhei Hardziyevich—to prison terms ranging from six to 24 months over their reporting on peaceful protests.

Authorities targeted dozens of journalists as witnesses and suspects in trumped up criminal cases and subjected them to house searches, interrogations, and harassment. At least four journalists reported beatings and ill-treatment while in custody, including inhumane detention conditions and denial of medical assistance, in reprisal for their work.

Authorities also cracked down on online media outlets that reported on public protests and exposed human rights violations. The government stripped them of media licenses, raided their offices and the homes of their employees, blocked their websites and banned some of the outlets as extremist. The crackdown on the leading news outlet in the country TUT.by and Poland-based broadcaster Belsat was particularly brutal. Authorities banned them as extremist and subjected dozens of their employees to searches and detentions under criminal and administrative charges.

Belarusian state-owned printing houses refused to print at least five independent newspapers.

In June, a set of amendments to the law on mass media entered into force, further expanding official grounds for revoking accreditations and blocking media websites. Amendments prohibited livestreams of unauthorized mass protests and outlawed publications that "discredit" the state, effectively banning all forms of criticism.

Human Rights Defenders, Civil Society Groups, and Lawyers

In the months following peaceful protests after the 2020 presidential election, authorities escalated the crackdown against human rights groups. Human rights defenders and their family members faced repeated intrusive searches, arbitrary detention and being held in inhumane detention conditions, beatings, interrogations, smear campaigns, as well as petty and cruel forms of harassment. Dozens of human rights defenders were jailed on trumped up criminal charges.

In February, law enforcement officials carried out a nationwide wave of raids targeting human rights defenders and journalists. Authorities claimed the searches of homes and offices were part of their investigation into alleged financing of protests by those organizations. Human rights defender Dzmitry Salauyou was severely beaten by law enforcement officers during and immediately after the search of his home.

In July, authorities carried out an even harsher wave of raids, detaining 11 human rights defenders. Leading local human rights organization Viasna was hit particularly hard. At time of writing, the group's leader Ales Bialiatski, vice-chair Valentin Stefanovich, lawyer Uladzimir Labkovich, and four other members remained behind bars on trumped up criminal charges, including of "tax evasion," "actions violating public order," and "participation in criminal organization."

On November 3, court in Homiel sentenced the head of Viasna's Homiel office Leanid Sudalenka and Viasna's volunteer Tatsiana Lasitsa to three and two-and-a half-years in prison, respectively.

By mid-November 2021, authorities initiated the process of closing 278 human rights groups and organizations, including BAJ. In September, the Belarusian Supreme Court upheld the Ministry of Justice's lawsuit for the liquidation of the Belarusian Helsinki Committee, one of the oldest and most prominent rights groups in the country.

Authorities also shut down the Office for the Rights of Persons with Disabilities, the leading disability rights organization in Belarus. Director Siarhei Drazdouski and lawyer Aleh Hrableuski spent six months under house arrest and in detention, respectively, on spurious fraud charges. They remain suspects in the case.

Over the past year, authorities have increasingly targeted lawyers in retaliation for speaking out on rights issues or representing clients in politically motivated cases. The Ministry of Justice arbitrarily disbarred or revoked the licenses of at least 27 lawyers. Lawyers also faced criminal and administrative charges, searches, and harassment.

Authorities violated fundamental due process protections including interfering with the work of lawyers by recording their confidential conversations with clients and sharing those video recordings with governmental broadcasters, forcing them to sign overly broad nondisclosure agreements, arbitrarily denying them access to their clients, and questioning clients without them present.

In November, amendments to the law on the bar and advocates entered into force, requiring all practicing lawyers to be employed by regional bar associations controlled by the Ministry of Justice, further undermining the independence of the legal profession in the country.

Arrest and Harassment of Political Opposition Members and Supporters

Authorities continued to prosecute political opposition members and their supporters detained before and after the 2020 presidential elections.

In July, the Supreme Court sentenced Viktar Babarika, one of the former presidential contenders, to 14 years in prison on charges of "grand bribery" and "large-scale laundering of illicit funds." In March, authorities indicted Siarhei Tsikhanouski, also a former presidential contender and the husband of Sviatlana Tsikhanouskaya, current leading representative of political opposition in exile, on charges of "mass riots," "inciting hatred," "obstructing the work of central election commission," and "organizing activities violating public order." Siarhei Tsikhanouski has been detained since May 2020. In September, a Minsk court sentenced Maryia Kalesnikava and Maksim Znak, members of the presidium of the opposition's Coordination Council, to 11 and 10 years' imprisonment, respectively, on charges of "conspiracy to seize power" and "calls for actions aimed at harming national security.," Their trial was not open to the public. While in pretrial detention, Kalesnikava reported threats and ill-treatment.

Death Penalty

Belarus remains the only country in Europe to carry out the death penalty. Currently, at least one person, Viktar Syarhel, convicted of murder, is on death row in Belarus.

In 2021, Belarusian authorities allegedly executed two people. In September, state TV channel STV reported the execution of Viktar Skrundzik who had been sentenced to death having been convicted of murder and attempted murder. In June, Viktar Paulau, who had been sentenced to death following a conviction for murdering two people, was executed, according to his sister. However, at time of writing, Skrundzik's and Paulau's families have received no official confirmation of their respective executions. In Belarus, families of executed persons are typically informed by the authorities about the execution several weeks after it had taken place.

In April, Lukashenko granted a "clemency" (replacement of death sentence with life imprisonment) to two brothers, Stanislau and Illia Kostseu, who had been on death row since January 2020, convicted of murder. This is the second known "act of clemency" in Lukashenko's 27 years in office.

In September, Lukashenko said he would consider holding a referendum on the death penalty.

Key International Actors

In March, the United Nations Human Rights Council (UNHRC) condemned the ongoing grave violations of human rights in Belarus and tasked the UN high commissioner for human rights—with assistance from relevant experts—to report on the situation and collect and preserve evidence of human rights violations. As a result, the Office of the High Commissioner for Human Rights (OHCHR) appointed three experts and set up the OHCHR examination on Belarus to monitor the situation, assess evidence and advance accountability.

In July, UNHRC extended the mandate of the special rapporteur on the situation of human rights in Belarus for a period of one year and urged Belarusian authorities to cooperate with the mandate. The annual report by the current rapporteur, Anaïs Marin, documented the unprecedented human rights crisis in Belarus, including police violence against peaceful protesters, cases of enforced disappearance, allegations of torture and ill-treatment, and the repressions against civil society.

Over the past year, Marin and other UN human rights mandates repeatedly called on Belarus to end the excessive use of force, arrests, arbitrary detention and ill-treatment against protesters and the repression of journalists and media personnel. UN Secretary-General António Guterres condemned the use of force against protesters.

In March, 14 Belarusian and international human rights organizations launched the International Accountability Platform for Belarus with the support of numerous governments. The platform collects evidence of alleged human rights crimes in Belarus for future prosecutions.

Some European states, including Lithuania, Germany, Poland, and the Czech Republic opened criminal investigations under the principle of universal jurisdiction into the gross human rights violations perpetrated by Belarusian authorities.

In response to the forced landing of the Ryanair flight, Pratasevich's arrest and egregious human rights abuses in Belarus, the European Union, the United States, the United Kingdom, and Canada imposed further sanctions against Belarusian individuals and entities deemed responsible for the human rights violations and repression, as well as targeted economic sanctions.

The UN Human Rights Office and UN human rights experts expressed outrage over the Ryanair flight's forced landing. Guterres called for a "full, transparent and independent investigation" into the forced landing of the plane and Pratasevich's subsequent detention. The European Parliament also adopted a resolution condemning the forced landing of the flight and the political crackdown in Belarus. EU High Representative Josep Borrell repeatedly criticized the attacks against critics of the government, journalists, and protesters.

In January, the general rapporteur of the Parliamentary Assembly of the Council of Europe (PACE) condemned the death sentence handed down in the case of Skrundzik, calling on Belarus to abolish capital punishment. In June, the EU condemned the likely execution of Paulau, calling for transparency in the Belarusian penal system.

Bolivia

Political interference has plagued Bolivia's justice system for years. The Jeanine Áñez government (November 2019-2020) pursued baseless charges against political opponents. The Luis Arce government (November 2020 to date) supports unsubstantiated and excessive charges of terrorism and genocide against former President Áñez, and in February 2021, issued an amnesty for crimes related to the country's 2019 political crisis that appeared designed to favor his supporters. In response to a report issued in August by a group of international experts, President Arce revoked the amnesty and promised to reform the justice system.

The international experts documented serious human rights violations during the Áñez interim government, including two brutal massacres by security forces and acts of violence "instigated" under the preceding government of Evo Morales (January 2006-November 2019). They exposed failures by the Attorney General's Office to conduct adequate investigations and ensure accountability for these crimes.

Women and girls remain at high risk of violence. Prison overcrowding and excessive pretrial detention continue. Indigenous communities face obstacles to exercise their right under international law to free, prior, and informed consent to measures that may affect them, and are severely affected by fires set by farmers that spread to Indigenous lands.

Judicial Independence

Former President Evo Morales weakened judicial independence during his almost 14 years in power. The 2009 constitution empowered voters to elect high court judges from lists created by the Plurinational Assembly; legislators from Morales' party—the Movement toward Socialism (MAS, in Spanish)—packed the lists with its supporters. In 2010, all judges appointed before 2009 were deemed "temporary." Scores were summarily removed.

During Morales' government, prosecutors filed what appeared to be politically motivated charges against several of his political rivals.

About 80 percent of judges and prosecutors remain "temporary," heightening the risk that, in order to remain in their positions, they will issue decisions to please the authorities.

To further its interests, the government of President Áñez publicly pressured prosecutors and judges, leading to criminal investigations, many apparently politically motivated, of more than 150 people linked to the Morales government, for sedition, terrorism, or membership in a criminal organization.

After winning the October 2020 presidential election, Luis Arce, from MAS, said the justice system should be independent from politics. In November 2020, he established a commission of experts to propose reforms.

However, in February 2021, President Arce decreed an amnesty that opened the door to impunity for serious crimes and appeared designed to favor his supporters. In March, authorities detained Áñez and two of her former ministers on terrorism and other charges for their alleged participation in a coup against Morales in November 2019. In August, the attorney general accused Áñez of genocide in connection with two massacres that occurred during her government. Human Rights Watch examined the charging documents and did not find evidence that she had committed terrorist acts or genocide.

Áñez remained in pretrial detention as of November 3. In August, the United Nations Office in Bolivia called on the government to provide suicide prevention and other services to ensure her health.

Also in August, the Interdisciplinary Group of Independent Experts (GIEI, in Spanish), which was established under a government agreement with the Inter-American Commission on Human Rights, issued a report exposing the lack of independence in the judicial system. In response, the Arce administration revoked the February 2021 amnesty decree. In October, his government signed an agreement with UN agencies to reform the justice system that includes receiving recommendations from national and international experts.

Protest-Related Violence and Abuses

The GIEI report documented the deaths of 37 people in the context of protests over contested October 2019 elections. It concluded that, during the Áñez government, security forces had executed 20 pro-Morales protesters and injured more than 170 people in massacres in Sacaba (Cochabamba) and Senkata (La Paz). The report provided robust evidence of illegal detentions, sexual violence, and "systematic" torture by police forces in the predominantly Indigenous city of El Alto, as well as other abuses throughout the country. It also asserted that the police had failed to protect people from violence committed by both pro- and anti-Morales supporters, and in some locations it had encouraged and collaborated with violent groups of anti-Morales supporters that acted as "para-police" forces. The report also documented acts of violence "instigated" by the Morales administration, such as injuries, abductions, and torture of anti-Morales protesters.

The GIEI highlighted major flaws in the investigations into those abuses and called on the Attorney General's Office to reopen cases it had closed without taking important investigative steps.

Authoritarian-Era Abuses

Bolivia has only prosecuted a few of the officials responsible for human rights violations committed under authoritarian governments between 1964 and 1982, partly because the armed forces have at times refused to share information.

A truth commission created in 2016 presented its final report to President Arce in March 2021, documenting killings, forced disappearances, and torture during that period, allegedly by state agents. The 11-volume report calls for the prosecution of those responsible. As of November 3, only the executive summary was available online.

Covid-19

Bolivia had more than half-a-million confirmed Covid-19 cases and nearly 20,000 deaths as of October 27, although government data is likely to significantly undercount deaths. About 30 percent of the population had been fully vaccinated and an additional 29 percent had received one shot of a two-dose vaccine, as of October 27.

The Áñez government closed schools in March 2020. In August, it cancelled the rest of the school year, which was scheduled to end in December. Classes restarted in February 2021, mostly online. Thousands of students could not access classes for lack of devices or internet. By September, 77 percent of schools had resumed some in-person classes, the government said.

Detention Conditions

In April 2020, to reduce severe prison overcrowding in response to Covid-19, the Áñez administration issued a decree releasing certain categories of detainees. In February 2021, the Arce administration issued a similar decree. The decrees led to the release of 1,162 and 787 detainees, respectively, by July 2021, the Ombudsperson's Office said.

However, the impact on the total number of people in detention has been very small. Bolivian prisons and jails held 18,126 people in January 2020; 17,863 people in February 2021; and 17,908 in August 2021. Detention centers hold more than 2.5 times more detainees than they were built to accommodate, making social distancing virtually impossible.

Bolivia's justice system continues to use pretrial detention excessively. Sixty-five percent of detainees are awaiting trial, the Ombudsperson's Office reported.

In November 2020, the Ombudsperson's Office documented overcrowding in 4 of Bolivia's 16 juvenile detention centers, and inadequate access to health care, education, and sanitation.

Freedom of Expression and Access to Information

The GIEI report documented dozens of physical attacks against journalists by police, soldiers, and demonstrators during the 2019 election-related protests. The report concluded authorities had failed to conduct adequate investigations of these attacks.

The National Press Association, which represents the country's main print media, reported several cases of violence by police or demonstrators against reporters in 2021.

In August 2021, the government accused media outlets of "lying" and serving foreign interests, and singled out several newspapers because of their criticism of the administration. The National Press Association rejected the accusations and defended freedom of the press.

The constitution asserts the right of access to information, but Bolivia lacks a law to implement that right. The government said it was working on an access to information bill but had not presented it as of November 3, 2021. Comunidad Ciudadana, the largest opposition party in Congress, introduced its own bill in February.

Indigenous Rights

The 2009 constitution includes comprehensive guarantees of Indigenous peoples' rights to collective land titling, intercultural education, prior consultation on development projects, and protection of Indigenous justice systems.

Yet Indigenous peoples continue to face barriers to exercise their right to free, prior, and informed consent regarding measures that may affect them.

The Center for Legal Studies and Social Research (CEJIS), a Bolivian non-governmental organization, estimates that more than 5 million hectares of land in Indigenous territories in the Amazon and other lowland ecosystems—about 42 percent of such territories—were burned between 2010 and 2020. CEJIS reported that farmers set the fires to clear land near the Indigenous territories, a practice facilitated by legislation that extended the area of the Amazon Forest available for agricultural use, granted amnesties for illegal deforestation, and only established a small fine for setting fires without a permit.

Women's and Girls' Rights

Women and girls remain at high risk of violence, despite a 2013 law establishing comprehensive measures to prevent and prosecute gender-based violence. The law created the crime of "femicide," which it defines as the killing of a woman under certain circumstances, including domestic violence.

The attorney general reported 113 femicides in 2020—a 3 percent drop from 2019—and 95 from January through October 31, 2021.

Under Bolivian law, abortion is not a crime when a pregnancy results from rape or it is necessary to protect the life or health of a pregnant woman or girl. However, most staff interviewed by the Ombudsperson's Office in 39 health centers that should perform abortions in those circumstances either did not know the requirements for a legal abortion or cited more requirements than those provided for by the law. In addition, half of those centers lacked adequate facilities to perform abortions and 77 percent lacked multidisciplinary teams mandated by law.

Sexual Orientation

In December 2020, the national civil registry abided by a court order and registered a gay couple's relationship as a "free union." In June 2021, however, it denied the same right to a lesbian couple, which has since filed an administrative appeal. The gay couple's case is pending before the Constitutional Court, which is expected to determine whether all same-sex couples can join in "free unions."

Key International Actors

In 2017, Bolivia's Constitutional Court revoked the existing constitutional limit on reelection, arguing that it violated the human rights of then-President Evo Morales. In August 2021, the Inter-American Court of Human Rights issued an advisory opinion requested by Colombia, which concluded that barring unlimited presidential reelection did not violate human rights but rather ensured plurality and prevented the perpetuation of power in the hands of one person. Although not binding, the court's advisory opinions are authoritative interpretations of regional human rights law.

In December 2020, Bolivia, along with Mexico, voted against an Organization of American States (OAS) resolution condemning "fraudulent" elections in Venezuela. In March 2021, Bolivia voted against a UN Human Rights Council resolution urging Nicaragua to repeal or amend legislation that may unduly restricts freedom of expression and association. In June, it voted against an OAS resolution calling on Nicaraguan President Daniel Ortega's government to release illegally detained presidential opposition candidates, and in October it abstained from another OAS resolution making the same call.

Bosnia and Herzegovina

There was little visible progress on human rights in Bosnia and Herzegovina (BiH) in 2021. Public officials stirred xenophobia, failed to tackle discrimination, and put pressure on journalists. War crimes prosecutions slowed. Protections for women and lesbian, gay, bisexual and transgender (LGBT) people are inadequate.

Discrimination and Intolerance

In December 2020, the first local elections in 12 years were held in Mostard. Due to disagreements about election law among the main ethnic parties, voters last had the chance to elect the city government in 2008. Additional disagreements between the main parties meant it took two additional months and a joint intervention by diplomats before the city council elected a new mayor.

In March 2021, the Council of Europe Committee of Ministers criticized the 11-year failure of political leaders in BiH to implement a European Court of Human Rights ruling to amend the constitution and election laws to end political discrimination against Jews, Roma, and others.

In April, the Roma Information Center, Kali Sara, reported that Roma were especially impacted during the Covid-19 pandemic because about 35-40 percent had no insurance needed to access health care. In the 2020/21 school year, Roma, people living in poverty, and children with disabilities experienced greater obstacles in accessing online education due to lack of devices, reliable internet, and special assistance.

A June European Parliament resolution called on the government to adopt a de-institutionalization strategy for people with disabilities and condemned a law allowing them to be deprived of their legal capacity, or the right to make decisions for themselves.

In July, the Constitutional Court of BiH found the practice of "two schools under one roof" discriminates against children because it physically segregates children at school based on ethnicity.

The Organization for Security and Co-operation in Europe (OSCE) recorded 98 hate crimes between January and August 2021, mainly based on ethnicity or religion. At time of writing, there were seven ongoing trials against perpetrators.

Accountability for War Crimes

The Revised National War Crimes Processing Strategy adopted in 2020 called for the most serious war crimes to be processed by the end of 2023. However, in 2021, the OSCE documented a decline in the number of prosecuted cases generally. In the first six months of 2021, the state prosecutor indicted only two people for war crimes, one of whom was already in prison.

As of August, 250 war crimes cases involving 502 defendants were pending before courts in BiH, according to the OSCE. A lack of willingness in the region to extradite those on war crimes charges means that 80 of the defendants outside of BiH cannot be brought to trial.

According to the OSCE, in the first six months of 2021, courts in BiH rendered first instance judgments in 12 cases against 22 defendants, of whom 14 were found guilty. In the same period, 5 cases against 10 defendants ended with final judgments being rendered, and 10 found guilty.

There are currently 57 pending cases against 125 defendants involving allegations of conflict-related sexual violence. In the first six months of 2021, first instance judgments were rendered in 4 cases against 8 defendants, of whom 3 were convicted, and 1 final judgment was rendered with 1 defendant convicted before Court of BiH.

The Bosnian state failed again to financially compensate a woman raped in the war as recommended by the UN Committee Against Torture (CAT) in 2019.

In June, an appeals panel of the International Residual Mechanism for Criminal Tribunals upheld the 2017 genocide conviction and life sentence of Bosnian Serb wartime military commander Ratko Mladić.

The same month, in a press release by the United Nations High Commissioner for Human Rights and the UN special adviser on prevention of genocide, the special adviser warned against increasing glorification of convicted war criminals in Bosnia.

Asylum Seekers and Migrants

The Service for Foreigner's Affairs between January and August registered 10,075 irregular arrivals with 9,057 persons expressing an intention to apply for asylum; a slight decrease compared to the same period in 2020.

According to the UN Refugee Agency (UNHCR), in the first half of 2021, 67 persons submitted asylum applications and 31 were issued decisions, with 1 granted refugee status, and 4 subsidiary protection. Average processing time nearly doubled since 2018, from 223 to 419 days in 2021. According to UNHCR, this has led many people to abandon the process before a decision is issued.

Five state-operated reception centers are mostly overcrowded and around 1,500 migrants had to be accommodated elsewhere. Routine violent pushbacks into Bosnia by Croatian police exacerbate the poor situation for migrants, who often depend on civil society for medical care and basic needs.

Hostility against migrants was amplified during the local elections with some mayoral candidates in border towns running on an anti-migrant and refugee platform. People working on migration issues faced attacks and threats.

Domestic and Other Gender-Based Violence

After delays and criticism by the EU Delegation in Bosnia, the Federation of BiH entity adopted a draft law on protection from domestic violence. The draft was sent for a 60-day public discussion at the time of writing.

Ombudswoman Jasminka Dzumhur stated in March 2021 that criminal legislation in Bosnia does not align with obligations to combat gender-based violence in the Convention on Preventing and Combating Violence against Women and Domestic Violence, known as Istanbul Convention, which Bosnia ratified in 2013.

The European Parliament in September urged the Bosnian authorities to harmonize and implement legislation in line with the Istanbul Convention. The body responsible for monitoring compliance with the Istanbul Convention visited Bosnia in October to evaluate its implementation.

Sexual Orientation and Gender Identity

Research published in June by the Sarajevo Open Center, an LGBTI and women's rights group, found that lesbian, gay, bisexual, transgender and intersex people face discrimination in education, employment, and housing. According to the Ombuds Office report in May, there has not been much concrete progress in ensuring equality for people in same-sex partnerships.

The third Sarajevo Pride march went without incident despite an anti-LGBT protest on the same day. In 2021, local cantonal government provided over US$15,000 for security during the event, a cost march organizers previously had to cover.

Between January and September 2021, the Sarajevo Open Center recorded seven hate incidents against LGBTI people, two of which were physical attacks.

Freedom of Media

According to information provided to Human Rights Watch by the journalists' association BH Novinari, between January and July 2021, there were 42 threats against journalists, of which one was a physical attack. BH Novinari recorded several complaints from journalists against police and officials in Lipa migrant camp including threats, improper denial of access and forcing journalists to delete recorded material. An employee of the Ministry for Human Rights and Refugees was disciplined for threatening a journalist.

A September survey by BH Novinari involving 440 media professionals showed that in the last three years, over 40 percent of respondents indicated they had been subject to threats and intimidation, in most cases by politicians and public officials.

Following smears against journalist Tanja Topic by the Chairman of the BiH Presidency Milorad Dodik in May 2021, diplomats in Bosnia called on public officials to refrain from threats and misogynistic comments against media professionals.

BH Novinari registered increased gender-based violence against women in the media, with 70 incidents over five years, including death threats, verbal and physical threats, and discrimination at work.

Brazil

President Jair Bolsonaro has threatened democratic rule in Brazil by attempting to undermine trust in the electoral system, free speech, and judicial independence. In a forceful response, the Supreme Court in 2021 rejected "threats to its independence and intimidation."

President Bolsonaro continued to flout scientific recommendations to prevent the spread of the Covid-19 virus. A congressional investigation uncovered evidence of corruption in the purchase of vaccines.

Police killings reached the highest number on record in 2020. About 80 percent of the victims were Black.

Deforestation continued to ravage the Amazon rainforest. Indigenous people and others who defended it suffered threats and attacks.

Threats to Democratic Rule

President Bolsonaro has harassed and tried to intimidate the Supreme Court, which is overseeing four criminal investigations into his conduct, including whether he interfered with federal police appointments to further his personal interests and whether he committed malfeasance in a corruption case involving the purchase of Covid-19 vaccines.

In August 2021, he threatened to respond to the investigations with actions "not within the bounds of the constitution" and asked the Senate to impeach Justice Alexandre de Moraes, who is overseeing most of them. The Senate president rejected the petition.

In September, President Bolsonaro said he would not obey Justice Moraes' decisions. The Supreme Court responded that insulting justices and encouraging non-compliance with judicial decisions "are anti-democratic, illegal, and intolerable practices." President Bolsonaro later retracted his statement about Justice Moraes.

President Bolsonaro has sought to discredit Brazil's electoral system, making unproven claims of electoral fraud. Congress rejected changes he promoted to the system. He later signaled that he might try to cancel elections unless his proposals are implemented.

Freedom of Expression and Access to Information

The Bolsonaro administration has pursued prison sentences against at least 17 critics, including by using a military-era National Security Law. Although many of the cases have been closed, such actions send the message that criticizing the president can lead to persecution.

In August 2021, Congress revoked the National Security Law, but it has not revoked similar penal code provisions that punish defamation with prison terms and can be used to stifle free speech.

President Bolsonaro harassed and insulted the media and individual reporters 87 times during the first half of 2021, Reporters without Borders, a nongovernmental organization (NGO), reported.

He routinely blocks critics on the social media accounts he uses to discuss matters of public interest, violating their free speech rights. In September 2021, he issued a decree that would have impeded social media platforms from eliminating harmful misinformation. After the Senate rejected the decree and the Supreme Court suspended it, he sent a bill with similar provisions to Congress.

In February 2021, the Bolsonaro administration created a working group—without participation from Congress, judicial authorities, or civil society—to propose changes to the National Human Rights Program, the most important instrument of human rights policy in Brazil. The government told Human Rights Watch it could not provide information about these discussions because they were secret.

Covid-19

Brazil had 21 million confirmed Covid-19 cases and 609,447 deaths as of November 7—the second largest death toll in the world in absolute numbers.

President Bolsonaro continued to flout World Health Organization (WHO) recommendations and to promote ineffective drugs against Covid-19. The Supreme Court rejected two petitions he had filed to strike down decrees by governors that established social distancing measures. At an event in June 2021, the president, who frequently joins crowds without a mask, asked a child to remove her mask, and took off another child's mask.

A congressional inquiry into the Covid-19 response found that the federal government and local officials had failed to ensure provision of oxygen to hospitals in Amazonas state, leading to dozens of deaths in January 2021. It also found evidence of corruption in the purchase of vaccines and other failures in the government response.

The Brazilian government has failed to address the huge impact of the Covid-19 pandemic on education. Brazilian schools were mostly closed for 69 weeks between March 2020 and August 2021 due to Covid-19, UNESCO reported. Lack of access to adequate devices and internet connectivity necessary for online education excluded millions of children from schooling, particularly Black and Indigenous children, and those from low-income households.

Detention Conditions

The cramped quarters, poor ventilation, and inadequate health care services prevalent in Brazil's detention centers created an increased risk of Covid-19 outbreaks. As of December 2020, about 670,000 adults were being held in jails and prisons, exceeding maximum capacity by 47 percent, and another 139,000 were under house arrest, the Justice Ministry reported. In February 2021, the National Mechanism for the Prevention and Combat of Torture (MNPCT, in Portuguese) reported up to 13 people were being held in cells designed for one person in a prison in Acre state.

Since 2020, the National Council of Justice (CNJ, in Portuguese), which regulates the judicial system, has recommended that judges reduce pretrial detention during the pandemic and consider house arrest or early release for certain detainees.

Yet a study by the NGO Institute for the Defense of the Right to a Defense (IDDD, in Portuguese) showed that São Paulo state judges only released 1 out of 4 detainees who met the CNJ's conditions in 2020.

The state of São Paulo told Human Rights Watch that about 9,800 detainees had been released in response to the pandemic up to September 2021.

More than 92,800 detainees and staff had contracted Covid-19 and 582 had died as of October 31, the CNJ reported. The MNPCT said the number of deaths is likely an underestimate.

The government told Human Rights Watch that about 10,500 children and young adults were being held in juvenile detention centers as of September 2021, but the figure excludes five states for which it did not have data. More than 2,900 children and about 8,400 staff had been infected with Covid-19 as of October 31, the CNJ reported. The virus had killed 113 staff but no children.

Public Security and Police Conduct

After two years in decline, the number of homicides rose almost 5 percent in 2020.

Police killed more than 6,400 people in 2020—the last year for which data is available—the highest number of any year on record, the NGO Brazilian Forum for Public Security (FBSP in Portuguese) reported.

While some police killings are in self-defense, many result from illegal use of force. Police abuses contribute to a cycle of violence that undermines public security and endangers the lives of civilians and police alike. In 2020, 194 police officers were killed, 72 percent while off duty, the FBSP reported.

In March 2021, Rio de Janeiro's new attorney general dissolved the prosecutor unit specialized in police abuse. Despite a Supreme Court ruling that only allowed raids in Rio's impoverished neighborhoods during the pandemic in "exceptional cases," police conducted the deadliest raid in the state's history on May 6, leaving an officer and 27 residents dead. Witnesses said police executed at least three suspects and destroyed crime scene evidence. Police classified the report and other important information about the raid as secret for five years. Media reported that police refused to provide the victims' clothing to prosecutors, forcing them to seek a judicial order to search police facilities. In October, prosecutors charged two officers with tampering with crime scene evidence, and one of them with homicide.

Rio police killed 1,096 people from January through September 2021, a 17 percent increase from the same period in 2020.

On-duty police in São Paulo killed 353 people from January through September, a 39 percent decrease. In June, the Superior Court of Justice reinstated the convictions against 73 police for the 1991 killing of 111 inmates in Carandiru prison, which a São Paulo court had overturned in 2018.

Military-Era Abuses

President Bolsonaro and members of his cabinet have repeatedly praised the military dictatorship of 1964-1985, which was marked by widespread torture and killings.

A 1979 amnesty law has shielded perpetrators from justice. The Supreme Court upheld the law in 2010, but the Inter-American Court of Human Rights ruled that it violated Brazil's international legal obligations.

Since 2010, federal prosecutors have brought charges against about 60 former agents of the dictatorship. Courts have dismissed most cases, citing either the amnesty law or the statute of limitations. But in June 2021, in a case involving the enforced disappearance of a naval officer who opposed the 1964 coup, a judge issued the first criminal conviction of an agent of the dictatorship, ruling that kidnapping is not subject to the amnesty law.

Sexual Orientation and Gender Identity

About 30 trans people were elected to office in the 2020 local elections—up from only 8 in 2016. Several reported threats after taking office in 2021, including a Rio de Janeiro councilwoman who had to leave the country temporarily.

The national Human Rights Ombudsperson's Office received about 1,100 complaints of violence, discrimination, and other crimes against lesbian, gay, bisexual, and transgender (LGBT) persons between January and October 2021. In Ceará state, two trans girls, aged 13 and 16, were brutally killed in January and April.

Women's and Girls' Rights

The adoption of the 2006 "Maria da Penha" law against gender-based violence was an important step, but implementation has lagged.

In 2020, more than one million cases of domestic violence and about 5,500 cases of femicide—defined under Brazilian law as the killing of women "on account of being persons of the female sex"—were pending before the courts.

Reports of attacks against women resulting in injuries filed at police stations fell 7 percent in 2020, while calls to a police hotline to report domestic violence increased 16 percent, suggesting women may have had difficulty going to police stations during the Covid-19 pandemic. In 2020, 3,913 women were reported killed, about the same number as in 2019.

Abortion is legal in Brazil only in cases of rape, to save a woman's life, or when the fetus has anencephaly, a condition that makes survival difficult.

Only 42 hospitals were performing legal abortions in 2020, the NGO Article 19 and the news websites AzMina and Gênero e Número reported, compared to 76 in 2019.

The Health Ministry issued a regulation allowing telemedicine during the pandemic, but in a later "informative note," it called on health providers to exclude abortion care. Some health professionals were still providing such care as of October.

Women and girls who have unsafe and illegal abortions not only risk injury and death but face up to three years in prison, while people who perform illegal abortions face up to four years in prison.

Disability Rights

Thousands of adults and children with disabilities are confined in institutions, where they may face neglect and abuse, sometimes for life. Brazil lacks a comprehensive plan to progressively deinstitutionalize adults and children with disabilities.

In April 2021, the National Council of Prosecutor's Offices, a government body, adopted a resolution requiring prosecutors to oversee and inspect institutions for adults with disabilities yearly and take legal action in cases of abuse.

In August, the Minister of Education defended a new national policy that appeared to be aimed at establishing segregated schools for certain children with disabilities, arguing they "disturbed" other students. As of September, the Supreme Court was examining whether the policy is constitutional.

Indigenous Rights

President Bolsonaro and his allies in Congress promoted a bill to prevent Indigenous peoples from obtaining legal recognition of their traditional lands if they were not physically present on them on October 5, 1988—when Brazil's constitution was enacted—or if they had not, by that date, initiated legal proceedings to claim them. A case similarly seeking to block Indigenous land rights was pending before the Supreme Court, as of November 2021.

Meanwhile, Indigenous territories continued to suffer illegal encroachment. The area occupied by illegal mining grew five-fold from 2010 to 2020, the NGO Map Biomas reported.

"Wildcat" miners sought to impede a law enforcement operation in Munduruku Indigenous territories and attacked a Munduruku women's association and a leader's home in May 2021. In the Yanomami Indigenous territory, miners fired at Indigenous people and Federal Police in several incidents. Two Yanomami children who escaped a shooting alone were found drowned in May, and a plane used by miners hit and killed an Indigenous man in July.

Environment

Since taking office in January 2019, the Bolsonaro administration has weakened environmental law enforcement, effectively encouraging criminal networks that are driving deforestation and have used threats and violence against forest defenders. The average number of fines for deforestation in the Amazon paid in 2019 and 2020 was 93 percent lower than the average number paid in the previous five years, a study by the Federal University of Minas Gerais showed.

Between August 2020 and July 2021, 13,235 square kilometers of Amazon rain-forest were clear-cut, a 22 percent increase over the same period last year and the highest number since 2006. Brazil's space research agency had its defor-estation report ready on October 27, four days before the COP26 climate summit in Glasgow, but the government only released it on November 18, after the sum-mit ended, in an apparent attempt to preclude criticism.

In deforested areas, criminal groups often set remaining vegetation ablaze after they have extracted valuable timber, in order to clear land for pasture or land speculation. A study by InfoAmazônia and other organizations said smoke from forest fires, which can cause respiratory diseases and make people vulnerable to complications from Covid-19, was linked to an 18 percent increase in serious Covid-19 cases in the Amazon during the fire season in 2020.

The government promoted bills that would encourage deforestation by providing amnesty for land invasions, easing environmental licensing, and opening Indige-nous territories to mining and other projects with high environmental impact.

In response to criticism, the government announced in September 2021 that it would hire hundreds of new staff at its federal environmental agencies. But the Climate Observatory, a coalition of environmental NGOs, warned that only 157 of them would be agents with university degrees who have the mandate to lead en-vironmental law enforcement operations.

Climate Change Policy and Impacts

As one of the world's top 10 emitters of greenhouse gases, Brazil contributes to the mounting toll that the climate crisis is taking on human rights around the globe.

In its December 2020 climate action plan, Brazil pledged a smaller reduction of its overall greenhouse gas emissions than it had in its original 2016 plan, a re-gression in violation of its obligations under the Paris Agreement. The Climate Action Tracker, which provides independent scientific analysis, rated that plan as "highly insufficient" to meet the Paris Agreement goal to limit global warming to 1.5°C above pre-industrial levels. If all countries' plans fell this short, warming would reach over 4°C by the end of the century.

In November 2021, the Brazilian delegation to the global climate summit in Glasgow, COP26, announced a new plan that still does not represent an increase in ambition in relation to its initial plan submitted in 2016. The delegation also committed to ending illegal deforestation by 2028, but the federal government is yet to adopt an operational plan to deliver on this pledge.

Increased deforestation in the Amazon enabled by the Bolsonaro government has driven up overall emissions and may cause vast portions of the rainforest to turn into dry savannah in coming years, releasing billions of tons of stored carbon.

Migrants, Refugees, and Asylum Seekers

Thousands of Venezuelans, including unaccompanied children, have crossed the border into Brazil in recent years, fleeing hunger, lack of basic health care, or persecution. About 261,000 Venezuelans lived in Brazil as of October 2021.

In June 2019, Brazil issued a legal recognition of "serious and widespread violation of human rights" in Venezuela, which makes it easier for Venezuelans to obtain asylum. Brazil granted refugee status to about 50,000 Venezuelans from June 2019 to June 2021.

In response to the Covid-19 pandemic, Brazil barred foreign nationals from entering the country by land or water, except for permanent residents and some other foreigners with links to Brazil, who could still enter from all countries but Venezuela. In June 2021, the government started allowing the entrance of permanent residents and some other foreigners coming from Venezuela.

The government ordered the deportation of people who entered Brazil in violation of border restrictions, even if they intended to seek asylum, an infringement of Brazil's international obligations. Federal police told Human Rights Watch they deported 2,091 people in 2020—compared to only 36 in 2019—and 1,198 from January through July 2021.

In September 2021, Brazil announced that it would issue humanitarian visas allowing Afghans to travel to Brazil and apply for temporary residency or refugee status, but Brazilian media reported that embassies required prior proof that an organization would pay for all their expenses for at least six months. Brazil has not committed to resettling Afghan refugees on its territory or to assisting with the humanitarian response in Afghanistan and neighboring countries.

Key International Actors

In June 2021, the UN high commissioner for human rights highlighted police violence in Brazil in a landmark report to the UN Human Rights Council, urging countries to take steps toward eradicating systemic racism against people of African descent and to hold police accountable for abuses.

The high commissioner also expressed concern about threats against Brazil's Supreme Court. In September 2021, the chairman of the US Senate Foreign Relations Committee and three other senators called on the administration of US President Joe Biden to support Brazil's democratic institutions in response to President Bolsonaro's threats of "a rupture with Brazil's constitutional order."

Also in September, the UN Committee on Enforced Disappearances asked Brazil to ensure justice for enforced disappearances during the military dictatorship and to prosecute all cases, including current ones, before civilian courts.

Throughout 2021, the high commissioner, several UN rapporteurs, and the Inter-American Commission on Human Rights denounced illegal encroachment into Indigenous territories and attacks against Indigenous people.

The Organization for Economic Co-operation and Development cancelled a discussion about upgrading Brazil's status in its environment committee because of President Bolsonaro's poor environmental record. Several European leaders said they would not ratify a pending trade agreement between the European Union and Mercosur unless Brazil reduced Amazon deforestation and forest fires. The European Commission is negotiating an additional instrument with Mercosur to address deforestation.

In April 2021, 15 US senators urged President Biden to condition financial assistance to Brazil on reducing deforestation and ending impunity for environmental crimes and attacks against forest defenders.

Foreign Policy

In international forums, Brazil continued to oppose references to "sexual and re-productive" rights.

At the UN Human Rights Council, Brazil abstained from a resolution to launch an investigation into crimes committed during the conflict between Israel and Hamas in Gaza. Brazil also opposed a WHO resolution to provide health support to Palestinians, including Covid-19 vaccines.

At the World Trade Organization, Brazil opposed waiving certain intellectual property rights to increase Covid-19 vaccine manufacturing and allow fairer access for low-income countries; in June 2021, authorities indicated they might reassess that position.

In May 2021, Brazil ratified the Inter-American Convention against Racism, Racial Discrimination and Related Forms of Intolerance.

Burkina Faso

During 2021, there was a marked deterioration in Burkina Faso's human rights and security situation as attacks and atrocities by armed Islamist groups surged, unlawful killings by state security forces and pro-government militias during counterterrorism operations continued, and the humanitarian situation worsened.

The government of President Roch Marc Kaboré, elected in November 2020 to a second term, struggled during 2021 to address the overlapping crises. The violence, including the June massacre of over 135 civilians in Solhan, the single deadliest attack in the country since the outbreak of armed conflict in 2016, led to demonstrations calling for an end to the bloodshed. Several activists and members of the political opposition were questioned or detained after criticizing the government's response to the growing insecurity.

There was scant progress toward providing justice for the alleged killings of hundreds of suspects during past security forces operations, though a few trials of crimes by alleged Islamist fighters took place. Rule-of-law institutions remained weak; however, the government took steps to reduce the numbers of suspects in pre-trial detention.

Attacks by armed groups caused over 237,000 people to flee their homes in 2021, bringing the total number of internally displaced people since 2016 to over 1.4 million, or 6 percent of the population. The government struggled to care for the growing number of displaced.

A 2019 law criminalizing some aspects of reporting on security force operations dampened media freedom, with journalists reluctant to report on allegations of abuses by pro-government forces. The government implemented a de facto ban on visits by journalists to internally displaced camps, and pressured journalists and victims for reporting on allegations of sex in exchange for humanitarian relief.

Burkina Faso's international partners including the European Union, France, the United Nations, and the United States readily denounced abuses by Islamist armed groups but were largely reluctant to denounce or push for investigations into those by pro-government forces.

Abuses by Islamist Armed Groups

Islamist armed groups allied with Al-Qaeda and the Islamic State (ISIS) in the Greater Sahara killed over 350 civilians. Their presence and attacks on military targets and civilians expanded from Burkina Faso's north and east into the south and west. Their attacks largely targeted communities which had formed local civil defense groups.

On November 1, armed Islamists killed around 10 civilians from Dambam village on their way to a local market near the border with Niger. On August 18, armed Islamists ambushed a convoy of traders near Arbinda, northern Burkina Faso, killing 59 civilians and numerous pro-government security force members. On June 4 and 5, they killed at least 137 civilians during an attack on Solhan village, in northern Burkina Faso.

On May 3, armed Islamist fighters killed 30 villagers during an attack on Kodyel village. On April 26, they ambushed an anti-poaching patrol, killing two Spanish journalists and an Irish conservationist. During a separate attack the same day, armed Islamists killed 18 villagers in the northern village of Yattakou. Between February and May, they killed at least 30 civilians in northern Oudalan Province, including traders on their way to a market in February, and 15 during a baptism in May.

Throughout 2021, armed Islamist groups abducted scores of civilians from villages, public vehicles, and displacement camps. Victims included religious and health workers, village chiefs, traders, and displaced people. Many of the abducted, including a priest, were later killed, while at least 27 villagers abducted from public vehicles between the towns of Dablo and Barsalogho in June and July were unaccounted for at time of writing.

Islamist group fighters also burned villages, markets, and businesses; abducted and raped dozens of women; imposed their version of Sharia (Islamic law) via courts that did not adhere to international fair trial standards; and prevented farmers from accessing their fields.

Abuses by State Security Forces and Pro-Government Militias

There were several allegations of extrajudicial executions of suspects by the Burkinabé security forces during counterterrorism operations, most targeting ethnic Peuhl. However, the number of unlawful killings was lower compared to 2019 and 2020.

In response to the growing number of Islamist armed attacks, the president removed the defense minister after a cabinet reshuffle and by decree created a special force to fight terrorism whereby special force members "may not be prosecuted for acts committed in the exercise of their functions."

State-sponsored self-defense groups, notably the Volunteers for the Defense of the Homeland (VDP), created in 2020, were implicated in numerous grave crimes including arbitrary detentions, torture, and unlawful killings targeting suspected armed Islamists and criminals.

Some allegations involved the VDPs and security forces working together, including the alleged killing in mid-September of six men, including a university student, and the enforced disappearance of five others during a joint operation in the western Cascades region.

Accountability for Abuses

There was little progress with investigations into past atrocities by the security services—notably the 2018 and 2019 killings of scores of suspects in Burkina Faso's Sahel region; the deaths of over 200 men in Djibo in 2020; and the deaths of 12 men in gendarme custody in Tanwalbougou.

The military justice directorate, mandated to investigate incidents involving the security forces, continued to be underfunded.

The high-security prison for terrorism-related offenses remained overcrowded – with about 876 people detained in a prison made for 448, at time of writing. The vast majority had been detained far beyond the legal limit. The government took steps to address the backlog and to ensure due process by releasing scores of suspects accused of terrorism-related offenses against whom there was insufficient evidence and by beginning trials. Very few detainees had access to defense lawyers.

A court dedicated to terrorism-related offenses was established and started to hear cases in mid-2021. One trial, in August, led to the conviction of two members of the Islamist armed group Ansaroul Islam for a 2018 attack on a primary school; however, the proceeding raised due process concerns, including that defendants were not informed of their legal right to counsel.

The long-awaited trial of those implicated in the 1987 assassination of President Thomas Sankara and 12 others began on October 11. The 14 men standing trial include former President Blaise Compaoré, who fled to Côte d'Ivoire in 2014 after being ousted in a popular uprising. He and several others will be tried in absentia. In July, France approved an extradition request from Burkina Faso for François Compaoré, brother of the former president, for his alleged involvement in the 1998 murder of prominent investigative journalist Norbert Zongo.

Children's Rights and Attacks on Education

Armed groups, notably armed Islamists, increased their recruitment and use of children. At least 15 children were among those detained in the high security prison. Over 300,000 children were out of school due to the closure of 2,244 schools as a result of insecurity as of May, approximately 10 percent of the country's schools, according to the United Nations Children's Fund (UNICEF.) During 2021, at least 30 education-related attacks by Islamist armed groups, including damaging or pillaging schools and abducting, detaining, or threatening teachers, were documented by Human Rights Watch or reported by Burkina Faso's Education Ministry or the Armed Conflict Location and Event Data (ACLED) Project.

Key International Actors

The rapidly deteriorating security and humanitarian situation garnered significant attention from Burkina Faso's key international partners. They issued several statements denouncing abuses by Islamist armed groups but were reluctant to denounce abuses by pro-government forces or publicly press the national authorities to investigate the allegations.

Donors, notably France, the Netherlands, the UN, and the US, supported programs to improve the justice sector, address prison overcrowding and extended pretrial detention of terrorism suspects, and provide human rights training for the security forces.

G5 Sahel, a regional counterterrorism force created in 2017 that includes Burkina Faso, Chad, Mali, Mauritania, and Niger, conducted operations along Burkina Faso's northern borders with Mali and Niger, some of which involved French troops.

In October, the UN Office of the High Commissioner for Human Rights signed an agreement to open a country office mandated to monitor the conduct of security force operations during G5 Sahel operations and, more widely, to support the national human rights commission and civil society.

The US provided US\$2 million in training programs to counter improvised explosive devices (IEDs), as well as \$5 million in counterterrorism funding to develop the law enforcement capacity to investigate complex terrorism cases. As of July, the US had committed \$69 million to Burkina Faso's humanitarian assistance, health, peace and security, program support, and economic development sectors.

The EU provided €188.6 million in humanitarian assistance to the Sahel and €4.5 billion in support for the G5 Sahel joint counterterrorism force, including for the human rights due diligence framework, which presses governments to ensure their forces respect human rights during operations.

France, Burkina Faso's leading bilateral donor, provides military training to Burkinabé troops and supported security operations in the Sahel region through its 5,100-strong Operation Barkhane counterinsurgency operation, which is set to draw down in 2022.

In response to the gravity and number of attacks on schools and the killing and maiming of children, the UN secretary-general included Burkina Faso as a situation of concern for the UN's monitoring and reporting mechanism on grave violations against children during armed conflict.

Burundi

Since President Évariste Ndayishimiye came to power in June 2020, there have been limited improvements in Burundi's human rights situation. His administration released four journalists and two human rights defenders, jailed on baseless charges. The authorities lifted some restrictions on media and civil society, while promises were made to rein in the ruling party's youth league, the Imbonerakure.

However, many of Ndayishimiye's repeated promises to deliver justice and promote political tolerance remain unfulfilled. The president has appointed ruling party hardliners to key positions. Sanctions against the prime minister and three other individuals were lifted by the United States in November. The minister of interior, community development, and public security remains under European Union targeted sanctions. Killings, disappearances, torture, ill-treatment, arbitrary arrests and detention, and sexual and gender-based violence were documented by international and Burundian rights groups. Unidentified dead bodies, often mutilated or tied up, were regularly found in different parts of the country, often buried by local authorities, Imbonerakure members, or police, without investigation.

Ndayishimiye has shown greater openness than his predecessor toward the international community. In February 2021, the Burundian government and representatives of the European Union and its member states resumed a political dialogue, on hold since 2016. The Burundian government has produced a technical roadmap regarding human rights and other reforms, but it is vague and noncommittal and avoids addressing impunity for the many crimes committed since 2015.

Security Situation and Political Repression

Since August 2020, there have been several reports of security incidents involving clashes between security forces and armed groups, as well as attacks by unidentified assailants. Attacks by armed groups were reported in Cibitoke and other provinces bordering the Democratic Republic of Congo. In some of these attacks, Imbonerakure members supported the national army. Groups of unidentified armed men are also reported to be responsible for random attacks resulting in civilian casualties. The Burundian authorities denounced these as "terrorist" or "criminal" acts and committed abuses against alleged perpetrators and civilians.

According to the report of the Commission of Inquiry on Human Rights in Burundi, men suspected of belonging to, or assisting, armed groups were executed by police or national intelligence agents throughout 2021. Dozens of real or suspected members of opposition groups have been victims of enforced disappearances. Many people were also detained by the National Intelligence Service and allegedly subjected to severe torture, rape, and ill-treatment.

Local and international monitoring groups, including Human Rights Watch, documented cases of torture of people suspected of collaborating with armed groups. The Commission of Inquiry on Burundi documented cases where victims died in detention.

Despite a lull in abuses against opposition members after the May 2020 elections, killings, disappearances, torture, arbitrary detention, and harassment of those perceived to oppose the government continued throughout 2021. There have been limited attempts by authorities to rein in the Imbonerakure. Some members were prosecuted, although rarely because of serious criminal offenses, in trials that often lacked transparency. Fabien Banciryanino, a former member of parliament and outspoken human rights advocate was convicted of abusive security-related charges on May 7 and sentenced to a year in prison and a fine of 100,000 Burundian Francs (US$51). He was released after time served on October 1.

On March 5, a presidential decree announced the pardon or early release of more than 5,000 prisoners. However, the decree excluded many prisoners in pretrial detention or accused of security-related offenses, many of whom were arrested in the aftermath of protests over the former President Pierre Nkurunziza's 2015 bid for a third term and are held on political grounds.

Civil Society and Media

Many members of civil society or journalists who fled in 2015 remain in exile. During former President Nkurunziza's third and final term, independent civil society and media were relentlessly attacked, and their members killed, disappeared, jailed, and threatened.

Although Ndayishmiye's government has lifted some restrictions, including the suspension of the anti-corruption organization PARCEM (Parole et Action pour le Réveil des Consciences et l'Évolution des Mentalités), the authorities continue to exercise undue interference in and oversight over the operations of civil society and the media.

Since Ndayishimiye's election, several unfairly imprisoned journalists and human rights defenders were released. Four journalists working for Iwacu, the popular news website, were pardoned and released on December 24, 2020. Their pardon does not acquit them of the politically motivated conviction for complicity in an "impossible attempt" to undermine the internal security of the state.

Nestor Nibitanga, a human rights defender arrested in November 2017 and convicted on security charges, was pardoned and released on April 27. The conviction of Germain Rukuki, a member of ACAT-Burundi, arrested in July 2017 and sentenced to 32 years in prison in April 2018 for "rebellion," "threatening state security," "participation in an insurrectional movement," and "attacks on the head of state," was overturned on appeal in June. Rukuki was released on June 21, the same day the EU's head of delegation announced that the process of lifting sanctions on Burundi had been initiated.

Despite these welcome releases, the space for civil society and the media to operate remains severely restricted. A lawyer and former human rights defender, Tony Germain Nkina, was sentenced to five years in prison in June, likely due to his past human rights work. On September 29, his conviction was maintained on appeal. On February 2, Burundi's Supreme Court published the guilty verdict—dated June 23, 2020—in the case against 34 people accused of participating in a May 2015 coup attempt, including 12 human rights defenders and journalists in exile. After a trial, during which the defendants were absent and did not have legal representation, the group was found guilty of "attacks on the authority of the State," "assassinations," and "destruction."

On February 11, the CNC lifted the ban on public comments on Iwacu, which had been in place since April 2018, and pledged to restore access to the website in

Burundi. On February 22, the CNC lifted the ban on Bonesha FM, which was required to sign an agreement similar to one the private radio station Isanganiro and Rema FM, a pro-ruling party station, signed when they resumed broadcasts in February 2016. On April 21, the CNC authorized several new radio and television channels to begin operating. However, international media are still restricted, and the BBC and the Voice of America remain suspended since 2018.

Lesbian, Gay, Bisexual and Transgender Rights

Burundi punishes consensual same-sex sexual relations between adults with up to two years in prison under Article 567 of the penal code.

Refugee Rights

Burundian authorities have repeatedly spoken of the need for refugees to return from exile. As of September 30, 269,330 Burundians officially remain refugees in neighboring countries with over 170,000 Burundian refugees being repatriated under the tripartite voluntary repatriation program launched in 2017. Human Rights Watch has documented how Tanzanian authorities have forced or coerced refugees into signing for "voluntary" repatriations.

In its September 2021 report, the Commission of Inquiry on Burundi said that although the climate of hostility toward returnees had abated under Ndayishimiye, some who had been politically active in the past have been accused of collaborating with armed groups, arbitrarily arrested and detained, and tortured in detention. Some refugees who had returned fled Burundi again during 2021 for fear of being targeted. A group of eight Burundian refugees who were tortured and forcibly returned to Burundi by Tanzanian security officials were acquitted of security-related charges in August. At time of writing, the prosecution has appealed the verdict.

Covid-19

Although the government's response to the Covid-19 pandemic was initially marked by repression and misinformation, since Ndayishimiye came to power, the authorities have taken steps to curb the spread of Covid-19. In July, the government announced that it would begin vaccinating the population, and the vaccination program began in October.

Cooperation with the World Health Organization (WHO) resumed with the arrival of its new representative in April 2021. In 2020, Nkurunziza's government had refused to follow WHO guidelines to prevent the spread of the virus and declared the WHO's country director and three of its experts persona non grata.

Key International Actors

The UN Commission of Inquiry on Burundi, established in September 2016 to document grave human rights violations in the country, concluded on September 16, 2021, that grave human rights violations continued to be committed in Burundi and that "no structural reform has been undertaken to durably improve the situation."

Despite these findings, the EU tabled a resolution at the September session of the UN Human Rights Council, adopted by a vote, which ended the mandate of the commission and instead created a special rapporteur mandate. Burundian authorities announced that they would not cooperate with even this more limited mandate and continue to refuse to cooperate with other international or regional human rights mechanisms.

In 2021, the EU and the Burundi government proceeded to hold several rounds of a political dialogue aimed at developing a "roadmap" for reforms, as the government presses the EU to lift its 2016 suspension of direct budgetary support. Although the government has yet to meet many of the benchmarks set by the EU in 2016, including those relating to media and civil society, in June, the EU's head of delegation announced that the process to lift the measures had been initiated.

Despite the lack of substantive progress on human rights issues, on April 27, the African Union Peace and Security Council ended its human rights observer mission and called for lifting all international sanctions against Burundi, and in December 2020, the UN Security Council ended its Burundi-specific briefings.

Cambodia

In anticipation of upcoming commune and national elections in 2022 and 2023, Prime Minister Hun Sen made use of a worsening Covid-19 pandemic to expand authoritarian control by further restricting civil and political rights and failing to protect the social and economic rights of marginalized groups. His government adopted a new, overbroad Covid-19 law, allowing for up to 20-year-prison sentences for violations of Covid-19 measures.

To silence dissent, Cambodia's politicized courts held a series of mass trials against over 100 political opposition members and dozens of human rights defenders for exercising their rights to freedom of expression and peaceful assembly. At time of writing, Cambodia had more than 60 political prisoners behind bars.

The government's harsh Covid-19 lockdowns were imposed without ensuring access to adequate food, medical, and other basic needs. The authorities also resorted to beating people on the streets in Phnom Penh with bamboo canes for leaving their homes in defiance of the Covid-19 edicts. The government also failed to take sufficient steps to prevent major Covid-19 outbreaks among the prison population in a penal system plagued by massive overcrowding.

The government adopted a sub-decree that tightens control of the internet and expands online surveillance of internet users critical of the government, while infringing privacy rights. Independent journalists and media outlets, as well as critical social media users, faced continued government intimidation and attacks.

New Rights-Abusing Laws and Bills

The government adopted new measures that further clamp down on human rights.

In February, the authorities enacted the Sub-Decree on the Establishment of the National Internet Gateway, which, after coming into effect in February 2022, will allow the government to monitor all internet activities and grant the authorities broad powers to block and disconnect internet connections.

In March, the government followed with the rights-abusing Law on Measures to Prevent the Spread of Covid-19 and other Serious, Dangerous and Contagious

Diseases. The law provides that violations of Covid-19 measures can be punished by up to 20-year prison sentences and other disproportionate penalties. The law contains overly broad provisions without independent oversight or procedural safeguards. By May, the authorities had criminally charged over 100 people with violating the law.

Other draconian laws are still awaiting finalization of drafting or adoption, such as a cybercrime bill, which poses further threats to online speech, and a draft public order law that seeks to control people's daily lives by prohibiting a vast array of public and private actions. Cambodia has no data protection law or safeguards to ensure official requests for data are necessary and proportionate.

Human Rights Watch obtained in March a copy of a draft disability law that fails to adopt a human rights-based approach to ensure equal rights for people with disabilities. The draft law reinforces stigma against people with disabilities rather than ensuring equal access to education, employment, transportation, social and legal services, and independent living.

Human Rights Defenders Behind Bars

At time of writing, the government held at least 24 human rights defenders in jail.

In August, the authorities convicted trade union leader Rong Chhun of incitement, together with former political opposition members Sar Kanika and Ton Nimol. Their sentences ranged from 20 months to two years in prison and a large fine of 400 million riel (nearly US$100,000), which must be paid to the government's Border Affairs Committee. Rong Chhun's arrest followed his public comments on communities' land loss because of the demarcation of the Cambodia-Vietnam border. The two other activists had peacefully protested for Chhun's release. The authorities arrested nineteen activists, artists, and human rights defenders for participating in similar protests.

In August, a Phnom Penh court convicted nine activists and former opposition members of incitement and sentenced them to between 12 and 20 months in prison. They had peacefully protested near the Chinese Embassy in Phnom Penh as part of a 2020 campaign to commemorate the Paris Peace Accords anniversary.

Attacks Against Environmental Activists

Starting in 2020, the authorities stepped up their attempts to intimidate peaceful environmental activists, accusing them of attempting to use foreign funds to topple the government. In May 2021, a Phnom Penh court convicted five Mother Nature Cambodia (MNC) activists of incitement and sentenced them to between 18 and 20 months in prison. The activists had publicly raised concerns over the filling-in of a lake in Phnom Penh and its expected negative environmental impacts. In July, the authorities imposed additional charges of conspiracy against three of the activists.

In June, the authorities charged four other MNC activists for documenting the government's destruction of the environment and prosecuted them on charges including conspiracy and insulting the king. Authorities detained three of them and remanded them to pre-trial detention; the fourth remained outside the country.

Attacks Against Political Opposition Members

With upcoming elections in 2022 and 2023, harassment intensified against members of the political opposition. Many leaders and senior members of the dissolved opposition Cambodia National Rescue Party (CNRP) were forced to flee the country and remained abroad out of fear of being arrested.

After issuing court summons in November 2020, the authorities started mass trials in 2021 against over 100 persons connected with CNRP, as well as political activists. In March, the authorities convicted nine exiled CNRP leaders in absentia based on attempted "attack" charges, including CNRP leader Sam Rainsy, and sentenced them to up to 25 years in prison. The case against them is based on false allegations that the CNRP attempted to stage a coup by announcing their plans to return to Cambodia in November 2019.

The head of the CNRP, Kem Sokha, continues to face trumped-up treason charges. His three-month-long trial was interrupted in March 2020 due to Covid-19. In January 2021, the court informed him that his case was no longer a "priority" and unlikely to resume in 2021 because the authorities were pursuing new cases against hundreds of opposition members.

Impunity

July 2021 marked five years since the unlawful killing of prominent political commentator and human rights defender Kem Ley. To date, there has been no credible, independent investigation into his killing in broad daylight in downtown Phnom Penh. There has also been no progress made to uncover the facts around the abduction of prominent Thai activist Wanchalearm Satsaksit. Both cases have yet to see justice, despite evidence and witness testimony pointing to likely government involvement that requires an effective and transparent investigation.

Freedom of Media

In 2021, the authorities used the pandemic to further stifle independent media by labelling independent reporting as "fake news" and imposing de facto bans on independent reporting.

In January, Phnom Penh authorities announced a directive that seeks to ban filming, recording, and livestreaming of police actions.

In May, the Ministry of Information announced that only state media or media "invited" by the government would be permitted to report from areas under harsh Covid-19 lockdowns. Following livestreaming of long queues of Covid-19 patients outside government treatment centers, the ministry issued a letter warning journalists not to disseminate information that could "provoke turmoil in society," and threatened legal action against those that disobeyed.

In July, Phnom Penh police questioned three journalists who covered a land protest and coerced them into signing an agreement, pledging not to report again on the land situation. These intimidatory efforts are common tactics by the authorities to silence independent voices.

The government's campaign to silence critical commentary extends also to social media platforms. In August, the government sent senior officials to Bangkok to ask Thai authorities to block or otherwise stop the critical social media broadcasts of opposition activists residing in Thailand.

Lack of Adequate Standard of Living

As a result of a rapid spike in Covid-19 cases, authorities in April introduced a color-based zoning system under which lockdown measures were imposed in areas with higher case counts. Residents in so-called "red zones," disproportionately low-income populations, faced the most restrictive lockdown measures, including a ban on leaving their homes. For over a month, many residents were unable to work and had inadequate access to food, medicine, and other basic necessities. The authorities denied access to aid groups and United Nations agencies to distribute aid to those urgently needing it. Protesting residents were accused of being affiliated with the opposition.

The pandemic revealed the absence of a robust social protection system, leaving low-income households disproportionately harmed by Covid-19's economic impact and lockdowns without a safety net. Sporadic one-off cash transfers and an unaddressed micro-loan debt crisis failed to guarantee Cambodians' rights to social security and an adequate living standard.

Key International Actors

Cambodia continued to strengthen its ties with China during the pandemic. While the European Union had partially suspended Cambodia's trade preferences in August 2020 after finding systematic rights violations, bilateral trade between Cambodia and China increased by 20 percent to US$3 billion during the first quarter of 2021. Cambodia is a key "Belt and Road Initiative" partner; however, rights abuses continue to mar large-scale development projects in Cambodia.

Cambodia ranks among countries with the highest percentages of people fully vaccinated. In September, China pledged US$270 million in aid and 3 million Sinovac Covid-19 vaccine doses—adding to 3.2 million Sinovac and Sinopharm vaccine doses already provided. In mid-2021, through COVAX, Japan, the United States and the United Kingdom donated other Covid-19 vaccines.

In March, the European Parliament adopted a strongly worded resolution condemning the mass trials against opposition members as well as the intensifying clampdown on independent media and civil society, while calling for sanctions against rights-abusing Cambodian leadership. An EU statement also condemned the mass trials.

The United States, in part because of the ongoing harassment of environmental activists, announced on June 17 that it halted over $100 million in funding to the government regarding the forestry-protection "Greening Prey Lang" project.

In October, the UN Human Rights Council adopted a weakly worded resolution extending the mandate of the special rapporteur on the situation of human rights in Cambodia, mandating a one-time oral update in March 2022 in addition to ordinary reporting by the special rapporteur.

Cameroon

Armed groups and government forces committed human rights abuses, including mass killings, across Cameroon's Anglophone regions and in the Far North region.

As the crisis in the Anglophone regions continued unabated for the fifth year, over 712,000 people were internally displaced in the Anglophone regions and in the Francophone Littoral, West, and Centre regions as of August 2021, and at least 2.2 million people were in need of humanitarian aid.

Separatists, who have violently enforced a boycott on education since 2017, continued to attack students and education professionals. Separatists, who have violently enforced a boycott on education since 2017, continued to attack students and education professionals. Separatists, who have violently enforced a boycott on education since 2017, continued to attack students and education professionals.

The Islamist armed group Boko Haram increased its attacks in the Far North region from January to April, killing at least 80 civilians, with over 340,000 internally displaced as of August 2021. In responding to the armed conflict, government forces have also been responsible for violations of international humanitarian and human rights law, including unlawful killings and arbitrary arrests.

The government continued to restrict freedom of expression and association, while state-sanctioned persecution of lesbian, gay, bisexual and transgender (LGBT) people intensified. Government forces subjected Cameroonian asylum seekers deported from the United States to serious human rights violations following their return, including physical assault and abuse, arbitrary arrest and detention, extortion, and confiscation of identity documents, thus impeding freedom of movement, ability to work, and access to public services. The government's response to the Covid-19 pandemic lacked transparency and was marred by allegations of corruption and misappropriation of funds.

Anglophone Crisis

Based on Human Rights Watch's field and open source research, at least 4,000 civilians have been killed by both government forces and armed separatist fighters since late 2016 in the North-West and South-West regions, as separatists seek independence for the country's minority Anglophone regions.

Abuses by Government Forces

Security forces responded to separatist attacks with a heavy hand, often targeting civilians across the Anglophone regions.

On January 10, army soldiers killed at least nine civilians, including a woman and a child, in Mautu village, South-West region. The soldiers also looted scores of homes and threatened residents.

In Gom village, North-West region, on June 8, two soldiers broke into the house of *fon* (the local traditional authority) and harassed eight people there, including a 72-year-old man whom they beat. They also shot and killed Nwang Lydia, a 60-year-old woman, after she failed to provide information about a separatist fighter.

On June 9, soldiers from the regular army and the elite Rapid Intervention Battalion (*Bataillon d'Intervention Rapide*, BIR) killed a 58-year-old man and raped a 53-year-old woman during a security operation in and around Mbuluf village, North-West region. They also broke into, damaged, and looted at least 33 shops and homes, including the residence of the fon in Ndzeen village.

On October 14, a gendarme shot and killed Caroluise Enondiale, a 4-year-old girl, on her way to school in Buea, South-West region. An angry mob responded by lynching the gendarme.

On November 10, an improvised explosive device was thrown on to the roof of a lecture hall at the University of Buea, South-West region, wounding at least 11 students. At time of writing no one had claimed responsibility for the attack, but authorities blamed separatist fighters.

HUMAN
RIGHTS
WATCH

"They Are Destroying Our Future"
Armed Separatist Attacks on Students, Teachers, and Schools
in Cameroon's Anglophone

Abuses by Armed Separatists

Separatist fighters continued to kill, torture, assault, and kidnap civilians. They also continued their attacks against education. According to the United Nations, 700,000 students were out of school in March 2021 as a result of the crisis.

On January 9, suspected separatist fighters killed the principal of a high school in Eyumojock, South-West region, and wounded a principal from another high school in Tinto, South-West region. On January 12, separatist fighters shot and injured a female public-school teacher in Bamenda, North-West region.

Separatist fighters killed three tribal chiefs in Essoh Attah village, South-West region, on February 13. On February 27, armed separatists kidnapped a medical doctor in Bali, North-West region and threatened to kill him before releasing him the same day after a ransom payment.

On June 6, separatist fighters attacked a religious center in Mamfe, South-West region, killing a 12-year-old boy and wounding a 16-year-old boy. Separatist fighters killed Fuh Max Dang, a physics teacher at Government Bilingual High School in Kumba, South-West region, on July 1. On August 29, armed separatists kidnapped Julius Agbortoko, a Catholic priest of the Mamfe diocese in the South-West region and asked for 20 million CFA (around US $34,000) ransom for his release.

Restrictions on Humanitarian Access and Abuses against Aid Workers

Humanitarian access is severely restricted and humanitarian workers have been victims of attacks by both government forces and groups separatist armed groups. In December 2020, the Cameroonian authorities suspended all activities of Médecins Sans Frontières (MSF, Doctors Without Borders) in the North-West region, accusing the organization of being too close to Anglophone separatists. The move forced MSF to withdraw from the region, leaving tens of thousands of people without access to vital health care.

Separatist fighters have also hindered aid agencies' access in the areas under their control. On February 4, a nurse working with an international nongovernmental organization (NGO) was shot and injured as her ambulance was caught in the crossfire during a separatist attack on Mbalangi village, South-West region. On June 25, fighters from the separatist armed group Ambazonia Defense Forces (ADF) stopped a humanitarian vehicle in Guzang, North-West region, kidnapped the four staff members, beat one, and released them the following day.

Attacks in the Far North by Boko Haram

In the first half of 2021, attacks and raids by the Islamist armed group Boko Haram increased in the Far North Region, with at least 80 civilians killed. On January 8, a Boko Haram suicide attack killed at least 14 civilians, including 8 children, and wounded 3 others, including 2 children. The presumed death in May of Abubakar Shekau, the leader of Boko Haram, in a confrontation in Nigeria with the splinter faction Islamic State West Africa Province (ISWAP), helped consolidate ISWAP's power and increased insecurity in Cameroon's Far North region.

Crackdown on Political Opposition, Dissent

The government limited the ability of the political opposition to function freely. Authorities prohibited a demonstration by the country's main opposition party, Cameroon Renaissance Movement (*Mouvement pour la renaissance du Cameroun*, MRC), planned for July 25 in Yaoundé, the capital, citing concerns around Covid-19 and general public order. On the same day, a demonstration by supporters of the ruling party took place in Bertoua, Eastern region.

On August 9, gendarmes arbitrarily arrested prominent tech entrepreneur, human rights campaigner, and vocal critic of President Paul Biya, Rebecca Enonchong, in Douala. She was held in custody for "contempt of a magistrate" until August 13, when she was released and all charges against her dropped.

At least 124 opposition party members and supporters arrested in September 2020 during peaceful demonstrations remained in detention on politically motivated charges, including Olivier Bibou Nissack and Alain Fogué Tedom, two prominent MRC members.

Sexual Orientation and Gender Identity

Cameroon's penal code punishes "sexual relations between persons of the same sex" with up to five years in prison. Security forces arbitrarily arrested, beat, or threatened at least 24 people, including a 17-year-old boy, for alleged consensual same-sex conduct or gender nonconformity. Some were subjected to forced anal examinations. On May 11, a Cameroonian court sentenced Shakiro and Patricia, two transgender women, to five years in prison and fines of 200,000 CFA (US$370) for alleged same-sex relations.

Justice and Accountability

Since January, seven hearings were held in the trial of three security force members accused of involvement in the killings of 21 civilians in Ngarbuh village, North-West region. The trial is being held before a military court in Yaoundé, about 380 kilometers from Ngarbuh, making it difficult for family members of victims to attend. The defendants are charged with murder, arson, destruction, violence against a pregnant woman, and disobeying orders. Seventeen members of a vigilante group and a former separatist fighter have also been charged but remain at large.

In June 2020, the French ambassador to Cameroon told the media that President Biya had assured him that an investigation would be opened into the death in custody of journalist Samuel Wazizi in August 2019. However, there has not been any progress on the investigation.

On July 26, the Special Criminal Court, which oversees cases relating to the misappropriation of public funds, adjourned for the 74th time the trial of journalist Amadou Vamoulk̈e, arrested in 2016 for alleged embezzlement. In 2020, the United Nations Working Group on Arbitrary Detention found his detention to be arbitrary.

On September 7, a military court in Buea, South-West region, sentenced 4 people to death by firing squad for the killing of 7 children and the injuring of at least 13 others last year at a school in Kumba, South-West region. Defense lawyers said the trial was marred by serious procedural irregularities, starting with the use of military courts to try civilians, and including that the entire prosecution case was based on statements from alleged witnesses, none of whom were brought to court to be examined on their statements. In addition to those obstacles preventing the accused from being able to present a defense, there was no translation from English or French into Cameroonian Pidgin English, the language spoken by the majority of the defendants.

In an October 14 press release, the army spokesperson acknowledged the "disproportionate reaction" of a gendarme who shot and killed a 4-year-old girl on her way to school in Buea, South-West region, and said an investigation has been opened.

Women's Rights

Discrimination against women is prevalent within Cameroonian society and incorporated in laws that subordinate women's status to men. The civil code, which applies in Francophone regions, provides that men are the head of households (Article 213), husbands have the right to choose the place of residence (Article 215), men and women do not have equal rights to immovable property (Article 1428), and spouses do not have equal administrative authority over assets during marriage (Articles 1421 and 1428). Domestic violence is endemic. There is no legislation that specifically criminalizes domestic violence or provides for preventative measures nor measures to promote protection of survivors.

Corruption

The government did not publish meaningful information about its Covid-19 spending, and many health care workers reported receiving little or no support to aid their pandemic response. The International Monetary Fund (IMF) approved two emergency loans and a multiyear program to Cameroon totaling over US$1 billion, despite the government failing to meet several of the transparency commitments in those loans.

On May 19, Cameroonian media published a summary of an audit by a Supreme Court investigative body, the *Chambres des Comptes*, which detailed findings of large-scale corruption and mismanagement involving 180 billion CFA ($333 million) dedicated to the Covid-19 response. It recommended "initiating 10 judicial cases regarding findings that likely violate criminal law." Cameroonian authorities have not yet commissioned or published an independent audit of Covid-19 spending, despite promising the IMF to do so by December 31, 2020.

Key International Actors

In January, the Vatican's secretary of state visited Cameroon and expressed the Roman Catholic Church's willingness to facilitate dialogue between the government and separatists.

On June 7, US Secretary of State Antony Blinken announced visa restrictions "on individuals who are believed to be responsible for, or complicit in, undermining the peaceful resolution of the crisis in the Anglophone regions of Cameroon" and condemned "human rights violations and abuses, and threats against advocates for peace or humanitarian workers."

Although Cameroon is not formally on the agenda of the UN Security Council, council members discuss the country during periodic sessions on the work of the UN Regional Office for Central Africa (UNOCA). Human Rights Watch and other organizations have called on the council to formally add the crisis in Cameroon's Anglophone regions to its agenda.

In November, the European Parliament adopted a resolution deploring human rights abuses in Cameroon and urging the European Union to step up action to address them. The EU repeatedly raised concerns about Cameroon at the UN Human Rights Council.

Canada

Since assuming office in 2015, the government of Prime Minister Justin Trudeau has made notable efforts to advance human rights in Canada. Despite progress, serious domestic and foreign policy challenges remain. These include wide-ranging abuses against Indigenous peoples and immigration detainees, including persons with disabilities. Canada's failures to mitigate the impact of climate change and provide adequate government support are also leading to violations in Indigenous communities across the country while compounding risks for people with disabilities and older people. Canada also grapples with serious human rights issues abroad relating to the lack of accountability for abuses by Canadian mining companies and meaningful action to repatriate Canadian nationals unlawfully detained in northeast Syria for suspected Islamic State (ISIS) ties.

Rights of Indigenous Peoples

Wide-ranging abuses against Indigenous peoples persist across Canada with significant challenges remaining to undo decades of structural and systemic discrimination.

Inadequate access to clean, safe drinking water continues to pose a major public health concern in many Indigenous communities—and continues to impede efforts to advance Indigenous rights in Canada, one of the world's most water-rich countries.

The government committed to end all drinking water advisories on First Nations reserves by 2021 but, as of September, more than 30 First Nations communities across Canada remained subject to long-term water advisories, which alert communities when their water is not safe to drink. In July, an CDN$8 million settlement agreement was reached in two class action lawsuits against the federal government brought by First Nations communities living under drinking water advisories.

In September, the Canadian Human Rights Tribunal rejected the federal government's request for judicial review of two decisions relating to Indigenous children. In 2019, the tribunal found that Ottawa "willfully and recklessly discriminated against Indigenous children on reserve by failing to provide funding for child and family services." The tribunal ordered the government to provide up to CDN$40,000 to each Indigenous child who was unnecessarily taken into government care on or after January 1, 2006.

From May to July, hundreds of unmarked graves were found at former government-funded and church-run residential schools in the provinces of British Columbia and Saskatchewan. Approximately 150,000 Indigenous children were removed from their families and communities and placed in residential schools, where they were forbidden to speak their own languages or practice their culture. Many also suffered physical and sexual abuse at residential schools, which operated until the 1990s.

Prime Minister Trudeau called on the Roman Catholic Church, which ran residential schools across Canada, to make a formal apology and publish their records. Indigenous groups and the former chair of the Truth and Reconciliation Commission called for an independent investigation and resources from the federal government to continue forensic investigations of burial sites at former residential schools.

In June, the Canadian government passed Bill C-15, establishing a framework for implementing the United Nations Declaration on the Rights of Indigenous Peoples (UNDRIP) into federal legislation. The legislation requires that all levels of government affirm Indigenous rights as protected by international human rights standards.

Violence against Indigenous Women and Girls

New data released by Statistics Canada in May found that more than six out of 10 Indigenous women reported experiencing physical or sexual assault at some point in their lifetime. The report further found that 83 percent of Indigenous women who identify as lesbian, bisexual, or transgender had experienced intimate partner abuse.

In June, the federal government released a report promising a series of "transformative changes" to address persistent discrimination and violence against Indigenous women and gender-diverse people. In June, Prime Minister Justin Trudeau promised $2.2 billion in new spending over five years to address the root causes of violence against Indigenous women and girls. Canada has yet to release a federal action plan to address violence against Indigenous women and girls.

Immigration Detention

Following the onset of the Covid-19 pandemic, the government released immigration detainees at unprecedented rates due to public health concerns. However, a joint Human Rights Watch and Amnesty International report released in June found that Canada continues to detain people on immigration grounds in often abusive conditions. People in immigration detention, including persons with disabilities as well as those fleeing persecution and seeking protection in Canada, are regularly handcuffed, shackled, and held with little to no contact with the outside world. With no set release date, they can be held for months or years. Many are held in provincial jails with the regular jail population and are also sometimes subjected to solitary confinement.

The Canada Border Services Agency (CBSA) remains the only major law enforcement agency in Canada without independent civilian oversight. CBSA's unchecked exercise of its broad mandate and enforcement powers has repeatedly resulted in serious human rights violations in the context of immigration detention.

Corporate Accountability

Canada is home to half of the world's mining companies, with operations in nearly 100 countries around the world. Despite its extensive reach, the government has consistently failed to implement promised reforms to hold Canadian mining companies accountable for abuses committed abroad. The Canadian Ombudsperson for Responsible Enterprise (CORE) established in 2018 still lacks the authority to independently investigate or publicly report on human rights abuses involving Canadian extractive companies and has limited capacity to hold responsible parties accountable.

In June, the House of Commons Subcommittee on International Human Rights tabled a report calling on the government to introduce legislation requiring Canadian companies to conduct human rights due diligence to "identify, prevent, mitigate and account for any potential adverse human rights, environmen-

"I Didn't Feel Like a Human in There"

Immigration Detention in Canada and its Impact on Mental Health tal and gendered impacts" caused by their supply chains and operations. The committee also asked the government to consider strengthening the powers of the CORE by granting it the authority to compel witnesses and documents.

In February, a Canadian member of parliament filed a petition in the House of Commons calling on the government to investigate the role of Canadian mining companies in the extrajudicial killings of environmental and human rights defenders in the Philippines.

In March, a Canadian law professor filed a lawsuit against the federal government alleging that it improperly withheld information about its diplomatic interventions on behalf of a Canadian mining company accused of human rights violations at its mine in Guatemala.

In May, over 80 civil society organizations released a letter calling on Canadian mining company Barrick Gold, as well as the government of the Dominican Republic, to reconsider the planned expansion of the Pueblo Viejo gold mine due to concerns about environmental and human rights impacts.

Counterterrorism

Nearly four dozen Canadian men, women, and children remain unlawfully and indefinitely detained in northeast Syria in locked desert camps and prisons for Islamic State (ISIS) suspects and their families. The government of Prime Minister Trudeau continues to fail to take adequate steps to assist and repatriate these nationals, who have spent over two years in filthy, deeply degrading, life-threatening and often inhuman conditions. None of the Canadians has been charged with any crime or brought before a judge to review the legality and necessity of their detention.

In March, Canada with the assistance of a former US diplomat repatriated a 4-year-old Canadian child from one of these camps, but refused to bring her Canadian mother home. The mother was able to leave northeast Syria, but at time of writing remained stuck in the Kurdistan Region of Iraq awaiting travel documents that Canada needed to provide her in order for her to come home. At time of writing, Covid-19 was rapidly spreading across northeast Syria with nearly 30,000 cases reported in the region in September alone. The World Health Organization has warned of "significant risk" of high transmission in the camps.

In June, the Standing Committee on Foreign Affairs and International Development released a report following a parliamentary hearing on the impact of Covid-19 on children in crisis settings and called on the government to "pursue all options possible" to repatriate Canadian children detained in northeast Syria. The committee urged the government to "make every effort" to provide consular assistance to all detained Canadians. Opposition MPs on the committee tabled a supplementary report, recommending that the government act immediately to facilitate the swift repatriation of Canadian children and provide consular services to the detainees.

In September, 26 detainees in northeast Syria and their families in Canada filed an application in federal court against the government for failing to repatriate or help secure the release of these citizens. In September, Kimberly Polman, one of the Canadian detainees, began a hunger strike to protest her lack of medical care.

Climate Change Policy and Impacts

As a top 10 global greenhouse gas emitter Canada is contributing to the climate crisis taking a growing toll on human rights around the globe. Since being elected in 2015, the Trudeau government has repeatedly pledged to pursue ambitious action to reduce greenhouse gas emissions.
However, Canada remains the only G7 country whose greenhouse gas emissions have increased substantially since the adoption of the Paris Agreement.

Canada is also the top per capita public financer of fossil fuels in the world and projects increased oil production through 2050. According to the Climate Action Tracker, Canada's commitment to reduce emissions by 40-45 percent below 2005 levels by 2030 is not sufficient to meet the Paris Agreement goal to limit global warming to 1.5°C above pre-industrial levels. And Canada is not on track to meet its target.

World governments' failure to tackle climate change is already taking a growing toll on marginalized populations in Canada. Warming temperatures and increasingly unpredictable weather are reducing the availability of First Nations' traditional food sources, and increasing the difficulty and danger associated with harvesting food from the land.

Federal and provincial climate change policies have failed to put in place adequate measures to support First Nations in adapting to current and anticipated impacts of climate change and have largely ignored the impacts of climate change on First Nations' right to food. While the federal government made historic funding commitments in 2021 to support Indigenous food security and Indigenous-led climate monitoring, much more is needed to address the impact of the climate crisis on First Nations and to ensure that appropriate food subsidies and health resources are available to all who need them.

Inadequate government support also compounded risks for people with disabilities and older people during the June 2021 "heat dome," an extreme and foreseeable heatwave that killed hundreds of people in the Canadian province of British Columbia. Lack of proper heat planning and lack of access to cooling and targeted support for at-risk populations contributed to unnecessary suffering and possibly deaths.

Key International Actors

UN Secretary-General António Guterres has repeatedly called for countries to repatriate their nationals held as ISIS suspects and family members from northeast Syria and in March called it "absolutely essential" that Canada do so. In February, the UN special rapporteur for the protection and promotion of human rights while countering terrorism had placed Canada on a 57-country "list of shame" for its failure to repatriate Canadian nationals from northeast Syria. The US has also repeatedly called on all countries to repatriate their nationals. Syria. The US has also repeatedly called on all countries to repatriate their nationals.

Foreign Policy

Prime Minister Trudeau has acknowledged the need for negotiations at the World Trade Organization to "resolve" intellectual property issues constraining supply of Covid-19 health products globally, but Canada has not supported the proposal of India and South Africa for a waiver of certain provisions of the TRIPS agreement, only going as far as supporting text-based negotiations for a consensus-based outcome.

In January, Canada issued a business advisory to Canadian companies outlining the legal and reputational risks of working in Xinjiang, China, where their supply chains may be tainted by forced labor. At the June session of the United Nations Human Rights Council, Canada delivered a joint statement on behalf of 44 countries, expressing concerns at abuses in Xinjiang, as well as the deteriorating rights situations in Hong Kong and Tibet.

At the February session of the United Nations Human Rights Council, Canada as a member of a core group on Sri Lanka supported the adoption of a resolution establishing a new accountability mechanism to collect, analyze, and preserve evidence of international crimes for use in future prosecutions.

In March, Canada joined more than 30 countries in supporting a joint declaration condemning human rights abuses in Egypt, including the crackdown on civil society and political opposition, and called for "accountability and immediate end of impunity."

In April, Canada announced additional sanctions on individuals and entities affiliated with the Myanmar military and issued an advisory for Canadian companies doing business with Myanmar-related entities. In July and August, Canada also imposed targeted sanctions on individuals in Nicaragua and Belarus respectively in response to ongoing human rights violations.

Central African Republic

Violence involving attacks on civilians continued across the country as govern-ment forces, with support from the Rwandan military and Russian mercenaries, fought the remnants of a rebel coalition that controls significant parts of the country. The Coalition of Patriots for Change (*Coalition des patriotes pour le changement*, CPC) attacked major towns in late 2020, preventing hundreds of thousands of people from voting in the December 27 presidential election won by President Faustin Archange Touadéra. Legislative elections, held in March, were more successful with only some parts of the country experiencing violence due to the counteroffensive against the CPC.

A January 13 CPC offensive on the capital, Bangui, was thwarted, and the city re-mained relatively stable. Much of the countryside, especially the northwest and the east, remained contested territory, with civilians often caught between the rebels and the government forces with their foreign allies.

Groups allied to the CPC, notably the Union for Peace in the Central African Re-public (UPC) in the east and 3R in the northwest, committed widespread abuses, including deliberately targeting civilians. Credible reports, including from the United Nations, indicated that security forces and Russian mercenaries also committed serious human rights abuses. On July 21, unidentified assailants car-ried out an attack in Ouham province, outside of Bossangoa, killing at least 13 people. The government committed to investigate the crime via a special com-mission of inquiry.

More than 2,000 Russian mercenaries, possibly from Wagner—a mercenary out-fit affiliated with Yevgeniy Prigozhin, a Russian oligarch said to be close to Russ-ian President Vladimir Putin—are deployed in the Central African Republic. While officially in the country to serve as military instructors, the UN has documented several instances in which these mercenaries participated in active fighting and were implicated in human rights abuses and violations of international humani-tarian law.

In April, Sidiki Abass, the leader of 3R, who was sanctioned by the UN and the United States, was killed in combat.

Several investigations remained pending at the Special Criminal Court (SCC), a war crimes court based in Bangui staffed by national and international judges and prosecutors. In September, the SCC announced charges against a high-ranking member of the presidential guard under former President François Bozizé. The International Criminal Court (ICC) started a trial of two anti-balaka suspects and held a confirmation of charges hearing in the case of a Seleka leader.

The country remained one of the most dangerous places in the world for humanitarians to work, with over 261 attacks on humanitarians registered between January and October.

Attacks on Civilians by Rebel Fighters

From December 15 to June 21, CPC fighters killed at least 61 civilians, according to the UN. Many of them appear to have been targeted because they participated in or were suspected of voting in the presidential election. In one case, in March, UPC fighters affiliated with the CPC in Ouaka province tied up, tortured, and killed three men before leaving their bodies on a road with electoral cards hanging around their necks, according to the UN.

Human Rights Watch also received credible reports throughout 2021 of dozens of civilians who were killed by fighters from the UPC in the Ouaka province and 3R in the Ouham Pende province. Landmines placed by 3R fighters, in an apparent attempt to ward off attacks by national forces and their foreign allies in Ouham Pende province, killed at least 20 civilians, including a worker from a Catholic mission and a humanitarian worker.

Abuses by National Forces and Foreign Allies

Members of the national army, the *Forces armées centrafricaines* (FACA), allegedly committed serious human rights violations including the extrajudicial executions of eight suspected CPC members in Ombella M'Poko province between late December and mid-January 2021. In the course of military operations, they also attacked civilians, occupied schools, and looted private property, according to the UN.

Human Rights Watch heard accounts from victims, witnesses, and other credible sources about human rights abuses committed by alleged Wagner mercenary fighters in the northwest and the east. In one instance, alleged Wagner fighters collaborated with troops from FACA to keep men suspected of being CPC combatants in inhuman detention conditions in Basse-Kotto province. Three former detainees from Basse-Kotto told Human Rights Watch that Wagner fighters committed extrajudicial executions of other detainees.

A Central African Republic government report published in October accused Russian trainers of committing human rights abuses.

Shrinking Political Space

Opposition leaders, including the former Interim President Catherine Samba-Panza, were forbidden from leaving the country at the beginning of the year due to "ongoing judicial investigations" into alleged links to armed groups affiliated with the CPC. A January judicial proceeding against Bozizé and other members of Bozizé's party also loosely implicated other opposition leaders without clear justification.

Some programs on Radio Centrafrique and all radio programs that allow listeners to call in—on both state and private radio stations—were suspended by the High Communication Council during the presidential electoral period. Officially due to security concerns, the authorities restricted the movement of journalists outside Bangui throughout the year, limiting their ability to accurately report on abuses by rebels, national forces, and international forces aligned with the government.

Justice for Serious Crimes

In January, Seleka commander Mahamat Said Abdel Kani was transferred to ICC headquarters in The Hague. Said is accused of war crimes and crimes against humanity committed in Bangui in 2013. He is the first Seleka leader to face charges before the ICC. The ICC held a hearing on whether to confirm the charges in October, which will determine whether there is sufficient evidence for the case to go to trial.

In February, the ICC opened the trial in the case of anti-balaka leaders Patrice-Edouard Ngaïssona and Alfred Yékatom. The charges against both include war crimes and crimes against humanity committed between December 2013 and December 2014. Ngaïssona was arrested in France and transferred to the ICC in December 2018. Yékatom was transferred to the ICC by Central African Republic authorities in November 2018.

On September 10, the SCC announced that it had charged Eugène Ngaïkosset with crimes against humanity, but did not specify details of the charges. Ngaïkosset, a former captain in the presidential guard, led a unit that was implicated in numerous crimes, including the killing of at least dozens of civilians and the burning of thousands of homes in the country's northwest and northeast between 2005 and 2007. He is also alleged to have committed crimes as a leader of the anti-balaka movement.

Despite some advances in terms of rendering justice, Human Rights Watch received credible accounts from victims of crimes committed by FACA or alleged Wagner members who said they were too scared to make judicial complaints.

In response to a joint report from the UN peacekeeping mission, MINUSCA, and the Office of the UN's High Commissioner for Human Rights (OHCHR) in July, the government of the Central African Republic, which disputed some of the report's findings on abuses by FACA forces, reiterated that it was ready to initiate judicial proceedings against perpetrators of serious crimes in order to put an end to human rights violations.

Refugees and Internally Displaced People (IDPs)

The total number of displaced people rose as a result of renewed fighting. Over 1.4 million people, according to the UN, were either refugees in neighboring countries (710,000) or internally displaced (712,000) as of September 2021. Over 233,000 people, 70,000 of whom are children, were newly internally displaced, including 131,000 who became refugees due to electoral violence. Conditions for IDPs and refugees, most of whom stay in camps, remained harsh. Assistance to IDPs was seriously hampered by attacks on humanitarians and general insecurity in the country.

About 2.8 million people, out of a population of 4.6 million, needed humanitarian assistance. The humanitarian response plan was underfunded, with a budget gap of around US$176 million as of October 2021.

Key International Actors

The UN peacekeeping mission, MINUSCA, deployed 11,938 military peacekeepers and 2,182 police across many parts of the country. Under Chapter VII of the UN Charter, the mission is authorized to take all necessary means to protect the civilian population from threat of physical violence and to "implement a mission-wide protection strategy." In November, the UN Security Council extended the mandate of the mission for an additional year.

On September 15, the mission announced the repatriation of the 450-strong contingent from Gabon after internal investigations revealed cases of sexual exploitation and abuse of five girls. The UN Secretariat called on the Gabonese authorities to appoint a national investigator to conduct an investigation within 90 days, and launched its own investigation through the Office of Internal Oversight Services. Allegations of sexual violence and abuse against the Gabonese contingent had been made over the past several years.

In March, a group of UN experts, including those from the Working Group on the use of mercenaries, expressed concern about reports of crimes and human rights abuses attributable to fighters from Wagner, working jointly with state security forces (and in some instances, UN peacekeepers), including extrajudicial executions, torture, arbitrary detention, enforced disappearances, and forced displacement. In October, the same group of UN experts expressed concern about intimidation and violent harassment by "Russian instructors" from Wagner of civilians, including peacekeepers, journalists, aid workers, and minorities.

Chad

On April 19, the Chadian electoral commission announced that President Idriss Déby Itno had won a sixth term in the April 11 presidential elections. The pre-election period was marred by a ruthless government crackdown on protesters and the political opposition. On April 20, a spokesperson for the Chadian army announced that President Déby, 68, had died of injuries suffered in clashes between government forces and rebels from the Front for Change and Concord in Chad (FACT), based in southern Libya. The exact circumstances of Déby's death remain unclear. The government and parliament were dissolved, and a Transitional Military Council (TMC) headed by Mahamat Idriss Déby Itno, Déby's son, took control of the country and promised an 18-month transition.

The period following elections and Déby's death was characterized by violence. During protests in late April and May, security forces used excessive force against opposition-led demonstrations, and arrested more than 700 people, many who reported ill-treatment, including torture, in detention. On October 2, security forces fired teargas canisters, rubber bullets, and potentially live ammunition at protesters in N'Djamena, injuring about 40 to 45 people and damaging private property.

On June 10, the authorities released Baradine Berdei Targuio, a prominent human rights defender, arrested in January after he posted a Facebook message about President Déby's alleged poor health.

On August 10, the transitional president invited rebel groups, with whom he had previously refused to negotiate, to participate alongside other stakeholders in a national dialogue which started on November 5. In a November 2 joint statement, Chad's main rebel groups, including the Union of Resistance Forces (UFR) and the FACT said they are willing to participate in the national dialogue under "certain conditions," such as the release of members of their groups from prison, and a general amnesty. Opposition and civil society groups criticized the proposed national dialogue but called on transitional authorities to ensure it is inclusive.

Former Chadian dictator Hissène Habré died of Covid-19 on August 24 in Dakar, Senegal's capital, where he was serving a life sentence for serious international crimes. In September, a delegation from the African Union visited N'Djamena, Chad's capital, to finalize a trust fund aimed at compensating 7,396 victims of Habré's crimes.

The armed Islamist groups Boko Haram and the Islamic State in West Africa Province (ISWAP) continued their attacks in the Lake Chad area, targeting both civilians and military forces, and causing restrictions in humanitarian access. On August 21, Chad announced it will recall half of its 1,000 troops from the G5 Sahel Joint Force, a military force created to counter Islamist armed groups in the tri-border area of Mali, Burkina Faso, and Niger.

According to the United Nations, at least 309 people were killed, 182 injured, and more than 6,500 were internally displaced during intercommunal violence in Chad in 2021.

Pre-Election Violence

Chad's security forces cracked down on protesters and the political opposition in the lead-up to the country's April 11 presidential election. In the capital N'Djamena, they used teargas to disperse peaceful protesters who called for political change and an end to social and economic injustices on February 6, February 15, March 20, and March 27, injuring dozens of protesters and human rights activists, including Mahamat Nour Ibedou, Secretary General of the Chadian Human Rights Convention, a local rights group, and bystanders. They also arbitrarily arrested at least 112 opposition party members and supporters and civil society activists, subjecting some to severe beatings and other ill-treatment.

In an attack on the home of a political opposition leader and presidential candidate, Yaya Dillo, on February 28, security forces killed his 80-year-old mother and wounded five other family members.

Opposition parties accused the government of using Covid-19 regulations to block their campaigns and ban political gatherings, including a strict lockdown that was imposed in N'Djamena from January 1 to March 10.

Post-Election Violence

Security forces used excessive force, including indiscriminate live ammunition, to disperse opposition-led demonstrations across Chad in the aftermath of the April 11 election and Déby's subsequent death.

Members and supporters of opposition parties and civil society organizations united under a coalition known as *Wakit Tamma* ("the time has come" in Chadian Arabic) and other residents demonstrated in N'Djamena, Moundou, Doba, and other cities across the country, on April 27 and 28, and May 8 and 19, challenging the transitional military council's ban on demonstrations and demanding a transition to civilian rule.

During protests, at least seven people were killed, dozens were wounded, and security forces arrested more than 700 people, many who reported ill-treatment and torture in detention. Among those whom security forces and other authorities arrested, threatened, and intimidated were injured persons being treated at health facilities. All those arrested were released in the following months.

On October 2, hundreds of N'Djamena residents joined members and supporters of Wakit Tamma to protest the TMC's rule and seek amendments to Chad's transitional charter. Although the authorities had authorized this demonstration, anti-riot police—and in at least one case, gendarmes—fired teargas canisters, rubber bullets, and potentially live ammunition at the protesters, injuring about 40 to 45 people and damaging private property.

Abuses by Armed Groups

Boko Haram and ISWAP continue to commit serious human rights abuses against civilians in the Lake Chad area, leading to dozens of deaths and a major humanitarian crisis. The UN said over 400,000 people were internally displaced in September in the region.

International media reported that on September 19, Boko Haram fighters killed nine people and burned several homes in Kadjigoroumave village, Lake Chad region.

International Justice

Former Chadian dictator Hissène Habré died on August 24 in Dakar, where he was serving a life sentence following his conviction for serious international crimes. This followed a landmark effort to ensure justice for his role in serious human rights violations.

Habré's government was responsible for widespread political killings, systematic torture, thousands of arbitrary arrests, and targeting of particular ethnic groups. Habré himself was involved in the abuses during his rule in Chad from 1982 to 1990, principally by maintaining tight control over his feared political police, the Documentation and Security Directorate (DDS), whose members tortured and killed those who opposed Habré or simply belonged to the wrong ethnic group.

An appeals court confirmed Habré's conviction in April 2017 and awarded 82 billion CFA francs (approximately US$150 million) to 7,396 victims, mandating an African Union Trust Fund to raise the money by searching for Habré's assets and soliciting contributions. In September, a delegation from the African Union visited N'Djamena, Chad's capital, to finalize the establishment of the Trust Fund, which could help pave the way for victims of his crimes to receive long sought reparations.

Intercommunal Violence

Intercommunal and inter-ethnic violence intensified across Chad, especially in the eastern region, primarily in areas where availability of natural resources, including water and land, is limited. Local human rights groups accused the government of ignoring these conflicts and failing to prevent the violence and protect the population. According to the UN, at least 309 people were killed, 182 injured, and more than 6,500 internally displaced in intercommunal violence in Chad in 2021.

On April 14 and 15, intercommunal clashes between herders and farmers in Am-Barid and Siheb, Salamat province, led to over 100 deaths and 100 injured, according to the UN. On August 7 and 8, intercommunal clashes caused by a conflict over land between local farmers and herders in Hadier Lamis province led to the death of at least 25 people, according to international media. Inter-communal violence between sedentary farmers and nomadic herders killed at least 28 people on September 19 and 20 in the villages of Kidji-Mina and Tiyo, eastern Chad, according to international media and local human rights groups.

Chile

Chile has taken initial steps to reform the national police, the Carabineros, prompted by complaints of serious abuses against protesters in 2019. Substantial changes to the police disciplinary system and protocols are still needed.

In October 2020, Chileans voted to establish a convention to write a new constitution. Members began work in July 2021 and have a year to present a new text, which is to be submitted to popular plebiscite.

Chile faces important human rights challenges related to prison conditions, accountability for past abuses, and protecting the rights of migrants, refugees, women, children, Indigenous people, and lesbian, gay, bisexual, and transgender (LGBT) people.

Police Reform

Hundreds of complaints of use of excessive force against protesters and ill-treatment of detainees since 2019 have prompted efforts to reform the police.

The Chilean National Human Rights Institute (INDH) reported 460 cases of eye injuries allegedly caused by police from October 2019 through March 2020. The Salvador Hospital in Santiago reported treating 182 cases of ocular trauma caused by kinetic impact projectiles that appeared to have been fired by police anti-riot guns between October and November 2019.

In November 2019, at Human Rights Watch's recommendation, the Carabineros temporarily suspended the use of anti-riot shotguns—which use less lethal ammunition— except when there was risk to life. In July 2020, however, the Carabineros updated its protocol on these shotguns in a way that leaves ample room for abuse. The protocol says their use should be "preferably," but not exclusively, defensive; it also allows the use of shotguns in defense of police stations, which could include when protesters throw rocks at a police building. The protocol does not specify what type of less lethal ammunition may be used, thus allowing the same type of kinetic impact projectiles that caused hundreds of eye injuries in 2019 and 2020; does not say at what distance from protesters police should shoot; and in some circumstances even allows shooting anywhere on the body.

In January 2020, the Carabineros adopted a protocol on body cameras that gives officers complete control to start and stop recording. It requires them to start recording right before they open fire with an anti-riot shotgun, meaning they would not record a video of the prior situation, which could show whether the use of force was permissible or not. The protocol also establishes that recordings are to be kept secret, even from victims of excessive police force, unless prosecutors or judges request access within a short 30-day period, after which most recordings will be deleted.

The Ministry of Interior has met with nongovernmental organizations (NGOs), experts, and the Carabineros to discuss amending police protocols, including a 2019 protocol that allows the police to add teargas to water cannons without having previously performed a public study on its health impact.

The government has also introduced several police reform bills that would increase oversight and transparency but do not overhaul the Carabineros' disciplinary regime, which does not guarantee independent and impartial investigations.

The Attorney General's Office launched 8,581 investigations on alleged police abuses committed from October 2019 to March 2020. By January 2021, it had closed more than 35 percent of them without pressing charges. As of September, only five Carabineros had been convicted, the National Human Rights Institute reported.

Carabineros opened 1,433 administrative investigations for involvement "in acts of violence," which resulted in 158 disciplinary punishments, including the firing of 22 police officers, it said in July. Carabineros said it is considering firing another 21 officers.

Confronting Past Abuses

Chilean courts continue to try agents of Augusto Pinochet's dictatorship (1973-1990) for human rights abuses. In January 2021, four former military officers and a former police officer were convicted and sentenced to 15 years in prison for two murders and five attempted murders of detainees poisoned in 1981, which the court considered part of a "systematic" policy of repression and crimes against humanity.

Migrants and Refugees' Rights

In April 2021, Congress passed a new immigration law that allows authorities to issue deportation orders without hearing migrants or giving them the chance to present evidence. Although the law decriminalizes undocumented entry into the country, it allows for the immediate expulsion of migrants who crossed the border or were trying to cross the border, raising concerns about due process. Some of the law's provisions have already entered into effect, while others require the Ministry of Interior to issue regulations.

From January through April, the government had deported 294 people, most without judicial review, and announced plans to deport a total of 1,500 by year's end.

A series of rulings by Chile's Supreme Court and appeal courts have ordered authorities to stop hundreds of deportations. The rulings have exposed violations of due process in deportations.

Most people deported in 2021, up to October, were Venezuelans. More than 457,000 Venezuelans are estimated to be living in Chile, most with legal status. But migration policies since 2019 have made it increasingly difficult for Venezuelans to obtain visas or asylum. Chile only granted refugee status to 3 Venezuelans, out of 325 applications, in 2020, and to 4 out of 987 in 2021, as of September. The relatively low number of applications appears to be the result of obstacles to apply and border closures.

From January through November 10, 20 migrants had died crossing the high-altitude border from Bolivia to Chile.

In September, Carabineros evicted Venezuelans from a square in the northern city of Iquique, during which there were some acts of violence. The next day, anti-migrant protesters burned personal belongings of Venezuelans living in the streets.

Women's and Girls' Rights

Chile's 28-year total abortion ban ended in 2017, when the Constitutional Court upheld a law decriminalizing abortion when the life of a pregnant woman is at risk, the fetus is unviable, or a pregnancy results from rape.

However, people seeking safe and legal abortions continue to face multiple barriers. The latest government data available, from 2019, shows that 18 percent of obstetricians in public hospitals refuse to perform abortions when the life of a woman is at risk; 25 percent when the fetus is unviable; and almost 50 percent in cases of rape.

In November 2021, the House of Representatives rejected a bill to decriminalize abortion until the 14th week of pregnancy.

According to the coalition of NGOs Mesa de Acción por el Aborto, the public health system restricted access to comprehensive sexual and reproductive health services like pap tests, mammograms, and medical care for sexually transmitted infections for some periods of the pandemic, but resumed providing them at the beginning of 2021.

Thirty-three women and girls were victims of femicide from January through mid-September 2021, the NGO Women's Network Against Violence Against Women reported. Legislation in 2020 expanded the definition of femicide to a killing committed for "gender motives," without requiring a relationship between the perpetrator and the victim, as was previously the case.

Indigenous Rights

In May 2021, 1.2 million Indigenous voters selected representatives for 17 seats at the constitutional convention reserved for Indigenous people.

In July, the constitutional convention chose as its president Elisa Loncón of the Mapuche people, the largest Indigenous group in Chile, with more than 1 million members.

Indigenous movements want the new constitution to recognize Indigenous peoples as nations within a plurinational Chile, as well as their rights to land and resources.

Long-standing conflict between the government and some Mapuche land-rights activists in the south continues. In October, a former Carabinero colonel was found guilty of killing a 17-year-old Mapuche boy, almost two decades after the death had taken place.

In October, President Sebastián Piñera declared a state of emergency in four southern provinces, citing increasing violence linked to drug trafficking, terrorism, and organized crime. More than 2,000 military personnel were sent to support police activities.

Sexual Orientation and Gender Identity

In December 2021, Congress approved a bill, prioritized by President Piñera, which legalizes marriage between same-sex couples and also recognizes rights enjoyed by heterosexual couples, like the right to adopt children.

In August, a law eliminating "homosexual conduct" as grounds for divorce came into effect.

Children's Rights

In August 2021, a judge presented before the Senate commission on children's rights complaints of sexual exploitation and human rights violations in a shelter for children separated from their families run by the National Service for Minors (SENAME) in Santiago.

In October, a new National Specialized Protection Service for Children and Adolescents took over SENAME's child protection programs. A pending bill would also create a new agency to handle children in conflict with the law, replacing SENAME. Human rights organizations have raised concerns that, despite institutional changes, substantial reform to improve care for children is lacking.

Covid-19

More than 80 percent of Chileans were fully vaccinated against Covid-19 as of November 8, 2021, one of the highest rates in the world.

In March 2020, schools closed to curb the spread of the Covid-19 virus, affecting 3.5 million students. The Ministry of Education provided educational content through an online platform, but acknowledged that only 27 percent of low-income students had access to online education. In-person education resumed in July 2021, although, as of October, attendance was not mandatory and remained low.

Disability Rights

Chile's civil code uses derogatory language about people with disabilities and in many cases strips them of their legal capacity, including by providing for full guardianship of them.

The government has not updated data about the number of people with disabilities since 2015.

Prison Conditions and Pretrial Detention

Overcrowding in some detention centers and prison violence endangered Chile's detainee population of 39,000 as of October 31, 2021. Homicides in prisons increased by 75 percent from 2017 through 2020, the Attorney General's Office said in September 2021.

In May, the government reported that around 1,800 detainees belonging to groups at higher risk from Covid-19 had been granted house arrest based on an April 2020 law.

The number of pretrial detainees has increased by about a third since 2012. As of August, 37 percent of detainees were awaiting trial. Chile's criminal code allows pretrial detention in broad circumstances and does not establish a maximum period for detention.

In December 2020, the Minister of Justice acknowledged that pretrial detention is used excessively. He said that about 40 percent of pretrial detainees are later found innocent or given sentences not compatible with pretrial detention.

Freedom of Speech

In November 2020, the Constitutional Court ruled unconstitutional a bill passed by the House of Representatives to criminalize speech of people who "justify," "approve of," or "deny" human rights violations during the dictatorship, finding it violated the freedom to express opinions without prior censorship. The Senate then had to drop the bill.

Key International Actors

In April 2021, the UN Committee on the Protection of the Rights of All Migrant Workers and Members of Their Families expressed concern that Chile had expelled migrants en masse in February, failing to examine each case and making appeals materially impossible.

Chile strongly criticized abuses by the Nicolás Maduro government in Venezuela and, with other members of the Lima Group, a group of Latin American countries calling to restore democracy in Venezuela, refused to recognize the flawed legislative elections of December 2020.

Chile denounced arbitrary detention of presidential candidates, students, and members of civil society organizations in Nicaragua, and called for free and fair elections there.

President Piñera committed, in August, to receiving 10 Afghan women with their families in the context of the crisis affecting their country. The Foreign Ministry told the press it was working to receive up to 300 Afghans.

China

With President Xi Jinping at the helm, the Chinese government doubled down on repression inside and outside the country in 2021. Its "zero-tolerance" policy towards Covid-19 strengthened the authorities' hand, as they imposed harsh policies in the name of public health.

Beijing's information manipulation has become pervasive: the government censors, punishes dissent, propagates disinformation, and tightens the reins on tech giants. The once-cacophonous internet is now dominated by pro-government voices that report to the authorities on people whose views they deem insufficiently nationalistic.

The Chinese government pushed for more conservative values in 2021, shrinking space for lesbian, gay, bisexual and transgender (LGBT) and women's rights—issues previously considered less sensitive. Beijing grew less tolerant of criticism from private entrepreneurs. In July, courts imposed a sentence of 18 years on Sun Dawu, an agricultural tycoon supportive of rights activists, for vague crimes, after handing down a similarly harsh sentence to Ren Zhiqiang, an outspoken real estate mogul.

Xi's latest promise to tackle inequality and deliver "common prosperity" rings hollow as his government suffocates grassroots voices. After the self-immolation of a delivery truck driver in January, the government tightened regulatory controls to protect gig workers, yet also cracked down on their activism. China's rapidly expanding inequality led some young people to advocate a form of passive resistance known as "tang ping"—opting out of consumption and demeaning work—a concept that the government condemned and censored.

Authorities devastated human rights protections and civil liberties in Hong Kong, recasting much of the peaceful behavior that had undergirded Hong Kong life, such as publishing news, as acts of subversion. An April 2021 report by Human Rights Watch found authorities were committing crimes against humanity as part of a widespread and systematic attack on Uyghurs and other Turkic Muslims in Xinjiang, including mass detention, torture, and cultural persecution. Tibetans continued to be subjected to grave abuses, including harsh and lengthy imprisonment for exercising their basic rights.

"Break Their Lineage, Break Their Roots"

Chinese Government Crimes against Humanity Targeting Uyghurs and Other Turkic Muslims

**H U M A N
R I G H T S
W A T C H**

MillsLegalClinic
StanfordLawSchool

The Chinese government's rights record and its "wolf warrior" diplomacy resulted in increasingly negative public perceptions of the government in some countries abroad. New research from AidData revealed US$385 billion in "hidden debt" owed by developing countries to Chinese authorities. Some foreign governments took more concrete measures to press the Chinese government to improve its rights record, at home and abroad, but those remained inadequate to effectively challenge the scope and scale of Beijing's abuses.

Hong Kong

Beijing and Hong Kong authorities moved aggressively to roll back rights in Hong Kong.

Pro-democracy activists were arbitrarily arrested and detained. In January, authorities arrested 53 politicians for "subversion" for their involvement in a July 2020 public opinion poll. In September, three members of the group Student Politicism were arrested for "conspiracy to incite subversion" for delivering snacks to imprisoned protesters. Ordinary people were arrested for public defiance, such as for displaying flags bearing the banned 2019 protest slogan, "Reclaim Hong Kong, Revolution of Our Times."

At time of writing, over 150 people had been arrested for violating the draconian National Security Law (NSL) since it was imposed on June 30, 2020. Some NSL suspects held in custody were mistreated; pro-democracy activist Tam Tak-chi has been held in solitary confinement since he was detained in September 2020.

Authorities turned Hong Kong's quasi-democratic institutions into rubber-stamp bodies. In March, Beijing imposed "electoral reforms," requiring that only those loyal to the Chinese Communist Party could win a seat in Hong Kong's legislature. In April, following citizens' calls to cast blank ballots to protest the changes, the government revised the electoral laws to prohibit "incitement of others to cast blank ballots," with sentences of up to three years in prison. In September, when the government required elected members to the District Council—a consultative body that advises the government on local issues—to take a loyalty oath, about half resigned as they anticipated being disqualified by the government for their pro-democracy views.

Authorities banned the annual Victoria Park vigil commemorating victims of the 1989 Tiananmen Square massacre in Beijing. On the day of the vigil, police arrested the vice-chair of the organizing group, Hong Kong Alliance, cordoned off the park, and stationed officers throughout the city to prevent remembrances. In September, police froze the Alliance's HK$2.2 million (US$283,000) in assets, closed its June 4th Museum about the massacre, revoked its registration, deleted its social media accounts, and arrested its four leaders for "inciting subversion."

Dozens of civil society organizations disbanded in 2021, including protest organizer Civil Human Rights Front in August and the legal aid group 612 Humanitarian Relief Fund in November. Major labor groups, including the Hong Kong Professional Teachers' Union and Hong Kong Confederation of Trade Unions (HKCTU), disbanded in August and September respectively.

Throughout 2021, Beijing's newspapers smeared the Hong Kong Bar Association and its chairperson, Paul Harris, and called for his resignation. In August, citing threats to himself and his family, a pro-democracy candidate withdrew from a council election of the Law Society, a solicitors' association. Candidates with Beijing ties later won.

Authorities attacked press freedom. They forced the city's second most popular newspaper, *Apple Daily,* to close in June, after arresting its owner, Jimmy Lai, top executives, and editors, freezing Lai's HK$500 million (US$64 million) worth of assets, and raiding the paper's headquarters. Lai was also sentenced to a total of 14 months in prison in April for attending protests; he faced an additional six charges in four other cases.

The government also transformed the previously independent Radio Television Hong Kong (RTHK). In May, it replaced the head of RTHK with Li Pak Chuen, who had no prior media experience. Li then censored current affairs programs, prohibited staff from attending press award events that honored their coverage of the 2019 protests, and fired journalists and talk show hosts for their views critical of the government.

Police censored the internet through website blocking for the first time. In January 2021, the police ordered internet service providers to block access to HKChronicles.com, a website that documents police abuse but had also revealed personal information about police officers. In June, an Israeli hosting company took down the website of a Hong Kong exile initiative, 2021 Hong Kong Charter, at the request of the Hong Kong police, though it reinstated the site following an international outcry. In September, Hong Kong police blocked the website of the June 4th Museum.

Academic freedom deteriorated. University administrations were hostile towards student unions throughout 2021, while a number of academics were fired, or their contracts were not renewed, because of their pro-democracy views.

Authorities censored art, forcing theaters to pull a documentary about the 2019 protests in March, and forcing a new museum, M+, to pull a work by Chinese dissident-artist Ai Weiwei from its opening in November.

Xinjiang

The Chinese authorities are committing crimes against humanity against Uyghurs and other Turkic Muslims in Xinjiang. Abuses committed included mass arbitrary detention, torture, enforced disappearances, mass surveillance, cultural and religious persecution, separation of families, forced returns to China, forced labor, and sexual violence and violations of reproductive rights. Little news trickled out of Xinjiang in 2021, however, as the authorities maintained tight control over information, and as access to the region, already limited, was further constrained due to Covid-19 movement restrictions.

Some Uyghurs who disappeared into Xinjiang's abusive "Strike Hard Campaign against Violent Terrorism" were confirmed imprisoned, including prominent academic Rahile Dawut, though her alleged crime, length of sentence, and location of imprisonment remained unclear. There were also reports of Uyghurs dying in detention, including biotech researcher Mihriay Erkin, 31, businessman Yaqub Haji, 45, and poet and publisher Haji Mirzahid Kerimi, 82.

A report by the Uyghur Human Rights Project showed the Xinjiang government dispossessed Uyghurs by confiscating $84.8 million worth of assets from 21 jailed Uyghurs and auctioning the assets online.

Neighboring governments continued to facilitate Beijing's abuses. In September, Kazakh authorities banned a Russian-American researcher, Yevgeniy Bunin, from the country in apparent efforts to stymie his work documenting Xinjiang's abuses. Also in September, Turkey denied entry to Dolkun Isa, president of the Uyghur exile organization Uyghur World Congress. Uyghurs abroad from Afghanistan to Morocco feared deportations to China as the Chinese government continued to seek their return for alleged terrorism, a term vaguely defined under Chinese law that encompasses peaceful expression and advocacy.

Businesses continued to be subjected to heightened scrutiny over their Xinjiang involvement. In March, Chinese consumers boycotted international clothing brands for vowing to stop purchasing cotton from Xinjiang due to reports of forced labor. In April, Shenzhen police shut down the Chinese affiliate of a US labor auditing nonprofit, Verite. In July, US photography company Kodak deleted from Instagram a photographer's post calling Xinjiang "dystopian." The US Customs and Border Protection agency issued numerous import bans related to Xinjiang, including cotton and tomatoes from Xinjiang, and all downstream products that use Xinjiang cotton and tomatoes manufactured outside the region. There are growing calls for other countries to impose similar bans on Xinjiang imports.

Tibet

Authorities in Tibetan areas continue to severely restrict freedoms of religion, expression, movement, and assembly. They also fail to address popular concerns about mining and land grabs by local officials, which often involve intimidation and unlawful use of force by security forces.

Following a November 2020 announcement tightening controls on online communications that "undermine national unity," there was a surge of reported detentions of Tibetans in 2021 for alleged online offenses. In particular, Tibetans who communicated with people outside China were harassed and punished, regardless of the content of their communications.

The government stepped up coercive assimilationist policies. Chinese language classes were already compulsory for schoolteachers, local officials, and vocational trainees. In July, authorities announced that kindergartens in ethnic minority areas must use Chinese as a medium of instruction. In August, President

Xi emphasized the subordination of minority identities to a single national identity at the national "Ethnic Work" conference.

Authorities' heightened surveillance and intimidation at all levels, from online to neighborhoods to schools, and have rendered protests—such as those over the downgrading of minority language in Inner Mongolia in 2020—virtually impossible in Tibetan areas.

At least eight Tibetan prisoners or suspects were released due to ill health, some due to torture, four of whom died soon after, though the true number is unknown due to extreme information controls in Tibet.

Covid-19

Authorities continued to detain or prosecute people for criticizing the government's handling of the Covid-19 pandemic. Between January 2020 and June 2021, the Twitter account SpeechFreedomCN recorded at least 663 arrests for Covid-19-related speech. In March, retired professor Chen Zhaozhi was put on trial on charges of "picking quarrels and provoking trouble" for posting on social media, "The Wuhan pneumonia is not a Chinese virus, but Chinese Communist Party virus."

In August, a Beijing court sentenced activists Chen Mei and Cai Wei to 15 months in prison after convicting them of "picking quarrels and provoking trouble." They were detained in April 2020, for archiving censored online articles and social media posts about the pandemic. In the same month, imprisoned citizen journalist Zhang Zhan became seriously ill following a hunger strike. In December 2020, Zhang was sentenced to four years in prison after travelling to Wuhan to document the pandemic in February. Citizen journalist Fang Bin, who was detained in April 2020 in Wuhan, remained missing.

In 2021, authorities launched a nationwide vaccination campaign. Though the central government insists that the scheme is voluntary, many complained online about local authorities' abusive tactics to drive up vaccination rates. In some cases, the police physically restrained people to forcibly inoculate them; in others, authorities announced that they would suspend government benefits for anyone who refused vaccination or conditioned school enrollment on the vaccination of the student's entire family. Vaccine safety activist He Fangmei, taken

into custody by Henan authorities in October 2020, remained forcibly disappeared.

Human Rights Defenders

Authorities continued to crack down on human right defenders. Police in Hunan province detained activist Ou Biaofeng in December 2020, and later charged him with "inciting subversion." Ou has been an outspoken critic of the Chinese government and a supporter of Dong Yaoqiong, who was held in a psychiatric hospital for over a year after she splashed ink on a poster of President Xi in 2018. In February, Dong was reportedly taken into a psychiatric hospital again after she posted on Twitter about being subjected to police surveillance.

In January 2021, a court in Guizhou province sentenced former journalist Zhang Jialong to one-and-a-half years in prison for "picking quarrels and provoking trouble" for criticizing the government's censorship and urging the US to help "tear down" the Great Firewall in a 2014 meeting with then-US Secretary of State John Kerry.

In April, Beijing police detained food delivery worker and labor activist Chen Guojiang, accusing him of "picking quarrels and provoking trouble" after he tried to unionize delivery workers, undermining the government's vow to protect gig workers from dangerous working conditions.

In May, Guangzhou police detained human rights activist and writer Wang Aizhong on suspicion of "picking quarrels and provoking trouble."

In July, a court in Hebei province sentenced outspoken agricultural mogul Sun Dawu to 18 years in prison on charges including "picking quarrels and provoking trouble" and "assembling a crowd to attack state agencies." Sun was also a longtime supporter of human rights activists and lawyers.

In August, a court in Anhui province sentenced activist Zhou Weilin to three-and-a-half years in prison for his tweets critical of the government and articles he wrote for the overseas-based Rights Defense Network website.

Also in August, Cheng Yuan, Liu Yongze, and Wu Gejianxiong, the founder and two staff members of the anti-discrimination group Changsha Funeng, were sentenced to between two and five years in prison in a secret trial. Authorities detained the three in July 2019, on charges of "subversion."

In September, prominent rights lawyers Ding Jiaxi and Xu Zhiyong were indicted for "subversion." Authorities detained the activists in late 2019 and early 2020, for participating a gathering where attendees discussed human rights and China's political future. In February, Beijing police detained Li Qiaochu, a women's and labor rights activist, and partner of Xu, charging her with "subversion." While in detention, Li was taken to a hospital several times for treatment of mental and physical illnesses.

Also in September, the authorities forcibly disappeared Huang Xueqin, a journalist and leading voice in China's #MeToo movement, and Wang Jianbing, a labor activist. In the same month, detained human rights lawyer Chang Weiping was allowed by authorities to meet with his lawyer for the first time since he was forcibly disappeared in 2020.

Freedom of Expression

Authorities harassed, detained, or prosecuted numerous people for their online posts and private chat messages critical of the government, bringing trumped-up charges of "spreading rumors," "picking quarrels and provoking trouble," and "insulting the country's leaders." A 2021 *Wall Street Journal* report found that 58 Chinese users were punished with prison sentences between six months and four years since 2017 for their posts on Twitter, Facebook, and YouTube—all platforms banned in China.

An increasing number of people were punished for speeches deemed "unpatriotic." In February, at least seven people were detained for comments in relation to the border clash with Indian troops. In March, the government passed a provision stipulating that slandering "heroes and martyrs" could be punished with up to three years in prison. Former journalist Qiu Ziming was sentenced to the an eight-month prison term for suggesting the real death toll of Chinese soldiers in the clash was higher than the official figure.

Authorities continued to suppress online content not in line with "core socialist values." They targeted "misbehaving" celebrities and their online fan groups, and banned some reality shows. In April, censors deleted from WeChat and other websites an article penned by former premier Wen Jiaobao in which he wrote, "China, in my vision, should be a country of justice and fairness."

In December 2020, the Beijing police detained Haze Fan, a journalist for Bloomberg News, on suspicion of endangering national security. In July, the Communist Youth League encouraged the harassment and doxing of foreign journalists who were covering the flood disaster in Zhengzhou.

Freedom of Religion

Chinese law allows people to practice only five officially recognized religions in officially approved premises, and authorities retain control over personnel appointments, publications, finances, and seminary applications. Since 2016, when President Xi called for "Sinicization" of religions—which aims to ensure that the Chinese Communist Party is the arbiter of people's spiritual life—state control over religion has strengthened.

In 2021, police arrested those who worshipped outside of state-sanctioned parameters. In May, a Shenzhen court sentenced four employees from a company that sold audio devices broadcasting the Bible to between 15 months and six years for "operating an illegal business." In July, five members of an unauthorized "house church" in Shanxi province were detained on suspicion of "illegally crossing the border" after they went to a January 2020 religious conference in Malaysia. In August, police took nine people involved with the Golden Lamp Church, an unauthorized "house church" in Linfen, Shanxi province, into custody.

Authorities continued efforts to alter the architectural style of mosques and landmarks to make them look more "Chinese" across the country, while Hui Muslim activists said police had harassed them for criticizing the policy.

Mass Surveillance

Authorities devoted resources to expanding mass surveillance systems nationwide, in the absence of meaningful legal protections against unlawful or abusive government surveillance. Chinese companies with reported links to the government continue to draw global scrutiny for their data collection practices.

HUMAN RIGHTS WATCH

"Take Maternity Leave and You'll Be Replaced"

China's Two-Child Policy and Workplace Gender Discrimination

The Standing Committee of the National People's Congress passed the Personal Information Protection Law (PIPL) in August, making significant progress to regulate companies' collection of consumer data. While it could potentially empower citizens to hold companies accountable by filing a complaint with the government or getting a government-approved organization to file a lawsuit, it will unlikely check the state's use of mass surveillance.

Women's and Girls' Rights

March marked the fifth anniversary of the landmark Anti-Domestic Violence Law, yet victims continued to face an uphill battle in seeking authorities' protection and accountability for their abusers. In February, an article by former journalist Ma Jinyu on the violent abuses she suffered by her husband ignited a heated discussion on social media about the government's persistent failure to prosecute domestic violence.

Women's rights issues continued to face online censorship. In April, dozens of social media accounts run by women's rights activists, including those of prominent feminists Xiao Meili and Liang Xiaomen, were abruptly shut down after they were attacked and reported by nationalistic trolls online.

In June, the Chinese government announced that it would further relax the country's birth quotas from two to three children after the previous strict "one-child" policy led to a demographic crisis—and human trafficking. Many women expressed concerns that without measures to increase access to equitable parental leave and caregiving, the policy change could further exacerbate gender inequality. Human Rights Watch research shows that the two-child policy, in effect from 2016 to 2021, had worsened workplace gender discrimination.

In September, the State Council, China's cabinet, in its "Chinese Women's Development Guidelines" for 2021-2030, identified "reducing non-medically necessary abortions" as a step toward women's development. Many expressed concerns that the Chinese government could further restrict reproductive rights.

The #MeToo movement gained new traction in 2021, after more women came forward to accuse well-known men of sexual harassment. In August, the Beijing police arrested Chinese-Canadian singer Kris Wu for rape. Authorities in Hangzhou investigated a manager at the online commerce giant Alibaba after rape allega-

HUMAN
RIGHTS
WATCH

Underwater
Human Rights Impacts of a China Belt and Road Project in Cambodia

tions surfaced online. In September, a Beijing court dismissed a landmark sexual harassment case brought against a prominent TV host at the state broadcaster CCTV, after the judge refused the plaintiff's requests to retrieve corroborating evidence, including security camera footage.

Sexual Orientation and Gender Identity

While China decriminalized same-sex conduct in 1997, it still lacks laws protecting people from discrimination on the basis of sexual orientation or gender identity, and same-sex partnerships are not legal. The Chinese government showed greater rigidity towards sexual orientation and gender norms in 2021.

In February, a court in Jiangsu province ruled in favor of a publisher that described homosexuality as a "psychological disorder" in a university textbook. In July, social media platform WeChat removed dozens of LGBT accounts run by university students, claiming some had broken rules on online information. In September, the Chinese government banned "sissy" effeminate men and "abnormal esthetics" in the entertainment sector. It called for media to establish "correct beauty standards" and spread "positive values."

Belt and Road Initiative

The Belt and Road Initiative (BRI), announced in 2013, is the government's trillion-dollar infrastructure and investment program stretching across some 70 countries. Some BRI projects have been criticized for lack of transparency, disregard of community concerns, and negative environmental impacts.

Human Rights Watch published a report, in August, that documented economic, social, and cultural rights violations in Cambodia resulting from the Lower Sesan 2 dam's displacement of nearly 5,000 people between 2013 and 2018 and impacts on the livelihoods of tens of thousands of others upstream and downstream. The dam was a BRI project funded mainly by a Chinese-state owned bank and built by a Chinese-state owned electricity generation company.

China Labor Watch, an NGO, reported, in April, that overseas Chinese workers working on BRI infrastructure projects in Algeria, Indonesia, Pakistan, and other countries were victims of human trafficking and forced labor, including being deceived into working illegally, held against their will, and forced to work while infected with Covid-19 in early and mid-2020.

Climate Change Policies and Actions

China is by far the largest emitter of greenhouse gases globally, making a major contribution to the climate crisis that is taking a mounting toll on human rights around the globe. China accounts for nearly 70 percent of global emissions in 2018, although its per capita emissions put it only in the top 40 countries. Much of the considerable energy that has fueled China's economic growth comes from coal, driving these emissions. It produces half of the world's coal and is also the largest importer of oil, gas, and coal.

China is the world's largest funder and builder of overseas coal projects, some of which are through the BRI. President Xi announced at the UN General Assembly in October, that China would no longer "build new coal-fired power projects abroad." China continues to develop coal projects domestically.

In September 2020, Xi announced China would reach carbon neutrality by 2060, and reach peak carbon emissions before 2030. Despite these improved targets, the Climate Action Tracker rates China's domestic target as "highly insufficient" to meet the Paris Agreement goal to limit global warming to 1.5°C above pre-industrial levels.

China also leads the world in renewable energy use and is the largest funder of overseas renewable projects, some of which, however, have been linked to human rights abuses. China has much of the global production capacity for the materials needed for a global transition to renewable energy including wind turbines, solar panels, and minerals. Some of these materials are reportedly processed in Xinjiang, raising concerns about the use of forced labor.

China's imports of agricultural commodities drive more deforestation globally than those of any other market—including the imports of all 27 member states of the European Union combined. This deforestation is largely illegal. In November, in a joint China-US statement issued in the context of the global climate summit in Glasgow, the two countries said they would contribute to eliminating global illegal deforestation by enforcing their respective laws that ban illegal imports of timber. China has yet to enforce a restriction on illegal timber imports it adopted in 2019.

Key International Actors

Canada, the European Union, the United Kingdom, and the United States imposed coordinated and bilateral targeted sanctions on Chinese government officials and companies responsible for serious human rights violations, including international crimes, in Xinjiang. The US also imposed sanctions on several senior Hong Kong officials for imposing the National Security Law. In August, the US gave Hong Kong people in the US a temporary 18-month "safe haven."

In September, UN High Commissioner for Human Rights Michelle Bachelet expressed "regret" that the authorities had not given her meaningful access to Xinjiang, and said that her office would issue an assessment of human rights in that region. Her announcement followed a joint statement of concern by 44 governments at the 47th session of the UN Human Rights Council. A similar statement was delivered by 43 governments at the UN General Assembly in October 2021.

Parliamentarians in Belgium, Canada, the Czech Republic, Lithuania, the Netherlands, and the UK passed resolutions accusing the Chinese government of committing genocide against Uyghurs; some also called on their governments to limit participation in the 2022 Beijing Winter Olympics. The UK Parliament passed a non-binding motion supporting a diplomatic boycott of the Games. Members of the European Parliament halted the EU's proposed Comprehensive Agreement on Investment with China, citing human rights concerns, and freezing consideration of the deal for as long as they are subject to Beijing's counter sanctions. In September, they also adopted a recommendation for a new, more assertive, and better coordinated EU strategy on China, placing human rights at its core.

EU member states continued to issue strong statements of condemnation of China's human rights abuses at the UN. In July, the European Commission issued a guidance note to help businesses address the risk of forced labor, and, in September, Commission President Ursula von der Leyen pledged that the EU would introduce legislation banning goods produced through forced labor to enter the EU market.

Multinational companies came under greater pressure to withdraw operations from Xinjiang over concerns about forced labor. Those who publicly expressed concerns about that issue, including H&M and Nike, were then targeted for a boycott by consumers in China.

International technology companies continued to facilitate censorship in their operations in China. According to a May *New York Times* report, Apple created a mechanism to proactively reject or remove apps the company believes could run afoul of government censors. In June, Apple announced that it would not roll out its new privacy measure, Private Relay, in China. (Apple declined to respond on the record to a Human Rights Watch letter regarding the issues.) Also in June, the *New York Times* reported that the search engine Bing, owned by Microsoft, blocked image and video results for the phrase "tank man" in countries including the US, Germany, and Switzerland. Microsoft attributed the incident to "accidental human error." LinkedIn, also owned by Microsoft, citing the need to comply with local laws, blocked the profiles of some Chinese government critics and people associated with organizations deemed critical of the government, including a Human Rights Watch employee. In October, LinkedIn announced it was shutting down its professional networking service in China, citing "challenging operating environment."

Few universities in democracies took steps to protect their students' and scholars' free speech involving criticism of the Chinese government. In Australia, Human Rights Watch research showed only weak efforts to push back against such problems. At the same time, none of the universities with ties to academia in Hong Kong publicly challenged Hong Kong authorities' clear assault on academic freedom—including harassing student unions and firing pro-democracy faculty—in the territory.

Foreign Policy

The Chinese government confirmed its use of "hostage diplomacy" when it released two Canadians, Michael Kovrig and Michael Spavor, within hours of Canada allowing Huawei executive Meng Wanzhou—detained for alleged violations of US sanctions law—to return to China.

At the United Nations, Chinese authorities continued to push back against criticism of its human rights violations. The government advanced a resolution on "combating legacies of colonialism," and continued to present other resolutions—prioritizing economic development, "mutually beneficial cooperation," and "realizing a better life for everyone" (the last of which was withdrawn due to lack of support)—that would weaken international norms by shifting focus away from accountability for rights violations. It also blocked access to UN forums for civil society groups that referred to Taiwan as an independent country.

In August and September, the Chinese government moved quickly to offer support to Afghanistan's new, abusive Taliban-controlled government, making clear its concerns that instability in that country should not allow for security threats to Xinjiang or the BRI.

New research shows that Chinese government-linked disinformation campaigns have spread in scope, languages used, and platforms globally, including in 2021 on the origin of Covid-19.

In response to sanctions imposed on Chinese government officials, companies, and agencies, in March, Chinese authorities accused several EU officials and civil society groups of "maliciously spread[ing] lies and disinformation," and imposed vague sanctions on them. In July, Beijing announced another round of sanctions on US-based individuals and organizations, including Human Rights Watch.

HUMAN
RIGHTS
WATCH

LEFT UNDEFENDED
Killings of Rights Defenders in Colombia's Remote Communities

Colombia

The peace accord in 2016 between the Revolutionary Armed Forces of Colombia (FARC) and the government ended a five-decades-long armed conflict and brought an initial decline in violence. But conflict-related violence has since taken new forms, and abuses by armed groups, including killings, massacres, and massive forced displacement increased in many remote areas of Colombia in 2021.

Civilians in various parts of the country suffered serious abuses at the hands of National Liberation Army (ELN) guerrillas, FARC dissidents, and paramilitary successor groups. Human rights defenders, journalists, Indigenous and Afro-Colombian leaders, and other community activists face pervasive death threats and violence. The government has taken insufficient and inadequate steps to protect them.

Between late April and mid-June, tens of thousands of people took to the streets across Colombia to protest a range of issues, including a proposed tax reform, economic inequality, police violence, and little protection for vulnerable communities in remote areas. Police officers repeatedly and arbitrarily dispersed peaceful demonstrations and used excessive, often brutal, force, including live ammunition and gender-based violence.

The Covid-19 pandemic and measures in place to control it had a devastating impact on poverty and inequality in Colombia. Almost half-a-million people fell into poverty in 2020, according to the government's multi-dimensional poverty index, and the number of households with children who did not attend school increased by almost 14 percent.

Impunity for past abuses, barriers to land restitution for displaced people, limits on reproductive rights, and the extreme poverty and isolation of Indigenous and Afro-Colombian communities remain important human rights concerns.

Guerrillas and FARC Dissidents

A minority of FARC guerrilla fighters, known as FARC dissidents, rejected the terms of the peace agreement, refused to disarm, and continue to commit abuses.

Other FARC dissidents disarmed initially but joined or created new groups, partly in response to attacks by armed groups and others against former fighters. As of late September 2021, more than 290 former FARC fighters had been killed in these attacks.

FARC dissidents and other armed groups, including the ELN and paramilitary successors, have committed multiple "massacres," defined in Colombia as the killing of three civilians or more in the same incident. OHCHR documented 76 massacres in 2020—the highest figure since 2014—and received reports of 82 more between January and September 2021.

The ELN continued in 2021 to commit war crimes and other serious abuses against civilians, including killings, forced displacement, and child recruitment.

In the southern municipality of Argelia, Cauca state, the ELN and FARC dissident groups committed multiple abuses including killings, massacres, and kidnappings, forcing thousands to flee. Similarly, on the Pacific coast of the southern state of Nariño, fighting among various FARC dissident groups displaced over 23,000 people between January and mid-August.

In Chocó state, on the western coast, fighting continued between the ELN and the Gaitanist Self-Defense Forces of Colombia (AGC), a group that emerged from right-wing paramilitaries. Fears of antipersonnel landmines, threats by armed groups, and the hazards of crossfire prevented more than 33,000 people in Chocó from leaving their communities between January and September, a situation known as "confinement."

Paramilitaries and Successors

Between 2003 and 2006, right-wing paramilitary organizations with close ties to security forces and politicians underwent a deeply flawed government demobilization process during which many members remained active and reorganized into new groups. These successor groups, most notably the AGC, continue to commit violations of the laws of war and serious human rights abuses including killings, disappearances, and rape.

In late July 2021, fighting between the AGC and a FARC dissident group, as well as threats by armed groups, forced over 4,000 people to flee the municipality of Ituango, in the north of Antioquia state.

Implementation of the Justice and Peace Law of 2005, which offers reduced sentences to demobilized paramilitary members who confess to their crimes, has been slow. Of the more than 30,000 paramilitary troops that officially demobilized, 4,000 have sought to exchange a confession for a reduced sentence. As of October 2020, roughly 650 had been sentenced.

Violations by Public Security Forces

Police officers committed serious human rights violations in response to largely peaceful protests across Colombia between late April and mid-June 2021. Human Rights Watch identified evidence linking the police to 25 killings of protesters and bystanders, in most cases with live ammunition.

Hundreds of protesters were injured, some suffering likely permanent loss of vision in one eye, apparently from teargas cartridges, stun grenades, or kinetic impact projectiles fired from riot guns.

In June, the Ombudsperson's Office reported receiving complaints of 5 cases of rape and over 100 cases of gender-based violence by police officers, including slapping and verbal abuse. Victims included lesbian, gay, bisexual, and transgender (LGBT) people.

Police officers arbitrarily detained hundreds of people, in some cases misusing a provision under Colombian law that allows them to "transfer" a person to an "assistance or protection center" to "protect" them or others.

While most demonstrations were peaceful, some individuals engaged in serious acts of violence, including attacking police officers and stations. On April 29, several people beat up and sexually abused a woman officer when they attacked a police station in Cali. Some protesters blocked roads for prolonged periods, at times limiting or impeding distribution of food or circulation of ambulances.

Cuba

The Cuban government continues to repress and punish virtually all forms of dissent and public criticism. At the same time, Cubans continue to endure a dire economic crisis, which impacts their social and economic rights.

In July, thousands of Cubans took to the streets in landmark demonstrations protesting long-standing restrictions on rights, scarcity of food and medicines, and the government's response to the Covid-19 pandemic. The government responded with brutal repression.

Arbitrary Detention and Short-Term Imprisonment

The government employs arbitrary detention to harass and intimidate critics, independent activists, political opponents, and others.

Security officers rarely present arrest warrants to justify detaining critics. In some cases, detainees are released after receiving official warnings, which prosecutors may use in subsequent criminal trials to show a pattern of what they call "delinquent" behavior.

Over 1,000 people, mostly peaceful demonstrators or bystanders, were detained during the July protests, Cuban rights groups reported. Officers prevented people from protesting or reporting on the protests, arresting critics and journalists as they headed to demonstrations or limiting their ability to leave their homes. Many were held incommunicado for days or weeks, violently arrested or beaten, and subjected to ill-treatment during detention.

Gabriela Zequeira Hernández, a 17-year-old student, was arrested in San Miguel de Padrón, Havana province, as she was walking past a demonstration on July 11. During detention, two female officers made her strip and squat naked five times. One of them told her to inspect her own vagina with her finger. Days later, a male officer threatened to take her and two men to the area known as the "pavilion," where detainees have conjugal visits. Officers repeatedly woke her up at night for interrogations, asking why she had protested and who was "financing" her. Days later, she was convicted and sentenced to eight months in prison for "public disorder," though she was allowed to serve her sentence in house arrest. She was only permitted to see her private lawyer a few minutes before the hearing.

In October 2021, Cuban authorities said that a demonstration being organized by a group of artists and dissidents for November 27 was "unlawful." Later that month, the Attorney General's Office released a statement "warning" people that they would face criminal prosecution if they "insisted" on carrying out a demonstration on November 27.

Cuban officers have also systematically detained independent journalists and artists. Victims include members of the coalition of artists known as the "San Isidro," "27N," and "Archipelago" movements, two coalitions of independent artists, as well as those involved in "Motherland and Life"—a viral song that repurposes the Cuban government's old slogan, "Motherland or Death" (Patria o Muerte) and criticizes repression in the country.

In many cases, police and intelligence officers appeared at critics' homes, ordering them to stay there, often for days or weeks, in what amounted to arbitrary deprivations of liberty.

Officers have repeatedly used regulations designed to prevent the spread of Covid-19 to harass and imprison government critics.

Freedom of Expression

The government controls virtually all media in Cuba and restricts access to outside information.

In February and August 2021, the Cuban government expanded the number of permitted private economic activities, yet independent journalism remained forbidden.

Journalists, bloggers, social media influencers, artists, and academics who publish information considered critical of the government are routinely subject to harassment, violence, smear campaigns, travel restrictions, internet cuts, online harassment, raids on homes and offices, confiscation of working materials, and arbitrary arrests. They are regularly held incommunicado.

Freedom of Expression, Peaceful Assembly, and Media

Journalists, activists, whistleblowers, and critics of government policies were intimidated and threatened, beaten, arrested, and in some cases prosecuted by the authorities and security forces.

In January, a military court acquitted eight members of Lucha (*Lutte pour le Changement*, Struggle for Change), a citizens' movement, after they spent a month in detention for peacefully marching in Beni territory. In July, two other members, Elisée Lwatumba and Eric Muhindo, who had been detained for three months following a peaceful march in Butembo, were provisionally released. Authorities arrested Parfait Muhani and Ghislain Muhiwa, also members of Lucha, in July and August respectively. They were both detained at Goma's central prison before being released on bail on November 6. Their trial on criminal defamation and criminal association charges was started on November 5 after their group denounced misappropriation of aid allegedly involving staff from Congo's first lady's foundation.

In February, authorities arrested three members of the citizens' movement Jicho ya Raiya in North Kivu's Masisi territory, after they criticized the mismanagement of local health structures. At time of writing, Claude Lwaboshi Buhazi, Serge Mikindo Waso, and Faustin Ombeni Tulinabo remained in pretrial detention in Goma's central prison.

In late February, it was revealed that authorities had sentenced whistleblowers Gradi Koko and Navy Malela to death in absentia in September 2020. The two former bank employees exposed alleged illegal financial practices and money laundering. In July, exiled anti-corruption whistleblower Jean-Jacques Lumumba faced threats and intimidation in Europe and Kinshasa.

Jacky Ndala, a youth leader for the political party Ensemble pour la République (Together for the Republic), was sentenced on appeal to 22 months in prison for "incitement to civil disobedience" after publicly opposing the discriminatory "Congolité Bill."

Authorities also banned demonstrations, while security forces used excessive force to break them up. In April, police killed five people and wounded at least eight others during peaceful protests in Goma, Butembo, and Beni territory. Following the protests, security forces and violent mobs in Nyiragongo territory, North Kivu, killed at least 10 people and injured at least 50 others.

On April 29, dozens of students calling for peace were violently accosted and rounded up by police forces in Beni. Tshisekedi later apologized to all children involved, but only after he appointed the police commander in charge of the round-up, François Kabeya, as mayor of Goma.

Attacks on Civilians by Armed Groups and Government Forces

Around 120 non-state armed groups were active in eastern Congo's Ituri, North Kivu, South Kivu, and Tanganyika provinces. Many of their commanders have been implicated in war crimes, including massacres, sexual violence against women and girls, forced recruitment of children, and pillage.

Various armed personnel, some unidentified, killed at least 1,600 civilians in South Kivu, North Kivu, and Ituri provinces, according to data collected by the Kivu Security Tracker, which documents violence in eastern Congo. This includes at least 172 civilians killed by Congolese security forces.

Congolese security forces conducted operations against armed groups in eastern Congo, with mixed results and at times using militia as proxy forces against other groups. United Nations peacekeepers supported national troops in joint operations against the ADF.

Tension remained high in South Kivu's highlands, with fighting involving several armed groups, some backed by neighboring countries.

On February 22, armed assailants ambushed a World Food Programme (WFP) convoy on the road north of Goma, killing one Congolese driver and the Italian ambassador to Congo as well as his bodyguard. In June, UN experts said they could not establish the identity of the attackers, and that national and international investigations were ongoing.

In July, the Tshisekedi administration launched a new Disarmament, Demobilization, Community Recovery, and Stabilization program. However, many Congolese activists publicly raised concerns over the appointment of the program's coordinator, Tommy Tambwe, a former leader of major Rwandan-backed rebel groups that have been responsible for countless abuses over the past 25 years.

Justice and Accountability

In January, French authorities arrested former Congolese rebel leader Roger Lumbala on charges of participating in a group formed to plan crimes against humanity and complicity in crimes against humanity. The investigation focuses on abuses featured in the 2010 UN Mapping Report, which documented the most serious crimes committed across Congo between 1993 and 2003.

In February, at least 67 Indigenous people, ethnic Iyeke, were killed and more than 1,200 houses burned by ethnic Nkundo villagers, across a dozen villages sitting on the edge of the Salonga National Park in the western Tshuapa province. Although four suspects were arrested, the investigation into the killings made no progress.

In March, the International Criminal Court's appeals chamber confirmed the conviction and sentence of Bosco Ntaganda, a former rebel leader and subsequently general in the Congolese army, to 30 years in prison on 18 counts of war crimes and crimes against humanity.

Starting in May, civilians in North Kivu and Ituri, both under martial law, were prosecuted for criminal offenses before military courts, contrary to principles of the African Commission on Human and Peoples' Rights.

In August, the Tshisekedi administration established a commission tasked with delivering a roadmap for transitional justice, but it has yet to fully commit to ending impunity for serious crimes. Military courts and other tribunals adjudicating cases of war crimes and crimes against humanity have made little progress in filling the wide accountability gap in the country. These cases continue to highlight severe shortcomings in the domestic justice system.

The trial, which opened in 2017, continued for the murders of United Nations investigators Michael Sharp and Zaida Catalán, and the disappearance of their three Congolese moto drivers and their interpreter. In September 2021, human rights organizations and foreign diplomats denounced the arrest of Congolese journalist Sosthène Kambidi, who was interrogated over the origin of a video showing the killing of the two investigators. Kambidi was granted conditional release on October 12.

The trial for the December 2018 Yumbi killings in the country's west, in which at least 535 people were killed, started before a military court in May 2021 but little progress was made.

Following revelations by international media, authorities made several arrests linked to the 2010 murder of prominent human rights defender Floribert Chebeya and his driver Fidèle Bazana. A new trial began in September 2021 for defendants Christian Kenga Kenga and Jacques Mugabo, both senior police officers. Meanwhile, Gen. John Numbi, who was also implicated in the double murder, reportedly fled Congo and was officially declared a deserter in June.

Congolese authorities made no apparent progress investigating and providing adequate medical or psychological support to victims of the September 2020 prison riot at Kasapa Central Prison in Lubumbashi. During three days of violence, inmates repeatedly raped several dozen female detainees, including a teenage girl.

Gédéon Kyungu, a notorious warlord responsible for atrocities in the southern region of Katanga who escaped from house arrest in Lubumbashi in March 2020 remained at large at time of writing.

Militia leader Guidon Shimiray Mwissa, wanted by Congolese authorities since 2019 for serious crimes, including rape and child soldier recruitment, remained active in North Kivu, commanding a faction of the Nduma Defense of Congo-Rénové (NDC-R). The Congolese army used a separate faction of the NDC-R, led by Gilbert Bwira, as a proxy to fight other armed groups, UN experts said in June. Bwira was eventually arrested in October.

Environment and Climate Change

Congo contains the world's second largest rainforest. Scientists estimate that the forest's soil alone holds billions of tons of carbon, as much as 20 years' worth of the fossil fuel emissions of the United States. If released through increased deforestation or other disturbances it could have catastrophic effects on efforts to contain climate change.

Successive governments continued to grant multiple logging contracts, despite imposing a moratorium on new logging concessions in 2002. In February, civil society organizations filed a lawsuit against the former environment minister for reportedly breaching the prohibition by granting logging concessions to Chinese companies in 2020.

In July, the Tshisekedi administration set out a plan that includes ending the moratorium on logging, but an agreement reached at the COP26 conditions lifting the moratorium on the planning of forest allocations based on a consultative process.

In April, President Tshisekedi pledged to restore forest cover to 63 percent by 2030 at a climate summit hosted by the US.

During the same month, a bill that would recognize Indigenous peoples' rights over their traditional territories was adopted in the National Assembly but it had yet to be voted by the Senate before it could be passed into law. Ending the moratorium on logging without a domestic legal framework that protects Indigenous rights could undermine communities' access to their forests, as they would have little recourse against businesses that claimed them.

Key International Actors

In January 2021, the UN Human Rights Committee, which monitors state compliance with the International Covenant on Civil and Political Rights, found that Congo violated the right to life of human rights defender Pascal Kabungulu, who was killed in an extrajudicial execution, in front of his family in 2005.

An independent commission, prompted by reporting of investigative journalists, found in September that more than 80 aid workers, including some employed by the World Health Organization, were involved in sexual abuse and exploitation of dozens of women during an Ebola outbreak in Congo between 2018 and 2020.

In October, the UN Human Rights Council decided to renew the mandate of the Team of International Experts on the situation in the Kasai and to extend its mandate to cover the entire country.

Ecuador

In May, President Guillermo Lasso took office. The 137 lawmakers of the National Assembly, where Lasso lacks a majority, started their four-year term in May, and elected the assembly's first Indigenous president. One of Lasso's first actions was to introduce a new bill aimed at undoing the severe damage to free speech caused by former President Rafael Correa during his decade in power.

Corruption, inefficiency, and political interference have plagued Ecuador's judiciary for years. Reforms under former President Lenín Moreno to repair the Correa administration's damage to democratic institutions improved the independence of key institutions but reports of trial delays and allegations of improper pressure on courts and lack of due process in high-profile corruption cases continued.

Poor prison conditions and violence, security agencies' indiscriminate use of force, restrictions on women's and girls' access to reproductive health care, and limited protection of children's and refugee rights remained serious concerns.

Several allegations of corruption marred the Covid-19 pandemic response.

Judicial Independence

Under President Moreno, a transitional Council of Citizen Participation was appointed to repair the Correa administration's damage to key institutions by dismissing authorities after evaluating their performance, and appointing new members to the Judiciary Council, Constitutional Court, and Prosecutor's Office, among other institutions.

In August 2020, Ecuador's Constitutional Court significantly limited the Judiciary Council's powers to interfere in judges' work.

However, during 2021, allegations persisted of unjustified delays during trials, government officials improperly pressuring courts, and lack of due process in high-profile corruption cases.

Use of Force by Security Forces

On May 6, the Constitutional Court nullified a May 2020 Defense Ministry resolution giving the military broad powers to participate in security operations at demonstrations and meetings, and to use lethal force. Security forces had used excessive force against demonstrators in October 2019. The role of the armed forces in law enforcement must be exceptional, temporary, limited to what is strictly necessary, and complementary to that of law enforcement agents, the court held.

The Constitutional Court instructed the National Assembly to consider its relevant findings—and international standards—during debate of a bill, pending at time of writing, to regulate use of force by security agencies.

In August, the Ombudsperson's Office found that police officers used excessive force in the rural town of La Merced de Buenos Aires when they dispersed residents who were blocking a road and protesting a government mining concession to an Australian mining company.

In March, a truth commission created by the Ombudsperson's Office to investigate excessive use of force during 2019 demonstrations attributed the deaths of six protesters to security forces. It attributed around 75 percent of human rights violations during the protests to police and 13 percent to the military.

Prison Conditions

Overcrowding and other poor conditions, violence, and inadequate health care are longstanding problems in prisons.

Over 600 detainees contracted Covid-19 in 2020 and fell ill in overcrowded cellblocks. Several reportedly died.

In September, a prison uprising in Guayaquil city left over 118 detainees dead and 52 injured. For the second time since taking office, President Lasso decreed a state of emergency in prisons, this one for 90 days.

Two other uprisings, in February and July, left over a hundred detainees dead and injured dozens of detainees and security officers, including a female officer who was raped.

In all three uprisings, police officers and soldiers intervened against armed criminal groups inside the facilities.

Women's Rights

On April 28, the Constitutional Court ruled abortion decriminalized in all cases in which the pregnancy results from rape. To comply, the Ombudsperson's Office introduced a bill on June 28 to guarantee access to abortion for victims of rape; six months are allowed for legislative debate at the National Assembly.

Until April, women and girls could seek an abortion only when they had a "mental disability" and had been raped or when the pregnancy endangered their health or life.

Stigmatization, mistreatment by health professionals, fear of criminal prosecution, and a narrow interpretation of the health exception remain barriers to abortion access. Low-income women appear more likely to be prosecuted.

The Attorney General's Office reported 49 femicides—defined as murders of women based on their gender—between January and September. But civil society organizations reported over 100 cases of killings of women in just the first six months of 2021.

Children's Rights

Sexual violence is a longstanding, pervasive problem in public and private schools. Between January 2014 and February 2021, Ecuador's Education Ministry registered 3,777 complaints of school-related sexual violence by teachers, administrative staff, and other students, including online.

On August 14, Ecuador commemorated its first national day against sexual violence in schools, complying with a 2020 Inter-American Court of Human Rights ruling in the Paola Guzman Albarracín case. Paola, who was 14 when her vice principal raped and abused her, took her own life in 2002. At time of writing, Ecuador had not complied fully with measures ordered by the court, including publishing data on school-related sexual violence, and training education staff on how to treat and prevent situations of sexual violence and assist victims of school-related sexual violence and their families.

HUMAN
RIGHTS
WATCH

"Why Do They Want to Make Me Suffer Again?"

The Impact of Abortion Prosecutions in Ecuador

In March, the National Assembly changed Ecuador's education law, adding mechanisms against violence in schools and guaranteeing free access to information about sexuality and sexual and reproductive rights.

The government's pandemic response included nationwide school closures, starting in April 2020. Ecuador ranked 13th, worldwide in total days of school closures, UNICEF reported, with 169 as of February 2021. Almost 4.5 million students have missed at least three-quarters of a year of classroom instruction. During the pandemic, only 4 out of 10 households with children under 5 have had access to early childhood development services, including pre-primary education.

Disability Rights

A substitute decision-making model for people with disabilities still prevails, failing to recognize their full legal capacity in all areas of life, including the right to informed consent to health treatment.

On March 26, the Inter-American Court of Human Rights ruled that Ecuador failed to properly inform Luis Eduardo Guachalá Chimbo, a 23-year-old with an intellectual disability, and his mother, about his treatment at a public psychiatric hospital and did not adopt all measures to obtain his full consent. Guachalá disappeared from the hospital in 2004, and Ecuador did not fulfill its obligation to search for him, the court ruled. He has never been found.

Sexual Orientation, Gender Identity, and Sex Characteristics

In June 2019, the Constitutional Court ruled in favor of same-sex marriage, declaring the country's marriage legislation unconstitutional.

The National Assembly has not yet complied with Constitutional Court rulings to revise legal provisions on civil marriage to include same-sex couples, reform the legal gender recognition procedure for transgender people to be based on self-determination, regulate assisted reproduction methods, and allow for same-sex couples to register their children with their surnames.

On June 28, the Secretary for Human Rights created a subsecretary office for diversity, charged with developing policies to prevent violence against lesbian, gay, bisexual, and transgender (LGBT) people. The office will not have its own budget.

Rights of Indigenous Peoples

Indigenous peoples are entitled, in the constitution, to communal possession of ancestral lands and consultation regarding resources and projects on them. These rights are not fully protected, human rights organizations and community leaders report.

Several communities have filed complaints seeking protection for their ancestral lands. In one case, the National Court will decide whether to uphold a lower court's order to evict loggers and farmers trespassing on the Siekopai Indigenous people's territory in the Amazonian province of Sucumbíos. Trespassers occupy half of the territory and have cleared a quarter of the forests, community leaders said.

In August, the Constitutional Court ruled against pretrial detention of members of uncontacted Indigenous tribes; it also ruled that pretrial detention of members of recently contacted tribes could not be ordered without first engaging in appropriate inter-cultural dialogue, including about alternatives to detention.

Indigenous people were impacted by Covid-19. On June 18, 2020, Waorani Indigenous communities successfully sued the government for its inaction. The judge ordered the Ministry of Health to send medical personnel and equipment to respond to an outbreak. In July this year, 126 Waoranis were vaccinated.

Refugees, Asylum Seekers, and Migrants

Ecuador has passed some of the most progressive laws in the region protecting migrants and refugees. As of September, Ecuador was sheltering 451,093 Venezuelan migrants and refugees. As of August, 1,151 people from all countries were recognized as refugees in 2021.

Although Ecuador promises free health care regardless of migratory status, Venezuelans experience limitations.

Venezuelans have various options for obtaining a visa, but with elevated costs and long processes, slowed by Covid-19. On June 17, President Lasso announced a regularization process that could benefit around 450,000 Venezuelans.

Right to Privacy

On May 10, the National Assembly adopted a data protection law, introduced under former President Moreno after a major breach of citizens' personal data. The law protects, under certain circumstances, citizens' rights to access, correct, and erase incorrect data about them stored in databases

Freedom of Expression

Soon after taking office, President Lasso introduced a bill to replace the Communications Law that former President Correa wielded to undermine free speech.

In 2018, legislators eliminated the agency known as SUPERCOM, which the Correa administration had used to harass and punish media. In 2020, they rescinded a problematic provision identifying communication as a public service.

On May 6, the lame duck National Assembly approved a Law to Prevent Violence, Digital Harassment, and Violation of Privacy. Though intended to address online gender-based violence, it threatened to severely restrict the ability of journalists and others to document and expose misconduct and human rights violations. President Lasso vetoed some problematic provisions on criminal defamation and disclosure of secrecy. However, legislators retained an overly broad definition of criminal defamation, which can be committed "through any of the information and communication technologies."

Accountability for Past Abuses

In 2010, a truth commission to investigate government abuses from 1984 to 2008 documented gross human rights violations against 456 people. Final rulings have been rendered in only two prosecutions. Others appear to be stalled.

Covid-19 and Corruption

The pandemic hit Ecuador hard, with 513,026 reported cases and 32,899 deaths as of October. In June 2020, amid allegations that corpses of people who died after getting Covid-19 had disappeared, a judge ordered authorities to identify them in hospital and police morgues in Guayaquil City. At time of writing, dozens of families were still looking for relatives' bodies.

Despite some improvements, the transparency of the government's spending in response to the pandemic has gaps, particularly related to beneficial ownership and publication of emergency procurement contracts. The Attorney General's Office has investigated allegations of corruption related to Covid-19 such as embezzlement and overpriced purchases of medical supplies.

President Lasso's administration accelerated roll-out of vaccines, bringing the percentage of people fully vaccinated to over 57, as of October.

Key International Actors and Foreign Policy

On June 14, the Inter-American Court of Human Rights held a hearing on allegations of human rights violations in the 2011 convictions of journalist Emilio Palacios and three members of the board of the newspaper El Universo for criminal defamation in an opinion piece criticizing then-President Correa. At time of writing, a decision was pending.

On July 13, the National Assembly ratified the Inter-American Convention Against All Forms of Discrimination and Intolerance, which disallows discrimination regarding gender expression, migratory circumstances, and genetic characteristics.

In August, the office of the United Nations High Commissioner for Refugees (UNHCR) released a survey showing that 82 percent of migrants and refugees in Ecuador would face significant risks if returned to their country of origin. Since a humanitarian visa program ended, UNHCR noted, regularization has become "difficult" in Ecuador for the Venezuelan population.

During the UN General Assembly in September, President Lasso expressed concern for fleeing Venezuelans. His administration has criticized the human rights situation in Venezuela and Nicaragua.

Ecuador joined 70 other countries in highlighting the need for a safe exit for fleeing Afghans. The 5,000 Afghans whom Ecuador volunteered to receive temporarily appear to have been relocated to other countries by the United States instead.

Egypt

In 2021, authorities escalated the use of the abusive Emergency State Security Courts to prosecute peaceful activists and critics who joined thousands of dissidents already in Egypt's congested prisons. Courts issued death sentences in mass trials, adding to the sharply escalating numbers of executions.

The government in January issued implementing regulations for the 2019 NGO law that codified draconian restrictions on independent organizations. The authorities failed to appropriately investigate a high-profile gang-rape, and key witnesses remain under extrajudicial travel bans after being jailed for months in apparent retaliation for coming forward.

The army continued to impose severe restrictions on movement and demolish hundreds of buildings in North Sinai in the name of fighting *Wilayat Sina'*, a local affiliate of the Islamic State (also known as ISIS). These demolitions likely amount to war crimes.

Egypt's prolonged human rights crisis under President Abdel Fattah al-Sisi's government was subject to rare international criticism at the United Nations Human Rights Council.

Police and Security Forces Abuses

In 2021, Interior Ministry police and National Security agents arbitrarily arrested dozens, likely hundreds, for peaceful activism, forcibly disappearing many for days or weeks. National Security officers also routinely required newly released activists to report to their offices regularly, in addition to other forms of extrajudicial coercion and summons. On February 1, police arrested Ahmed Samir Santawy, a Central European University student, and held him incommunicado for five days during which, his lawyer said, he was severely beaten.

Authorities failed to investigate incidents of torture and mistreatment, which remain widespread. On April 18, security forces arrested the mother, father, and sister of jailed dissident Abdelrahman Gamal Metwally al-Showeikh after his family filed a complaint about al-Showeikh's alleged torture and sexual assault

in a Minya prison. His mother, Hoda Abdel Hamid, remained in pretrial detention in a Cairo prison as of October, deprived of seeing her family or lawyers, after prosecutors accused her of "spreading false news" and "joining a terrorist organization" because of the video she posted on Facebook detailing the alleged torture of her son.

Security forces intimidated and harassed families of dissidents who live abroad. On February 13, authorities raided the homes of six members of the extended family of Mohamed Soltan, a US-based human rights advocate. They arrested two of his cousins and another relative at their homes. They were released five days later. Soltan's father, Salah, jailed since 2013 in several cases for opposing the military removal of former President Mohamed Morsy, has been held in incommunicado detention since June 2020 in reprisal for Mohamed Soltan's human rights advocacy in Washington.

The National Security Agency in recent years killed dozens of alleged "terrorists" across the country in extrajudicial executions the authorities contended were "shootouts." A Human Rights Watch report released in September 2021 found that the alleged armed militants killed posed no imminent danger to security forces or others when they were killed, and in many cases had already been in custody.

The army continued to impose severe restrictions on freedom of movement in North Sinai, where the military have for years been battling the armed group *Wilayat Sina'*, an ISIS affiliate. Despite an apparent decrease in violent attacks by armed militants, the army demolished hundreds of homes and razed most of the farmland in the governorate. The government failed to compensate thousands whose houses and livelihoods were destroyed in the name of creating buffer zones. The massive demolitions, including over 12,300 buildings, likely amount to war crimes, absent in many cases evidence of an "absolute" military necessity.

President al-Sisi issued a decree on October 2 transferring unchecked powers to the Defense Ministry in North Sinai, including the power to evict residents from any areas, impose curfews, and ban transportation or communication. The six-month decree can be renewed indefinitely as long as the government claims a continuing "terrorist" threat.

Prison Conditions and Deaths in Custody

The dire conditions in Egyptian prisons and detention centers remained shielded from independent oversight. Authorities routinely deprived sick prisoners from access to adequate health care. According to the Committee for Justice, an independent organization, 57 prisoners, most of them jailed on political grounds, died in custody in the first eight months of 2021.

On July 25, the family of 69-year-old Abd al-Moniem Abu al-Fotouh, the former presidential candidate and leader of the Strong Egypt Party, said he had suffered symptoms resembling a heart attack while in prolonged solitary confinement in Cairo's Tora Prison. Abu al-Fotouh, unjustly detained without trial since 2018, had suffered several heart attacks in detention, his family said, but prison authorities rejected their pleas to have him admitted to a hospital.

Prominent activist Alaa Abdel Fattah has been in solitary confinement without trial in Tora's maximum-security prison since September 2019. His family said a National Security Agency officer has been depriving prisoners of visits, exercise, sunlight, and books and newspapers. In October, authorities referred Abdel Fattah along with human rights lawyer Mohamed al-Baqr to trial in another case on charges of "spreading false news" before an Emergency State Security Court.

On September 15, President al-Sisi said that the government would soon inaugurate Egypt's largest prison complex, which he described as built according to an "American model." We Record, an independent group, reported in October that the new complex, northwest of Cairo, will have a capacity exceeding 30,000 prisoners.

Fair Trials, Due Process, Death Penalty

In 2021, Egypt continued to escalate its use of the death penalty and executions, in many cases following unfair proceedings and mass trials. The Egyptian Front for Human Rights said that in the first six months of 2021, the authorities executed 80 people, roughly half in cases of alleged political violence. Amnesty International said that Egypt ranked third worst in numbers of executions worldwide. On June 14, the Court of Cassation, Egypt's highest appellate court, upheld death sentences for 12 Muslim Brotherhood leaders, members, and sympathizers as well as long prison sentences for hundreds of others convicted in a mass unfair trial of over 700 dissidents, including 22 children, charged with involvement in the 2013 Rab'a sit-in that opposed the military ouster of President Mohamed Morsy.

Authorities increasingly employed the extraordinary Emergency State Security Courts, the decisions of which are not subject to appeal, to prosecute dissidents. Former President Hosni Mubarak's government had abolished them in 2007 but al-Sisi's government reinstated them in 2017.

According to lawyers and detainees' families, judges and prosecutors routinely remanded thousands of detainees in custody without presenting evidence, often in brief hearings that did not allow them to present a defense. Even when courts ordered detainees released, Supreme State Security prosecutors routinely added them to new cases with the same charges to detain them beyond the two-year limit on pretrial detention in Egyptian law.

Freedom of Association and Attacks on Human Rights Defenders

In January 2021, the government issued implementing regulations for the 2019 NGO Law, confirming its restrictive nature and extensive government interference. Existing nongovernmental organizations (NGOs) must register under the new law by January 2022 or face being dissolved.

Under international and domestic pressure, authorities dropped investigations against several critical organizations and defenders in the decade-old Case 173 of 2011 in which dozens of NGOs were prosecuted for receiving foreign funds. However, punitive travel bans and asset freezes have not been lifted despite the judge's orders in August and September to do so. Several other organizations and staff members remain accused in the case, including Gamal Eid, director of the Arab Network for Human Rights Information, and Hossam Bahgat, director of the Egyptian Initiative for Personal Rights.

In September, authorities referred to trial before an Emergency State Security Court Patrick Zaki, a gender-rights researcher at the Egyptian Initiative for Personal Rights, on charges of "spreading false news." Authorities had detained him since February 2020 and officers allegedly tortured him in custody.

Also in September, a mass trial began before an Emergency State Security Court that included lawyer Ezzat Ghoniem, director of the Egyptian Coordination for Rights and Freedoms, and about two dozen activists that authorities linked to the group, including lawyer Hoda Abdel Moniem and activist Aisha al-Shater. Security forces have detained Ghoniem since March 2018. They face criminal charges of joining and financing an unlawful group as well as "spreading false news."

The trials of Zaki, Ghoniem and the others began the same week that President al-Sisi announced the government's "national strategy" for human rights and claimed that 2022 would be the "year of civil society."

Freedom of Expression

The authorities released several detained journalists such as Khaled Dawood and Esraa Abdel Fattah, but detained others. On February 22, National Security officers at Cairo Airport arrested columnist and journalist Gamal al-Gamal, known for his critical views, and held him incommunicado for five days upon his return from Turkey. Authorities released him without trial in July.

In May, authorities arrested veteran journalist Tawfiq Ghanim on terrorism charges. He remained in pretrial detention at time of writing. In July, authorities arrested Abdel Nasser Salama, a former chief editor of the government-owned *al-Ahram* newspaper following an article he posted on his Facebook page criticizing President al-Sisi and calling on him to step down.

Freedom of Belief

Authorities detained independent activists working on societal and governmental discrimination against Egypt's Christian minority, such as Ramy Kamal, the head of Maspero Youth for Human Rights. He has been held without trial since November 2019, accused of joining and financing a "terrorist group."

The Egyptian Initiative for Personal Rights said in October that since 2016 the authorities have approved legalization of only 1,958 churches and service buildings among more than 5,540 Christian worship buildings that lack proper legal status. The government also issued no licenses to build new churches except in new desert cities that are subject to different rules.

Women's Rights, Gender Identity, Sexual Orientation

In 2021, courts sentenced at least four women social media influencers to two and five years in prison for morality-related offences for their online videos and posts.

On May 11, Prosecutor General Hamada al-Sawy said his office had terminated investigations into the high-profile 2014 "Fairmont" gang-rape case for "insufficient evidence" and ordered the release of the four accused men. This came after the main witnesses, who came forward to support the rape survivor in 2020, had been unlawfully arrested and two of them spent months in arbitrary detention. At time of writing, all five key witnesses remain arbitrarily banned from travel abroad despite closure of the case.

On September 25, a criminal court in al-Qaliubya governorate sentenced a father and a nurse to three and ten years respectively in prison for carrying out female genital mutilation (FGM) of a young girl that led to long-term disability. In March, the Egyptian parliament amended the penal code to impose tougher penalties for medical professionals and others who perform FGM. Earlier increases in sentences have done little to stem the practice of FGM, which remains rampant.

In March, women launched the social media #GuardianshipIsMyRight campaign to oppose amendments to the Personal Status Law, proposed by the government, which would have added to deeply entrenched discrimination against women.

Social, Economic, and Health Rights

Authorities used abusive terrorism laws to crack down on businesses and workers. In late September, National Security agents arrested three workers from an electrical appliances factory in western Cairo for participating in a sit-in. Supreme State Security prosecutors released them a week later after filing terrorism-related charges against them, the independent Center for Trade Union and Workers Services reported. The authorities arrested well-known businessman

Safwan Thabet in December 2020 and his son, Seif Thabet, in February 2021 and kept them in pretrial detention in conditions amounting to torture on terrorism-related charges. Their arrest came after they refused security officials' requests to relinquish control of their company's assets, the family said.

The government's plan for Covid-19 vaccine rollout that began in March has been inefficient and vague. By mid-October, roughly 15 per cent of the population received one dose of the vaccine despite the government claim that it had millions of additional doses. A study cited by a World Bank report, published in August, found that Egyptian authorities underreported Covid-19 related deaths by tens of thousands.

Most children in Egypt experience corporal punishment at home or at school. Egypt promised to ban corporal punishment in all settings during its UN Universal Periodic Review in 2019 but did not revise the penal code or other laws that exempt the practice from penalty.

Key International Actors

In 2021, two major factors worried the Egyptian government: the change of administrations in the United States, and a long overdue joint condemnation of Egypt's record by 32 states at the UN Human Rights Council in Geneva in March.

Despite US President Joe Biden promising that he would give President al-Sisi "no more blank checks," in September his administration released $170 million out of $300 million in military financing that the US Congress had suspended pending human rights improvements. The remaining $130 million will be released pending progress on nontransparent conditions set by the administration.

European Union member states continued to cite Egypt in their Joint Item 4 statement at the UN Human Rights Council, but weapon sales, military assistance and political support continued to be the rule at the bilateral level for many of those states. The negotiation of EU-Egypt partnership priorities has been stalled due to Egypt's resistance to linking assistance to human rights conditions.

French President Emmanuel Macron said in December 2020 that his government would not condition weapon sales to Egypt on human rights improvements. In

May, the French government announced a €3.75 billion (US$4.5 billion) sale of 30 Rafale fighter jets to Egypt, financed through French loans that add to Egypt's external debt burden.

In October, an Italian court suspended the trial in absentia for four Egyptian police and National Security Agency officers charged by Italian prosecutors with the abduction and torture of Guilio Regeni, an Italian researcher who was murdered in Egypt in 2016, because of Egyptian authorities' persistent lack of cooperation.

El Salvador

In 2021, President Nayib Bukele and his allies in the legislature undermined basic democratic checks and balances, including by summarily dismissing and replacing Supreme Court judges they disagreed with and passing laws to dismiss hundreds of lower-level judges and prosecutors.

In September, the Constitutional Chamber of the Supreme Court allowed President Bukele to run for re-election, despite a constitutional prohibition on immediate re-election.

President Bukele's government has indicated he plans to introduce a proposal to reform the constitution, including by extending the presidential term from five to six years and overhauling some democratic institutions.

Gangs continue to exercise territorial control over some neighborhoods and extort residents throughout the country. They forcibly recruit children and sexually abuse women, girls, and lesbian, gay, bisexual, and transgender (LGBT) people. Gangs kill, disappear, rape, or displace those who resist.

Historically, security forces have committed extrajudicial executions, sexual assaults, enforced disappearances, and torture.

From 2011 to October 2020, 71,500 people were internally displaced, mostly due to violence perpetuated by gangs and security forces, according to the Office of the United Nations High Commissioner for Refugees.

Girls and women accused of having abortions have been imprisoned for homicide and aggravated homicide. LGBT individuals face discrimination and police violence.

Judicial Independence

During the campaign for the February 2021 parliamentary elections, President Bukele repeatedly accused members of the Supreme Electoral Court of organizing a "fraud," with no evidence.

President Bukele's party won the elections, obtaining a two-thirds majority. On May 1, the day his supporters were seated in the National Assembly, they summarily removed and replaced all five judges of the Supreme Court's Constitutional Chamber, as well as the attorney general.

In late June, the Legislative Assembly appointed five new judges to the Supreme Court, in violation of the process established in the constitution. The Assembly had appointed 10 of a total 15 Supreme Court judges by September, although Salvadorean law only allows each newly constituted legislature to appoint five.

On August 31, lawmakers passed two laws dismissing all judges and prosecutors over 60 years of age or with 30 or more years of service, allowing the Supreme Court and the attorney general to grant exceptions extending their terms "due to reasons of necessity or specialty." The law affects one-third of all judges.

Abuses by Security Forces

President Bukele continued using the military in public security operations, although the 1992 peace accord bars it. In February 2020, President Bukele entered the Legislative Assembly with armed soldiers in an apparent effort to intimidate legislators into approving a loan for the security forces. Between March and May 2020, the police arbitrarily detained individuals accused of violating Covid-19 measures.

In November 2020, during an investigation into allegedly irregular purchases related to Covid-19, police blocked prosecutors from executing a court order to raid the offices of the Health Ministry.

Between 2015 and 2020, the police committed 179 extrajudicial killings, the Ombudsperson's Office reported. Twenty-five resulted in convictions.

Education

Between March 2020 and April 2021, the government closed schools to prevent the spread of Covid-19. Approximately 1.4 million students missed "almost all classroom instruction" between March 2020 and February 2021, according to UNICEF. The government implemented a range of distance learning initiatives, including online classes.

Prison and Police Barracks

Prisons held over 36,600 detainees in March, twice the official capacity, the World Prison Brief revealed. Approximately 23 percent of inmates were in pretrial detention.

Overcrowding and poor sanitation endangered the health of prisoners and risked accelerating the spread of Covid-19.

Gangs and Violence

Approximately 60,000 gang members operate in El Salvador, media report. They exert control over parts of the territory and commit serious abuses, including killings and rape.

According to media reports, numerous security and elected officials have collaborated with gangs in criminal operations, and many political parties have negotiated with the groups, including in exchange for gang members' support during elections.

In August 2021, the digital outlet *El Faro* reported that Attorney General Raúl Melara had been investigating alleged negotiations between the government and the country's three largest gangs prior to his removal on May 1. According to the article, the government had offered jail privileges to imprisoned gang members and increased employment opportunities for members outside of prison in exchange for the gang's commitment to lower homicide rates.

The National Police reported 1,322 homicides from January to December 2020, compared to more than 2,398 during the same period in 2019, a 46 percent drop. Homicide data for 2021 had not been published at time of writing.

Disappearances

From January 2014 to November 2020, authorities reported more than 13,000 disappearance victims (including more than 400 children)—which exceeds the estimated 8,000 to 10,000 disappeared during the civil war (1979-1992). Disappearances are committed by a range of actors, including gangs and the police. Few cases are investigated.

Government Accountability

Impunity for government abuses is the norm.

A trial of former military commanders accused in the 1981 El Mozote massacre started in 2016 and continued at time of writing. Soldiers committed mass rape and killed 978 civilians at El Mozote, including 553 children. In September 2020, soldiers—with President Bukele's backing—refused to comply with a court order that allowed a judge to review military records about the massacre. In September 2021, Jorge Guzmán, the judge investigating the massacre, was ousted because he was over 60 years of age. His removal is likely to cause further delays in the trial.

Between March and June 2020, the Access to Public Information Agency, charged with implementing the Access to Public Information Law, suspended all hearings and processes, invoking the Covid-19 state of emergency. The decision undermined access to information of public interest. In May, legislators granted government officials and contractors "immunity" from criminal and administrative charges related to Covid-19 policies, including acquisition of medical supplies and services. In October, the Assembly reformed the law to "clarify" that the "immunity" would not cover "corruption," "bribing," or any "similar crimes." At the time of his removal also in May, Attorney General Melara was investigating six government officials, including the health minister, for alleged corruption and improper emergency purchases related to Covid-19.

In June, the Attorney General's Office ended a cooperation agreement with the International Commission Against Impunity in El Salvador (CICIES), a body backed by the Organization of American States (OAS) to fight corruption. CICIES had been investigating alleged irregularities in emergency purchases related to Covid-19.

Former President Mauricio Funes (2009-2014), who has been living in Nicaragua since 2016, faces criminal charges including corruption, embezzlement, and money laundering. Nicaraguan President Daniel Ortega granted Funes Nicaraguan citizenship in July 2021.

Women's Sexual and Reproductive Rights

Abortion is illegal under all circumstances. Women face two to eight years in prison for having an abortion. Providers face prison sentences of 6 months to 12 years.

In September, President Bukele said that the government-backed constitutional reform would not help ease the country's prohibition on abortion.

Many women, including women who suffered miscarriages or obstetric emergencies, have been sentenced to up to 40 years in prison on charges of violating the law. As of June 2021, 17 women who said they had suffered obstetric emergencies remained imprisoned on charges of abortion, homicide, or aggravated homicide. suffered obstetric emergencies remained imprisoned on charges of abortion, homicide, or aggravated homicide.

Disability Rights

El Salvador's legislative framework remains inconsistent with international disability rights law, with restrictions on legal capacity for people with intellectual and psychosocial disabilities, as well as insufficient measures to improve physical and communication accessibility. Criminal gangs have attacked women and girls with disabilities, with high levels of impunity.

LGBT Rights

LGBT people remain targets of homophobic and transphobic violence by police, gangs, and the general public. In many cases, LGBT people flee persecution at home, including to the United States. Salvadorean authorities, which in 2017 acknowledged anti-LGBT violence committed by public security officials, reported 692 cases of violence against LGBT and intersex people from January 2015 to June 2019.

El Salvador does not have comprehensive civil non-discrimination legislation that covers discrimination on the basis of sexual orientation and gender identity, nor a legal gender recognition procedure for transgender people. In September, President Bukele said that the government-backed constitutional reform would not legally recognize same-sex relationships.

Attacks on Journalists

The Association of Journalists of El Salvador (APES) reported 173 press freedom violations between January and August 2021, including attacks, digital harassment, and restrictions on journalists' work and access to public information.

In September 2020, a few weeks after *El Faro* reported that President Bukele had negotiated with MS-13, the president announced criminal investigations accusing the newspaper of "money laundering" and "tax evasion." *El Faro* has also been subject to tax audits that appear selective and abusive.

Since taking office, President Bukele has undermined the credibility of independent media outlets, accusing them of spreading "fake news" or serving political interests. In June, the security minister said authorities "were following" journalists he had accused, without providing any evidence, of "advocating for the commission of crime." In October, Vice President Félix Ulloa said that "some journalists should be prosecuted on slander and defamation charges" for criticizing the government.

In July, immigration authorities denied Daniel Lizárraga, a Mexican journalist working for *El Faro*, a work permit. According to media reports, police interrogated Lizárraga prior to his appointment at the immigration office, asking whether he intended to "report on political issues." He did not attend the appointment because, he told authorities, he had been exposed to Covid-19. A day later, he was expelled from the country.

Key International Actors

During fiscal year 2021, the US appropriated over US$65 million in bilateral aid to El Salvador, particularly to reduce extreme violence and strengthen state institutions. In May, in response to growing concerns "about transparency and accountability," the US Agency for International Development redirected assistance away from the National Police and the Institute for Access to Public Information, toward civil society and human rights groups.

Between July and September, the administration of US President Joe Biden included 19 Salvadorans—including President Bukele's legal advisor and his cabinet chief, and all of the judges of the Constitutional Chamber—on the "Engel List" of individuals identified as having engaged in "significant corruption."

More than 178,000 Salvadorans were seeking asylum in other countries at the end of 2019, mostly in the United States. In fiscal year 2019, the last year data is available for, the US granted asylum to 3,212 Salvadorans—the third highest nationality ranking for asylum grants in the US. From 2013 through 2019, 138 Salvadorans were killed following deportation from the US; more than 70 were beaten, sexually assaulted, extorted, or tortured.

In May, UN Secretary-General António Guterres flagged continuing concerns about "the procedures used in the removal of the members of the constitutional chamber of the Supreme Court of Justice and its impact on the control mechanisms in El Salvador," and urged the government to "respect constitutional provisions, rule of law and separation of powers."

Also in May, UN High Commissioner for Human Rights Michelle Bachelet expressed concern about the "the decision by El Salvador's Legislative Assembly to dismiss the magistrates of the Constitutional Chamber of the Supreme Court of Justice and the Attorney General" as this "seriously undermines democracy and the rule of law in the country." Similarly, the OAS Secretariat "reject[ed]" these dismissals.

In February, the Inter-American Commission on Human Rights granted precautionary measures to 34 members of *El Faro*, considering that they were facing "alleged harassment, intimidation, threats and stigmatization … related to the exercise of their freedom of expression in matters of public interest to their country."

Eritrea

Eritrean government forces committed war crimes, possible crimes against humanity, and other serious violations against Tigrayan civilians during the ongoing conflict in Ethiopia's Tigray region. Eritrean forces also forcibly disappeared dozens of Eritrean refugees living there, raped several, coercively repatriated hundreds, and destroyed two Eritrean refugee camps. Eritrean forces also committed widespread pillaging with much of the plunder taken back to Eritrea.

At home, government repression persisted, including through forced conscription, mass roundups to fill the army's ranks and widespread forced labor. The government also severely restricted freedom of expression, opinion, and faith.

Eritrea has been ruled by its unelected president, Isaias Afewerki, since independence in 1993, with no legislature, no independent civil society organizations, and no independent judiciary. The transitional constitution, which guarantees civil rights, has never been implemented—removing all checks on Isaias's arbitrary rule.

September marked the 20th anniversary of the beginning of the government's clampdown on perceived critics, including the arrest of 11 high ranking government officials and 10 journalists, and the closure of privately owned media outlets. There has been no information on the whereabouts of 20 of the 21.

War Crimes and Other Abuses in Tigray

Eritrean Defense Forces (EDF) committed widespread abuses against civilians during its involvement in the conflict in Ethiopia's Tigray region alongside the Ethiopian National Defense Forces (ENDF) against forces aligned to the Tigray People's Liberation Front (TPLF).

On November 9, 2020, Human Rights Watch documented artillery attacks launched from Eritrea hitting the Tigrayan town of Humera, in western Tigray. Eritrean forces have carried out large-scale massacres, summary executions, widespread sexual violence including rape, gang rape, and sexual slavery, widespread pillage, attacks on refugee camps, and destruction and pillaging of crops.

Indefinite Military Conscription and Forced Labor

Human Rights Watch received credible reports of new roundups ("giffas" in Tigrinya the most widely spoken language) to help fill the army's ranks due to losses suffered during the war in Tigray, during which security forces reportedly block off certain areas and round up individuals perceived as being of military age or trying to evade conscription. Relatives of those forced to fight in the Tigray region did not receive official feedback on the fate of their loved ones.

A diaspora human rights organization reported that a 16-year-old boy was picked up outside his home in Eritrea's capital, Asmara, and trained for two months in Eritrea before disappearing. His family heard about his whereabouts a month later when he was named as a prisoner of war by Tigrayan forces.

Forced conscription and deployment to the military also continued through the country's infamous indefinite national service system. Mostly men and unmarried women were sent indefinitely into the military or civil service for low pay and with no say in their profession or work location. Conscripts are often subjected to inhuman and degrading punishment, including torture, without recourse. Conscientious objection is not recognized; it is punished. Discharge from national service is arbitrary and procedures are opaque.

For secondary students, some as young as 16, conscription begins at the Sawa military camp where students finish secondary school and undergo compulsory military training. Students are under military command, with harsh military punishments and discipline, and female students have reported sexual harassment and exploitation.

The government continued to rely on poorly trained national service teachers, which affects the quality of primary and secondary education, and teacher retention.

Unlawful, Prolonged, and Abusive Detentions

Thousands of prisoners languish in the country's extensive prison network, held in overcrowded places of detention with inadequate food, water, and medical care. Many are held incommunicado and detained indefinitely, denied basic due process rights, without access to legal counsel, judicial review, or family visits, some for decades.

In September 2001, Eritrean authorities arrested 11 government officials who had called on Isaias to introduce political reforms and 10 prominent journalists who reported on this. Among those detained was journalist Dawit Isaak, a dual Eritrean-Swedish citizen, who was briefly released from jail in 2005, and remains in incommunicado detention. At least 10 of the 21 initially arrested are reported to have died in detention.

Other high profile detainees remain in incommunicado detention, including Ciham Ali Abdu, daughter of a former information minister, held since December 2012 when she was just 15 years old, and former finance minister and critic of the president, Berhane Abrehe, detained since September 2018. The country's massive prison population also includes draft evaders or "deserters," some of whom were detained while trying to flee the country, and individuals detained for their religious beliefs and practices.

The US-based Public Broadcasting Service (PBS) released a documentary in May which included footage that was reportedly recorded by a former prisoner in Abi Abeito, one of the country's military detention facilities, offering an insight into the horrific conditions. The film shows cells that are so overcrowded that prisoners lie one on top of each other, unable to stretch out.

Freedom of Religion

For over two decades, the government has denied religious liberty to anyone whose religious affiliation does not match the four denominations that the government "recognizes:" Sunni Islam, Eritrean Orthodox, Roman Catholic, and Evangelical (Lutheran) churches. People affiliated with "unrecognized" faiths continue to be imprisoned, and torture has been used to force them to renounce their religion.

Positively, in the first two months of the year, the government released dozens of Evangelical and Orthodox Christian detainees held for their religious beliefs and practices, who had reportedly been detained for between 2 to 12 years. In addition, since late 2020, 32 Jehovah Witnesses were released, including three conscientious objectors who had been detained since 1994. Despite these releases,

20 Jehovah Witnesses are still detained, and the government continued to severely restrict religious freedoms and arrest people because of their religious
practices.

Refugees

Eritrea's ongoing rights crisis continues to drive Eritreans into exile, including
children and youth escaping conscription.

For decades, Ethiopia's northern Tigray region, just south of the border with Eritrea, had been one of the main destinations for Eritrean refugees. At the start of
the conflict in November 2020, around 96,000 Eritrean refugees were registered
in Tigray.

Between November, 2020 and January, 2021 Eritrean forces twice occupied Hitsats and Shimelba camps hosting Eritrean refugees in Tigray near the country's
border and subjected camp residents to enforced disappearances, rape, and coercive repatriations before destroying the camps. During these two months Eritrean forces also targeted Tigrayans living in the surrounding communities,
including through killings and widespread pillaging, resulting in significant tensions between Tigrayans and the Eritrean refugee community. As of September,
over 7,500 refugees from both camps remained unaccounted for.

Covid-19

Eritrea refused to join the UN-led COVAX initiative to receive Covid-19 vaccine
supplies and is reportedly yet to start a vaccination campaign.

Covid-related restrictions kept schools largely closed during the first three
months of the year, disrupting education for more than 600,000 students. However, the government continued to force final year high-school students to attend Sawa, where dormitories are crowded, and water supplies and health
facilities limited. Students were not released from Sawa despite concerns that
the virus that causes Covid-19 could easily spread in the cramped and unsanitary
conditions.

Key International Actors

Media reported in February that the United Arab Emirates had begun to dismantle parts of its military base near the port of Assab. The base, established in 2015, had supported UAE's intervention in the Yemen conflict.

In March, the European Union designated Eritrea's national security agency, under its global human rights sanctions regime, for serious human rights abuses including killings, arbitrary arrests, enforced disappearances, and torture committed by its agents. The European Commission announced that around €1 million (US$1.1 million) funds allocated to Eritrea under the EU's Emergency Trust Fund for Africa (EUTF) would be reallocated, citing a lack of interest on the part of Eritrea. This followed fierce criticism in 2020, including by the European Parliament, of the EU's funding of the procurement of materials for the construction of a road in Eritrea that employed conscript forced labor.

In August, the US imposed targeted sanctions on General Filipos Woldeyohannes, the chief of staff of the Eritrean Defense Forces (EDF), for serious human rights abuses committed by the Eritrean forces in Tigray.

In September, the Biden administration issued an executive order enabling the United States to sanction individuals "responsible for, or complicit in, prolonging the conflict in Ethiopia, obstructing humanitarian access, or preventing a ceasefire." On November 12, the U.S. Department of the Treasury's Office of Foreign Assets Control (OFAC) designated four Eritrean entities and two individuals.

The EU, US, and African members on the UN Security Council repeatedly called on Eritrea to withdraw its troops from Ethiopia. repeatedly called on Eritrea to withdraw its troops from Ethiopia.

Eswatini

In 2021, Eswatini, an absolute monarchy ruled by King Mswati III since 1986, was rocked by waves of protests amid a drastic deterioration in the human rights situation and lack of reforms. The authorities responded by banning protests and deployed police and soldiers who shot at protesters indiscriminately with live ammunition. A 1973 decree banning political parties remains in force. Despite the adoption of the 2005 constitution which guarantees basic rights and the country's international human rights commitments, the king continues to exercise absolute power to appoint the prime minister and cabinet, and to dissolve the Parliament.

Conduct of Security Forces

In June, violent protests triggered by the king's decree banning petitions to the government calling for democratic reforms broke out across the country. According to media reports at least 50 people were killed and property worth an estimated R3 billion (US$19.4 million) was looted or damaged. The waves of protests began in May 2021, when students and teachers protested the killing of Thabani Nkomonye, a law student at the University of Swaziland. The killing was allegedly committed by the police. The authorities initiated an investigation into the killing, but protests escalated in late June when about 500 youths took to the streets in the Manzini district, 30 kilometers from the capital, Mbabane.

The government has yet to ratify the Optional Protocol to the Convention Against Torture, despite previously agreeing to do so.

Freedom of Association and Assembly

Restrictions on freedom of association and assembly continued in 2021. The Eswatini authorities have used the Suppression of Terrorism Act of 2008 (Terrorism Act) and the Sedition and Subversive Activities Act of 1938 (Sedition Act) to suppress free speech and stifle criticism of the monarch. On July 25, the police arrested two Eswatini members of parliament (MPs), and charged them with terrorism for allegedly encouraging the protests and calling for a democratically elected prime minister and other reforms. The two MPs, Mduduzi Bacede

Mabuza and Mthandeni Dube, remain in custody after the High Court of Eswatini denied their bail application twice. At the time of writing, the trial had yet to commence.

Rule of Law and Media Freedoms

There has been no progress on essential rights reforms, including the removal of all legislative and practical restrictions to free exercise of civil and political rights. This would include the repeal or amendment of laws that obstruct the rights to freedom of association and expression, that would allow the registration and operation of political parties; introducing greater political freedoms through free, fair, transparent democratic elections; ensuring the right to health without discrimination on the basis of sexual orientation or gender identity; abolition of the death penalty; and decriminalization of same-sex relations and the prevention of discrimination based on marital status and sexual orientation.

Restrictions on freedom of association and assembly remained in place and there were no remedies for violations that occurred in previous years. On October 20, 2020, the High Court heard a challenge by the Eswatini Sexual and Gender Minorities (ESGM), a human rights community-based advocacy organization which aims to advance the protection of human rights of lesbian, gay, bisexual, transgender, and intersex persons. In September 2019, the Eswatini Registrar of Companies had refused to register ESGM as a company saying that "ESGM's objectives were unlawful because same-sex sexual acts are illegal in the country." At the time of writing the court has not rendered its judgment.

In 2021, Eswatini ranked 141 out of 180 countries in the Reporters Without Borders' world press index on media freedom, based partly on constraints journalists face under the absolute monarchy and because courts are not permitted to prosecute crimes and abuses against representatives of the monarchy. In June, the Eswatini Communications Commission allegedly ordered network providers, Eswatini Post and Telecommunications, Eswatini MTN and Eswatini Mobile to shut down the internet to prevent protesters from mobilizing online. Local activists in Eswatini told Human Rights Watch that the internet was shut down for several hours, from about 4:30 p.m. local time on June 29 until around 9 a.m. on June 30.

On June 30, media groups African Freedom of Expression Exchange (AFEX), Collaboration on International ICT Policy for East and Southern Africa (CIPESA), International Freedom of Expression Exchange (IFEX), Panos Institute Southern Africa, and the Media Institute of Southern Africa (MISA) sent a joint petition to the acting Prime Minister Themba Masuku calling on him to ensure that the internet, social media platforms, and all other communication channels are open, secure, and accessible regardless of the protests then taking place in the country.

Women's Rights

The under-representation of women in leadership and decision-making positions in both public and private sectors continued, with little effort to implement provisions of the 2018 Election of Women Act. The Act is designed to ensure the fulfillment of the constitutional requirement of representation quotas for women and marginalized groups in parliament.

While it is yet to ratify the Protocol to the African Charter on Human and Peoples' Rights on the Rights of Women in Africa (Maputo Protocol), Eswatini has ratified some regional and international instruments to promote gender equality. These include the Convention for the Elimination of All Forms of Discrimination Against Women (CEDAW), which Eswatini ratified without reservation and the Southern African Development Community (SADC) Declaration on Gender and Development. Article 20 of the Constitution provides for equality before the law and non-discrimination on several protected grounds, but does not include discrimination on the basis of language, sexual orientation, or gender identity. Eswatini's dual legal system where both the common law, which is based on Roman Dutch law and Eswatini unwritten customary law operate side by side, has resulted in conflicts, resulting in numerous violations of women's rights over the years.

Children's Rights

Schools were closed for 237 days, and partially open to certain ages or in certain areas, for 159 days since the pandemic's start in 2020. In 2021, 350,000 students were affected. Before the pandemic, 16 percent of children were out of primary school.

Key International Actors

In July, the Southern African Development Community (SADC) Chairperson of the Organ Troika on Politics, Defence and Security, deployed two fact finding missions to investigate the causes of the protests and help find peaceful resolution to the political crisis in the country. SADC appealed for calm and restraint from all the stakeholders in Eswatini, and encouraged national dialogue.

South Africa's Minister of International Relations and Cooperation, Naledi Pandor, who was part of the delegation, expressed disappointment over the Eswatini fact-finding mission. Pandor said, "I was quite disappointed, we were on a fact-finding mission and what we found in Swaziland [Eswatini] was that our colleagues in government essentially wanted government to brief us when we wanted a wider set of briefing as we wished to speak to the broader stakeholders including non-government stakeholders." The reports of the SADC fact-finding missions were not made public.

In July, the Commonwealth secretariat issued a statement calling for calm and restraint and urging all political and civic leaders to demonstrate tolerance, to promote unity, and give a chance to peaceful channels to address any grievances. It said its Secretary-General will continue to work with regional and international partners to encourage constructive dialogue and appropriate demarches founded on the rule of law as a means to foster sustainable peace.

Also in response to the violent protests, the United Nations Secretary-General António Guterres called on the Eswatini authorities to ensure people are able to exercise their civil and political rights peacefully and urged the security forces to exercise utmost restraint. The UN office of the high commissioner for human rights urged the government to "ensure that there are prompt, transparent, effective, independent and impartial investigations into all allegations of human rights violations."

HUMAN
RIGHTS
WATCH

"I Always Remember That Day"
Access to Services for Survivors of Gender-Based Violence
in Ethiopia's Tigray Region

Ethiopia

The human rights and humanitarian situation in Ethiopia deteriorated further in 2021, with civilians impacted by the devastating Tigray conflict, security force abuses, attacks by armed groups, and deadly ethnic violence in other regions. The government's actions in Tigray contributed to growing international pressure to address accountability for rights abuses.

In Tigray, government forces and allies committed forcible displacement, large-scale massacres, widespread sexual violence, indiscriminate shelling, pillage, and attacks on schools and hospitals. By mid-year, these abuses had left an estimated 350,000 people facing starvation. After government forces withdrew from many parts of Tigray in late June, it imposed an effective siege on Tigray, blocking virtually all humanitarian aid from reaching the region, violating international humanitarian law and possibly committing the war crime of using starvation as a weapon of war. The conflict spread into the Amhara and Afar regions resulting in large-scale displacement. Tigrayan forces were also implicated in serious abuses against Amhara civilians.

Elections took place in an environment marred by restrictions on free expression and association, and insecurity in several regions. In June, the ruling political party was re-elected for a five-year term.

In western Oromia, government counterinsurgency campaigns against armed rebel groups resulted in serious abuses committed by all sides against communities. Attacks against Amhara communities by armed groups and unidentified gunmen also increased.

Accountability for past and present abuses remained minimal. In Tigray, the prime minister admitted forces engaged in looting and sexual violence but downplayed the severity of abuses. For months, the government denied the presence of Eritrean forces and resisted international investigations. A joint investigation into abuses in Tigray by the state-appointed Ethiopian Human Rights Commission and the United Nations Office of the High Commissioner for Human Rights (OHCHR) concluded that there have been widespread violations of international human rights, humanitarian and refugee law by all parties to the conflict in Tigray, some of which may amount to international crimes, in particular, war crimes and crimes against humanity.

Tigray Conflict

Ethiopian federal and allied forces committed widespread abuses in Tigray.

In western Tigray, Amhara regional forces and militias carried out numerous abuses and forcibly displaced thousands of Tigrayans in what the US secretary of state in March characterized as "ethnic cleansing."

In January, Ethiopian and Eritrean forces rounded up and executed dozens of un-armed men after attacking several villages surrounding Mahbere Dego, in central Tigray. On March 23, Ethiopian soldiers forced passengers off a public bus in northeastern Tigray, separated the men from the women, and executed at least four men. On June 22, a government airstrike hit a market in Togoga village, cen-tral Tigray, reportedly killing at least 51 people and injuring scores. Government strikes in Tigray continued in October.

Ethiopian authorities blocked roads into the region and only allowed sporadic humanitarian access. The destruction and pillage of health facilities prevented survivors of conflict-related sexual violence from accessing health services.

On June 28, after the defeat of Ethiopian government forces in Tigray, Ethiopian authorities declared a . Retreating Ethiopian soldiers raided UNICEF and World Food Programme offices in the regional capital, Mekelle, and looted communica-tions equipment. Since then, the government has imposed what the UN has called a de facto blockade on Tigray. Electricity and fuel supplies reached dan-gerous lows in September, communications and banking remained shut, and ac-cess to cash was severely limited.

In August, Ethiopia suspended three nongovernmental organizations (NGOs), in-cluding the Norwegian Refugee Council, Médecins Sans Frontières (MSF), and Al Maktoume Foundation for three months. On September 30, Ethiopia expelled seven senior UN officials. Twenty-three aid workers have been killed since the conflict began, including three MSF workers murdered on June 24.

The conflict expanded into the neighboring Amhara and Afar regions in July, dis-placing hundreds of thousands. Tigrayan forces summarily executed Amhara civilians and were implicated in the pillage of civilian property. On August 5 in

Galikoma, Afar, dozens of civilians were reportedly killed and injured near a school and health facility. In the Amhara region, fighting between Tigrayan forces and Ethiopian and allied forces intensified. In August and September, Tigrayan fighters summarily executed Amhara residents in Chenna and Kobo, and committed rape, including gang rape in Nifas Mewcha and Geregera in the Amhara region.

Outside Tigray, Ethiopian authorities arbitrarily detained, forcibly disappeared, and arbitrarily closed businesses of scores of ethnic Tigrayans in Addis Ababa. Arrests of Tigrayans increased following the government's declaration of a sweeping state of emergency on November 4.

Security Force Abuses, Attacks by Armed Groups, Communal Violence

Extrajudicial killings, mass arrests, arbitrary detentions, and violence against civilians occurred in other regions facing unrest and insecurity.

In Oromia, reports of arrests, detention, and summary executions of Oromo civilians accused of supporting the armed rebel group, the Oromo Liberation Army (OLA), continued. In May, security forces in Dembi Dollo, western Oromia, violently apprehended a 17-year-old boy and then summarily executed him in public.

Armed groups carried out attacks against officials, police, and civilians, including killings and lootings in western Oromia. In late March, OLA rebels reportedly killed at least 28 Amhara civilians and injured over a dozen in Babo Gembel West Wellega zone.

Tensions over politics and land administration in Benishangul-Gumuz fueled violence, with summary executions of Amharas and other ethnic groups by armed militias, particularly in Metekel zone, escalating.

In the Amhara region, an imam's killing in March triggered inter-communal violence in the North Shewa and Oromia Special zones. Hundreds of Amhara and Oromo residents were reportedly killed, over 200,000 people displaced, and large-scale property damaged. Thousands of minority Qimant residents also fled to Sudan mid-year after Ethiopian military forces and Amhara militias reportedly attacked villages.

Conflict between Afar and Somali communities over disputed boundaries intensified, with the reported involvement of regional armed forces on both sides, killing hundreds in March and July and displacing thousands.

Elections and Political Space

Ethiopia's sixth national elections were held in two stages, after two initial postponements. The first on June 21, was held in most electoral constituencies; the second in the Somali and Harari regions on September 30 after reported voting irregularities, and in 12 constituencies in the Southern Nations, Nationalities, and People's (SNNPR) region. Voting did not take place in Tigray or in parts of Oromia, Amhara, Afar, and Benishangul-Gumuz regions due to insecurity.

On July 10, Ethiopia's electoral board declared Prime Minister Abiy Ahmed's Prosperity Party the winner, after securing most seats in Ethiopia's parliament. On October 4, Prime Minister Abiy was sworn in for a new five-year term.

More parties and candidates competed than in the past, and internally displaced persons (IDPs) were able to cast their vote in some areas, but the pre-electoral period was marred by violence and insecurity in several regions and accusations by opposition parties of a repressive operating environment.

Two opposition candidates, Girma Moges of EZEMA and Berihun Asferaw of NAMA, were assassinated in Oromia and Benishangul-Gumuz region in February and April.

In Oromia, the country's biggest regional constituency, the ruling Prosperity Party ran unopposed, after the main opposition parties, the Oromo Federalist Congress (OFC) and the Oromo Liberation Front (OLF), boycotted the election, citing intimidation of supporters and the detention of party leaders.

In the Somali region, on September 17, the Ogaden National Liberation Front (ONLF) withdrew from the elections alleging attacks on candidates and members and blocks on registration.

The incumbent party faced stiff competition in the Amhara region, but opposition parties submitted several complaints to the National Election Board alleging voter and observer intimidation by local officials and militias.

Due Process Rights and Fair Trial

On January 27, Ethiopian authorities arrested dozens of supporters of detained Oromo politicians in Addis Ababa outside a court hearing. Twenty senior Oromo political detainees began a hunger strike in protest. Oromo politician Bekele Gerba's health worsened. In February, authorities defied a court clearance to transfer him to a private hospital, forcibly took him to an army hospital, and briefly detained his doctor.

Authorities also blocked Lidetu Ayalew from the Ethiopian Democratic Party (EDP) from leaving the country for medical purposes three times, citing several reasons, including Lidetu's objection to the Tigray war.

On February 14, security forces arrested Oromo Mohammed Deksisso, a graduating student in Jimma, after calling for the release of Oromo politicians and justice for murdered Oromo singer Hachalu Hundessa. Mohammed was held for five months, faced serious due process violations before his release.

Freedom of Expression, Media, and Association

Government attacks and restrictions on the media and free expression increased.

In January, government forces shot dead Tigrayan journalist Dawit Kebede Araya in Mekelle. In May, Sisay Fida, a journalist with Oromia Broadcasting Network, was killed in western Oromia.

Journalists and outspoken public figures reporting or critiquing rights abuses linked to the Tigray conflict faced intimidation, expulsion from the country, and arrest. On July 15, the Ethiopia Media Authority temporarily suspended Addis Standard, a leading news outlet in Ethiopia "claiming it was advancing the agenda of the TPLF."

In March, Ethiopian security forces briefly detained three media workers and one journalist in Tigray in a military camp. In early July, police arrested 10 Awlo Media journalists and media workers and two EthioForum journalists; they were held incommunicado for weeks before their release in August.

On September 30, security forces arrested Abraha Desta, a former official in Ethiopia's interim administration in Tigray, after he published an open letter denouncing arbitrary arrests and discrimination against ethnic Tigrayans in Addis Ababa.

Ethiopian authorities passed a nationwide state of emergency November 4, granting the government far-reaching powers that heighten the risks of arbitrary arrest and detention against at-risk communities, but could have a chilling effect on humanitarian activities, induce self-censorship by the media, activist groups, and human rights organizations, and risk emboldening abusive elements within the security forces.

The government maintained an internet shutdown in Tigray throughout the year. Telephone connections were sporadic through June when they were shut off again.

Refugees

Between November 2020 and January 2021, Eritrean forces and Tigrayan militia alternatively occupied Hitsats and Shimelba refugee camps in Tigray and committed killings, sexual violence, arbitrary detention, forcible disappearances, and looting against scores of the 20,000 Eritrean refugees living in these camps. In January, Eritrean forces destroyed large parts of the camps, which were empty of refugees by March. Fighting in mid-July in Mai Aini and Adi Harush, the region's two other functioning camps, left Eritrean refugees in urgent need of protection and assistance.

Until August, Eritrean refugees fleeing to Addis Ababa from Tigray received no protection. Finally, ARRA with UNHCR began issuing three-year temporary identification documents to Eritrean refugees who had relocated to Addis from Tigray, enabling them to access assistance and services.

Key International Actors

Ethiopia's relations with some of its regional neighbors and donors significantly worsened, particularly over the conflict in Tigray. The UN Security Council's ability to address the crisis was largely nullified by China, Russia, and India. Kenya, Niger, and Tunisia, in July called for a comprehensive ceasefire, humanitarian access, and expressed support for an inquiry led by the African Commission on Human and Peoples' Rights (ACHPR). These calls did little to encourage substantive Security Council action.

The US repeatedly condemned the human rights abuses committed by warring parties in Tigray. In March, Secretary of State Antony Blinken characterized the Ethiopian government's actions in Western Tigray as "ethnic cleansing." On September 18, President Joe Biden issued an Executive Order that established a sanctions regime on individuals and entities responsible for human rights abuses in northern Ethiopia and for obstructing humanitarian aid.

On January 15, the European Union announced US$107 million and the UK committed £75 million in humanitarian assistance. The UK and EU leadership repeatedly condemned abuses. The EU urged member states to consider imposing "restrictive measures" on Ethiopia. In May, the EU withdrew its elections observers, citing a failure to agree with the government, including over its ability to operate independently. On October 4, the European Parliament adopted a resolution urging sanctions against those responsible for abuses and for obstructing humanitarian aid, for an arms embargo, and for a robust international investigative mechanism. On October 18, EU foreign ministers agreed to prepare ground for targeted sanctions on Ethiopia.

The African Union remained the only international body to monitor the June elections and declared them to be "credible," despite irregularities and insecurity in several regions.

In November, the Office of the UN High Commissioner for Human Rights (OHCHR) and the EHRC published the report of their joint investigation into human rights violations and abuses committed by all parties in the context of the Tigray conflict between November 3, 2020, and June 28, 2021. The report acknowledges it was not a comprehensive investigation and calls for further independent investigations and for accountability.

In June, the ACHPR launched a commission of inquiry into violations committed in Tigray. In response, Ethiopian authorities urged it to "immediately cease," proposing a joint probe with the national EHRC instead, which the inquiry rejected citing concerns around independence.

Relations with Egypt and Sudan remained tense. Disputes between Ethiopia and Sudan over the contested territory of al-Fashaga increased, resulting in several open clashes.

European Union

The European Union and most member states continue to espouse a commitment to human rights and democratic values. In practice, however, the policies and actions of the union and member states often fall short.

On migration, the response to the crisis in Afghanistan, the humanitarian emergency at the Poland-Belarus border, and pushbacks at that and other external EU borders exemplified a focus on sealing borders and externalizing responsibility for refugees, migrants, and asylum seekers at the expense of human rights. State responses to racism, violence, and discrimination, affecting women, ethnic and religious minorities, lesbian, gay, bisexual and transgender (LGBT) people, and people with disabilities, are often inadequate and in some cases exacerbate rights abuse.

The Covid-19 pandemic exacerbated deep inequality and poverty in the European Union, despite some state measures to mitigate it. EU member states used stronger rhetoric to criticize attacks on the rule of law and democratic institutions inside the EU, but fell short of taking decisive action available under the EU treaties or fully activating financial conditionality mechanisms.

Migrants, Refugees, and Asylum Seekers

EU member states evacuated thousands of Afghans from Kabul in August after the Taliban takeover but subsequently focused largely on measures to keep people fleeing Afghanistan in neighboring countries. During a high-level EU forum on providing protection to Afghans at risk, convened in October, EU member states did not make any concrete resettlement pledges.

In May, Spain summarily returned thousands of people, including unaccompanied children, from Ceuta after an estimated 10,000 people entered the Spanish North African enclave within 24 hours with alleged facilitation by Morocco.

Lithuania, Latvia, and Poland declared states of emergency, deployed troops, and unlawfully pushed people back into Belarus after saying that Belarus authorities were facilitating people, including Iraqis and Afghans, entering EU states. In August, the European Court of Human Rights ordered Latvia and Poland to provide assistance to groups of Iraqi and Afghan asylum seekers, respectively, stuck at the Belarus border, but reserved for a full hearing the question of whether they should be admitted to their territory. The situation escalated significantly in November, with thousands of people in dire wintery conditions at the Poland-Belarus border, and estimates that at least nine people had died in the area.

According to the UN refugee agency, over 103,889 people arrived irregularly at the EU's southern borders by mid-November 2021, most by sea, while at least 1,319 died or went missing in the Mediterranean Sea, almost as many (1,401) as in all of 2020. The International Organization for Migration (IOM) estimates that 1,563 people died at the Mediterranean, and recorded 785 dead or disappeared in the Atlantic Ocean on their way to Spain's Canary Islands in the first eight months of 2021. The death toll may be much higher; the nongovernmental organization (NGO) Walking Borders said almost 2,000 had died in the first six months alone.

The EU and member states continued to cooperate with Libya, including to facilitate interceptions at sea and disembarkation in Libya, despite known risks of arbitrary detention, torture, and other abuses. At least 27,551 people—well over double the total for 2020—were disembarked in Libya in the first 10 months of 2021. A UN inquiry published in October said the litany of inhumane acts against migrants in Libya may amount to crimes against humanity, adding that the responsibility of other countries needs to be investigated.

The Council of Europe commissioner for human rights and the UN high commissioner for human rights, in March and May respectively, urged the EU to conduct search and rescue in the Mediterranean Sea, stop obstructing the work of nongovernmental rescue organizations, and condition cooperation with Libya on respect for human rights. As of September, only five NGO rescue vessels were operational, with groups alleging obstruction by Italy and Malta.

In June, Denmark amended its immigration law so it can send asylum seekers to another country for examination of their claim, without any guarantee of relocation to Denmark if successful. The African Union strongly condemned the move in August, and to date no country is on record as agreeing to host offshore processing.

A European Parliament investigation concluded in July that the EU Border and Coast Guard Agency, commonly known as Frontex, failed to take action to stop unlawful pushbacks, ignoring reports and deliberately delaying hiring rights monitors. Despite having numerous accountability mechanisms, Frontex has failed to credibly investigate or mitigate pushbacks where they were operating. In late October, the European Parliament froze part of the agency's budget until it makes improvements related to human rights.

In September, the European Commission noted slow progress on implementing its 2020 Pact on Migration and Asylum, with notably limited momentum to create more safe and legal migration pathways and towards more equitable sharing of responsibility for asylum seekers. Steps towards creating independent border monitoring mechanisms envisioned in the pact fell short of guarantees to ensure such mechanisms would contribute to accountability and to ending illegal pushbacks.

Discrimination and Intolerance

The Covid-19 pandemic fuelled discrimination and hate crimes particularly against migrants and Roma people, according to a June EU Fundamental Rights Agency report.

The European Committee of Social Rights of the Council of Europe (CoE) said in a March report that the pandemic had a dire impact on schooling during the 2020-2021 academic year, including in EU member states. Inequalities were exacerbated particularly for marginalized and socially disadvantaged children and those in greater need of educational support such as children with disabilities.

A June report by the EU's Fundamental Rights Agency (FRA) found in some countries asylum seekers and undocumented migrants faced difficulties in accessing Covid-19 vaccines, but other countries waived formal requirements to facilitate access.

In response to increasing antisemitism and attacks on Jews in many parts of Europe, including online hate speech, the CoE's European Commission against Racism and Intolerance issued a General Policy Recommendation in September calling on European countries including EU states to tackle the issue and in October, the European Commission published a strategy on combatting anti-semitism.

A May survey by the FRA on police stops across the EU found that overall ethnic minorities, Muslims, and those who do not identify as heterosexual were among those most often stopped. It also found that those who experience ethnic profiling place less trust in public authorities than those who do not.

The pandemic highlighted a stark rise in abuse and hate speech against lesbian, gay, bisexual, transgender and intersex (LGBTI) people, problems accessing health care including for LGBTI people with disabilities. A survey published in April found increased vulnerability to homelessness for LGBTI young people linked to the pandemic.

The FRA called in July on EU countries to remove barriers that prevent hate crime victims from coming forward, and to encourage reporting by tackling structural discrimination and prejudice in society, eliminating discriminatory policing, publicly condemning hate crime and raising victims' awareness of their rights and support available.

In March, the Council of Europe commissioner for human rights, Dunja Mijatović, expressed concern about people of African descent's continued exposure to racist violence, racial profiling or other grave forms of racism and racial discrimination in Europe including in EU states.

Violence and harassment on the grounds of gender and sex, including for LGBTI people, remained widespread. A FRA survey published in March found that 83 percent of women and girls aged between 16 and 29 limit where they go or who they spend time with to protect themselves; over 1 in 4 women (28 percent) reported having been victims of harassment in the year before the survey, and women were significantly more likely to experience sexual harassment than men; when women face non-sexual physical violence, they said it is most often by a family member or a relative (32 percent) and frequently in their own homes (37 percent). More than two thirds of respondents said they did not report incidents of violence to the police. At time of writing, six member states and the EU had yet to ratify the CoE Istanbul Convention on combatting and preventing violence against women; some member states were actively opposing ratification or threatening to withdraw from the convention.

A March study by the European Institute for Gender Equality found that while all 27 EU countries had taken steps to support and protect women victims of intimate partner violence and their children in the context of Covid-19, only a handful had comprehensive action plans to address the situation.

In March, the European Commission adopted a strategy for the rights of persons with disabilities 2021-2030, prioritizing accessibility; deinstitutionalization and independent living; countering discrimination and achieving equal access in employment, justice, education, health, and political participation; and promoting disability rights globally. The 2021 Fundamental Rights Agency annual report noted particular risks for people with disabilities in institutions during the Covid-19 pandemic, as well as increased obstacles to accessing essential services, education, and healthcare.

The European Court of Human Rights (ECtHR) ruled in July to permit employers to discriminate against people who wear religious dress, raising concerns about protection of religious freedom for Muslim women in particular.

Poverty and Inequality

Official estimates suggested that 91.4 million people across the EU (around a fifth of the population), of whom 17.9 million were children, are at risk of poverty or social exclusion (defined as living with severe material deprivation or chronic underemployment), with inequality levels static or worsening since the 2008-9 financial crisis.

The European Food Banks Federation estimated in September that its member organizations were providing food aid to 12.8 million people in need, an increase of 34.7 percent compared to pre-pandemic situation, highlighting a sharp increase in aid provided to people who had lost their jobs. Temporary financial relief from governments in many EU states helped partly mitigate the negative impact of the Covid-19 pandemic on inequality, which nonetheless widened.

The UN special rapporteur on extreme poverty concluded a visit to EU institutions in January warning that national governments and regional institutions needed to prioritize socioeconomic rights and "rethink [their] fundamental economic rules" to make meaningful headway on reducing poverty in the coming decade, and noting the disproportionate impact of poverty on women, people with disabilities, older people, and Roma.

In March, the European Commission adopted the European Child Guarantee, spurred by concerns of increasing child poverty during the pandemic, setting out specific steps on children's right to food and right to an adequate standard of living. The European Commission proposal for the European Council calls on Member States "to guarantee for children in need effective access to healthy nutrition and adequate housing."

In May, EU member states signed the Porto Declaration committing to the implementation of a European Pillar of Social Rights, confirming a target to remove 15 million people from poverty by 2030, and setting out a need to modernize minimum incomes schemes across the EU. The UN special rapporteur on extreme poverty assessed the Porto Declaration's targets as "insufficiently ambitious."

Anti-poverty and environmental groups criticized the European Commission's announcement in July of a legislative package on energy for failing to protect people on low-incomes from fluctuating energy prices and for insufficiently addressing emission reduction targets. As energy prices rose, by October researchers estimated some 80 million households would struggle to meet energy costs during the winter.

Roma people remained at disproportionate risk of living in poverty and social exclusion. Roma rights activists documented anti-Roma discrimination and segregation in housing, evictions and lack of access to water, sanitation and essential public services in some EU countries, including Bulgaria, the Czech Republic, France, Hungary, Ireland, Italy, Romania, and Slovakia. The European Roma Rights Center reported that Roma children were overrepresented in state care in Bulgaria, the Czech Republic, Hungary, Italy, Romania, and Slovakia, often as a byproduct of discriminatory policy, poverty, and social exclusion.

Rule of Law

Hearings on Poland and Hungary under Article 7—the EU treaty procedure to scrutinize threats to EU values on rights and rule of law—took place in the EU Council in June 2021.

In June, 18 EU member states jointly condemned the Hungarian legislation discriminating against LGBT people. In a June resolution, the European Parliament called on the Council to issue concrete rule-of-law recommendations to Hungary and Poland under Article 7.

In July, the European Parliament condemned Hungary's anti-LGBT law and other attacks on the rule of law. In September, it criticized the deterioration of media freedom and the erosion of judicial independence in Poland. In October, it called on the Commission to launch an infringement against Poland on the functioning and composition of the Constitutional Tribunal, following a decision by the tribunal that undermines EU law.

In October, the EU Court of Justice imposed a daily €1 million (approximately US$1,132,000) penalty on Poland for failing to respect a CJEU request in July to block a 2020 law undermining judges' independence. In September, the EU Commission opened a follow-up procedure against Poland for failing to implement a separate CJEU ruling that found the disciplinary regime against judges was illegal. In July, the commission initiated another legal procedure against Poland over "LGBT-ideology free zones" in several municipalities. In October, EU Commission President Ursula Von der Leyen stated she was deeply concerned by the ruling of Poland's compromised Constitutional Tribunal on the unconstitutionality of EU law, and committed to use all the powers under the treaties to protect the binding nature of CJEU rulings.

The commission opened a follow-up case in February against Hungary for failing to implement 2020 CJEU ruling finding illegal the law on foreign-funded NGOs, and requested in November that the CJEU orders financial penalties on Hungary for failing to implement a December 2020 Court ruling finding the asylum law illegal. In November, the CJEU ruled that Hungary's 2018 asylum law that restricted access to international protection and criminalized legitimate activities in support of migrants breached EU law. The commission opened new legal infringements against Hungary for forcing independent station Klubradio off air, and in July for the law violating the rights of LGBT people.

A European Parliament Monitoring Group continued to assess situations in other EU countries, including Bulgaria, Slovakia, Slovenia, and Malta.

In July, the European Commission released its second rule of law report covering all 27 EU states. In September, Commission President Von Der Leyen announced that from 2022, the rule of law reports would come with specific recommendations to member states, and committed to introduce a media freedom legislation within a year.

At time of writing, the commission had not yet started using the new rule of law conditionality mechanism for EU funding, prompting a legal challenge by European Parliamentarians. The commission in September explained that delays in approving Poland's and Hungary's Covid recovery funds were justified by rule of law concerns. In September, four Polish regions revoked their anti-LGBT declarations for fear of losing EU funds earmarked to the regions.

Lack of accountability for the killing of journalists for their work remains a concern. In an April resolution, the European Parliament urged Malta to bring to justice the perpetrators of the 2017 murder of journalist Daphne Caruana Galizia. In February, one of the three accused of the murder was sentenced to 15 years of prison; the other two were awaiting trial. In August, Malta's attorney general called for life sentence against Yorgen Fenech, for his involvement in planning the murder. In July, the report of an independent judicial inquiry flagged the responsibility of the state for the climate of impunity that led to Caruana Galizia's killing.

In June, Slovakia's Supreme Court acquitted and ordered the retrial of a man accused of being involved in the murder of journalist Ján Kuciak and his fiancée, Martina Kušnírová, in 2018. In Athens, Greece, investigative journalist Giorgos Karaivaz was shot in April 2021. The investigation was ongoing. In the Netherlands, investigative journalist Peter R. de Vries was shot in Central Amsterdam on July 6 and died nine days later; two people were in custody for their alleged involvement. According to investigators, the murders of Karaivaz and de Vries are linked to organized crime networks.

In its annual Rule of Law report, the European Commission identified that civil society organizations face serious challenges in some EU states. In Hungary, civil society groups continue to face smear campaigns and laws criminalizing legitimate activities. In Poland, human rights defenders face harassment and defunding, with women's human rights defenders facing escalating threats. France's top administrative court confirmed in September the government-ordered dissolution of an anti-discrimination group. In Greece, Cyprus, and Italy, civil society groups working on migration face a hostile environment.

Climate Change Policy and Impacts

The 27 member states of the European Union are among the top 10 greenhouse gas emitters globally, making a major contribution to the climate crisis that is taking a mounting toll on human rights around the globe. In July, the European Commission adopted a series of legislative proposals laying out how it intends to achieve climate neutrality by 2050, the target set in the 2020 European Climate Law adopted in June, including the intermediate target of an at least 55 percent net reduction in greenhouse gas emissions by 2030. According to Climate Action Tracker, the 2030 commitment is "almost sufficient" to meet the Paris Agreement goal to stay below 1.5°C of warming.

Despite committing to phase out environmentally harmful subsidies, including subsidies for fossil fuels, by 2020, European Parliament members voted in 2021 to prolong gas subsidies until 2027, undermining emissions reduction efforts.

Several European officials, including the French president and the then-German chancellor, have said they opposed or had strong reservations about the EU-Mercosur free trade agreement due to Brazil's disregard for its commitments under the Paris Climate Agreement and failure to curb illegal deforestation in the Amazon, a "carbon sink" critical for mitigating climate change.

Foreign Policy

The European Commission continued to oppose temporarily waiving some intellectual property and trade rules in the Agreement on Trade-Related Aspects of Intellectual Property Rights (TRIPS Agreement) that would facilitate the world-wide production of Covid-19 tests, treatments, and vaccines needed for the pandemic response.

Hungary repeatedly used the EU's unanimity rule to prevent the adoption of several EU statements on human rights, as well as of EU foreign ministers' conclusions on China's crackdown in Hong Kong.

Highlighting major double-standards in foreign policy, the EU and its member states failed to take decisive action to address serious human rights abuses in Egypt, the Gulf countries, Israel and Palestine, and India. Trade, migration-management, and perceived geostrategic interests ostensibly took precedence over human rights concerns in EU relations with these and other countries, leading to a reluctance to publicly denounce abuses or to condition military, budgetary, or political support to states responsible for grave human rights violations. Similarly, the EU raised concerns on rule of law and human rights in Turkey but failed to make it a priority in the relationship. When unanimity was secured, the EU managed to take bold steps, including notably on Russia, Nicaragua, Venezuela, Myanmar, and Belarus.

The EU collectively and several of its member states continued to play an important role on several initiatives at the UN, and sponsored, co-sponsored, or supported important resolutions including on Afghanistan, Belarus, Ethiopia, Sudan, Syria, Sri Lanka, Myanmar, Nicaragua, North Korea, and climate change. But EU member states' support for joint statements on Egypt and on China was fragmented, and none supported the establishment of a commission of inquiry on Israel.

The failure to seriously address human rights violations by EU member states, and EU double standards continued to risk devaluing important EU declarations and human rights policies including the new EU Action Plan on Human Rights and Democracy.

In February, the EU revised its guidelines for human rights dialogues with third countries, recognizing the need to maximize their impact. Human rights dialogues have often been unproductive undertakings, often held just ahead of higher-level engagements by EU leaders with their counterparts, giving the appearance of being no more than a box ticking exercise.

In April, EU foreign ministers adopted a new strategy for the Sahel region, recognizing the urgent need for security sector reform, improved governance, and accountability, including justice for violations committed by the security forces. Concerns remain over its implementation in a changing scenario and uncertainties over the EU's presence in the region.

In March, under the new EU global human rights sanctions regime, the EU designated a total of 15 individuals and 4 entities from Russia, China, North Korea, Libya, South Sudan, and Eritrea. At the time of writing these were the only designations under the new EU global human rights sanctions regime. The sanctions against Chinese officials deemed responsible for what Human Rights Watch and others has determined to be crimes against humanity in Xinjiang were the first restrictive measures against the Chinese government since the 1990 Tiananmen massacre. Beijing retaliated with countersanctions against several EU and European entities and Members of the European Parliament; in response, the European Parliament froze any consideration of a bilateral trade deal with China. Existing sanctions regimes and arms embargoes were confirmed or strengthened, including those on Myanmar, Belarus, Syria, and Venezuela, among others.

In March, the European Parliament adopted a legislative initiative report paving the way for EU legislation on sustainable corporate governance. The proposed legislation should put in place binding provisions for companies to conduct human rights and environmental due diligence throughout their value chain, foreseeing penalties in case of failure to comply and establishing legal remedies for affected individuals and communities. In September, the Commission's President, Ursula von der Leyen, also announced upcoming legislation to ban products produced by forced labor from entering the EU market.

In September, the European Commission proposed a new regulation to replace the current Generalised Scheme of Preferences (GSP) when it expires in 2023. The scheme provides beneficiary countries with tariff benefits for their exports to the EU against varying degrees of human rights conditionality. While the new proposal includes some improvements, several human rights groups, including Human Rights Watch, urged the European Parliament and the European Council to address some of the scheme's longstanding key weaknesses.

Current GSP beneficiaries include countries with very serious shortcomings in their human rights records, including Sri Lanka, the Philippines, Pakistan, Bangladesh, and Myanmar. In April, the EU granted GSP+ to Uzbekistan despite persistent serious human rights concerns. Pressure from the European Parliament ahead of the EU's assessment of Sri Lanka's compliance with its obligations under the GSP scheme helped build momentum to secure reform of parts of the country's abusive counter-terrorism legislation and responses.

The European Parliament continued to play an important role as a watchdog of EU foreign policy, often denouncing abuses committed by governments that the EU and its member states were unwilling to publicly criticize, including Egypt, Rwanda, India, Saudi Arabia, Bahrain, the United Arab Emirates, and Vietnam. Unfortunately, calls by European parliamentarians for concrete EU action often were ignored by the European Commission, the European External Action Service, the European Council, and EU member states. The European Parliament awarded the 2021 Sakharov Prize to Russian dissident Alexei Navalny.

France

Despite government measures to mitigate its economic impact, the Covid-19 pandemic exacerbated poverty and inequality. Police targeted minority youth for discriminatory police identity checks. Child protection authorities often failed to provide unaccompanied migrant children with appropriate care and services. Migrants and asylum seekers faced inhumane living conditions and police abuse. Racist violence remained a concern. Persons with disabilities faced discrimination. The forced dissolution of a leading anti-discrimination group and the increased use of accelerated procedures in the legislative process raise rule of law concerns.

Poverty and Inequality

According to the National Institute of Statistics and Economic Studies and the National Council for Poverty and Social Exclusion Policies, the Covid-19 crisis exacerbated the precariousness of the poorest people, despite government support and safeguard measures. The pandemic led to more people experiencing food insecurity and seeking food aid, and exacerbated domestic violence.

According to government data, vaccination rates were lower among people in poverty. Although vaccination is open to all, in practice many obstacles remained for the most marginalized populations, such as far distances from health care centers or lack of access to information.

The annual winter evictions moratorium, including a ban on suspending gas and electricity for non-payment, was extended by two months, to the end of May. A coalition of nongovernmental groups (NGOs) warned in mid-July against an increase in evictions from informal settlements since June 1.

Migrants and Asylum Seekers

Throughout the year, adults and children living in informal encampments in Paris and in and around Calais in northern France were subjected to repeated mass evictions, police harassment, and restrictions on humanitarian assistance. The CNCDH denounced in February the living conditions and rights violations of migrants in northern France hoping to travel onward to the UK. Irregular boat cross-

HUMAN
RIGHTS
WATCH

Enforced Misery

The Degrading Treatment of Migrant Children and Adults
in Northern France

ings in the Channel more than doubled in 2021 compared to 2020. France criticized a UK plan to push boats back as contrary to maritime law and the obligation to safeguard life at sea.

French border police unlawfully expelled migrants, including unaccompanied children, at the French-Italian border.

In April, France deported a Chechen who was an important witness in a torture case to Russia despite a decision by the national asylum court prohibiting his expulsion; he was arbitrarily detained by Chechen security officials two days after his deportation. In a separate April case, the European Court of Human Rights (ECtHR) urged France to assess in a "complete and precise" way the risks that a Chechen national would face before being deported to Russia.

In July, the ECtHR ruled that the 2018 detention pending deportation of a Malian woman and her four-month-old daughter violated their rights to liberty and security and the prohibition of inhuman and degrading treatment.

By the end of August, France had evacuated 2,600 Afghans from Kabul. French authorities opened a dedicated office to process their asylum claims, which will undergo expedited processing.

Rule of Law

In September, the Council of State, France's highest administrative court, approved the December 2020 dissolution by decree of the Collective against Islamophobia in France (CCIF), disappointingly accepting the government's argument that the prominent anti-discrimination group engaged in incitement to discrimination, hatred, and violence. The dissolution of CCIF is part of a broader crackdown on liberties in response to attacks attributed to Islamist extremists.

The CNCDH and the European Commission expressed concerns that the law "consolidating the principles of the Republic" intended to "fight against separatism and attacks on citizenship," adopted in August, might violate fundamental rights, including freedom of association, information, and education.

In March, the French defender of rights warned against the proliferation of laws in response to Covid-19 that the pandemic did not always justify, and the multiplication of norms regulating individual freedoms without judicial control. In its

July report on European rule of law, the European Commission noted that the use of accelerated procedures, including for laws with a significant impact on individual freedoms, has become the norm and denounced the shrinking space for civil society.

A new security law enacted in May prompted concerns over its potential impact on freedom of expression and information, and on the right to protest.

The state of health emergency introduced in March 2020 in response to Covid-19 was successively extended during the year. Concerns were raised about the risks to individual liberties under the state of emergency. The defender of rights pointed to the potential for discrimination, violations of children's rights, the risks to vulnerable populations, and data protection in relation to the creation of an obligatory health pass in August.

Law Enforcement and Police Abuse

In July, six civil society groups including Human Rights Watch filed an unprecedented case before the Council of State over systemic racial discrimination by the police with respect to unlawful ethnic profiling during identity checks.

In April, Reporters Without Borders (RSF) warned against police attacks on journliasts covering protests. Similarly, in its July rule of law report, the European Commission noted attacks on journalists and media workers, both by protestors and police, despite France's solid legal framework to ensure media pluralism and independence.

In May, the Constitutional Council declared unconstitutional some provisions included in a "global security law," in particular one that would have made it an offense to disseminate images of law enforcement officers in the exercise of their duties.

Children's Rights

The French defender of rights raised concerns about the placement of unaccompanied children in closed reception facilities, in some departments across France, and called on authorities to house children in adequate and dignified facilities.

At time of writing, a draft law on child protection that would prohibit the placement of unaccompanied children in hotels, where they face overcrowding, isolation, weak surveillance, and proximity to places of trafficking, was pending before the Senate. NGOs have criticized some provisions as contrary to the best interest of the child, including the imposition of biometric registration of unaccompanied children.

By September, France had relocated 379 unaccompanied children and 366 other asylum seekers deemed vulnerable from Greece.

The National Assembly adopted a law in April defining as rape any act of sexual penetration between an adult and a child under the age of 15, punishable by up to 20 years in jail, without having to prove coercion.

In a February report, the controller general of places of deprivation of liberty expressed concerns about the increase in detention of children, the frequent failure to strictly separate children and adults in prisons and in police custody cells, and the lack of access of children deprived of their liberty to education and mental and physical care.

Discrimination and Intolerance

According to official data published in July, overall bias crimes decreased by 26 percent in 2020 compared to 2019 but anti-Muslim acts increased by 52 percent. The interior ministry registered 5,086 victims of offenses due to ethnicity, nationality, religion, or race in 2020, a 5 percent decrease compared to 2019. According to the same report, Roma and Travellers continued to be stigmatized, with polls compiled by the CNCDH showing that 75 percent of respondents consider Roma people as a "separate group" in society.

In a July report, the CNCDH suggested that, while there had been fewer serious bias acts during Covid-19 lockdowns, there had been an increase in online hate speech.

A law on bioethics allowing fertility treatments for lesbian couples and single women was adopted in August. Transgender people continued to be legally excluded from these treatments.

In a May report, the nongovernmental group SOS Homophobie concluded that violence targeting lesbian, gay, bisexual and transgender (LGBT) people, particularly youth, by their families and their communities increased during the pandemic as measures to try to prevent the spread of Covid-19 were enforced.

Women's Rights

The National Assembly voted to ratify the Violence and Harassment at Work Convention of the International Labour Organization (ILO) in July; it was voted by the Senate in October. France's minister of labor said that the current legal framework is sufficient to address sexual harassment at work, but feminist groups and labor unions argue further reform is necessary, in accordance with the convention and its standards.

In September, the government announced that free contraception, previously available only to girls under 18, would be extended to women up to the age 25, beginning in 2022.

In August, France's interior minister announced a series of measures to address domestic violence, including the appointment of officers specializing in domestic violence to each police station and each gendarmerie brigade across France. He noted that domestic violence "is becoming the primary reason for police and gendarme intervention," with 400,000 police interventions in 2020. France's femicide rate remains among the highest in Europe, and failures by police in high-profile cases led to protests and calls for improvements in authorities' response to violence against women.

A study commissioned by the European Parliament found that female employment was disproportionately impacted by the Covid-19 pandemic.

Disability Rights

In its September concluding observations, the UN Committee on the Rights of People with Disabilities expressed concerns about discrimination; limited implementation of accessibility in public services and facilities; deprivation of legal capacity and the lack of supported decision-making; deprivation of liberty on grounds of disability; the high number of children with disabilities in segregated education settings; and barriers in access to justice.

It also criticized inhuman and degrading conditions, including violence, humiliation and sexual abuse in residential and mental health facilities, forced psychiatric treatment, and the use of solitary confinement, seclusion, chemical and physical restraints, including on children.

The committee also noted the lack of a disability-inclusive response to the disproportionate impact of the Covid-19 pandemic on persons with disabilities. Among other things, it called on the government to initiate emergency deinstitutionalization and ensure safe and independent living in the community and to actively consult with people with disabilities and their representative organizations in public decision-making.

Counterterrorism

Several civil society organizations criticized a counterterrorism law, adopted in July, for permanently renewing emergency measures adopted in 2015 and 2017 and giving intelligence services new powers of mass surveillance, including the possibility of using algorithms to scan internet connections and browsing data, and the interception of satellite communications. The law also empowers the government to close places of worship where terrorism, hatred, or discrimination is promoted, as well as spaces affiliated with these places of worship.

The trial opened in September of 20 suspects of the extremist armed group Islamic State (ISIS), charged with involvement in the November 2015 Paris attacks, which killed 130 people and injured hundreds more.

Climate Change Policy and Impacts

As one of the EU's biggest greenhouse gas emitters, France is contributing to the climate crisis taking a growing toll on human rights around the globe. France committed to reducing emissions by 40 percent by 2030. From January 2020 through March 3, 43 percent of the almost US$57 billion Covid-19 recovery were subsidies for fossil fuels. In a February report, the High Council for the Climate said that, while progress has been made, the government's efforts remain too slow to achieve the 2030 target. France has already warmed by 1.7 degrees and severe climate impacts such as heat waves and forest fires will become more frequent and intense.

In February, the Paris Administrative Court held in a landmark ruling that climate change constitutes environmental damage to which state inaction has contributed. In October, the court issued an additional ruling in this case finding that France has to make up for its past failures and achieve additional emission reductions by December 2022. In June, the Senate adopted the "climate and resilience" law. Despite some positive measures, it has been severely criticized for its lack of ambition. In July, the Council of State ordered the government to take additional measures by March 2022 to put France on track to meet its commitment to reduce greenhouse gas emissions.

Despite poor implementation by the government, civil society groups are increasingly using the French Duty of Vigilance Law to hold private actors to account for harming the climate. In February, the Nanterre civil court held that it had jurisdiction over a case against Total, an energy company, claiming it had not taken adequate measures to prevent human rights, health, and environmental damage resulting from its contribution to climate change.

Foreign Policy

France continued to support scrutiny under Article 7—the European Union mechanism to deal with EU members putting the union's values at risk—to address rule of law concerns in Hungary and Poland. The European Affairs Minister claimed he was denied access to an "LGBT-free" zone by Polish authorities during an official visit in March. In June, he called the anti-LGBT law adopted in Hungary "a scandal."

In February, France condemned the jailing of Russian opposition leader Alexei Navalny, supported EU sanctions against Russia and stated that President Putin and Russian authorities would be held responsible and face further sanctions if Navalny died.

In May, France condemned the unlawful forced landing of a Ryanair flight by the Belarus authorities, calling it an "act of state piracy," and the consequent arbitrary arrest of a prominent blogger and political activist and his partner, and called for "a strong and united response from the EU."

Although France signed on to a joint declaration at the UN Human Rights Council condemning the human rights situation in Egypt in March, in May it announced a deal, financed through French loans, for the sale of 30 Rafale fighter jets to Egypt. A few months before, President Emmanuel Macron said he would not make the sale of weapons to Egypt conditional on human rights.

Despite mounting evidence of war crimes by the Saudi and UAE-led coalition in Yemen and lack of accountability for these crimes, Saudi Arabia was France's biggest arms buyer in 2020. In December, France concluded with the UAE what the government characterized as its largest arms contract ever, totaling US$19 billion, including the sale of 80 Rafale fighter jets.

In May, French Foreign Minister Jean-Yves Le Drian warned of "a risk of apartheid" in Israel's treatment of Palestinians, noting that "even the status quo produces this." France, though, abstained at the Human Rights Council on a resolution that established a commission of inquiry into violations in Israel and the Occupied Palestinian Territory (OPT).

In August, France announced €100 million in humanitarian aid for the Lebanese people during a donors' conference it co-sponsored with the UN, but has not yet supported calls from victims and civil society for an international independent investigation into the Beirut blast.

In May, in Kigali, Macron said he recognized France's "responsibilities" in the genocide in Rwanda and hoped for forgiveness, while indicating that "France was not complicit" in the massacres. In March, a report commissioned by Macron concluded that France had "heavy and overwhelming responsibilities" in the 1994 genocide.

In February, the foreign minister denounced "institutionalized repression" of Uyghurs by China's authorities and called for an impartial, independent mission to Xinjiang under the auspices of the UN High Commissioner for Human Rights. In October, France led a cross-regional joint statement at the UN General Assembly's Third Committee condemning the Chinese government's widespread violations in Xinjiang.

France failed to show leadership in pushing for sanctions on Myanmar's oil and gas revenues. Like the US and the UK, it also failed to push for a global arms embargo at the UN Security Council in response to the February 1 military coup in Myanmar and the junta's atrocities.

Georgia

Setbacks in several areas of human rights occurred during 2021 against the backdrop of a dramatic political standoff between the ruling Georgian Dream (GD) and opposition parties that dominated much of the year in Georgia.

Lack of accountability for law enforcement abuses persisted. Other areas of concern included police interference in freedom of assembly, attacks against journalists and declining media freedom, institutionalization of children, violence against lesbian, gay, bisexual, and transgender (LGBT) people, and threats to labor safety.

In August, the European Union said Georgia failed to qualify for a €75 million (around US$86 million) in assistance conditioned on judicial reforms.

Municipal Elections

After the October 2020 general elections, opposition parties boycotted their seats in parliament, alleging electoral fraud. In April, the EU mediated an agreement between the GD and opposition parties that ended the boycott, envisaged electoral and judicial reforms, and proposed early parliamentary elections if GD failed to garner 43 percent of votes in October 2021 municipal elections. This prompted the opposition to frame municipal elections as a "referendum" on holding snap parliamentary elections. GD abandoned the agreement in July, citing the refusal by the main opposition party, United National Movement (UNM) to sign it and ruling out snap polls.

GD won a significant majority in the municipal elections in October. The opposition rejected the results and called for street protests.

International observers, led by the Organization for Security and Co-operation in Europe (OSCE), found that the elections were competitive and "technically well-administered," but "marred by allegations of pressure on voters, vote-buying and an unlevel playing field." Following the run-offs later in October, they also said that "sharp imbalances in resources, and an undue advantage of incumbency further benefited the ruling party and tilted the playing field."

On October 1, a day before the polls, police detained ex-President Mikheil Saakashvili after his return to Georgia following an eight-year absence. In 2018, a court convicted him in absentia on two counts of abuse of office and sentenced him to six years. The Interior Ministry launched an investigation into illegal border crossing in addition to two other pending charges. Saakashvili denied all charges and said they were politically motivated.

Lack of Accountability for Law Enforcement Abuses

Impunity for abuses by law enforcement remained a persistent problem. By September 2021, the Ombudswoman's Office received 133 complaints of ill-treatment by prison staff or police and petitioned the State Inspector's Office, an independent body investigating abuses by law enforcement, to launch investigations in all cases. At time of writing, the investigations were ongoing.

Police interfered with the right to freedom of assembly by preventing protesters from installing tents outside the parliament building in Tbilisi. In February, police arrested over 20 protesters on misdemeanor disobedience charges after law enforcement officers seized a tent, which led to skirmishes with the gathered activists.

On February 23, police stormed UNM's headquarters to detain its leader, Nika Melia, over his failure to pay additional bail fees. Police used teargas, detained 21 people on disobedience charges, and seized computer servers. The Georgian Young Lawyers' Association (GYLA), a leading nongovernmental group, said that the use of tear gas was disproportionate and criticized the police for failing to explain the grounds for seizing the computer hardware. Melia continued to face charges for inciting violence during 2019 protests in Tbilisi and refusing to pay increased bail after he discarded an ankle monitor during November 2020 rally.

GYLA also criticized the police use of misdemeanor disobedience charges to detain people protesting the raid as a means "to suppress peaceful protests."

In April, the parliament rushed amendments to the code of administrative offenses, toughening penalties for petty hooliganism and police disobedience. The amendments doubled or tripled fines (up to approximately US$1,300), increased administrative detention from 7 to 15 days, and stripped the judicial discretion for more lenient sanctions for repeat offenders. Georgian human rights groups criticized the amendments as making "room for arbitrary use of repressive police mechanisms and sanctions." They emphasized that court rulings on administrative offenses are often based solely on the testimonies of police officers and disregard fair trial norms.

In September, an anonymous source claiming to have worked for the state intelligence agency, leaked thousands of documents to media containing compromising information on Georgian clergy, including information on their intimate relationships, sexual orientation, or illegal drug use. The documents were gathered allegedly through illegal surveillance and wiretapping, The files also included conversations of Georgian journalists, opposition politicians, civil servants, and foreign diplomats. The prosecutor's office launched an investigation into the leak.

Freedom of Media

Journalists and other media professionals endured numerous threats and attacks throughout 2021. In February, police arrested three people for assaulting Vakho Sanaia, an independent Formula TV anchor in Tbilisi. Sanaia said the assailants recognized him and shouted insults at him during the attack. In August, a court convicted the assailants and sentenced them to time served on remand.

On July 5, amid homophobic violence against a planned Pride March, hate groups verbally and physically assaulted at least 53 media workers in Tbilisi, including journalists and cameramen from television channels TV Pirveli, Formula TV, Mtavari Arkhi, Rustavi 2, Imedi TV, Public Broadcaster, Radio Liberty's Georgia service, and several online media outlets. The attackers smashed and destroyed media equipment. Several journalists sustained physical injuries and required brief hospitalization.

Police appeared to be present but failed to prevent the violent incidents. (See below).

TV Pirveli cameramen Alexandre Lashkarava, who sustained facial bone fractures, a concussion, and contusions, and underwent surgery, was found dead in his apartment two days later. The day after Lshkarava was found, before the cause of death was fully established, the authorities publicly alleged he had died from a drug overdose, based on what they called "interim forensic results" of a blood test. No final forensic results have been issued at time of writing. Lashkarava's family and civil society groups questioned the rushed findings. Police launched an investigation into incitement to suicide.

On July 22, the culture minister grabbed and confiscated the microphone from a journalist with the pro-opposition television channel, Mtavari Arkhi, in response to uncomfortable questions.

Sexual Orientation and Gender Identity

Organizers of Tbilisi Pride had to cancel the planned march on July 5 after far-right groups stormed their headquarters and attacked journalists. Mobs climbed onto the balcony of the Tbilisi Pride headquarters, broke windows, tore a rainbow flag, and ransacked the offices. They also attacked and injured over 50 journalists (see above) and broke into the offices of several nongovernmental groups that hid Pride organizers as violent mobs chased them throughout the city.

Instead of ensuring the safety and freedom of assembly of the Pride organizers and participants, the authorities appeared to blame them. Prime Minister Irakli Garibashvili said that it was "unreasonable" to hold the demonstration in a public place that could lead to "civil confrontation." The Interior Ministry also warned against holding such marches in a public space. According to numerous media reports, police were present in small numbers and failed to effectively intervene. In the aftermath of the violent spree, police launched investigation and arrested at least 27 people for participating in organized violence. The ombudswoman criticized the authorities for failing to prosecute any of the organizers of the violence.

In March, authorities allowed the first-ever legal gender recognition for a transgender person, changing the gender marker from "male" to "female," but only after she provided a medical certificate proving she had undergone surgery. Medical certification is required for transgender people to obtain legal gender recognition in Georgia. This represents a serious obstacle in the daily lives of transgender people, encouraging their marginalization, and raising unemployment and poverty risks.

Children's Rights

In May, a foster care home in Ninotsminda for 56 children, including eight with disabilities, run by the Georgian Orthodox Church, drew media attention after the office of the ombudswoman was twice denied a monitoring visit, prompting the UN Committee on the Rights of the Child to issue an emergency temporary measure. The measure called on the authorities to immediately ensure state monitoring.

The ombudswoman publicized information about four ongoing criminal investigations related to physical and sexual abuse against children in the Ninotsminda institution. After a public outcry, in June, a court ruled to remove children with disabilities from the institution. State social workers facilitated the transfer of over 30 children, including children without disabilities. Over a dozen children remained there under close state scrutiny. The church also replaced the establishment's director. The new director claimed to have dismissed over two dozen staff and expressed readiness to cooperate with the office of the ombudswoman.

In July, UNICEF hosted a two-day workshop with Georgian officials and all partners working on children's rights to assist the government in developing an action plan for deinstitutionalization for children with and without disabilities residing in state and private institutions.

In July, a court ruled that forcibly separating children from families due to poverty is illegal. It ordered the government to pay GEL35,000 (US$11,000) in damages to each of three children who had been forcibly separated from their mothers two years earlier due to poverty, without the state first attempting to provide support to the family.

Schools were closed for 155 days, and partially closed to certain ages or in certain areas, for another 84 days since the pandemic's start in 2020. UNICEF estimated that at least 50,000 children lost access to education when Georgia switched to online schooling. Many students faced barriers to accessing remote education, primarily due to limited internet access in mountainous regions, the lack of suitable electronic devices among families living in poverty, and the lack of teachers' experience with online education.

Labor Rights

Sweeping labor reforms came into effect on January 1, 2021, expanding the Labor Inspectorate's mandate to monitor all labor standards and introducing new regulations for work hours, overtime, and time off.

Despite these reforms, fair labor conditions remain a persistent concern. Social protections are minimal, unions lack legal guarantees that would allow them to effectively bargain for systemic changes, and the Labor Inspectorate's effectiveness has been hampered by a shortage of resources. A June report by the independent trade union Solidarity Network found that nurses earn less than a living wage.

Workplace safety also remains a persistent problem. According to the Labor Inspectorate, 20 workers died and 189 were injured in work-related accidents from January through September. App-based food delivery services, which boomed during the Covid-19 pandemic, emerged as a new battleground for workplace safety. In early 2021, more than 100 delivery couriers turned off their apps to protest unrealistic performance targets, which they said made their jobs more dangerous.

Key International Actors

The EU, US, and Georgia's other Western partners engaged throughout the year to assist in resolving the political crisis. European Council President Charles Michel mandated a Swedish diplomat, Christian Danielsson, to broker mediation efforts. (See above).

In February, the EU released its Association Implementation report, highlighting that Georgia broadly continued alignment to European standards, but noted challenges regarding the independence of the judiciary and the need for further electoral reforms.

In March, the EU-Georgia Association Council assessed the implementation of the Association Agreement. The EU urged Georgia to further implement the anti-discrimination law, ensure protection for minority groups, and safeguard gender equality. It also urged Georgia to continue efforts to create an effective labor inspectorate "to further improve working conditions." During their human rights dialogue in July, the EU and Georgia condemned the violent attacks leading to the cancellation of the Pride march, and Georgia committed to investigate such attacks.

In February, following opposition leader Nika Melia's detention, the US embassy expressed regret that the authorities ignored international partners' call for restraint and dialogue and the EU stated that the political polarization following his arrest undermines Georgia's democracy.

In January, the European Court of Human Rights issued a ruling in the inter-state complaint lodged by Georgia finding Russia's conduct in the aftermath of the 2008 war breached six articles of the European Convention of Human Rights. (See Russia chapter).

The International Criminal Court continued its investigation into war crimes and crimes against humanity committed during the August 2008 Russia-Georgia war over South Ossetia.

Germany

Right-wing extremism, antisemitism, and racism appeared to be on the rise. Media freedom, which deteriorated during the Covid-19 pandemic, was further affected by new surveillance laws. Following the Taliban takeover in Afghanistan, Germany halted repatriations of Afghans, but largely failed to evacuate at-risk Afghans in time. A new law obligates large companies to address human rights risks in their direct supply chains. Germany apologized for the 1904-1908 genocide in Namibia.

Discrimination and Intolerance

Official statistics published in May showed an increase in politically motivated crimes in 2020, particularly hate crimes carried out by right-wing extremists. Anti-immigrant and antisemitic crimes increased by 72 and almost 16 percent, respectively, over the previous year. In August, Germany's Federal Anti-Discrimination Agency published figures showing a 78 percent increase in calls reporting a racist incident in 2020.

Tareq Alaows, a Syrian human rights activist and the first refugee in Germany to run for parliament, withdrew in March citing racist attacks and personal threats.

There were several high-profile criminal cases. In January, a Neo-Nazi was sentenced to life in prison for fatally shooting pro-refugee politician Walter Lübcke in 2019.

In May, a German army officer with alleged right-wing affinities was put on trial for planning to murder at least one politician in 2017 using the fake identity of a Syrian asylum seeker to provoke anti-migrant sentiment.

Germany's domestic intelligence agency put the Alternative für Deutschland (AfD) party under formal surveillance for potential extremist links in February 2021. The agency's chief identified far-right extremism as the biggest threat to democracy in Germany.

Authorities took steps against far-right infiltration in security forces. A special police unit in Frankfurt was disbanded after an investigation found in June 2021 that some of its officers had been involved in far-right extremist chat groups.

In February, illegal weapons, ammunition, and explosives were found in a house of a soldier from an elite army unit, *commando special forces* (KSK), prompting the Defense Ministry to suggest a change in the law for quicker dismissal of soldiers in the event of serious offenses. The defense minister had dissolved part of the controversial KSK unit in 2020 over right-wing extremism in its ranks.

In June, Germany decided to repatriate a Bundeswehr army platoon stationed in Lithuania due to concerns of antisemitism and right-wing extremism.

German President Steinmeier condemned an increase in attacks on Jewish institutions in German cities following the escalation in conflict between Israel and Palestine in May.

An April report commissioned by the European Commission found a considerable increase in online antisemitic hate speech during the Covid-19 pandemic. In the first two months of 2021 alone, the study recorded a thirteen-fold increase in antisemitic comments in German compared to the same period in 2020.

The June report by an independent commission set up by the German Bundestag in 2019 found that the effects of the Nazi genocide and the failure to counter anti-Roma racism are still evident today with discrimination in public spheres including education, social services, and policing.

A new law entered into force in September 2021 making private hate-motivated insults a criminal offense punishable as incitement to racial hatred.

Parliament rejected bills to reform the onerous procedure for transgender people to modify their registered name and gender.

For the first time, people with disabilities who had previously been denied the right to vote due to court-imposed restrictions on their rights voted in the September federal elections, as per a 2019 Constitutional Court ruling finding their exclusion from voting unconstitutional.

International Justice

In the first known trial dealing with state-sponsored torture in Syria, and making use of Germany's universal jurisdiction laws, a Koblenz court sentenced in February 2021 a former Syrian intelligence officer to four-and-a-half years in prison for his role in the torture of protestors in Syria in 2011. A verdict in the ongoing trial of a second defendant, also an alleged former Syrian intelligence officer charged with crimes against humanity, was expected by the end of 2021.

Progress was also made in other cases brought under Germany's universal jurisdiction laws. In March, German authorities arrested a former Gambian "death squad" member suspected of crimes against humanity in the 2000s. In July, German prosecutors filed torture and murder charges against a suspected Syrian military intelligence agent accused of torturing an inmate in a prison where he worked as a doctor.

In August, another Syrian man was arrested in Berlin on war crime charges for firing a tank grenade into a crowd of people awaiting food distribution in Damascus in 2014, killing at least seven.

Using Germany's universal jurisdiction laws, Reporters Without Borders (RSF) filed a lawsuit in March with a German prosecutor against Saudi Crown Prince Mohammed bin Salman and his aides for the murder of journalist Jamal Khashoggi. RSF claims that the killing constitutes a crime against humanity and that Saudi officials are responsible for "widespread and systematic" persecution of journalists in the kingdom. At time of writing, the prosecutor had not decided whether to open an investigation.

In May, Germany acknowledged and apologized for the 1904-1908 genocide in today's Namibia, where the German colonial government killed 80,000 Herero and Nama people. Some groups argued that Herero and Nama people were not consulted enough in the negotiation and that US$1.34 billion that Germany committed for social projects in Namibia is not same as paying reparations directly to the families.

Business and Human Rights

In January, a new law entered into force granting better protections to foreign workers in the meat processing industry. The law was adopted after Covid-19 outbreaks in meat processing plants in 2020 exposed horrific working conditions in the industry.

In June, parliament adopted a new law on supply chains requiring large companies to identify and address human rights and environmental risks in their direct supply chains. Though a step forward, the law does not incorporate the highest international standards.

Also in June, the Federation of German Industries urged local companies to monitor for forced labor when doing business with companies in the Chinese region of Xinjiang, where about one million Turkic Muslims have been detained in "political reeducation" labor camps.

Migrants and Asylum Seekers

In the first eight months of 2021, 85,230 people applied for asylum in Germany, an increase of 33.2 percent compared to the same period last year. Most applicants came from Syria, Iraq, and Afghanistan. By the end of August, 75,579 applications were pending.

Undocumented migrants in Germany had difficulties accessing Covid vaccines according to Doctors of the World Germany because of a lack of a national plan. Federal states applied different rules in some cases creating risk of deportation for undocumented people because of a lack of a firewall between social welfare and healthcare services and law enforcement.

In April, Germany ended the program, set up in 2020, to relocate asylum seekers from Greek islands through which more than 2,700 people were transferred to Germany.

A Berlin court ruled in June that Germany's Federal Office for Migration and Refugees (BAMF) had violated the rights of an asylum seeker by demanding access to her cell phone data early in her application and unnecessarily storing the information obtained during the search. The ruling could set a precedent for similar cases pending in German courts and have an important impact on efforts to abolish the problematic 2017 law that permits authorities to analyze asylum seekers' phone data.

In July, a court in North Rhine-Westphalia ruled that Germany should take responsibility for the asylum applications of two men even though they had first entered the European Union via Italy because they could face inhumane and degrading treatment if returned to Italy under EU rules.

The Federal Ministry of the Interior reported one attack per week on centers housing asylum seekers and refugees in the first half of 2021. While fewer than in the previous year, the attacks were more violent.

After initially signing a letter with five other EU member states in early August arguing that forced returns to Afghanistan should continue, Germany suspended repatriations of Afghan migrants following the Taliban takeover in that country.

Surveillance and Freedom of Media

In June, parliament adopted a law allowing federal police and intelligence services to use spyware to hack devices and access encrypted data, raising privacy concerns.

In May, parliament amended the controversial Network Search Act (NetzDG) to better counter hate speech online but the amendments still fail to address concerns regarding the impact of the law on freedom of expression.

In 2021, Germany fell two points in the Reporters Without Border's ranking of press freedom. The organization recorded attacks on journalists by protesters during protests against Covid-19 restrictions—including in Stuttgart and Kassel, and a brutal attack on the manager of the journalists' union DJU during the protest in Berlin—and cited a climate of mistrust fomented by populist politicians.

Women's Rights

According to a May report commissioned by the European Parliament, the Covid-19 crisis could exacerbate already-existing gender inequalities in Germany because women engage more than men in unpaid care, are over-represented in part-time work, and experience lower salaries, increasing the likelihood of female poverty.

In May, a court fined a gynecologist €3,000 ($3,650) for providing factual information on his abortion services on his website under a law that criminalizes "advertising abortion."

Climate Change Policy and Impacts

As the EU's biggest greenhouse gas emitter, Germany is contributing to the climate crisis which is taking a growing toll on human rights around the globe. In 2021, the constitutional court held that the 2019 climate change law does not adequately regulate emission reductions and violates the government's obligation to protect rights. Since the ruling, the government pledged to reduce emissions by 65 percent by 2030 compared to 1990 levels and reach net zero by 2045. According to the Climate Action Tracker, this commitment is not sufficient to meet the Paris Agreement goal to stay below 1.5°C of warming, necessary to limit the most catastrophic climate outcomes.

Continued government support for fossil fuels will make it difficult to meet these new targets. From January 2020 through March 3, 2021, 38 percent of the almost $70 billion Covid-19 recovery were subsidies for fossil fuels. Germany is still among the world's top 10 coal producers and has only committed to a phase out by 2038.

Germany is experiencing increasingly frequent and extreme heat events that threaten human health. Record-breaking floods linked to climate change in July resulted in the deaths of at least 189 people, including 12 people with disabilities living in a group home.

Foreign Policy

In its Action Plan for Human Rights 2021/22, the German government pledged to mainstream human rights in all its policy areas. Germany's foreign policy should be measured against this principle.

Germany stepped up its engagement at the UN Human Rights Council in Geneva, leading or supporting action on countries such as Belarus, China, Egypt, Ethiopia, and Russia—except for Israel where Germany with other Western states opposed a commission of inquiry in the Occupied Palestinian Territory and Israel. The German government was also a driving force on several thematic issues in the council, such as the right to privacy in a digital age and climate change and environmental issues.

In March, the German government pledged to do more to uphold the rights of lesbian, gay, bisexual, transgender and intersex (LGBTI) people abroad through its Inclusion Strategy, a multifaceted scheme for foreign policy and development cooperation.

Within the EU, Germany strongly condemned legislation against the rights of LGBT people in Hungary and discrimination against LGBT people in Poland. It also supported continued scrutiny under Article 7—the EU mechanism to deal with EU governments putting the union's values at risk—to address rule of law concerns in both countries.to address rule of law concerns in both countries.

On China, Germany was amongst the few states willing to use diverse opportunities at the United Nations to call out the country for human rights violations. In New York, it played a central role in organizing a high-level virtual event on Xinjiang in May 2021. Outside the UN, however, German policy supporting human rights in China appeared compromised, particularly in Chancellor Angela Merkel's strong support for an EU-China investment deal ignoring the problem of forced labor in Xinjiang.

Germany was a strong supporter of human rights defenders and critics in Russia and Belarus. Chancellor Merkel continued to stand up for the imprisoned Russian opposition politician Alexej Navalny. The Foreign Ministry launched an action plan for civil society in Belarus including supporting access to humanitarian visas for government critics and the documentation of abuses in the country.

In Afghanistan, Germany widely ignored the needs of human rights defenders, journalists, and local employees to leave the country ahead of the withdrawal of international troops. Shifting responsibilities between government authorities, lack of attention, and wrong assessments put many Afghans at risk. While the German government pledged to evacuate local staff after the Taliban took over, it avoided any general commitment for the resettlement of Afghan refugees.

While being a strong voice in the fight against impunity in the international arena, Germany's engagement in specific countries could have been more active. In Libya, the Foreign Office continued its important mediation efforts for a political settlement but could have done more to publicly address widespread impunity; in Sudan, much needed support for economic development and political cooperation trumped a stronger focus on accountability.

In the international effort to curb Covid-19, Germany strongly supported the international vaccine platform COVAX, and pledged to donate millions of vaccine doses; they also pledged to donate other diagnostic tools and medicine worldwide and provided funds for vaccine production in the Global South. Yet, the German government was one of the main opponents of waiving some intellectual property and trade rules to speed up the production of Covid-19 vaccines and other health products.

The Human Rights Committee in Parliament scrutinized the German government's human rights performance and prominently raised human rights violations in Xinjiang, China. The Human Rights Commissioner was an important voice for civil society and human rights defenders worldwide.

Greece

Greece hosts large numbers of asylum seekers while failing to protect their rights, including by pushing new arrivals back to Turkey. Migrant children face homelessness and lack of access to adequate healthcare and education. Victims of hate crimes are reluctant to report attacks to the police. Authorities failed to address rising violence against women and instituted measures that could heighten risks for some domestic violence survivors. Curbs on civil society groups assisting migrants and interference with independent media raised concerns about the state of rule of law in the country.

Migrants and Asylum Seekers

The government continued its heavy-handed and often abusive immigration controls. There was a mounting chorus of criticism of Greece's practice of summarily returning thousands of people to Turkey, including through violent pushbacks.

In April, the Greek ombudsman released an interim report as part of an investigation launched in 2017, criticizing authorities for failing to adequately respond to multiple allegations of pushbacks at the Greek-Turkish land border. In May, Council of Europe (CoE) Commissioner for Human Rights Dunja Mijatović urged authorities to end pushbacks at both the land and sea borders with Turkey, and to ensure independent and effective investigations. In July, EU Commissioner for Home Affairs Yilva Johansson warned Greece to end pushbacks, describing them as "violations of our fundamental European values."

Greek officials deny the allegations, and authorities regularly fail to carry-out proper investigations into pushbacks. The media reported in September that the European Commission asked Greece to set up an independent mechanism to monitor abuses at borders before it releases €15.83 million (around $18 million) in EU migration funding.

In May, the office of Greece's Supreme Court prosecutor transmitted a criminal complaint concerning 147 pushbacks between March and December 2020, filed by Helsinki Monitor, to 16 first instance prosecutors across Greece for investigations. Several other complaints regarding pushbacks and violations by Greece border forces are pending before the European Court of Human Rights.

In June, Greece expanded the use of inadmissibility procedures on the basis that Turkey is a "safe third country" to asylum seekers from Afghanistan, Somalia, Pakistan, and Bangladesh threatening to leave thousands of people in limbo, denied protection in the EU, and unable to return to Turkey as the country has not accepted returns from Greece since March 2020. These nationals represent more than 65 percent of asylum seekers in the country. Syrians have been subject to the same rules since 2016.

Nongovernmental groups (NGOs) said in July the new rules had already resulted in people being denied protection within days of their arrival, following perfunctory asylum interviews, without legal representation. More than 2,800 people were denied protection on that basis in 2020. On August 25, an appeals committee rejected the return of an Afghan family which had been refused asylum, ruling that Turkey could not be considered a safe third country for them. In June, Commissioner Johansson urged the Greek authorities to reverse the inadmissibility decisions for those who cannot be returned and examine cases on their merits.

A law that threatens asylum seekers' rights was adopted in September. NGOs and the CoE commissioner for human rights raised the alarm over the law, which undermines the right to asylum and weakens safeguards against detention and return to the risk of persecution or other human rights abuse.

During the year, the European Court of Human Rights issued interim measures for at least 13 cases regarding living conditions for vulnerable people trapped in migrant camps on the Aegean islands, requesting the urgent transfer of individuals and their families into safer accommodation, and their immediate access to urgently needed medical care. In most of the cases, authorities have failed to act.

One year after the Moria camp on Lesbos burned down, there was little progress towards improving living conditions for migrants there. Although thousands were relocated to other parts of Greece, more than 4,000 remained at time of writing on the Aegean islands, including 3,819 contained in camps. In May, the CoE commissioner for human rights warned that the government's plan to build new closed reception centres created a risk of large-scale, long-term detention. The first such center opened on Samos at the end of September.

In January, limited government soil testing confirmed dangerous levels of lead in some areas of one of the camps on Lesbos, Mavrovouni, built on of a former military shooting range. Despite the government taking some positive steps to address the situation, including fencing off an area with elevated lead levels, at time of writing, dozens of residents continued to live in tents in areas contaminated by lead. Authorities ignored calls to conduct comprehensive testing and remove all residents living near lead-contaminated areas.

By mid-October, 1,047 unaccompanied children and 3,416 others deemed vulnerable had been relocated from Greece to other EU and associated countries, including 2,812 to Germany.

Migrant Children

In a January landmark decision, the European Committee of Social Rights found that Greece violates the rights of asylum-seeking children, citing inadequate, unhealthy, and dangerous living conditions, homelessness, and inadequate access to healthcare and education.

Data on school closures in Greece linked to Covid-19 underscored significant disruption to education for children in the country during 2021. According to the ombudsman for children's rights, only one in seven asylum-seeking children living in camps on the mainland, and none on the islands, was able to attend school in the 2020-2021 school year. During school closures, no Wi-Fi hotspots, tablets, or laptops were provided to children in camps. Some camps were locked down to prevent the spread of Covid-19, with children unable to leave for school and no alternative education provided. In some cases, local officials prevented children from enrolling in public schools in nearby communities. There were persistent delays in opening classes for children who do not speak Greek.

By mid-August, 21 unaccompanied children were detained in police-run facilities despite Greece's abolition of the so-called "protective custody" regime in December 2020. No government statistics have been published since then on child detention.

Attacks on Civil Society

Greek authorities' use of criminal investigations to harass and intimidate groups that investigate abuses against migrants at Greece's border continued.

News emerged in July that 10 individuals, including 4 members of NGOs, are facing criminal investigation for allegedly facilitating the irregular entry of foreign nationals from Turkey to Lesbos. No indictment was issued following a similar investigation announced in September 2020, suggesting that it was a form of state harassment.

In March, three UN special rapporteurs addressed a joint letter to the government expressing concern about 2020 regulations hampering the work of NGOs focused on asylum and migration. According to a May report from NGO Refugee Support Aegean (RSA), since December 2020, 78 groups have had their applications rejected and another 97 have pending applications on the NGO Registry. Most provide services in camps for asylum seekers. Judicial review applications challenging the legal framework are pending before the Council of State.

In its July EU-wide rule of law report, the European Commission expressed concern about the narrowing space for civil society groups working with migrants and asylum seekers. It also said that despite reforms in the judicial system, concerns remain around the procedure of appointinga senior judges and prosecutors.

In September, the CoE human rights commissioner urged the Greek parliament to reconsider legislative proposals that hinder "life-saving" work and human rights monitoring by NGOs. The bill, which was adopted on September 3, introduces restrictions and conditions on NGOs active in areas of competence of the Greek Coast Guard, at the threat of heavy sanctions and fines.

Freedom of Media

At the end of 2020, journalist Dimitra Kroustalli resigned from the daily newspaper To Vima, citing "suffocating pressure" from the prime minister's office following a story she had written on the government's flawed monitoring of Covid-19 cases.

The European Commission flagged concerns about attacks and threats against journalists in Greece in its July rule of law report, in particular the killing of Greek investigative journalist Giorgos Karaivaz. At time of writing, no arrests had been made related to Karaivaz's murder.

In January, the citizen protection minister unveiled guidelines to implement a controversial 2020 law regulating demonstrations, which journalists are concerned will restrict their ability to report effectively.

In April, Reporters Without Borders (RSF) raised concerns about restrictions on media freedom in Greece, including the withholding of government advertising from critical outlets, accusations of government censorship, as well as violence and harassment of journalists by police during demonstrations.

Racism and Intolerance

Statistics on hate crimes for 2020, released in April by the nongovernmental Racist Violence Recording Network (RVNR), showed an increase in incidents of racist violence against refugees and migrants, and attacks on civil society groups working with them. The RVNR recorded racist incidents in the context of police enforcement of Covid-19 movement restrictions. The RVRN also recorded 30 incidents of verbal assault, physical violence, or sexual assault against individuals based on their sexual orientation or gender identity. Of the 107 incidents of hate crimes documented by the RVRN, only 35 were reported to the police. In 46 incidents, the victims said that they would not take further actions due to fear, lack of trust in the authorities, or bureaucratic obstacles.

Police statistics published in May on fines for breaches of Covid-19 measures on the islands of Lesbos, Chios, and Samos showed that between March 23, 2020 and May 24, 2021 74 percent of the fines were issued against foreigners, despite the fact foreign nationals make up a small percentage of the islands' population, raising concerns about the use of ethnic profiling, a long-standing issue in Greece. Covid-19 movement restriction measures in camps across the country were stricter than for the general population.

The trial of six people, including four police officers, for causing fatal bodily harm in the 2018 killing of 33-year-old queer activist and human rights defender Zak

Kostopoulos resumed in October after being postponed in October 2020 due to Covid-19.

Women's Rights

Violence against women was the subject of heated debate during the year, after Olympic medalist Sofia Bekatorou alleged in January she had been sexually assaulted in 1998 by an official of the Greek sailing federation, triggering a national "#MeToo" movement.

In May, government passed a controversial family law, despite the risk that the law poses to women and children who are victims of domestic violence.

In March, nongovernmental group Diotima noted that during the pandemic there was an increase in reported incidents of domestic and other gender-based violence. At least 11 women have been murdered by their current or former husbands or partners in the first nine months of the year. The killings shocked the public, opening a debate on the issue of domestic violence. Women face multiple barriers to reporting domestic violence and seeking help from the state.

Guatemala

Judicial independence has been threatened by corruption, delays in appointments of judges, refusal by Congress to swear in the head judge of the Constitutional Court, removal of the chief of the Special Prosecutor's Office against Impunity (FECI), and spurious complaints against judges and prosecutors investigating high profile cases.

Harassment and violence against human rights defenders and journalists remain major concerns. Authorities have restricted access to information, including about vaccine purchases and other measures to address the Covid-19 pandemic.

Guatemala faces challenges in protecting the rights of migrants; human rights defenders; women and girls; and lesbian, gay, bisexual, and transgender (LGBT) people.

Judicial Independence and Corruption

In recent years, investigations by the United Nations-backed International Commission against Impunity in Guatemala (CICIG)—terminated in 2018—and the Attorney General's Office have exposed corruption schemes in all three branches of government. However, measures adopted recently by Congress, the Attorney General's Office and other authorities are impeding accountability and threatening judicial independence.

Congress has flouted a Constitutional Court order to proceed with selecting judges and justices, for the period 2019 through 2024, for 13 seats on the Supreme Court and 135 seats on the Courts of Appeals. The seats remain vacant. The selection process has been marred by corruption allegations based on an investigation by the Special Prosecutor Against Impunity (FECI) that revealed evidence of possible influence peddling in the selection of judicial nominees.

In April, Congress refused to swear in the re-elected Constitutional Court Judge Gloria Porras who had led anti-corruption cases, because of allegations of irregularities in her selection process. The Council of the University of San Carlos, which selected Porras, ratified its decision after reviewing the challenges and, in

July, asked Congress to swear her in. At time of writing, Congress had not complied. Fearful of reprisals and spurious investigations, Porras fled Guatemala.

On June 21, judges investigating high-profile cases asked the Attorney General's Office to review and dismiss old and spurious complaints filed to harass them. The Inter-American Commission on Human Rights (IACHR) had issued precautionary measures ordering Guatemala to protect the judges, but the government failed to comply with them. Judge Erika Aifán, who convicted high-profile people in corruption cases, for example, faces more than 70 complaints that the government has failed to investigate. Instead, the Constitutional Court ruled that the Supreme Court can move forward with an attempt to strip her immunity.

On July 23, Attorney General Consuelo Porras, who is not related to Judge Gloria Porras, removed Special Prosecutor's Office against Impunity (FECI) Chief Juan Francisco Sandoval, alleging he humiliated her and citing lack of trust. Sandoval, whose office is probing several corruption cases originally handled by the CICIG, said Porras blocked or tried to block several that implicated high-ranking officials.

Weeks before Sandoval's removal, President Alejandro Giammattei described his work as politicized and biased. A group of lawyers, seeking to dismantle the FECI, filed two complaints asking the Constitutional Court to declare it unconstitutional.

In September, the Constitutional Court struck down a provision of the criminal code that prohibited allowing people sentenced to five or more years of incarceration for corruption from serving their sentences outside jail. They can now serve corruption sentences under house arrest, for example.

Accountability for Past Human Rights Violations

The limited progress that Guatemala was making in recent years in adjudicating major crimes seems to have come to a standstill. Challenges persist in searching for and identifying the disappeared during the armed conflict, mainly Indigenous Mayans.

In September, authorities and the Guatemalan Forensic Anthropology Foundation, a nongovernmental organization (NGO), began efforts to recover the bodies of at least 116 Indigenous children believed to have been buried at a former military garrison in the 1980s. Efforts were suspended at time of writing.

In June, legislators presented a bill for Peace and Reconciliation, seeking to end proceedings for crimes committed during the armed conflict. It is similar to a 2019 bill shelved in April, after a Constitutional Court judgment that held that pardons for crimes against humanity and serious human rights violations are unconstitutional and contrary to human rights standards.

Freedom of Expression

Guatemala is ranked 116 of 180 countries on the World Press Freedom Index because of constant violence against the press and impunity for perpetrators. Since taking office in 2020, President Giammattei's government has unleashed verbal attacks and imposed restrictions on the press. Authorities have restricted access to information during the pandemic.

The Journalists' Association of Guatemala reported 149 physical or verbal attacks or restrictions on journalists and media workers in 2020. As of August 2021, the organization had counted 79 attacks. Investigations into threats, attacks, and killings of journalists have made little progress.

On July 30, Pedro Alfonso Guadrón Hernández, founder of the Facebook news page "Concepción Las Minas mi Tierra," was shot dead in Chiquimula department. Guadrón covered local news, including anti-government protests, corruption, and drug trafficking. He had reportedly received death threats.

Human Rights Defenders

Attacks on human rights defenders and social leaders increased in 2020, the NGO Unidad de Protección a Defensoras y Defensores de Derechos Humanos de Guatemala (Udefegua) reported, counting 1,004 attacks and 15 killings from January to December 15, 2020.

In June, a law limiting the work of NGOs took effect, after the Constitutional Court struck down challenges to it. The law includes overly broad language that allows the executive to cancel the legal status of NGOs when they conduct activities contrary to "public order."

Women's and Girls' Rights

The Observatory for Sexual and Reproductive Rights reported 57,578 pregnancies of adolescents and girls as of June, including 2,737 in girls between 10 and 14 years old. Guatemalan law considers that all girls under 14 who have sexual relations are victims of sexual violence.

Abortion is legal only when a pregnant person's life is in danger.

When President Giammattei, in July, announced a policy to develop inter-institutional work on programs focused on "life and family protection," he also emphasized that Guatemala protects life starting from conception.

Guatemala's civil code limits the sexual and reproductive rights of women and girls with disabilities, including by forcing sterilization and other contraceptive treatments without their consent.

Sexual Orientation and Gender Identity

Guatemala has no comprehensive civil legislation protecting people from discrimination on the grounds of sexual orientation and gender identity, nor a legal gender recognition procedure for transgender people.

A 2021 Human Rights Watch report on violence and discrimination against LGBT people in Guatemala revealed that perpetrators included public security agents, gangs, and members of the public, including LGBT people's family members. The report found that the government is failing to protect LGBT people adequately.

Guatemalan civil society organizations reported that, as of September, at least 21 LGBT people had been killed in 2021. One gay man and two transgender women—including Andrea González, legal representative of the advocacy group OTRANS Queens of the Night—died in separate attacks during one week in June. Months earlier, González had asked the Attorney General's Office for protection from death threats she was receiving.

Disability Rights

Children with disabilities with high support requirements are forced to live in institutions in Guatemala. There are few if any policies that would enable them to live in a family household.

Asylum Seekers and Refugees

In February, the United States ended the Asylum Cooperation Agreement (ACA), implemented in July 2019 by former President Donald Trump, which allowed the US to deport Honduran and Salvadoran asylum seekers to Guatemala on the false premise that Guatemala was capable of examining their asylum claims fully and fairly.

As part of US efforts to address the root causes of migration, Guatemala and the US reached several agreements, including to increase the number of Guatemala's border security officers. In July, President Giammattei and US Homeland Security Secretary Alejandro Mayorkas opened the first reception center for returned migrants.

Since at least April, Guatemala has been receiving groups of migrants trying to reach the US that are being expelled from Mexico. Between August 22 and October 18, the Guatemalan Institute for Migration registered in El Ceibo, at the border with Mexico, 15,387 returnees, including 4,117 children. Most people sent to Guatemala are from Honduras and El Salvador. Between January and October 19, 4,072 unaccompanied Guatemalan minors were returned from Mexico to Tecún Úman, according to the institute.

Covid-19

As of early October, Guatemala counted more than 581,498 cases of Covid-19 and more than 14,118 deaths. The collapse of Guatemala's public hospital system and limited access to mass vaccinations are likely contributing factors.

The vaccination program has lacked transparency. As of September, only 1.7 million of Guatemala's 17 million people—10 percent—had been fully vaccinated. The Sputnik vaccines the government purchased, in a contract never made public, were not delivered by a March deadline. In July, a renegotiated contract reduced the number of doses to be delivered by half.

From March 2020 through February 2021, 4.2 million students missed at least three-quarters of classroom instruction due to Covid closures, according to UNICEF. Schools partially opened in January 2021.

Key International Actors

In February, the United Nations High Commissioner for Human Rights reported that Guatemala continues to face systemic and structural human rights challenges, in particular poverty, inequality, discrimination, impunity, and insecurity, exacerbated by Covid-19.

In June, United States Vice President Kamala Harris visited Guatemala. Following a bilateral meeting with President Giammattei, Harris announced the creation of an anticorruption task force that will include US prosecutors and law enforcement experts and a regional task force to prevent migrant smuggling and human trafficking. In September, the United States sanctioned Consuelo Porras and her secretary by including them in the Undemocratic and Corrupt Actors List.

In July, United Nations and Organization of American States experts expressed concern regarding the new NGOs law, claiming it violates international human rights standards and could criminalize human rights defenders. Also in July, UN rights experts expressed concern over violations of due process and health rights in the spurious prosecution of Indigenous activist Bernardo Caal Xól, who opposed the Oxec hydroelectric project.

In August, the IACHR expressed concern over actions jeopardizing judicial independence, including the government's firing of FECI's chief prosecutor, Congress's refusal to swear in the Constitutional Court's re-elected president, and investigations against judges and prosecutors in high profile cases, some of whom are beneficiaries of the IACHR's precautionary measures.

The IACHR held public hearings on two cases against Guatemala, one alleging persecution by state agents and the arbitrary installation of a police substation on the complainant's land, the other alleging that shots fired by Guatemalan authorities to detain a boat killed and wounded people, and that authorities failed to investigate.

Guinea

On September 5, Guinean army officers staged a coup and arrested President Alpha Condé, who won the October 2020 presidential election after a year-long effort to secure a third term in office. Col. Mamady Doumbouya, head of Guinea's special forces and of the putschists, who called themselves the National Committee for Reconciliation and Development (*Comité national du rassemblement et du développement*, CNRD), proclaimed the dissolution of the government and constitution and announced a transition period. On September 28, the new military authorities adopted a transitional charter outlining the missions and duties of the transitional government and appointed Doumbouya as head of the transition. The international community widely criticized the coup. The Economic Community of West African States (ECOWAS) suspended Guinea's membership on September 8 and imposed targeted sanctions, including travel bans and asset freezes, on the coup leaders and their families on September 16.

The coup came after a period of political instability following a March 2020 constitutional referendum that allowed Condé to run for a third term and the October 2020 presidential election, which were marred by violence. Security forces used excessive force during opposition-led demonstrations and arrested and detained over 350 leaders and members of the National Front for the Defense of the Constitution (*Front national pour la défense de la Constitution*, FNDC), a coalition of civil society groups and opposition parties, during the period surrounding the presidential vote. In April, Condé's government released 40 of them. In September, the new military authorities released 79 others and allowed 4 opponents in exile to return to Guinea.

Members of the security forces continued to enjoy almost total impunity for the excessive use of force and other human rights abuses, with the 2019 conviction of a police captain still the only known conviction of a member of the security forces for the dozens of protest deaths that occurred since Condé came to power in 2010.

Condé's government failed to meet a self-imposed June 2020 deadline for the trial of alleged perpetrators of the 2009 stadium massacre. There was some modest renewed progress toward the trial in mid-2021. While the coup may disrupt progress, Doumbouya announced on September 5 that "justice will be the compass that will guide every Guinean citizen," making a symbolic appearance at this year's commemoration of the stadium massacre.

Guinea lost privileged access to the US market offered under the African Growth and Opportunity Act (AGOA). On November 2, the Biden administration announced it intends to cut trade benefits for Guinea by January 1, 2022, "for not having established, or not making continual progress toward establishing, the protection of the rule of law and of political pluralism."

Guinea's penal code punishes undefined indecent acts or acts against nature with six months to three years in prison.

Covid-19

The health state of emergency, imposed by former President Condé in March 2020 to curb the spread of Covid-19, is still in place. In July 2021, following increased confirmed cases, Condé imposed more restrictive measures, including a ban on large gatherings, and curfew at 10 p.m. instead of midnight, which had been maintained by the new military authorities. The political opposition and civil society have expressed concerns about the use of the state of health emergency as an excuse to quell dissent and violate rights.

School closures due to the Covid-19 pandemic affected 2.6 million children. After the pandemic's start in 2020, schools were closed for 151 days, but reopened in September 2020 and remained open through 2021.

Release of Political Prisoners

On April 29, authorities under former President Condé ordered the release of 40 people after the Dixinn court in Conakry found no grounds for prosecution. They had been in pretrial detention since October 2020, when they were arrested on various charges following opposition-led demonstrations during the election period. On May 5, authorities released journalist Amadou Diouldé Diallo, who was arrested in March after he criticized President Condé in one of his articles. On June 18 and 22, Condé granted pardons to two political opponents, Souleymane Condé, FNDC coordinator, and Youssouf Diabaté, a FNDC member.

On September 7, the new military authorities released 79 political prisoners. They included leaders and members of the main opposition party, the Union of Democratic Forces of Guinea (*Union des forces démocratiques de Guinée*, UFDG), including Abdoulaye Bah, and FNDC's Oumar Sylla, alias Foniké Mengué.

Foniké Mengué—arrested on September 29, 2020, in Conakry while preparing to participate in an FNDC-led protest against President Condé's decision to run for a third term—was sentenced to three years in prison for "communication and disclosure of false information, and threats of violence or death" during his appeal trial on June 10, 2021. On August 2, he was transferred to a hospital as his health deteriorated. He was on hunger strike between December 25, 2020, and January 8, 2021, protesting repeated adjournments of his trial. He was also infected by Covid-19 in March while in detention at Conakry's central prison. His relatives accused the government of denying him access to adequate medical treatment.

Abdoulaye Bah was among a group of four opposition members released on health grounds in July by authorities under former President Condé, along with Ibrahima Cherif Bah, Ousmane Goudal Diallo, and Cellou Balde. The four had been arrested in November 2020 for alleged involvement in post-election violence. However, on August 10, Abdoulaye Bah was returned to prison for "violating the conditions of his release."

On September 18, the new military authorities allowed four exiled political opponents to return to Guinea, including FNDC member Sékou Koundouno. Guinean judicial authorities had issued an international arrest warrant against Koundouno in August, for criminal association, arson, insurrection, and disturbing the state through killing, destruction, and looting.

Deaths in Custody, Arbitrary Arrests, and Restrictions on the Opposition

Four suspected political opposition supporters died in custody between November 2020 and January 2021. Mamadou Oury Barry, 21, detained as a suspected political opposition supporter, died on January 16. His family and lawyer said he died in his cell and did not receive proper medical attention for ill-treatment and an illness he suffered in detention, but authorities stated that he died at the hospital of "natural causes."

On February 3, the Dixinn Court of First Instance in Conakry ruled that the head-quarters of the main opposition party, the UFDG, which had been shut down in October 2020, should remain closed. On March 17, Conakry's airport authorities prevented Cellou Dalein Diallo, leader of the UFDG, from traveling to Ivory Coast and seized his passport. On May 24, the prosecutor of the Dixinn Court of First Instance said his travel ban had been maintained and could be further extended. Authorities did not provide any explanation for the ban. The new military authorities lifted the travel ban in September and allowed Diallo to access his offices.

On July 9, judicial authorities sentenced Ismaël Condé, a former member of the ruling party who joined the opposition, to three years and four months in prison for "insulting the head of state," after he declared that only weapons could drive Alpha Condé from power.

Accountability for Serious Abuses

Although Condé's government announced investigations into alleged security force abuses during demonstrations—including the establishment of a pool of judges to investigate the "serious provocations, abuses, and destruction" committed in Conakry during the March 2020 legislative elections and referendum—a lack of political will, limited investigative capacity, and witnesses' unwillingness to come forward meant that most investigations did not result in charges against members of the security forces. The trial of several police officers for using a woman as a human shield to protect themselves from protesters in January 2020, which opened in March 2020, stalled.

Twelve years after security forces massacred over 150 peaceful opposition supporters and raped dozens of women at a stadium on September 28, 2009, those responsible have not been tried.

Even before the coup, concerns over an evident lack of will for the trial to go forward in Guinea increased amid stagnation in the organization of the trial by the justice sector. Nevertheless, in mid-2021, there were some new developments, with renewed meetings of a strategic committee established to plan the trial, construction of the courtroom underway, and training of magistrates planned. Several people charged in the case have been in detention beyond the legal limit while they wait for the trial to start.

In December 2020, the International Criminal Court, which is conducting a preliminary examination of the 2009 massacre, expressed its disappointment in the fact that the trial had not yet opened and stated it was looking to Guinean authorities to demonstrate their willingness and ability to fight impunity in the coming months.

Natural Resources

Guinea's natural resources, notably bauxite, the ore needed to produce aluminum, remained central to the economy. The bauxite sector continued to expand rapidly in the Boké and Boffa regions, leading to thousands of farmers losing their land to mines, often for inadequate compensation, and damaging vital water sources in the area. A coalition of car manufacturers, who are increasing their demand for aluminum as they transition to electric vehicles, in January 2021 expressed concern about bauxite mining companies' practices in Guinea.

A Chinese-backed consortium continued preparations for development of the massive Simandou iron ore deposit in southeastern Guinea. The consortium, which is already Guinea's largest bauxite exporter, has in the past failed to respect international human rights and environmental standards.

Guinea's new military government on September 16 reassured mining companies that they could continue their operations, but said it would ensure mining revenues improve living standards and that mining companies respect strong environmental and social standards. The Extractive Industries Transparency Initiative (EITI), a global resource revenue transparency initiative that counts Guinea as a member, warned that the coup could undermine accountable governance.

On May 8, a landslide at a clandestine gold mine in Guinea's north-eastern Siguiri region killed 15 people. The government announced the opening of an investigation to ascertain the circumstances and causes of the incident. There are hundreds of unofficial artisanal mines around Siguiri.

Haiti

The Covid-19 pandemic and associated economic crisis, the assassination of President Jovenel Moïse in July 2021, and a 7.2 magnitude earthquake in August exacerbated Haiti's existing challenges of political instability and violence by gangs often tied to state actors. Haiti has continuously struggled to meet the basic needs of its people and resolve long-standing human rights problems.

Since the government's announcement in 2018 that it would eliminate fuel subsidies, widespread civil unrest has paralyzed Haiti. Demonstrations intensified in 2019, amid evidence of embezzlement of funds intended for infrastructure and healthcare under the last three governments. Demonstrations increased again in 2021, against Moïse's government and his proposed constitutional referendum. Police responded with excessive force. Impunity for gang and police violence continued.

The earthquake, followed by Tropical Storm Grace, affected 2 million people in Haiti's southern peninsula—77 percent of which lived below the poverty line—and left 2,246 dead, more than 12,700 injured, up to 26,000 displaced, and at least 329 missing.

Political Crisis

Haiti's Superior Council of the Judiciary ruled on February 6, 2021, that Moïse's presidency would end the next day, but Moïse argued his term would end on February 7, 2022, five years after he took office. He had been ruling by decree since January 2020, due to the inexistence of a seated parliament given postponed legislative elections.

On February 7, 2021, police detained Supreme Court Justice Yvickel Dieujuste Dabrésil, whom the political opposition was allegedly poised to nominate as provisional president. The following day, Moïse decreed Dabrésil's retirement, along with those of Justices Joseph Mécènes Jean-Louis, whom the opposition appointed as provisional president after Dabrésil's arrest, and Wendelle Coq Thélot, who had opposed Moïse's appointment by decree of all members of the Provisional Electoral Council (CEP) in September 2020.

Moïse charged the CEP with carrying out presidential and legislative elections and a constitutional referendum in 2021, despite a constitutional prohibition on modifying the constitution through a referendum.

Demonstrators who opposed the referendum and planning for elections demanded that the president step down and that a transitional government be put in place.

On July 7, a group of armed people burst into President Moïse's private residence in Port-au-Prince, killed him, and injured his wife. On July 20, Ariel Henry, whom Moïse had appointed prime minister days before the assassination, was installed as head of a new government. Some civil society organizations said his installment as head of state was unconstitutional.

In September, an Independent Advisory Committee created by Moïse in 2020 presented the draft of a new constitution to Ariel Henry, who signed a political agreement with the opposition to carry out general elections in 2022.

Investigation of President Moïse's Assassination

A day after the assassination, Haitian police engaged in a shootout with suspected assassins, killing several and taking others into custody.

In late July, two judges and two clerks of the Court of Peace who conducted judicial proceedings regarding the murder of President Moïse were threatened.

On August 9, Justice Mathieu Chanlatte was appointed to lead the judicial investigation into President Moïse's killing. In circumstances still under investigation, his clerk died on August 11. Two days later, the judge withdrew from the case, citing personal reasons. On August 22, Justice Garry Orélien was designated to replace him.

As of August, the Haitian National Police (HNP) and the National Human Rights Defense Network (RNDDH) reported 3 people killed and 44 arrested—including former Colombian military officers—in connection with President Moïse's assassination. Officials of the Colombian Ombudsperson's Office who visited the Colombian ex-military detainees in Port-au-Prince reported that they had not been presented to a judicial authority, had not had access to legal assistance, and were being held incommunicado in a six-by-two-meter cell without sunlight, handcuffed, and sleeping on the floor. Some of the detainees claimed they had been tortured by police.

Violence and Displacement

Violence is escalating. The United Nations Integrated Office in Haiti (BINUH) reported 1,074 intentional homicides and 328 kidnappings from January to August 2021. Intentional homicides increased by 14 per cent, compared with 944 cases in the same period of 2020, and kidnappings continued to rise, compared with 234 for all of 2020. According to the Bureau des Avocats Internationaux (BAI) and the Institute for Justice & Democracy in Haiti (IJDH) gender-based violence is chronically under-reported.

Some 95 gangs are fighting over territory in Port-au-Prince, where approximately 1.5 million people live, displacing 19,100. Haitian civil society groups say insecurity is exacerbated by alleged complicity between politicians and gangs.

Under Moïse, since 2018, the IJDH, the RNDDH, and the Fondasyon Je Klere (FJKL), three nongovernmental organizations, documented 18 massacres in Port-au-Prince. In 2021, in Martissant, according to the UN Office for the Coordination of Humanitarian Affairs, gang members killed 4 people and injured 2 more; in Cité Soleil, gang clashes killed a minor and 10 gang members; and in Delmas 32 and other neighborhoods armed individuals killed 19 people. At time of writing, no one had been charged or convicted for these massacres. Former policeman Jimmy Chérizier, who leads the "G9" gangs federation, is allegedly implicated in most cases and remains free.

Human Rights Defenders

BINUH documented 32 cases of attacks, threats, and intimidation against judges, human rights defenders and journalists, from February to August 2021.

RNDDH Director Pierre Espérance received a death threat from the "G9" in June. Diego Charles, an anticorruption activist and reporter, and Antoinette Duclaire, a feminist, political activist, and journalist, were both killed on June 29 by armed individuals at the Christ-Roi neighborhood.

At time of writing, eight people had been detained in connection with the August 2020 killing of Monferrier Dorval, head of the Port-au-Prince bar association, but no one had been charged.

In 2019, Charlot Jeudy, the President of Kouraj, an organization advocating for the rights of lesbian, gay, bisexual, and transgender (LGBT) people, was found dead in his home. Circumstances surrounding his death and the results of an autopsy remained publicly unknown at the time of writing.

Criminal Justice System

Haiti's prisons remain severely overcrowded, with many detainees living in inhumane conditions. Overcrowding is largely attributable to pretrial detentions, BINUH and OHCHR reported in 2021.

As of September, prisons housed nearly 11,000 detainees, 82 percent of whom were awaiting trial. New criminal and criminal procedure codes set to enter into force in June 2022 provide alternative measures to pretrial detention and establish detention of children as a measure of last resort.

Abuses by Security Forces

Protests against the government continued to be repressed with excessive use of force. The RNDDH, in January 2021, reported at least 8 journalists injured, 10 demonstrators and 13 political activists arbitrarily arrested, and 2 students beaten by police during several protests. In February, the Inter-American Commission on Human Rights (IACHR) reported two cases of journalists injured with rubber bullets.

On February 25, a prison breakout at the Croix-des-Bouquets penitentiary left the prison director and 29 prisoners dead. BINUH reported law enforcement agents arbitrarily killed 25.

From February to May, BINUH reported 238 cases of human rights violations by police, including 42 killings and indiscriminate use of tear gas.

Accountability for Past Abuses

In 2014, a court of appeal ordered investigations re-opened into arbitrary detentions, torture, disappearances, summary executions, and forced exile during Jean Claude Duvalier's presidency (1971-1986). As of September 2021, investigations remained pending.

In 2020, former Haitian death squad leader Emmanuel "Toto" Constant was deported from the US. In 2000, he had been convicted in absentia for involvement in a 1994 massacre in Gonaïves. He remained in detention at time of writing.

Rights to Health, Water, and Food

The country's most vulnerable communities face dramatic floods and soil erosion caused by deforestation that has nearly eliminated forest cover in the country, leading to reduced agricultural productivity.

Over a third of the population lacks access to clean water and two-thirds have limited or no sanitation service. More than a third of Haitians—4.4 million—live with food insecurity, international agencies report, and 217,000 children suffer moderate to severe malnutrition.

Without appropriate adaptation, decreased rainfall and rising temperatures driven by climate change will increasingly negatively impact agriculture and access to water.

After the 2021 earthquake, water and sanitation infrastructure suffered extensive damage. Of 159 health facilities, 88 had been reportedly affected. Displaced people are exposed to a heightened risk of infectious diseases and the virus that causes Covid-19.

Inequality and Barriers to Education

Just under half of Haitians aged 15 and older are illiterate. The country's education system is highly unequal. The quality of public education is generally very poor, and 85 percent of schools are private, charging fees that exclude most children from low-income families.

Over 3 million children had been unable to attend school for months at a time during the past two years, for security reasons, as well as Covid-19 related restrictions.

The 2021 earthquake destroyed or heavily damaged 308 schools, affecting 100,000 children. Schools were set to open on September 21, but the opening delayed until October 4 in the affected area. Before the earthquake, UNICEF estimated that 500,000 children were at risk of dropping out.

Women's and Girls' Rights

Gender-based violence is common. Rape was only explicitly criminalized in 2005, by ministerial decree. Gender-based violence was already one of the highest risks for girls and women in the southern province even before the earthquake, with sexual exploitation prevalent in some areas; these risks were expected to rise in the wake of the 2021 earthquake.

A new penal code set to enter into force in June 2022 lists sexual harassment and gender-based violence as punishable offenses. The code will legalize abortion in all circumstances until the twelfth week of pregnancy, in cases of rape or incest, or if the mental or physical health of the woman is in danger. It will lower the legal age for consensual sex to 15.

Disability Rights

Around 15 percent of the Haitian population lives with a disability, the World Health Organization reports.

Although Haiti ratified the Convention on the Rights of Persons with Disabilities, its legislative framework has not been harmonized and includes offensive and discriminatory provisions against people with disabilities. People with disabilities continue experiencing discrimination in access to public services such as health, education, and justice and are at higher risk of suffering violence due to the significant social stigma and exclusion they face. Civil legislation restricts legal capacity for people with certain types of disabilities.

The new penal code includes provisions prohibiting violence or incitement against people with disabilities.

Sexual Orientation and Gender Identity

LGBT people continue to suffer high levels of discrimination in Haiti, and no comprehensive legal framework forbids it.

The new penal code, not yet in force, will make any crime motivated by its target's real or perceived sexual orientation an aggravated offense. The code punishes any murder motivated by a victim's sexual orientation with up to life imprisonment.

In 2017, the Senate passed two anti-LGBT bills, which remained pending in the Chamber of Deputies at time of writing. One bans same-sex marriage and public support or advocacy for LGBT rights. The other establishes homosexuality as a one of the possible reasons for denial of a Certificat de Bonne Vie et Mœurs (a certificate of good standing required as proof that a person has not committed a felony).

Migration

In September 2020, the Dominican Republic restarted deportations of undocumented Haitians, ending a pandemic moratorium. In January 2021, Dominican Republic President Luis Abinader and Jovenel Moïse agreed to address irregular migration and improve border security. The precarious status of Dominicans of Haitian descent and Haitian migrants in the Dominican Republic remains a serious concern.

In February 2021, Abinader announced construction of a wall on the border. In August, the Dominican Ministry of Defense reported more than 178,000 Haitians forcibly repatriated.

On September 28, the Dominican Republic's National Migration Council adopted a policy that prevents any foreign person who "would result in an unreasonable burden on public finances" from entering the country, including women who are at least six months pregnant.

In May 2021, the US extended a Temporary Protected Status 18-month designation for Haitians in the US for another 18 months. However, the US has continued to carry out expulsions of arriving Haitian migrants and asylum seekers to Haiti throughout the pandemic and, in September, it deployed border agents on horseback against Haitians seeking to enter the US through the US-Mexico border. Between taking office on January 20, 2021, and late November, the Biden administration expelled approximately 12,000 Haitians, a dramatic increase from 2020, when 895 Haitians were expelled from the country.

Mining and Access to Information

Haiti is one of the most densely populated countries in the Western Hemisphere, and environmental degradation is a concern. In the past decade, foreign investors have pursued the development of the mining sector. Resistance is widespread, as communities fear the industry will destroy their farmland and further contaminate their water.

A 2017 draft mining law is silent on the rights of those displaced by mining activities, the Global Justice Clinic of New York University School of Law reports, and it grants insufficient time for review of the environmental impacts of new mining projects. It contains provisions that could render company documents, including environmental and social impacts, confidential for 10 years, preventing meaningful consultation with communities. The draft remained under consideration as of September 2021.

Key International Actors

In November 2020, the International Federation of Football Association (FIFA) Ethics Committee sanctioned Haitian Football Federation (FHF) President Yves Jean-Bart with a lifetime ban, following its investigation into evidence of systematic sexual abuse of female players. As of July 2021, FIFA had suspended four additional senior FHF officials in connection with the abuses and banned another one from the sport for life.

After the August 2021 earthquake, the UN appealed for US$187.3 million to provide relief including shelter, water and sanitation, emergency healthcare, food, protection, and early recovery. In August, the US Agency for International Development announced $32 million in humanitarian assistance in response to the earthquake.

The US government and the Organization of American States supported Ariel Henry and his aim to hold elections in 2022, though activists warned that conditions were not conducive to free and fair elections.

Haiti's political and humanitarian situation continue being discussed at the UN Security Council. UN Secretary-General António Guterres called on all member states to support Haiti in overcoming the humanitarian crisis. BINUH's mandate was extended to July 15, 2022.

Honduras

Violent organized crime continues to disrupt Honduran society and push many people to leave the country. Journalists; environmental activists; human rights defenders; lesbian, gay, bisexual, and transgender (LGBT) individuals; and people with disabilities are among the groups targeted for violence.

Impunity remains the norm. Efforts to reform public security institutions have stalled. Marred by corruption and abuse, the judiciary and police remain largely ineffective. Support and resources from a four-year Organization of American States (OAS) mission to strengthen the fight against corruption and impunity, concluded in January 2020, have not produced lasting reforms. Anti-corruption prosecutors have been left defenseless.

Gangs

Gang violence is widespread in and around urban areas. Estimates of the number of active gang members range from 5,000 to 40,000. From 2015 through 2019, authorities arrested 4,196 gang members, the National Police reported.

Gangs exercise territorial control over some neighborhoods and extort residents throughout the country. They forcibly recruit children and sexually abuse women, girls, and LGBT people. Gangs kill, disappear, rape, or displace those who resist.

Gangs, particularly the Mara Salvatrucha (MS-13) and the 18th Street Gang (Barrio 18), are considered largely responsible for Honduras' murder rate, and are infamous for extortion and drug peddling. Although Honduras has reduced its homicide rate by half since 2011, it remains one of the world's highest, with 44.8 murders per 100,000 population in 2019.

Historically, governments have responded to organized crime with iron-fist security strategies. In 2018, the government created a special force to fight gangs (Fuerza Nacional Anti Maras y Pandillas), with members from the police, military, and Attorney General's Office.

Weak state institutions and abuses by security forces have contributed to persistent gang violence. There have been repeated allegations of collusion between security forces and criminal organizations.

Criminal Justice System and Impunity

The criminal justice system regularly fails to hold accountable those responsible for crimes and abuses.

Judges face interference—including political pressure, threats, and harassment—from the executive branch, private actors with connections to government, and gangs. Prosecutors and whistleblowers have received death threats. The Supreme Court, particularly its president, exerts excessive control over the appointment and removal of judges, and career instability limits judges' independence.

In January 2020, the government shut down the Mission to Support the Fight against Corruption and Impunity in Honduras (MACCIH). Established in 2016 by the government and the OAS, MACCIH contributed to the prosecution of 133 people, including congresspeople and senior officials, 14 of whom stood trial.

Since MACCIH left, the Attorney General's Office has harassed and intimidated the head of its own anti-corruption criminal enterprise office, Prosecutor Luis Javier Santos, and members of his team. International organizations, the United States, and the United Kingdom have expressed their support for Santos' work.

Human Rights Defenders

In 2019, the UN special rapporteur on the situation of human rights defenders called Honduras one of the most dangerous countries for them in Latin America. Activists say the government's Mechanism for the Protection of Journalists, Human Rights Defenders, and Justice Activists, created in 2015, is ineffective.

In June 2021, the Inter-American Commision on Human Rights (IACHR) estimated a 90 percent rate of impunity for crimes committed against human rights defenders in Honduras. The IACHR received information on frequent threats of lawsuits and prosecutions, including for slander and libel, hindering human rights work in Honduras.

In July, the Office of the High Commissioner of Human Rights (OHCHR) and the IACHR urged the government to refrain from charging Garifuna women with damage, threats, theft, and usurpation of lands. Honduras has failed to uphold the Garifuna's right to collective tenure over their lands and to promptly and adequately investigate threats and acts of harassment against community leaders, the IACHR stated in 2020.

In August, a former director of the Honduran hydroelectric company DESA was convicted of organizing the 2016 assassination of environmental and Indigenous rights defender Berta Cáceres, who opposed construction of a hydroelectric dam on the Gualcarque river. In 2019, seven others were convicted for carrying out the killing. The trial has been marred by irregularities.

Attacks on Journalists

Honduras is one of the Western Hemisphere's deadliest countries for journalists, with security forces representing their biggest threat, Reporters Without Borders noted in 2021. Since 2010, 42 journalists have been killed, UNESCO reported. According to the Inter-American Press Association, 29 journalists were beneficiaries of official protective measures.

In February, journalist Henry Fiallos and his family received anonymous death threats after he covered a femicide in which police officers were implicated. In August, he reported having been brutally beaten by police officers while doing his job.

Internal Displacement, Migration, and Asylum

As of December 2020, internally displaced people in Honduras represented almost 80 percent of the internally displaced population in Central America and Mexico. Around 191,000 people were internally displaced because of violence between 2004 and 2018, the government reported. In 2020, hurricanes Eta and Iota forced more than 55,000 to move into temporary shelters, according to the Red Cross.

The groups most likely to be internally displaced are children subjected to forced gang recruitment, professionals and business owners who face extortion, domestic violence survivors, and LGBT people and members of ethnic minorities who face violence and discrimination, the IACHR has reported. Rural communities subject to increased food insecurity due to prolonged drought and extreme weather events are also vulnerable to displacement.

A bill was introduced in 2019 to prevent, assist, and protect people internally displaced by violence. In June 2020, Congress passed a new penal code that introduced the crime of internal displacement, punishing, with prison sentences of six to nine years, those who, through violence or intimidation, force someone to abandon or change their place of living.

In January 2021, the IACHR and the UN special rapporteur on the human rights of internally displaced persons urged the government to adopt a law protecting internally displaced people.

From January to September 2021, 31,894 Hondurans requested asylum in Mexico, the Mexican Commission for Refugee Aid (COMAR) reported—filing more than 35 percent of Mexico's total asylum petitions. From January to July, 7,007 accompanied and 676 unaccompanied Honduran children requested asylum. In a 2020 survey by UNHCR and UNICEF, half of Hondurans interviewed in Mexico named violence as the main reason for their leaving.

As of October 17, 42,357 Hondurans were deported in 2021 to Honduras—more than the total throughout 2020—the government reported. Of those, 37,114 were deported from Mexico and 4,689 from the US. Human Rights Watch documented mass expulsion of migrants and asylum seekers, including Hondurans, from Mexico to a remote jungle in Guatemala.

Sexual Orientation and Gender Identity

LGBT people are frequently targets of discrimination, extortion, and violence from gangs, the national civil police and military police, and members of the public. Discrimination is also common in schools, the workplace, and in the home. Violence against LGBT individuals displaces many internally and forces others to leave the country to seek asylum.

In June, the Inter-American Court of Human Rights held that Honduras violated the rights to life and personal integrity of Vicky Hernández, a transgender woman killed during the 2009 coup. The court found that Hernández suffered harassment by police the night before she was killed, the police and military had effective control of the streets on the night she died, and Honduras conducted no effective investigation into her killing. The court ordered Honduras to train security forces to investigate anti-LGBT violence and to adopt a process allowing people to change the gender listed on their documents to match their identity.

In January, Congress voted to increase the majority needed to amend Honduras's constitutional ban on same sex marriage from two-thirds to three-quarters, thereby further entrenching the prohibition.

In September, President Hernández accused those who advocate for same-sex marriage of "attacking Christian principles" and "the notion of the family."

Women's and Girls' Rights

Honduras has the highest rate of femicide—defined as the killing of a woman by a man because of her gender—in Latin America, the UN Economic Commission for Latin America and the Caribbean reports.

As of August 5, 174 femicides have been committed in Honduras in 2021 according to the Women's Rights Center, a Honduran nongovernmental organization. In 2013, Honduras reformed the penal code to recognize femicide as a crime.

Women with disabilities are not included in general policies to prevent violence against women. Honduras lacks a comprehensive legislative framework that includes women with disabilities and policies to combat domestic violence.

Abortion is illegal in Honduras under all circumstances, with prison sentences of up to six years. The law also sanctions abortion providers. In January, legislators increased the majority needed to amend the provision banning abortion from two-thirds to three-quarters.

Girls and adolescents younger than 19 carry 15 percent of all pregnancies, the Monitoring Mechanism of the Belém do Pará Convention reported in 2016. Thirty-four percent of women ages 20 to 24 had married when they were 15 to 19, a UN Population Fund study conducted from 2005 to 2019 found.

Children's Rights

Honduras' fragile institutions fail to protect the rights of children, including adolescents, and ensure that they have access to basic services such as education and healthcare, the IACHR reported in 2019.

In 2019, more than 360,000 children between 5 and 17 years old worked, and only half of children under 18 years old attended school, according to the National Statistics Unit.

The Covid-19 pandemic has further limited access to education. Schools were closed in March 2020 and had not yet returned to full in-person classes by September 2021.

Child recruitment by gangs has caused many children to flee and abandon school. The average age of first contact with gangs is 13 years old, a 2020 UN Development Programme report found.

Prison Conditions

As of September, more than 20,000 people were detained in prisons with capacity for under 11,000. More than half of the men and two-thirds of the women were in pretrial detention, according to official statistics.

Overcrowding, inadequate nutrition, poor sanitation, beatings, intra-gang violence, and killings are endemic in prisons.

After 37 detainees were killed in a 2019 wave of gang violence, President Juan Orlando Hernández declared a state of emergency—extended to December 2021—and put prisons under military control. Assassinations and violence continue under military supervision. From January to June, the OV-UNAH documented eight violent deaths in prisons.

To reduce overcrowding in response to the pandemic, the legislature approved alternatives to pretrial detention and judges have released more than 1,600 people. However, many petitions for pandemic release have been rejected.

Key International Actors

In February, the US announced suspension and planned termination of the "asylum cooperative agreement" signed with Honduras in 2019, whereby Honduras had agreed to receive non-Honduran asylum-seekers transferred from the US.

Several UN special rapporteurs and the Working Group on Enforced or Involuntary Disappearances warned, in April, of growing numbers of migrants from Honduras, Guatemala, and El Salvador who have disappeared in Mexico, including 741 Hondurans from March through August 2019. They called for implementation of protective measures.

Honduras voted in favor of an OAS resolution rejecting Venezuela's December 2020 elections, which have been widely considered fraudulent. However, in June and October 2021 it abstained from OAS resolutions condemning arrests of Nicaraguan presidential opposition candidates and critics and demanding their release.

In July, the US released the "Engel List," listing individuals from Honduras, El Salvador, and Guatemala allegedly associated with corruption and undemocratic acts. It named 21 from Honduras, including former President Porfirio Lobo Sosa (2010-2014), who became ineligible for visas and admission to the US.

In September, the OAS and Honduras signed an agreement to allow an OAS electoral observation mission to the November elections to elect president, legislators, and local authorities.

In October, Honduras was elected as a member of the UN Human Rights Council for the 2022-2024 term.

Hungary

The government continued its attacks on the rule of law and democratic institutions in 2021. It also prolonged a state of emergency due to the Covid-19 pandemic, allowing it to rule by decree on matters related to public health, including by imposing restrictions on freedom of assembly and access to public information.

The government continued its attacks on members of the lesbian, gay, bisexual and transgender (LGBT) community, harassment of independent media, and its discrimination of the Roma minority and undercut women's rights. Access to the asylum procedure remains close to impossible.

Attacks on Rule of Law

The "state of danger"—a special legal order granting overwhelming power to the executive to rule by decree—initiated in March 2020 in the context of the Covid-19 pandemic and extended in December 2020 and June 2021 was effectively still in place at time of writing. Under the special legal order, government may use decrees to suspend application of acts of parliament, derogate from provisions of acts, and take other extraordinary measures. Since March 2020, the government issued over 250 decrees, most, but not all of them, related to the pandemic. A law adopted in May 2020 in the context of the Covid-19 pandemic gives the government power to unilaterally declare future public health emergencies, which would allow it to rule indefinitely by decree by prolonging the emergency every six months with minimal or no parliamentary or judicial oversight.

Freedom of Media

The government continued its harassment of independent media and freedom of expression. Most media outlets are directly or indirectly controlled by the government which has a chilling effect on independent journalism.

In June, the Supreme Court upheld a September 2020 decision by the Media Council, and revoked the frequency for Klubradio, an independent radio station in Budapest. Klubradio was pushed off air in February. In August, the radio station turned to the Constitutional Court, arguing that the stripping of its frequency by the Media Council was unconstitutional. The case was pending at time of writing.

In July, Hungarian independent journalists who report critically on the Hungarian government were named on a leaked list of targets for Pegasus phone spyware, and at least one journalist's phone was subsequently determined to have been compromised by the software.

Academic Freedom

The government continued its attacks on academic freedom during the year. In May, the government pushed through a law to privatize public resources and public universities by creating "public trust funds performing a public function" and designated 32 entities, of which most manage higher education institutions, as universities. The entities receive large amounts of public funds and assets, members of governing bodies are loyal to the ruling party, and public scrutiny is impossible.

Right to Health

Long-standing neglect of the public health care system and deficiencies in Hungarian hospitals, including lack of basic items such as hand soap and sanitizer, during spikes in Covid-19 cases may have contributed to high death rates—the highest per capita rate in the EU in the period from January/February 2020 to September 2021. By September, over 30,000 Covid-19 deaths were recorded. The vaccine rollout, which started in December 2020, alongside lockdowns and other restrictions, curbed the spread, drastically reduced cases, hospitalizations, and Covid-19 related deaths.

Discrimination against Roma

Workplaces and schools continued to discriminate against Roma and many Roma live in abject poverty. At the early stages of vaccine rollout, authorities effectively excluded many Roma as registration for vaccine appointments was only available online and many Roma lack internet connectivity or have inadequate technical knowledge and digital literacy to navigate the internet. Local authorities in many cases failed to provide proper information and assistance to Roma for vaccine registration; instead, local activists in Roma communities aided residents to register online. The lack of devices and connectivity significantly impacted Roma children's ability to access distance learning during school closures, further entrenching existing education inequalities.

Gender Identity and Sexual Orientation

The government continued to restrict the rights of LGBT people. Transgender people are not legally allowed to change the gender markers on their identification documents. In December 2020, the parliament adopted a constitutional amendment that states that only married couples will be eligible to adopt children, with the minister in charge of family policies able to make exceptions on a case-by-case basis. It effectively excludes same-sex couples, single people, and unmarried different-sex couples from adopting children. The amendment includes language that stigmatizes transgender people, stating that "children have the right to their identity in line with their sex at birth" and rejects diversity and inclusivity by mandating that children's upbringing should be "in accordance with the values based on our homeland's constitutional identity and Christian culture."

In June, a new law falsely conflated pedophilia and homosexuality, prohibiting discussion of gender identity and sexual orientation. The law targets content "promoting" or "portraying" sexual and gender diversity, putting health providers, educators, artists, and broadcasters at risk of sanctions, including financial and administrative penalties. An implementation decree in August put restrictions on shops selling products "promoting" or "portraying" sexual and gender diversity, banning all such sales within 200 meters of places frequented by children, and in all other cases required shops to separate those products in sealed packages.

Migration and Asylum

The country saw a significant decline in asylum applications in 2021 due to border closures. Pushbacks from Hungary to Serbia, sometimes violent, continued. The two transit zones on Hungary's border with Serbia remained closed. In August, Hungary airlifted at-risk Afghans from Afghanistan, and per Covid-19 protocols, quarantined them in the non-operational transit zones. Activists reported that instead of processing airlifted Afghans under asylum law, authorities consider their cases under the aliens policing act, as illegal migrants.

In June, the European Court of Human Rights ruled that pushbacks on Hungary's border with Serbia were a breach of the prohibition of collective expulsion. According to official police statistics, border officials have carried out at least 72,000 pushbacks since July 2016.

Human Rights Defenders

The government and ruling party members continued to smear human rights defenders, using government friendly media to claim they are part of a wider Soros network and describe them "Soros mercenaries" or "national security risks."

In April, in response to a 2020 Court of Justice of the EU ruling that held a 2017 law forcing civil society organizations receiving more than €20,000 (around $23,000) to declare themselves as foreign funded to be in violation of EU law, the governing majority adopted a bill to repeal it. The repeal bill however failed to address the criminalization of organizations aiding asylum seekers and migrants, also part of the Court of Justice ruling.

India

Critics of the Bharatiya Janata Party (BJP)-led government in India including activists, journalists, peaceful protesters, and even poets, actors, and businesses increasingly risked politically motivated harassment, prosecutions, and tax raids. Authorities shut down rights groups using foreign funding regulations or allegations of financial irregularities.

The government adopted laws and policies that discriminated against religious minorities, especially Muslims. This, coupled with vilification of Muslims by some BJP leaders and police failure to take action against BJP supporters who commit violence, emboldened Hindu nationalist groups to attack Muslims and government critics with impunity.

A devastating second wave of Covid-19 in April exposed systemic weaknesses in India's health infrastructure and the government's mishandling of the pandemic. The authorities threatened action against criticism of its pandemic response, and allegedly suppressed data to downplay the threat of the pandemic.

Jammu and Kashmir

In February, the government finally lifted an 18-month internet shutdown in Kashmir imposed in August 2019 when it revoked the state's constitutional autonomy and split it into two federally governed territories.

In September, after the death of separatist leader Syed Ali Shah Geelani, the government once against imposed restrictions on movement and a near-total communications' blackout for two days to prevent a mass gathering at his funeral. Geelani's family alleged that they were denied the right to conduct proper final rites.

In July, four UN human rights expert mandates wrote to the Indian government urging an inquiry into the death in custody of separatist leader Muhammad Ashraf Khan Sehrai, who was detained in July 2020 under the Public Safety Act, a preventive detention law. In March, five UN expert mandates wrote to the government seeking information about the detention of Kashmiri politician Waheed Para, the alleged custodial killing of a shopkeeper Irfan Ahmad Dar, and the enforced disappearance of Naseer Ahmad Wani. They raised concerns about "the repressive measures and broader pattern of systematic infringements of fundamental rights used against the local population, as well as of intimidations, searches and confiscations committed by national security agents."

Journalists in Kashmir faced increased harassment by the authorities, including raids and arrests on terrorism charges. In September, the police raided the homes of four Kashmiri journalists and confiscated their phones and laptops. In June, the UN special rapporteur on freedom of expression and the Working Group on Arbitrary Detention expressed concerns over "alleged arbitrary detention and intimidation of journalists covering the situation in Jammu and Kashmir."

Impunity for Security Forces

Allegations of torture and extrajudicial killings persisted with the National Human Rights Commission registering 143 deaths in police custody and 104 alleged extrajudicial killings in the first nine months in 2021.

After BJP leader Himanta Biswa Sarma became chief minister of Assam in May, his government's "zero tolerance policy" on crime led to an increase in police killings. By September, the police had reportedly killed 27 people in alleged extrajudicial killings and injured 40 others. In September, Assam police opened fire during a protest against forced evictions, killing a man and a 12-year-old boy. In a video shared on social media, police were seen beating the man after he was shot and a photographer hired by the local authorities stomping on the body of the injured man. The victims were Bengali-speaking Muslims, a community the BJP government has frequently vilified as "illegal Bangladeshis."

The authorities continued to use section 197 of the Criminal Procedure Code, which requires government approval to prosecute police officials, to block accountability even in cases of serious abuses. In March, the Gujarat state government refused to give permission to prosecute three police officials accused in the 2004 extrajudicial killing of a Muslim woman, Ishrat Jahan.

The Armed Forces (Special Powers) Act, which remained in effect in Jammu and Kashmir and several northeastern states, provides effective immunity from prosecution to security forces, even for serious human rights abuses.

The Border Security Force frequently used excessive force against irregular immigrants and cattle traders from Bangladesh.

Dalits, Tribal Groups, and Religious Minorities

Hindu mobs beat up Muslims, often working class men, with impunity while pro-BJP supporters filed baseless complaints against critics, especially religious minorities.

In January, a Muslim stand-up comic, Munawar Faruqui, and five of his associates were arrested on a complaint brought by the son of a BJP politician who accused him of hurting Hindu sentiments in jokes Faruqui apparently did not utter. Police subsequently admitted they had no evidence of the performance.

In October, over 200 men and women allegedly belonging to the BJP youth wing and affiliated Hindu nationalist groups Vishwa Hindu Parishad (VHP) and Bajrang Dal attacked a church in Uttarakhand state, vandalizing property and injuring several churchgoers. The attack came soon after the VHP allegedly threatened to demolish churches in Madhya Pradesh state's Jhabua district, claiming they were doing illegal religious conversions. Hindu nationalist groups also attacked churches in Chhattisgarh state. Several states enacted or amended laws ostensibly to prevent forced religious conversions, but these laws have been largely used to target minority communities, particularly Christians, Muslims, Dalits, and Adivasis.

In September, the National Crime Records Bureau reported that 50,291 cases of crimes against Dalits were reported in 2020, an increase of 9.4 percent over the previous year. Crimes against tribal communities also increased by 9.3 percent, at 8,272 cases.

Civil Society and Freedom of Association

In July, the death of jailed tribal rights activist Stan Swamy, 84, was emblematic of the ongoing persecution of rights activists. Swamy was arrested on politically motivated terrorism charges in the Bhima Koregaon case, related to caste violence in Maharashtra state in 2017. Fifteen other prominent human rights defenders are charged in this case. The UN special rapporteur on human rights defenders said Swamy's death "will forever remain a stain on India's human rights record."

In February, Prime Minister Narendra Modi described people participating in various peaceful protests as "parasites."

Hundreds of thousands of farmers, many of them from the minority Sikh community, protesting amendments to farm laws since November 2020, were accused by BJP leaders and pro-government media of having a separatist agenda.

Following violent clashes on January 26, 2021 between the police and protesting farmers in which one protester died, the authorities filed baseless criminal cases against journalists, shut down the internet at multiple sites, prevented journalists from entering protest sites, and ordered Twitter to block hundreds of accounts. In February, the authorities arrested a climate activist, Disha Ravi, accusing her of sedition and criminal conspiracy for allegedly editing a document providing information on the protests, and issued warrants against two others. In March, several UN human rights experts raised concerns over government's measures to restrict the protests, intimidate those involved, and stifle public debate about them.

In October, police arrested the son of a BJP minister on accusations that he ran over and killed four protesting farmers in Uttar Pradesh state with his car. An angry mob, in retaliation, then killed three men in the car, including the driver. A journalist also died in the violence.

In September, government financial officials raided the home and office of Harsh Mander, an activist, in Delhi, alleging financial and administrative irregularities. In July, the government restricted funding for 10 international nongovernmental organizations working on climate change, environment or child labor, using the Foreign Contribution Regulation Act.

In June, the Delhi High Court, while granting bail to three student leaders arrested on terrorism charges in relation to communal violence in Delhi in February 2020, said, "in its anxiety to suppress dissent, in the mind of the State, the line between the constitutionally guaranteed right to protest and terrorist activity seems to be getting somewhat blurred."

UN human rights experts repeatedly raised concerns over misuse of counterter-rorism laws to bring criminal charges against human rights defenders. In April, UN rights experts wrote to the Indian government on the alleged arbitrary deten-tion of Adivasi human rights defender Hidme Markam on terrorism charges, say-ing the arrest appeared to be in response to her human rights work, and in particular her work to highlight instances of sexual violence against women by state security forces.

Freedom of Expression and Privacy Rights

The authorities continued to intimidate and harass journalists and news outlets critical of the government through politically motivated lawsuits and tax raids. In July, the Indian news website The Wire reported that at least 300 Indian phone numbers, including those of human rights defenders, journalists, lawyers, gov-ernment officials, and opposition politicians, were included on a list of potential targets for advanced Israeli spyware Pegasus. Phone numbers of several ac-tivists arrested in the Bhima Koregaon case, as well as some of their family mem-bers were also on the leaked Pegasus list. In October, the Supreme Court, in response to several petitions related to the use of Pegasus spyware, appointed an independent panel to investigate the allegations of illegal surveillance.

In February, the government enacted the Information Technology (Intermediary Guidelines and Digital Media Ethics Code) Rules, 2021, which target internet in-termediaries, including social media services, digital news services, and curated video streaming sites. While the government said they aimed to curb the spread of "fake news," they allow greater governmental control over online content, threaten to weaken encryption, and would seriously undermine rights to privacy and freedom of expression online. In June, three UN human rights experts said the rules did not conform with international human rights norms.

Women's and Girls' Rights

The alleged rape and murder of a 9-year old Dalit girl in Delhi in August once again spotlighted that Dalit women and girls are at heightened risk of sexual vio-lence. In August, a 24-year-old woman and her male friend from Uttar Pradesh died after setting themselves on fire in front of the Supreme Court, alleging harassment by state police and judiciary in retaliation for her rape complaint against a member of parliament.

In February, former BJP minister M.J. Akbar lost his defamation case against journalist Priya Ramani, who among several other women, had accused him of sexual harassment in the workplace. The ruling by a Delhi court, the first major legal victory in India's #MeToo movement, noted that "a woman cannot be punished for raising her voice against sexual abuse." However, the law addressing sexual violence in the workplace remained poorly enforced, especially for women in the informal sector.

The Covid-19 pandemic exacerbated existing challenges women faced in workforce participation, pushing even more women out of jobs and into poverty. Studies showed more women than men lost jobs; a 2021 study said 47 percent of women lost their jobs as compared to 7 percent of men during the first lockdown in 2020, and they had not returned to work by the end of the year. In the informal sector, women fared even worse. Between March and April 2021, women in informal jobs in rural India accounted for 80 percent of job losses.

Children's Rights during Covid-19 Pandemic

By September 2021, several states in India began to reopen schools that had been shut for the most part since March 2020, affecting around 320 million children in India. An August report by a parliamentary standing committee noted that children's learning had "suffered immensely and because education sector also provides help, nutrition and psychological services, the overall welfare of the children has declined substantially." The report noted that 77 percent of students were deprived of attending online classes, while 40 percent of students had not accessed any remote learning.

A February study by Azim Premji University covering approximately 16,000 students across grade 2 to 6 in five states found significant learning losses. Another report led by some economists found devastating impact of school closures on children's learning, especially in rural areas and in poor and marginalized households.

School disruptions accompanied by declines in earnings and loss of jobs, particularly in marginalized communities, resulted in an increase in child labor, early marriage, and trafficking. A UNICEF report said about 10 million students are at risk of never returning to school.

Disability Rights

Disability rights groups welcomed two court judgments recognizing barriers to justice for persons with disabilities and calling for an end to abuses in mental health institutions. In September, the Supreme Court recognized that the rights of people with disabilities in mental hospitals are being violated and called on the government to monitor state-run institutions more closely. It also ordered states to make Covid-19 vaccinations available to everyone detained in a mental health facility and to the staff. In April, the Supreme Court issued a ruling, echoing calls from the Indian disability rights movement to make concrete reforms to make the criminal justice system more accessible for people with disabilities.

Sexual Orientation and Gender Identity

In June, the Madras High Court issued guidelines for the safety of lesbian, gay, bisexual, transgender, queer, and intersex persons and for prevention of harassment by the state authorities. The ruling recognized widespread discrimination and also recommended several measures towards addressing prejudices against them in society, including through training and sensitization programs for police and judiciary.

In January, the Delhi Commission for Protection of Child Rights recommended a ban on medically unnecessary "normalizing" surgeries on children born with intersex variations. In August, a rights group filed a public interest litigation in Delhi High Court asking the Delhi government to declare a ban, citing the state's child rights agency's stance on the matter.

Key International Actors

In April, the European Union held a local human rights dialogue with India. To date, the EU's foreign policy branch has refrained from publicly expressing concerns over India's human rights record, as have EU leaders during a summit with their Indian counterparts in May. The European parliament remains the only EU body that raised concerns on human rights in India, including in a recommendation adopted in April.

In September, India and Australia held the inaugural 2+2 Ministerial Dialogue where they discussed cooperation on cyber and critical technology and called for international counterterrorism efforts in Afghanistan.

In September, Prime Minister Modi attended the first in-person Quad summit in Washington, DC with leaders of Japan, Australia, and the United States. The leaders reiterated their commitment for a free and open Indo-Pacific, with an eye on China, and boosting global vaccine supply. The US deputy secretary of state visited Delhi in October to discuss India's security concerns with the spillover effects from the Taliban takeover in Afghanistan.

Foreign Policy

Following the military coup in Myanmar in February, even as India condemned the violence and called for the release of detained leaders, it abstained on a UN General Assembly resolution in June that called for the release of those arbitrarily detained, stopping the flow of arms into the country, and the Myanmar military to respect the outcome of the 2020 election.

In August, under India's month-long presidency, the UN Security Council adopted a resolution on Afghanistan that called on the Taliban to ensure safe passage for Afghan nationals who want to leave the country, allow humanitarian access, and uphold human rights. India, reflecting Pakistan's ties to the Taliban, pushed for commitments from the Taliban to ensure the country is not used by extremist groups to carry out attacks on India. In August, the Indian ambassador to Qatar met the head of the Taliban's political office in Doha.

India did not raise rights protections publicly with other neighbors including Bangladesh, Nepal, and Sri Lanka.

India gifted 10.7 million vaccines to 47 countries, commercially exported 35.7 million vaccines to 26 countries, and supplied 19.8 million vaccines to Covax, the global vaccine initiative that procures and distributes vaccines to low-and middle-income countries. Covax is largely supplied by AstraZeneca, which in turn has relied on only one manufacturing partner in India, the Serum Institute.

As India struggled with a huge surge in deaths and infections with the second wave of Covid-19, the government halted all vaccine exports, causing shortages in countries that depended on Covax. In September, the government said it would restart the exports, including to Bangladesh, Nepal, and the Maldives.

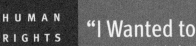

HUMAN
RIGHTS
WATCH

"I Wanted to Run Away"
Abusive Dress Codes for Women and Girls in Indonesia

Indonesia

Covid-19 cases surged in Indonesia in mid-2021, prompting the government to lock down most of Java, Bali, and many other parts of the archipelago in July and August. At time of writing, the government had confirmed more than 4.2 million cases and 142,000 deaths. Because many people self-isolated and did not report their symptoms or seek testing, public health researchers believe the actual death toll is much higher.

President Joko Widodo's government further weakened Indonesia's Corruption Eradication Commission, screening its employees and later firing 57 staff, including some leading investigators. The president's ruling coalition also continued to push through a new criminal code with many rights-violating articles.

Religious minorities continue to suffer from discriminatory regulations, including the 1965 blasphemy law and the so-called religious harmony regulation that makes it difficult for minorities in this predominantly Sunni Muslim country to build houses of worship, including non-Sunni minorities (Ahmadiyah, Shia) as well as non-Muslim minorities (Christians, Hindus, Buddhists, and Confucians, as well as followers of local religions such as Sunda Wiwitan).

Women's and Girls' Rights

On May 3, a panel of three male judges at the Supreme Court ruled that a new government regulation issued in February, which allowed millions of girls and women in thousands of state schools a basic freedom—to choose whether or not to wear a *jilbab* (Muslim apparel that covers the head, neck, and chest)—had "violated four national laws." The ruling stated that children under 18 have no right to choose their clothes.

The government adopted the regulation after a father in Padang, West Sumatra, publicized his daughter being forced to wear a jilbab. A Human Rights Watch report documented widespread bullying of girls and women into wearing a jilbab, and the deep psychological distress it can cause. Girls who do not comply have been forced to leave school or withdraw under pressure, while female civil servants, including teachers and university lecturers, have lost their jobs or resigned. Many Christian, Hindu, Buddhist, and other non-Muslim students and teachers have also been forced to wear the jilbab. Human Rights Watch is aware of at least 64 mandatory jilbab regulations in Indonesia.

In July, Army Chief Gen. Andika Perkasa told army commanders that the required medical check-up in the recruitment process for female officers should be similar to the check-up used for male officers, ending the abusive and unscientific "virginity test." Applicants should be assessed only on their ability to take part in physical training, he said. He also clarified that male army personnel seeking army permission to get married should no longer be required to submit medical check-ups for their fiancées.

Freedom of Religion

In June, members of Nahdlatul Ulama protested the construction of a Muhammadiyah mosque in Banyuwangi, prompting the local government to stop construction, invoking the 2006 religious harmony regulation. The two Sunni groups are Indonesia's two largest Muslim organizations.

In August, the National Police separately arrested and detained two clergymen on blasphemy charges. Muhammad Kece, a Christian preacher, was arrested for alleged blasphemy against Islam; Yahya Waloni, a Muslim imam, was arrested at his Jakarta house after allegedly saying in a sermon that the Bible was fake.

On September 3, more than 200 ethnic Malay men attacked an Ahmadiyah mosque in Sintang, West Kalimantan. Police arrested 22, charging them with arson and destruction of private property. Governor Sutarmidji supported the Muslim militants, meeting their two top leaders, cleric Mohammad Hedi and political operative Zainudin, in the detention center. Sutarmidji later asked the Sintang government to demolish the Ahmadiyah mosque.

Sexual Orientation and Gender Identity

On January 28, 2021, authorities in Aceh province publicly flogged two gay men 77 times each after a vigilante mob raided their apartment the previous November, allegedly caught them having sex, and handed them over to the police.

The Jakarta-based LGBT group Arus Pelangi has identified 45 anti-LGBT regulations in Indonesia, including the 2008 Anti-Pornography Law that categorizes homosexuality as "deviant sex."

In Semarang, policeman Tri Teguh Pujianto is challenging his 2018 dismissal from the Central Java Police because of his sexual orientation. He filed his case in March 2019. A documentary entitled "Teguh," meaning "firm," was produced supporting his case. In September, the Medan district court granted a transgender man permission to legally change his name to match his identity.

Land Rights

The Indonesian government is failing to protect the rights of communities living on or near land allotted to commercial agriculture. Due to minimal ongoing monitoring and oversight, some of these plantations degrade the environment they operate in and, in some cases, cause almost irreparable damage to peatlands, one of the world's most important carbon sinks.

PT Sintang Raya, a subsidiary of South Korean Daesang Corporation, has established and expanded its plantations in peatlands in three tidal villages in West Kalimantan without genuine consultation with local residents and without adequate compensation for loss of their farmland or livelihoods.

West Papua

Sporadic fighting between Indonesian security forces and the West Papua National Liberation Army continued in the central highlands area, killing at least 25 civilians in 2021, including Reverend Yeremia Zanambani, who had translated the Bible into the Nduga language.

On May 9, Indonesian police arrested Victor Yeimo, a spokesman for the West Papua National Committee, in Jayapura. Police charged him with treason for a 2019 statement made during anti-racism protests and ensuing riots in Papua and West Papua calling for a referendum on independence.

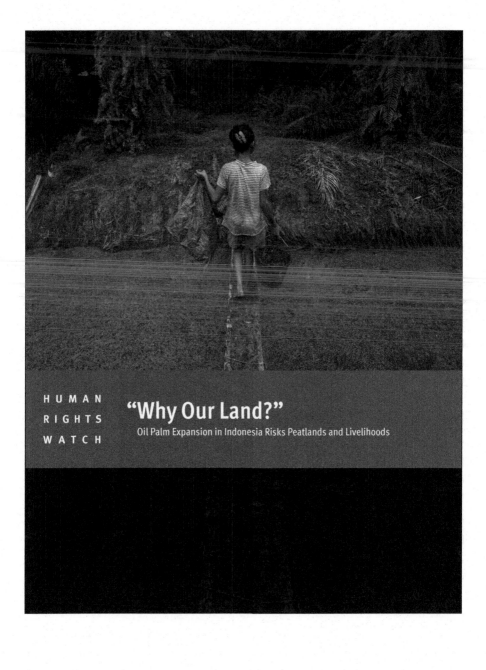

HUMAN
RIGHTS
WATCH

"Why Our Land?"
Oil Palm Expansion in Indonesia Risks Peatlands and Livelihoods

Climate Change Policy and Impacts

Indonesia, one of the world's top 10 emitters of greenhouse gases, is contributing to the climate crisis taking a mounting toll on human rights around the globe. In its 2021 update to its national climate action plan, Indonesia reiterated its 2016 goals, rather than establishing more ambitious targets as required by the Paris Agreement. Its climate plan is "critically insufficient" to meet the agreement's goal to limit global warming to 1.5°C above pre-industrial levels, according to The Climate Action Tracker. If all countries' commitments were in this range, the global temperature increase would exceed 4°C by the end of the century.

Government data released in March suggests deforestation dropped significantly between 2019 and 2020. Alternative estimates by Global Forest Watch (GFW) confirm a downward trend. In September, a government-mandated moratorium on new oil palm plantations lapsed. Despite an official ban on primary forest clearing in force since 2011, the latest GFW data indicates Indonesia lost 250,000 hectares in 2020. In November 2021, at the global climate summit in Glasgow, the Indonesian government signed a global pledge to end forest loss by 2030 – but its environment minister promptly criticized the pledge and vowed to continue clearing forests as part of 'development' plans.

Indonesia has taken few steps to move away from reliance on coal for electricity generation, a major contributor to greenhouse gas emissions. In May, the government said it would build more coal-fired power stations but would shut them all down in 2060. Indonesia could prevent tens of thousands of premature deaths linked to air pollution by rapidly reducing its reliance on coal-fired electricity.

Floods, droughts, sea level rise, changes in rainfall patterns, and warmer temperatures induced by climate change are expected to take a toll, requiring Indonesia to take steps to protect at-risk populations from their foreseeable harms. In January 2021, South Kalimantan and Borneo declared a state of emergency after heavy rainfall and flooding displaced tens of thousands.

Key International Actors

US President Joe Biden said in a speech in Washington, DC, on July 27: "What happens in Indonesia if the projections are correct that, in the next 10 years, they may have to move the capital because they will be underwater? That's important. It's a strategic question as well as an environmental question." The Indonesian government is finalizing a plan to move the capital from Jakarta to North Penajam Paser in Kalimantan, estimating 15 to 20 years for the relocation.

On September 17, UN Secretary-General António Guterres wrote in his annual report that between May 2020 and April 2021, five individuals in Indonesia seeking to cooperate with UN human rights agencies—Wensislaus Fatubun, Yones Douw, Victor Mambor, Veronica Koman, and Victor Yeimo—were "subject to threats, harassment and surveillance by government, non-state and private actors, including business enterprises and local political actors."

Indonesia played a role in excluding Myanmar junta leader Min Aung Hlaing from the Association of Southeast Asian Nations (ASEAN) summit on October 26-28. ASEAN said that a lack of progress on a peace roadmap that the junta had agreed on in April has prompted the group to exclude the junta. The move was unprecedented, as ASEAN usually works with compromises.

Iran

Iranian authorities continued their crackdown on peaceful dissent, prosecuting human rights defenders and dissidents while serious human rights violators enjoyed impunity.

Ebrahim Raeesi, who became president in unfree and unfair elections in June, previously oversaw the country's abusive judiciary and is accused of overseeing the mass extrajudicial execution of political prisoners in 1988.

Deteriorating economic conditions due to US unilateral sanctions and the impact of the Covid-19 pandemic have increased poverty and reduced living standards for millions in Iran. The government's response to the pandemic, especially its mismanaged national vaccine procurement plan, has been criticized for its opacity and politicization.

Freedom of Assembly and Expression, Right to Participate in the Conduct of Public Affairs

Iranian authorities severely restricted freedoms of assembly and expression. Over the past three years, security forces have responded to widespread protests stemming from economic rights issues with excessive and unlawful force, including lethal force, and have arrested thousands of protestors.

On February 16, authorities arrested photojournalist Noushin Jafari and transferred her to Qarchak prison to serve a revolutionary court sentence for charges of "spreading propaganda against the state" and "insulting the sanctities." Journalists and media activists currently in prison include Keyvan Samimi and Aliayeh Matlabzadeh, the chair and co-chair of the local nongovernmental organization (NGO) the *Society* for *Defending Press Freedom*. Both have been sentenced to imprisonment for their peaceful activism.

On February 22, according to the Baluchi Activists Campaign, Iran's Islamic Revolutionary Guard Corps (IRGC) blocked the road residents used to transport fuel to Pakistan at the Eskan border area in the town of Saravan, in Sistan and Baluchistan province. The security forces then apparently opened fire at those attempting to open the road, killing at least 10 people.

On June 19, Ebrahim Raeesi, former head of Iran's judiciary, became president after unfree and unfair elections. In the period before the election, the Guardian Council, a body of 12 male religious jurists and legal experts tasked with vetting elections, disqualified many candidates without providing a reason, including several prominent government officials. Raeesi, who has had a career for over three decades in the judiciary, reportedly served on a committee that decided the fate of prisoners in 1988, when the Iranian government summarily and extra-judicially executed thousands of political prisoners held in Iranian jails, in what amounted to crimes against humanity.

On July 15, people in dozens of towns and cities in Khuzestan and Lorestan provinces, which have a large ethnic Arab minority population, took to the streets for several nights to protest not having clean water for days. Human rights groups have verified the identities of at least nine people who were shot dead or died of injuries during the protests, including a 17-year-old boy. Videos shared on social media from protests in cities in Khuzestan show security officials shooting firearms and tear gas toward protesters.

Iran's parliament has been working on a draft bill that seeks to impose further restrictions on internet access for people in Iran. The bill includes a provision requiring international technology companies to have a legal representative in Iran to comply with Iranian law and cooperate with authorities. Iranian authorities have long surveilled users and prosecuted them for views they expressed online and censored online spaces. The bill also seeks to criminalize production and distribution of censorship circumvention tools (VPNs) commonly used in Iran to access a wide range of websites that are blocked by authorities.

Human Rights Defenders and Civil Society Activists

Scores of human rights defenders remain behind bars while authorities continue to harass, arrest, and prosecute those seeking accountability and justice, including human rights lawyers Nasrin Sotoudeh, Mohamad Najafi, and Amirsalar Davoudi.

On August 14, Iranian authorities arrested six prominent human rights lawyers and activists working on filing a complaint against Iranian authorities for their abject mismanagement of the Covid-19 crisis. As of November 8, they continued to detain three of them: Arash Keykhosravi, Mostafa Nili, and Mehdi Mahmoudian. Mahmoudian's lawyer said that authorities are implementing a four-year prison sentence his client previously received for his human rights activism.

On September 26, prominent human rights defender Narges Mohammadi announced that authorities summoned her to serve a 30-month prison sentence for charges including "signing a letter opposing the death penalty," "staging a sit-in at the prison office," "refusing order (to end the sit in)," and "property damage." Authorities previously released Mohammadi on October 5, 2020, after she served five years in prison for her rights activism.

Since the IRGC's downing of Ukraine International Airlines Flight 752 in January 2020 that killed 176 people, authorities have harassed the families of victims and restricted their rights to seek truth and justice.

In July, an Iranian court sentenced Manoucher Bakhtiari, the father of Pouya Bakhtiari, 27, who was fatally shot during the crackdown on protesters in November 2019, to three and a half years in prison and two and a half years in internal exile to a remote area on unclear charges.

Seven members of the Persian Wildlife Heritage Foundation, a local NGO focused on preserving biodiversity, remained behind bars on the charge of "collaborating with the hostile state of the US." Iranian authorities have failed to produce any evidence to support their charges nor have they investigated allegations of torture against them.

Execution, Right to Life

Iran continues to be one of the world's leading implementers of the death penalty. According to rights groups, in 2021 Iran had executed at least 254 people as of November 8, including at least seven people on alleged terrorism-related charges.

The judiciary also executed at least one individual sentenced to death for crimes they allegedly committed as a child. Under Iran's current penal code, judges can use their discretion not to sentence to death individuals who committed their alleged crime as children. However, several individuals who were retried under the penal code for crimes they allegedly committed as children have then been sentenced to death again.

Iranian law considers acts such as "insulting the prophet," "apostasy," same-sex relations, adultery, drinking alcohol, and certain non-violent drug-related offenses as crimes punishable by death. The law also prescribes the inhumane punishment of flogging for more than 100 offenses, including "disrupting public order," a charge that has been used to sentence individuals to flogging for their participation in protests.

More than two years after a brutal crackdown against widespread protests in November 2019, authorities have failed to conduct any transparent investigation into the use of excessive and unlawful force against protestors.

Iranian authorities' criminal investigation into the January 2020 shooting down of the Ukrainian plane has been handled by the judicial organization of the armed forces and remains shrouded in secrecy, with families of victims receiving very few details. On August 31, the association of families of flight PS752 said that they received a government notification that the military prosecutor's office had indicted 10 officials, ranging from a commander of a Tor M1 air defense missile system to operators deemed "worthy of punishment" for charges that include participating in unintentional murder, negligence, imprudence, and not following the protocol.

Covid-19 Vaccine Access

Authorities' prohibition on procuring US and UK-produced vaccines, lack of transparency, and mismanagement exacerbated the already devastating impact of Covid-19 in Iran, with an official death toll at 127,299 as of November 8.

In January, Ayatollah Khamenei placed a ban on the import of US and UK-produced vaccines. It appeared that authorities also sought to prioritize domestic production but fell behind in delivering promised quotas. Faced with widespread criticism, authorities have said that the ban has been reversed. The pace of national vaccination has picked up since mid-August. According to official statistics, as of November 8, more than 46 percent of the population had received two doses of Covid-19 vaccines.

Due Process Rights, Fair Trial Standards, and Prison Conditions

Iranian courts, and particularly revolutionary courts, regularly fall far short of providing fair trials and use confessions likely obtained under torture as evidence in court. Authorities have failed to meaningfully investigate numerous allegations of torture against detainees. Authorities routinely restrict detainees' access to legal counsel, particularly during the initial investigation period.

The IRGC's Intelligence Organization continues to arrest Iranian dual and foreign nationals on vague charges, such as "cooperating with a hostile state."

There have been numerous reports of suspicious deaths in Iranian prisons, which authorities have failed to properly investigate. According to Amnesty International, in 2010 at least 72 people had died in custody in Iranian prisons, while authorities have failed to provide accountability despite credible reports of torture and ill-treatment. Moreover, over the past year, there have been at least two reported deaths of prisoners, with families alleging that delayed or improper medical care contributed to their deaths. In many cases, Iranian authorities have restricted access of prisoners to medical care, particularly outside prison.

On March 1, a group of formerly imprisoned political activists and human rights defenders filed a complaint against the authorities use of prolonged solitary confinement in Iranian prisons, particularly for vaguely defined national security crimes.

Women's Rights, Children's Rights, Sexual Orientation, and Gender Identity

Women face discrimination in personal status matters related to marriage, divorce, inheritance, and decisions relating to children. Under the Passports Law, a married woman may not obtain a passport or travel outside the country without the written permission of her husband who can revoke such permission at any time. Under the civil code, a husband is accorded the right to choose the place of living and can prevent his wife from having certain occupations if he deems them against "family values." Iranian law allows girls to marry at 13 and boys at age 15, as well as at younger ages if authorized by a judge.

At least five activists are currently behind bars for their peaceful protests against compulsory hijab laws.

While cases of femicide are increasingly reported in media and social media, Iran has no law on domestic violence to prevent abuse and protect survivors. On January 3, the cabinet approved the draft bill on violence against women. While a step forward in providing legal definitions surrounding violence against women and measures to support victims, the bill lacks provisions for criminalizing marital rape and child marriage. With the change in the administration, it is unclear whether the bill will be introduced to parliament for a vote.

Iran's criminal law exempts parents and guardians from penalty for inflicting corporal punishment "within the customary limit."

On November 1, the Guardian Council passed the "rejuvenation of the population and support of family" bill that offers numerous incentives for childbearing and seeks to further limit access to contraception and abortion.

The draft bill outlaws voluntary sterilization and free distribution of contraceptives in the public health care system unless pregnancy threatens the woman's health. The draft law also mandates the Health Ministry to establish a committee that includes doctors, Islamic jurists, and representatives of the judiciary and the parliamentary health committee to draft new bylaws for abortion that could lead to further restrictions on access to abortion.

Under the current law, abortion can be legally performed during the first four months of pregnancy if three doctors agree that the pregnancy threatens a woman's life or the fetus has severely physical or mental deformities that would create "extreme hardship" for the mother. In October, a letter, issued by the crime prevention deputy at the judiciary in Iran's Mazandaran province, was leaked on Twitter mandating local laboratories to report on women with positive pregnancy tests to prevent "criminal abortions."

Under Iranian law, extramarital sex is criminalized with flogging if the person is unmarried or death if married, impacting women in particular as pregnancy serves as evidence of sexual relations and women who report sexual violence can find themselves prosecuted if authorities believe it to be consensual. Same-sex conduct is also punishable by flogging and, for men, the death penalty. Although Iran permits and subsidizes sex reassignment surgery for transgender people, no law prohibits discrimination against them.

Treatment of Minorities, Refugees, and Migrants

Iranian law denies freedom of religion to Baha'is and discriminates against them. Authorities continue to arrest and prosecute members of the Baha'i faith on vague national security charges and to close businesses owned by them. Iranian authorities also systematically refuse to allow Baha'is to register at public universities because of their faith.

The government also discriminates against other religious minorities, including Sunni Muslims, and restricts cultural and political activities among the country's Azeri, Kurdish, Arab, and Baluch ethnic minorities. Minority activists are regularly arrested and prosecuted on vaguely defined national security charges in trials that grossly fall short of international standards.

It appears that over the past year, authorities have increased the crackdown against Kurdish political activists. On September 9, IRGC forces launched missile attacks against the bases of Kurdish opposition forces (Kurdistan Democratic Party of Iran or KDPI) in the Kurdistan Region of Iraq.

Iran hosts a long-staying population of about 780,000 registered Afghan refugees and another estimated 850,000 undocumented Afghans. In mid-August, the government set up three temporary tent camps for refugees fleeing Afghanistan, but its border remained closed to most Afghan asylum seekers, as entry was limited to people with valid passports and visas. During September, about 2,000 Afghans per day were estimated to enter Iran irregularly, but a comparable number of Afghans were deported from Iran.

Right to Water and Impact of Climate Change

As one of the world's top 10 emitters of greenhouse gases, Iran is contributing to the climate crisis taking a mounting toll on human rights around the globe. Most of its emissions are from the energy sector: 94 percent of Iran's electricity comes from fossil fuels. Iran is the eighth largest producer of crude oil and the third largest producer of natural gas but also has significant renewable energy potential. Energy costs are heavily subsidized, one of the factors leading to a high energy intensity per capita. Iran has taken few steps to reduce reliance on fossil fuels, regularly citing international sanctions as a barrier to transitioning towards cleaner energy. Iran is one of six countries that has not yet ratified the Paris Agreement.

There are longstanding concerns across Iran, and Khuzestan in particular, over mismanagement of water resources and pollution from oil development. For decades, environmental experts have warned that development projects in oil-rich Khuzestan, including the construction of hydroelectric dams, irrigation schemes, and water transfers to neighboring provinces are causing environmental harm and leading to water shortages affecting a range of rights.

Climate change is a serious threat to Iranian livelihoods including from increased temperatures, more frequent and intense forest fires, dust storms, inland flooding, and sea level rise. In 2021, droughts exacerbated long-standing pressures on water resources. The increasing frequency and intensity of droughts is projected to continue, diminishing agricultural productivity compromising food security.

Key International Actors

While several rounds of indirect negotiations have taken place between Iran and the US for a return to compliance with the 2015 Joint Comprehensive Plan of Action (JCPOA), the US has maintained its broad sectoral economic and financial sanctions on Iran. Although the US government has built exemptions for humanitarian imports into its sanctions regime, Human Rights Watch found that in practice US and European companies and banks continue to refrain from exporting or financing exempted humanitarian goods and services for fear of legal action and sanctions from the US government.

On June 17, the US Department of Treasury's Office of Foreign Assets Control (OFAC) issued an additional general license that expanded an existing humanitarian exemption to transactions and activities involving the delivery of face masks, ventilators and oxygen tanks, vaccines and the production of vaccines, Covid-19 tests, air filtration systems, and Covid-19-related field hospitals, among others.

On July 27, Swedish prosecutors announced their decision to prosecute an Iranian citizen for "committing grave war crimes and murder in Iran during 1988." The trial opened on August 10 and is expected to last through April 2022.

Iraq

In 2021, the government failed to deliver on its promises to hold to account those responsible for the arbitrary arrests, enforced disappearances, and extra-judicial killings of protesters, activists, journalists, and others openly critical of political and armed groups in the country.

Iraq's criminal justice system was still marred by the widespread use of torture, including in order to extract confessions. Despite serious due process violations in trials, authorities carried out at least 19 judicial executions of defendants sentenced to death.

No ISIS defendants have been convicted of international crimes such as war crimes, crimes against humanity, or genocide. In March Iraq's parliament passed the Law on Yazidi Female Survivors, which recognized crimes committed by ISIS against women and girls from the Yezidi, Turkman, Christian, and Shabaks minorities as genocide and crimes against humanity, but little progress has been made towards applying the law.

In a brazen attack on November 7, unnamed armed actors tried but failed to assassinate the prime minister in his home using three armed drones.

Accountability for Abuses against Critics

During protests that began in October 2019 and continued into late 2020, clashes with security forces, including the Popular Mobilization Forces (PMF or *hashad*) nominally under the control of the prime minister, left at least 560 protesters and security forces dead in Baghdad and Iraq's southern cities. In May 2020, when Prime Minister Mustafa al-Kadhimi took office, he formed a committee to investigate the killings of protesters. It had yet to announce any findings as of September 2021.

In July 2020, the government announced it would compensate the families of those killed during the protests. As of September 2021, the six families of activists killed whom Human Rights Watch contacted had not received any compensation. In February 2021, the government announced the arrest of members of a "death squad" that had allegedly been responsible for killing at least three activists in the southern city of Basra. Baghdad authorities announced in July that they had arrested three low-level security forces officers linked to abuses against protesters, and one man allegedly responsible for the 2020 killing of political analyst Hisham Al-Hashimi.

A United Nations Assistance Mission to Iraq (UNAMI) report published in May found that not one of several arrests related to targeted killings appeared to have moved beyond the investigative phase. As of late September, it appeared that none of the arrests had led to any charges being brought.

Torture, Fair Trial Violations, and the Death Penalty

UNAMI released a report in August based on interviews with more than 200 detainees, over half of whom shared credible allegations of torture. The report found that the authorities acquiesce in and tolerate the use of torture to extract confessions, a finding consistent with Human Rights Watch reporting on the systemic use of torture in Iraq.

Criminal trials of defendants charged under Iraq's overbroad terrorism law, most often for alleged membership in the Islamic State (ISIS), were generally rushed and did not involve victim participation. Convictions were based primarily on confessions including those apparently extracted through torture.
Authorities systematically violated the due process rights of suspects, such as guarantees under Iraqi law that detainees see a judge within 24 hours, have access to a lawyer throughout interrogations, and that their families are notified and be able to communicate with them.

Based on the criminal age of responsibility in the penal code,
authorities can prosecute child suspects as young as 9 on terrorism charges in Baghdad-controlled areas and 11 in the Kurdistan Region of Iraq. This violates international standards, which recognize children recruited by armed groups primarily as victims who should be rehabilitated and reintegrated into society, and call for a minimum age of criminal responsibility of 14 years.

According to a Ministry of Justice statement in September, authorities were detaining close to 50,000 people for suspected terrorism links, over half of them sentenced to death. Informed sources told Human Rights Watch that at least 19 executions had been carried out as of September. Those imprisoned for ISIS affiliation reportedly include hundreds of foreign women and children, though children are not sentenced to death.

Many defendants were detained because their names appeared on wanted lists of questionable accuracy or because they were family members of listed suspects.

In the Kurdistan Region, the Kurdistan Regional government (KRG) has maintained a de facto moratorium on the death penalty since 2008, banning it "except in very few cases which were considered essential," according to a KRG spokesperson.

ISIS Crimes Against the Yezidi Community

Despite ISIS's systematic rape, sexual slavery, and forced marriage of Yezidi women and girls, prosecutors neglected to charge ISIS suspects with rape—which carries a sentence of up to 15 years—even in cases where defendants admitted to subjecting Yezidis to sexual slavery. Instead, Iraqi judges routinely prosecuted ISIS suspects solely on the overbroad charge of ISIS affiliation. No ISIS defendants have been convicted of international crimes such as war crimes, crimes against humanity, or genocide, despite the apparent genocide by ISIS against the Yezidis.

On March 1, 2021, Iraq's parliament passed the Law on Yazidi Female Survivors, which recognized crimes committed by ISIS including kidnapping, sexual enslavement, forced marriage, pregnancy, and abortion against women and girls from the Yezidi, Turkman, Christian, and Shabaks minorities as genocide and crimes against humanity. The law provides for compensation for survivors, as well as measures for their rehabilitation and reintegration into society and the prevention of such crimes in the future. In September 2021, the parliament passed the necessary regulations to implement the law but by November, little progress had been made towards applying the law.

Collective Punishment

In March 2020, the government endorsed a National Plan to Address Displacement in Iraq calling for a thoughtful and sustainable approach to assisting Iraq's

protracted displaced population. However, the government closed 16 camps between October 2020 and January 2021, leaving at least 34,801 displaced people
without assurances that they could return home safely, get other safe shelter, or
have access to affordable services. Many residents were female-headed households displaced by fighting between ISIS and the Iraqi military from 2014 to
2017, and many of these families were being labeled ISIS-affiliated.

Only three camps remain open in Baghdad-controlled territory, two in Nineveh
and another in Anbar.

In July, the Iraqi army unlawfully evicted 91 families from a village in Salah al-Din
to one of the Nineveh camps in an apparent family feud involving a government
minister.

In 2021, security forces continued to deny security clearances, required to obtain
identity cards and other essential civil documentation, to thousands of Iraqi
families the authorities perceived to have ISIS affiliation, usually based on accusations that an immediate family member of theirs had joined the group.
This denied them freedom of movement, their rights to education and
work, and access to social benefits and birth and death certificates needed to inherit property or remarry.

Authorities continued to prevent thousands of children without civil documentation from enrolling in state schools, including state schools inside camps for displaced people.

The government allowed some families to obtain security clearances if they filed
a criminal complaint disavowing any relative suspected of having joined
ISIS, after which the court issues them a document to present to security
forces enabling them to obtain their security clearances.

At least 30,000 Iraqis who fled Iraq between 2014 and 2017, including some who
followed ISIS as it retreated from Iraqi territory, were held in and around al-Hol
camp in northeast Syria. In May, the Iraqi government repatriated 95 Iraqi families from al-Hol and in September at least another 20 families. Authorities have
prevented some of them from leaving the camp freely, retaining cell phones, or
returning home.

The KRG continued to prevent thousands of Arabs from returning home to villages in the Rabia subdistrict and Hamdaniya district, areas where KRG forces

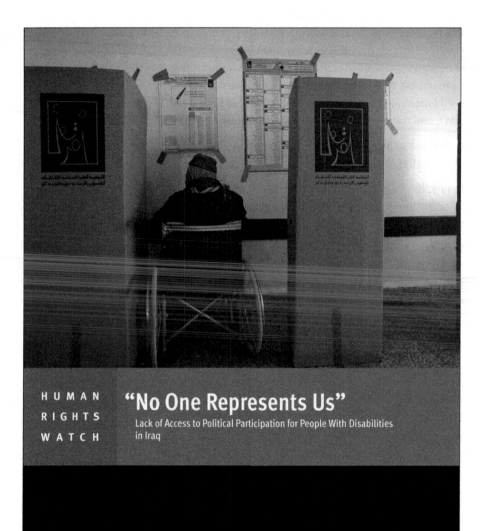

HUMAN
RIGHTS
WATCH

"No One Represents Us"
Lack of Access to Political Participation for People With Disabilities
in Iraq

had pushed ISIS out and taken territorial control in 2014 but allowed local Kurdish villagers to return to those same areas.

Elections

On October 10, Iraqis voted for a new parliament with a voter turnout of 36 percent. Prominent Shia cleric Moqtada al-Sadr's movement secured the largest number of seats in peaceful elections.

People With Disabilities

Iraq failed to secure political rights, in particular the right to vote, for Iraqis with disabilities. People with disabilities are often effectively denied their right to vote due to discriminatory legislation that strips the right to vote or run for office for people considered not "fully competent" under the law, inaccessible polling places, and legislative and political obstacles, like requirements for a certain level of education that many people with disabilities are unable to attain. In 2019, the UN's Committee on the Rights of Persons with Disabilities said that Iraq, plagued by decades of violence and war, including the battles against ISIS from 2014-2017, has one of the world's largest populations of people with disabilities.

KRG Prosecution of Critics

In 2021, the Erbil Criminal Court sentenced three journalists and two activists to six years in prison, based on proceedings marred by serious fair trial violations as well as high-level political interference. The court rejected the defendants' claims of torture and ill-treatment, citing a lack of evidence. Another journalist was sentenced to one year for misuse of his cell phone and defamation charges in June and September. Another four activists and journalists arrested in 2020 were awaiting charge as of October 2021.

Women's Rights, Gender Identity, Sexual Orientation, Morality Laws

While Iraq's penal code criminalizes physical assault, Article 41(1) allows a husband to "punish" his wife and parents to discipline their children "within limits prescribed by law or custom." UNICEF surveys have found more than 80 percent of children are subjected to violent discipline. The penal code also provides for mitigated sentences for violent acts, including murder, for "honorable motives," and catching one's wife or female relative in the act of adultery or sex outside of marriage.

Such discriminatory laws expose women to violence. Cases of domestic violence were reported throughout 2021, including killings of women and girls by their husbands or families.

Parliamentary efforts to pass a draft law against domestic violence has stalled since 2019. The 2019 version seen by Human Rights Watch included provisions for services for domestic violence survivors, restraining orders, penalties for their breach, and establishment of a cross-ministerial committee to combat domestic violence. The bill had several gaps and provisions that would undermine its effectiveness, such as prioritizing reconciliation over protection and justice for victims.

In 2021, Iraqi security forces arbitrarily arrested lesbian, gay, bisexual, and transgender (LGBT) people based solely on their gender non-conforming appearance, and subjected them to ill-treatment including torture, forced anal exams, severe beatings, and sexual violence, in police custody. Security forces also physically, verbally and sexually harassed people they perceived as LGBT at checkpoints. Human Rights Watch documented cases of digital surveillance by armed groups against LGBT people on social media and same-sex dating applications. The government has failed to hold accountable members of armed groups who have abducted, raped, tortured, and killed LGBT Iraqis with impunity.

Article 394 of Iraq's penal code makes it illegal to engage in extra-marital sex, a violation of the right to privacy that disproportionately harms LGBT people as well as women, as pregnancy can be deemed evidence of a violation. Women reporting rape can also find themselves subject to prosecution under this law. Iraq's criminal code does not explicitly prohibit same-sex sexual relations, but Article 401 of the penal code holds that any person who commits an "immodest act" in public can be imprisoned for up to six months.

Key International Actors

On January 3, 2020, a US drone strike killed Lt. Gen. Qassem Soleimani, the commander of Iran's Islamic Revolutionary Guards Corps, at Baghdad airport. Two days later, Iraqi parliamentarians passed a non-binding resolution to expel US-led coalition troops from the country. In mid-2021, President Biden said that by December 31, US troops would end their combat mission in Iraq but would continue to provide training and advice to Iraqi forces.

Turkish airstrikes continued in 2021, targeting the Iranian Kurdish Party for Free Life of Kurdistan (PJAK) and Kurdistan Workers' Party (PKK) members based in northern Iraq, in some cases killing civilians. Human Rights Watch was unaware of any investigations by the Turkish military into possible unlawful attacks it had carried out in northern Iraq or compensation of victims.

In 2017, the UN Security Council created an investigative team, UNITAD, to document serious crimes committed by ISIS in Iraq. Given the deeply flawed Iraqi criminal proceedings against ISIS suspects and ongoing fair trial concerns in the country, it remained unclear to what extent the team has supported the Iraqi judiciary in building case files in line with international standards.

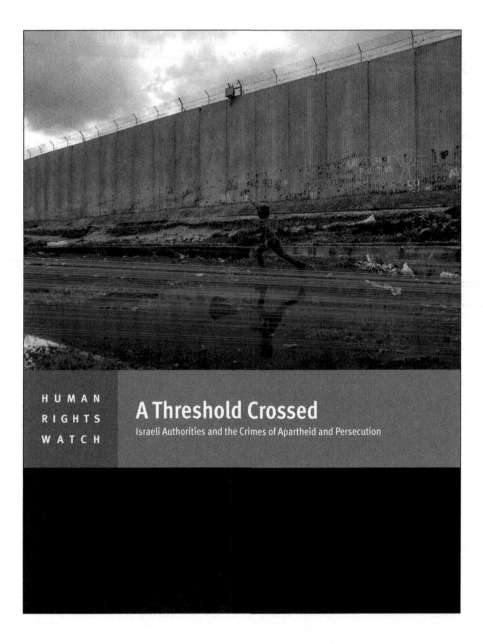

HUMAN
RIGHTS
WATCH

A Threshold Crossed
Israeli Authorities and the Crimes of Apartheid and Persecution

Israel and Palestine

Across two governments, each in power for roughly half of 2021, Israeli authorities doubled down on policies to repress Palestinians and privilege Jewish Israelis. The government's policy of maintaining the domination of Jewish Israelis over Palestinians across Israel and the Occupied Palestinian Territory (OPT), coupled with the particularly severe repression against Palestinians living in the OPT, amounts to the crimes against humanity of apartheid and persecution.

In May, amid discriminatory efforts to force Palestinians out of their homes in occupied East Jerusalem, 11 days of hostilities broke out between the Israeli government and Palestinian armed groups in Gaza. The Israeli military said it struck about 1,500 targets in Gaza with ground- and air-launched munitions, which, according to UN figures, killed at least 120 Palestinian civilians. Palestinian armed groups, including Hamas, launched more than 4,000 rockets and mortars towards Israel, resulting in the deaths of 12 civilians in Israel and at least 7 Palestinians in Gaza.

Human Rights Watch documented serious violations of the laws of war and apparent war crimes during the hostilities, including Israeli strikes that killed scores of civilians and destroyed four high-rise Gaza towers full of homes and businesses, with no evident military targets in the vicinity, as well as indiscriminate rocket attacks fired by Hamas and other Palestinian armed groups towards Israeli cities.

These attacks took place amid Israel's sweeping restrictions on the movement of people and goods into and out of Gaza. With rare exceptions, Israel's closure policy, which is not based on an individualized assessment of security risk and is exacerbated by Egyptian restrictions on its border with Gaza, rob the more than two million Palestinians of Gaza of their right to freedom of movement, severely limit their access to electricity, health care, and water, and have devastated the economy. More than 80 percent of Gaza's population depend on humanitarian aid.

In June, a broad range of political parties formed a new Israeli coalition government, with Naftali Bennett as prime minister. This government continued to facilitate the transfer of Israeli citizens into settlements in the occupied West Bank, a war crime. In October, it advanced plans and issued tenders for more than 4,000 new settlement units.

During the first eight months of 2021, Israeli authorities demolished 666 Palestinian homes and other structures in the West Bank, including East Jerusalem, displacing 958 people, a 38 percent increase compared to the same period in 2020, according to the UN Office for the Coordination of Humanitarian Affairs (OCHA). Most buildings were demolished for lacking building permits, which authorities make nearly impossible for Palestinians in these areas to obtain. In July, Israeli authorities razed for the sixth time in less than a year the homes of most residents of the Palestinian community of Khirbet Humsah in the Jordan Valley for being in a designated "firing zone," displacing 70 people, 35 of them children.

Israeli authorities in late 2021 designated six prominent Palestinian civil society organizations as "terrorist" and "illegal" organizations, moves that permit closing their offices, seizing their assets, and jailing their staff and supporters.

The Palestinian Authority (PA) manages affairs in parts of the West Bank, where it systematically arrests arbitrarily and tortures dissidents. In April, the PA postponed planned parliamentary and presidential elections, which would have been the first in 15 years. In June, PA critic Nizar al-Banat died in custody shortly after PA forces arrested and beat him outside a relative's home. The PA violently dispersed popular protests and rounded up scores of Palestinians demanding justice for al-Banat's death.

GAZA STRIP

During the May hostilities, 260 Palestinians were killed, including 66 children, and 2,200 were wounded, "some of whom may suffer a long-term disability requiring rehabilitation," according to OCHA. Authorities in Gaza said that 2,400 housing units were made uninhabitable and over 50,000 units were damaged. 8,250 people remained internally displaced as of October 14, OCHA said. The fighting also damaged 331 educational facilities, 10 hospitals, and 23 primary health clinics. The World Bank estimated $380 million in total physical damage and $190 million in economic losses.

Israeli Closure

For a 14th consecutive year, Israeli authorities blocked most of Gaza's population from traveling through the Erez Crossing, the sole passenger crossing from Gaza into Israel through which Palestinians can travel to the West Bank and abroad. A generalized travel ban applies to all, except those whom Israeli authorities deem as presenting "exceptional humanitarian circumstances," mostly persons needing vital medical treatment and their companions, as well as prominent business people. Even the few seeking to travel under these narrow exemptions, including those seeking urgent medical care outside Gaza, often face denials or failures to respond to in a timely manner to their requests.

Israeli authorities tightened the closure amid the Covid-19 pandemic. During the first nine months of 2021, an average of 86 Palestinians in Gaza exited via Erez each day, just 17 percent of the daily average of 500 in 2019 and less than 1 percent the daily average of more than 24,000 before the beginning of the Second Intifada or Palestinian uprising in September 2000, according to the Israeli rights group Gisha.

Gaza's exports during this period, mostly produce destined for the West Bank and Israel, averaged 300 truckloads per month, compared to the monthly average of 1,064 truckloads prior to the June 2007 tightening of the closure, according to Gisha. During the May hostilities and up until August, Israeli authorities banned the entry of construction materials and other vital materials and limited access to Gaza's territorial waters for Palestinian fishermen, measures targeting Gaza's general civilian population that amount to unlawful collective punishment. Authorities continue to severely restrict the entry of construction materials and other items they deem "dual-use" materials that could also be used for military purposes. The list of such items also includes X-ray and communications equipment and spare parts.

The closure limits access to basic services. During the first nine months of 2021, families in Gaza on average had to make do without centrally provided electricity for more than 11 hours a day, according to OCHA. Chronic prolonged power outages encumber many aspects of everyday life, from heating and cooling and sewage treatment to health care and business, in particular for people with disabilities who rely on light to communicate using sign language or equipment powered by electricity, such as elevators or electric wheelchairs, to move. OCHA found that Gaza's groundwater, its sole natural water source, is "almost completely unfit for human consumption." According to the World Health Organization (WHO), 42 percent of "essential" medicines were at less than one month's supply as of June.

Egypt also restricts the movement of people and goods via its Rafah crossing with Gaza, at times fully sealing the crossing. In the first nine months of 2020, an average of 13,678 Palestinians crossed monthly in both directions, less than the monthly average of over 40,000 before the 2013 military coup in Egypt, according to Gisha.

Hamas and Palestinian Armed Groups

Rocket attacks by Palestinian armed groups resulted in the deaths of 13 people in Israel, all during the May hostilities.

Hamas authorities provided no information about two Israeli civilians with psychosocial disabilities, Avera Mangistu and Hisham al-Sayed, whom they have apparently held in violation of international law for more than six years after they entered Gaza.

Hamas authorities detained opponents and critics for their peaceful expression and tortured some in their custody. The Palestinian statutory watchdog, the Independent Commission for Human Rights (ICHR), received 75 complaints of arbitrary arrests and 72 of torture and ill-treatment against Hamas authorities between January and September 2020.

Since they took control in Gaza in June 2007, Hamas authorities carried out 28 executions following trials marred with due process violations, but none during the first nine months of 2021. Courts in Gaza had, as of October 24, sentenced 19 people to death this year and 161 since June 2007, according to the Gaza-based Palestinian Center for Human Rights.

In February, Hamas authorities issued new restrictions that allow male guardians to request local authorities to block unmarried women from leaving Gaza when such travel will cause "absolute harm," a broad term that allows men to restrict women's travel at will.

WEST BANK

Israeli Use of Force and Detentions

In the West Bank, including East Jerusalem, Israeli security forces, as of October 14, killed 67 Palestinians—nearly triple the figure for all of 2020 and including 14 children—and wounded more than 1,000 Palestinians with live ammunition, according to OCHA. This total includes non-violent demonstrators and bystanders, as well as those alleged to have attacked Israelis.

On July 28, Israeli officers shot and killed 11-year-old Mohammad Abu Sarah in the back of his father's car at the entrance to their village of Beit Ummar near Hebron in a situation where neither posed any apparent threat to Israeli soldiers, as documented in video footage published by the Israeli rights group B'Tselem.

Israeli settlers killed five Palestinians, wounded 137, and caused property damage in 287 incidents, as of October 22, according to OCHA. The number of incidents of settler violence against Palestinians in the first half of 2021 was more than double the figure for the first half of 2020 and more than all of 2019, according to government data. As of October 16, Palestinians killed one Israeli settler and wounded 37 Israeli soldiers and 72 settlers in the West Bank.

Israeli authorities have rarely held accountable security forces who used excessive force or settlers who attacked Palestinians.

Israeli authorities closely monitor online speech by Palestinians, in part relying on predictive algorithms to determine whom to target, and have detained Palestinians based on social media posts and other expressive activity.

While applying Israeli civil law to settlers, Israeli authorities govern West Bank Palestinians, excluding Jerusalem residents, under harsh military law. In so doing, they deny them basic due process and try them in military courts with a near-100 percent conviction rate.

As of October 1, Israel held 4,460 Palestinians in custody for "security" offenses, including 200 children, many for throwing stones, and 492 in administrative detention without formal charges or trial and based on secret evidence, according to figures by the Israeli human rights group HaMoked and Palestinian prisoner rights group Adameer. Israel incarcerates many Palestinians from the OPT inside

Israel, complicating family visits and violating international humanitarian law's prohibition against their transfer outside occupied territory.

In September, six Palestinian prisoners from the OPT escaped from an Israeli prison in northern Israel. In response, Israeli authorities temporarily cancelled family visits to all detainees. Lawyers for several of the men said the escaped prisoners were tortured upon their rearrest.

More than 1,300 complaints of torture, including of painful shackling, sleep deprivation and exposure to extreme temperatures, have been filed with Israel's Justice Ministry since 2001, resulting in two criminal investigations and no indictments, according to the Israeli rights group Public Committee Against Torture.

In August, the Israeli Supreme Court upheld the Israeli government's policy of withholding the bodies of Palestinians killed in what they consider security incidents, as leverage to secure Hamas's release of the bodies of two Israeli soldiers presumed killed in 2014 hostilities, as authorities have acknowledged. As of August, authorities held the bodies of 81 Palestinians killed since 2015, according to the Haifa-based human rights group Adalah.

Settlements and Home Demolitions

Israeli authorities provide security, infrastructure, and services for more than 667,000 settlers in the West Bank, including East Jerusalem.

The difficulty in obtaining Israeli building permits in East Jerusalem and the 60 percent of the West Bank under Israel's exclusive control (Area C) has driven Palestinians to build structures that are at constant risk of demolition or confiscation for being unauthorized. OCHA considers 46 Palestinian communities in the West Bank to be at "high risk of forcible transfer due to a 'relocation' plan advanced by the Israeli authorities," and more than 100,000 Palestinians in East Jerusalem at risk of displacement. Save the Children considered, as of February, more than 50 kindergartens and primary schools, serving more than 5,000 Palestinian kids in the West Bank, at risk of demolition.

International law prohibits an occupying power from destroying property unless "absolutely necessary" for "military operations."

In the East Jerusalem neighborhoods of Sheikh Jarrah and Silwan, Israeli settler organizations advanced efforts to take possession of Palestinian homes and evict their long-term residents. They have done so under a discriminatory law, upheld by Israeli courts, that allow these groups to pursue claims for land they claim Jews owned in East Jerusalem before 1948. Palestinians, including Sheikh Jarrah residents set to be displaced, are barred under Israeli law from reclaiming property they owned in what became Israel, and from which they fled in 1948. A final court ruling on many of these cases is pending.

Freedom of Movement

Israeli authorities continued to require Palestinian ID holders with rare exceptions to hold difficult-to-obtain, time-limited permits to enter Israel and large parts of the West Bank, including East Jerusalem. B'Tselem describes this as "an arbitrary, entirely non-transparent bureaucratic system" where "many applications are denied without explanation, with no real avenue for appeal." Israeli authorities, as of June 2020, maintained nearly 600 checkpoints and other permanent obstacles within the West Bank, in addition to nearly 1,500 ad-hoc "flying" checkpoints erected between April 2019 and March 2020, according to OCHA. Israeli forces routinely turn away or delay and humiliate Palestinians at checkpoints without explanation, while permitting largely unfettered movement to Israeli settlers.

The separation barrier, which Israel said it built for security reasons but 85 percent of which falls within the West Bank rather than along the Green Line separating Israeli from Palestinian territory, cuts off thousands of Palestinians from their agricultural lands. It also isolates 11,000 Palestinians who live on the western side of the barrier but are not allowed to travel to Israel and whose ability to cross the barrier to access their property and basic services is highly restricted.

Palestinian Authority

Following the death in custody of activist Nizar al-Banat in June, the PA detained activists on manifestly political charges, like insulting "higher authorities" and creating "sectarian strife," that in effect criminalized peaceful dissent. Between January and September 2021, the ICHR received 87 complaints of arbitrary arrests, 15 of detention without trial or charge pursuant to orders from a regional governor, and 76 of torture and ill-treatment against the PA.

PA personal status laws discriminated against women, including in relation to marriage, divorce, custody of children and inheritance. Women's rights groups have documented an increase in reports of domestic violence since the beginning of the Covid-19 pandemic, with five women killed across the OPT in 2021. Palestine has no comprehensive domestic violence law. The PA is considering a draft family protection law, but women's rights groups have raised concern that it does not go far enough to prevent abuse and protect survivors.

The penal code in force in the West Bank and Gaza permits corporal punishment of children by parents, which remains a widespread practice.

ISRAEL

During the May hostilities, intercommunal violence broke out in cities where both Palestinian and Jewish citizens of Israelis lived, leaving three people killed and hundreds wounded, including both Palestinians and Jews. According to the Haifa-based Mossawa Center, more than 2,000 people were detained in the aftermath, over 90 percent of them Palestinians. Human rights groups accused the Israeli government of failing to sufficiently protect Palestinians from attacks by armed Jewish mobs.

In July, the Israeli Supreme Court upheld the Nation State Law, a law with constitutional status that affirms Israel as the "nation-state of the Jewish people," declares that within that territory the right to self-determination "is unique to the Jewish people," and establishes "Jewish settlement" as a national value.

The Knesset in July failed to renew a temporary order that had been in place since 2003 barring, with few exceptions, the granting of long-term legal status inside Israel to Palestinians from the West Bank and Gaza who marry Israeli citizens or residents. Interior Minister Ayelet Shaked instructed authorities to continue to act as if the law was in place while the Interior Ministry examines the implications of its expiration, prolonging the separation of many families. Such a restriction does not exist for spouses of virtually any other nationality.

Israeli authorities continued to systematically deny asylum claims of the roughly 31,000 Eritrean and Sudanese asylum seekers in the country. Over the years the government has imposed restrictions on their movement, work permits, and access to health care and to education in order to pressure them to leave.

Covid-19

The Covid-19 pandemic continued to affect communities in Israel and the OPT.

The Israeli government had vaccinated more than two-thirds of its citizens and residents and begun offering third booster shots, as of October. Israeli authorities provided vaccines to Palestinian citizens of Israel and residents of occupied East Jerusalem, as well as Israeli settlers in the West Bank, but not to most of the more than 4.7 million Palestinians living under Israeli control in the occupied West Bank and Gaza.

Israeli authorities claim this responsibility falls on the PA, but the Fourth Geneva Convention obliges occupying powers to ensure medical supplies, including to combat the spread of pandemics, to the occupied population. More than 1 million Palestinians in the West Bank, excluding Jerusalem residents, and 466,000 Palestinians in Gaza, were vaccinated as of October 21, according to the WHO, largely through vaccines obtained from external sources and administered by Palestinian authorities.

Key International Actors

During the May fighting, the Biden administration criticized rocket attacks by Palestinian armed groups, but not Israeli conduct, and proceeded with the sale of $735 million in arms to Israel, including of the kind of precision-guided munitions used in unlawful attacks in Gaza. This funding supplemented the annual $3.7 billion in security assistance the US provides and an additional $1 billion authorized in October.

In May, the UN Human Rights Council established an ongoing Commission of Inquiry (COI) to address abuses arising from the May hostilities and their root causes, including systematic discrimination and repression based on group identity across Israel and the OPT, and to promote accountability for those responsible. All Western states on the council abstained or voted against creating the COI.

The European Union condemned Israel's settlement policy and Israeli and Palestinian abuses, but divisions among EU member states have frustrated attempts to adopt more forceful measures.

During the May hostilities, Facebook wrongfully removed and suppressed content by Palestinians and their supporters, including about human rights abuses.

In February, the International Criminal Court (ICC) ruled that it has jurisdiction over serious crimes committed in the OPT. In March, the ICC prosecutor's office announced the opening of a formal investigation into the situation in Palestine.

The American company Ben & Jerry's announced in June that it will stop selling its ice cream in Israeli settlements, explaining that "it is inconsistent with our values for our product to be present within an internationally recognised illegal occupation."

Italy

The Covid-19 pandemic continued to impact daily life, including access to education and employment. Italy renewed its migration cooperation with Libya and obstructed sea rescue organizations while nonetheless allowing disembarkations in Italy. The Senate rejected a bill to make incitement to violence or discrimination based on sex, gender, sexual orientation or gender identity an offense. Authorities failed to take steps to ensure access to abortion in areas where significant barriers to access, including high rates of conscientious objection remain. The European Commission noted rule of law concerns with respect to the judiciary and the media.

Covid-19

The government imposed restrictions on movement and activity periodically in different parts of the country due to elevated Covid-19 transmission rates. As of mid-September, only Sicily had significant restrictions in place though limits on numbers allowed to gather in public spaces and mask mandates remained throughout Italy. The state of emergency, declared at the end of January 2020, was set to expire at the end of 2021.

Schools throughout the country and at different grade levels adopted hybrid and entirely distance learning approaches, with elementary schools largely returning to in-person schooling. Approximately 3 million Italian students may not have been able to access remote learning during school closures due to a lack of internet connectivity or devices at home, according to estimates by the Italian National Institute of Statistics. Some schools adopted positive measures to ensure quality education for students with disabilities, including safe in-person learning, though organizations representing people with disabilities said that many children with disabilities did not receive a quality, inclusive education, or in some cases, any education at all during the pandemic.

Despite a slow start, Italy's vaccination campaign had reached 80 percent of the eligible population by mid-October. As of mid-October, possession of proof of vaccination, a negative test, or recovery from Covid—the "green pass"—was obligatory in virtually all public spaces and private workplaces. Undocumented migrants and people experiencing homelessness faced bureaucratic and other obstacles to accessing the vaccine, and even when vaccinated, faced obstacles to obtaining the green pass.

Despite early release programs to alleviate overcrowding in prisons during the pandemic, in June Italian prisons were at 113 percent capacity according to the quasi-independent ombudsman for people deprived of their liberty. Limits on prison visits, movement within facilities, and other activities, imposed during the pandemic, remained in place in some prisons. Vaccination rates in prisons were in line with national rates.

Migrants and Asylum Seekers

Italy evacuated 4,890 Afghans—individuals who had worked with the Italian military mission and their families—out of Kabul between June and August. At time of writing, it was unclear whether they would be processed under the normal asylum procedure or would be granted prima facie refugee status. The government was pursuing arrangements to allow municipalities, associations, and private citizens to host Afghan families due to lack of capacity in the state reception system. In November the government announced agreements with faith-based and civil society organizations to facilitate "humanitarian corridors" to Italy for 1,200 Afghans from countries neighboring Afghanistan.

In January, a court in Rome ruled that pushbacks to Slovenia under a decades-old readmission agreement violated the Italian Constitution, the European Convention on Human Rights, and the EU Charter on Fundamental Rights because of the risk of chain refoulement and inhuman and degrading treatment in neighboring countries along the Balkan route. Migrants faced dire humanitarian conditions in border regions with France, while French police summarily returned unaccompanied children and adults to Italy.

In July, parliament renewed funding for migration cooperation with Libya despite overwhelming evidence of brutality against migrants, the systematic use of arbitrary detention, and the complete absence of an asylum system in Libya. Libyan forces receiving support from Italy and the EU interdicted at sea and took back to Libya more than 27,500 people by late October.

According to government statistics, more than 52,770 people reached Italy by sea, including 7,190 unaccompanied children, by late October. There was an increase in boats arriving without the assistance of rescue ships to Lampedusa, an Italian island in the Mediterranean Sea, where the reception facility able to accommodate up to 250 people was periodically well over capacity, with more than 1,200 at one point in August.

Italian authorities allowed nongovernmental rescue ships to disembark, usually after some delay. However, they also often held ships in port for administrative reasons, inhibiting rescue efforts. The Council of Europe Commissioner for Human Rights expressed concern about Italy's use of ferries to quarantine people arriving by sea and called on the government to prioritize prompt disembarkation on land.

According to the International Organization for Migration, 1,224 persons died or went missing in the central Mediterranean by late October, many while attempting to cross to Italy.

In January, the UN Human Rights Committee found Italy responsible for contributing to the deaths in 2013 of an estimated 200 people, including 60 children, when it failed to respond adequately to distress calls about an overcrowded migrant boat in the Mediterranean.

Prosecutors in Agrigento opened an investigation in July against Libyan authorities for "attempted shipwreck" of a migrant boat following a complaint, with footage and photos, filed by the nongovernmental organization Sea-Watch of an incident in late June in which a Libyan coast guard boat maneuvered dangerously and appears to fire shots. In May, the same office dropped all charges against Carola Rackete, the Sea-Watch captain who had docked her rescue ship in Lampedusa without authorization in 2019.

In the first ruling of its kind against a commercial ship's captain, in October a court in Naples convicted and sentenced to one year in prison the captain of the Asso 28, a service ship for an Italian oil platform in the Mediterranean Sea, for returning more than 100 people to Libya in July 2018 following a rescue.

The trial of former Interior Minister Matteo Salvini for abduction and dereliction of duty over his handling of the disembarkation of 147 people from a rescue ship belonging to the Spanish NGO Open Arms in August 2019 began in October in Palermo. In May, a judge in Catania dismissed a similar case against Salvini involving a delay in disembarkation from an Italian military ship, also in 2019.

One year after a flawed program was launched to provide residency permits to undocumented migrants working in agriculture, domestic work, and home care, only 25 percent of the roughly 207,800 applications had been processed.

In September, a court in Calabria convicted and sentenced Domenico Lucano, the former mayor of Riace, to more than 13 years in prison—double what prosecutors had requested—on charges of abetting irregular immigration and irregularities in a program that settled and employed hundreds of asylum seekers in the small town.

Discrimination and Intolerance

At time of writing, the trial of four men was ongoing for the brutal beating to death in September 2020 of 21-year-old Willy Monteiro Duarte, a Black Italian, in a town on the outskirts of Rome. The men are accused of voluntary homicide; prosecutors did not charge them with the aggravating circumstance of racial bias.

One year after it was approved by the lower house of parliament, the Senate rejected a bill to make incitement to violence or discrimination "based on sex, gender, sexual orientation or gender identity" a crime. The bill would have broadened existing law on bias crimes in Italy, increased funding for projects to prevent and counter violence based on sexual orientation and gender identity, as well as for victim support, and instituted a national day against homophobia.

Women's Rights

The Council of Europe Committee of Social Rights said in January that Italy had failed to take adequate measures to ensure access to abortion under national law given the high number of conscientious objectors among healthcare workers. In its annual report on access to abortion, in July, the Ministry of Health provided data from 2019 indicating that 67 percent of gynecologists and 43.5

percent of anesthesiologists in Italy refuse to perform abortions, a slight decrease over the previous year.

Data published in May showed that calls to the national hotline for victims of gender-based violence and stalking increased by 79 percent in 2020, in particular during the months of lockdown, compared to the year before. The government said that reports of gender-based violence decreased by 8 percent in the first half of the year compared to the same period in 2020. The Interior Ministry reported that 86 women were killed by relatives or people they knew in the first ten months of the year, 59 of them by a partner or ex-partner.

At time of writing, the executive branch had yet to formally ratify International Labour Organization Convention 190 on violence and harassment in employment though parliament gave its approval in January.

Rule of Law

In its July European rule of law report, the European Commission noted the need to strengthen judicial independence and tackle excessive length of proceedings in Italy. The report cited the lack of an effective law regulating conflicts of interest in the media sector as reason for concern over political interference in media freedom and called physical attacks and intimidation against journalists in Italy "an issue of concern." Italy's Interior Ministry recorded a 19 percent increase in such cases in the first seven months of 2021 compared to the same period in 2020.

The revelation in April that prosecutors in Sicily secretly recorded hundreds of conversations between at least 15 journalists working on migration issues and NGO staff caused significant concern about violation of confidentiality.

HUMAN
RIGHTS
WATCH

#EqualityActJapan
日本にもLGBT平等法を

REPORTERS' GUIDE
For the 2020 Summer Olympic and
Paralympic Games in Tokyo, Japan

Japan

Japan is a liberal democracy with a vigorous civil society. In October, the Liberal Democratic Party's (LDP) Fumio Kishida became Japan's prime minister succeeding Yoshihide Suga, who served for about a year. The LDP secured a sole majority in the lower house election held on October 31.

Japan has no law prohibiting racial, ethnic, or religious discrimination, or discrimination based on sexual orientation or gender identity. Japan does not have a national human rights institution.

Covid-19

Japan declared states of emergency in response to the Covid-19 pandemic three separate times in 2021 (January-March, April-June , and July-September). In February, Japan revised its laws to allow authorities to impose administrative fines on businesses for not complying with business hour restrictions, as well as on individuals infected with Covid-19 who refuse hospitalization.

In May, Japan's government said it would not oppose, but also did not endorse, a temporary waiver at the World Trade Organization of intellectual property laws that would allow increased global production of Covid-19 vaccines and other medical products.

Tokyo 2020 Olympic and Paralympic Games

The Tokyo 2020 Olympic and Paralympic Games were hosted in Japan between July and September 2021 after being delayed for a year due to the Covid-19 pandemic. In February, Yoshiro Mori, the head of the Tokyo Olympics organizing committee, resigned after making sexist remarks about adding women to the Olympics Committee board. Keigo Oyamada, the music composer for the Olympics opening and closing ceremonies, resigned in July after a past interview resurfaced in which he admitted to bullying classmates with disabilities. Kentaro Kobayashi, the show director of the opening and closing ceremonies, was fired in July over his past comments about the Holocaust.

Refugees

Japan's asylum and refugee determination system remains strongly oriented against granting refugee status. In 2020, the Justice Ministry received 3,936 applications for refugee status, but recognized only 47 people as refugees, and categorized another 44 persons as needing humanitarian assistance, allowing them to stay in Japan.

In February, the government proposed an amendment to the Immigration Control and Refugee Recognition Act that would allow for supervised release upon payment of a deposit for people subject to a deportation measure as an alternative to detention. In March, four UN human rights experts said the amendment continued to embody a "presumption of detention," rather than treating detention as a measure of last resort. The amendment also introduced, for the first time, a provision in Japanese law for complementary protection for non-refugees who need protection, but still fell short of meeting Japan's nonrefoulement obligations, according to UNHCR.

Sri Lankan migrant Wishma Sandamali, 33, died in detention in March, after being denied access to adequate medical treatment by detention authorities. With intensified domestic and international criticism following her death, on top of existing criticism of the bill, the Japanese government, in a rare move, dropped the amendment in May.

Death Penalty

In December, Japan executed three people on death row. At the end of 2021, there were 107 people on death row. Concerns have long been raised about death-row inmates being notified of their execution only on the day it takes place and having inadequate access to legal counsel.

In November, two prisoners on death row sued the government seeking compensation for the "extremely inhumane" same-day notices and executions.

Women's Rights

In June, to encourage men to take childcare leave, Japan revised the Act on Childcare and Caregiver Leave. A new provision allows male employees to take up to four weeks of leave during the first eight weeks after their child is born on top of benefits already offered by the childcare leave system. The revised law also requires corporations to proactively confirm with their employees, regardless of their gender, whether they are interested in using childcare leave benefits. The use of childcare leave by men remained low, at less than 10 percent in 2019.

Following a 2015 decision, Japan's Supreme Court, in June, again ruled the country's lack of a dual-surname system for married couples is constitutional. Some 96 percent of married couples end up using their husband's surname, partly due to social norms and socioeconomic inequalities.

Children's Rights

In February, the Osaka District Court ruled that a public high school forcing a student to dye her hair black according to school rules was legal. In October, the Osaka High Court ruled against the student's appeal, judging the school's actions as legal. Many schools in Japan continue to dictate the color of their students' hair, clothes, and, in certain cases, their underwear.

In May, Japan's parliament passed a law to curb sexual abuse against children by teachers. The new law included the revision of the School Teacher's License Act to allow regional educational boards to refuse the reissuing of teaching licenses to teachers who lost their teaching licenses for sexually abusing children. Previously, the authorities were not able to do so if three years had passed since teachers' licenses were revoked.

Sexual Orientation and Gender Identity

In a landmark decision, the Sapporo District Court, in March, ruled that the government's failure to recognize same-sex marriages is unconstitutional and discriminatory in the country's first judicial ruling on marriage equality. Similar trials are pending at five district courts, including in Tokyo and Osaka.

HUMAN
RIGHTS
WATCH

"The Law Undermines Dignity"
Momentum to Revise Japan's Legal Gender Recognition Process

Japan failed to pass a national non-discrimination law to protect lesbian, gay, bisexual, and transgender (LGBT) people, despite widespread national support and strong global pressure to pass such a law before the Tokyo 2020 Games were held.

The government still requires sterilization surgeries before transgender people can be legally recognized.

Right to Health

In July, then-Prime Minister Yoshihide Suga said he would not appeal a Hiroshima High Court ruling extending recognition and benefits to a broader range of individuals affected by radioactive "black rain" caused by the US atomic bombings in Hiroshima and Nagasaki. Following the ruling, Suga issued a statement that effectively overturned Japan's previous position of not recognizing many victims of "black rain" as "Hibakushas," atomic bomb survivors entitled to government relief.

Forced Disappearances by North Korea

In August, the Tokyo District Court summoned North Korea's leader Kim Jong Un to face demands for compensation from five North Korean escapees in Japan, who say they suffered human rights abuses in North Korea after joining a resettlement program on false premises that North Korea was a "Paradise on Earth." The judgment is scheduled to be delivered on March 23, 2022. Approximately 93,000 ethnic Koreans (Zainichi) and Japanese migrated from Japan to North Korea under the program's auspices between 1959 and 1984.

Japan continues to demand the return of 12 Japanese citizens whom North Korea abducted in the 1970s and 1980s. Some Japanese civil society groups insist the number of abductees is much higher.

Climate Change Policies and Impacts

Japan is among the top 10 emitters of greenhouse gases responsible for the climate crisis that is taking a growing toll on human rights around the globe.

Then-Prime Minister Suga announced in October 2020 that Japan will cut emissions to net zero by 2050 and, in April 2021, announced an emissions reduction target of 46 percent by 2030, earning it an "almost sufficient" rating for its "Domestic Target" from the Climate Action Tracker.

Following the Fukushima nuclear accident in 2011, Japan increased its reliance on fossil fuels, including coal to generate electricity. In July 2021, Japan released a draft of its 2030 strategic energy strategy that stated Japan would aim to reduce coal to 19 percent of energy use by 2030, just a 13 percentage point reduction from current levels. Japan's government, financial institutions, and industrial companies are also major providers of finance and technical support for development of overseas coal plants, second only to China. Despite announcements restricting coal lending, loopholes in these policies mean Japan continues to be a lender to a variety of high-emitting coal plans, including in Bangladesh, Vietnam, and Indonesia.

Climate change is expected to have a significant impact on Japan due to sea-level rise, increased summer heat, shifting precipitation patterns, and more frequent and intense extreme weather events. In August, the heaviest rain since 1982 caused flooding and landslides in some locations that left at least 13 people dead.

Foreign Policy

Japan officially states it aims to "contribute to the improvement of the world's human rights environment," but has not played a leadership role.

After the Myanmar military staged a coup in February, Japan suspended new non-humanitarian aid to Myanmar and supported a Myanmar resolution at the UN General Assembly in June, a major shift from its continual abstention since 2017. Japanese business projects in Myanmar including Y-Complex, a high-end real estate project in Yangon, continued to face criticism for its connections to the Myanmar military.

After the Taliban returned to power in Afghanistan, Japan's response for fleeing Afghan civilians at risk has been to provide visas for a limited number of Afghans with past ties to Japan. Pledges for resettlement have not been announced. At time of writing, Afghans eligible for the scheme were those who worked directly with the Japanese government and their families, those who worked directly with private Japanese organizations, and Afghan students who studied in Japan, but not family members. Details of the scheme had not been publicly disclosed.

Japan again led the negotiation of a resolution at the UN Human Rights Council on the human rights situation in Cambodia. The adopted resolution was weak, and while it failed to sufficiently reflect the deteriorating human rights situation in the country, it did renew the mandate of the special rapporteur and increase international scrutiny ahead of the 2022 elections, through additional reporting to the Human Rights Council.

Jordan

In 2021, Jordanian authorities did not rescind a state of emergency declared in March 2020 in response to the Covid-19 pandemic, granting the prime minister sweeping powers to rule by decree.

In June, King Abdullah II convened a 92-member committee to make recommendations for reforming and modernizing Jordan's political system. In October, the committee, chaired by former Prime Minister Samir Rifai, issued recommendations for amending laws on political parties and elections, but it was unclear whether the recommendations would improve access to political participation across Jordanian society.

On July 12, Jordan's State Security Court convicted a former high-level official and a little-known royal family member of "sowing discord" and "inciting opposition to the political regime," sentencing both of them to 15 years in prison for allegedly undertaking a plot to "mobilize public opinion against the ruling regime in the kingdom and propose Prince Hamza [King Abdullah II's younger half-brother] as an alternative to take rule."

Freedom of Expression

Jordanian law criminalizes speech deemed critical of the king, foreign countries, government officials and institutions, Islam and Christianity, and defamatory speech.

Jordanian authorities further curtailed press freedom in 2021 by issuing arbitrary press gag orders prohibiting reporting on important local developments, including local reporting on the ongoing crackdown on the independent Teachers' Syndicate and the April arrests of individuals connected to Prince Hamza accused of undertaking a plot to undermine the country's leadership. Jordanian press outlets did not report on revelations about the king's real estate holdings in the United States and United Kingdom as part of the Pandora Papers reporting in October.

Freedom of Association and Assembly

In 2021 Jordan's Ministry of Social Development convened a committee to draft amendments to Jordan's Law on Associations (NGO law) but as of October 2021 the committee, which included representatives of local and international non-governmental organizations (NGOs), had yet to issue the draft amendments.

Under the Public Gatherings Law amended in March 2011, Jordan did not require government permission to hold public meetings or demonstrations, but organizations and venues continued to be required to obtain permission from the Interior Ministry or General Intelligence Department to host events. In August, Jordanian security authorities blocked a public book launch hosted in part by the Ministry of Culture.

Jordanian authorities in 2021 continued a crackdown on the independent Teachers Syndicate, keeping it shuttered on dubious legal grounds, and on December 31, 2020, a Jordanian court sentenced the syndicate leaders to one year in prison on vague charges after an unfair trial.

Refugees and Migrants

By late 2021, over 670,000 people from Syria had sought refuge in Jordan, according to the UN High Commissioner for Refugees (UNHCR). Over 85 percent of Syrians lived outside refugee camps in rented accommodation.

According to the UNHCR, Jordan also hosted asylum seekers and refugees from other countries in 2021, including 66,665 Iraqis, 12,866 Yemenis, 6,013 Sudanese, 696 Somalis, and 1,453 from other countries. Authorities continued to enforce a January 2019 decision banning the UNHCR from registering as asylum seekers individuals who officially entered the country for the purposes of medical treatment, study, tourism, or work, effectively barring recognition of non-Syrians as refugees and leaving many without UNHCR documentation or access to services.

Jordanian authorities in 2021 deported at least six Yemeni asylum seekers registered with UNHCR and issued deportation orders against others who made asylum claims. The authorities handed down most of the deportation orders after the Yemenis attempted to apply for work permits and regularize their immigration status in the country.

Authorities continued to implement the Jordan Compact, the 2016 agreement between the Jordanian government and donor countries, which aimed to improve the livelihoods of Syrian refugees by granting new legal work opportunities and improving the education sector. By the end of 2020, labor authorities had issued or renewed at least 215,668 work permits for Syrians since 2016, although many of these were renewals. The number of currently valid individual permits was not reported but was apparently much lower. Most professions remained closed to non-Jordanians, and many Syrians continued to work in the informal sector without labor protections.

The roughly 230,000 school-age Syrian refugees in Jordan face multiple obstacles to education that are most acute for children ages 12 and older, including poverty-driven child labor and child marriage, lack of affordable school transportation, government policies that limit access to education, and lack of inclusive education and accommodation for children with disabilities.

Only a quarter of secondary-school-age Syrian refugee children in Jordan were enrolled in school. Non-Syrians refugees and asylum seekers were in many cases prevented from enrolling their children in school in 2021. Children without official identification numbers were unable to access online learning platforms during Covid-19 school closures.

Authorities did not allow aid deliveries from Jordan to tens of thousands of Syrians at Rukban, an unofficial camp along Jordan's border with Syria. Authorities deported Syrians to Rukban in 2020 without permitting them to challenge their deportations.

The economic downturn and drastic lockdown measures have undermined the livelihoods of thousands of Syrian refugees. Syrian refugees who voluntarily returned to Syria between 2017 and 2021 from Jordan faced grave human rights abuses and persecution at the hands of Syrian government and affiliated militias, including torture, extra-judicial killings, and kidnappings. While Jordan does not impose a formal re-entry ban on Syrian refugees, Jordanian border guards said they could not re-enter Jordan for three to five years, denying returnees the right to claim asylum if, having returned to Syria, they again face persecution.

Jordan hosted an estimated 70,000 migrant domestic workers in 2021, mostly from the Philippines, Sri Lanka, and Indonesia. NGOs repeatedly referred domestic workers who had suffered multiple abuses to labor ministry investigators. Abuses included non-payment of wages, unsafe working conditions, long hours, document confiscation, and physical, verbal, and sexual abuse.

Women's and Girls' Rights

Jordan's personal status code remains discriminatory, despite amendments in 2019. Women need the permission of a male guardian to marry for the first time, and marriages between Muslim women and non-Muslim men are not recognized. Women cannot travel abroad with their children, as men can, without the permission of their child's father or male guardian or a judge. While women can travel outside the country without needing permission, authorities sometimes comply with requests from male guardians to bar their unmarried adult daughters, wives, and children from leaving the country. Authorities also arrest women reported as "absent" for fleeing their home by their male guardians under the Crime Prevention Law.

Article 98 of Jordan's penal code, amended in 2017, states that the "fit of fury" defense does not allow mitigated sentences for perpetrators of crimes "against women," but judges continued to impose mitigated sentences under article 99 if family members of victims did not support prosecutions of their male family members. Article 340 of the Penal Code also allows a man to receive a reduced sentence if he kills or attacks his wife or any of his female relatives in the alleged act of committing adultery or in an "unlawful bed."

Such discriminatory laws leave women exposed to violence. Jordan's Higher Population Council reported in October that it recorded a "dramatic increase" in domestic violence in 2020 with a total of 54,743 cases, with 82 percent perpetrated by husbands against their wives. In 2021, Tadamon (Sisterhood is Global Institute Jordan - SIGI), reported that men in Jordan had murdered more than 14 women between January and October 2021. Similarly, the penal code and Juve-

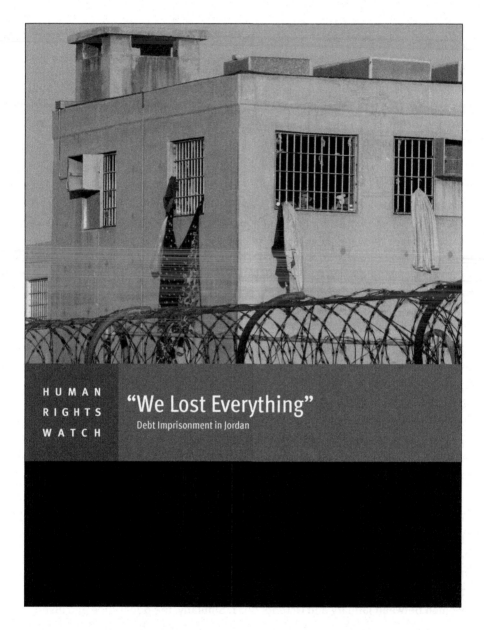

HUMAN
RIGHTS
WATCH

"We Lost Everything"
Debt Imprisonment in Jordan

niles Act do not prohibit corporal punishment and allow parents to punish children in accordance with "general norms."

Article 9 of Jordan's nationality law does not allow Jordanian women married to non-Jordanian spouses to pass on their nationality to their spouse and children. In 2014, authorities issued a cabinet decision purporting to ease restrictions on access to key economic and social rights for non-citizen children of Jordanian women, but the measures fell short of expectations. Non-citizen children of Jordanian women no longer require work permits for employment, but many professions in Jordan remained closed to non-Jordanians.

Sexual Orientation and Gender Identity

Jordan has no laws that explicitly criminalize same-sex relations. The penal code includes vague "immorality" provisions that could be used to target sexual and gender minorities. Jordanian law does not prohibit discrimination based on sexual orientation and gender identity.

Jordan summarily deports foreign nationals found to be HIV-positive, and LGBT people living with HIV have reported facing stigma and discrimination by medical professionals and employers, without any legal recourse.

Criminal Justice

In March, Jordanian authorities issued a suspension of detentions for failure to repay a debt until the end of the year. The announcement came shortly after Human Rights Watch issued a report documenting Jordan's harsh treatment of people unable to repay their debts. The report showed how in the absence of an adequate social security net, tens of thousands of Jordanians feel compelled to take out loans to cover utilities, groceries, school fees, and medical bills, often using unregulated informal lenders, and face months of detention when they fail to repay.

As of November, authorities had not carried out any executions in 2021.

Local governors continued to use provisions of the Crime Prevention Law of 1954 to place individuals in administrative detention for up to one year, in circumvention of the Criminal Procedure Law.

Key International Actors

In 2021, the US president requested US$1.275 billion in Foreign Military Financing, Economic Support, and other aid to Jordan. This exceeds the amount outlined in the 2018 Memorandum of Understanding between the United States and Jordan. The US did not publicly criticize human rights violations in Jordan in 2021, except in annual reports of the State Department and other agencies.

Jordan is a member of the Saudi Arabia and UAE-led coalition fighting the Houthi forces in Yemen, which continues to commit violations of international human rights and humanitarian law in Yemen.

Kazakhstan

The Kazakh government continued to claim it is pursuing human rights reforms, despite the absence of meaningful improvements in its rights record. Authorities cracked down on government critics using overbroad "extremism" charges, restricted the right to peaceful protest, suppressed free speech, and failed to address impunity for domestic violence and torture. The government did not extend Covid-19 related economic assistance into 2021, although the pandemic continued to affect living standards, employment, and schooling.

There was an increase in spontaneous strikes, with workers across the country demanding better pay and working conditions. In June, the International Labour Organization (ILO) heavily criticized Kazakhstan for violating international labor rights standards. In September, a Russian-American Xinjiang researcher was arbitrarily banned from Kazakhstan for five years. A new inclusive education law is a positive development, but many children with disabilities continue to be denied the right to education.

Parliamentary Elections

Kazakhstan held parliamentary elections on January 10, 2021. The Organization for Security and Co-operation in Europe Office for Democratic Institutions and Human Rights (OSCE/ODHIR) election monitoring mission concluded that the elections were "technically prepared efficiently," but "lacked genuine competition" and that the electoral process needed reform. The ruling Nur Otan Party retained its qualified majority in parliament.

Civil Society

In December 2020 and January 2021, tax authorities targeted over a dozen leading nongovernmental groups (NGOs) with fines and suspensions for allegedly violating rules for reporting on foreign grants. After sustained public outcry, authorities in February dropped the fines and suspension decisions. In February the United Nations Human Rights Commissioner Michele Bachelet called on the authorities to "eliminate far-reaching reporting requirements" affecting freedom of association.

The human rights defender, Max Bokaev, imprisoned for five years in 2016 for peacefully protesting against proposed land reforms, was released on February 4, but remains subject to heavy restrictions. On February 3, police temporarily detained the Uralsk-based journalist Lukpan Akhmedyarov to prevent him from meeting Bokaev.

Prison officials continued to target Elena Semenova, a Pavlodar-based rights defender who monitors prison conditions, with over a dozen spurious lawsuits in 2021 in response to her human rights activities.

The UN Working Group on Arbitrary Detention on May 28 found that imprisoned labor activist Erzhan Elshibaev had been arbitrarily detained. The group called for his immediate release and said he should be provided compensation and other reparations.

Freedom of Assembly

Authorities continued to routinely interfere and restrict the right to peaceful assembly by detaining, fining, or sentencing to short-term custodial sentences people who tried to exercise this right. Police also increasingly resorted to "kettling" protesters, de facto detaining groups on the street for up to 10 hours. On rare occasions, city authorities granted permission for protests, for example in Uralsk in late February, to a group of approximately 200 people calling for the release of political prisoners.

In February, a small group of ethnic Kazakhs began to gather daily outside the Chinese consulate in Almaty to demand that their detained or disappeared loved ones in Xinjiang, China, be released and reunited with them in Kazakhstan. In June and July police detained several protesters who were later sentenced to up to 17 days' administrative detention.

Orynbai Okhasov, an activist from Uralsk who was sentenced to a one-year parole-like sentence in mid-November for alleged participation in a banned "extremist" organization, spent 45 days in jail in July and August serving three consecutive administrative sentences for violating Kazakhstan's restrictive public assembly law.

Freedom of Expression

Journalists continue to face harassment, arrest, physical attack, and prosecution for carrying out their work. In September, parliament passed a draft law on the protection of children in its first reading that contains provisions threatening freedom of expression. The provisions, if adopted, would require foreign social media platforms to register locally and comply with content removal requests within 24 hours. In May, police initiated a criminal investigation on charges of "disseminating knowingly false information" against Temirlan Ensebek, a 25-year-old who ran a satirical Instagram account for less than a month before shutting it down.

In July, the Organized Crime and Corruption Reporting Project, a member of the international investigative journalism collaboration Pegasus Project, reported that the phone numbers of human rights defender, Bakytzhan Toregozhina, and journalists Serikzhan Mauletbay and Bigeldy Gabdullin appear to have been selected for targeting with spyware.

In March, the UN Human Rights Committee (UNHRC) found that the state had violated Dmitry Tikhonov's rights to freedom of expression and peaceful assembly by detaining him in February 2014 while he was trying to report on a peaceful protest.

In August, an Almaty court convicted the blogger Ermek Taichibekov on overbroad criminal charges of "inciting national discord through mass media" and sentenced him to seven years in prison.

OSCE Media Freedom Representative Teresa Ribeiro, upon concluding a visit to Kazakhstan on September 17, said she raised with government officials in Kazakhstan the issue of journalists' safety, disinformation, legislative developments, and other challenges.

Arrest and Harassment of Opposition Members

Kazakh authorities have continued their multi-year crackdown on government critics, targeting with criminal prosecution perceived or actual members of banned "extremist" groups, including for participating in peaceful rallies. Courts convicted dozens of people in 2021, subjecting them to restrictions including multi-year bans on engaging in political activities, and imprisoned at least seven people: Askar Kaiyrbek, Erbol Eskhozhin, and Ulasbek Akhmetov, as well as Askhat Zheksebaev, Kairat Kylyshev, Abai Begimbetov, and Noyan Rakhimzhanov.

On July 30, Aset Abishev, who was imprisoned in 2018 for alleged participation in the banned Democratic Choice of Kazakhstan, was released on parole after serving two-and-a-half years of a four-year sentence.

Labor Rights

In February 2021, a Shymkent court suspended the independent Industrial Trade Union of Fuel and Energy Workers for six months for allegedly failing to register in accordance with Kazakhstan's restrictive 2014 trade union law. The Congress of Free Trade Unions of Kazakhstan, Kazakhstan's largest independent trade union, remains unable to register.

There was an increase in spontaneous workers' strikes and local initiatives to unionize in 2021, including in Aktobe region, Nursultan, and Almaty. Authorities in some cases took legal action against workers for organizing "illegal" strikes.

In June, the ILO issued highly critical conclusions and recommendations on Kazakhstan's compliance with the Freedom of Association and Protection of the Right to Organise Convention, instructing the government to "stop judicial harassment practices of trade union leaders" and review the cases of individual union leaders.

Violence against Women and Girls

President Kasym-Jomart Tokaev has repeatedly noted that domestic violence is an acute problem and protection of women's rights is key. Yet in January, parliament suspended review of a new draft domestic violence law and has not, since then, proposed any new legislation offering strengthened protection to women from family abuse. Meanwhile, police and service providers lack appropriate training to identify, prevent, and adequately respond to domestic violence.

Hundreds of people participated in a march authorized by Almaty city authorities for the first time celebrating International Women's Day on March 8. Participants called for gender equality and criminalization of domestic violence.

Disability Rights

In June, Kazakhstan adopted a new inclusive education law that removed multiple references to a problematic medical and educational exam as a prerequisite for enrolment in a mainstream school and introduced new provisions that make it state responsibility to provide children with disabilities with reasonable accommodations.

In practice, many children do not have access to inclusive education and remain isolated in segregated special schools or residential institutions, where they can face violence, neglect, physical restraint, and overmedication. Kazakhstan has no national plan to close such institutions. Covid-related restrictions on in-person education in the first half of the year continued to negatively impact children with disabilities, because of poor internet connectivity and because digital learning platforms are not sufficiently adapted to their needs.

Sexual Orientation and Gender Identity

Kazakhstan does not have an anti-discrimination law, nor does its constitution prohibit discrimination on the basis of gender identity or sexual orientation. The process for changing one's legally recognized gender remains invasive and humiliating.

In May in Shymkent and again in July, in Karaganda, mobs of hostile men attacked small closed-door trainings on women's rights led by Feminita, a rights group that focuses on lesbian, bisexual, and queer women. In response, police detained Feminita co-leaders Zhanar Sekerbaeva and Gulzada Serzhan and escorted them out of each city.

On May 17, over a dozen ambassadors of embassies in Nursultan issued a joint statement on International Day Against Homophobia, Biphobia, and Transphobia expressing solidarity with lesbian, gay, bisexual, and transgender (LGBT) people and calling on the government to protect all citizens of Kazakhstan from discrimination.

Torture

Torture and ill-treatment occur with impunity in Kazakhstan. Radio Azattyk, the Kazakh branch of Radio Free Europe/Radio Liberty, reported in July that out of 120 torture allegations that prison facilities had registered between January and May, no cases had been sent to court.

After members of the National Preventive Mechanism (NPM), an anti-torture body, visited the 68-year-old poet and dissident Aron Atabek and reported that Atabek's health had significantly deteriorated, he was hospitalized. On October 1, Atabek, who was sentenced in 2006 to 18 years in prison for his alleged role in organizing mass riots outside Almaty, was released on parole on grounds of his ill-health. He was completely emaciated. Several weeks after his release, Atabek died in a hospital in Almaty.

Poverty and Inequality

Kazakhstan's economy recovered slightly in 2021, but following the economic downturn that occurred in 2020 in connection with the Covid-19 pandemic and a weak social safety net, Kazakhstan's poverty rate has increased to 12-14 percent, according to World Bank estimates. Mothers with multiple children across Kazakhstan continued in 2021 to intermittently protest for increased social and housing benefits.

Key International Actors

The European Parliament (EP) in February issued a strongly worded resolution on the human rights situation in Kazakhstan, focusing on the crackdown on civil society, torture, free speech, and politically motivated persecution. The EP called on the government to "end all forms of arbitrary detention, reprisals and harassment" against activists and other groups and to amend the new peaceful assembly law.

In Kazakhstan in August, the newly appointed European Union special representative on Central Asia, Terhi Hakala, discussed human rights and gender equality with the authorities. In October, the EU special representative on human rights,

Eamon Gilmore, met rights defenders and government officials, including President Tokaev, during his visit to Kazakhstan.

In October, Kazakhstan was elected to sit on the UN Human Rights Council from January 2022.

HUMAN RIGHTS WATCH

"We Are All Vulnerable Here"

Kenya's Pandemic Cash Transfer Program Riddled With Irregularities

Kenya

Kenya's human rights trajectory has remained a concern, with authorities failing to ensure accountability for serious abuses throughout 2021. Kenya, with a long history of violent elections, is set to hold general elections in August 2022. In the aftermath of the 2017 elections, police responded violently to opposition supporters' protesting alleged vote rigging, resulting in the death of over 100 people. Kenyan authorities have done little to ensure accountability for election-related abuses in the past.

In mid-2021, the authorities ordered the closure of both Daadab and Kakuma refugee camps by June 2022, although conditions in countries of origin, notably Somalia and South Sudan, were not yet conducive for safe returns.

The ongoing Covid-19 crisis has devastated many livelihoods across Kenya. A large number of individuals and families lost some or all of their sources of income, with business closures and job losses.

Extrajudicial killings by police, including during the enforcement of Covid-19 containment measures, have remained largely unaddressed. The two main police accountability institutions, the Independent Policing Oversight Authority (IPOA) and Police Internal Affairs Unit, have been unable, for various reasons, including lack of political will, to promptly investigate and prosecute incidents of police killings. IPOA started work in 2012 and, eight years later, has managed just nine successful prosecutions for various offences, mostly for murder, despite commencing investigations into more than 500 new incidents each year.

Abuses Related to Covid-19 Pandemic

In a July 2021 report, which focused on the socio-economic impact of the Covid-19 pandemic on informal settlements in the capital, Nairobi, Human Rights Watch found that the pandemic devastated many livelihoods, as thousands of individuals and families, who lost some or all of their sources of income, with business closures and job losses, faced the threat of hunger and eviction. Children went hungry and did not get needed urgent medical treatment.

The authorities were slow to respond to the needs of the vulnerable groups, including households in informal settlements. When the authorities finally created the eight-month cash transfer program, it was inadequate and short-lived. It provided no clear information about eligibility, how beneficiaries were identified, or why thousands of households that met the approved criteria were excluded.

The Kenyan government, which has a responsibility to ensure no one goes hungry, failed to design a social security program that would guarantee everyone, not just a few, an adequate standard of living during the pandemic. Only a small fraction of vulnerable families in Nairobi benefited from the program, which was characterized by lack of transparency, cronyism, nepotism, and outright favoritism. The authorities confirmed that the program reached just 29,000 out of over 600, 000 households in Nairobi's eight informal settlements. This amounts to approximately 4.8 percent of all the households in dire need of support.

Abuses by Security Forces

Despite public criticism, the police continued to use excessive force while enforcing coronavirus control measures in 2021. While the government had since eased most of the measures, save for the curfew that was lifted in October, police brutality has persisted.

On August 1, police in Kianjokoma town, Embu County, eastern Kenya, detained two brothers Emmanuel Marura Ndwiga, 19, and Benson Njiru Ndwiga, 22, for violating the 10 p.m. to 4 a.m. curfew. Relatives found their bodies at a local morgue three days later. The officers who arrested the duo claimed they fell from the moving police vehicle, but an autopsy found that the head and rib injuries found on the bodies were inconsistent with the alleged fall. These findings triggered public protests which the police violently suppressed, killing one person. On August 15, the Director of Public Prosecutions Noordin Haji charged six police officers with the killing of the two brothers.

In other instances, as in the case of Robert Mutahi, police extorted money from people arrested for violating the curfew. Mutahi told media that three police officers detained him on August 12 and forced him to transfer money from his phone to them. The three officers have since been charged with robbery with violence.

Refugee Rights

In March 2021, authorities issued a two-week ultimatum to the United Nations refugee agency, UNHCR, to draft a plan for closing both Daadab and Kakuma refugee camps, citing alleged security risks. The camps hosted over 433,000 refugees as of mid-2021, the majority Somali and South Sudanese.

In April, the government announced its intention to close both camps by June 2022, and UNHCR proposed a roadmap encompassing voluntary repatriation, some "departures to third countries," and "alternative stay options in Kenya for certain refugees from East African Community (EAC) countries." However, the latter does not include Somalia, previous "voluntary" repatriation efforts had proved involuntary and coercive, and the security situations in Somalia and South Sudan remained far from safe for return, as they risked being tortured or killed.

Kenya previously threatened in 2016 and 2019 to close the Dadaab camp on grounds that it allegedly harbored members of the Somalia-based Islamist armed group Al-Shabab. The authorities have never provided any evidence to support the allegation, and no one from the camp has ever been prosecuted for links with terrorism.

In May 2021, Selahaddin Gülen, a Turkish man who had requested asylum in Kenya, was forcibly returned to Turkey under suspicious circumstances. After entering Kenya in October 2020, Gülen was detained by Kenyan immigration authorities due to an Interpol Red Notice from Turkey. Kenyan authorities commenced extradition proceedings but later substituted this with a deportation order.

On May 3, 2021, during one of his court-mandated visits to the Directorate of Criminal Investigations in Nairobi, Gülen was reported missing. Another Turkish national who had accompanied Gulen to the agency headquarters and disappeared along with him was released by Kenyan authorities on May 5. On May 31, the Turkish authorities released a photo of Gülen in handcuffs in Ankara, Turkey, stating that he had been captured by agents of Turkey's National Intelligence Organization from a foreign country and was in the custody of their counterterrorism police. The deportation of Gulen, a registered asylum seeker in Kenya, violated Kenya's obligations to uphold the principle of non-refoulement under international and regional refugee law.

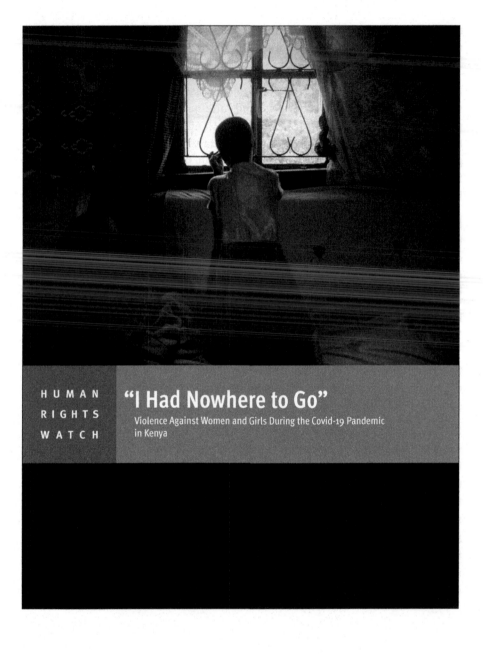

HUMAN
RIGHTS
WATCH

"I Had Nowhere to Go"
Violence Against Women and Girls During the Covid-19 Pandemic
in Kenya

Forced Evictions

On February 5, 2021, a state corporation forcefully evicted without notice about 3,500 members of the Nubian community from their homes in Kibos, Kisumu County. The Nubian community in Kenya are descendants of soldiers transported forcibly from Sudan by the British colonial government a century ago. Currently estimated to number over 100,000, the Nubians have been unable to access Kenyan citizenship and remain stateless. Armed police used teargas to force residents out of their homes despite a court order stopping the evictions as well as a May 1, 2020, presidential moratorium on evictions the during the coronavirus pandemic. A child was trapped under debris and killed as a bulldozer brought down their homes.

Women and Girls' Rights

In a September 2021 report on gender-based violence (GBV), Human Rights Watch found that Kenya, like other countries across the world, recorded an increase in violence against women and girls during its lockdown and ongoing nightly curfew introduced to curb the spread of the coronavirus. Despite a previous history of heightened incidences of violence against women and girls during crisis Kenyan authorities failed to institute measures to help prevent sexual and GBV; to properly investigate and prosecute cases; and to ensure survivors have access to timely medical treatment, psychosocial care, protection services, and financial assistance. In May, President Uhuru Kenyatta committed the country to ending GBV by 2026, pledging US$23 million by 2022 increasing to $50 million by 2026.

The Kenyan government has an obligation to prevent, counter, and provide redress for violence against women and girls at all times, including during crises and in humanitarian settings. In light of the ongoing Covid-19 pandemic, the government should rectify these failures and build a solid rights-based framework to anticipate future emergency-related sexual and GBV, including ahead of the planned general elections in 2022.

LGBTI Rights

On September 23, the Kenya Film Classification Board (KFCB) banned a gay-themed documentary, "I am Samuel," claiming that the film attempted to "promote same sex marriage. It is the second gay-themed film banned in Kenya, following a 2018 decision to stop cinemas from showing "Rafiki, "a lesbian love story which became the first Kenyan movie to premiere at the Cannes film festival. The ban on "Rafiki" ("friend" in Swahili) was later overturned by a court, and the film opened to sold-out audiences in Nairobi, "and the film opened to sold- but the ban was later reinstated.

Section 162 of Kenya's penal code punishes consensual same-sex relations with up to 14 years in prison. The High Court rejected a constitutional challenge to the ban in May 2019. Activists have appealed the ruling on grounds that section 162 violates rights to equality, non-discrimination, human dignity, security, privacy, and health, all protected under Kenya's constitution. They are currently awaiting a hearing at the Court of Appeal.

Key International Actors

Kenya currently occupies two key international and regional leadership roles. In January, Kenya began its two-year term as a non-permanent member of the United Nations Security Council (UNSC). President Kenyatta took over as chair of the East African Community (EAC) in February. With its forces in South Sudan and Somalia, Kenya joined other nations at the UNSC in July to endorse an African Union Commission of Inquiry into the alleged atrocities committed in Ethiopia's beleaguered Tigray region. Kenya's Permanent Representative to the UN Martin Kimani urged parties in Tigray to lay down arms. He said Kenya was looking forward to thorough investigations so that perpetrators could be held to account.

Kenya received significant support to address the challenging impact of the Covid-19 pandemic from both bilateral and multilateral partners. The United States, United Kingdom, China, European Union and individual European countries such as Germany provided material, technical and financial support to aid Kenya's response to the pandemic. The World Bank, International Monetary Fund (IMF) and the African Development Bank have variously provided Kenya with budgetary and project supports from the outset of the pandemic. In June 2021, the World Bank approved a $750 million budgetary support, in part to aid Kenya's pandemic response.

Kosovo

The Hague-based special court for Kosovo began its first war crimes trial in September while a Pristina court secured Kosovo's first conviction for wartime rape. Journalists continued to be targets of attacks, threats and intimidation, with perpetrators rarely held to account. Tensions between Serbia and Kosovo grew after Kosovo authorities ordered vehicles to remove Serbia license plates when entering Kosovo. Discrimination against Roma, Ashkali, and Balkan Egyptian communities remained a problem.

Accountability for War Crimes

In September, the Specialist Chambers for Kosovo in The Hague began its first war crimes trial. The defendant, former Kosovo Liberation Army unit commander Salih Mustafa, is charged with murder, torture, cruel treatment, and arbitrary detention during the 1999 Kosovo war.

In a landmark decision in July, the Pristina Basic Court convicted former Serb policeman Zoran Vukotic of wartime sexual violence and involvement in forced expulsions in 1999. Vukotic was sentenced to 10 years.

In March, Kosovo police arrested a Kosovo Albanian with Serbian citizenship on suspicion of war crimes against the civilian population during an operation by Serbian forces in 1999, in which 147 civilians were killed.

Also in March, the Basic Court in Pristina convicted two former police officers, Zlatan Krstic and Destan Shabanaj for their involvement in a 1999 attack that killed four members of an ethnic Albanian family. They were sentenced to fourteen-and-a-half-years and seven-years' imprisonment respectively.

Accountability of International Institutions

There was no progress during the year towards financially compensating members of the Roma, Ashkali, and Balkan Egyptian communities who were victims of lead poisoning in now-closed camps for displaced persons established by the United Nations Mission in Kosovo (UNMIK). The Human Rights Advisory Panel (HRAP), an independent international body set up to examine complaints of abuses by UNMIK, in 2016 recommended the United Nations pay individual compensation and apologize to victims—the UN has done neither. Since its establishment in 2017, only one state had contributed to the voluntary UN trust fund set up for community assistance projects.

Treatment of Minorities

Discrimination against Roma, Ashkali, and Balkan Egyptians in Kosovo remains a problem.

The prosecution of six defendants charged in the 2018 murder of Kosovo Serb politician Oliver Ivanovic, continued in the Basic Court in Pristina with the indictment confirmed in May and the trial starting in July following delays in 2020. Four defendants are accused of having been part of a criminal group that organized the murder of Ivanovic. Two defendants stand accused of evidence-tempering. Ivanovic was shot dead by unknown assailants outside of his office in Mitrovica, northern Kosovo.

Women's Rights

Domestic violence survivors continued to face obstacles in obtaining protection from abuse, with inadequate state response, few prosecutions, and continued failure by judges to issue restraining orders against abusive partners.

A 2018 mechanism set up to help provide financial compensation for the estimated 20,000 wartime survivors of sexual violence, continued to have limited reach. Between February 2018 and April 2021, only around 1,220 survivors sought financial compensation, with over 900 approved and over 230 rejected.

Asylum Seekers and Displaced Persons

During the first nine months of 2021, the United Nations High Commissioner for Refugees registered 261 voluntary returns of members of ethnic minorities to Kosovo from other countries, up from 245 during the same period in 2020. Fifty-four were children.

The Kosovo Ministry of Internal Affairs registered 467 deportations to Kosovo between January and September. The ministry claimed to lack data on the ethnicity of those returned.

Sexual Orientation and Gender Identity

The Centre for Equality and Liberty of the lesbian, gay, bisexual and transgender (LGBT) Community in Kosovo (CEL), in October expressed concern about inadequate investigations into threats and hate speech against LGBT people and activists, particularly on social media. In July, CEL reported that an LGBT activist in Pristina was approached by three unknown assailants, who spat in the activist's face, screaming, "We are going to kill you." A police investigation was pending at time of writing.

Freedom of Media

Between January and September, the Association of Journalists of Kosovo registered 18 cases of threats, intimidation and violence against journalists and media outlets. At least nine cases were under investigation at time of writing, but investigations and prosecutions have been slow.

One of the cases involves an assault on a journalist at *Gazeta Insajderi*, Visar Duriqi, who was physically attacked in Pristina in February by three unknown assailants. The attack is believed to be linked to his reporting. Duriqi suffered a broken nose and broken teeth due to the attack. Police were still investigating at time of writing.

Key International Actors

After tensions and movement restrictions following a September decision by Kosovo authorities to order the removal of Serbian licence plates from vehicles entering Kosovo, European Union High Representative Josep Borrell called on Kosovo and Serbia to de-escalate by withdrawing special police forces and dismantling roadblocks and the NATO led peacekeepers increased patrols. The parties reportedly reached a compromise in late September brokered by EU Special Representative Miroslav Lajcek.

The European Commission October progress report stated that more needs to be done to effectively guarantee the rights of minorities, including Roma, Ashkali, and displaced people and to ensure gender equality in practice. It further stated that concerns remain about freedom of expression, including threats and physical attacks on journalists and public smear campaigns.

Kuwait

Kuwaiti authorities use provisions in the penal code and the national security and cybercrime laws to restrict free speech and prosecute dissidents, particularly for comments made on social media.

The status of the Bidun, a community of stateless people who claim Kuwaiti nationality, remains in legal limbo while the government suppresses and penalizes peaceful activism by them.

Amid the Covid-19 pandemic, the government implemented restrictive measures that had a disproportionate impact on already marginalized migrants and undocumented communities.

Freedom of Expression and Assembly

Authorities prosecuted dissidents using penal code provisions and the cybercrime law that criminalize speech deemed insulting to religion or the emir, or peaceful dissent generally.

On July 5, State Security authorities arrested Jaber al-Sayer, an activist and poet who faces charges including "insulting the emir" and "broadcasting false news." Authorities reportedly released al-Sayer on July 13.

Authorities harassed activists who advocate for the rights of the Bidun community. The Gulf Centre for Human Rights reported that on March 29 the Ministry of Justice informed prominent human rights defender Hadeel Buqrais that there was a pending case against her on charges of public insults, defamation, and misuse of her mobile telephone in connection with two tweets from early August 2020. In November 2020, the Department to Combat Electronic and Cyber Crime had summoned and interrogated Buqrais about these tweets. In May 2021, the Public Prosecution dismissed the charges and closed the case.

On September 22, authorities released Abdollah Fairouz, who worked on Bidun issues, after serving two-and-half years of a five-year prison term for "insulting the emir."

Article 12 of the 1979 Public Gatherings Law bars non-Kuwaitis from participating in public gatherings. The Gulf Center for Human Rights reported that on August

11 and 12, the General Department of Criminal Investigation at the Ministry of Interior summoned 19 Bidun activists for questioning after they participated in weekly Saturday evening gatherings in Al-Erada Square. In 2021, the authorities also deported at least two non-Kuwaiti residents for peaceful dissent.

Women's Rights, Children's Rights, Sexual Orientation, Gender Identity

Kuwait's personal status law applies to Sunni Muslims, who make up most Kuwaitis. It discriminates against women in matters of marriage, divorce, and child custody, including a stipulation that women need permission of a male guardian to marry and they can lose their right to financial maintenance from their husbands if they refuse to live with their husband without justification. Women can only apply to the courts for a divorce on limited grounds while men can divorce women without any restrictions. The personal status rules that apply to Shia Muslims also discriminate against women. Kuwaiti women married to non-Kuwaitis cannot pass citizenship to their children or spouses on an equal basis with Kuwaiti men.

Although a record number of female candidates ran in the December 2020 National Assembly elections, none were elected.

According to the study by the Kuwait Society for Human Rights in May 2021, gender-based violence increased during the Covid-19 pandemic and consequent restrictions. In February, Kuwaiti women activists launched a nationwide online campaign called Lan Asket ("I will not be silent") to speak out against harassment, discrimination, and violence against women. Dozens of women's testimonies about being stalked, harassed, or assaulted emerged online.

In April 2021, outrage and protests followed reports that Farah Hamza Akbar had been killed after being kidnapped from her car during the day by a man her family had previously reported to the authorities for harassment.

Domestic violence continues to remain pervasive. Women and girls who need to flee abuse have nowhere to turn. They can be reported to local police for "absence" if they leave their homes without their family's or guardian's permission. Kuwait still has no shelters for survivors of domestic violence, despite Kuwait's national assembly passing in 2020 a Law on Protection from Domestic Violence, which included a provision that the state provide assistance for survivors including establishing a shelter. Although the law provides penalties to combat domestic violence and assistance for survivors, it falls short of criminalizing domestic violence as such and does not cover people in relationships outside of marriage, including engaged couples or former partners.

Kuwait's penal code provides reduced sentences for male violence against women. Article 153 allows men who kill their wife, daughter, sister, or mother upon finding them in the act of extra-marital sex to receive a reduced sentenced of a maximum of three years in prison or a fine of 3,000 Kuwaiti dinars (approximately US$9,820). Article 182 also allows an abductor who uses force, threat, or deception with the intention to kill, harm, rape, prostitute or extort the victim to avoid punishment if he marries the victim with the permission of her guardian.

The penal code also criminalizes sexual relations outside marriage and consensual same-sex relations between men. Transgender people can face one year in prison, a 1,000 Kuwaiti dinar fine ($3,293), or both, under a 2007 penal code provision that prohibits "imitating the opposite sex in any way." Transgender people have been subjected to arbitrary arrest, degrading treatment, and torture while in police custody. On October 3, a court sentenced Maha al-Mutairi, a transgender woman, to two years in prison and a fine of 1,000 Kuwaiti dinars for "misusing phone communication" by "imitating the opposite sex" online under article 70 of the telecommunication law and article 198 of the penal code.

The criminal code and the Child Rights Act permit corporal punishment of children by their parents or legal caregivers.

Stateless People

The Bidun are a group of between 88,000 and 106,000 stateless people who claim Kuwaiti nationality, dating back to the foundation of the state in 1961. Rejecting their claims to Kuwaiti nationality, the government refers to them as "illegal residents," resulting in them facing obstacles to obtaining civil documentation, receiving social services, and impairing their rights to health, education, and work.

The Central System for the Remedy of Situations of Illegal Residents, the administrative body in charge of Bidun affairs, has been issuing temporary ID cards since 2011. These ID cards often state that the cardholder possessed Iraqi, Saudi, Iranian, or other citizenship, but it was unclear how the agency determined the individual's alleged nationality and what due process procedures are available for Bidun to challenge the Central System's determination. Over the past year there have been at least two reports of Bidun youth committing suicide after what Bidun activists claim was the Central System's refusal to renew their ID cards or due to their difficult living conditions.

Article 12 of the 1979 Public Gatherings Law bars non-Kuwaitis from participating in public gatherings. The Gulf Centre for Human Rights reported that on August 11 and 12 that the General Department of Criminal Investigation at the Ministry of Interior summoned 19 Bidun activists for questioning after they participated in weekly Saturday evening gatherings in Al-Erada Square.

Migrant Workers

Two-thirds of Kuwait's population is comprised of migrant workers, who remain vulnerable to abuse, largely due to the *kafala* (sponsorship) system which ties migrants' visas to their employers and requires that migrants get their employers' consent to leave or change jobs. Migrant domestic workers continue to face additional forms of abuse including being forcibly confined in their employers' homes, and verbal, physical and sexual abuse.

As a result of the Covid-19 pandemic, many migrant workers found themselves dismissed without their wages, trapped in the country, unable to leave due to travel restrictions and more expensive flight tickets, or dismissed from their jobs and deported. In April 2021, Migrant-rights.org reported that migrant workers in the food and beverage sector were among those most affected, with many losing jobs, facing denial of wages for months or severe salary deductions.

In 2020, the government said that it seeks to reduce the number of migrant workers from 70 to 30 percent of the population. In January, the Public Authority for Manpower reportedly began implementing a 2020 administrative decision to prohibit issuing or renewing work permits for migrants aged 60 and above who hold only high school diplomas or below. On July 14, local papers reported that the authorities decided to allow for the renewal of work permits of migrant workers over age 60 but for a high fee of 2,000 Kuwaiti dinar ($6,650) per year. Following citizens and residents taking to social media to oppose the decision critiquing it as extortion of the elderly, in August, local media reported that officials were considering halving the fee to 1,000 Kuwaiti dinar (approximately $3,300).

Government's Response to the Covid-19 Pandemic

Since April 2021, in response in the Covid-19 pandemic, Kuwaiti authorities imposed various restrictions, including general lockdowns. Several of these government actions have had a disproportionate impact on already marginalized communities.

In June 2020, Amnesty International reported that the official contact tracing mobile application used in Kuwait to track reported Covid-19 cases uses one of the most invasive centralized approaches, posing a threat to privacy. There are no general data protection laws in the country.

Morbidity rates during Covid have been higher among migrant workers. Reports indicate that migrant workers were not given equal access to Covid-19 vaccines based on the same health criteria as Kuwait citizens.

The closure of schools and shift to online education in response to Covid-19 affected the education of 800,000 students. Bidun children, who are already socially marginalized, reportedly have more difficulty accessing devices for online education. In September and October the government started reopening private and public schools.

There have been several reports of Covid-19 outbreaks in Kuwait prisons. According to the US State Department, the authorities released more than 1,000 prisoners and asked several other countries to repatriate any of their nationals who had served more than half of their prison terms and have them serve the remainder of their sentences at home to reduce prison overcrowding during the pandemic.

Climate Change Polices and Impacts

Kuwait, the world's seventh-largest exporter of crude oil, has the sixth-highest greenhouse gas emissions per capita globally, a considerable portion from air conditioning. As one of the world's hottest and most water-stressed countries, Kuwait is particularly vulnerable to the impacts of climate change. The increasing frequency and intensity of heat waves, decreased precipitation, and rising sea levels pose risks to the right to health, life, water, and housing, especially of migrant workers.

Kuwait generates two-thirds of its electricity from burning oil but has no national climate change plan and has yet to submit its second Nationally Determined Contribution (NDC), a Paris Agreement-mandated, five-year, national climate change action plan due at the end of 2020. Its first NDC contained no quantitative targets.

Key International Actors

Kuwait has a bilateral defense cooperation agreement with the United States, and the US uses military bases in the country. Kuwait is a member of the Saudi-led coalition conducting military operations in Yemen. Kuwait has not responded to Human Rights Watch inquiries regarding what role, if any, it has played in unlawful attacks in Yemen.

Kyrgyzstan

In a year marked by Sadyr Japarov's win at a snap presidential election in January, Kyrgyzstan adopted a new constitution that includes provisions undermining human rights norms and engaged in a short border conflict with Tajikistan.

Throughout the year, Kyrgyzstan's caretaker parliament adopted several problematic bills including one imposing unnecessary financial reporting requirements on nongovernmental organizations (NGOs), and another overly broad bill penalizing "false" information. In February, the government initiated a massive legal review that was rushed and failed to involve a proper consultation process.

In late April, a border conflict between Kyrgyzstan and Tajikistan killed at least 41 people, injured hundreds, and displaced thousands.

Measures put in place to protect women and girls have yet to end impunity for domestic violence, which remains widespread. An investigation into the death in custody of the wrongfully imprisoned human rights defender Azimjon Askarov in July 2020 was improperly closed in May, but the case was re-opened on order of a court. Several foreign human rights workers and a foreign media correspondent remain banned from Kyrgyzstan. In March, Kyrgyzstan repatriated 79 children, who were held in prisons in Iraq together with their mothers as Islamic State suspects. The returnees reportedly underwent rehabilitation before being placed with family members.

Parliamentary Elections

Two days after the disputed parliamentary elections on October 4, 2020, and ensuing protests, Kyrgyzstan's Central Election Committee (CEC) annulled the outcome and scheduled a rerun for December 20. However, on October 22, the caretaker parliament adopted amendments postponing new parliamentary elections until sometime in 2021 to allow for constitutional reforms initiated by the then acting president Sadyr Japarov. The amendments were adopted in violation of procedural norms, rushed through three readings in parliament in one day. This allowed the caretaker parliament to continue passing numerous laws, including many that violate the country's international human rights obligations—such as the modified editions of the criminal and criminal procedural codes, with excessive criminalization and decrease in the rights of detainees. Elections were scheduled for November 28, 2021.

Constitutional Reform

The Council of Europe's (CoE) Venice Commission and the Organization for Security and Co-operation in Europe's (OSCE) Office for Democratic Institutions and Human Rights issued a joint opinion concluding that the constitution—adopted by referendum on April 21—contains provisions threatening the necessary balance of power and the protection of individual freedoms, essential to democracy and rule of law.

Several provisions directly violate international human rights standards. Article 10 prohibits activities, public events, and dissemination of information contrary to "moral values and the public consciousness of the people of Kyrgyzstan" and is incompatible with fundamental human rights to freedom of expression, assembly, and association. Another provision includes a requirement to obtain advance permission from the authorities to hold peaceful assemblies.

Civil Society

In June, parliament adopted a bill on NGOs that imposes additional burdensome financial reporting requirements on civil society groups. President Japarov signed the bill into law in July.

In May 2020, the State Committee on National Security (GKNB) brought dubious forgery charges against the rights defender, Kamil Ruziev, after he spent two days in detention for interrogation as a witness. Ruziev had filed a lawsuit against the GKNB and the prosecutor's office for failing to investigate his complaint that officials had psychologically abused him and threatened him, including at gunpoint, during his detention. The case against Ruziev was sent to court in September 2020 and is ongoing after numerous postponements.

On July 25, 2020, the human rights defender Azimjon Askarov died in custody. Askarov had served 10 years of a life sentence imposed after an unfair trial on politically motivated charges. The Kyrgyz Investigative Department of the State Penitentiary Service was tasked with investigating his death, which was problematic as the Penitentiary Service also oversaw his detention. The inquiry that closed on May 28 concluded that Askarov died from Covid-19-related complications and denied that he was mistreated in prison. A Bishkek city district court ruled in August that the decision to close the investigation was unfounded and that the investigation should be re-opened. In September, the prosecutor general tasked the GKNB with the new investigation, under its supervision.

Conflict at the Kyrgyzstan-Tajikistan border

A two-day border conflict between Kyrgyzstan and Tajikistan in late April—the worst in Central Asia in decades—killed over 40 people, most of them civilians, and injured hundreds.

The conflict began over control of a crucial water-intake facility which diverts to Kyrgyzstan a small part of a river that flows naturally into Tajikistan, in line with a water-sharing protocol. About 58,000 people in Kyrgyzstan and Tajikistan fled their homes or were evacuated. Dozens of houses and at least three schools were damaged or destroyed. The two countries quickly called a ceasefire and committed to rebuilding houses damaged during the conflict in their respective territories.

As of September, three nationals of Kyrgyzstan, ethnic Tajiks, and two nationals of Tajikistan were on trial in Kyrgyzstan for looting private property during the conflict. There are no reports of an impartial investigation by Kyrgyzstan into whether its military violated the laws of war during the conflict.

Freedom of Expression

In 2021, journalists continued to be harassed by law enforcement, and in some cases threatened with criminal sanctions for critical reporting. Police detained at least four journalists covering the April constitutional referendum in Osh and Bishkek. In May, GKNB officers allegedly harassed Kanat Kanimetov, a reporter and presenter at independent television broadcaster "Aprel," and his family, in connection to a criminal case on which he had reported.

On August 23, president Sadyr Japarov signed into law a vague and overly broad bill on protection from "false information" that allows authorities, without judicial oversight, to order the removal of information that officials consider "false" or "inaccurate" from internet platforms.

In September, police detained activist and blogger Orozayym Narmatova for "excessive and unfair criticism of the government", releasing her later following the intervention of the human rights ombudsman and civil society protests.

Labor Rights

Parliament twice tried to push a restrictive trade union bill that had been stalled in parliament since 2019. The bill would grant the Federation of Trade Unions a monopoly over all federal-level union activity and require industrial and regional trade unions to affiliate with the federation. It would undermine trade union pluralism and the right of trade unions to freely determine their structures and statutes. The International Labour Organization (ILO) and IndustriALL Global Union criticized the proposed law. President Japarov vetoed the bill twice, in May and August.

Violence against Women and Girls

Despite legislation, including amendments to the Criminal Procedural Code adopted in 2020, which provides better protections for victims of domestic violence and other violence against women and girls, authorities do not fully enforce protective measures or hold perpetrators accountable. Impunity for domestic violence—the vast majority of which is committed by male perpetrators against women and girls—is still the norm.

Police registered 7,665 cases during the first eight months of 2021, a 30 percent increase over the same period in 2020. Cases of violence against women and girls remain underreported and survivors face multiple barriers to accessing services and justice, such as insufficient shelters and other essential services, dismissive response by authorities, stigma, and attitudes that perpetuate harmful stereotypes and practices, including by police, judicial officials, and government and religious leaders.

In April, the murder of Aizada Kanatbekova, a young woman who was killed by a man who had kidnapped her for forced marriage, sent shock waves through the country, triggering public protests and renewed commitments by authorities to tackle so-called bride-kidnapping and domestic violence.

Sexual Orientation and Gender Identity

In the second half of 2020, parliament amended the law on civil registry, deleting a paragraph that previously allowed for transgender people to change their gender markers on official documents on the basis of medical certification. Civil registry workers now have the discretion to refuse applications for gender marker change.

Lesbian, gay, bisexual and transgender (LGBT) issues in Kyrgyzstan are often used as a scaremongering tactic by politicians to taint their opponents. In the run-up to the failed parliamentary elections in Kyrgyzstan in October 2020, a gay couple working for an opposition party was outed as part of a smear campaign against it.

While there is no direct discrimination on the basis of sexual orientation and/or gender identity in Kyrgyz legislation, Article 10 of Kyrgyzstan's new constitution allows for indirect censorship of any LGBT-rights related activities, public events, or information as they may be deemed contrary to "moral values and the public consciousness of the people of Kyrgyzstan."

Disability Rights

Despite ratification of the United Nations Convention on the Rights of Persons with Disabilities in 2019, the government has yet to adopt a comprehensive plan on its implementation. A September 2021 presidential decree increased the monthly social benefit payments to people with disabilities, primarily benefiting various groups of children with certain types of disabilities. Children with disabilities face significant barriers to inclusive education, with only 1,067 enrolled in mainstream schools since the beginning of the year as part of a pilot project run by an NGO. Others remain in segregated schools and residential institutions, or out of education altogether.

Torture

Impunity for torture and ill-treatment remains the norm. According to statistics of the Kyrgyz National Center for Prevention of Torture, 77 allegations of torture were registered in the first eight months of 2021. In September, the center reported that conditions in pretrial detention centers in Osh, Batken and Jalal Abad oblasts violated the human rights of detainees under the Kyrgyz law on "Order and conditions of detention of suspects"—where four beds in a cell were shared by seven or eight detainees, some of whom spent months or years in such conditions. Women in the Jalal-Abad detention center complained about harassment by officers.

Abduction of Orhan Inandi

Between May and June, Orhan Inandi, a dual Turkish-Kyrgyz national living in Bishkek was abducted, forcibly disappeared, and extrajudicially transferred to Turkey. The actions included egregious violations of international and domestic law. Inandi is the director of Sapat network of prestigious schools in Kyrgyzstan.

On July 5, 2021, President of Turkey Recep Tayyip Erdogan alleged on a Turkish state TV channel that Inandi is part of the movement run by US-based cleric Fethullah Gülen, which Turkey deems a terrorist organization responsible for the July 2016 failed coup in the country. He stated that Inandi had been captured and taken to Turkey. Authorities in Kyrgyzstan said in September they were investigating aspects of his enforced disappearance and were seeking access to him in jail in Turkey.

Key International Actors

In March, the special representative of the United Nations secretary-general for Central Asia, Natalia Gherman, visited Kyrgyzstan and during the meeting with President Sadyr Japarov noted that it is important to "conduct reforms in an inclusive and transparent manner," based on the principles of rule of law, human rights, and good governance.

In May, after the escalation of border conflict between Kyrgyzstan and Tajikistan, the European Union, OSCE, and the UN all offered their assistance in resolving the conflict and responding to the immediate consequences for the livelihoods of people on both sides of the border.

In September, during its annual Human Rights Dialogue with the Kyrgyz Republic, the EU recalled the need to conduct an impartial and transparent investigation into the death of Azimjon Askarov and expressed its concerns over the controversial legislative initiatives that limit civil society and freedom of information in contravention of the country's obligations under relevant international conventions. In July, the US State Department spokesperson expressed deep concern over the new law imposing burdensome requirements on civil society groups.

In November, the UN Committee on the Elimination of Discrimination against Women urged Kyrgyzstan to review the law "On protection and defense against domestic violence" to ensure that it covers all forms of gender-based violence, taking into account the special needs of marginalized groups of women, including women with disabilities and lesbian, bisexual, and transgender women; to pursue efforts to prevent, protect and assist victims, as well as to prosecute and adequately punish perpetrators, of bride kidnapping; and to reinstate the right of transgender persons, including women, to change the gender marker on their passport and other identity documents and in their personal identification number, including by repealing the amendments of August 1, 2020, to the Law on Civil Registry.

HUMAN
RIGHTS
WATCH

"They Killed Us from the Inside"
An Investigation into the August 4 Beirut Blast

Lebanon

The human rights situation in Lebanon deteriorated further in 2021. More than 80 percent of the country's residents did not have access to basic rights, including health, education, and an adequate standard of living, such as adequate housing and electricity, according to the United Nations. The World Bank has described Lebanon's crisis as a "deliberate depression," due to Lebanese leaders' mismanagement and lack of effective policy actions, and ranked it among the top three most severe global financial crises since the mid-nineteenth century.

The Lebanese pound has lost 90 percent of its value since October 2019, eroding people's ability to access basic goods, including food, water, health care, and education. Fuel shortages have caused widespread electricity blackouts, lasting up to 23 hours per day, and private generators—a costly alternative—have not been able to fill the gap, leaving large portions of the country in darkness for several hours per day. Hospitals, schools, and bakeries have struggled to operate amid these energy shortages.

The Lebanese government removed or decreased subsidies on fuel, wheat, medicine, and other basic goods, but it has failed to implement an adequate social protection scheme to shield vulnerable residents from the impact of steep price rises. Marginalized communities, including refugees, people with disabilities, migrant workers, and LGBTQ people, have been disproportionately impacted.

No one has yet been held accountable for the catastrophic explosion in Beirut's port on August 4, 2020, which killed at least 219 people and devastated half the city.

Security forces continued to use excessive and even lethal force to suppress protests, often with impunity.

Women face systematic discrimination and violence due to the archaic nationality law and multiple religion-based personal status laws. Although Lebanon criminalized sexual harassment, the law falls short of international standards.

On September 10, Prime Minister Najib Mikati formed a government, ending the 13-month vacuum.

Beirut Blast

Following decades of government mismanagement and corruption at Beirut's port, on August 4, 2020, one of the largest non-nuclear explosions in history pulverized the port and damaged over half the city. The explosion resulted from the detonation of tons of ammonium nitrate, a combustible chemical compound commonly used in agriculture as a high nitrate fertilizer, but which can also be used to manufacture explosives. The Beirut port explosion killed at least 219 people, wounded 7,000 people, and left hundreds with permanent disabilities.

Human Rights Watch's review of hundreds of pages of official documents strongly suggests that some government officials were aware of the fatal disaster that the ammonium nitrate's presence in the port could result in and tacitly accepted the risk to human life. This amounts to a violation of the right to life under international human rights law.

Lebanese leaders have continued to obstruct and delay the ongoing domestic investigation, shielding high-level officials from accountability. In February 2021, a court dismissed the judge appointed to lead the investigation after two former ministers whom he had charged filed a complaint against him. While judge Tarek Bitar was appointed a day later, the political establishment has similarly started a campaign against him after he made requests to charge and summon for questioning senior political and security officials. In October, seven people were killed and dozens injured after gunfire erupted during a demonstration that Hezbollah and its allies called for to demand the removal of Bitar.

Human Rights Watch has also documented a range of procedural and systemic flaws in the domestic investigation that render it incapable of credibly delivering justice, including flagrant political interference, immunity for high-level political officials, lack of respect for fair trial standards, and due process violations.

Families of the victims and local and international rights groups have called for a Human Rights Council-mandated international, independent investigation, into the Beirut Blast.

In December 2020, the World Bank, United Nations, and European Union announced an innovative model for disbursing aid to Lebanon in the aftermath of the Beirut Blast, the Reform, Recovery, and Reconstruction Framework (3RF), that aims to disburse funds dir*ectly to nongovernmental groups and businesses.*

Financial and Economic Crisis

Lebanon's financial and economic crisis is caused by the Lebanese authorities' "deliberately inadequate policy responses," according to the World Bank.

Between June 2019 and June 2021, the inflation rate was 281 percent. Food prices alone increased by 550 percent between August 2020 and August 2021. Meanwhile, the national currency lost 90 percent of its pre-crisis value, and banks continue to impose arbitrary restrictions on cash withdrawals.

In 2019, the government decided to subsizide vital imports, such as fuel, wheat, and medicine. But in 2021, the central bank ran out of money to finance these imports, causing residents to experience severe shortages. Fuel shortages have caused widespread electricity blackouts, lasting up to 23 hours per day. Hospitals, schools, and bakeries have struggled to operate amid these supply and electricity shortages, and residents had to endure hours-long queues for necessities, such as fuel and bread.

The impacts of the crisis on residents' rights have been catastrophic and unprecedented. The UN estimates that by March 2021, 78 percent of Lebanon's population was in poverty—triple the estimated number in 2020. Thirty-six percent of the population live in extreme poverty—up from 8 percent in 2019 and 23 percent in 2020.

The Lebanese government provided almost no support to families struggling to cope with the economic crisis, exacerbated by the Covid-19 pandemic, fumbling a World Bank loan intended to provide emergency relief to vulnerable Lebanese and repeatedly delaying a ration card program to help families cope with the lifting of subsidies.

Healthcare Crisis

The economic crisis has had a devastating impact on the healthcare sector. Medicines and medical supplies, most of which are imported, are in short supply, leading to several deaths due to lack of medication and threatening the lives of patients with illnesses, such as cancer. The fuel and electricity shortages in the country have pushed hospitals to "imminent disaster," with hospitals permanently closing or warning that they will be forced to cease their operations, threatening the lives of hundreds.

The value of nurses and doctors' salaries has declined rapidly, triggering a mass exodus, placing a heavy burden on the remaining workforce. The Covid-19 pandemic also placed an additional strain on a healthcare sector already in crisis. Lebanese authorities have shown a callous disregard for the protection of healthcare workers at the front lines of the pandemic.

Despite the enormous pressures facing hospitals, the government is not disbursing billions of dollars that it owes them.

A national vaccination campaign was rolled out in mid-February and, as of November 15, around 30 percent of the population had been vaccinated against Covid-19. However, the government's program risks leaving behind marginalized communities, including refugees and migrant workers.

Freedom of Assembly and Expression

Anti-government protests, which began in October 17, 2019, continued amid the rapidly deteriorating economic and political situation.

In January, the Internal Security Forces (ISF) used force to disperse protests that turned violent over the rapidly deteriorating economic conditions, exacerbated by Covid-19 lockdown measures, in one of Lebanon's poorest cities, Tripoli. They fired teargas, rubber bullets, and live ammunition at protesters, injuring hundreds and killing one protester.

Military Intelligence forcibly disappeared and allegedly tortured detainees who were participating in these protests. The military prosecution charged at least 35 of the protesters, including two children, with terrorism before the military courts, which are inherently unfair.

Journalists, media workers, and activists in Lebanon—especially critics of the ruling elite and established political parties—are coming under increasing threat both by private actors, with the authorities unwilling or unable to protect them, and directly by government authorities, often acting with impunity.

Lokman Slim, a prominent intellectual and Hezbollah critic, was assassinated in February by unidentified assailants. There has been no meaningful progress in the investigation.

Women's Rights

Women continue to face discrimination under 15 distinct religion-based personal status laws. Discrimination includes inequality in access to divorce, child custody, and inheritance, and property rights. Unlike men, Lebanese women cannot pass on their nationality to foreign husbands and children.

In December 2020, parliament passed a law criminalizing sexual harassment which provided important protections by making sexual harassment a crime and outlining whistleblower protections, but the law fails to meet international standards including that it should have sought to tackle harassment at work through labor laws, occupational safety and health laws, and equality and nondiscrimination laws. Parliament also amended the domestic violence law to expand its scope to include violence related to—but not necessarily committed during—marriage, enabling women to seek protection from their ex-husbands. But it still does not criminalize marital rape.

Migrant Workers

An estimated 250,000 migrant domestic workers, primarily from Ethiopia, the Philippines, Bangladesh, and Sri Lanka, are excluded from Lebanon's labor law protections, and their status in the country is regulated by the restrictive *kafala* (sponsorship) system, which ties migrant workers' legal residency to their employer.

Abuse against migrant domestic workers has increased amid Lebanon's economic crisis and the Covid-19 pandemic, including employers forcing domestic workers to work without pay or at highly reduced salaries, confining them to the household, to work long hours without rest or a day off, and verbal, physical and sexual abuse. The International Labour Organization has warned that migrant workers in Lebanon now face conditions that "greatly increase their risk of entering forced or bonded labor."

Sexual Orientation and Gender Identity

LGBTQ people participated prominently in the nationwide protests that began on October 17, 2019. By taking their struggle to the streets, through chants, graffiti, and public discussions, lesbian, gay, bisexual, and transgender (LGBT) people have moved demands of their rights from the margins to mainstream discourse.

However, Article 534 of the penal code punishes "any sexual intercourse contrary to the order of nature" with up to one year in prison. Transgender women in Lebanon face systemic violence and discrimination in accessing basic services, including employment, health care, and housing. The economic crisis, compounded by Covid-19 lockdown measures, disproportionately affected LGBT people.

General Security forces issued entry bans, which remain in effect to date, to the non-Lebanese attendees of a 2018 conference that advances LGBT rights.

Refugees

Lebanon hosts nearly 900,000 registered Syrian refugees, and the government estimates another 500,000 live in the country informally. Only 20 percent of Syrian refugees have legal residency, making most of them vulnerable to harassment, arrest, detention, and deportation.

The government continues to pursue policies designed to coerce Syrian refugees to leave, and the acute economic crisis and staggering inflation have made it exceedingly difficult for refugees to afford the most basic necessities; 90 percent of Syrian families in Lebanon live in extreme poverty, relying on increasing levels of debt to survive.

Although the Lebanese government continues to publicly state its commitment to the principle of nonrefoulement, it has deported more than 6,000 Syrians in recent years.

According to the Lebanese Palestinian Dialogue Committee, there are approximately 174,000 Palestinian refugees living in Lebanon, where they continue to face restrictions, including on their right to work and own property.

Syrian refugees who returned to Syria from Lebanon between 2017 and 2021 faced grave human rights abuses and persecution at the hands of the Syrian government and affiliated militias.

Childrens' Rights

Many Lebanese and nearly all Syrian refugee children received no meaningful education as the government closed schools due to the Covid-19 pandemic without ensuring access to distance learning. Children with disabilities were particularly hard hit, as they could not access remote education on an equal basis with others amid a lack of government support.

The authorities' planning failures delayed the start of the 2021-22 school year to October 11 and led to concerns public schools would not remain open.

Corporal punishment of children was widespread and permitted under the criminal code.

Legacy of Past Conflicts and Wars

Despite a 2018 law creating an independent national commission to investigate the fate of the estimated 17,000 Lebanese kidnapped or disappeared during the country's civil war, the government has yet to allocate a budget for the commission to commence its work.

The Special Tribunal for Lebanon, which in 2020 convicted a member of Hezbollah for his role in the killing of former Lebanese Prime Minister Rafik Hariri and 21 others in 2005, risked shutting down amid funding difficulties. Although tribunal officials announced in October that they had secured sufficient funding to handle a prosecution appeal of the acquittal of two other suspects in the Hariri case, the tribunal's operations remain uncertain after that due *to funding constraints.*

Key International Actors

Syria, Iran, and other regional powers maintain influence in Lebanon through their support of local political allies and proxies.

Tensions with Israel along Lebanon's southern border remain high, and hostilities flared up in May and August. A Lebanese man was shot and killed by Israeli forces after he tried to cross a security fence on the border with Israel. Israel continues to frequently violate Lebanese airspace.

In July, the EU adopted a framework for targeted sanctions against Lebanese officials responsible for obstructing the formation of a government, the improvement of accountability and good governance, and for serious financial mismanagement, but no individual or entity has been designated.

The United States has continued to sanction individuals for links to Hezbollah, and in October, sanctioned two Lebanese businessmen and one lawmaker for contributing to "the breakdown of good governance and the rule of law in Lebanon."

On September 16, the European Parliament adopted a resolution describing the dire situation in Lebanon as a "man-made disaster" and calling for the establishment of an international fact-finding mission into the Beirut Blast and targeted sanctions against corrupt Lebanese officials.

In October, several Gulf states, led by Saudi Arabia, expelled the Lebanese ambassadors and banned all Lebanese imports in response to critical comments made by a Lebanese minister about the Saudi-led military intervention in Yemen.

Lebanese security agencies continue to receive assistance from a range of international donors, including the United States, European Union, United Kingdom, France, and Saudi Arabia.

Libya

After five months of UN-brokered political talks between Libyan stakeholders, the country's House of Representatives swore in on March 15 a new interim authority, the Government of National Unity (GNU).

As of October, the first round of a two-round presidential election was due to take place on December 24. Parliamentary elections were due to take place 52 days after the first round of presidential elections.

The country reeled from continued mass displacement, dangers caused by newly-laid landmines, and the destruction of critical infrastructure, including healthcare and schools. Hundreds of people remain missing, including many civilians, and the authorities made grim discoveries of mass graves containing dozens of bodies that remain unidentified.

Migrants, asylum seekers, and refugees in Libya faced arbitrary detention, during which many experienced ill-treatment, sexual assault, forced labor, and extortion by groups linked with the Government of National Unity's Interior Ministry, members of armed groups, smugglers, and traffickers.

Political Process and Elections

UN-facilitated political talks involving 75 Libyan stakeholders at the Libyan Political Dialogue Forum (LPDF) since November 2020 culminated in the nomination of the GNU. The new interim authority replaced the Government of National Accord and the Interim Government in eastern Libya.

While members of a joint military commission known as the 5+5 were negotiating the merging of Libyan fighters into a unified force, the Libyan Arab Armed Forces (LAAF), the armed group under the command of General Khalifa Hiftar, remained in control of eastern Libya and parts of the south.

The GNU's core mandate is to conduct presidential and parliamentary elections on December 24 and to implement a ceasefire agreement from October 2020 between parties. As of October, the House of Representatives (HOR) passed a law for electing a president on December 24, and a separate law on electing a new parliament, paving the way for national elections. The High Council of the State, mandated to approve elections laws per political agreements, contested the legislation citing lack of consultation.

Libya remains without a permanent constitution, with only the 2011 constituent covenant in force. A draft constitution proposed by the elected Libyan Constitution Drafting Assembly in July 2017 has yet to be put to a national referendum. As of October, no date had been scheduled for the referendum.

The constitutional chamber of the Supreme Court has remained shuttered since 2014 due to armed conflict. The lack of a constitutional court to review and revoke legislation deemed unconstitutional, including elections-related legislation, only deepens Libya's constitutional crisis.

Armed Conflict and War Crimes

The October 2020 ceasefire agreement between former Government of National Accord and Hiftar's LAAF stipulated the departure of all foreign fighters from the country. According to the UN mission in Libya, as of September, thousands of foreign fighters from Syria, Russia, Chad, and Sudan, including members of private military companies, remained in Libya.

Since the discovery of mass graves in the town Tarhouna after the end of the armed conflict in June 2020, Libyan authorities said they had retrieved more than 200 bodies from more than 555 mass graves as of October. The Public Authority for Search and Identification of Missing Persons as of October had yet to confirm how many individuals were identified based on DNA matching or other means, such as clothing.

The use of landmines during the armed conflict in Tripoli and surroundings, reportedly by the Wagner Group, a Russian government-linked company, has killed and maimed dozens of people and deterred families from returning to their homes. In September, eight members of one family were injured when a landmine exploded near their home in southern Tripoli. According to a March report by the UN Panel of Experts on Libya, internationally banned antipersonnel landmines manufactured in Russia and never before seen in Libya were brought into the country and used in Libya in 2019 and early 2020.

Judicial System and Detainees

Libya's criminal justice system remained dysfunctional in some areas due to years of fighting and political divisions. Where prosecutions and trials took place, there were serious due process concerns and military courts continued to try civilians. Judges, prosecutors and lawyers remained at risk of harassment and attacks by armed groups. Libyan courts are in a limited position to resolve election disputes, including registration and results.

Libya's Justice Ministry as of August held 12,300 detainees, including women and children, in 27 prisons under their control and other detention facilities "acknowledged" by the GNU, according to the UN Support Mission in Libya (UNSMIL). Forty-one percent of the detainees were held in arbitrary, long-term pre-trial detention, according to UNSMIL. Armed groups held thousands of others in irregular detention facilities. Prisons in Libya are marked by inhumane conditions such as overcrowding and ill treatment.

Libyan authorities in March deported to Tunisia 10 Tunisian women and 14 children held in Libyan prisons, some for more than 5 years, for having ties to suspected members of ISIS.

The Libyan Supreme Court in May annulled a 2015 verdict against Gaddafi-era officials whose prosecution and trials for their roles during the 2011 revolution had been marred by due process violations. Muammar Gaddafi's son Saif al-Islam was among nine sentenced to death. The Supreme Court ordered a retrial, yet at time of writing none of the defendants had appeared in court.

Authorities in western Libya on September 5 released eight detainees linked with former leader Muammar Gaddafi held since 2011, including one of Gaddafi's sons, Al-Saadi, held since 2014 after his extradition from Niger. A Tripoli appeals court in April 2018 had cleared Al-Saadi of all charges, including first degree murder, yet he remained held in arbitrary detention and subjected to ill-treatment for three more years.

International Justice and the ICC

The International Criminal Court's (ICC) former prosecutor in May reported to the Security Council that members of her office had travelled to Libya and inter-

425

viewed witnesses but she did not announce any new arrest warrants against Libyan suspects.

Saif al-Islam Gaddafi, wanted by the ICC since 2011 for serious crimes during the 2011 uprising, remains a fugitive and Libya remains under legal obligation to surrender him to the Hague.

Al-Tuhamy Khaled, former head of the Libyan Internal Security Agency and wanted by the ICC for crimes he allegedly committed in 2011, reportedly died in Cairo in February; Mahmoud el-Werfalli, a commander linked with the LAAF and wanted by the ICC for multiple killings in eastern Libya, was reportedly killed in March in Benghazi by unidentified armed men.

Khalifa Hiftar faces three separate lawsuits filed in a US District Court in Virginia by families who allege their loved ones were killed or tortured by his forces in Libya after 2014. In July, the judge ruled that Hiftar cannot claim head-of-state-immunity in his defense.

The Libya Fact-Finding Mission (FFM) established by the UN Human Rights Council (HRC) in June 2020 to investigate alleged violations and abuses since 2016 only became fully operational in June due to delays caused by the Covid-19 pandemic. On October 3, the FFM issued its report, which found that "several parties to the conflicts violated International Humanitarian Law and potentially committed war crimes."

On October 11, the HRC renewed the mission's mandate for an additional nine months to allow completion of its investigations.

Death Penalty

The death penalty is stipulated in over 30 articles in Libya's penal code, including for acts of speech and association. No death sentences have been carried out since 2010, although both military and civilian courts continued to impose them.

Freedom of Association

Libya's Penal Code levies severe punishments, including the death penalty, for establishing "unlawful" associations, and prohibits Libyans from joining or establishing international organizations unless they receive government permission.

Presidential Decree 286 on regulating NGOs, passed in 2019 by the former Presidential Council of the GNA, includes burdensome registration requirements and stringent regulations on funding. Fundraising inside and outside Libya is prohibited. The decree mandates onerous advance notification for group members wanting to attend events. The Tripoli-based Commission of Civil Society, tasked with registering and approving civic organizations, has sweeping powers to inspect documents and cancel the registration and work permits of domestic and foreign organizations.

Freedom of Speech and Expression

Authorities in eastern Libya on September 11 released freelance photojournalist Ismail Abuzreiba al-Zway, who had been detained since December 2018. In May 2020, a Benghazi military court had sentenced him in a secret trial to 15 years in prison for "communicating with a TV station that supports terrorism." The General Command of the LAAF reportedly granted al-Zway amnesty, but the conditions of his release were not publicized.

In October, the Libyan parliament passed a cybercrime law. The final text is not available but an earlier draft contains overbroad provisions and draconian punishments including fines and imprisonment that could violate freedom of speech.

A number of provisions in Libyan laws unduly restrict freedom of speech and expression including criminal penalties for defamation of officials, the Libyan nation and flag, and insulting religion. The penal code stipulates the death penalty for "promoting theories or principles" that aim to overthrow the political, social or economic system.

Human Rights Defenders

In April, the Committee on the Elimination of Discrimination against Women (CEDAW), responding to a complaint filed in 2017 by Libyan human rights defender Magdulien Abaida, found that Libya had violated the human rights of an activist "by failing to investigate and prosecute her unlawful arrest and torture by a militia group affiliated with the government." In August 2012, the armed group Martyrs of 17 February Brigade, had seized Abaida from a hotel in Benghazi during a workshop and over the course of five days moved her between different military compounds while subjecting her to threats, harassment, insults and beatings. Abaida fled Libya soon after the group released her and was granted asylum in the United Kingdom.

Mansour Mohamed Atti al-Maghribi, a civic activist and head of the Red Crescent Society in the eastern town of Ajdabiya, has been missing since June 3 when unidentified armed men seized him while he was driving in the town. According to a joint submission to the GNU in July by two United Nations special rapporteurs and the Working Group on Enforced Disappearances, the Internal Security Agency (ISA) in Ajdabiya had previously harassed al-Maghribi and subjected him to intimidation. ISA agents in December 2020 and in February had summoned him for questioning on his civil society work, and in April the ISA briefly arrested him for "promoting foreign agendas." As of October, the GNU had yet to respond.

Women's Rights, Sexual Orientation, Gender Identity

Libyan law does not specifically criminalize domestic violence. Corporal punishment of children remains common. Libya's Family Code discriminates against women with respect to marriage, divorce, and inheritance.

The penal code allows for a reduced sentence for a man who kills or injures his wife or another female relative because he suspects her of extramarital sexual relations. Under the penal code, rapists can escape prosecution if they marry their victim. The 2010 nationality law stipulates that only Libyan men can pass on Libyan nationality to their children.

Online violence against women has reportedly grown steadily in recent years, often escalating to physical attacks, with no laws in place to combat the problem.

The penal code prohibits all sexual acts outside marriage, including consensual same-sex relations, and punishes them with flogging and up to five years in prison.

Internally Displaced Persons

As of October, the International Organization for Migration (IOM) estimated there were 212,593 internally displaced people in Libya, or 42,506 families, with the largest number in Benghazi, followed by Tripoli and then Misrata.

They include many of the 48,000 former residents of the town of Tawergha, who were driven out by anti-Gaddafi groups from Misrata in 2011. Despite reconciliation agreements with Misrata authorities, massive and deliberate destruction of the town and its infrastructure and the scarcity of public services by consecutive interim governments have been the main deterrent for the vast majority to return to their homes.

Migrants, Refugees, and Asylum Seekers

Between January and September, at least 46,626 people arrived in Italy and Malta via the Central Mediterranean Route, most of whom had departed from Libya, according to the International Organization for Migration (IOM), which said arrivals in Malta and Italy in 2021 had been consistently higher when compared with the same period in 2019 or 2020. The organization recorded 1,118 deaths off the shores of Libya between January and September 30.

The IOM identified 610,128 migrants in Libya as of October. According to the UN refugee agency, UNHCR, over 41,000 including more than 15,000 children were registered asylum seekers and refugees as of October. Between January and September, UNHCR assisted 345 vulnerable refugees and asylum seekers to depart Libya, and more than 1,000 refugees and asylum seekers had been identified as a priority for humanitarian evacuations.

The European Union continued to collaborate with abusive Libyan Coast Guard forces, providing speedboats, training, and other support to intercept and return thousands of people to Libya. As of October, 27,551 people were disembarked in Libya after the LCG intercepted them, according to UNHCR.

Migrants, asylum seekers and refugees were arbitrarily detained in inhumane conditions in facilities run by the GNA's Interior Ministry and in "warehouses" run by smugglers and traffickers, where they were subjected to forced labor, torture and other ill-treatment, extortion, and sexual assault. At least 5,000 were held in official detention centers in Libya as of August, according to IOM.

429

In June, Doctors Without Borders (MSF) reported that its staff had witnessed shooting by guards in one facility as well as repeated incidents of ill-treatment, physical abuse, and violence in two migrant detention centers in Tripoli, in Al-Mabani and Abu Salim, leading MSF to temporarily withdraw from these centers.

On October 1, authorities conducted raids in Hay al-Andalous municipality in Tripoli on houses and other shelters used by migrants and asylum seekers to curb irregular migration, arresting 5,152 people including women and children, according to IOM. One man was reportedly killed and 15 people injured during the raids. On October 8, during a riot in al-Mabani prison in Tripoli that resulted in a mass break-out of thousands of detainees, guards shot to death at least six migrants and injured at least 24, according to the IOM. As of October, thousands remained in front of the closed UNHCR headquarters in Tripoli protesting conditions and demanding shelter and evacuations outside of Libya.

UNHCR resumed resettlements of refugees and humanitarian evacuations to Niger as of November 3.

Key International Actors

The UN Sanctions Committee's Panel of Experts report from March found that all Libyan parties as well as Egypt, the United Arab Emirates, Jordan, Syrian Arab Republic, Russia and Turkey had violated the arms embargo. The panel said "violations are extensive, blatant and with complete disregard for the sanctions measures. Their control of the entire supply chain complicates detection, disruption or interdiction."

In March, the European Union put on its sanctions list the brothers Mohammed and Abderrahim al-Kani, and their Kaniyat Militia, for extrajudicial killings and disappearances in the town of Tarhouna between 2015 and 2020. Mohamed al-Kani was reportedly killed during a raid by armed men on his dwelling in Benghazi in July. In April, the EU lifted sanctions against Khalifa Ghwell, a former prime minister. In June, the EU extended for two years the mandate of the European Integrated Border Management Assistance Mission in Libya (EUBAM Libya), tasked with assisting Libyan authorities in border management, law enforcement and criminal justice.

In June high representatives, including from Germany, the UN, Egypt, France, Italy, Russia, Turkey, the United Arab Emirates, the United States, and the European Union, convened for the Second Berlin Conference on Libya, which aimed to ensure implementation of the previously negotiated political roadmap and ceasefire agreement. Among the conclusions was a call on Libyan authorities to conduct judicial reviews of all detainees and the immediate release of all those unlawfully or arbitrarily detained.

US Congress in October passed two amendments to the National Defense Authorization Act for 2022 requiring the president to review violations of the Libya arms embargo for sanctions per Executive Order, and another requiring the US Department of State to report on war crimes and torture committed by US citizens in Libya. Hiftar is believed to hold US citizenship.

UN Security Council in October added Osama al-Kuni Ibrahim to the Libya sanctions list in his capacity as de facto manager of the Al-Nasr Migrant Detention Center in Zawiya for directly engaging in, or providing support to commit acts that violate international humanitarian law and human rights abuses. Violations include torture, sexual and gender-based violence, and human trafficking.

Malaysia

Faced with political instability, the Malaysian government resorted to heavy-handed tactics, investigating and arbitrarily arresting those critical of the government and its policies, pursuing a hardline anti-migrant policy, and threatening enhanced action against lesbian, gay, bisexual, and transgender (LGBT) people. In August, Prime Minister Muhyiddin Yassin resigned and was replaced by Ismail Sabri, but there was little change in the government's approach to human rights.

Attacks on Human Rights Defenders

The government continued to use a range of broad and vaguely worded laws, including the Sedition Act and section 233 of the Communications and Multimedia Act (CMA), to prosecute critical speech.

On April 23, 2021, police arrested graphic artist and activist Fahmi Reza for a Spotify playlist he had created as a satirical response to a controversial tweet by Malaysia's queen. After a four-month sedition investigation, the police dropped the case. Reza was arrested again on October 4 in connection with a caricature of the Malaysian prime minister.

In May 2021, the authorities opened an investigation into political cartoonist Zulfikar Anwar Ulhaque, known as Zunar, for alleged violations of the CMA and penal code section 505(c) for a satirical drawing that mocked the Kedah state chief minister.

In July, the authorities opened investigations into the creators of a short animated film depicting the abuse that one boy said he suffered in police custody, for criminal defamation and other violations of the penal code. The same month, authorities formally charged activist Heidy Quah with violating the CMA for a June 2020 Facebook post alleging poor treatment of refugees at an immigration detention center.

Those participating in peaceful protests have also been the target of police investigations.

On April 24, authorities arrested activist Mukmin Nantang and six others for protesting the 14-day extension of strict movement control orders in a village in Sabah. On July 6, police announced they were investigating for sedition and other offenses the "black flag" campaign, which urged people to display black flags to voice their disappointment with the government. At least 31 people who participated in a black flag vehicle convoy on July 24 were summoned for questioning.

On July 21, a youth coalition announced it would hold a protest on July 31 against the government's handling of the Covid-19 pandemic. On July 29, police arrested youth activist Sarah Irdina at her home. On the same day, police questioned three coalition members under the CMA and a penal code section criminalizing "making statements conducive to public mischief."

On August 19, 31 people who were holding an outdoor candlelight vigil for those who died of Covid-19 were forcibly detained by police. At least one participant subsequently filed a police report over physical injuries allegedly caused by the police.

Freedom of Media

Freedom of the press declined during the year. On February 18, the country's highest court held online news portal Malaysiakini in contempt of court for five comments posted by readers, even though the portal removed the comments shortly after being notified of their presence. The court imposed a fine of RM500,000 (US$124,000). The authorities opened a contempt investigation into the outlet's editor-in-chief, Steven Gan, for commenting on the court's ruling.

In May, the police summoned two Malaysiakini journalists for questioning about their coverage of allegations that police brutality was the cause of a death in detention. In July, they summoned Boo-Su Lyn of health care news portal Code Blue for questioning over an article about a Covid-19 outbreak at a vaccination center.

On July 2, the Federal Court upheld a defamation ruling against Malaysiakini in a decision that narrowly construed the common law public interest defense, posing a serious risk to media freedom. The case, brought by Raub Australian Gold

Mining Company, related to articles and videos posted by Malaysiakini about the possible impact of air pollution from a gold mine.

Police Abuse and Impunity

Police abuse of suspects in custody continues to be a serious problem, as does a lack of accountability for such offenses. The standard of care for those in detention is problematic, with detainees dying of treatable illnesses. According to the home minister, as of August, 42 people had died in custody, with 28 of those deaths in immigration detention centers.

Refugees, Asylum Seekers, and Trafficking Victims

Malaysia has not ratified the 1951 Refugee Convention. Over 179,000 refugees and asylum seekers, mostly from Myanmar, are registered with the United Nations High Commission for Refugees (UNHCR) office but are not granted legal status and remain unable to work or enroll in government schools.

The government has denied UNHCR access to immigration detention centers since August 2019, and the home minister has rejected calls for access. Malaysia's Home Ministry reported that, as of October 26, 2020, 756 children were being held in immigration detention facilities nationwide, including 326 from Myanmar who are detained without parents or guardians. In May, the Suhakam child commissioner expressed concern that Rohingya girls who had been trafficked to Malaysia as child brides were being detained in an immigration detention center. In February, Malaysia deported 1086 Myanmar nationals just weeks after a coup overthrew that country's elected government.

The immigration authorities conducted repeated raids and detained thousands of undocumented workers, despite concerns that doing so would discourage them from seeking vaccination or treatment for Covid-19.

The United States downgraded Malaysia to Tier 3 in its annual Trafficking in Persons report, noting that the government was "not making significant efforts" to eliminate trafficking.

Freedom of Religion

Malaysia restricts the rights of followers of any branches of Islam other than Sunni, with those following Shia or other branches subject to arrest for deviancy.

In March, the government appealed a High Court ruling that struck down a 1986 directive forbidding non-Muslims from using the word "Allah" and other Islamic words.

In September, the government announced it was drafting a new law to restrict the propagation of non-Islamic religions in the Federal Territories.

Criminal Justice

Malaysia permits the death penalty for various crimes and makes the sentence mandatory for 11 offenses.

Malaysia detains individuals without trial under restrictive laws. The Security Offenses (Special Measures) Act, or SOSMA, allows for preventive detention of up to 28 days with no judicial review for a broadly defined range of "security offenses." On September 1, the home minister stated that individuals "issuing statements that could incite others to the point of causing public fear" could face action under SOSMA.

Both the 1959 Prevention of Crime Act and the 2015 Prevention of Terrorism Act give government-appointed boards the authority to impose detention without trial for up to two years, renewable indefinitely, to order electronic monitoring, and to impose other significant restrictions on freedom of movement and association. No judicial review is permitted for these measures.

Sexual Orientation and Gender Identity

Discrimination against LGBT people remains pervasive in Malaysia. Federal law punishes "carnal knowledge against the order of nature" with up to 20 years in prison and mandatory whipping. Numerous state Sharia laws prohibit both same-sex relations and non-normative gender expression, resulting in frequent arrests of transgender people. In February, the Federal Court ruled that section

28 of Selangor's Shariah Criminal Offences Enactment, which criminalizes sexual intercourse "against the order of nature," was invalid.

Authorities have proposed a range of changes to Sharia regulations that, if passed, would negatively impact LGBT people. These include harsher sentencing for same-sex conduct and gender expression. In September, the Perlis state fatwa committee announced that those in gender-nonconforming clothing were banned from entering mosques.

In January, Islamic authorities arrested Nur Sajat, a cosmetics entrepreneur and social media personality, on charges of "insulting Islam" by dressing in clothing typically associated with women at a religious event. On February 23, after she failed to appear in court, the Sharia court issued an arrest warrant for her. On February 25, the Islamic authorities announced the deployment of at least 122 law enforcement officers "to find and arrest Nur." In October, Malaysia filed extradition requests for Nur with Thailand and Australia. On October 18, Nur Sajat announced that she was in Australia, where she has been granted asylum.

Women's Rights

In September, the High Court ruled children born overseas to Malaysian mothers and foreign fathers are automatically entitled to Malaysian citizenship, overturning a discriminatory practice in which only children born abroad to Malaysian fathers were entitled to citizenship. The government appealed the decision.

Female students have described being subjected to "period spot checks" in some schools to prove that they are menstruating and can be excused from fasting. A student who reported on social media that her teacher made jokes about rape in class was threatened with expulsion, harassed on social media, and investigated for "intentional insult with intent to provoke a breach of the public peace."

Children's Rights

Malaysia continues to permit child marriage under both civil and Islamic law. Girls ages 16 and 17 can marry with the permission of their state's chief minister. For Muslims, most state Islamic laws set a minimum age of 16 for girls and 18 for boys, but permit marriages below those ages, with no apparent minimum, with the permission of a Sharia court. Widespread school closures due to Covid-19 may have increased risks of child marriage, as research shows that leaving education is highly correlated with girls being married off.

Children in Malaysia were unable to attend in-person classes due to Covid-19 restrictions for most of the year. The government began a phased reopening of school starting in October. The prolonged closure exacerbated existing inequalities, as many underprivileged students did not have the tools to access online learning.

Key International Actors

Malaysia was one of the first countries to call for the Association of Southeast Asian Nations (ASEAN) to play a role in resolving the crisis in Myanmar, and strongly supported the decision to exclude the Myanmar commander-in-chief from the annual ASEAN summit in October. Malaysia has also been supportive of calls for equitable distribution of Covid-19 vaccines. The country has been elected to a seat on the United Nations Human Rights Council for the 2022-2024 term.

Maldives

The Maldives government of President Ibrahim Mohamed Solih took steps to end repressive restrictions on the media and speech in 2021, and made some progress addressing protection needs of migrant workers. However, the government failed to reform abusive laws, including on freedom of assembly, and blocked a number of protests.

The authorities also failed to ensure justice in cases of violence against women and girls, which rights groups criticized.

Authorities have also done little to address threats posed by extremist Islamist groups that have targeted politicians and activists. On May 6, 2021, parliament speaker and former President Mohamed Nasheed, accused of being an apostate by his opponents, was targeted in a bomb attack. Nasheed survived critical injuries from the explosion that also injured bystanders and members of his security detail.

Lack of Accountability

A government-appointed commission investigating deaths and enforced disappearances failed to make significant progress in investigating violent attacks on activists and politicians, including journalist Ahmed Rilwan who disappeared in 2014 and blogger Yamin Rasheed who was killed in 2017. The commission recommended that the police file charges against former Vice President Ahmed Adeeb for interfering in the investigation and protecting alleged perpetrators. However, as of November the police had not charged Adeeb. The authorities appeared to stall prosecutions in other cases investigated by the commission.

In January 2021, the government established the Ombudsperson's Office for Transitional Justice, tasked with conducting criminal investigations and prosecutions for state-led atrocities from 1953 to 2018. As of October, there were no updates regarding its investigations.

Migrant Workers

Roughly one-third of the population in the Maldives comprises foreign migrant workers, at least 60,000 of them undocumented. The vast majority work in the construction and tourism industries.

In August, Member of Parliament Ahmed Riza was charged with human trafficking for the purpose of labor exploitation. The case first came to light in July 2020 when workers on Bodufinolhu island, a tourist resort, protested months of non-payment.

While the Maldives made progress on its anti-human trafficking efforts and was upgraded to Tier 2 on the US State Department's Trafficking in Persons report in 2021, the government failed to implement adequate measures to identify and support trafficking victims or investigate and prosecute perpetrators. A draft bill is pending in parliament to bring the existing Anti-Human Trafficking law in compliance with the United Nations Protocol to Prevent, Suppress and Punish Trafficking in Persons.

Freedoms of Expression, Association, Assembly

The Solih government has taken steps to end repressive restrictions on the media and speech. According to the Reporters Without Borders' World Press Freedom Index, Maldives rose to a ranking of 72 in 2021 from 120 in 2018.

However, the government has not effectively confronted threats by Islamist groups targeting activists and civil society organizations. In August 2021 a social media campaign targeted the local chapter of Transparency International, Transparency Maldives, calling for it to be banned and accusing the government of colluding with civil society to "make the Maldivian education system secular." This followed an announcement by Ministry of Education that it was partnering with Transparency Maldives.

Covid-19

The Maldives experienced a surge in Covid-19 cases in 2021. About 18 percent of the confirmed cases were among migrant workers, who also had to cope with economic hardship due to non-payment of wages.

The government provided vaccinations free of charge to everyone residing in the Maldives, including migrant workers, including those without documentation.

Despite the findings by an expert committee pointing to unhealthy conditions and overcrowding in prisons, the government did not enforce its recommendations to improve hygiene. In September, Maafushi Prison was brought under a state of emergency after a corrections officer contracted Covid-19, leading to fear of an outbreak.

Environmental Harm

Although it acknowledged increased threats from climate change, the Solih government failed to adequately enforce environmental protection laws and launched reclamation projects that risked environmental harm, something the ruling party had criticized while in opposition. In September, the citizen-led environmental group Save Maldives sought a civil injunction to stop the government's development project in Gulhifalhu lagoon, arguing that it would destroy environmentally protected areas in violation of Maldivian law.

The government has yet to fulfill its pledge to restore the Environmental Protection Agency as an independent entity. Environmental impact assessments for new projects often lack genuine consultations with communities and proposed mitigation measures are rarely implemented.

Torture and Ill-Treatment

The Human Rights Commission of the Maldives (HRCM) launched an investigation into claims that a suspect arrested on terrorism allegations was tortured in prison. The police admitted that they had used pepper spray on him.

While hundreds of complaints of torture and ill-treatment have been filed with government commissions since the Anti-Torture Act was passed in 2013, none have led to the prosecution of officials or redress for victims.

Women's and Girls' Rights

A March 2021 UN report analyzing reporting of gender-based violence in 2020 found that confinement in the home with abusers, financial insecurity, and other problems exacerbated by lockdown restrictions contributed to an escalation of reported cases of abuse. In April, protests broke out across Malé, the capital, in response to an increase in reported incidents of sexual assault and domestic violence.

In February, Gender Minister Aishath Mohamed Didi and four women parliamentarians joined civil society groups in condemning the authorities for allowing the former tourism minister, Ali Waheed, to travel to the United Kingdom despite the fact that he was on trial at the time for multiple charges of sexual assault against ministry employees. Waheed was arrested and is currently detained in the UK.

Sexual Orientation and Gender Identity

The Maldivian penal code criminalizes adult, consensual same-sex sexual conduct; punishment can include imprisonment of up to eight years and 100 lashes, and applies equally to men and women. Same-sex marriage is outlawed and punishable by up to a year in prison. Extremist groups in the Maldives use social media to harass and threaten those who promote the rights of lesbian, gay, bisexual, and transgender (LGBT) people.

Key International Actors

United States Ambassador to Maldives Alaina Teplitz made an official visit in January 2021; in the same month the US and Maldives held their first ever meeting on defense and security cooperation. In June, US Under Secretary of Defense Policy Colin Kahl spoke by phone with Maldivian Foreign Minister Abdulla Shahid about furthering security cooperation and countering the threat of violent extremism.

In a phone call with Chinese President Xi Jinping in June, President Solih committed to continuing cooperation on development projects. China agreed to a Covid-19 related postponement of loan repayments; the Maldives is significantly in debt to China.

In August, India signed a contract to build a series of bridges linking Malé with neighboring islands. The $500 million Greater Malé Connectivity Project is described as the "largest-ever" infrastructure project in the Maldives.

In July, the Maldives was taken off the "Human Rights Priority Countries" list compiled by the Foreign, Commonwealth and Development Office of the United Kingdom.

In September, the Maldives endorsed the intergovernmental Safe Schools Declaration.

Mali

Human rights and security deteriorated in Mali in 2021 as abuses by armed Islamist groups spiked, a political crisis deepened, and impunity for past and ongoing atrocities by all armed groups persisted. Mali's transition to civilian rule following the 2020 military coup suffered a setback after another coup in May, the third in under 10 years.

Armed Islamist attacks on civilians and government forces intensified, while the Malian security forces summarily executed numerous suspects. The number of internally displaced people increased significantly, bringing the total to over 385,000.

The authorities made scant progress addressing rampant banditry or restoring state authority and services, including the judiciary, in the north and center, undermining the rule of law and confidence in the state. They made some progress delivering justice in terrorism cases, but not for large-scale atrocities implicating ethnic militias and soldiers during counterterrorism operations.

Political Crisis

On May 24, the vice-president, Col. Assimi Goïta, detained transitional President Bah N'Daw, Prime Minister Moctar Ouane, and other members of a transitional government installed after the August 2020 military coup. After stripping them of their powers, Goïta was sworn in as head of state in June.

Goïta initially promised to abide by the 18-month transition to civilian rule and organize free and fair parliamentary and presidential elections by February 2022, as agreed after the 2020 coup, but later announced the timeline could not be met. At writing several key electoral deadlines had not been met, including updating voter rolls and a planned October 31 constitutional referendum.

Abuses by Islamist Armed Groups

Islamist armed groups allied to Al-Qaeda or the Islamic State (ISIS) in the Greater Sahara killed scores of civilians, as well as at least 19 United Nations peacekeepers and over 120 government security force members.

On August 8, armed Islamists massacred around 50 ethnic Songhai during an attack on several villages in Gao region. On June 3, they killed 11 ethnic Tuaregs near Menaka. At least 33 civilians were killed by improvised explosive devices planted on roadways, including 16 people on May 22 in Gao region. On December 3, they killed at least 31 traders after firing on a bus bringing them to the Bandiagara market in Mopti region.

The number of civilians abducted or kidnapped by armed Islamists increased significantly during 2021, with those abducted including local officials, village and religious leaders, aid workers, and Chinese construction workers. French journalist Oliver Dubois was taken hostage near Gao. A Swiss missionary and at least one Malian aid worker were executed while in the custody of armed Islamists.

In areas under their control, Islamist armed groups imposed *zakat* (forced taxation), beat civilians refusing to adhere to their strict behavioral and dress code, and implemented Sharia (Islamic law) via courts that did not adhere to fair trial standards. They also contributed to food insecurity by attacking farmers and besieging villages. In May, Islamist armed groups amputated the arms and legs of three men accused of banditry in Gao region.

Abuses by State Security Forces

Malian security forces were implicated in over 40 unlawful killings of suspects and civilians, and at least 20 enforced disappearances from December 2020 to October 2021. Most killings took place during counterterrorism operations in the Mopti and Ségou regions and targeted ethnic Peuhl.

In January, soldiers unlawfully killed eight people and disappeared two others near Mali's border with Burkina Faso. On March 23, soldiers in Boni beat dozens of bus passengers after finding suspicious material in the baggage compartment. The bodies of at least 13 of the passengers are believed to be buried in a common grave. At least seven other men were unlawfully killed by soldiers from the Boni military camp in March and April. Several men were allegedly killed or subjected to enforced disappearance after their arrest by soldiers in Sofara and N'Dola villages in October.

The detention, in Bamako, of former government officials and others by the military government raised due process concerns. Five men, including a former prime minister and journalist, were detained in December 2020 for allegedly plotting a coup against the Malian transitional government. They were released in April for lack of evidence.

Following the May coup, the deposed interim president and prime minister were unlawfully detained under house arrest for three months. In July, a man accused of attempting to stab interim President Goïta died in custody under suspicious circumstances. At least three high-level government officials arrested in Bamako by the security forces in September and October were held incommunicado for several weeks and tortured in unauthorized detention facilities.

Violations of Children's Rights

The United Nations reported that at least 60 children were killed and 71 were maimed by armed groups in 2021. Armed groups also recruited and used over 200 children as child soldiers. As of June 2021, insecurity forced the closure of 1,595 schools, leaving more than 478,000 children out of school.

Women and Girls Rights

An estimated 91 percent of Malian women and girls continued to undergo female genital mutilation and numerous women were subjected to sexual abuse by different armed groups. During 2021, seven officials with Mali's Basketball Federation were fired or suspended, and the head coach was indicted, for their involvement in the sexual abuse of teenage players with Mali's national youth team.

Communal Violence

Dogon and Bambara militias increasingly targeted members of their own communities, apparently for their failure to provide recruits and support their military objectives. In central Mali, militias kidnapped dozens of civilians for whom they demanded considerable ransoms. These groups killed several hostages and others, including people they had detained at unauthorized checkpoints in central Mali.

Accountability for Abuses

Hundreds of detainees were held in extended detention awaiting court trials. The Specialized Judicial Unit against Terrorism and Transnational Organized Crime (SJU), whose mandate was expanded in 2019 to include human rights violations, made progress investigating terrorism and a few atrocity cases. At least 14 terrorism-related trials, including for 2015 attacks on a night club and two hotels which killed 37 people, were adjudicated in late 2020 and 2021.

The transitional government pursued a few other cases involving human rights abuses that involve high-profile suspects. In July, Moussa Diawara, a former intelligence chief, was arrested and charged with involvement in the 2016 torture and disappearance of journalist Birama Touré. In connection with the same case, Interpol issued an international arrest warrant for Karim Keita, the former president's son, who fled to Côte d'Ivoire after the 2020 coup.

In August, a former defense minister and a former finance minister were arrested on corruption charges linked to the 2014 fraudulent purchase of a presidential plane. In September, the judiciary indicted and detained the commander of an elite police unit in connection with excessive use of lethal force which left several protesters dead in 2020.

The minister of defense signed 10 prosecution orders against alleged perpetrators of four atrocity cases involving soldiers in 2018 and 2020. At year's end, trials had yet to be held.

On March 15, a Bamako court dropped charges against 16 soldiers, including former coup leader Amadou Sanogo for the 2012 killing of 21 elite soldiers. The court cited the 2019 Law of National Understanding which grants amnesty for some domestic offenses but not for international crimes.

Justice for communal violence was hindered by the reluctance of members of the security forces to help gendarmes arrest suspects. Only a few cases of communal violence were tried by the Mopti High Court, including, in June, a trial which led to the conviction, in absentia, of 12 Dogon men for the 2019 killing of 37 Peuhl villagers in Koulogon.

The report of the International Commission of Inquiry, established under the 2015 peace accord to investigate serious violations between 2012 and January

2018, was presented to the United Nations Security Council in December 2020. The report documented evidence of war crimes by Malian security forces and crimes against humanity by armed Islamists and ethnic militias.

Public hearings by the Truth, Justice and Reconciliation Commission, established in 2014 to investigate crimes and root causes of violence since 1960, continued in 2021. Over 22,500 people have provided testimony to the Commission.

Key International Actors

In the wake of the May coup, the Economic Community of West African States (ECOWAS) and the African Union suspended Mali from their decision-making bodies. In October, Mali's transitional government expelled the ECOWAS special representative and, in November, ECOWAS imposed sanctions, including travel bans and asset freezes, on members of the transitional government.

Aid from the United States remains suspended pending free and fair elections.

Operation Barkhane, the 5,100-member French counterterrorism force, conducted numerous operations, but in June, France announced a significant reduction, notably a halving of personnel and the closure of military bases in northern Mali by early 2022.

A French airstrike on January 3 in central Mali killed at least 22 people. A United Nations investigation concluded that the majority of those killed were civilians attending a wedding. French authorities rejected the findings, insisting that the victims were armed Islamist fighters and characterized the UN investigation as "biased."

The European Union Training Mission in Mali (EUTM) and the EU Capacity Building Mission (EUCAP) continued to train and advise Mali's security forces. In January 2021, EUCAP's mandate was adjusted to include the restoration of government presence in central Mali. Task Force Takuba, comprised of 600 European special forces, engaged in military operations throughout 2021.

In May, June, and September, the EU condemned the coup and urged the government to organize elections by February 2022. At the UN Human Rights Council (HRC), the EU also stressed the importance of fighting impunity for abuses committed by terrorist groups, armed militias, and Mali's security forces.

In June, the UN Security Council renewed for one year the mandate of the UN Multidimensional Integrated Stabilization Mission in Mali (MINUSMA) and expanded it to support Mali's return to democratic rule. During a visit by the UNSC in October, members pressured the government to promptly restore democratic rule.

In March, the HRC renewed the mandate of the UN independent expert on Mali for another year. During a visit to Mali in August, the expert, Alioune Tine, noted that the security situation had deteriorated to the extent that the "very survival of the state" is threatened. In August, the Security Council renewed for one year the Mali Sanctions Committee Panel of Experts.

The International Criminal Court trial continued against a former leader of the Islamist armed group Ansar Dine on charges of war crimes and crimes against humanity, including rape and sexual slavery committed in 2012-2013.

Mexico

Human rights violations—including torture, enforced disappearances, abuses against migrants, extrajudicial killings, gender-based violence, and attacks on independent journalists and human rights defenders—have continued under President Andrés Manuel López Obrador, who took office in December 2018. Impunity remains the norm. Legal reforms enacted in 2017 and 2018 have been slow and ineffective in addressing torture and impunity.

President López Obrador has greatly expanded the scope of the armed forces' activities, deploying them for law enforcement and customs enforcement, and to control irregular immigration, run social programs, and build and operate mega projects.

The National Search Commission (CNB) has increased transparency about the number of "disappeared" persons, but prosecutors make little effort to investigate disappearances or identify those responsible.

In November 2019, the Senate named Rosario Piedra Ibarra to head the National Human Rights Commission (CNDH). Many human rights defenders called her appointment unconstitutional, saying that, as a former senior member of the president's party, she is too close to the administration to be autonomous and apolitical.

In August 2021, President López Obrador held a referendum on whether "past political actors" since 1988 should be tried for "crimes" including electoral fraud, corruption, and loss of lives to neoliberalism. Low turnout invalidated the results.

The president has collaborated with the US in abusive anti-immigration policies, including illegal expulsion of migrants and asylum seekers by plane and bus to Central America.

Criminal Justice System

The criminal justice system routinely fails to provide justice to victims of violent crimes and human rights violations. Only 5.2 percent of crimes committed in Mexico are solved, the nongovernmental group México Evalúa reports. Causes of failure include corruption, inadequate training and resources, and complicity of prosecutors and public defenders with criminals and other abusive officials.

The justice system regularly fails to ensure due process for those accused of crimes. Police and prosecutors commonly use torture to obtain confessions. Pre-trial detention is mandatory for many offenses, violating international human rights standards. Prisons are notoriously unsanitary and overcrowded. Prosecutors continue to use arraigo detention, a mechanism allowing them to obtain judicial authorization to detain anyone for up to 40 days without charge, for interrogation.

The attorney general never properly implemented a 2018 reform intended to make the office more independent from the government and more accountable to victims and their families, human rights and rule-of-law groups report. In 2021, Congress repealed many of the human rights provisions of the 2018 reform.

In April 2021, pro-government legislators passed a law extending the terms of the Supreme Court Chief Justice and members of the Federal Judiciary Council, which controls hiring and firing of judges. The chief justice declined the extension, and opposition legislators have challenged the law before the Supreme Court.

Military Abuses and Extrajudicial Killings

Mexico has relied heavily on the military to control drugs and fight organized crime, leading to widespread human rights violations. From 2013 through 2020, the CNDH received 3,799 complaints of military abuses.

President López Obrador has vastly expanded the scope of the military in public security, often supplanting civilian law enforcement. In 2019, he created the National Guard to replace the Federal Police as the government's principal law enforcement body. The National Guard is led by military officers, trained by the military, and composed largely of military troops. In May 2020, the president formally deployed the military to assist the National Guard in civilian law enforcement. The military can now legally detain civilians, take charge of crime scenes, and preserve evidence. Under past governments, charging the military with these tasks has contributed to serious cover-ups of human rights abuses. In July

2021, the president proposed formally placing the National Guard under military control.

In 2014, Congress reformed the Code of Military Justice, requiring abuses by members of the military against civilians to be prosecuted in civilian, not military, courts. However, pursuit of justice remains elusive.

In July 2020, 12 civilians were killed in a shootout with soldiers in Tamaulipas state. A video leaked to the press in August showed a soldier giving the order to kill a civilian. In September, the Secretary of Defense announced that only military police—no civilian prosecutors—were investigating. In March 2021, a lawyer for the families of victims told Reuters that no soldiers had yet been detained, despite the video evidence.

In September 2021, the Defense Ministry admitted that at least 47 people had been killed in "collateral damage" by the armed forces during the López Obrador presidency, according to information obtained through transparency requests by Mexican journalists. The Defense Ministry has paid compensation to families but has not sanctioned any soldiers or reported the cases to police or prosecutors for criminal investigation.

Torture

Torture is widely practiced to obtain confessions and extract information. It is most frequently applied after victims are detained, often arbitrarily, but before they are handed to civilian prosecutors. Victims are often held incommunicado at military bases or illegal detention sites. A 2017 law made it illegal to use confessions obtained through torture as evidence at criminal trials. However, authorities often fail to investigate allegations of torture.

In 2016—the last year for which data is available—Mexico's national statistics office surveyed more than 64,000 people incarcerated in 338 prisons. Almost two-thirds (64 percent) reported physical violence at the time of arrest, including electric shocks, choking, and smothering.

Disappearances

Thousands of people disappear every year in Mexico. Police, the military, and criminal groups are responsible for many disappearances.

Prosecutors and police rarely attempt to find the disappeared or identify those responsible. Families of the disappeared have formed more than 130 "search collectives" to investigate disappearances, including, frequently, by digging up mass graves.

In 2019, a well-respected human rights defender was appointed to head the government's National Search Commission (CNB). The CNB searches mass graves across the country. It has also taken steps to determine and publish the true number of people disappeared, gathering information from authorities and creating an online platform to report disappearances anonymously and show real-time numbers of those disappeared, excluding personally identifying information.

As of September 2021, the platform had recorded over 90,000 people disappeared, mostly since 2006. Authorities have publicly acknowledged the real number is likely higher. The majority are between 15 and 30 years old, from lower income families, the CNB reports. More than 23,000 are listed as having disappeared since President López Obrador took office in December 2018.

From 2006 to 2020, at least 50,000 bodies passed through the custody of state and local forensic medical services without being properly identified. Most are now buried in mass graves. From 2006 to 2021, authorities reported having found at least 4,000 mass graves.

In August 2021, the government named a group of seven international forensic and legal experts to lead the Extraordinary Forensic Identification Mechanism, which will be tasked with identifying bodies recovered from mass graves.

In November, the UN Committee on Enforced Disappearances visited Mexico—its first visit to any country. The committee first requested permission to visit Mexico in 2013 but was denied access by the previous government. In August 2020, the López Obrador government recognized the committee's jurisdiction to consider cases from Mexico, allowing families of victims to submit cases to the committee once they have exhausted their legal options domestically.

Attacks on Journalists and Human Rights Defenders

Journalists and human rights defenders—particularly those who criticize public officials or expose the work of criminal cartels—often face attacks, harassment, and surveillance by government authorities and criminal groups.

Mexico is one of the most dangerous countries in the world for journalists, on par with war zones like Syria and Afghanistan in number of journalists killed, according to the Committee to Protect Journalists and Reporters Without Borders. In 2020, journalists registered 692 threats, attacks, or other forms of aggression—reportedly the highest year on record. Article 19 reported five journalists killed in relation to their work from January to September 2021.

Authorities routinely fail to investigate crimes against journalists adequately, often preemptively ruling out their profession as a motive. Since its creation in 2010 through August 2021, the federal Special Prosecutor's Office to investigate crimes against journalists has opened more than 3,362 investigations, brought 265 charges for crimes, and obtained 25 convictions. In the face of uninvestigated violence, many journalists self-censor.

Mexico is also one of the most dangerous countries in the world for human rights defenders. From January through September 2021, the Mexico Office of the UN High Commissioner for Human Rights reported 10 human rights defenders killed. As with journalists, violence against human rights defenders is rarely investigated or prosecuted.

In 2012, the federal government established the Protection Mechanism for Human Rights Defenders and Journalists, which provides bodyguards, armored cars, and panic buttons, and helps journalists temporarily relocate in response to serious threats. A 2019 study by the Office of the United Nations High Commissioner for Human Rights documented the Mechanism's problems in coordinating protective measures, providing resources, and establishing clear procedures. Six journalists have been killed under the program's protection, four since President López Obrador took office. In October 2020, the government eliminated the independent fund that paid for protection measures, putting the mechanism in a precarious financial situation.

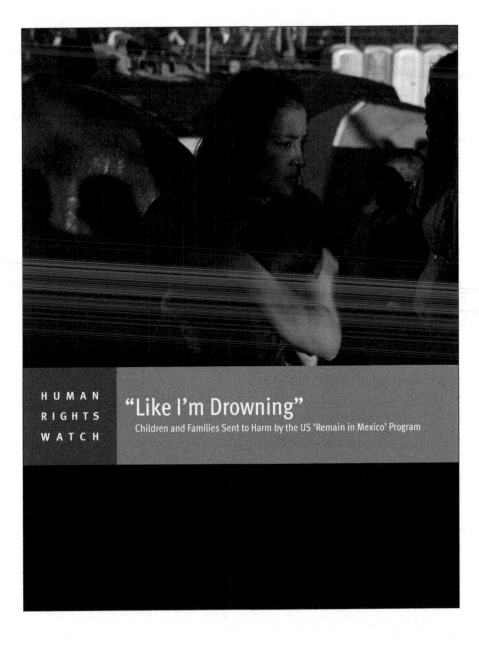

HUMAN
RIGHTS
WATCH

"Like I'm Drowning"
Children and Families Sent to Harm by the US 'Remain in Mexico' Program

Women's and Girls' Rights

Mexican laws do not adequately protect women and girls, including those with disabilities, against gender-based and sexual violence. Some provisions, including those that peg the severity of punishments for sexual offenses to the "chastity" of the victim, contradict international standards.

Abortion access varies by state. All 32 states allow abortion in cases of rape. Six allow it for any reason up to 12 weeks of pregnancy. Women and pregnant people face many barriers when trying to access abortion, even when it is legal. Doctors and nurses regularly attempt to dissuade them from undergoing the procedure or refuse to perform it.

In September, the Supreme Court made three rulings that set important precedents for reproductive rights. The court found that absolute criminalization of abortion is unconstitutional and that women should not be criminally prosecuted for undergoing the procedure. It ruled that state governments do not have the authority to legislate that life begins at conception. And it ruled that medical staff's right to conscientiously object to performing abortions is subject to limits.

Women and girls continue to face alarming rates of gender-based violence. In 2020, the government reported nearly 1,000 femicides—killings of women because of their gender. Women's rights groups say femicide is likely under-reported.

Migrants and Asylum Seekers

Criminal cartels, common criminals, and sometimes police and migration officials regularly target people migrating through Mexico to rob, kidnap, extort, rape, or kill them. These crimes are rarely reported, investigated, or punished.

The López Obrador administration has actively participated in abusive US immigration policies. It failed to provide police protection or access to justice, work, health care, and education for the over 71,000 asylum seekers, including many families with children, sent to Mexico under the "Remain in Mexico" policy. Many suffered abuses from criminal cartels or Mexican authorities. President López Obrador said the program had produced "very good results."

The López Obrador administration has been illegally expelling thousands of asylum seekers to Guatemala without due process, including many who were first expelled from the US into the custody of Mexican authorities.

In 2019, President López Obrador deployed the National Guard for migration enforcement. The government says soldiers only support migration officials. However, in a leaked audio recording from 2019, a senior migration official told her team they were now "under the instruction and supervision of the National Guard." In September 2021, National Guard troops and Mexican immigration agents violently detained a series of caravans of asylum seekers in Chiapas state, leaving many injured.

Mexican immigration officials have refused to follow court rulings ordering them to prevent the spread of Covid-19 in immigration detention centers. Detained migrants have said they were not given masks or soap and were denied medical treatment when they had symptoms of Covid-19.

Mexico's asylum system is severely overstretched. Since 2013, the number of applications received has nearly doubled every year. Officials expect to receive more than 100,000 applications in 2021. From January through August 2021, Mexico received nearly 78,000 asylum applications but resolved just over 23,000.

Sexual Orientation and Gender Identity

Twenty-four of 32 states have legalized same-sex marriage. Elsewhere, same-sex couples must petition for an injunction (amparo) to be allowed to marry. In 2019, the Supreme Court ruled that a lesbian couple from Aguascalientes state should be allowed to register a child born to one of the women as a child of both. The ruling was based on the best interest of the child and the principles of equality and non-discrimination.

Seventeen states have passed laws creating a procedure permitting transgender people to change their names and gender markers on birth certificates through a simple administrative process. In 2018, the Supreme Court ruled in favor of a transgender person from Veracruz who contended that in refusing to change their name and gender marker on their birth certificate, the municipal Civil Registry had violated their rights. In 2019, the Supreme Court issued a similar ruling arising from a case in Jalisco.

Disability Rights

Under the López Obrador administration, serious gaps remain in protecting the rights of people with disabilities. They lack access to justice, education, legal standing, legal capacity, protection from domestic violence, and informed consent in health decisions. In 2019, Human Rights Watch documented cases of state-run hospitals and private individuals who shackled people with disabilities. They lack access to buildings, transportation, and public spaces. Women with disabilities suffer disproportionate violence.

The only policy to assist people with disabilities is a non-contributive disability pension that reaches only 933,000 people of the 6,179,890 who live in the country. Its distribution is opaque and discretionary.

In many states, people with disabilities have no choice but to depend on their families for assistance or to live in institutions, which is inconsistent with their right to live independently and be included in the community under the Convention on the Rights of Persons with Disabilities. People with disabilities receive little government protection or support and are at higher risk of abuse and neglect by their families.

In October 2021, following a CRPD committee recommendation, the government publicly apologized to a man with intellectual and psychosocial disabilities who had been imprisoned for four years although there was no evidence he had committed a crime and a judge had found him unfit to stand trial, leaving him without the opportunity to defend himself.

Since President López Obrador took office, the National Council on People with Disabilities, the principal government body coordinating efforts to implement disability rights, has been effectively non-operational.

Covid-19

The López Obrador administration has failed to take many of the basic steps recommended by global health authorities to limit the spread of Covid-19. The official leading Mexico's response has called large-scale testing "useless" and "a waste of time," despite the World Health Organization's insistence on the importance of testing. As a result, Mexico has one of the lowest rates of Covid-19 testing—and highest rates of positive test results—in the world. Officials and experts agree that the real number of Covid-19 infections and deaths is likely many times higher than the official count.

As of September 2021, 30 percent of Mexicans had been fully vaccinated against Covid-19 and 47 percent had received at least one dose of the vaccine. Mexico has made the vaccine eligible by regions and age groups, from older to younger people. Proof of address is required to receive the vaccine. Anyone over the age of 18 was eligible to receive at least the first dose of the vaccine by September.

Schools were closed in Mexico from March 2020 to August 2021, and classes were broadcast on television and radio. Although 94 percent of Mexican households have television, a lack of affordable internet access left many children, especially those in low-income households or with disabilities, unable to fully participate in education. Many teachers protested the re-opening, at the height of the third wave of reported Covid-19 deaths.

Climate Policy and Impacts

As one of the world's top 15 emitters of greenhouse gases, Mexico is contributing to the climate crisis that is taking a growing toll on human rights around the globe.

López Obrador has openly opposed wind and solar energy production. He has promised to rescue Mexico's coal and oil industries and has introduced reforms that favor state-owned fossil-fuel power plants over renewable energy sources. He has vowed to amend the constitution to overcome legal challenges to these policies.

López Obrador's initiative "Sowing Life," which he touts as a major component of his strategy to cut greenhouse gas emissions, may have caused 72,000 hectares of forest loss, with inadequate monitoring enabling beneficiaries to clear forests and then be paid by the government to plant trees. (López Obrador falsely claimed in November 2021 that a deal to end forest loss by 2030 reached at the global climate summit in Glasgow was inspired by "Sowing Life".) Law enforcement actions to curb illegal deforestation drastically diminished in recent years.

In its December 2020 climate action plan, Mexico increased the baseline against which its emissions reductions are calculated but maintained its 2015 emissions reduction commitments. This will allow Mexico to increase its emissions while technically meeting its targets. The plan is "insufficient" to meet the Paris Agreement goal of limiting global warming to 1.5°C, according to the Climate Action Tracker. If all countries' commitments were in a similar range, warming would reach up to 3°C by the end of the century.

Climate change is expected to increase the severity of extreme weather events, requiring steps by the government to protect at-risk populations from their foreseeable harms, including food insecurity due to rising temperatures and droughts impacting crops. In August 2021, hurricanes Grace and Nora caused flooding, landslides, and power outages in multiple states, killing at least nine people.

Key International Actors and Foreign Policy

Mexico's foreign policy regarding human rights under the López Obrador administration has been based on the principle of "non-intervention." In June, Mexico criticized other countries in the region that had condemned the jailing of critics and opposition candidates in Nicaragua, saying that they were intervening in Nicaragua's internal affairs.

In June 2020, Mexico was elected as a non-permanent member of the UN Security Council for 2021 to 2022. Mexico highlighted that one of its priorities on the council would be the protection of children. Mexico endorsed the Safe Schools Declaration in May 2021.

In October 2020, Mexico was re-elected to the UN Human Rights Council.

In 2020, Mexico appointed itself as one of 23 "Champion countries" of the Global Compact for Safe, Orderly and Regular Migration.

In August and September 2021, Mexico hosted negotiations between representatives from the Venezuelan government and opposition groups mediated by Norway.

Mexico endorsed the World Health Organization's Solidarity Call to Action for the Covid-19 Technology Access Pool, an initiative to "realize equitable global access to COVID-19 health technologies through pooling of knowledge, intellectual property and data."

Morocco and Western Sahara

Morocco cracked down on journalists and critics, including via apparently politically motivated prosecutions for criminal offenses. Laws restricting individual freedoms remained in effect, including laws that discriminate against women and lesbian, gay, bisexual and transgender (LGBT) persons. In Western Sahara, authorities continued to severely constrain activities and speech of independence activists.

Criminal Justice System

The Code of Penal Procedure gives a defendant the right to contact a lawyer after 24 hours in police custody, extendable to 36 hours. But detainees do not have the right to have a lawyer present when police interrogate or present them with their statements for signature. In recent years, police agents often coerced or tricked detainees into signing self-incriminating statements, which judges later relied on to convict even when the defendants repudiated those statements in court.

Freedom of Association and Assembly

Authorities continued to impede the work of the Moroccan Association for Human Rights (AMDH), the country's largest independent human rights group. The AMDH said that, as of September 15, 2021, authorities had declined to process the administrative formalities for 84 of the 99 AMDH local branches, impeding the ability of these branches to carry out basic functions like opening new bank accounts or renting space. These obstructions persisted even when administrative courts ruled in favor of the AMDH.

Freedom of Expression

On July 30, several global media reported that Pegasus, a potent spyware developed by Israeli firm NSO Group, might have been used to infiltrate the smartphones of many individuals in Morocco. Pegasus, which NSO Group claims is exclusively sold to governments, is capable of accessing contact lists, reading emails and text messages, tracking calls, collecting passwords, mobile phone tracking, and hijacking the target device's microphone and video camera to turn it into a surveillance device. Journalists and Moroccan human rights activists and journalists were among the targets.

Morocco's penal code punishes with prison and fines nonviolent speech offenses, including "causing harm" to Islam or the monarchy, and "inciting against" Morocco's "territorial integrity," a reference to its claim to Western Sahara. While the Press and Publication Code does not provide prison as a punishment, journalists and people who speak out on social media have been prosecuted under the penal code for their critical, nonviolent speech.

Those included Moroccan-American YouTube commentator Chafik Omerani and protester Noureddine Aouaj, sentenced to three months and two years in prison, respectively, for "defaming constitutional institutions" after they criticized King Mohammed VI. Omerani was freed on May 6 after completing his term. YouTube commentator Mustapha Semlali, also known as Allal Al-Qadous, was sentenced to two years for "undermining the monarchy" after he allegedly defamed Prince Moulay Rachid, the king's brother; Moroccan-Italian student Ikram Nazih, was sentenced to three years for "harming the Islamic religion" after she shared a Facebook post deemed to be making light of a Quranic verse. She was freed on August 23 after an appeals court reduced her sentence to two months. YouTube commentator Jamila Saadane was sentenced to three months for "insulting organized institutions and distributing false allegations" after she claimed that authorities protected sexual tourism activities in Marrakech.

In other cases, Morocco has arrested, prosecuted, and imprisoned several critics not overtly for what they said but instead for offenses related to sex or embezzlement, where the evidence was either scant or dubious, or the trial involved clear fair-trial violations.

On January 27, a Rabat Court of First Instance sentenced historian and free speech advocate Maati Monjib to one year in prison for "receiving funds from a foreign organization in order to undermine Morocco's internal security." The basis for the charge was that a nongovernmental organization (NGO) set up by Monjib to defend free speech received grants from European NGOs to organize trainings for local journalists in a way that "harmed Morocco's internal security."

The trial of Monjib took place on January 20 in his absence, even though he had been in the same tribunal that day to answer a prosecutor's questions in another case, for which he was in pretrial detention. Monjib's lawyers say the court notified neither Monjib nor them about the trial, which the authorities denied. Monjib was released on March 23, after hunger striking for 19 days. The case, in which three co-defendants were sentenced to one year in absentia, was pending at time of writing appeal.

On July 9, a court of first instance in Casablanca sentenced popular critical columnist Soulaiman Raissouni to five years in prison for "indecent assault." Raissouni was placed in pretrial detention on May 2020, days after a man accused him in a Facebook post of sexually assaulting him two years earlier, while he was visiting Raissouni's home. Raissouni spent a year in pretrial detention without the court ever providing a substantive basis for denying him bail for such an extended period. He was denied access to his own case file until late in the trial.

Raissouni, who waged a long hunger strike to protest the conditions of his trial, requested to be transported to the courtroom in an ambulance and attend the sessions in a wheelchair, under medical supervision. The judge denied his request, and thus Raissouni did not attend the last four sessions of his own trial. His defense withdrew from the trial in protest. After the verdict, Raissouni stopped his hunger strike, which had lasted 118 days. The case was pending appeal at time of writing.

Taoufik Bouachrine, the director of the now-defunct independent daily *Akhbar al-Yaoum*, where Raissouni worked as editor-in-chief, is serving a 15-year sentence for sexual assault on several women. The verdict was handed down by an appeals court in 2019 after a trial that the United Nation's Working Group on Arbitrary Detention said was marred by due-process violations and part of a "judicial harassment attributable to nothing other than [Bouachrine's] investigative journalism."

On July 19, a court of first instance in Casablanca sentenced investigative journalist Omar Radi to six years in prison on multiple charges, including espionage and rape of a female co-worker, and his colleague, journalist Imad Stitou, to one year in prison, with six months suspended, for "participation" in the alleged rape because he "failed to intervene to stop it." Radi testified that the sex with the complainant was consensual.

Radi, an outspoken critic who has long been subject to state harassment, has been in detention since his arrest on July 29, 2020. Stitou remained free pending appeal.

Examining the facts in the case on which the espionage charges against Radi are based, Human Rights Watch found that they consist of nothing but standard journalistic work, corporate due-diligence studies that Radi performed as a paid consultant, and his routine meetings with foreign diplomats. The case file, which Human Rights Watch reviewed, included no evidence that Radi had provided classified information to anyone or that he even had access to such information.

Several due process violations were recorded during the trial, which Human Rights Watch observed. The court never provided a substantive justification for holding Radi for one year in pretrial detention. The court refused to hear a defense witness, and admitted written statements by prosecution witnesses but refused to summon them, thus denying the defense's right to cross-examine them. While Radi had to fight in court for months to get his case file, websites closely tied with security services obtained leaked copies even before the trial started, and based on those leaks, published scores of articles affirming Radi's guilt. The case was pending appeals at time of writing.

Monjib, Raissouni, Radi, and others were subjected to relentless character assassination efforts in scores of articles published in websites known locally as "slander media" because of their incessant and seemingly coordinated attacks against critics of the authorities. Known for their proximity to security services, these websites have published in past years thousands of articles including personal information on targeted individuals. The information included banking and property records, screenshots of private electronic conversations, allegations about sexual relationships, and intimate biographical details.

Western Sahara

The United Nations-sponsored process of negotiations between Morocco and the Polisario Front, the liberation movement that seeks self-determination for Western Sahara, remained stalled after the resignation in May 2019 of Horst

Kohler, the envoy of the UN secretary-general. Staffan De Mistura was appointed as a new envoy on October 6.

Most of Western Sahara has been under Moroccan control since Spain, the territory's former colonial administrator, withdrew in 1975. In 1991, both Morocco and the Polisario, the liberation movement for Western Sahara, agreed to a UN-brokered ceasefire to prepare for a referendum on self-determination. That referendum never took place. Morocco considers Western Sahara to be an integral part of the kingdom and rejects demands for a vote on self-determination that would include independence as an option.

In November 2020, Moroccan security forces established a near-constant heavy presence outside the house of independence activist Sultana Khaya, in Boujdour, Western Sahara. They have provided no justification and have prevented several people, including family members, from visiting. According to Khaya, police forces raided her house several times, beating her and relatives, and smearing the house with a foul-smelling liquid. Khaya is locally known for her public displays of vehement opposition to Morocco's control of Western Sahara. The arbitrary blockade of her house was still in place at time of writing.

Moroccan authorities systematically prevent gatherings supporting Sahrawi self-determination, obstruct the work of some local human rights NGOs, including by blocking their legal registration, and on occasion beat activists and journalists in their custody and on the streets, or raid their houses and destroy or confiscate their belongings. Human Rights Watch documented some of these beatings and raids, including of the house of independence activist Hassana Duihi in May 2021.

In 2021, 19 Sahrawi men remained in prison after they were convicted in unfair trials in 2013 and 2017 for the killing of 11 security force members, during clashes that erupted after authorities forcibly dismantled a large protest encampment in Gdeim Izik, Western Sahara, in 2010. Both courts relied almost entirely on their confessions to the police to convict them, without seriously investigating claims that the defendants had signed their confessions under torture. The Cassation court, Morocco's highest judicial instance, upheld the appeals verdict on November 25, 2020.

Women's and Girls' Rights

The Family Code discriminates against women with regard to inheritance and procedures to obtain divorce. The code sets 18 as a minimum age of marriage but allows judges to grant "exemptions" to marry girls aged 15 to 18 at the request of their family.

While Morocco's 2018 Violence against Women law criminalized some forms of domestic violence, established prevention measures, and provided new protections for survivors, it required survivors to file for criminal prosecution in order to obtain protection, which few can do. It also did not set out the duties of police, prosecutors, and investigative judges in domestic violence cases, or fund women's shelters.

Morocco's law does not explicitly criminalize marital rape, and women who report rape can find themselves prosecuted instead for engaging in sexual intercourse outside marriage if authorities do not believe her.

In July, an Instagram post showing a hotel in Marrakech denying access to Moroccan women unaccompanied by either their husbands or families, went viral.

Morocco bans hotels from accommodating unmarried couples in a shared room, but there is no known law denying access to unaccompanied women from any facility.

In July, authorities appointed the first female head prosecutor at a court of first instance. While Morocco does have female judges, women overall continue to remain heavily underrepresented in judicial positions.

In May, Morocco's National Human Rights Council reported that sexual harassment and gender-based violence are widespread against female staff and students at Moroccan universities, and a lack of mechanisms and means to adequately deal with harassment, and provide assistance to victims in universities.

Sexual Orientation and Gender Identity

Consensual sex between adults who are not married to one another is punishable by up to one year in prison. Moroccan law also criminalizes what it refers to as acts of "sexual deviancy" between members of the same sex, a term that authorities use to refer to homosexuality more generally, and punishes them with prison terms of up to three years.

In a memorandum published in October 2019, the National Human Rights Council, a state-appointed body, recommended decriminalizing consensual sex between non-married adults. More than 25 NGOs expressed support for the recommendation. The Moroccan government did not act upon it.

Refugees and Asylum Seekers

The government has yet to approve a draft of Morocco's first law on the right to asylum, introduced in 2013. A 2003 migration law remained in effect, with provisions criminalizing illegal entry that failed to provide an exception for refugees and asylum seekers. As of September 2021, the Ministry of Foreign Affairs had granted, or started the administrative process for granting, refugee cards, along with special residency permits and work authorizations to 856 persons, most of them sub-Saharan Africans, whom the UN High Commissioner for Refugees (UNHCR) had recognized in recent years. All of the 8,853 refugees recognized by UNHCR as of September 2021 had access to health services and where applicable public education, but only about half of them had regular residency permits and work authorizations, according to UNHCR. Morocco also hosted 6,902 registered asylum seekers as of September.

Human rights violations against migrants by Moroccan authorities, as reported by the media and non-governmental organizations during 2021, included abusive raids targeting sub-Saharan migrants for forced internal displacements, usually toward the south of the country, and arbitrary detention of migrants, including children. In a positive step, the Moroccan government stated it would include refugees, migrants and asylum seekers in its national Covid-19 vaccination campaign, which launched in January 2021. As of September, 547 refugees had been vaccinated.

On July 19, Idris Hasan, an Uyghur activist who had been living in Turkey, was arrested upon landing in Casablanca airport. A court agreed to China's extradition request on December 15 but he had not been extradited yet at time of writing. Extraditing Hasan would violate Morocco's obligations under the 1951 Refugee

Convention and the 1984 Convention against Torture, which prohibit forcibly sending anyone to a place where they would risk persecution and torture.

Key International Actors

On September 29, the European Court of Justice (ECJ) annulled two trade agreements on agriculture and fishing between the European Union and Morocco. The court said that Western Sahara, which was included in those bilateral agreements, should be considered a third party and as such, its people had to give its "full consent" for the agreement to be valid. The ECJ ruled that the consultations with stakeholders in Western Sahara, in which the Polisario refused to take part, did not meet the threshold of "consent." Morocco and the EU had not appealed the ECJ ruling at time of writing.

Mozambique

The human rights situation in Mozambique worsened in 2021, largely because of the ongoing violence in the northern Cabo Delgado province. The humanitarian crisis in the province also deteriorated due to insecurity and violence, causing the displacement of over 800,000 people. The armed group locally known as Al-Shabab or Al-Sunna wa Jama'a (ASWJ), which is linked to the Islamic State (ISIS), continued to attack villages, kill civilians, kidnap women and children, as well as to use boys as soldiers in its fight against government forces. State security forces were implicated in human rights abuses, including intimidation, sexual exploitation of displaced women, and the unlawful use of force against civilians.

International partners, including Rwanda, the Southern African Development Community (SADC), Portugal, the United States, and the European Union responded to the Mozambican government's request for military assistance in operations against ASWJ in Cabo Delgado.

Humanitarian Crisis in Cabo Delgado

The humanitarian situation in Cabo Delgado province continued to deteriorate due to intensified fighting between government security forces and ASWJ. As of September 2021, the Mozambican government and the United Nations Refugee Agency, UNHCR, estimated that over 800,000 people had been internally displaced. Of these, about 48 percent were children, and over 84 percent lived in temporary accommodation and host communities across the country, while over 9 percent were in camps in Cabo Delgado, Niassa and Nampula provinces. The number of internally displaced people (IDPs) increased considerably in March, when more than 88,000 people fled Palma town, following a major attack by ASWJ. Many of the fleeing civilians sought refuge in Quitunda village, about five kilometers from Palma, where they lacked water, food, and other basic services.

In July, the UN World Food Programme (WFP) warned that northern Mozambique's displacement crises risked becoming a hunger emergency as more families continued to flee violence. As in the previous year, humanitarian groups were unable to reach communities most affected by the violence. The WFP suspended food distribution to Palma district in March due to security risks. Provision of assistance to displaced people in isolated areas in Palma, Macomia, Mocimboa da Praia, Muidumbe, and Quissanga districts only resumed in September, when access to the region improved.

In September, allegations reemerged of sexual exploitation and abuse of women in exchange for humanitarian aid. An investigation by Mozambique's Centre for Investigative Journalism found that some aid workers demanded money or sex before distributing food parcels to women in various internally displaced persons' camps across Cabo Delgardo province. As of October, the government had not shown any public commitment to investigate these allegations.

Abuses by Government Forces

State security forces were implicated in human rights violations during counterterrorism operations in northern Cabo Delgado province, including intimidation, ill-treatment of displaced people, and use of unlawful force against civilians. Government soldiers prohibited people who fled the ASWJ Palma attack to Quitunda from leaving the village, and physically assaulted those caught trying to flee. A number of displaced people also accused government forces deployed to Palma of forcing distressed residents to pay bribes to get space on rescue flights. As of October, the government had not taken any publicly known step to investigate those abuses or punish those implicated.

State security forces were also implicated in abuses outside the conflict zone, including against imprisoned women. In July, a commission of inquiry set up by the Ministry of Justice confirmed sexual exploitation and other rights violations against female inmates by guards at the Ndlavela Women's Prison in Maputo. The commission was set up following a report by the Centre for Public Integrity (CIP), a Mozambican anti-corruption organization that reported that prison guards took women inmates outside the prison and forced them "to have sexual relations with strangers outside the prison." The Commission recommended, among other things, prison legislation reform that explicitly criminalizes sexual relations between inmates and guards, and that women prisoners should be supervised only by women guards.

Abuses by Islamist Armed Groups

ASWJ continued to attack villages, kill civilians, kidnap women and children, and train boys to fight government forces. On March 24, the group raided the town of Palma, killing and injuring an unknown number of civilians, some in their homes, and displacing thousands. The group was also implicated in the kidnapping of boys and subsequently using them to fight government forces in violation of the international prohibition on the use of child soldiers. On October 5, the United Nations Children's Fund, UNICEF raised concerns that the insurgents were training and indoctrinating boys to fight in Cabo Delgado.

Human Rights Watch found evidence that ASWJ fighters are using hundreds of kidnapped women and girls, in child and forced marriages, and as sex slaves. The group released others after their families paid huge sums of money in ransom. In October, the British Broadcasting Corporation reported that joint Mozambican and Rwandan forces had freed an unknown number of women who were rescued from captivity.

Attacks on Refugees and Asylum Seekers

In June, the Mozambican government announced that Tanzania would not create a refugee camp to accommodate Mozambicans fleeing violence in Cabo Delgado. The government spokesman said the two governments had agreed that fleeing citizens would be repatriated to Mozambique. These people have continued to be forcibly returned by Tanzanian authorities. As of September, according to UNHCR, more than 10,300 asylum seekers had been sent back to Mozambique since the start of the year. Tanzania's actions violated the principle of non-refoulement, which prohibits forcibly returning people to threats to their lives or freedom.

Mozambican authorities failed to protect Rwandan asylum seekers in the country from attacks, and on at least one occasion were implicated in the enforced disappearance of a Rwandan national. Although the authorities denied knowledge of the whereabouts of Cassien Ntamuhanga, a Rwandan asylum seeker who disappeared on May 23, four witnesses told Human Rights Watch that they saw seven uniformed agents of the Mozambican National Criminal Investigation Service (SERNIC) arrest and take Ntamuhanga to the local police station on Inhaca island. Ntamuhanga's whereabouts remained unknown at time of writing.

On September 13, Révocat Karemangingo, a prominent member of the Rwandan refugee community in Mozambique, and former Rwandan army official, was shot dead by unknown individuals. In October, the Mozambican Human Rights Defenders Network, (RMDDH), denounced threats from unknown individuals against a Rwandan refugee known as Innocent Abubakar. In September, members of the Rwandan community in Mozambique told journalists that they lived in fear following the killing of Karemangingo.

Unresolved Kidnappings

The number of unresolved cases of kidnappings, including of businesspeople or their relatives, continued to increase in 2021, and police officers were implicated in at least one case. In June, according to media reports, the National Criminal Investigation Service (SERNIC) announced the detention of five people including one SERNIC agent and a policeman, in connection with the kidnapping of a businessman, Kapil Rajas. The ransom of US$600,000 demanded had not been paid when the police rescued Rajas and arrested three of his kidnappers. In August, the National Human Rights Commission reportedly urged the purging of Defense and Security Forces (FDS) ranks to prevent security forces from facilitating or covering up kidnapping crimes.

At least six other kidnapping cases remained unresolved as of October, with three of them, including the case of a Portuguese national, happening within five days. The police said families of the victims refused to cooperate with authorities, choosing to pay ransom for their release while police investigation was ongoing. Earlier in April, Mozambique's attorney general, Beatriz Buchilli, expressed concerns about increasing numbers of kidnapping cases, noting difficulties in resolving the existing 16 cases reported in 2020. In October, the Confederation of Business Associations of Mozambique (CTA), said kidnappings were "negatively affecting the business environment and private investment in Mozambique."

Key International Actors

Various international partners responded to the Mozambican government request for support in its military operations against ASWJ in Cabo Delgado. In May, Portugal signed a five-year military cooperation agreement with Mozambique that includes a training mission of 60 troops.

In July, Rwanda responded with the deployment of 1,000 soldiers and policemen to Cabo Delgado. A month later, the two governments reported that their joint forces had recovered control of Mocimboa da Praia, a town seized and occupied by insurgents since August 2020. Also in July, the European Council adopted a decision setting up an European Union military training mission in Mozambique to support government forces in the protection of civilians and restoration of safety and security in the Cabo Delgado province.

In September, United States special forces conducted an exercise with Mozambican troops which the US said incorporated components of human rights, the laws of war, protection of civilians, and engagement with civil society.

In October, SADC extended indefinitely its SADC Mission in Mozambique (SAMIM), which it launched in July for an initial three-month term. The mission's troop contributing countries include South Africa, Botswana, Tanzania, and Angola.

Myanmar

The military coup on February 1, 2021, effectively ended the democratic transition under Aung San Suu Kyi's National League for Democracy (NLD). The NLD was poised to return to power for another five years after winning landslide general elections in November 2020. Instead, under the military State Administration Council (SAC) junta led by Senior Gen. Min Aung Hlaing, soldiers and police rounded up hundreds of members of parliament, including Aung San Suu Kyi and senior NLD party members, and held them in arbitrary detention for months, many of them in undisclosed locations.

The military seized power making unfounded claims of widespread and systematic election and voter irregularities, although international and domestic election observers found that the election was "credible and reflected the will of the majority of the voters."

The junta brought multiple charges against Aung San Suu Kyi, including for corruption, incitement, and breaching the Official Secrets Act. Three of her deposed cabinet ministers and an Australian economic adviser also faced charges under the Official Secrets Act.

Millions took to the streets across the country in largely peaceful protests to call for the military to relinquish power, while members of parliament, ethnic minority representatives, and civil society activists formed the opposition National Unity Government (NUG). The security forces responded by committing offenses amounting to crimes against humanity against the civilian population, including torture, severe deprivation of liberty, enforced disappearances, rape and other sexual abuse, and inhumane treatment. Journalists, lawyers, medical personnel, anti-junta protesters, civil society activists, women, and many others continue to be at high risk of arbitrary arrest.

Between February 1 and November 1, the police and military killed at least 1,200 protesters and bystanders, including approximately 75 children, and have detained over 8700 government officials, activists, journalists, and civil servants.

On March 14, the junta imposed martial law in several townships across Yangon and began to enforce additional restrictions in other parts of the country. On May 13, the junta also imposed martial law in Chin State's Mindat township after clashes between security forces and lightly armed opposition militias. Under martial law orders, direct authority over the townships was transferred to the respective regional military commanders.

Since the coup, the military has intensified military operations against ethnic armed groups in some areas, such as Chin State. The military's indiscriminate use of artillery and airstrikes has reportedly injured and killed civilians, damaged villages, including schools, and forced thousands to flee.

Post-Coup Crimes against Humanity

The security forces have engaged in widespread and systematic attacks on civilians throughout Myanmar, including killing protesters, enforced disappearance of opposition supporters, torture, sexual abuse, rape of some detainees, and mass political detentions. On February 21, 2021, the junta stated in the state's *Global New Light of Myanmar*: "Protesters are now inciting the people, especially emotional teenagers and youth, to a confrontation path where they will suffer the loss of life."

Many of the 1,200 people killed by police and military since the coup were protesters and bystanders in cities and towns across Myanmar, including Yangon, Mandalay, Bago, Monywa, and other townships in Sagaing Region, Mindat township in Chin State, and many other locations. International human rights standards permit law enforcement officials to use lethal force only as a last resort when there is an imminent threat to life. But in numerous cases in 2021 reported by the United Nations, Human Rights Watch, other human rights organizations, and media, security forces fired on demonstrators who were unarmed and posed no apparent threat.

The UN reported that on March 3, security forces across the country fired live rounds at protesters, killing at least 38 and wounding more than 100. Killings were also reported in one day in Monywa, Sagaing Region; Myingyan and Mandalay, Mandalay Region; Salin, Magway Region; and Mawlamyine, Mon State, according to media reports. On March 13, authorities killed at least nine protesters, including five in the Sein Pan area of Mandalay, when security forces shot into a crowd. On March 14 in Hlaing Tharyar township, Yangon, security forces killed an estimated 66 people, according to the Assistance Association for Political Prisoners.

The MRTV news channel announced the day before Armed Forces Day, on March 27, that demonstrators "should learn from the tragedy of earlier ugly deaths that you can be in danger of getting shot to the head and back." On March 27, security forces followed through on that threat by carrying out violent crackdowns on protesters in at least 40 towns and cities, killing dozens.

On April 9, military personnel killed an estimated 82 people in Bago in a dawn assault on protesters' barricades and encampments; exact figures have been difficult to determine due to a strong security presence and lack of access to the area by reporters or independent investigators.

Many persons detained for taking part in pro-democracy demonstrations said after their release that security personnel tortured and otherwise ill-treated them and others in custody. Methods of torture included beatings, mock executions with guns, burning with cigarettes, and rape and threatened rape.

The junta has taken into custody more than 100 politicians, election officials, journalists, activists, and protesters, and refused to confirm their whereabouts or conditions of detention in violation of international law. Security forces frequently detained family members, including children and older people, when they were unable to find the individual they sought to arrest.

Threats to Rohingya

Authorities have been committing the crimes against humanity of apartheid, persecution, and severe deprivation of liberty against 600,000 Rohingya remaining in Rakhine State. Most Rohingya had fled the country following the military's campaign of killings, rape, and arson that resulted in crimes against humanity and genocidal acts in 2017.

Approximately 130,000 Rohingya have been confined to open-air detention camps in central Rakhine State since being displaced by ethnic cleansing in 2012, in violation of their fundamental right to return home. They are denied freedom of movement in what amounts to arbitrary and discriminatory deprivation of liberty.

Following the coup, restrictions on humanitarian access increased, leading to preventable deaths and illnesses in Rohingya camps and villages. In late May, nine children reportedly died Rakhine State following an outbreak of acute watery diarrhea.

Threats to Women's and Girls' Rights

Women have led and taken part in mass protests as part of the Civil Disobedience Movement (CDM) against the junta. Female protesters were some of the first killed by security forces and arbitrarily detained. Many women reported being beaten by security forces during their arrests, and some reported credible allegations of sexual violence and humiliating treatment by security forces during their detention.

Trafficking of women and girls remains a serious problem in Shan and Kachin States, where conflict and economic desperation has made them vulnerable to being lured to China under false promises and sold into sexual slavery and forced reproduction as "brides."

The NLD government, prior to the coup, was unable to pass the Prevention of Violence Against Woman Law. While the law had been criticized for falling well short of international standards, the absence of targeted legislation has stalled efforts to prevent gender-based violence, assist survivors, and bring perpetrators to justice.

Freedom of Expression and Media

As of October 25, Myanmar's junta had arrested 98 journalists, 46 of whom remained in detention, according to the Assistance Association for Political Prisoners. Six journalists had been convicted, including five for violating section 505A of the penal code, a new provision that makes it a crime to publish or circulate comments that "cause fear" or spread "false news." In such prosecutions, "false news" appears to be any news that the authorities do not want to reach the public.

On March 8, the junta stripped media licenses from five local outlets: Democratic Voice of Burma (DVB), Khit Thit Media, Mizzima, Myanmar Now, and 7Day.

On May 4, authorities banned two other outlets, the Kachin-based 74 Media and the Shan-based Tachileik News Agency, and also banned satellite television.

Also, on May 4, authorities arrested US journalist Danny Fenster, the managing editor of *Frontier Myanmar*, and detained him on politically motivated charges. On November 12, a court sentenced him to 11 years' hard labor, but he was permitted to leave the country on November 15.

On June 30, the Ministry of Information issued a warning to journalists to stop describing the SAC as a "junta" or face prosecution.

Internet Shutdowns

In the weeks following the coup, the junta imposed nationwide internet shutdowns from 1 a.m. to 9 a.m., which were later lifted, but authorities continued to block many websites and throttled internet speeds throughout the year. Blocks to mobile data and networks also continued across 22 townships where anti-junta opposition resulted in heavy clashes between the Myanmar military and pro-democracy militia groups.

Threats to Humanitarian Aid

Increased fighting between the Myanmar military and ethnic armed groups in the border areas in Chin, Kachin, Karen, Kayah, and Shan States has increased strain on access and limited humanitarian aid to those areas. The UN said, in July, at least 3 million people needed humanitarian aid—an increase of 2 million since February 1—and food shortages were reported in parts of Chin and Rakhine States.

Anti-Junta Militias

Militias have formed around the country since the coup to oppose the junta and target security forces. Many of the militias have adopted the title of People's Defense Forces, the same name the NUG adopted for the nationwide force it created. However, not all the recently formed People's Defense Forces are linked to the NUG or take orders from its command structure.

These militias began conducting small-scale attacks against the military in July. In Sagaing and Magway Regions and Chin State, intense fighting between the militias and the military reportedly killed hundreds of troops. The military responded with increased raids and by burning villages. Some militias have carried out unlawful bombings of buildings and targeted killings of civilian supporters of the military.

On September 7, acting NUG President Duwa Lashi La declared a "defensive war" against the military junta.

Sexual Orientation and Gender Identity

Myanmar's penal code punishes "carnal intercourse against the order of nature" with up to 10 years in prison and a fine.

The opposition NUG reported that lesbian, gay, bisexual, and transgender (LGBT) people have been particularly vulnerable to sexual violence in custody. One transgender woman recounted after her release that she was raped in custody with an object, tortured, and severely beaten.

Covid-19 and Attacks on Healthcare Workers

By November 2021, just 13 percent of Myanmar's 54 million population was fully vaccinated. A total 17,998 deaths were recorded by the Ministry of Health between March 2020 and October 2021, although the actual numbers are likely much higher.

The junta has harassed, arbitrarily arrested, and attacked medical professionals, sometimes as they treated injured protesters. Healthcare workers were early leaders of the opposition Civil Disobedience Movement and refused to work in government hospitals as a form of protest. In the nine months following the coup, at least 260 healthcare workers were attacked while trying to administer medical aid, and 20 killed. The AAPP said 76 remained in detention in September, and as many as 600 healthcare workers had outstanding arrest warrants against them. Many have been forced to work underground in makeshift mobile clinics to treat Covid-19 patients or have gone into hiding to evade arrest. The UN Country Team in Myanmar has said that attacks on healthcare workers have jeopardized the Covid-19 response and prevented patients from receiving health care.

Key International Actors

In February, the UN Human Rights Council held a special session and adopted by consensus a resolution deploring the removal of the elected government and calling for the unconditional release of all those arbitrarily detained. A further resolution was adopted at the council's March session "condemning in the strongest terms" the military deposition of the civilian government, and highlighting the need for accountability.

In June, the United Nations General Assembly passed a resolution strongly condemning the February 1 coup. The General Assembly also made several important recommendations, including calling for all members states to prevent the flow of arms into Myanmar. The UN Security Council did not follow up and pass a legally binding resolution of its own that would impose a global ban on the transfer of weapons and dual-use technologies to Myanmar.

Canada, the European Union, the United Kingdom, and the United States have imposed targeted sanctions against Myanmar's top military officials and members of the junta, conglomerates, and companies owned or controlled by the military. However, foreign governments did not impose sanctions on oil and gas revenues, the junta's main source of revenues.

In October, the US Congress introduced the BURMA Act 2021, supporting authorization of further targeted sanctions and recommended the US government make a Rohingya genocide determination. The European Parliament also supported recognizing the NUG as the legitimate government of Myanmar and urged further EU sanctions against military-owned businesses. While the EU expressed support for the Association of Southeast Asian Nations (ASEAN) as a mediator with the Myanmar military, it also condemned the coup in "the strongest terms."

The UN-backed Independent Investigative Mechanism for Myanmar (IIMM) is mandated to build case files to support efforts to hold individuals legally accountable for serious international crimes. The IIMM is "closely monitoring" events and is collecting evidence of such crimes committed following the coup, and said if substantiated, the alleged violations could amount to crimes against humanity.

On April 24, ASEAN negotiated a five-point consensus plan with the military, and appointed Brunei diplomat Erywan Yusof as special envoy. The military's failure to implement the five-point plan led ASEAN to exclude junta leader Senior Gen. Min Aung Hlaing from its October summit.

At the International Criminal Court, the prosecutor is investigating Myanmar for the crimes against humanity of deportation and persecution, based on the completion of these crimes in Bangladesh, an ICC member, following the 2017 ethnic cleansing campaign against the Rohingya. In July, citing Article 12(3) of the ICC Statute, the NUG lodged a declaration with the ICC accepting the court's jurisdiction over crimes committed in Myanmar since July 1, 2002.

Gambia's case alleging Myanmar's violation of the Genocide Convention continued before the International Court of Justice, with Myanmar raising preliminary objections to the court's jurisdiction and the admissibility of Gambia's application.

"I Must Work to Eat"

Covid-19, Poverty, and Child labor in Ghana, Nepal, and Uganda

Nepal

Inadequate and unequal access to health care in Nepal was exacerbated in 2021 by government failures to prepare or respond effectively when the Covid-19 pandemic surged, leading to many preventable deaths.

A pervasive culture of impunity continues to undermine fundamental human rights in the country. Ongoing human rights violations by the police and army, including cases of alleged extrajudicial killings and custodial deaths resulting from torture, are rarely investigated, and when they are, alleged perpetrators are almost never arrested.

Serious rights challenges remained unaddressed for months in 2021 during internal political infighting, the government was largely paralyzed by a struggle over the post of prime minister and repeated dissolutions of parliament. After the Supreme Court ordered in July that Sher Bahadur Deuba replace K.P. Oli as prime minister, the positions of health and education minister were left vacant for three months.

Both the Oli and Deuba governments continued to block justice for conflict-era violations. The mandates of the two transitional justice commissions were once again extended, although neither has made progress since being established in 2015 to provide truth to victims, establish the fate of the "disappeared," and promote accountability and reconciliation.

In March the government signed a peace agreement with a banned Maoist splinter group, the Nepal Communist Party (NCP), after it agreed to renounce violence.

Health and Education

During a major wave of Covid-19 infections, which peaked in May, senior health officials described a system at the breaking point, with patients dying due to lack of bottled oxygen.

The government had failed to prepare for the scale of the outbreak. The situation was made worse by a shortage of vaccines, reflecting both global scarcity—wealthy governments blocked an intellectual property waiver that would have allowed for increased international production of vaccines and failed to require

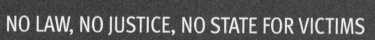

NO LAW, NO JUSTICE, NO STATE FOR VICTIMS
The Culture of Impunity in Post-Conflict Nepal

HUMAN
RIGHTS
WATCH

ADVOCACY
FORUM

more widespread technology transfers—and delays in procurement by the government amid allegations of corruption. Those living in poverty, and members of marginalized social groups, were often least able to obtain treatment, and most vulnerable to economic hardship resulting from lockdowns.

After decades of progress in maternal and neonatal health, there was a substantial drop in the number of births at health facilities, which were overstretched by the pandemic. This was accompanied by increases in neonatal deaths, still births, and pre-term births.

Nepal had made progress in reducing child labor in recent years, but the economic impact of the Covid-19 pandemic, together with school closures and inadequate government assistance, pushed children back into exploitative and dangerous child labor.

Transitional Justice

The Truth and Reconciliation Commission (TRC) and the Commission of Investigation on Enforced Disappeared Persons (CIEDP) were established in 2015, but despite receiving over 60,000 complaints of abuses committed during the 1996-2006 conflict, they have made no progress.

Successive governments have promised to bring the Enforced Disappearances Enquiry, Truth and Reconciliation Commission Act (2014) into conformity with international law as directed by the Supreme Court in 2015 but have failed to do so. The Office of the UN High Commissioner for Human Rights (OHCHR) has criticized the act for failing to comply with Nepal's international legal obligations by giving the commission powers to recommend amnesties for gross violations of international human rights law and serious violations of international humanitarian law, avoiding or delaying criminal prosecutions, and failing to ensure independence and impartiality. The United Nations and international community therefore do not support these commissions.

Meanwhile, the authorities have prevented cases of conflict era violations from being heard in the regular courts on the grounds that they will be addressed by the transitional justice process, although no meaningful or credible transitional justice process exists. Victims' groups have long called for the government to consult with victims before reappointing commissioners, but one of the first actions of Sher Bahadur Deuba upon becoming prime minister in July 2021 was to extend the commissioners' terms for another year.

Survivors of sexual violence committed during the conflict suffered from a particular lack of support or interim relief.

Rule of Law

Impunity for human rights abuses extends to ongoing violations, undermining the principles of accountability and rule of law in post-conflict Nepal. In October, police shot dead four people in Rupandehi district while attempting to evict landless settlers from government land. UN rights experts have repeatedly raised cases of killings by the security forces but none have led to prosecutions, although the government acknowledged that one victim had been tortured in police custody.

A partial exception was the case of Rajkumar Chepang, who died in July 2020 after being tortured by soldiers guarding Chitwan National Park. In July 2021 a soldier was found guilty by Chitwan district court, in what is believed to be the first successful prosecution for torture in Nepal since it was criminalized in domestic law in 2018. However, he was sentenced to only nine months in jail.

In December 2020, the then government of K.P. Oli amended the law governing the Constitutional Council, which makes appointments to the National Human Rights Commission, and then appointed new human rights commissioners without proper consultation with opposition members. Because parliament was dissolved, the new commissioners were sworn in without parliamentary approval.

The same process was used to make other appointments, including to the Election Commission.

In October 2021 police detained a human rights defender, Ruby Khan, on false charges of "polygamy," and initially defied a Supreme Court habeas corpus order to release her, after she led a protest demanding police investigate the alleged murder of two women.

Women's and Girls' Rights

Nepal has one of the highest rates of child marriage in Asia, with 33 percent of girls marrying before 18 years and 8 percent married by age 15. Among boys, 9 percent marry before the age of 18. This situation worsened during the pandemic, as children were pushed out of education and families faced increased poverty.

Nepal's 2006 Citizenship Act, as well as the 2015 constitution, contain provisions that discriminate against women. A draft bill to amend the Citizenship Act, first presented to parliament in 2018, retains several discriminatory provisions. In September 2020, three UN human rights experts wrote to the government raising concerns that "the bill would continue to discriminate systematically against women, regarding their ability to transmit citizenship through marriage and to their children." Due to flawed citizenship laws, an estimated 5 million people are forced to live without citizenship and are at risk of statelessness.

Reported cases of rape continued to sharply increase in 2021, but the police were often reluctant to register cases and investigations were frequently ineffective, resulting in widespread impunity for sexual violence.

Following Nepal's Universal Period Review, the government began consultations to update the criminal code to better safeguard the recognized right to abortion.

Sexual Orientation and Gender Identity

The bill to amend the Citizenship Act also contains a clause that would require transgender people to provide "proof" of their transition to access citizenship documents according to their gender identity—which violates international human rights law and a 2007 Nepal Supreme Court judgment mandating that gender identity be recognized based on "self-feeling."

While Nepal was among the first countries in the world to protect social and political rights for LGBT people—including legal recognition of a third gender—cases of discrimination and police abuse continue.

Treatment of Minorities

Caste-based violence and discrimination against Dalits are rarely investigated or prosecuted, despite the adoption of the Caste-based Discrimination and Un-touchability (Crime and Punishment) Act in 2011. Two emblematic cases of caste-based killings committed on May 23, 2020, are yet to be prosecuted. One involved the death of a 12-year-old Dalit girl a day after she was forced to marry her alleged rapist, and the second, the killing of six men in Rukum West district after a young Dalit man arrived to marry his girlfriend from another caste.

Key International Actors

Nepal's most important international relationships are with neighbors India and China, which compete for influence in Nepal. Both provided vaccine and other assistance to help Nepal cope with the pandemic, although India failed to keep up supplies during a surge in cases in early 2021 as it battled a devastating second wave of its own.

Nepal is a participant in the Chinese government's "Belt and Road Initiative." It continues to restrict free assembly and expression rights of its Tibetan community under pressure from Chinese authorities.

The Nepal government remains dependent for much of its budget on international development aid. Several of Nepal's donors have funded programs for many years intended to support respect for human rights, police reform, access to justice, and respect for the rule of law, but have not pressed the government to advance transitional justice or end the impunity of the security forces.

Nepal is serving a second consecutive term on the UN Human Rights Council from 2021-2023.

Nicaragua

Since taking office in 2007, the government of President Daniel Ortega has dismantled nearly all institutional checks on presidential power. The Electoral Council, stacked with the president's supporters, removed opposition lawmakers in 2016 and has barred opposition political parties ahead of the 2021 presidential elections. A constitutional amendment approved by President Ortega's party, which controls the National Assembly, abolished term limits in 2014. President Ortega was elected to a fourth consecutive term in November amid government repression of critics and the political opposition. Many governments from the region and Europe said the elections had not met minimum guarantees to be considered free and fair.

To pave the way for his re-election, authorities arbitrarily arrested and prosecuted government critics and political opponents, including presidential candidates, journalists, lawyers, and leaders of community, business, and student groups.

Police abuses committed during a brutal crackdown by the National Police and armed pro-government groups in 2018 have gone unpunished.

Persistent problems include severe restrictions on freedom of expression and association, political discrimination, and stringent restrictions on abortion.

Detention and Prosecution of Critics

Between late May and October 2021, authorities arbitrarily detained 7 presidential candidates and 32 prominent government critics. Prosecutors opened investigations against most on alleged "treason" charges.

Since February, an amendment to the Code of Criminal Procedure has allowed prosecutors to request detentions of up to 90 days without charge; in most cases involving critics, courts have permitted them.

In August, the Attorney General's Office filed charges against most of the detainees, in criminal proceedings that lacked basic due process guarantees. Charges, carrying prison sentences of 15 to 25 years, ranged from money laundering to, most commonly, "conspiracy to undermine national integrity." Prosecutors failed to identify specific acts by the defendants to support the charges in at least 14 cases.

Most critics have been held incommunicado and subjected to abuses in detention, including daily interrogations, prolonged solitary confinement, and insufficient food. Authorities have barred critics' lawyers from participating in public hearings, assigning public defenders instead. Despite repeated requests, most lawyers had no access to court documents for months.

Right to Vote and Run for Office

Election-related changes and laws adopted between October 2020 and February 2021 have been used to deter critical speech, inhibit opposition participation in elections, and keep critics in prison without formal charges, to prevent or limit their political participation.

In December 2020, the National Assembly passed the Law for the Defense of People's Rights to Independence, Sovereignty, and Self-determination for Peace, prohibiting so-called "traitors" from running for or holding public office. The law defines "traitors" in sweeping terms to include, for example, people who "undermine independence, sovereignty and self-determination" or "damage the supreme interests of the nation."

In May 2021, the National Assembly approved a legal reform consolidating government control of the electoral process. The reform codifies troubling new grounds for excluding candidates; does not require independent domestic or international electoral observation, which the Organization of American States and the United Nations Human Rights Council deemed essential to ensure credible scrutiny of the elections; and allows the National Police to authorize demonstrations in public spaces, including public campaign events.

After the National Assembly, which is allied with Ortega, appointed new Supreme Electoral Council members in May, the Council stripped legal registration from the main opposition parties.

Covid-19 Response

Denial, inaction, and opacity have characterized the government's response to the Covid-19 pandemic. The government took no emergency measures in response to the pandemic, kept schools open, and fired doctors critical of the government who disagreed with its management of the Covid-19 response.

While the government reported over 13,000 cases and more than 200 deaths, as of September 2021, the nongovernmental organization (NGO) Covid-19 Citizen Observatory registered almost twice as many suspected cases and 4,500 suspected deaths. The government has accused the organization and critical doctors of promoting "health terrorism." The Inter-American Commission on Human Rights (IACHR) reported that "state agents" were persecuting and harassing members of the Observatory, as well as from the medical associations Nicaraguan Medical Unit (UMN) and Interdisciplinary Scientific Committee.

As of October 2021, just over 8 percent of the population was fully vaccinated.

During the 2018 crackdown, at least 405 doctors, nurses, and other health workers were fired from public hospitals, seemingly for providing care to protesters or criticizing the government.

No specific policies to diminish the negative economic impact of the pandemic were enacted.

Crackdown on Protesters

Police, in coordination with armed pro-government groups, brutally repressed massive anti-government protests in 2018, leaving at least 328 dead, some 2,000 injured, and hundreds detained. Authorities reported 21 police officers killed in the context of demonstrations.

Many protestors were detained for months, subjected to torture and ill-treatment including electric shocks, severe beatings, fingernail removal, asphyxiation, and rape. Serious violations of due process and other rights marred prosecutions.

A broad amnesty that released many protestors in 2019 has contributed to immunity from prosecution for those responsible for human rights violations related to the crackdown. In 2019, President Ortega promoted top officials

HUMAN
RIGHTS
WATCH

Critics Under Attack
Harassment and Detention of Opponents, Rights Defenders,
and Journalists ahead of Elections in Nicaragua

implicated in abuses. Impunity for human rights violations by the police contin-ues.

In addition to the 39 detentions carried out since late May 2021, Nicaraguan rights groups reported that over 100 perceived critics detained earlier remained under custody as of October. Many had been held for over a year, under abusive conditions.

Attacks on Human Rights Defenders and Independent Media

Human rights defenders and other critics are targets of death threats, assaults, intimidation, harassment, surveillance, online defamation campaigns, and arbi-trary detention and prosecution. Police frequently station themselves outside the houses of government critics, preventing them from leaving, in what amounts to arbitrary arrest. Those harassed are unable to visit friends and fam-ily, attend meetings, go to work, or participate in protests or political activities. Some have been detained repeatedly—sometimes being abused during deten-tion—for periods ranging from several days to several months.

The government restricts freedom of expression for journalists and media outlets through threats, physical attacks, detentions, arbitrary financial investigations, arbitrary prosecutions, and forced closures.

Between July 28 and August 26, 2021, authorities ordered the closure of 45 NGOs, including women's groups, international aid organizations, and several medical associations. Ten others had been closed since 2018. In 2019, Army Commander in Chief Julio César Avilés Castillo called NGOs "coup-plotters".

Other organizations have announced their suspension of activities after the Law for the Regulation of Foreign Agents went into effect in 2020, requiring the regis-tration of people and groups receiving foreign funding as "foreign agents" and preventing them from running for office.

Police raided the offices of the newspaper *Confidencial* in May 2021, confiscat-ing equipment and detaining a journalist for several hours without providing warrants for the detention or raid. The newspaper *La Prensa* ended its print edi-tion in August, when the Customs Authority withheld newsprint and ink supplies it had imported. National Police and the Public Prosecutor's Office later raided its facilities, seizing items and arresting the newspaper's general manager.

Between January and October 2021, authorities had arbitrarily arrested and prosecuted three journalists and brought charges or initiated investigations against several journalists who were abroad. At least 16 journalists have been summoned as witnesses in a money laundering investigation into Cristiana Chamorro, a detained presidential candidate who, until its closure, headed an NGO dedicated to press freedom.

Doctors and journalists have been threatened with charges under Nicaragua's cybercrime law during interviews with prosecutors, according to news media. The law, passed in October 2020, criminalizes a wide range of online communications, including by punishing with sentences of up to five years the "publication" or "dissemination" of "false" or "distorted" information on the internet that is "likely to spread anxiety, anguish or fear."

On September 7, 2021, the Attorney General's Office charged activist Amaru Ruíz under the cybercrime law. He was accused of "dissemination of false information" to "instill instability and insecurity that endangers national sovereignty" after he allegedly said "the state and its institutions had deliberately failed to investigate" the murders of Indigenous persons in the North Caribbean Coast in 2020 and 2021.

Defense lawyers have experienced escalating harassment and prosecutions. Some remain in the country, facing threats, and others have fled. Two were arrested and prosecuted for "conspiracy to undermine national integrity."

The Human Rights Collective "Nicaragua Nunca +", an NGO based in Costa Rica that documents human rights abuses in Nicaragua, reported that the Ortega government's sustained "persecution, harassment, and prosecution" had forced at least 100 journalists into exile, including 25 in 2021.

In August 2021, at least nine Indigenous persons were reportedly killed, and two women sexually abused, in an attack related to a dispute over gold mining in the Mayangna Sauni As Indigenous territory. The government granted the mining concession without prior consultation with the community. Homicides and aggressions "related to territorial disputes" in the area since January 2020 "remain unpunished," the United Nations Office of the High Commissioner for Human Rights (OHCHR) reported. Both OHCHR and the IACHR point to a larger, persistent failure of the Nicaraguan government to title and protect Indigenous territories from invasions.

Women and Girls' Sexual and Reproductive Rights

Nicaragua has prohibited abortion under all circumstances since 2006, even when a pregnancy is life-threatening or results from rape or incest. Those who have abortions face prison sentences of up to two years; medical professionals who perform them can face up to six years. The ban forces women and girls confronting unwanted pregnancies to seek illegal and unsafe abortions, risking their health and lives.

Rates of domestic abuse, violence against women, and femicide, defined in Nicaraguan law as a crime committed by a man who murders a woman "in the public or private sphere," have increased since 2019, OHCHR reported in February 2021.

Nicaraguan Asylum Seekers

From April 2018 through June 2021, more than 110,000 people fled Nicaragua, the UN High Commissioner for Refugees reported. Costa Rica hosts some 80,000 Nicaraguan refugees and asylum seekers. Thousands more live in Mexico, Panama, Europe, and the United States.

Key International Actors

No international monitoring bodies have been allowed into the country since 2018, when the government expelled the IACHR Special Monitoring Mechanism for Nicaragua, the IACHR-appointed Interdisciplinary Group of Independent Experts, and OHCHR.

In February 2021, OHCHR urged the government to enact meaningful electoral reforms, end arbitrary arrests, guarantee freedoms to civil society, investigate and prosecute rights abuses in the context of protests, and amend laws that seriously restrict rights to freedom of expression and association and could undermine free and fair elections. The IACHR has also continued to monitor the situation from afar.

The UN Human Rights Council adopted a resolution in March urging the government to repeal or amend legislation that undermines fundamental rights and to adopt electoral reforms to ensure free and fair elections with international oversight.

In June, the OAS Permanent Council expressed concern that the Ortega regime had not implemented electoral reforms consistent with international standards before a deadline set for May. The resolution condemned harassment and arbitrary restrictions on presidential candidates, opposition parties, and independent media. In November, the OAS Permanent Council condemned the elections saying they "were not free, fair or transparent, and lack[ed] democratic legitimacy."

As of September, the US Treasury Department had imposed targeted sanctions on 26 Nicaraguans for abuses or corruption, including 23 pursuant to Executive Order 13851 and 3 pursuant to the Global Magnitsky Act of 2016, which allows for sanctions against human rights violators. Of the 26, 6 were also sanctioned pursuant to the Nicaraguan Human Rights and Corruption Act of 2018. The Treasury Department has also sanctioned nine entities, including financial and state security institutions.

In November, the US Congress passed the RENACER Act to monitor, report on, and address corruption by the Ortega government, as well as human rights abuses by Nicaraguan security forces. The law had been approved by the Senate in August.

The European Parliament, in July, condemned the Ortega government's repression of opposition groups and other opponents and called for the release of arbitrarily detained political prisoners, including presidential candidates. In August, the EU imposed targeted sanctions on eight more Nicaraguans accused of "serious human rights violations" and undermining democracy, including Vice President Rosario Murillo, for a total of 14 Nicaraguans sanctioned since 2020. Sanctions against all 14 were renewed for another year in October 2021. Following EU foreign ministers' discussions in October, EU foreign policy chief Josep Borrell once again condemned the Nicaraguan government's repression, referring to it as 'one of the worst dictatorships in the world', whose scheduled elections were going to be 'fake'.

In July, Canada imposed targeted sanctions on 15 government officials implicated in human rights violations, for a total of 24 sanctioned.

"Between Hunger and the Virus"

The Impact of the Covid-19 Pandemic on People Living in Poverty in Lagos, Nigeria

HUMAN
RIGHTS
WATCH

jei
JUSTICE &
EMPOWERMENT
INITIATIVES · NIGERIA

Nigeria

The Nigerian government's ban on Twitter in June, after the social media company deleted a tweet by President Muhammed Buhari for violating its rules, signaled a worsening repression of fundamental rights in the country. The ban was widely condemned by citizens who rely on the platform for critical social and political discourse.

The reported death of Boko Haram leader Abubakar Shekau in June changed the dynamics of the conflict in the northeast and strengthened the breakaway Islamic State West Africa Province (ISWAP). In September, the Nigerian air force admitted that it had carried out an airstrike on a village in Yobe State that killed 10 civilians and injured 20. A spokesperson claimed the civilians were struck erroneously while the air force was responding to reported Boko Haram and ISWAP activities in the area, and that it had set up a board of inquiry to investigate. Authorities have not released any information on the progress or outcome of the investigation.

The International Criminal Court (ICC) determined in December 2020 that an ICC investigation is warranted for crimes committed in the Boko Haram-related conflict given inadequate domestic efforts to deliver justice for the crimes and after finding "reasonable basis to believe" the group, its breakaway factions, and Nigerian security forces had committed war crimes and crimes against humanity.

Communities in the northwest witnessed a spate of mass kidnappings of schoolchildren for ransom. Over 1,000 children were kidnapped between January and August 2021 by armed groups popularly known as bandits, according to Save the Children International.

There has yet to be accountability for violence and other abuses against protesters during the October 2020 #EndSARS protests against police brutality, including when security forces shot at peaceful protesters at the Lekki Toll Gate in Lagos.

Nigerians continue to grapple with the devastating economic impact of Covid-19, as the number of citizens experiencing hunger more than doubled during the pandemic. Although authorities sought to respond by introducing or expanding measures such as cash transfers and food assistance, only a tiny fraction of those needing support received it. This is largely due to the absence of a robust social protection system that recognizes and protects people's right to an adequate standard of living.

Violence in the Northwest

Armed groups known locally as bandits carried out widespread killings, kidnappings, and looting across several states in Nigeria's northwest region. These groups emerged following years of conflict between nomadic herdsmen and farming communities. According to SBM Intelligence, a Nigerian research organization, 519 people were kidnapped and 22 people killed in kidnapping-related incidents in northwestern Zamfara State alone between January and June. The activities of these groups have also caused massive displacement.

In response to the insecurity, President Buhari ordered airstrikes on the camps of suspected bandits, while some governors in the region have attempted amnesty deals resulting in pardons for criminal acts by bandits in exchange for peace, but most have failed. In September, authorities imposed a telecommunications shutdown in parts of the northwest to disrupt communication among the bandits.

Separatist Agitations in the South

Simmering separatist agitations from the Indigenous People of Biafra (IPOB) in the southeast and the Yoruba Nation in the southwest highlighted the worsening divisions and tensions in the country, to which the authorities sometimes responded with excessive use of force. IPOB leader Nnamdi Kanu was arrested abroad and brought to stand trial in Nigeria for charges including treason and terrorism. The authorities have not revealed where and how he was arrested, amid questions about the legitimacy of his arrest as his representatives claim he was abducted in Kenya. Kanu was previously arrested and charged in 2015. He fled the country in 2017 after he was released on bail.

Abuses by Armed Islamists in the Northeast

In March, suspected ISWAP fighters attacked a United Nations base and humanitarian hub in the Dikwa Local Government Area of Borno State, burning aid workers' offices, destroying government facilities and hospitals, and abducting at least seven humanitarian workers. In a series of attacks in April, suspected ISWAP fighters set ablaze the facilities of three international aid organizations in Damasak town in Borno State. Eight people were killed, over a dozen were injured, and about 65,000 people were displaced. The UN suspended humanitarian operations in these areas to ensure safety of humanitarian staff.

The Borno State governor continued to relocate internally displaced persons from camps in the state capital, Maiduguri, to volatile areas, despite security concerns raised by humanitarian actors. In August, 11 civilians were killed, and several others injured during clashes between suspected ISWAP fighters and security forces in Ajiri Local Government Area of Borno State. Ajiri is one of the first locations to which internally displaced people were returned in 2020. The authorities also relocated more people to Ajiri in August just days before the deadly clashes there.

Accountability for Serious Crimes

In December 2020, the chief prosecutor of the ICC announced that the Boko Haram- related conflict in the northeast warranted a full ICC investigation after finding "reasonable basis to believe" that the group and its breakaway factions, as well as Nigerian security forces, had committed war crimes and crimes against humanity.

The ICC reached this conclusion after considering the lack of progress on efforts to investigate and prosecute these crimes nationally. In response, Nigeria's information minister accused the ICC of having "colluded" with civil society groups to "exacerbate" Nigeria's security challenges, using threats of prosecution to demoralize security forces.

Trials for hundreds of Boko Haram suspects have been repeatedly postponed since 2019, and those that took place in the two preceding years were fraught with irregularities. Most of the charges against the more than 200 defendants in the flawed July 2018 trials were based on alleged confessions and involved vague accusations of supporting Boko Haram by repairing members' vehicles, laundering their clothes, or supplying them with food and other items. Some of the defendants arrested in 2019 are still in being detained.

The Lagos Judicial Panel of Inquiry investigating the shooting of #EndSARS protesters by military officers at the Lekki Toll Gate in Lagos held its final hearing on October 19. Its final report and recommendations have not been made public. Recommendations from the panel have no force of law except that they are adopted by the Lagos State Governor, after which they can be enforced as a judgment of the State High Court. Courts cannot however automatically assume jurisdiction over police and military officers. Charges can only be brought against them after internal disciplinary processes lead to their being fired.

Military officers who were at the scene during the Lekki Toll Gate shooting on October 20, 2020, refused to appear before the panel. A military representative told the panel that officers at the scene only shot blank bullets after they were attacked by "hoodlums" who pelted them with stones and injured a soldier on the lip. The military had initially denied claims that officers shot at protesters. Human Rights Watch found that at least 15 people lost consciousness and appeared dead after the shootings at the Lekki Toll Gate; 10 of these bodies were then taken away from the scene by military officers.

Freedom of Expression, Media, and Association

After the Twitter ban was announced in June, the Nigerian Communications Commission (NCC), the telecommunications regulator, directed to suspend access to Twitter. Nigerians responded by using virtual private networks (VPNs) to circumvent the ban. The justice minister announced that those circumventing the ban will be prosecuted but this has yet to happen.

On June 22, the Court of Justice of the Economic Community of West African States (ECOWAS) ordered the Nigerian authorities to refrain from imposing sanctions, harassing, arresting, or prosecuting those using Twitter in Nigeria. The preliminary order was granted pending the determination of a case brought against the Nigerian government by a group of civil society groups challenging the Twitter ban. Hearing of the substantive case is still ongoing.

Despite repeated claims by the authorities that the ban would soon be lifted, the platform remained inaccessible through local internet service providers at time of writing.

In July, Nigerian media organizations launched a campaign against controversial media bills being considered at the national assembly aimed at bringing internet broadcasting under the control of the federal government's broadcast regulator and empowering the president to appoint officials of the board of the Nigerian Press Council, which ensures the professional standards of the press, upon the recommendation of the information minister.

Later that month, Nigeria's broadcasting authority asked broadcast stations to stop reporting details of insecurity issues or details of victims so as not to jeopardize the efforts of the Nigerian military and other security agents.

Security forces continued to disrupt #EndSARS related gatherings and protests. In February, police officers arrested people protesting a decision to reopen the Lekki Toll Gate in Lagos where military officers opened fire during the protests against police brutality in 2020. Following the arrests, a video surfaced showing over a dozen arrested protesters tightly packed together in a small yellow bus with their hands tied behind their backs in a position which appeared similar to a torture style known as 'tabay.' Tabay is a form of punishment used by the Nigerian security forces in which a person's elbows are tied together behind his back, and the rope is pulled tighter and tighter until their rib cage separates.

In response to this, the Lagos State police authorities issued a statement denouncing the treatment of protesters and announcing an investigation to ensure officers responsible are held accountable. The authorities have yet to provide further information on the investigation. The protesters were charged with crimes including conduct likely to cause a breach of peace and violation of Covid-19 protocols and later granted bail.

Sexual Orientation and Gender Identity

In July, five men accused of homosexuality were arrested in Kano State by the state Hisbah Board, a religious police unit that enforces Sharia (Islamic law). Kano is among 10 Nigerian states that practice Sharia alongside Nigerian secular law. Both laws criminalize same-sex relations. If the men are found guilty under Nigerian law, they may face up to 14 years in prison. If found guilty under Sharia, they may face the death penalty.

Children

Schools were open in 2021 following extended closures in 2020 to control the spread of Covid-19. Before the pandemic, an estimated 10.5 million children were out of school, although primary education is supposedly free and compulsory. Successive kidnappings of school children in northern parts of the country have also seriously impacted education. Girls who are not in school are often married off at an early age and the varied adoption or lack of legislation against child marriage presents opportunities for families to force their daughters into early marriage. In October, the Nigerian government hosted the fourth international Safe Schools Conference, which aimed to galvanize action on protecting education from attack.

Key International Actors

In August, Nigeria received the first 6 of 12 "Super Tucano" light attack aircrafts sold by the United States government. The sale is the largest foreign military sales program in Sub-Saharan Africa by the US, valued at almost US$500 million. It was approved by the Trump administration in 2017 after the Obama administration held up the deal due to human rights concerns. In July 2021, US lawmakers paused another proposed sale of 12 AH-1 Cobra attack helicopters and accompanying defense systems to the Nigerian military, worth about $875 million, citing human rights concerns.

In August, Nigeria and Russia signed a military cooperation deal which provides a legal framework for the supply of equipment and the training of troops in Nigeria.

Foreign Policy

Nigeria condemned the October military coup in Sudan and called on those behind it to urgently restore constitutional order. Nigerian authorities previously condemned the military coup in Guinea in September and Mali in May.

During his address at the UN General Assembly, President Muhammadu Buhari pledged his support to the efforts of ECOWAS to address the trend of coups in West Africa and called on leaders to adhere to their countries' constitutional term limits, noting that failure to do so generates crises and political tensions.

North Korea

The Democratic People's Republic of Korea (DPRK) remains one of the most repressive countries in the world. Ruled by the authoritarian leader Kim Jong Un, the government responded to international challenges and the Covid-19 pandemic in 2021 with deepened isolation and repression, and maintained fearful obedience in the population through threats of execution, imprisonment, enforced disappearances, and forced hard labor in detention and prison camps.

In 2021, the North Korea government extended extreme and unnecessary measures under the pretext of protecting against the spread of Covid-19 by closing its borders, and tightly restricting domestic travel as well as distribution of food and other products within the country.

The government does not tolerate pluralism, bans independent media, civil society organizations, and trade unions, and systematically denies all basic liberties, including freedom of expression, public assembly, association, and religion. Fear of collective punishment is used to silence dissent. Authorities in North Korea routinely send perceived opponents of the government to secretive political prison camps (*kwanliso*) in remote regions where they face torture by guards, starvation rations, and forced labor.

The government systematically extracts forced, unpaid labor from its citizens to build infrastructure and conduct other government-ordered campaigns and public work projects. The government fails to protect the rights of numerous at-risk groups, including women, children, and people with disabilities.

North Korea has taken no meaningful steps to advance economic, social and cultural rights. When the impact of the almost two-year-long Covid-19 lockdown intensified as the country was hit by major droughts in July, followed by flooding in August, Kim Jong Un in September acknowledged North Korea's dire economic and food situation and called for self-reliance and "unspecified" tightened measures against Covid-19, even though the country was reporting zero positive cases of Covid-19. Meanwhile, the government continued to prioritize weapons development, conducting missile tests in March, September, and October.

Freedom of Movement

Moving from one province to another, or traveling abroad, without prior approval remains illegal in North Korea. The government continues to strictly enforce a ban on "illegal" travel to China. Border buffer zones set up in August 2020, which extend one to two kilometers from the northern border, operated continuously in 2021 with guards ordered to "unconditionally shoot" on sight anyone entering without permission. There were reports of border guards shooting dead North Koreans trying to cross the border.

During the year, the government banned nearly all international travel, suspended all international flights, and closed down its official land border crossings with China. The government also imposed extreme measures on resident diplomats and international organization workers. It prohibited travel outside of Pyongyang and stopped the receipt of diplomatic pouches. Diplomatic missions, United Nations agencies, and international nongovernmental organizations were permitted to repatriate staff but were unable to bring staff back into the country. The DPRK also implemented quarantines of over a month for all reentry into the country. These measures led almost all diplomats to leave the country, along with all UN and nongovernmental organization (NGO) aid workers.

The government also enhanced restrictions on domestic travel because of Covid-19, granting permits to travel only for movement of essential personnel and goods. Authorities increased road checkpoints, blocked inter-district movements, and enhanced enforcement to prevent "illegal" travel. These measures severely hurt people's livelihoods and their ability to access food, medicines, and other essential goods.

Activist networks in China and South Korea that help North Koreans flee to a safe third country said they faced major obstacles because increased numbers of random checks on roads, and surveillance. Many North Koreans in China remained hidden in safe houses for months as the Chinese government sought to detain North Korean refugees and return them to the DPRK, violating China's obligations as a state that has ratified the UN Refugee Convention. North Koreans fleeing into China should be recognized and protected as refugees sur place because of the certainty of persecution on return. China forcibly returned a group of nearly 50 North Koreans to the DPRK in July.

North Korean law states that leaving the country without permission is a crime of "treachery against the nation," punishable by death. The 2014 UN Commission of Inquiry (COI) on human rights in the DPRK found Pyongyang committed crimes against humanity against those forcibly returned by China to North Korea.

Very few North Koreans are escaping the country. Just over 1,000 North Koreans fled to the south in 2019, but only 229 escaped in 2020. Between January and September 2021, only 48 North Koreans successfully reached South Korea where their rights are protected.

Freedom of Expression and Information

The North Korean government does not respect the rights to freedom of thought, opinion, expression or information. All media is strictly controlled. Accessing phones, computers, televisions, radios or media content that are not sanctioned by the government is illegal, and considered "anti-socialist behavior" to be severely punished. The government regularly cracks down on unsanctioned media consumption. It also jams Chinese mobile phone services at the northern border, and arrests those communicating with people outside of the country, or connecting outsiders to people inside the country.

The North Korean government adopted the "DPRK Law on rejecting reactionary ideology and culture" in December 2020. The law bans people from distributing media originating from South Korea, the US, or Japan, and sets out punishments up to the death penalty. Simply watching such media content can result in a sentence of 15 years in an ordinary crimes prison camp (*kyohwaso*). Under the law, speaking, writing, or singing in South Korean style can be punished with two years of hard labor. In April 2021, Kim Jong Un published a letter about "dangerous poisons," setting out his policy to stop young North Koreans from adopting foreign speech, hairstyles, and clothes.

The law also criminalizes possession of unsanctioned foreign mobile phones, setting out penalties of three months or more of forced labor. Media with contacts inside North Korea reported increased inspections and crackdowns on student text messages that contain South Korean slang, mass arrests of users of foreign cell phones, and a propaganda campaign depicting foreign phone users as "evil" enemies of the state who must be reported to the authorities.

Forced Labor

The North Korean government routinely and systematically requires forced labor from much of its population to sustain its economy. The government's forced labor demands target women and children through the Women's Union or schools; workers at state-owned enterprises or deployed abroad; detainees in short-term hard labor detention centers (*rodong dallyeondae*); and prisoners at long-term ordinary prison camps (*kyohwaso*) and political prison camps (*kwan-liso*).

At some point in their lives, a significant majority of North Koreans must perform unpaid hard labor, often justified by the state as "portrayals of loyalty" to the government. Since punishment for crimes in North Korea is arbitrary, and depends on a person's record of loyalty, personal connections, and capacity to pay bribes, any refusal of a government order to work as a "volunteer" can result in severe punishment, including torture and imprisonment.

The government routinely compels North Koreans to join paramilitary labor brigades (*dolgyeokdae*) that the ruling party controls and operates, working primarily on buildings and infrastructure projects. In theory, these workers are entitled to a salary worth around three to five kilograms of rice a month, but in almost all cases, the *dolyeokdae,* like most state-owned enterprises, do not financially compensate their workers. This forces workers to find other jobs to survive while paying bribes not to go to their officially assigned workplace. Failing to show up for work without permission is a crime punishable by three to six months of unpaid hard labor in detention centers (*rodong dallyeondae*).

North Korea remains one of only seven United Nations member states that has not joined the International Labour Organization.

Marginalized Groups and Women and Girls

North Korea uses *songbun*, a socio-political classification system that groups people into "loyal," "wavering," or "hostile" classes, and is used to justify politically determined discrimination in employment, residence, and schooling. Pervasive corruption allows some maneuvering around the strictures of the *songbun* system, with government officials accepting bribes to grant permissions, permit certain market activities, or avoid possible punishments.

In addition to the violations suffered by the general population, women and girls in North Korea are the target of a range of sexual and gender-based abuses. Government officials both perpetrate and fail to effectively respond to rights violations including widespread gender discrimination, sexual and gender-based violence, and constant exposure to stereotyped gender roles.

Key International Actors

North Korea has ratified five core human rights treaties, but the government has made no apparent effort to implement these treaties or otherwise demonstrate respect for human right. A 2014 COI report found the government committed crimes against humanity, including extermination, murder, enslavement, torture, imprisonment, and rape, forced abortion, and other forms of sexual violence. It recommended the UN Security Council refer the situation to the International Criminal Court. The North Korean government has repeatedly denied the COI's findings and refuses to cooperate with the Seoul-based Office of the UN High Commissioner for Human Rights or the UN special rapporteur on the situation of human rights in North Korea.

On March 23, 2021, the UN Human Rights Council adopted by consensus a resolution extending its accountability efforts and mechanisms. In November, the UN General Assembly's third committee passed a resolution by consensus condemning human rights in North Korea.

Every year from 2014 to 2017, the UN Security Council placed North Korea's human rights violations on its formal agenda and held open meetings on how the violations threaten international peace and security. However, this effort faltered for three years in a row during the US Trump administration. The US government currently imposes human rights-related sanctions on North Korean government entities, as well as on Kim Jong Un and on several other top officials.

Despite North Korea's rejection of any diplomatic engagement, South Korean President Moon Jae-in's administration continued to seek political dialogue with Pyongyang in 2021. The South Korean government has not adopted a clear policy on North Korean human rights issues. Since 2019, it has declined to co-sponsor key resolutions on North Korea's human rights record at the UN Human Rights Council or the General Assembly.

Pakistan

In 2021, the Pakistan government intensified its efforts to control the media and curtail dissent. Authorities harassed, and at times detained, journalists and other members of civil society for criticizing government officials and policies. Violent attacks on members of the media also continued.

The authorities expanded their use of draconian sedition and counterterrorism laws to stifle dissent, and strictly regulated civil society groups critical of government actions or policies. Authorities also cracked down on members and supporters of opposition political parties.

Women, religious minorities, and transgender people continue to face violence, discrimination, and persecution, with authorities failing to provide adequate protection or hold perpetrators to account. The government continues to do little to hold law enforcement agencies accountable for torture and other serious abuses.

Attacks by Islamist militants, notably the Tehrik-i-Taliban Pakistan, targeting law enforcement officials and religious minorities killed dozens of people.

Freedom of Expression, Attacks on Civil Society Groups

A climate of fear impedes media coverage of abuses by both government security forces and militant groups. Journalists who face threats and attacks have increasingly resorted to self-censorship. Media outlets have come under pressure from authorities not to criticize government institutions or the judiciary. In several cases in 2021, government regulatory agencies blocked cable operators and television channels that had aired critical programs.

Several journalists suffered violent attacks in 2021. On April 20, an unidentified assailant shot and wounded Absar Alam, a television journalist, outside his house in Islamabad. Alam has been a prominent critic of the government. On May 25, Asad Ali Toor, a journalist, was assaulted by three unidentified men who forcibly entered his apartment in Islamabad, bound and gagged him and severely beat him. Toor said that they identified themselves as being from a security agency, interrogated him about the "source of his funds," and took away his cell phone and other electronic devices. The government ordered an investigation into the incident, but no findings were made public. On May 29, the news channel, Geo, "suspended" Hamid Mir, one of Pakistan's best-known television talk show hosts, after he spoke at a protest in solidarity with Toor.

Nongovernmental organizations (NGOs) reported intimidation, harassment, and surveillance of various by government authorities. The government used the "Regulation of INGOs in Pakistan" policy to impede the registration and functioning of international humanitarian and human rights groups.

Freedom of Religion and Belief

Members of the Ahmadiyya religious community continue to be a major target for prosecutions under blasphemy laws as well as specific anti-Ahmadi laws. Militant groups and the Islamist political party Tehreek-e-Labbaik (TLP) accuse Ahmadis of "posing as Muslims." The Pakistan penal code also treats "posing as Muslims" as a criminal offense.

According to a Pakistani human rights organization, the Centre for Social Justice, at least 1,855 people were charged under Pakistan's blasphemy laws between 1987 and February 2021.

On May 17, dozens of people attacked a police station in Islamabad to lynch two brothers charged with blasphemy, breaking into the facility and battling with police officers before the station was brought under control. The two brothers were physically unharmed. The police arrested a number of individuals who were part of the mob, but none were prosecuted.

On June 4, the Lahore High Court acquitted a Christian couple, Shafqat Emmanuel and Shagufta Kausar, of blasphemy after spending seven years on death row. The couple was convicted in 2014 of sending "blasphemous" texts to a mosque cleric.

In August, an 8-year-old Hindu boy in Rahim Yar Khan, Punjab, became the youngest person to ever be charged with blasphemy in Pakistan after he was accused of defiling a carpet at a religious seminary. Following his release on bail, a mob attacked a Hindu temple, causing damage. All charges against the child were subsequently dropped.

Abuses against Women and Girls

Violence against women and girls—including rape, murder, acid attacks, domestic violence, and forced marriage—is endemic throughout Pakistan. Human rights defenders estimate that roughly 1,000 women are killed in so-called honor killings every year.

In July, the torture and murder of Noor Muqadam, 27, in Islamabad led to nationwide protests. A childhood friend of Muqadam, Zahir Jaffer, whose marriage proposal she had spurned, was arrested and charged with the murder. Earlier in July, Pakistan's Parliament did not pass a bill that sought to criminalize domestic violence; women rights activists criticized the government's decision to refer the bill to the Council of Islamic Ideology (CII) for review. The CII criticized the bill saying that it contained "un-Islamic injunctions" and would destroy the institution of the family.

In August, a viral video of a young woman being assaulted by more than 400 men in a Lahore park while she and her companions were filming a TikTok video led to domestic and international condemnation. The government vowed to find the perpetrators, but no arrests were made public.

Child marriage remains a serious problem in Pakistan, with 18 percent of girls marrying before age 18, and 4 percent marrying before 15. Women from religious minority communities remain particularly vulnerable to forced marriage. The government has done little to stop such marriages.

Pakistan ranked 153 out of 156 nations on the Global Gender Gap 2021 index issued by the World Economic Forum.

Children's Rights to Education

Even before the Covid-19 pandemic, over 5 million primary school-age children in Pakistan were out of school, most of them girls. Human Rights Watch research found girls miss school for reasons including lack of schools, costs associated with studying, child marriage, harmful child labor, and gender discrimination. School closures to protect against the spread of Covid-19 affected almost 45 million students for most of the year; Pakistan's poor internet connectivity hampered online learning.

Police and Security Forces Abuses

The Tehrik-Taliban Pakistan (TTP), Al-Qaeda, Balochistan Liberation Army (BLA), and their affiliates carried out suicide bombings and other indiscriminate attacks against security personnel that caused hundreds of civilian deaths and injuries during the year. In July, an attack on a bus carrying workers at the Dasu Hydroelectric project in Khyber-Pakhtunkhwa killed nine Chinese engineers. In August, a grenade attack in Karachi killed 12 people, including six women and children. No group claimed responsibility for either incident.

Pakistan law enforcement agencies were responsible for numerous human rights violations, including detention without charge and extrajudicial killings. In March, Pakistan Prime Minister Imran Khan met with families of people who had been forcibly disappeared, allegedly by Pakistani security forces, and pledged that their concerns would be addressed. However, his government announced no investigations in any cases.

Pakistan has still not enacted a law criminalizing torture despite Pakistan's obligation to do so under the UN Convention against Torture. In July, the Pakistan Senate unanimously approved a critically important bill outlawing police torture and otherwise seeking to prevent deaths in police custody. The law had not been passed by the National Assembly at time of writing. The law if passed would be the first time that Pakistan enacts a comprehensive definition of torture in line with Convention Against Torture. The bill also proposes criminal liability for death caused in police custody,

Pakistan has more than 4,600 prisoners on death row, one of the world's largest populations facing execution. Those on death row are often from the most marginalized sections of society.

In June, the intergovernmental Financial Action Task Force (FATF) retained Pakistan as a jurisdiction under "Increased Monitoring"–a so-called gray list of countries that fall short of FATF standards for countering terrorism financing and money laundering. Pakistan has been on the gray list since 2018. The FATF noted that Pakistan had made progress by largely addressing 26 of 27 goals, but still needed to show that its investigations into terrorism financing and prosecutions "target senior leaders and commanders of UN-designated terrorist groups

In October, Pakistan's Senate approved a bill that would decriminalize suicide; parliamentary approval was still pending at time of writing. Disability rights and mental health advocates welcomed the move as an important first step.

Sexual Orientation and Gender Identity

Pakistan's penal code criminalizes same-sex sexual conduct, placing men who have sex with men and transgender people at risk of police abuse and other violence and discrimination. In July, activists claimed that the transgender community in Karachi was being targeted in an organized social media campaign to instigate violence against its members. On April 6, a 60-year-old transgender resident of Karachi's Korangi neighborhood was shot and killed by unidentified assailants who broke into their home.

Key International Actors

The European Union is Pakistan biggest trading partner. In April, the European Parliament passed a resolution deploring human rights violations in Pakistan and calling for an immediate review of Pakistan's eligibility for GSP+ status, which grants Pakistan trade benefits conditional on its compliance with human rights obligations. In June, the EU and Pakistan held human rights talks. The EU's report on Pakistan's compliance with its human rights obligations to retain GSP+ status is scheduled to be published in early 2022.

In April, a ruling party member tabled a resolution in the National Assembly demanding a debate on whether to expel the French ambassador for "anti-Islamic" remarks made by President Emmanuel Macron.

In April, Pakistan secured membership on three United Nations panels: the Commission on Crime Prevention and Criminal Justice, the Commission on the Status of Women, and the Commission on Population and Development.

Pakistan's relationship with United States, the country's largest development and military donor, remained volatile in 2021. The United States acknowledged Pakistan's significant role as one of the stakeholders in resolving the Afghanistan conflict. However, in September, US Secretary of State Antony

Blinken said that the United States would reassess its relationship with Pakistan in formulating a policy on the future of Afghanistan. He also called on Pakistan not to recognize the Taliban government in Afghanistan unless it meets international demands. Pakistan's Ministry of Foreign Affairs said Blinken's remarks were "not in line with the close cooperation" between the two countries.

After the Taliban took control of Afghanistan in August, Pakistan signaled that it was prepared to recognize the Taliban government.

Pakistan and China deepened their extensive economic and political ties in 2021, and work continued on the China-Pakistan Economic Corridor, a project consisting of construction of roads, railways, and energy pipelines. In October, Pakistan carried out joint counterterrorism military exercises with China.

Papua New Guinea

Although a resource-rich country, almost 40 percent of Papua New Guinea's (PNG) population lives in poverty. The Covid-19 pandemic highlighted ongoing challenges with government inaction, economic mismanagement, and a severely under-resourced health care system. Before Covid-19 started spreading, PNG was already struggling with outbreaks of measles, drug-resistant tuberculosis, and polio with poor vaccination rates. Weak implementation of laws on violence against women and children foster a culture of impunity. Prime Minister James Marape has committed to reforms to address gender-based violence, but real progress has yet to be seen.

Women's and Girls' Rights

Violence against women and girls is rampant. Over 1.5 million people experience gender-based violence each year.

In May, a Special Parliamentary Committee examined measures to prevent violence against women and girls. The inquiry found a lack of support, funding, and coordination from the government contributed to an inadequate response to the high volume of cases of violence against women and girls.

In 2020, approximately 15,000 cases of domestic violence were reported, but only 300 people were prosecuted, and 100 people were convicted. Police officials admitted at the inquiry that the police force cannot currently keep women and children safe and lack resources for thorough investigations.

PNG laws designed to protect women and children, including the Lukautim Pikinini (Child Welfare) Act 2015 and the Family Protection Act 2013, are rarely enforced. Initiatives such as Family Sexual and Violence Units within the police force remain limited. A lack of services for survivors of gender-based violence compounds the problem.

In 2021, instances of domestic violence continued to spark outrage. In May, the body of a 31-year-old woman, Imelda Tupi Tiamanda, was found wrapped in tarpaulin in her husband's vehicle at a police checkpoint. Police arrested and charged three men, including her husband. In September, the three men were released from prison and the magistrate dismissed the charges citing a lack of evidence.

Between May and June, five women were violently attacked following accusations of practicing "sorcery," one of whom was killed. In May, attackers accused Mary Kopari of sorcery and tied her up and burned her to death in Komo-Magarima District. The attack was filmed and while police know the identity of some of the attackers, no arrests have been reported.

PNG has one of the highest maternal mortality rates in the world. More than 2,000 women and girls die in childbirth in PNG each year. These deaths are largely preventable. The risk of maternal death is increased by limited access to hospitals, with 80 percent of the population living outside urban centers.

Children's Rights to Health and Education

One in 13 children die each year of preventable disease. Children living in rural areas are twice as likely to die in their first five years of life compared to children living in urban areas. Covid-19 has put child health outcomes at risk due to interrupted vaccination and other health programs.

In March, 2.1 million children were affected by a four-week school closure. Before the pandemic, 7 percent of children—over 86,000 children—were out of primary, and 14 percent were out of lower-secondary school, because of barriers to access including remoteness, gender inequality, and a lack of learning resources.

Police Abuse

Police violence, including against children, is an ongoing problem in PNG. In April, police entered the residence of lawyer Laken Lepatu Aigilo without an arrest or search warrant and assaulted him before detaining him. PNG Police Minister David Manning ordered his release the following day. Police authorities conducted an internal investigation into the incident and police confirmed with Human Rights Watch that the officer involved was arrested, suspended, and that the matter was before the criminal court.

PNG police are severely understaffed, chronically underfunded, and often lack resources such as petrol, stationery, and vehicles.

Asylum Seekers and Refugees

At time of writing, about 124 refugees and asylum seekers remained in Papua New Guinea, transferred there by the Australian government since 2013. In October, Australia said it would end offshore processing in the country by December 2021 and those who remained in PNG could stay there or be transferred to Nauru or giving them the option to remain in PNG with a promise of a "permanent migration pathway." In April, attackers robbed and assaulted around 15 asylum seekers at gunpoint. At least three required medical attention.

Refugees and asylum seekers in PNG continue to endure violence and harassment, with little protection from authorities. Medical facilities in PNG are woefully inadequate and have proven unable to cope with the complex medical needs of asylum seekers and refugees, particularly their mental health needs.

Land and Environmental Rights

In July, Australian mining company Rio Tinto agreed to fund an independent assessment of the human rights and environmental impacts following the closure of its Panguna copper and gold mine in the autonomous region of Bougainville. One hundred and fifty-six Bougainville residents petitioned the Australian government in 2020 to investigate Rio Tinto's involvement in human rights abuses. Petitioners said that polluted water from the mine pit flowed into rivers and polluted fields.

In 2020, the PNG government refused an application to extend the Porgera gold mine lease in Enga Province with Prime Minister Marape citing long standing environmental and resettlement issues. In April of that year, the PNG government and local Porgera landholders took a majority share of the Porgera gold mine in Enga province, with the remainder held by joint venture partners Canadian company Barrick Gold and Chinese company Zijin Mining Group. At time of writing, the mine had been closed for over a year, with negotiations continuing between the parties.

In March, a report by Jubilee Australia Research Centre and Project Sepik detailed environmental and social risks associated with a proposed gold, copper, and silver mine to be built on the Frieda River in the Sepik region. The mine, if approved, would be the largest in PNG's history.

While contributing very little to global emissions that are driving the climate crisis, coastal and island communities in PNG are facing serious climate impacts as sea-level rise and coastal erosion limit access to food and water and force residents to relocate. Carterets Islanders, some of the world's first communities displaced by the effects of climate change, have said that more than 50 percent of their land has already been lost due to sea level rise.

PNG is also working to reduce its own emissions. Deforestation and forest degradation drive a significant portion of the country's emissions, and PNG has committed to reducing emissions from these sources by 2030. However, PNG has increased export of harvested timber in recent years and struggles to contain regulation and enforcement, and a failure to respect local land rights.

Disability Rights

Approximately 1.2 million people in PNG are living with a disability according to the World Health Organization. Despite the existence of a national disability policy, PNG has yet to pass comprehensive disability legislation.

People with disabilities are often unable to participate in community life, attend school, or work because of lack of accessibility, stigma, and other barriers. Access to mental health services and other support services are limited, and many people with psychosocial disabilities and their families often consider traditional healers to be their only option. Covid-19 has disproportionately affected people with disabilities who are left out of government Covid-19 policies and communications.

Sexual Orientation and Gender Identity

Same-sex relations are still punishable by up to 14 years of imprisonment in PNG's criminal code. While there is little information on actual convictions, the law is sometimes used as a pretext by officials and employers to harass or extort money from gay and lesbian people in Papua New Guinea, including gay refugees.

Covid-19

According to the PNG government's National Control Centre, as of November, more than 34,000 people had tested positive for Covid-19, and more than 520 people had died; inadequate testing means that the actual number of cases is likely far higher. Vaccination rates are extremely low with only 3 percent of the population vaccinated as of November. As of November, only about 770,000 vaccine doses had been delivered to the country—enough to vaccinate approximately 6 percent of the population, according to UNICEF. Over 130,000 vaccines delivered by the global facility COVAX expired before they could be administered.

Key International Actors

Australia is the biggest provider of aid and investment to PNG, and at time of writing had given Covid-19 support including 8,000 vaccine doses, 200,000 face masks, and 1 million surgical masks in 2021.

In 2021, Australia committed to refinancing an existing AUD$410 million loan (US$300 million), and to provide a further AUD$130 million loan (US$100 million loan) to assist PNG to continue the delivery of core government services. Australia's official development commitment to PNG during 2020 and 2021 is around AUD$600 million (US$430 million).

It is estimated that Australia has spent AUD$268 million (US$200 million) on offshore processing in PNG in 2019-2020, and approximately AUD$1.6 billion (US$1.2 billion) since the PNG Supreme Court ruled that Australia's detention of asylum seekers there was illegal in 2016.

China also provides significant development and economic support to PNG. In June, PNG's Foreign Minister Soroi Eoe visited China and signed a US$22 million loan to support the creation of a 'special economic zone' in Kikori, in the Gulf of PNG. Later that month, the Chinese government provided PNG with 200,000 doses of Covid-19 vaccine.

In November, at the UN Human Rights Council's Universal Periodic Review of PNG, countries urged the PNG government to improve gender-based violence, LGBT rights, and access to education for all children, including children with a disability. Fifteen nations questioned PNG's retention of the death penalty and called for its abolition.

Peru

On June 6, Peruvians elected Pedro Castillo as president in what international observers described as free and fair elections. Castillo's opponent, Keiko Fujimori, made unsubstantiated claims of voter fraud and sought to have the elections annulled through litigation and political pressure. Fujimori's appeals were dismissed, and Peruvian electoral authorities proclaimed Castillo president on July 19.

Criminal investigations into grave abuses committed during the 20-year internal armed conflict that ended in 2000 remain slow and limited. Violence against women, abuses by security forces, and threats to freedom of expression are also major concerns.

Covid-19 and measures imposed to prevent its spread have had a devastating impact on poverty and inequality, negatively impacting social and economic rights.

Right to Vote and Run for Office

International observers, including from the Organization of American States and the European Union, described Peru's June 6 presidential runoff elections as free and fair.

When rapid-count results indicated Castillo had won, Fujimori alleged voter fraud and filed hundreds of baseless lawsuits seeking to annul hundreds of thousands of ballots cast by mostly poor and rural Castillo voters. Keiko Fujimori and her party, Fuerza Popular, failed to provide credible evidence to support their claims.

Members of the JNE and other authorities repeatedly endured intimidation efforts during the electoral campaigns and vote counting process. In July, the Inter-American Commission on Human Rights (IACHR) issued precautionary measures in favor of JNE President Jorge Luis Salas Arenas and José Domingo Pérez, a prosecutor overseeing high-profile corruption cases, including against Keiko Fujimori.

As votes were being counted, several political parties, including Fujimori's Fuerza Popular, sped up a process to appoint six judges to the Constitutional Tribunal outside the regular session of Congress and without complying with legal standards, a move that many described as an attempt to pack the high court in preparation for seeking judicial annulment of the election, amongst other objectives. In July, a court granted a provisional measure ordering Congress to suspend the selection. Many lawmakers announced they would not comply with the ruling, but they were unable to gather the majority needed to appoint new judges.

Confronting Past Abuses

Efforts to prosecute grave abuses committed during the armed conflict have had mixed results.

Almost 70,000 people were killed or subject to enforced disappearance by the Shining Path, other armed groups, or state agents, during an armed conflict lasting from 1980 to 2000, Peru's Truth and Reconciliation Commission estimates. The vast majority of those killed were low-income peasants; most spoke Indigenous languages.

Authorities have made slow progress in prosecuting abuses by government forces during the conflict. As of September 2021, courts had issued 48 convictions in 90 cases, Peruvian human rights groups reported.

Former President Alberto Fujimori was sentenced in 2009 to 25 years in prison on charges of crimes against humanity, in connection with kidnappings and two massacres, and various corruption-related offenses.

In March, prosecutors indicted Fujimori and three former health ministers on charges related to the forced sterilizations of mostly poor and Indigenous women during his presidency. The case remains pending. As of June 2021, 6,103 people had registered as victims of these forced sterilizations, the Ministry of Women reported.

At time of writing, criminal investigations continued into the role of former President Ollanta Humala (2011-2016) in killings and other atrocities committed in 1992 and in their cover-up.

In 2018, then-President Martín Vizcarra established a genetic profile bank to help search for those disappeared during the armed conflict. Implementation has been sluggish.

Abuses by Armed Groups

A Shining Path offshoot known as the Militarized Communist Party of Peru (MPCP) continues to operate in the Apurímac, Ene, and Mantaro valleys, in alliance with drug cartels. On May 23, the Peruvian Joint Chiefs of Staff reported that the MPCP committed a massacre, killing 16 civilians in San Miguel del Ene, including four children.

Police Abuse

Police used excessive force in Lima against largely peaceful demonstrators protesting the removal of President Vizcarra in November 2020. Over 200 people were injured and two protesters were killed in the protests.

Security forces have also used excessive force when responding to largely peaceful protests that sometimes turned violent over mining and other large-scale development projects. According to the Ombudsperson's Office, 17 protesters or bystanders died in the context of protests between June 2020 and June 2021.

Law 30151, passed in 2014, granting immunity to police who kill in "fulfilment of their duty," may make it impossible to hold accountable police who use excessive force resulting in death, despite Decree 1186, issued in 2015, limiting police use of force.

In addition, in March 2020, Congress approved a so-called Police Protection Law, which revokes the provision in Decree 1186 requiring that any use of force be proportionate to the gravity of the threat.

In November 2021, the government deployed soldiers in Lima and Callao to support police efforts to address drug trafficking and organized crime.

Freedom of Expression

Threats to freedom of expression continue to be a concern in Peru, with some journalists facing prosecution for their work under Peru's criminal defamation laws.

Since late 2018, journalists Paola Ugaz and Pedro Salinas have been repeatedly accused of defamation in connection with their reporting on sexual abuse scandals involving a Catholic lay organization. Currently, Ugaz is facing four apparently spurious lawsuits, all pending at time of writing.

In May, reports emerged that the producer of a popular Sunday news show, "Cuarto Poder," had been fired because she had refused to take sides in her electoral coverage. This prompted a letter of protest to the television network's board of directors from the journalists who had been working with her. Soon after, two producers were fired and seven journalists resigned in protest, citing pressure to cover the elections in ways favorable to presidential candidate Keiko Fujimori.

In August, the Castillo administration's caucus in Congress introduced a bill declaring of "public necessity" the "fair and equitable distribution of the electromagnetic spectrum." The bill would allow the government to issue undefined "temporary measures" in cases of emergency (such as the Covid-19 pandemic), including taking over telecommunication services on a "transitory and exceptional basis."

Women's and Girls' Rights

Gender-based violence is a significant problem in Peru. The Ministry of Women reported 131 "femicides"—defined as the killing of a woman in certain contexts, including domestic violence—in 2020, and 73 from January through June 2021.

Access to legal abortion in Peru is still very limited. Women and girls can legally access abortions only in cases of risk to the life or health of the pregnant person. In 2014 the Ministry of Health adopted national technical guidelines for legal therapeutic abortions, but many health service providers have failed to implement them, leading to barriers to access to legal abortion. These guidelines have since been challenged in two separate court filings by anti-abortion groups. Both cases were dismissed but appeals remained pending at time of writing.

On April 28, 2021, Promsex, a sexual rights organization, petitioned courts to declare a 2009 Constitutional Court ruling that had banned free distribution of emergency contraception pills inapplicable. The case remained pending at time of writing.

Disability Rights

Peru has a legal framework recognizing full legal capacity for people with disabilities, but the country's civil registry has failed to take action to include people with disabilities who were previously under guardianship on the national voting register. This deprives them of their right to vote. At time of writing, the Peruvian executive branch had not issued enabling legislation fully to implement legal capacity for people with disabilities.

Sexual Orientation and Gender Identity

President Castillo opposes legalizing same-sex marriage. In a speech on the campaign trail, he said that recognition of trans people was an "idiosyncrasy" that "should be thrown in the garbage." He has also expressed opposition to including a gender focus in school curricula, which fosters tolerance around gender and sexual diversity.

In July, President Castillo appointed Guido Bellido as prime minister. Media reported a long history of misogynist, homophobic, and transphobic statements from Bellido, prompting calls that he be replaced. In October, Castillo forced Bellido to resign as part of a cabinet shake-up.

Same-sex couples in Peru are not allowed to marry or enter into civil unions. Some courts have begun recognizing same-sex marriages contracted by Peruvians abroad. In November 2020, the Constitutional Court denied recognition to a same-sex couple married abroad.

In August 2020, a judge ordered the civil registry to allow transgender Peruvians to change their name and gender marker on national identity documents. The registry's appeal remained pending at time of writing.

Human Rights Defenders and Community Leaders

Human rights defenders, environmental defenders, and community leaders, have been threatened and killed in recent years. In 2019, the Ministry of Justice established an inter-agency mechanism for the protection of human rights defenders.

In February, Herasmo García and Yenes Ríos Bonsano, two Cacataibo Indigenous environmental defenders who participated in their communities' efforts to repel illegal logging, were killed in the Amazonian region of Ucayali. In March, Estela Casanto, an Asháninka Indigenous leader and environmental defender, was killed in the central region of Junín; her community's territory is allegedly experiencing land invasions, which she opposed. In July, Mario Marcos López, an Asháninka Indigenous environmental defender who leads a local organization that administers a protected area, was shot in an Amazonian part of the region of Pasco, and later died from his injury. At the time of writting, nobody had been charged in connection with the crime.

Refugees, Asylum Seekers, and Migrants

More than 496,000 Venezuelans were seeking asylum in Peru at time of writing.

In his inauguration speech, President Castillo issued a "72-hour ultimatum" to "foreign criminals" to leave the country. Xenophobia continues to be a problem, particularly against Venezuelans, who have at times been victims of violent attacks.

In July, the government reintroduced temporary residence permits in a bid to regularize the situation of undocumented migrants, after having eliminated them in 2019. Regulations gave undocumented immigrants 180 days to request a permit allowing them to perform undefined "activities" for a year.

Economic and Social Rights

The Covid-19 pandemic, and measures in place to control it, had a devastating impact on poverty and inequality in Peru. In May, government authorities reported that poverty had increased by 9.9 percent in 2020, despite some state measures to mitigate it.

Schools have remained closed in Peru since March 2020 due to the Covid-19 pandemic at time of writing. While the government took some measures to ensure remote teaching, many students have not been able to attend. The Ministry of Education said in September 2020 that 230,000 students had dropped out of school and 200,000 others were not attending classes, despite being enrolled. The ministry had announced schools would start reopening in 2021, but implementation has been sluggish.

Key International Actors

In March, Peru ratified the Inter-American Convention on the Protection of the Human Rights of Older Persons, becoming the eighth country to do so.

In August, Peru announced it was withdrawing from the Lima Group, a coalition of states seeking to address the human rights crisis in Venezuela. Peru instead expressed its intention to promote initiatives by the EU-led Contact Group.

Philippines

Serious human rights abuses continued in the Philippines in 2021. On September 15, the International Criminal Court (ICC) agreed to open a formal investigation into possible "crimes against humanity" committed during President Rodrigo Duterte's "war on drugs" from 2016 to 2019, and extrajudicial executions committed in Davao City in the southern Philippines from 2011 to 2016, when Duterte was mayor.

In October, Maria Ressa, the co-founder and executive editor of the news website *Rappler*, won the Nobel Peace Prize for defending media freedom, specifically for resisting the Duterte government's attempts to muzzle the press.

In July, the Philippine government and the United Nations launched a joint "human rights program" to address human rights violations and accountability failings in the country, reflecting domestic and international concerns about "drug war" killings. Rights groups, including Human Rights Watch, consider the program inadequate, and continue to call for an independent international investigation.

Killings of civilians and "red-tagging"—accusing activists and others of being combatants or supporters of the communist New People's Army—are endemic to the government's counterinsurgency campaign. Many of those red-tagged are subsequently killed. Journalists covering the insurgency or investigating abuses and corruption also face harassment and violence.

"Drug War" Killings and the ICC

In September, a pre-trial chamber of the ICC granted the prosecutor's request to open a formal investigation into alleged crimes against humanity in the Philippines from the time the country ratified the ICC's Rome Statute on November 1, 2011, until its withdrawal from the treaty on March 16, 2019. In its decision to greenlight the investigation, the pre-trial chamber stated the government's anti-drug campaign "cannot be seen as a legitimate law enforcement operation, and the killings neither as legitimate nor as mere excesses in an otherwise legitimate operation." It further said there has been "a widespread and systematic attack against the civilian population" as part of a state policy.

The decision echoed claims by various rights groups that between 12,000 and 30,000 people have been killed in the "drug war." The government's own data shows more than 6,190 people were killed in police operations from 2016 to August 2021.

The Department of Justice, which announced, in June 2020, the creation of a panel that would review deaths in the "drug war" attributed to police officers, said, in September 2021, that it was now investigating 52 cases involving 154 police officers implicated in questionable killings. This followed its admission before the UN Human Rights Council, in February, that officers failed to follow protocols during these operations. In many cases, police made no effort to examine allegedly recovered weapons, verify ownership, or conduct ballistic examinations. In most of the cases the Department of Justice reviewed, police also failed to follow standard protocols in the coordination of drug raids and in the processing of crime scene evidence.

The Justice Department investigation has faced criticism for repeated delays, lack of transparency, and refusal to involve the national Commission on Human Rights in its review. Responding to this criticism, the department released in October a preliminary report affirming that police were culpable in at least 52 cases and promised to investigate further.

Killing of Activists, Rights Defenders

The country's 52-year-long communist insurgency continued in 2021. During counter-insurgency operations against the New People's Army (NPA), government security forces frequently targeted leftist activists, including peasant leaders, environmentalists, human rights lawyers, and Indigenous group heads, among others. Government and military officials often "red-tag" such individuals through announcements and social media, putting them at grave risk of attack.

In March, nine individuals belonging to different activist groups were killed during police raids in the Calabarzon region south of Manila. All those killed were previously accused of communist involvement. The simultaneous police raids occurred two days after President Duterte publicly ordered law enforcement officials to "finish off" communist insurgents. Human rights groups rejected claims that the victims were rebels or rebel supporters. In December 2020, police killed nine members of an Indigenous people's community on the island of Panay, in the central Philippines.

The counterinsurgency campaign has likewise targeted lawyers, including some representing clients who have been "red-tagged." In Cebu City in August, gunmen shot dead Rex Fernandez, a human rights lawyer whose group, the National Union of People's Lawyers, provides legal services to activists. Juan Macababbad, a human rights lawyer who worked on environment and Indigenous rights cases, was shot dead in September, by gunmen in South Cotabato province, in the southern Philippines.

The National Task Force on Ending Local Communist Armed Conflict is the main government agency engaged in "red-tagging." It is composed of officials from several government agencies, including the military and the police. In addition to activists and lawyers, the task force has "red-tagged" journalists, media groups, and even civilian food volunteers.

One of the tools the government has been using against activists is the Anti-Terrorism Act, a law Duterte signed in July 2020. Various groups denounced the law because, as the UN high commissioner for human rights noted, it "dilutes human rights safeguards" and creates a "chilling effect on human rights and humanitarian work." Since its passage, the law has been challenged but has also been used by the government against activists, Indigenous peoples, unionists, as well as alleged communist insurgents.

Covid-19

There were fewer serious Covid-19-related rights violations in the Philippines during the second year of the pandemic compared to the first, which had seen harsh treatment of quarantine violators by law enforcement. Age-based restrictions on movement for those under 18 and over 65 years of age prevented children and older people from leaving their homes, although in October, the government eased this restriction. Schools remained closed nationwide at time of writing, affecting the education of 28.5 million students.

Authorities imposed strict quarantine regulations across the country and had arrested tens of thousands of people for quarantine violations, some of whom spent time in detention while majority were given warnings, fined, or ordered to do community service. In November, the government eased these restrictions. Detention facilities in the Philippines have always been congested, posing considerable challenges for vaccination, with authorities reporting success in some pretrial or holding facilities but not in others.

Critics accused the government of mishandling its response to the pandemic, including inadequate initial vaccination roll-out. Vaccination for the general population began in November. There have also been complaints of inadequate financial support for communities affected by lockdowns, as well as failure to pay frontline health workers properly and on time, inducing some to quit. In September, a Senate committee uncovered alleged corruption in the government's purchase of medical supplies, favoring individuals identified with the administration.

Freedom of Media

Media freedom and freedom of expression received a big boost in October when Maria Ressa, the co-founder and executive editor of the news website *Rappler*, was awarded the Nobel Peace Prize, along with Russian editor Dmitry Muratov. Ressa and *Rappler* have been the target of reprisals from the Duterte government and its supporters for the website's reporting on "drug war" killings and for helping to expose what Ressa called Duterte's "weaponization of the Internet" to target government critics and dissidents.

The killing of journalists continues.

In October, Orlando Dinoy of *Newsline Philippines* and Energy Radio RM, was killed inside his home in Digos City. In July, an unidentified gunman shot dead Reynante Cortes, a radio broadcaster, as he was leaving his radio station in Cebu City, in the central Philippines. Cortes was known for his on-air commentary on local politics and corruption. In November 2020, gunmen killed newspaper columnist and radio commentator Virgilio Maganes in Villasis town, Pangasinan, a province north of Manila.

In April, journalists from *Northern Dispatch,* a weekly newspaper, were harassed by municipal police in Kalinga province, in the northern Philippines, for covering an event organized by leftist groups. Journalists of the same newspaper were later "red-tagged" by authorities. In September, leftist media organizations Bulatlat and AlterMidya accused the Philippine military of launching "denial of service" attacks on their websites.

Children's Rights

Philippine civil law sets out that a person can only be legally married at age 18. But this law does not apply to Muslims; under another law, a Muslim boy can marry at age 15 while a girl can be married off when she reaches puberty. The proposed "Girls Not Brides Act," passed by both houses of the Philippine Congress and now awaiting President Duterte's signature, will make it unlawful for anyone to marry a child (younger than 18) and make it a criminal offense to officiate such a union. According to the UN, one in six Filipino girls are married before age 18.

Another law awaiting the president's signature would raise the age of sexual consent to 16 years from the current 12 years. In September, the Senate passed its version of the statutory rape law after the House of Representatives passed its own version the year before. According to legislators, the Philippines currently "has the lowest age of sexual consent in Asia and one of the lowest in the world." In a 2015 study on violence against children in the Philippines, UNICEF said one in five Filipino children experienced their first sexual encounter at age 13 to 17.

Key International Actors

The United States continues to provide military assistance to the Philippines despite the Duterte government's poor human rights record. In June, the Biden administration notified Congress of a proposed sale of $2.5 billion in arms to the Philippines, including fighter jets and two kinds of missiles. In September, both countries announced that they would restart defense cooperation agreements that had been stalled by President Duterte's earlier threat to withdraw, including an agreement for building facilities for US troops in the Philippines.

In February, the EU and the Philippines held bilateral human rights talks. The Philippines continues to enjoy EU trade benefits pursuant to the Generalized System of Preferences Plus (GSP+), which are conditional on the ratification and implementation of 27 international conventions on human rights, labor rights, and governance. The EU postponed a GSP+ monitoring mission, citing Covid concerns. Negotiations for the EU-Philippines free trade agreement, on the other hand, have been frozen since 2019 over human rights concerns related to the "drug war."

In July, the Philippines and the United Nations signed a three-year joint program that aims to improve the human rights situation in the country. The program, which critics deem inadequate, was the UN's response to calls by members of the UN Human Rights Council to extend "technical cooperation" and "capacity building" to the Philippines, which has seen a deterioration of human rights through Duterte's "war on drugs." The program's components include the creation of a "national mechanism for reporting and follow-up" on human rights as well as "human rights-based approaches to drug control."

Poland

The Polish government continued to undermine rule of law by strengthening its control over the judiciary and smearing journalists and human rights activists critical of the government. An October decision by the politically compromised Constitutional Tribunal rejecting the supremacy of European Union law exacerbated the political and legal crisis in Poland's relationship with the EU. Attacks and harassment against lesbian, gay, bisexual and transgender (LGBT) and women's rights activists increased, with several arrested during the year. The government declared a state of emergency on its border with Belarus citing large numbers of migrants arriving through Belarus. Polish authorities have engaged in unlawful pushbacks, sometimes violent, as the numbers of irregular migrant border crossings increased.

Judicial Independence

The government continued its attacks on the independence of the judiciary. The Constitutional Tribunal, the composition and independence of which continues to be politically compromised, ruled in July that interim measures ordered in October 2020 by the Court of Justice of the European Union (CJEU) to protect the independence of the Polish judiciary were contrary to the Polish constitution. Also in July, the CJEU ordered the temporary suspension of the Polish Supreme Court's disciplinary body, ruling that the chamber could not be considered an impartial and independent judicial body as defined under EU law. In August, Poland's government notified the EU that it would dismantle the disciplinary chamber but failed to do so, prompting the European Commission in September to request that the CJEU issue daily fines for failing to comply with the court's order.

Judges and prosecutors continued to face arbitrary disciplinary proceedings for raising concerns about the rule of law and flawed judicial reforms—a direct interference with their judicial independence.

In April, the compromised Constitutional Tribunal ordered the removal, effective three months after the ruling, of the country's commissioner for human rights, Adam Bodnar, from his post despite the failure by parliament to appoint his successor following the end of his five-year term in September 2020. Bodnar, who frequently criticized the government's rule of law and human rights abuses during his mandate, should have stayed in his position until the appointment of a successor. The government instead turned to the Constitutional Tribunal, requesting the tribunal to rule the continuity provision unconstitutional, effectively ending Bodnar's term prematurely. In July, lawyer and academic Marcin Wiącek became commissioner for human rights after an eight-day vacancy following Bodnar's removal.

In October, following a motion filed by Poland's prime minster, the compromised Constitutional Tribunal ruled that CJEU's interpretation of Articles 1 and 19 of the EU Treaty was not compatible with the Polish Constitution, rejecting the binding nature of EU law and triggering the concerns of the European Commission and a number of other EU member states.

Freedom of Media and Pluralism

The government continued its attacks on independent media. According to Reporters Without Borders (RSF), since PiS came into power in 2015, Poland dropped from 18th to 64th place in its media freedom ranking. Smear campaigns and lawsuits against journalists and outlets remained a problem.

In April, the lower house in parliament, controlled by the ruling PiS party, passed a bill preventing non-European shareholders from owning a majority stake in Polish media companies, effectively impacting the US-owned independent station TVN and its 24-hour news station, TVN24. The approval of the bill followed the suspension of TVN's licence in July by the Broadcasting Council. In September, the upper house of the parliament rejected the bill and at time of writing, the law was back for consideration at the lower house of the parliament. Following EU criticism, late in September the Broadcasting Council extended the licence.

The state of emergency declared on Poland's border with Belarus in September following increasing numbers of migrants and refugees bans journalists from reporting from a two kilometer radius from the border, preventing reporters from covering stories of public interest.

Sexual Orientation and Gender Identity

The government continued its onslaught on LGBT rights as part of its "anti-gender ideology" rhetoric. LGBT activists reported an increasingly hostile environment making people feel unsafe. Many LGBT people left Poland during the year as a result of increased levels of homophobia and transphobia.

Hate crimes provisions in the criminal code do not include crimes committed on the basis of sexual orientation or gender identity and LGBT people reported that state response to reported threats or attacks is poor.

Some 100 local regions and governments in Poland continue to label themselves as "LGBT Ideology Free Zones." Following fears of losing EU funds, four Polish regions in September revoked their anti-LGBT declarations.

A local court in the city of Plock in August acquitted three LGBT activists, including Elzbieta Podlesna, charged with insulting religious feelings. The activists had publicly posted images of the Virgin Mary and baby Jesus with rainbows as halos. The judge held that the activists did not intend to offend anyone's beliefs but to show support for LGBT people and their equal rights.

Migration and Asylum

With increasing number of migrants irregularly crossing from Belarus to Poland since May, the Polish government in September declared a state of emergency on its border with Belarus, banning journalists, activists, humanitarian aid workers, and others from accessing the border area. As of August, credible reports of pushbacks of migrants and asylum seekers to Belarus by Polish border officials, sometimes violent, increased, with five migrant deaths confirmed in the woods on the Poland-Belarusian border.

Polish authorities sought to justify their abusive migration approach by arguing that they were responding to a deliberate policy by Belarusian President Aleksandr Lukashenko of allowing migrants to travel freely into Belarus and towards EU borders, in retaliation for EU sanctions against Belarus. Their justifications ignored the fact that Poland's actions violate its obligations under EU and international law and put migrants at risk of harm, including death, and the fact that its practice of migrant pushbacks predates those currently entering via Belarus.

Women's Rights

In January, an October 2020 Constitutional Tribunal decision virtually banning access to legal abortion, went into effect. Women's rights groups Abortion Without Borders, Abortion Dream Team, and the Federation for Women and Family Planning reported a significant increase in the number of women and girls contacting them for help in accessing abortion and other sexual and reproductive health care in the year since the ruling. Covid-19 pandemic restrictions continued to make cross-border travel to access abortion particularly difficult and costly.

In July, the European Court of Human Rights (ECtHR) announced that it will address complaints from Polish women who may be victims of violations of the European Convention on Human Rights and Fundamental Freedoms due to the Constitutional Tribunal's abortion ruling. Poland's government has failed to effectively implement previous ECtHR judgments concerning access to lawful abortion.

In September, a new bill that would criminalize people who have abortions with up to 25 years in prison was introduced. A draft bill essentially criminalizing sexuality education and supported by the government remains in parliamentary committee.

At time of writing, a July 2020 government request to the compromised Constitutional Tribunal to examine the compatibility with the Polish Constitution of the Istanbul Convention, a Council of Europe instrument to combat and prevent violence against women, was still pending consideration.

Threats and harassment of women's rights activists continued. Around International Women's Day in March, staff members from seven organizations reported bomb and death threats, due to their work for or perceived support for women's rights and abortion. Four groups filed reports to police but stated that, in many cases, police minimized the threats or did not effectively pursue investigations. In October, escalating threats against Marta Lempart, co-founder of Ogólnopolski Strajk Kobiet (All-Poland Women's Strike), led police to offer her protection during public appearances.

Women's rights groups reported an increase in reported domestic violence cases following Covid-19 lockdowns and movement restrictions, which resulted in some women and girls being trapped with abusers in the same household with limited possibilities to access help.

HUMAN
RIGHTS
WATCH

"Everything I Have to Do
is Tied to a Man"
Women and Qatar's Male Guardianship Rules

Qatar

Abuse and exploitation of the country's large migrant workforce persisted in 2021 despite the introduction of labor reforms, in part because of ineffective implementation and because certain elements of the kafala (sponsorship) system remained in place. Women in Qatar continued to face severe discrimination and violence due to abusive male guardianship policies.

In July, Qatar passed new laws to regulate its first legislative election, which took place in October; however, the laws effectively disenfranchised thousands of Qataris from voting or running because of their nationality by lineage. This led to debate among Qataris on social media as well as small-scale demonstrations led by members of one of Qatar's largest semi-nomadic communities. Politically motivated arrests and detentions followed.

Migrant Workers

Qatar's migrant labor force of over 2 million people comprises approximately 95 percent of its total labor force. Approximately 1 million workers are employed in construction, while around 100,000 are domestic workers.

In February, just six months after Qatar introduced significant labor reforms that allow migrant workers to change jobs without employer permission and set a higher minimum wage for all workers, regardless of nationality, Qatar's advisory Shura council pushed back with recommendations that would have effectively undone a crucial step forward in protecting migrant workers. The recommendations were not adopted. Qatar's labor minister earlier stressed to Shura council members, to alleviate concerns from Qatar's business community, that while the law allowed workers to submit a request to change employers, it was still "subject to approval or rejection after communicating with the concerned parties." The Shura council recommendations and labor minister comments indicated a willingness to backtrack on reforms and cast doubt on its effectiveness in promoting true job mobility.

In March, Qatar's minimum wage, which applies to all workers, came into force. In addition to the minimum monthly basic wage of 1,000 Qatari riyal (US$275), the legislation stipulates that employers must pay allowances of at least 300 and 500 Qatari riyal for food and housing respectively if they do not provide workers with these directly. However, employers across Qatar still frequently violate workers' right to wages paid in full and on time and the authorities' efforts to detect violations and enact swift and deterrent penalties have largely failed. Wage abuses only worsened during the Covid-19 pandemic.

Other abusive elements of the *kafala* system remain, namely that a migrant worker's legal status in Qatar remains tied to a specific employer, where an employer can apply, renew, or cancel a worker's residency permit, and that "absconding," or leaving an employer without permission, remains a crime. Workers, especially low-paid laborers and domestic workers, often depend on their employer not just for their jobs, but for housing and food. Passport confiscations, high recruitment fees, and deceptive recruitment practices remain largely unpunished. Workers are banned from joining trade unions or exercising their right to strike. Such impunity and remaining aspects of the *kafala* system continue to drive abuse, exploitation, and forced labor practices.

While Qatar introduced some tougher measures in May to protect workers from heat stress, the authorities continued to enforce a rudimentary midday summer working hours ban. Moreover, for seven years, Qatar has not made public any detailed or meaningful data on migrant worker deaths that would allow an assessment of the extent to which heat stress is a factor. Medical research published in July 2019 concluded that heatstroke is a likely cause of cardiovascular fatalities among migrant workers in Qatar. Climate change is expected to lead to further increased temperatures in Qatar.

In May, Qatari authorities forcibly disappeared a Kenyan security guard and labor activist, Malcolm Bidali, detaining him in solitary confinement for a month, after which they conditionally released him back to his company's worker accommodations. On July 14, Qatar's Supreme Judiciary Council handed down a criminal order stating that Bidali had broadcast and published "false news with the intent of endangering the public system of the state" under article 6 of the controversial cybercrime law, arising purely from the exercise of his right to freedom of expression. The court ordered him to pay a fine of 25,000 Qatari riyal (approximately US$6,800) and ordered the confiscation of his personal mobile phone and the blocking in Qatar of his Twitter and Instagram accounts through which "the crime was committed." On August 19, Human Rights Watch and other international organizations called on Qatari authorities to quash his conviction and to urgently reform its judicial processes, including the cybercrime law. Bidali left Qatar on August 16.

Women's Rights

In a report released in March, Human Rights Watch documented how the discriminatory male guardianship concept, which is incorporated into Qatari law, regulations, and practices, denies women the right to make many key decisions about their lives. Women in Qatar must obtain permission from their male guardians to marry, study abroad on government scholarships, work in many government jobs, travel abroad until certain ages, and receive some forms of reproductive health care. The discriminatory system also denies women the authority to act as their children's primary guardian, even when they are divorced and have legal custody, without regard to the child's best interests.

Single Qatari women under 25 years of age must obtain their guardian's permission to travel outside Qatar, and women can also be subject to travel bans at any age by their husbands or fathers. Qatari women are also required to have a guardian's permission in order to work for some government ministries and institutions, and women who attend Qatar University face restrictions on their movements. Some hotels also prohibit unmarried Qatari women under 30 years old from renting a hotel room, and Qatari women are prohibited from some events and bars that serve alcohol.

Qatar's Family Law also discriminates against women in marriage, divorce, child custody, and inheritance. Women are required to have a male guardian's permission to marry. Once married, a woman is required to obey her husband and can lose her husband's financial support if she works or travels or refuses to have sex with him, without a "legitimate" reason. Men have a unilateral right to divorce while women must apply to the courts for divorce on limited grounds. Under inheritance provisions, female siblings receive half the amount their brothers get.

While the family law forbids husbands from hurting their wives physically or morally, and there are general criminal code provisions on assault, Qatar has no law on domestic violence or measures to protect survivors and prosecute their abusers. No law explicitly prohibits corporal punishment of children either.

Women can be forced to return to their families by the police if they leave their home, including when fleeing abuse. In January, a Yemeni woman was killed by her former Qatari husband outside a family court that had ruled in her favor in a dispute concerning their child.

Qatar allows men to pass citizenship to their spouses and children, whereas children of Qatari women and non-citizen men can only apply for citizenship under narrow conditions. This discriminates against Qatari women married to foreigners, and their children and spouses.

Women continued to report that they faced intimidation by government cyber security for their tweets or other online actions about women's rights or other political issues, including through interrogations, being asked to sign pledges not to speak about these issues, and being asked to give officials access to their Twitter accounts or surrender their electronic devices to them.

Freedom of Expression

Qatar's penal code criminalizes criticizing the emir, insulting Qatar's flag, defaming religion, including blasphemy, and inciting "to overthrow the regime." Qatar's 2014 cybercrimes law provided for a maximum of three years in prison and/or a fine of 500,000 Qatari riyal (around $137,325) for anyone convicted of spreading "false news" (a term that is not defined) on the internet or for posting online content that "violates social values or principles," or "insults or slanders others."

In January 2020, Qatar amended its penal code to impose up to five years in prison for spreading rumors or false news with ill-intent and/or a fine of 100,000 Qatari riyal (around $27,465). The new text does not define who determines what is a rumor or "fake news," how to make such a determination, or what standards are to be used in doing so.

In August and September, newly introduced election laws that effectively disenfranchise thousands of Qataris from voting or running in Qatar's first legislative elections provoked controversy and debate among Qataris on social media as well as small-scale demonstrations. Qatari authorities responded to the criticism by referring seven people for prosecution on charges of "spreading false news" and "stirring up racial and tribal strife." Informed sources told Human Rights

Watch that Qatari authorities arrested and detained at least 15 people in the aftermath, some of whom remained detained without charge a month later.

Statelessness

Qatar's decision to arbitrarily strip families from the Ghufran clan of the Al Murra tribe of their citizenship starting in 1996 has left some members stateless 20 years later and deprived them of access to key human rights. In 2021, Qatar made no commitments to rectify their status.

Stateless members of the Ghufran clan are deprived of their rights to work, access to health care, education, marriage and starting a family, owning property, and freedom of movement. Without valid identity documents, they face restrictions accessing basic services, including opening bank accounts and acquiring drivers' licenses, and are at risk of arbitrary detention. Those living in Qatar are also denied a range of government benefits afforded to Qatari citizens, including state jobs, food and energy subsidies, and free basic healthcare.

Sexual Orientation and Morality Laws

Qatar's penal code criminalizes extramarital sex. Individuals convicted of *zina* (sex outside of marriage) can be sentenced up to seven years imprisonment. In addition to imprisonment, Muslims can be sentenced to flogging (if unmarried) or the death penalty (if married) for *zina*. These laws disproportionately impact women, as pregnancy serves as evidence of extramarital sex and women who report rape can find themselves prosecuted for consensual sex.

In addition to banning sex outside marriage for Muslims, Qatar punishes consensual sexual relations between men above sixteen, Muslim or not, with up to seven years imprisonment (article 285). It also provides penalties between one and three years (article 296) for any male who "instigates" or "entices" another male to "commit an act of sodomy or immorality." A penalty of ten years' imprisonment (article 288) is also imposed on anyone who engages in consensual sexual relations with a person above sixteen, outside marriage, which could apply to consensual same-sex relations between women, men, or heterosexual partners.

Journalists and printers operate under section 47 of the 1979 Press and Publications Law, which bans publication of "any printed matter that is deemed contrary to the ethics, violates the morals or harms the dignity of the people or their personal freedoms."

Climate Change Policy and Actions

As a significant contributor to the greenhouse gas emissions, Qatar is contributing to the climate crisis that is taking a growing toll on human rights around the globe. The country has the sixth highest greenhouse gas emissions per capita globally, a considerable portion from air conditioning. Qatar has taken few steps to move away from production and use of fossil fuels and instead is doubling down on producing liquified natural gas (LNG) for export. It has the world's third largest reserves of natural gas and until recently was the world's largest exporter of LNG. Qatar has yet to submit its second Nationally Determined Contribution (NDC), a Paris Agreement-mandated five-year national climate change action plan due at the end of 2020. Its first NDC contained no quantitative targets.

As one of the world's hottest countries, Qatar is particularly vulnerable to the impacts of climate change. Ninety-seven percent of Qatar's population lives along an exposed coastline making them particularly vulnerable to both sea level rise and extreme weather events.

Key International Actors

In January, Saudi Arabia ended its years-long isolation of Qatar, which began in 2017 when Saudi Arabia, Bahrain, Egypt, and the United Arab Emirates closed their borders to Qatar and expelled Qatari citizens over allegations of Qatar's support for terrorism and ties with Iran. All four countries restored their diplomatic relations when Qatar suspended its World Trade Organization case against the UAE's economic isolation efforts.

Qatar played a key role in Afghanistan after the United States military withdrawal in August propelled a Taliban takeover of Kabul, both by extensively aiding the US in evacuating tens of thousands of vulnerable people from Afghanistan and by operating daily flights starting in early September to deliver humanitarian aid to the country.

Russia

The legislative crackdown that started in November 2020 intensified ahead of the September 2021 general elections. Numerous newly adopted laws broadened the authorities' grounds to target a wide range of independent voices. Authorities used some of these laws and other measures, to smear, harass, and penalize human rights defenders, journalists, independent groups, political adversaries, and even academics. Many left Russia for their own safety or were expelled. Authorities took particular aim at independent journalism.

Amendments expanding and harshening "foreign agents" and "undesirable foreign organizations" legislation were among the newly adopted laws. Authorities continued to add more groups to the "foreign agents" registry, which imposes a toxic label and burdensome labelling and reporting requirements. They also expanded their registry of "undesirable organizations," blacklisting international and foreign organizations, including prominent rights group, and used the "undesirable" law to prosecute people.

After political opposition leader Alexey Navalny returned to Russia in January 2021, having received treatment in Germany for near-fatal poisoning, he was unjustly arrested, imprisoned and additionally prosecuted on new charges. This sparked countrywide protests that authorities suppressed. Authorities banned three groups affiliated with Navalny as "extremist."

Human Rights Defenders

In 2021, authorities continued to employ a variety of tools to harass human rights defenders and disrupt their work.

In December 2020, authorities revoked the residence permit of Vanessa Kogan, a US national, and ordered her to leave, based on the Federal Security Service's (FSB) claim that she was a national security threat. Kogan is the director of Stitching Justice Initiative (SJI), a nongovernmental organization (NGO) that successfully litigated hundreds of cases against Russia at international human rights bodies. In September, authorities initiated the forced closing of Astreya, SJI's Russian partner, on technical grounds.

In January, authorities interfered with the work of lawyers representing peaceful protesters and human rights defenders who monitored the January protests.

In March, Izzat Amon (Kholov), who for over 10 years provided legal services to migrants from Tajikistan, was stripped of his Russian citizenship and deported to Tajikistan, where authorities detained him on fraud charges reportedly pertaining to his work in Moscow.

In April, authorities opened a criminal case against Ivan Pavlov, a human rights lawyer and head of Team 29, an informal lawyers association that represented clients in highly sensitive cases. Pavlov was wrongly accused of disclosing classified information about one of his clients. In July, in order to protect its clients, team members, and supporters, the group closed after it learned authorities were equating it with a foreign organization blacklisted as "undesirable." Team 29 also represented Navalny's Foundation Against Corruption (FBK) in its legal challenge to the authorities' designating it an "extremist" group. In August, the Justice Ministry filed a complaint that may lead to Pavlov's disbarment. In September, Pavlov left Russia, stating that authorities had paralyzed his work, and in October, he learned that the authorities put him on a wanted list. In November, authorities designated him and four other Team 29 members as "foreign agent—foreign media."

In June, authorities opened a criminal case against Ernest Mezak, a human rights lawyer who litigates cases at the European Court of Human Rights (ECtHR). They charged him with insulting a judge in a social media post.

After a year under criminal investigation, in July, a court in Sochi sentenced rights defender Semyon Simonov to 250 hours of community service over supposed violations of the "foreign agents" law. In October, he was released from serving the sentence due to the expiration of statutory limitations.

In September, authorities barred human rights lawyer Valentina Chupik from re-entering Russia and stripped her of her refugee status, obtained in 2009. Chupik, a national of Uzbekistan, provided legal assistance to migrants in Russia and was an outspoken critic of the abuses she documented against them.

Also in September, authorities fined two human rights defenders, Alexey Glukhov and Igor Kalyapin, for mostly old social media re-posts with hyperlinks to an "undesirable" organization.

In October, Soldiers' Mothers of St Petersburg suspended work assisting servicemen because new FSB guidelines, issued following the expansion of the "foreign agents" law (see below), prohibited, among other things, disclosing information about the mood in the military.

In November, the prosecutors' office filed a lawsuit to close Memorial, one of Russia's oldest human rights organization, for alleged noncompliance with the foreign agents law.

Freedom of Expression

Since December 2020, the number of individuals and entities authorities branded "foreign media—foreign agent" exploded, reaching 94 by early November. Most are prominent investigative journalists and independent outlets.

In April, FSB raided the home of Roman Anin, editor-in-chief of iStories, several weeks after Anin published an article with allegations about a high-level FSB official. Also in April, the editorial team of DOXA, an independent university student magazine, faced criminal investigation on baseless accusations of encouraging the participation of students under 18 in unauthorized protests.

In July, authorities blacklisted Project Media, an investigative outlet behind high-profile anti-corruption investigations, as an "undesirable organization" and branded its Russian editor-in-chief, Roman Badanin and four other staff "foreign agents – foreign media," shortly after law enforcement searched Badanin's home and named him a suspect in a criminal defamation suit. Project Media evacuated some of their staff from Russia.

In May, authorities designated independent media outlet VTimes a "foreign agent", prompting it to close due to risks to its journalists.

In August, authorities also blocked the websites of two Open Russia media projects, MBKh-Media, and Open Media, and the entity's human rights project.

In July, police raided the apartments of Roman Dobrokhotov, editor-in-chief of investigative outlet The Insider, and that of his parents, apparently in relation to a criminal defamation case. Dobrokhotov left Russia in August. In September, authorities opened a criminal case against him on charges of illegal border crossing, and again raided his and his parents' apartments.

Police detained and in some cases physically assaulted journalists covering protests, despite their explicit compliance with official requirements to wear special identifying gear.

In February, a court in Moscow sentenced Sergei Smirnov, the editor-in-chief of Mediazona, to 25 days' detention for retweeting a post with imagery concerning a pro-Navalny protest.

In January, new legislative amendments came into effect imposing further restrictions on free expression. One amendment could allow authorities to institute misdemeanor proceedings on insult charges without a complainant and victim. Other amendments expanded the definition of criminal defamation and introduced imprisonment as a possible penalty.

Russian authorities continued to penalize artistic expression that criticized or shed light on sensitive issues.

In November 2020, Pavel Krisevich served 15 days' detention for a performance dedicated to political prisoners in front of the FSB building in Moscow, which also led to his expulsion from university. In June, Krisevich was detained and later indicted on criminal hooliganism charges after staging a performance against state repression and intimidation at Red Square. At time of writing, he remained in pretrial detention.

In December of that year, Moscow police detained Maria Alyokhina and Rita Flores of the punk collective Pussy Riot and two other people after they staged a performance that mocked authorities for prosecuting protesters. Alyokhina also spent several months under house arrest over a social media post supporting the January protest and was sentenced, in September, to one year of restricted freedom. In June and July, authorities repeatedly detained, for up to 15 days each time, several Pussy Riot activists on highly questionable charges of non-compliance with police orders. Three of the activists left Russia.

In March, a court fined civic activist Karim Yamadayev for "insulting authorities' and "incitement to terrorism" for a video of a mock corruption trial of President Vladimir Putin and two public officials. Yamadayev had spent more than a year in pretrial detention.

In August, police detained over two dozen attendees of an outdoor photography exhibition in St. Petersburg and questioned them regarding some of the photos, one of which included police, and another, a church. The exhibition organizers were charged with violating public assembly rules.

In September, authorities questioned a renowned actress, Liya Akhedzhakova, over a monologue her character delivers in a play which some groups claimed insulted war veterans and propagated same-sex relationships. In October, a popular rapper, Morgenshtern, in a media interview criticized the amount of money spent on the annual Victory Day celebration. Shortly after, authorities announced an inquiry into his statement that may lead to criminal prosecution. Also in October, authorities opened an inquiry into a St. Petersburg artist's painting depicting people carrying portraits of decomposing bodies. The complainants claimed it was an allusion to commemoration marches for World War II soldiers.

In October a couple was sentenced to 10 months in prison for insulting religious feelings over a photo in which the woman faked oral sex, with St. Basil's Cathedral in the background. The day after that trial, another woman was arrested on the same criminal charges for a photo showing her buttocks, across the street from a cathedral. A court released her pending trial. Earlier in 2021, several women served 2 to 14 days in detention for indecent exposure near police stations and Kremlin.

Throughout the year, authorities resorted to expelling or deporting foreigners in retaliation for their reporting, criticism, or activism. These included British BBC journalist Sarah Rainsford; Tajik activist Saidanvar Sulaimonov, barred from re-entry for 40 years; and Belarussian stand-up comic Idrak Mirzalizade, banned for life over a joke he told that authorities claimed was insulting to ethnic Russians.

Freedom of Assembly

Between January and April, six sets of legislative amendments entered into force, that further curtailed already restricted freedom of assembly.

Russian authorities also used Covid-19 as a pretext for blanket bans on public assemblies organized by civic and political activists and prosecuted organizers and participants for noncompliance. The pandemic did not deter the authorities from holding mass pro-government or state-sponsored events.

Navalny's arrest triggered countrywide protests in late January. Where organizers sought permission, authorities refused. Ahead of the protests, authorities detained and harassed presumed organizers and well-known activists. On several occasions, state universities threatened students with expulsion to prevent them from participating.

Police in some instances used excessive force to disperse crowds. Authorities detained thousands and in many instances denied them access to lawyers. Many were fined or jailed on administrative charges. Numerous criminal cases were opened. In late October a protester, Gleb Maryasov, was sentenced to 10 months in prison on allegations of organizing the blocking of traffic during the January 23 protest.

In March, authorities in Moscow raided a forum of municipal deputies, arresting around 200, claiming it was organized in collaboration with an "undesirable" organization. In May, a court fined activist Yuliya Galyamina and jailed her for seven days in relation to a similar gathering in Velikiy Novgorod, which authorities groundlessly claimed violated Covid-19 restrictions.

Authorities continued to hand down criminal penalties for peaceful protest. In December 2020, Galyamina received a two-year suspended sentence and in October 2021 Viacheslav Yegorov received a 15-month prison sentence, for repeated participation in peaceful albeit unauthorized protests.

Freedom of Association

In December 2020 and March 2021, parliament passed two laws to toughen Russia's "foreign agents" legislation. The December law drastically widened the scope of "foreign agents" to individuals and unregistered groups. It also expanded the definition of funding sources that could trigger a "foreign agent" designation, expanded the inspection regime, and introduced new labeling requirements. The other law expanded reporting requirements, allowed the Justice Ministry to ban any "foreign agent" organization's program or event, and set out additional grounds for unscheduled inspections.

By July, two new laws on "undesirables" also entered into force. One expanded the applicability of "undesirable" provisions, banning Russians' involvement with any such organization beyond Russia's borders and enabling authorities to ban any organization that assists an "undesirable" group's operations in Russia. The other substantially reduced the threshold for criminal liability for perceived members or supporters of "undesirable" groups.

As a result of these amendments, Open Russia civic movement—which authorities had targeted since 2019 with "undesirable"-related prosecutions—closed, citing risks to supporters and members. But at the end of May, authorities detained Andrey Pivovarov, the group's former director. At time of writing, he remained in detention facing up to six years in prison.

In February 2021, after two years under house arrest, a court sentenced Anastasiya Shevchenko to a four-year suspended sentence merely for being part of the Open Russia movement. In August, Mikhail Iosilevich was released after six months' pretrial detention for providing space for civil society events in his café. He still faces trial on "undesirable" and other trumped up charges.

Torture, Ill-Treatment in Custody, Police Accountability

Authorities regularly allowed cruel treatment, torture and suspicious deaths in custody to go unpunished by refusing to open criminal cases, explanations by law enforcement as justification to close or drop cases due to expiration of statutory limitations.

In January, a court in Moscow sentenced Azat Miftakhov to six years in prison on allegations of throwing a Molotov cocktail into an empty office of the ruling party. The investigation and trial were marred by allegations of torture, and reliance on "secret witnesses." The other two defendants pleaded guilty but repeatedly denied Miftakhov's involvement.

Also in January, a riot policeman was caught on camera kicking in the stomach a woman standing in his way. After public outcry, the authorities aired on television his staged apology to the victim while she was in hospital. Later, they claimed they were unable to identify the perpetrator.

In September, a court in Nizhny Novgorod jailed a man who a Russian anti-torture group said was severely beaten in police custody on charges of inflicting bodily harm on a police officer. Police pressed similar charges against a 66-year-old pensioner in Orenburg, whom police reportedly beat and tasered. At time of writing, authorities refused to investigate allegations of police misconduct in both cases.

Torture and ill-treatment of inmates continued in Russia's penitentiary system, despite official assurances following the publication of leaked, graphic videos of torture of inmates. In July, a number of inmates complained of intensified cruel treatment in retaliation for an April riot in a penal colony in Angarsk, reportedly sparked by ill-treatment.

In October, after new media reports about leaked videos documenting numerous incidents of rape and other ill-treatment of male inmates at a prison hospital in Saratov region, law enforcement announced they were opening an investigation. The person who leaked the videos fled the country.

In April and October, inmates rioted in penal colonies in Angarsk and Vladikavkaz, reportedly prompted by beatings.

Chechnya

Chechen leadership under governor Ramzan Kadyrov continued to ruthlessly quash all forms of dissent.

In February, Russian police forcibly returned Salekh Magamadov and Ismail Isaev who fled Chechnya fearing persecution for posting anti-government messages on social media. At time of writing, they remained in jail. In March, Chechen authorities temporarily detained and threatened their family members.

In April, Chechen security officials abducted Magomed Gadaev, an asylum seeker and key witness in a high-profile torture case against Chechnya's leadership, two days after France deported him to Russia. They took him to Grozny and apparently coerced him to refuse the services of his trusted lawyer. In June, a court sentenced him to 18 months' imprisonment on spurious weapons charges.

In May, Ibragim Selimkhanov was abducted from Moscow and forcibly returned to Chechnya, where authorities interrogated him about gay people in the region. He later managed to escape Chechnya.

Counterterrorism and Counter-Extremism

In June, a court approved authorities' request to ban three organizations affiliated with Navalny as extremist, including FBK, despite lack of any credible evidence that their activities were extremist, much less a security threat. Shortly before the ruling, parliament adopted a law retroactively banning staffers and founders of extremist organizations from running in parliamentary elections. The law was later expanded to ban them from any elections.

In September, authorities announced a new criminal case against Navalny and his allies over continuing "extremist group" activities. In November, authorities arrested Lilia Chanysheva, the former head of Navalny's team in Ufa, on charges of leading an extremist group.

Police continued to raid houses and open new criminal cases against Jehovah's Witnesses, banned as extremist in Russia since 2017. Russian courts convicted 92 people, 27 of whom were sentenced to prison terms of up to eight years. At time of writing, at least 15 people remained in prison, hundreds under criminal investigation, and 63 in pretrial detention. Those convicted and prosecuted included people in Russia-occupied Crimea. Authorities stripped two Jehovah's Witnesses of their citizenship and deported them.

Several persons were convicted for supposed affiliation with Nurdzhular, a group of followers of the late Turkish theologian Said Nursi that Russia banned as extremist in 2008, even though it has no history of incitement or violence. In October, authorities raided homes and arrested over 15 alleged Nursi followers.

In August, Yevgeniy Kim, who had been stripped of his Russian citizenship in 2019 following his prison sentence on charges of involvement with Nurdzhular, was released after more than two- and-a-half years in deportation custody. He remains stateless and without identification documents.

Since late 2020, at least 11 people were convicted for alleged affiliation with Tablighi Jamaat, an international Islamic missionary movement banned in Russia as extremist since 2009 although it disavows violence. At least 13 others were detained in 2021, with authorities pressing charges against five and deporting several others.

Since November 2020, at least eight people were sentenced, and several dozen detained over alleged involvement with Hizb-ut-Tahrir (HuT), a pan-Islamist movement that seeks to establish a caliphate but denounces violence to achieve that goal. Russia banned HuT as a terrorist organization in 2003. In May, an appeals court upheld verdicts against 10 people sentenced to 11 to 22 years in prison. According to Human Rights Center Memorial, as of October 2021, over 170 people served prison sentences upon conviction for involvement with HuT, 29 were on trial, at least 61 were under investigation and 27 more were wanted. Memorial's figures include Crimean Tatars.

Environment, Climate Change, and Human Rights

Environmental watchdogs continued to report physical attacks, harassment, intimidation, and prosecution of grassroot activists and environmental groups in different parts of the country.

In October authorities designated a prominent environmental defender, Yevgeniy Simonov, a "foreign agent."

As one of the world's top 10 emitters of greenhouse gases, Russia is contributing to the climate crisis that is taking a mounting toll on human rights around the globe. It is also the third largest producer of fossil fuels and a top gas exporter.

In its November 2020 update to its national climate action plan, Russia committed to reducing its emissions by 30 percent by 2030 compared to 1990 levels. The Climate Action Tracker rates Russia's domestic target as "highly insufficient" to meet the Paris Agreement goal to limit global warming to 1.5°C above pre-industrial levels.

Russia has failed to protect its forests that absorb and store carbon. Rising deforestation, driven by illegal logging; increasingly destructive wildfires exacerbated by climate change; and poor fire management, have increased overall emissions. In the summer months, smoke from record breaking wildfires in Siberia's Sakha (Yakutia) region resulted in air pollution threatening the health of thousands of residents.

Permafrost, ground that has been frozen continuously for a minimum of two years and currently covers about 65 percent of Russian territory, is rapidly degrading across Russia's north, due to warming temperatures and more intense fires. This poses a threat to livelihoods and infrastructure, increasing the risk of industrial accidents.

In February, a court ordered the Russian mining company, Norilsk Nickel, to pay a US$2 billion fine over an oil spill that caused massive environmental destruction. Norilsk Nickel said the spill resulted from the impact of climate change on permafrost, upon which all their infrastructure is located. But investigative reporters emphasized the role played by company's failure to invest in infrastructure.

Right to Asylum, Prohibition of Refoulement, Migration

In March and in April, numerous migrants were deported with multi-year re-entry bans for attending peaceful, unauthorized protests.

At least one asylum seeker was forcibly removed to Uzbekistan after "disappearing" from Russia; another—a Tajik political opposition group member— was refouled to Tajikistan in September 2020 under similar circumstances. In May, a member of the same group who was a naturalized Russian citizen "disappeared."

In October, a Belarussian journalist "disappeared" in Moscow and was later found in detention in Minsk. He had fled to Russia fearing persecution.

In spring, as authorities started lifting the special Covid-19 regime that had temporarily vacated the need for migrants' regular registration, many migrants became exposed to heightened risk of coronavirus due to extreme overcrowding at the processing centers, which resulted from the limited timeframe to regularize their status. Police renewed massive raids and mass arrests of migrants.

In June, Russia adopted new amendments to its migration law that mandate fingerprinting, photographing, and regular medical examination of all foreigners who spend more than 90 days in the country (30 days for migrant workers). Also, in July authorities developed a new bill that reforms migration legislation. The bill includes mandatory software and digital IDs for migrants that would aggregate private information—including biometric, health, and potentially location data. It would also require migrants to sign "loyalty agreements."

Sexual Orientation and Gender Identity

The government continued its trajectory of anti-lesbian, gay, bisexual and transgender (LGBT) discrimination and failed to investigate threats and attacks against LGBT people, in which their sexual orientation or gender identity was considered a motive.

In February, authorities in Khabarovsk region indicted Yulia Tsvetkova, a feminist and LGBT activist, on spurious pornography charges related to a group she administered on social media.

In April, an unidentified man in St. Petersburg assaulted and broke the nose of Ilya Bronsky, a gay blogger who earlier tweeted about living in Russia with HIV. The authorities failed to investigate. Bronsky later left Russia.

In July, a Russian supermarket chain retracted an advertising campaign that included a lesbian family and published an apology after being targeted by an online hate campaign and threats for boycott. The family received threats on social media that police failed to investigate, and later left the country citing safety concerns.

In November, authorities designated Russian LGBT Network as a "foreign agent" and LGBT activist Igor Kochetkov was designated a "foreign agent-foreign media"

Gender-Based Violence

Russia's systemic failure to properly address domestic violence continued to lead to tragic outcomes for victims deprived of state protection and support due to inadequate legislation, poor police response, and insufficient services, such as access to shelters.

In December 2020, the Justice Ministry added Nasiliu.net, a group that provides legal and psychological help to domestic violence survivors, to its "foreign agents" registry. In April, the authorities fined it for non-compliance with the "foreign agents" law.

In June, police raided a women's shelter in Dagestan and forcibly returned to Chechnya Khalimat Taramova, who identifies as bisexual and who had fled her parents' home to escape abuse. Several days later, she appeared on local TV stating on camera that she was "fine" and was being looked after by her family. In October, two women from Dagestan were forcibly taken, allegedly by police, from a shelter for domestic violence survivors in Tatarstan and forcibly returned to their families. Authorities opened an inquiry but denied police involvement.

Research published in 2021, covering nearly a decade, estimated that 66 percent of all murdered women in Russia were victims of domestic violence.

Rights of Older People

Approximately 25 percent of Russia's population are over pension age. Reforms have aimed to expand certain home services for older people. However, funding and delivery are inadequate and inconsistent, compelling many to enter nursing homes or other institutions. Journalists and advocates have documented serious human rights abuses in institutions, including use of restraints, inappropriate use of medication, and poor medical treatment.

In August, the government made one-off 10,000 rubles (US$135) payments to pensioners, in the face of rising inflation. Analysts believe this was to influence their vote in favor of the ruling party in the September elections.

Digital Rights, Right to Privacy

In 2021, Russia escalated pressure on foreign and Russian social media companies to strengthen its grip on free expression and curtail access to information online.

Several new laws encroaching on digital freedom entered into force. Amendments obliged social media platforms to take down content on request of the authorities and prohibited them from censoring the content of social media accounts affiliated with the Russian state. Another law entered into force in April, introducing penalties on manufacturers that do not pre-install designated

Russian software on relevant devices sold in Russia. In July, new provisions obliged popular foreign websites and apps to open representative offices in Russia. Sanctions for noncompliance include fines, advertisement bans, and blocking.

In February, following a wave of country-wide protests, authorities escalated pressure on social media companies to censor online content related to protests.

Throughout the year, authorities continued to slam social media platforms with large fines over noncompliance with regulations on content blocking and data localization, and eventually threatened to issue fines of up to 20 percent of the companies' annual revenue. The majority of fines against social media companies related to content about mass protests in January, February and April 2021.

In March, the government slowed access to Twitter over its alleged failure to censor calls for protests. Later, authorities stated that Twitter eventually complied, but threatened to block the platform entirely.

In May, authorities threatened to block VPNs for not complying with local regulations. By September, eight had been blocked.

In July, Russian authorities demanded that YouTube block channels linked to Navalny groups that had been designated "extremist." In August, they demanded that Apple and Google take down Navalny's app from their stores. The companies eventually complied but Google reinstated the app in October.

Authorities continued integrating public surveillance systems with facial recognition technology across the country, despite serious privacy concerns, lack of regulation, oversight, and data protection.

Russia and Crimea (see also Ukraine chapter)

Russian authorities continued to persecute critics of its actions in occupied Crimea.

In March, the authorities arrested freelance journalist Vladyslav Yesypenko, on apparently fabricated charges. Yesypenko alleged FSB officers tortured him to extract a false confession.

Russian authorities continued to target Crimean Tatars in Crimea with bogus terrorism charges related to involvement with HuT, which operates legally in Ukraine. In February and August, authorities raided homes and arrested a total of 12 men, 11 of them Crimean Tatars. In August, a court sentenced four Crimean Tatars to prison terms ranging from 12 to 18 years, and dozens more continued to serve baseless and harsh prison sentences.

Russia and Syria (see also Syria chapter)

Russia continued to play a critical role in the Syrian conflict. As part of a military alliance, it continues to support, and in some cases conduct, deliberate and indiscriminate attacks on civilians and civilian infrastructure, including schools, hospitals, markets, homes, and shelters, through what has become trademark tactics over the years, including the use of internationally banned weapons. Human Rights Watch has determined that the Syria-Russia alliance's attacks against civilian infrastructure in Idlib in northeast Syria are apparent war crimes and may amount to crimes against humanity.

In July 2021, the United Nations Security Council (UNSC) failed to reauthorize full cross-border operations into the region and authorize a resumption of aid flows from Iraq to northeast Syria, due to the threat of a Russian veto. Instead, the Security Council was able to extend the opening of one border crossing to Northwest Syria. Russia and the United States disagree regarding the duration of the authorization, which remains unclear.

Key International Actors

In January, the arrest of Navalny drew international outcry. Among others, top European Union (EU) institutions and a group of 45 states at the United Nations Human Rights Council (HRC) publicly condemned his imprisonment, the detention and prosecution of peaceful protesters, "shrinking civil society space" and Russia's use of the "tools of the state to ... to silence dissenting voices.

In February, the ECtHR requested that Russia release Navalny, and the Council of Europe's (CoE) Commissioner for Human Rights stated that Navalny's sentencing "contravenes Russia's international human rights obligations."

Following his first-ever visit to Russia in February, the EU high representative for foreign affairs, Josep Borrell, observed that "Russia is progressively disconnecting itself from Europe and looking at democratic values as an existential threat."

In March, the EU imposed sanctions over serious human rights violations as part of broader package of listings under the EU Global Human Rights Sanctions Regime.

In March, June, and October, UN-appointed human rights experts deplored the alleged involvement of individuals from the so-called Wagner group– a Russian military contractor with reported ties to the Kremlin–in indiscriminate killings, summary executions and widespread looting and sexual violence in the Central African Republic (CAR).

UN human rights experts and the UN human rights office repeatedly criticized Russia for Navalny's detention.

In September, 45 countries pressed Russia to urgently answer questions about Navalny's poisoning, under the rules of the Organization for the Prohibition of Chemical Weapons (OPCW).

In June, in its conclusions on Russia, the EU Foreign Affairs Council condemned the "limitations on fundamental freedoms … and the shrinking space for civil society." Also in June, the European Commission recommended that the EU "continues to push back against human rights violations and will speak up for democratic values."

Also in June, the European Parliament denounced the listing of German NGOs as "undesirable organizations" and Pivovarov's arrest. It called on Russian authorities to end all reprisals against political opposition.

In August, the Organization for Security and Co-operation in Europe (OSCE) Office for Democratic Institutions and Human Rights and the OSCE Parliamentary Assembly announced that the organization would not send observers to monitor the parliamentary, due to "limitations imposed by Russian Federation authorities on the election observation."

Rwanda

The ruling Rwandan Patriotic Front (RPF) continued to stifle dissenting and critical voices and to target those perceived as a threat to the government and their family members. The space for political opposition, civil society, and media remained closed. Several high-profile critics, including opposition members and commentators using social media or YouTube to express themselves, went missing, were arrested or threatened. Arbitrary detention, ill-treatment, and torture in official and unofficial detention facilities was commonplace, and fair trial standards were routinely flouted in cases deemed sensitive. There were credible reports of arbitrary detention and mistreatment of people accused of "deviant behaviors," including street children, sex workers and petty vendors.

Political Repression

The political and civic space in Rwanda remain closed. Christopher Kayumba, the former editor of *The Chronicles* newspaper, established a new political party, the Rwandese Platform for Democracy (RDP), in March. This followed the publication of an open letter in which Kayumba criticized President Paul Kagame's handling of the Covid-19 crisis, its impact on the population, and denounced the existence of "safe houses," where detainees are routinely held illegally and tortured. Shortly afterwards, allegations of rape and "sexual misconduct" were brought against him, and he was arrested in September. He began a hunger strike a few days after his arrest to protest the "politically-motivated" charges and had to be transferred to hospital for treatment. He was transferred to Nyarugenge prison in Kigali after his bail application was denied in October.

Other political opposition figures, such as Victoire Ingabire, continued to face obstruction in their work, including threats and harassment by authorities. Authorities detained 10 people around "Ingabire Day," an event scheduled for October 14 and organized by the unregistered opposition Dalfa-Umurinzi party to discuss, among other things, political repression in Rwanda. At the time of writing, seven party members, and a YouTube blogger were charged with several offenses including "spreading rumors", "spreading false information with intent to create a hostile international opinion against the Rwandan state," and "causing uprising or unrest among the population."

The September conviction and 25-year sentence of critic and political opponent Paul Rusesabagina on charges including murder and membership in a terrorist group after a flawed trial was emblematic of the government's overreach and manipulation of the justice system. Rusesabagina was forcibly disappeared and unlawfully returned to Rwanda in August 2020. His trial was marred with fair trial and due process rights violations.

Freedom of Expression

YouTube continued to be a contested space for free speech in Rwanda. In recent years, frustrated by the absence of critical debate in the media, some Rwandan bloggers and commentators have taken to the platform to publish videos on sensitive issues and discuss current matters. Such matters include evictions from poor neighborhoods of the capital Kigali, the strict lockdowns imposed in response to Covid-19, or the 1994 genocide commemorations.

On February 9, Innocent Bahati, a 31-year-old singer and poet, was reported missing to the Rwanda Investigation Bureau (RIB), two days after he was last seen in Nyanza, Southern Province. His poems, which he recited in videos posted on YouTube, focused on social issues such as growing poverty or criticism of the lockdown and its impact. Although the RIB spokesperson told the media an investigation into his whereabouts was ongoing, findings were never published and Bahati's whereabouts remain unknown.

Online commentators such as Yvonne Idamange and Aimable Karasira also used their videos to discuss the 1994 genocide, crimes committed by the ruling RPF in its aftermath, and the government's commemorations of the killings. On September 30, Idamange, a Tutsi genocide survivor who accused the government of monetizing the genocide and called for a protest, was found guilty of inciting violence and public uprising, denigrating genocide artefacts, and spreading rumors and violent assault, among other charges. Her trial was held behind closed doors and she was handed a 15-year sentence.

On May 31, Karasira was arrested on charges including denying and justifying the genocide and instigating divisions. For several months, he had repeatedly been harassed and summoned by Rwandan authorities for posting critical videos on YouTube speaking about his family's history and the genocide. He spoke out about killings by RPF soldiers in the aftermath of the genocide.

Dieudonné Niyonsenga, known as "Cyuma Hassan," the owner of Ishema TV, and his driver Fidèle Komezusenge, were arrested in April 2020 after reporting on the impact of the Covid-19 guidelines on vulnerable populations, and were accused of forgery, impersonating journalists, and hindering public works. Both were acquitted on March 12, 2021, after spending almost a year in detention. The prosecution appealed the verdict and Niyonsenga was rearrested on November 11, after the High Court in Kigali reversed his acquittal.

After his March release, Niyonsenga described in interviews on YouTube how the authorities held him in multiple unknown locations, where he was threatened and told to confess to working with an exiled opposition party that has reported ties to armed groups.

Bloggers and other YouTube commentators have said they were threatened or offered bribes to broadcast information that bolsters the government's line.

Repression Across Borders

Rwanda's government and those operating on its behalf continued to exert pressure on Rwandan refugee and diaspora communities, as far afield as Australia and Canada. Refugees who are known critics of the government have been threatened and harassed. In Africa, Human Rights Watch has documented and received credible reports of Rwandan refugees and asylum seekers being forcibly disappeared and returned to Rwanda, or killed.

Cassien Ntamuhanga, a Rwandan asylum seeker in Mozambique and founder of an opposition movement, was taken into custody by Mozambican police on May 23, in the presence of a suspected Kinyarwanda-speaker. He has not been seen since. Ntamuhanga was convicted in Rwanda after a highly politicized trial, alongside the singer and activist Kizito Mihigo, in February 2015. Rwanda's military intervention in Mozambique's devasted Cabo Delgado area, announced in July, raised concerns for the safety of Rwandan refugees and asylum seekers. Révocat Karemangingo, a former army officer in Rwanda, was shot dead in Maputo in September. The circumstances around his death are unclear. Other Rwandans in Mozambique reported being threatened.

In July, Amnesty International and Forbidden Stories reported that more than 3,500 activists, journalists, and politicians—both inside and outside Rwanda—were potential targets of the Rwanda authorities' use of NSO Group's Pegasus spyware. According to forensic analysis of her phone, they found that the spyware was used to infect the phone of Carine Kanimba, the daughter of Rusesabagina, living in Belgium. The list obtained by the group also reportedly contained Ntamuhanga's name and phone number, although it is not clear if his phone was infected.

Sexual Orientation and Gender Identity

Rwanda is one of a few countries in East Africa that does not criminalize consensual same-sex relations, and the government's policies are generally seen as progressive. However, in practice, lesbian, gay, bisexual, and transgender (LGBT) people have reported facing stigma. In 2021, Human Rights Watch documented how the authorities arbitrarily detained nine transgender or gay people at Gikondo transit center, in Kigali.

Several said the police or local security officers detained them after members of the public reported seeing them with their partners and other LGBT people, or wearing women's clothing if they were perceived not to be female. At Gikondo, police officers or guards accused them of being homeless, thieves, or delinquents and held them in a room reserved for "delinquent" men.

Covid-19

According to the World Bank, the Rwandan economy was one of the most affected by the pandemic in sub-Saharan Africa due to the government's failure to protect the right to an adequate standard of living through enhanced social protection as it imposed stringent lockdown measures, which "dramatically increase[ed] poverty." This particularly affected people in urban areas, children, and women. The police arbitrarily detained tens of thousands of people accused of violating public health measures, without legal grounds or due process, holding them in stadiums. The government perceives criticism of its response as particularly sensitive. Several people who publicly criticized the government's response to the pandemic and spoke about its impact on Rwanda's poorer population have been arrested and prosecuted.

The authorities continued throughout 2021 to operate Gikondo transit center, a facility where poor and marginalized people are arbitrarily detained and regularly beaten, often in crowded conditions. However, they failed to put in place measures to protect detainees from Covid-19.

School closures due to the Covid-19 pandemic affected 3.5 million children. After the pandemic's start in 2020, schools were closed or partially closed for 360 days, including several weeks in January and February 2021.

International Justice

Twenty-seven years after the 1994 genocide, a significant number of people responsible for the genocide, including former high-level government officials and other key figures, have been brought to justice.

On September 25, Malian officials announced the death of Théoneste Bagosora, a former Rwandan army colonel convicted of masterminding killings during the 1994 genocide. Bagosora, 80, was serving a 35-year sentence after being found guilty of crimes against humanity by the then International Criminal Tribunal for Rwanda (ICTR).

In recent years, the Rwandan government has requested or signed extradition treaties with dozens of countries in an attempt to have remaining genocide suspects returned for trial in Rwanda, although there are persistent concerns about failure to uphold fair trial standards in domestic atrocity trials. In July, Venant Rutunga, 72, was extradited from the Netherlands to Rwanda, to stand trial on three charges, including playing a role in the genocide, complicity in killing, and crimes against humanity, according to Rwanda's National Public Prosecution Authority.

In April, Beatrice Munyenyezi was deported by the United States after serving a prison term for lying on her naturalization application, and arrested upon arrival in Rwanda. She faces seven charges related to the 1994 genocide, including rape.

Key International Actors

The Commonwealth Heads of Government Meeting, scheduled to take place in Kigali in June 2020 and rescheduled for June 2021, was postponed again due to the pandemic. Poor and marginalized people were detained at Gikondo transit center in the lead up to June 2021 and detainees said the police told them they did not want them on the streets during the event.

After decades of tense relations between France and Rwanda, in March, a commission established by President Emmanuel Macron to investigate France's role in the 1994 killings published a 1,200-page report concluding that France has responsibilities it characterized as "serious and overwhelming," including for being blind to the preparation of the genocide and being slow to break with the government orchestrating it. A report commissioned by the Rwandan government concluded in April that the French government "bears significant responsibility for enabling a foreseeable genocide."

The European Parliament adopted two resolutions in February and October condemning Rusesabagina's enforced disappearance and unfair trial, and Rwanda's broader human rights record. However, other European Union institutions remained reluctant to publicly express concerns about human rights violations by Rwanda's authorities.

Saudi Arabia

Saudi authorities in 2021 carried out arbitrary arrests, trials, and convictions of peaceful dissidents. Dozens of human rights defenders and activists continued to serve long prison sentences for criticizing authorities or advocating political and rights reforms.

Saudi Arabia announced important and necessary reforms in 2020 and 2021, but ongoing repression and contempt for basic rights are major barriers to progress. The near-total repression of independent civil society and critical voices impedes the chances that reform efforts will succeed.

Freedom of Expression, Association and Belief

Saudi authorities in 2021 routinely repressed dissidents, human rights activists, and independent clerics. On April 5, Saudi Arabia's terrorism court sentenced an aid worker, Abdulrahman al-Sadhan, 37, to 20 years in prison followed by a 20-year travel ban on charges related to his peaceful expression. On April 20, the same court sentenced a human rights activist Mohammed al-Rabea to six years in prison on vague and spurious charges related to his activism. Sources close to both cases say that Saudi authorities tortured them in detention and compelled them to sign false confessions. A Saudi court sentenced Sudanese journalist Ahmad Ali Abdelkader, 31, to four years in prison in June on vague charges based on tweets and media interviews he shared to Twitter in which he expressed support for Sudan's 2018-19 revolution and criticized Saudi actions in Sudan and Yemen.

Saudi authorities released prominent women's rights activists from prison in 2021, including Loujain al-Hathloul, Samar Badawi, and Nassima al-Sadah. They remained banned from travel and were serving suspended sentences, allowing the authorities to return them to prison for any perceived criminal activity. In January, Human Rights Watch received text messages from persons identifying themselves as Saudi prison guards describing torture and ill-treatment they witnessed by Saudi interrogators against high-profile detainees in mid to late 2018, including Loujain al-Hathloul and Mohammed al-Rabia.

Capital trials continued against detainees on charges that related to nothing more than peaceful activism and dissent. As of September, those on trial facing the death penalty included prominent cleric Salman al-Awda, on charges alleging ties with the Muslim Brotherhood and public support for imprisoned dissidents, as well as Hassan Farhan al-Maliki on vague charges relating to the expression of his peaceful religious ideas. Al-Awda and al-Maliki have been in detention since September 2017 with multiple postponements of their trials, which began in 2018.

Prominent royal family members remained detained without any apparent legal basis in 2021. They include former Crown Prince Mohammed bin Nayef and former Saudi Red Crescent head Faisal bin Abdullah, both of whom were detained in early 2020 and have been held largely incommunicado.

In late 2020, a Saudi court following an unfair trial sentenced two children of former Saudi intelligence official Saad al-Jabri to nine and six-and-a-half years in prison respectively, for "money laundering" and "attempting to escape" Saudi Arabia, apparently in order to coerce their father to return from abroad. Authorities charged the two a month after al-Jabri filed a lawsuit against Crown Prince Mohammed bin Salman in a US court alleging that the crown prince had sent a hit squad to murder him in Canada in 2018. The authorities also detained up to 40 other al-Jabri family members and associates.

Over a dozen prominent activists convicted on charges arising from their peaceful activities were serving long prison sentences. Prominent activist Waleed Abu al-Khair was serving a 15-year sentence that the Specialized Criminal Court imposed after convicting him in 2014 on charges stemming solely from his peaceful criticism of human rights abuses in media interviews and on social media.

With few exceptions, Saudi Arabia does not tolerate public worship by adherents of religions other than Islam and systematically discriminates against Muslim religious minorities, notably Twelver Shia and Ismailis, including in public education, the justice system, religious freedom, and employment. A 2021 textbook review found that despite steps to purge school textbooks on religion of hateful and intolerant language, current texts maintain language that disparages practices associated with Shia and Sufi Muslims.

Yemen Airstrikes and Blockade

As the leader of the coalition that began military operations against Houthi forces in Yemen on March 26, 2015, Saudi Arabia has committed numerous violations of international humanitarian law. As of August, at least 8,773 civilians had been killed in the conflict and 9,841 wounded since 2015, according to the Yemen Data Project, although the actual civilian casualty count is likely much higher. Most of these casualties were a result of coalition airstrikes that have hit homes, markets, hospitals, schools, and mosques. Some of these attacks may amount to war crimes.

In September, the UN Group of Eminent International and Regional Experts on Yemen stated that it had "reasonable grounds" to believe that parties to the conflict in Yemen were responsible for grave human rights violations and reiterated its call to the UN Security Council to refer the situation in Yemen to the International Criminal Court. Saudi Arabia campaigned vigorously to end the mandate of the Group of Eminent Experts, which was not renewed at the September session of the UN Human Rights Council.

The conflict exacerbated an existing humanitarian crisis. The Saudi-led coalition has imposed an aerial and naval blockade since March 2015 and restricted the flow of life-saving goods and the ability for Yemenis to travel into and out of the country to varying degrees throughout the war. (See also Yemen chapter).

Criminal Justice

Saudi Arabia applies its uncodified interpretation of Sharia (Islamic law) as its national law. In the absence of a written penal code or narrowly worded regulations, judges and prosecutors can convict people on a wide range of offenses under broad charges such as "breaking allegiance with the ruler" or "trying to distort the reputation of the kingdom." Detainees, including children, commonly face systematic violations of due process and fair trial rights, including arbitrary arrest.

Judges routinely sentence defendants to floggings of hundreds of lashes. Children can be tried for capital crimes and sentenced as adults if they show physical signs of puberty. In 2021, judges based some capital convictions primarily on confessions that the defendants retracted in court and said had been coerced under torture, allegations the courts did not investigate. Saudi laws do not clearly prohibit the corporal punishment of children, which the UN Committee on the Rights of the Child concluded in 2016 "remains lawful in all settings".

Though Saudi authorities announced criminal justice reforms in 2020 that restated a 2018 legal change halting the death penalty for alleged child offenders for certain crimes, prosecutors can seek the death penalty against children for crimes such as murder. Abdullah al-Huweiti has been on death row since 2019 and could be executed even though he was 14 at the time of the alleged crime and his conviction followed a grossly unfair trial.

Saudi Arabia did not carry out any drug-related executions in 2021, in line with a moratorium on such executions that the Saudi Human Rights Commission said went into effect in 2020. According to Interior Ministry statements, Saudi Arabia executed 52 persons between January and September, mostly for murder, up from 24 executions total in 2020. Executions are carried out by firing squad or beheading, sometimes in public.

Women's and Girls' Rights

Despite recent important women's rights reforms, including allowing women over 21 to obtain passports and travel abroad without a guardian's permission, Saudi women still must obtain a male guardian's approval to get married, leave prison, or obtain certain healthcare. Women also continue to face discrimination in relation to marriage, family, divorce, and decisions relating to children, including child custody. Men can still file cases against daughters, wives, or female relatives under their guardianship for "disobedience," which have previously resulted in arrest, and forcible return to their male guardian's home or imprisonment.

In June 2021, the Saudi authorities amended the Legal Pleadings System, removing language that required the immediate enforcement of court decisions to send a woman to her mahram (husband or a male relative she cannot marry). This change suggests that there is no longer enforcement power for court orders to return women to a male relative as part of its judgement on disobedience cases. However, it does not prevent courts from penalizing women with losing their right to financial maintenance if they refuse to return to their marital home.

As of September 2021, there was no accompanying guidance issued to the police and other law enforcement agencies, suggesting women may still face arrests and forcible return home to their families.

In June 2021, Saudi authorities also allowed women citizens and residents to apply online for the limited hajj (Muslim pilgrimage) packages without a mahram (male relative).

Sexual Orientation, Gender Identity

Saudi Arabia has no written laws concerning sexual orientation or gender identity, but judges use principles of uncodified Islamic law to sanction people suspected of committing sexual relations outside marriage, including adultery, extramarital and same-sex relations. If individuals are engaging in such relationships online, judges and prosecutors utilize vague provisions of the country's anti-cybercrime law that criminalize online activity impinging on "public order, religious values, public morals, and privacy."

A Saudi court has used this law to sentence a Yemeni blogger and human rights activist to 10 months in prison, a fine of 10,000 Saudi Riyals (US$2,700), and deportation to Yemen after he posted a video on social media calling for equal rights, including for LGBT people. Security officers subjected him to a forced anal exam.

Migrant Workers

Millions of migrant workers fill mostly manual, clerical, and service jobs in Saudi Arabia despite government attempts to increase citizen employment. The Saudi Arabian Monetary Authority (SAMA) annual statistics for 2020 released in 2021 reflected that 49,600 foreigners worked in the public sector and 6.3 million in the private sector during that year.

Migrant workers routinely report abuse and exploitation. The abusive *kafala* (visa sponsorship) system gives their employers excessive power over their mobility and legal status in the country and underpins their vulnerability to a wide range of abuses, from passport confiscation to delayed wages and forced labor.

Saudi Arabia introduced labor reforms in March that, if implemented, will allow some migrant workers to change jobs without employer consent under certain narrow circumstances but do not dismantle the *kafala* system and exclude migrant workers not covered by the labor law, including domestic workers and farmers, who are among the most vulnerable to abuse. The reforms allow migrant workers to request an exit permit without the employer's permission but do not abolish the exit permit. The reform notifies employers of exit permit requests and allows them to lodge an inquiry into the request within 10 days. It remains unclear what criteria the ministry intends to use to determine whether to accept workers' exit requests and whether the employer's inquiry could be used to deny the worker the exit permit.

In July 2021, Saudi authorities began to terminate or not renew contracts of Yemeni professionals working in Saudi Arabia, leaving them vulnerable to arrest, detention and deportation to the conflict and humanitarian crisis in Yemen as a result of not having legal status in the country.

In November 2017, Saudi Arabia launched a campaign to detain all foreigners found to be in violation of existing labor, residency, or border security laws, including those without valid residency or work permits, or those found working for an employer other than their legal sponsor. By the end of 2019 the campaign had totaled over 4.4 million arrests, including for over 3.4 million residency law violations and over 675,000 labor law violations. Authorities did not publish updates in 2020, but in 2021 authorities began weekly updates. Between September 3 and 9, for example, the Interior Ministry announced that it had made 17,598 arrests, including 202 individuals apprehended while trying to cross the southern border from Yemen illegally.

In December 2020 Human Rights Watch reported that a deportation center in Riyadh was holding hundreds of mostly Ethiopian migrant workers in conditions so degrading that they amount to ill-treatment. Detainees alleged to Human Rights Watch that they were held in extremely overcrowded rooms for extended periods, and that guards tortured and beat them with rubber-coated metal rods, leading to at least three alleged deaths in custody between October and November 2020.

Saudi Arabia is not party to the 1951 Refugee Convention and does not have an asylum system under which people fearing persecution in their home country can seek protection, leading to a real risk of deporting them to harm.

Climate Change Policies and Actions

Saudi Arabia is the world's largest exporter of crude oil and among the top fifteen emitters of greenhouse gases contributing to the climate crises that is taking a growing toll on human rights around the world.

According to the Climate Action Tracker Saudi Arabia's current domestic targets are "critically insufficient" to limit global warming to 1.5°C above pre-industrial levels. If all countries' commitments were in this range, warming would reach over 4°C, risking catastrophic consequences for human rights around the world.

Saudi Arabia has shown no desire to move away from fossil fuels although in 2021 it announced it will join other major producers in forming a "Net Zero Producers Forum" in which oil and gas producers will discuss ways to achieve net zero carbon emission targets to limit global warming.

Climate change impacts, including more frequent and intense heat waves, decreased precipitation, and rising sea levels pose risks to right to health, life, water, and housing, especially of migrant workers. Saudi Arabia is particularly vulnerable to the impacts of climate change because it lacks permanent water resources relying on groundwater and energy-intensive desalination plants.

Key International Actors

As a party to the armed conflict in Yemen, the US provided logistical and intelligence support to Saudi-led coalition forces. In February, the Biden administration announced that it would end support for "offensive operations" in Yemen, but in April, Vox reported that the administration had authorized US defense contractors to continue to service Saudi warplanes. The administration also placed on hold some US arms sales and transfers to Saudi Arabia announced by the Trump administration.

The Biden administration did not hold the Saudi Crown Prince Mohammed bin Salman accountable, despite a US intelligence report released in February concluding that he had likely approved the 2018 murder of journalist Jamal Khashoggi. The US did, however, create the Khoshoggi Travel Ban, a new sanctions tool that allows the US State Department to impose visa restrictions on individuals "who, acting on behalf of a foreign government, are believed to have been directly engaged in serious, extraterritorial counter-dissident activities."

In July, the European Parliament adopted a resolution deploring Saudi Arabia's human rights record and urging tough action from EU and member states to address it, but those calls remained largely unheeded. In September, the EU and Saudi Arabia held their first ever human rights dialogue, shortly before a visit in October by EU foreign policy chief Josep Borrell, who made no public reference to Saudi Arabia's rights abuses. Rather, the EU's diplomatic efforts remain focused on strengthening trade and cooperation ties with the Gulf.

Senegal

Arbitrary arrests of opposition figures, use of excessive force by security forces, restrictive civic space, rape, and other serious human rights abuses continued in Senegal throughout the year. On June 25, Senegal's national assembly approved two flawed and overly broad counterterrorism laws with life imprisonment for those found guilty of flouting the laws.

Rape, sexual exploitation, and abuse of students remain serious concerns within Senegal's education system. Senegalese girls face high levels of sexual and gender-based violence, including sexual exploitation, harassment, and abuse by teachers and school officials. Some students were raped and sexually abused by their peers. Most of these cases go unreported, and perpetrators are seldom held to account. On June 29, a 19-year-old male student was detained by police and accused of raping a 15-year-old girl, also a student at the same school.

LGBT people and activists continued to be subjected to smear campaigns and abuse, including threats and physical assaults. Media and local rights groups reported dozens of incidents of assault on homosexual people in Senegal in the first half of the year.

Exploitation, abuse, and neglect of children living in Senegal's traditional Quranic schools continued. Thousands of them, known as talibés, live in conditions of extreme squalor, deprived of adequate food and medical care.

Excessive Use of Force

During protests in March and June, security forces used excessive force to maintain public order.

On March 3, demonstrations broke out across Senegal following prominent opposition leader Ousmane Sonko's arrest in Dakar. Security forces fired teargas and live bullets to disperse the protests and arrested 100 people, leaving hundreds injured. Sonko, leader of the political party, Patriots of Senegal for Work, Ethics, and Fraternity (PASTEF) was arrested after a woman accused him of rape, an allegation that he denied, saying it was politically motivated. His arrest sparked massive demonstrations with thousands of largely young people, members of opposition parties, and civil society members taking to the streets across the country. In a March 5 speech, Interior Minister Antoine Félix Abdoulaye Diome said the protests were "acts of terror," "insurrection," "vandalism," and "banditry," and were illegal due to the state of emergency for the Covid-19 pandemic.

Radio France Internationale (RFI) reported that at least 10 people died in the incident. International human rights organizations documented the deaths of at least eight people during the demonstrations, some "caused by the use of excessive force and firearms by security forces." Senegal's Red Cross reported that 6 people died and at least 590 were injured, including 232 who were transferred to health centers for treatment. Opposition groups reported that 11 people died.

On June 25, people took to the streets in Dakar, following a call by the Movement for the Defense of Democracy (*Mouvement pour la défense de la démocratie*, M2D), a group of opposition parties and civil society groups, to protest the national assembly's approval of two controversial counterterrorism laws. The media reported that the police responded by firing teargas and arresting at least 20 protesters. All those arrested have been released, with one alleging that the police beat and brutalized him.

Counterterrorism Laws

The two new flawed counterterrorism laws modify the penal code and Criminal Procedure Code and were approved by the national assembly by a vote of 70 to 11. The government said the laws are aimed at "strengthening the fight against terrorism, maritime piracy, and transnational organized crime," but civil society groups and opposition parties criticized them as overly broad and threatening fundamental rights and freedoms.

The laws define "terrorist acts" to include "seriously disturbing public order," "criminal association," and "offenses linked to information and communication technologies," all punishable with life in prison. The laws make it a criminal offense to "incite others" to carry out acts of terrorism, but does not define incitement, putting at risk of prosecution freedom of expression, including by the media.

The laws would make the leaders of associations, trade unions, or political parties criminally responsible for "offenses committed" by their organizations, threatening the right to association. If an organization is found guilty, the laws allow the confiscation of the leaders' and the organization's property. The laws also enhance law enforcement powers to surveil terrorism suspects without a judge's authorization.

On June 30, opposition party members filed an appeal with the Constitutional Council, arguing that the laws are unconstitutional and are contrary to Senegal's domestic and international legal obligations. On July 30, the Constitutional Council struck the appeal, ruling that the laws are not unconstitutional. However, it reduced to 12 months, instead of the initial 24, the administrative control and surveillance measures the laws allow for those convicted of acts of terrorism.

LGBT Rights

Lesbian, gay, bisexual, and transgender (LGBT) people and activists continued to be subjected to smear campaigns and abuse. Article 319 of Senegal's penal code punishes "acts against nature" with a person of the same sex with up to five years in prison. Media and local rights groups reported dozens of incidents of assault on LGBT people in Senegal in the first half of the year.

On May 23, the group "And Samm Jikko Yi," supported by the Senegal Islamic Association, organized an anti-LGBT demonstration in Dakar and called for legislation punishing "acts against nature" to be further toughened. In June, according to media reports, an employee of the Senegalese ministry of education was fired after he asked students taking an English exam at a Dakar high school to write about homosexuality.

Abuses against Talibé Children in Quranic Schools

Abuse, exploitation, and neglect of children attending Senegal's still-unregulated, traditional Quranic boarding schools (*daaras*) continued at alarming rates. Human Rights Watch has estimated that over 100,000 children known as "talibés" are forced by their Quranic teachers in Senegal to beg daily for money, food, rice, or sugar. Many Quranic teachers (also known as *marabouts*) and their assistants continue to set daily begging quotas enforced by beatings, and subjected talibés to neglect. Some committed other forms of abuse, such as chaining talibé children.

Each year thousands of talibés, including Senegalese and foreign children, migrate to major cities to attend Senegal's daaras. Thousands of talibés are victims of human trafficking. Trafficking under Senegalese law includes the act of exploiting children for money through forced begging, as well as the recruitment or transport of children for this purpose.

Despite strong domestic laws banning child abuse and human trafficking, and government efforts to address these issues, sustained commitment by Senegalese authorities to stop forced begging and abuse of talibés has proven elusive.. There were some prosecutions and convictions of Quranic teachers for abuses against talibé children in 2021, including for beating and chaining children and for the death of a boy following a beating in 2020, but enforcement of existing laws against exploitation through forced begging remained limited. The government continued its programs to "modernize" and support daaras. Some local governments continued efforts to reduce child begging and "remove children from the streets" in 2021, following the government's rollout of the third phase of this program nationally in 2020.

Sexual and Gender-Based Violence

Senegalese girls face high levels of sexual and gender-based violence, including sexual exploitation, harassment, and abuse by teachers and school officials, as well as rape and sexual abuse by other students.

On June 29, a 19-year-old male student was detained by police and accused of raping a 15-year-old girl, a student at the same school. The accused reportedly shared a video about the rape that has been widely distributed via WhatsApp and other channels, sparking the condemnation of the rape and the accused, as well as efforts to vilify and discredit the survivor's account of the rape. The government has not yet accepted the scale of school-related sexual violence or taken concrete actions to tackle school-related sexual violence and protect survivors when and after they report abuses.

Serbia

Journalists critical of authorities continued to face harassment, threats, violence, and intimidation. Most war crimes prosecutions involved low level perpetrators. Little progress was made to ensure people with disabilities can live independently in the community. Lesbian, gay, bisexual and transgender (LGBT) people continued to be subjected to attacks and threats with impunity.

Freedom of Media

Journalists continued to face threats with poor state response from Serbian authorities.

Between January and late August, the Independent Journalists' Association of Serbia (NUNS) registered 1 physical attack and 20 threats against journalists.

In April, Dasko Milinovic, a journalist and host of a satirical radio show, was attacked with tear gas by two men in Novi Sad on his way to work and suffered minor injuries as a result. Court proceedings against the assailants were pending at time of writing.

Journalist Vojislav Milovancevic, at Nova.rs news website, in January received threatening messages, including some death threats following the publication of his report on a rape allegedly by a member of clergy at the Orthodox Theological Faculty. Milovancevic reported the case to the Special Prosecutors' Office for High Tech Crime in January and an investigation was pending at time of writing.

In March, following an online column criticizing the involvement of convicted war criminals in popular culture in Serbia, journalist and professor Dinko Gruhonjic received death threats on Facebook.

Pro-government media continued smear campaigns against independent journalists and outlets.

Smears against the independent Crime and Corruption Reporting Network (KRIK), a website, put its journalists at risk. In March, pro-government channel TV Pink alleged KRIK was linked to a criminal gang. Several pro-government tabloids echoed the allegation. Members of the SNS ruling party and other members of parliament publicly discredited KRIK, including accusations it failed to pay taxes and is a criminal association.

The retrial of the four defendants accused of the 1999 murder of prominent journalist and editor, Slavko Curuvija, which started in October 2020, was marred by several delays and was ongoing at time of writing.

Social media platform Twitter in August labelled the Twitter accounts of some leading Serbian media outlets as state-affiliated, on grounds that the state exercises editorial and financial control over them through direct or indirect political pressure.

Accountability for War Crimes

Between January and August, the War Crimes Prosecutor Office launched 9 new investigations against 11 individuals and issued 3 indictments against a total of 4 individuals. An appeals court in Belgrade convicted one low-ranking official of war crimes. The first instance court in Belgrade handed down 7 convictions for war crimes in the same time period. As of August, 15 cases against 32 defendants were pending before Serbian courts.

The Appeals Court in Belgrade in July reduced the sentence of former Bosnian Serb Army soldier Dragomir Kezunovic from fourteen to five years for his role in the detention and killing of 28 civilians in Bosnia and Herzegovina (BiH) in June 1992. Kezunovic had been convicted and sentenced in absentia by the State Court in BiH before the case was taken over by the Serbian court.

In June, following a retrial, the High Court in Belgrade sentenced former Bosnian Serb soldier, Joja Plavanjac to 15 years' imprisonment and former serviceman Zdravko Narancic to seven years' imprisonment for their involvement in killing 11 civilian detainees in Bosanska Krupa, BiH, in 1992.

Also in June, the High Court in Belgrade opened trial proceedings against Branko Basara, a former Bosnia Serb commander, for war crimes against some 200 civilians in the Sanski Most area in BiH in 1992, including killings and forced relocations.

In May, the High Court in Belgrade convicted and sentenced to nine years imprisonment former Bosnian Serb army soldier, Dalibor Krstovic, for raping a woman prisoner detained in an elementary school in BiH town of Kalinovik in August 1992.

The UN International Residual Mechanism for Criminal Tribunals in the Hague in June sentenced former Serbian State Security Chief Jovica Stanisic and his deputy, Franko Simatovic, to 12 years in prison for aiding and abetting war crimes committed by a Serbian State Security Service special unit during the 1992 Bosnian war.

Migrants, including Asylum Seekers, Long-Term Displaced Persons, Refugees

Between January and August, 987 people lodged their intent to seek asylum in Serbia, a big drop from the 2,084 who lodged their intent to seek asylum during the same period in 2020. The asylum system remained flawed, with difficulties for asylum seekers accessing procedures, low recognition rates, and long delays. Between January and August, Serbia formally registered 107 asylum applications, granting refugee status to 3 and subsidiary protection to 6. In mid-October, none of the five government run camps were overcrowded.

By end of September, 20 unaccompanied children were registered with Serbian authorities compared to 37 during the same period in 2020. Serbia still lacks formal age assessment procedures for unaccompanied children, putting older children at risk of being treated as adults instead of receiving special protection.

Sexual Orientation and Gender Identity

A law change first promised in December 2020 to allow same sex couples enter into civil partnerships failed to progress during the year. The pride parade took place in Belgrade in September without incident. LGBT people continue to face violence and discrimination.

Disability Rights

Children with disabilities continue to be overrepresented in institutional settings (73.9 percent of children in institutions have disabilities) and lack access to inclusive education. The government has yet to adopt a time-bound deinstitutionalization strategy to move people with disabilities out of institutions and ensure independent living in the community.

Key International Actors

In February, OSCE representative on freedom of the media, Teresa Ribeiro, met with the Political Director of the Ministry of Foreign Affairs of the Republic of Serbia, Roksanda Ninčić, and highlighted the importance of safety for journalists, an independent public service broadcaster and media pluralism.

The October EU Commission progress report raised ongoing concerns with media freedom in Serbia and stressed the need to strengthen the overall environment for freedom of expression and journalists.

In September, Serbian President Aleksandar Vucic described the European Union's insistence on robust democratic institutions in EU candidate countries and member states as "rule of law jihad."

Singapore

The Singapore government uses overly restrictive criminal laws and civil defamation suits to harass and prosecute critical voices, including activists, bloggers, and journalists. There is little freedom of assembly. The rights of lesbian, gay, bisexual, and transgender (LGBT) people are severely curtailed, and sexual relations between men remain a criminal offense. There are no legal protections against discrimination on the basis of sexual orientation or gender identity.

Freedom of Assembly and Expression

In October 2021, Parliament passed the draconian Foreign Interference (Counter-Measures) Act (FICA). The law gives sweeping powers to the home minister to require removal or disabling of online content, publication of mandatory messages drafted by the government, banning of apps from being downloadable in Singapore, and disclosure of information by internet and social media companies, reinforced by severe criminal penalties and with judicial review limited to procedural matters.

The government can also designate individuals as "politically significant persons," after which they may be required to follow strict limits on sources of funding and to disclose all links with foreigners. The law's broad language encompasses a wide range of ordinary activities by civil society, academics, and journalists who engage with non-Singaporeans in doing their work.

The government maintains strict restrictions on the right to peaceful assembly through the Public Order Act (POA), requiring a police permit for any "cause-related" assembly if it is held in a public place or in a private venue if members of the general public are invited. The definition of what is treated as an assembly is extremely broad, and those who fail to obtain the required permits face criminal charges.

Even a single person standing alone holding a sign has been treated as an "assembly" requiring a permit. In March 2021, the police announced they were investigating Louis Ng, a member of parliament, for possible violation of the POA based on social media photos showing him alongside several food hawkers holding a sign saying, "support them." Ng said the posting was intended to encourage residents to support the hawkers.

The Public Order Act provides the police commissioner with authority to reject any permit application for an assembly or procession "directed towards a political end" if any foreigner is found to be involved. In February 2021, the police announced an investigation of three individuals who had held a brief protest outside the Myanmar embassy. The authorities said that permits would not be granted for any protest related to political issues in other countries.

Attacks on Human Rights Defenders

Singapore's restrictive laws are frequently used against activists and media critical of the government. Activist Jolovan Wham faced multiple charges under the POA for peaceful protests, including standing by himself with a sign. On February 15, 2021, Wham pleaded guilty to violating the POA for organizing a 2017 silent protest on the rapid transit system. He also pleaded guilty to vandalism for taping a piece of paper on the window and to refusing to sign a police statement. He was sentenced to a fine of S$8,000 (US$5,900) or imprisonment for 32 days. Wham paid the fine for refusing to sign the police statement but opted to serve the default jail term of 22 days for the other offenses.

In August 2021, Wham was tried on charges of holding an unlawful assembly for briefly holding up a sign in front of the courthouse, taking a photo, and leaving. Wham is also facing unlawful assembly charges, filed in November 2020, for standing in front of a police station holding a placard bearing a "smiley face" in support of two young activists under investigation.

In March 2021, the High Court of Singapore ordered blogger and activist Leong Sze Hian to pay Prime Minister Lee Hsien Loong S$133,000 (US$98,600) in damages for sharing a link on his Facebook page, without comment, to an article alleging that the prime minister was a target of a corruption investigation.

Lawyers defending inmates on death row have faced repercussions. In May 2021, the Court of Appeal fined lawyer M. Ravi S$5,000 (US$3,700) for making an "unmeritorious" application to reopen the case of a death row defendant.

Freedom of Media

Authorities have repeatedly targeted The Online Citizen, one of the few independent media outlets in Singapore, and its editor, Terry Xu. On August 19, 2021, the attorney general began contempt proceedings against Xu over the portal's January 2021 republication of a blog post on Singapore's legal system. Singapore's Administration of Justice (Protection) Act contains overly broad and vague powers to punish for contempt, with penalties of up to three years in prison or a fine of S$50,000 (US$37,000).

On September 3, 2021, Xu was found liable for defaming the prime minister by publishing an article about a dispute between Prime Minister Lee and his siblings about their family home. The author of the article was also found liable. The court awarded Lee S$160,000 (US$118,600) in general damages and S$50,000 (US$37,000) in aggravated damages, and, on October 13, ordered Xu to pay nearly S$88,000 (US$65,000) in legal fees and disbursements. On September 14, the InfoComm Media Development Authority suspended The Online Citizen's license for alleged violation of media funding rules.

New Naratif, an online media outlet focusing on issues in Southeast Asia, was accused of violating campaign regulations during the 2020 general election by paying to boost certain posts. After a year-long investigation in which the police twice interrogated New Naratif's founder and managing director, Dr. Thum Ping Tjin, raided his home, and seized his laptop and mobile phone, the police issued a "stern warning" in the case.

Criminal Justice System

Singapore retains the death penalty, which is mandated for many drug offenses and certain other crimes. However, under provisions introduced in 2012, judges have some discretion to bypass the mandatory penalty and sentence low-level offenders to life in prison and caning. There is little transparency on the timing of executions, which often take place with short notice.

In March 2021, the High Court confirmed that the Singapore Prison Service had forwarded private correspondence of 13 death row inmates to the attorney-general without their consent. The High Court dismissed an application brought by 22 death row inmates for information about disclosure of the letters.

Use of corporal punishment is common in Singapore. For medically fit males ages 16 to 50, caning is mandatory for a wide range of crimes. Such caning constitutes torture under international law.

Sexual Orientation and Gender Identity

The rights of LGBT people in Singapore are severely restricted. At time of writing, the Court of Appeal had yet to issue an opinion on appeals from a High Court decision rejecting three constitutional challenges to Criminal Code section 377A, which makes sexual relations between two male persons a criminal offense. There are no legal protections against discrimination on the basis of sexual orientation or gender identity. Singapore precludes LGBT groups from registering and operating legally.

In May 2021, the government warned the US Embassy "not to interfere" in domestic political or social matters, including "how sexual orientation should be dealt with in public policy," after the embassy co-hosted a webinar with a Singapore nongovernmental organization that supports LGBTIQ individuals.

Migrant Workers and Labor Exploitation

Foreign migrant workers are subject to labor rights abuses and exploitation through exorbitant debts owed to recruitment agents, non-payment of wages, restrictions on movement, confiscation of passports, and sometimes physical and sexual violence. Foreign women employed as domestic workers are particularly vulnerable to violence. In June 2021, an employer was sentenced to 30 years in prison for torturing and killing her domestic worker.

Work permits of migrant workers in Singapore are tied to a particular employer, leaving them extremely vulnerable to exploitation. Foreign domestic workers, who are covered by the Employment of Foreign Manpower Act rather than the Employment Act, are excluded from many key labor protections, such as limits on daily work hours and mandatory days off. In July 2021, the Ministry of Manpower announced limited new measures to protect migrant domestic workers from abuse, including one mandatory day off per month, post-placement interviews, and enhancement of required medical check-ups.

Many migrant workers in Singapore are housed in crowded dormitories, with up to 20 people sharing a room and communal bathrooms, in unsanitary conditions that increased the risk of Covid-19. Since April 2020, workers living in dormitories have been unable to leave them except for work under Covid-19 related restrictions. In September 2021, the government announced a pilot scheme to allow up to 500 fully vaccinated migrant workers per week to leave the dormitories to visit specific designated areas.

Key International Actors

Singapore is a regional hub for international business and maintains good political and economic relations with both the United States, which considers it a key security ally, and China. During visits to the city-state in 2021, neither US Vice President Kamala Harris nor US Secretary of Defense Lloyd Austin publicly raised Singapore's poor human rights record.

In May, Singapore underwent its third Universal Periodic Review at the UN Human Rights Council in Geneva. During the review, states made a large number of recommendations, including to address issues related to migrant workers, anti-discrimination legislation, and freedom of expression.

Somalia

During a year that marked the 30th anniversary of the collapse of the Somali state, domestic and international attention was focused on plans for the delayed parliamentary and presidential electoral process. Political tensions stalled reform efforts key to advancing human rights in the country, while conflict-related abuses, insecurity, and humanitarian and health crises took a heavy toll on civilians.

All parties to the conflict in Somalia committed violations of international humanitarian law, some amounting to war crimes. The Islamist armed group Al-Shabab conducted indiscriminate and targeted attacks on civilians and forcibly recruited children. Inter-clan and intra-security force violence killed, injured, and displaced civilians, as did sporadic military operations against Al-Shabab by Somali government forces, troops from the African Union Mission in Somalia (AMISOM), and other foreign forces.

Federal and regional authorities continued to intimidate, attack, arbitrarily arrest, and at times prosecute journalists, including by using the country's outdated penal code. Somalia continued to rely on military court proceedings that violated international fair trial standards; it did not hand over Al-Shabab cases from military to civilian courts.

Key legal and institutional reforms stagnated. The review of the country's outdated penal code stopped; there was no movement on the passing of federal legislation on sexual offenses or on key child's rights legislation. The government also failed to establish a national human rights commission; the appointment of commissioners has been pending since 2018.

Allegations that Somali soldiers were trained in Eritrea and deployed in Ethiopia's Tigray conflict added to the political tensions. The disappearance of the former intelligence official, Ikran Tahlil Farah, reportedly missing since late June, led to a standoff between President Mohammed Abdullahi "Farmajo" and Prime Minister Mohamed Hussein Roble, including over the control of the country's powerful national intelligence and security agency (NISA).

Attacks on Civilians

The United Nations Assistance Mission in Somalia (UNSOM) recorded at least 899 civilian casualties, including 441 killings, between late November 2020 and late July; a marked increase compared to the same reporting period the previous year. Most were killed during targeted and indiscriminate Al-Shabab attacks using improvised explosive devices (IEDs), suicide bombings, and shelling, as well as assassinations.

After the parliament extended the presidential term on April 25 by two years, armed confrontations between security forces linked to different political factions in various districts of Mogadishu, the capital, resulted in the displacement of between 60,000 and 100,000 people, according to the United Nations.

Federal and regional military courts continued to sentence people to death and carry out executions despite serious due process concerns. Puntland executed 21 men convicted by military courts of Al-Shabab membership and killings on June 27, in three separate locations.

Al-Shabab fighters killed dozens of individuals it accused of working or spying for the government and foreign forces, often after unfair trials.

The UN attributed six civilian casualties to AMISOM forces between late 2020 and late July. AMISOM established a board of inquiry into an August 10 incident involving Ugandan soldiers who were ambushed by Al-Shabab fighters around Golweyn, Lower Shabelle and responded by killing seven civilians. A Ugandan court martial found five soldiers responsible for the killings, sentencing two to death. Reports of civilian harm as a result of airstrikes in the Gedo region increased.

Despite federal and regional investigations into the May 2020 massacre of seven health workers and a pharmacist in the village of Gololey in Balcad District, the outcome of these investigations remains unknown.

Sexual Violence

The UN reported an increase in incidents of sexual and gender-based violence, including of girls, which often resulted in the victims being killed.

Key legal reforms stalled, notably the passing of progressive sexual violence legislation at the federal level. The Somali criminal code classifies sexual violence as an "offense against modesty and sexual honor" rather than a violation of bodily integrity; it also punishes same-sex relations. Article 4(1) of the Provisional Constitution (2012), places Sharia law above the constitution and it continues to be applied by courts in criminal cases. Consequently, the death penalty for consensual same-sex conduct could be enforced.

In Puntland, the first region to pass a sexual offenses law, the UN reported on government interference and blocking of investigations into sexual violence incidents.

Abuses against Children

Children continue to bear a heavy burden of ongoing insecurity, conflict, and lack of key reforms in the country. All Somali parties to the conflict committed serious abuses against children, including killings, maiming, recruitment and use of child soldiers, and attacks on schools.

Somali federal and regional security forces unlawfully detained children, notably for alleged ties with armed groups, undermining government commitments to treat children primarily as victims. The government failed to put in place child rights compliant justice measures.

The previous year, pending legal reforms sought to reduce the age of marriage, including a controversial draft law on sexual-intercourse related crimes—the status of which remained unknown—which would allow a child to marry at puberty regardless of their age.

When the Covid-19 pandemic started in early 2020, schools were closed or partially closed for 134 days, including several weeks in March and April 2021, affecting at least 1.2 million children.

Freedom of Expression and Association

Federal and regional authorities throughout Somalia repeatedly harassed, arbitrarily arrested, and attacked journalists. Moments of heightened tensions around the electoral process correlated with an uptick in incidents of harassment toward journalists.

The UN and Amnesty International reported an increase during the first quarter of the year in restrictions on journalist in Puntland. In March, the military appeals court in Puntland sentenced Kilwe Adan Farah, a journalist, to three years in prison under the outdated penal code for his coverage of anti-government protests. Earlier, a military court sentenced him to three months, despite the judge reportedly acknowledging a lack of evidence. The journalist received a presidential pardon.

Several journalists covering protests in Mogadishu were temporarily detained and harassed. On September 5, Bashiir Mohamud, producer at Goobjoog Media, was filmed being dragged through the streets by Somali police while he covered protests demanding justice for the killing of a former intelligence officer, Ikran Tahlil Farah. He was then held for a few hours at the Hodan police station.

Al-Shabab claimed responsibility for the March 1 killing of journalist Jamal Farah Adan in Galkayo.

Displacement and Access to Humanitarian Assistance

Over 2.6 million Somalis are internally displaced, increasingly because of conflict. The UN said over 570,000 people were displaced between January and August 2021. Droughts, flooding, and desert locust swarm—increasing in intensity and frequency due to climate change—exacerbated communities' existing vulnerabilities and contributed to displacement. The UN and Norwegian Refugee Council (NRC) reported that between January and August, droughts and floods displaced over 90,000 and 49,000 people respectively. Tens of thousands of internally displaced people were forcibly evicted, notably in Mogadishu.

Nearly 3.5 million people were expected to face acute food insecurity and need emergency food aid in the last quarter of the year.

Humanitarian agencies continued to face serious access challenges due to conflict, targeted attacks on aid workers, generalized violence, restrictions imposed by parties to the conflict, including arbitrary "taxation" and bureaucratic hurdles, and physical constraints due to extreme weather. Al-Shabab continued to impose blockades on some government-controlled towns, notably the town of Hudur, and occasionally attacked civilians who broke them.

An Amnesty International report documented Somalia's inadequate response to the Covid-19 pandemic, and highlighted the chronic underfunding of the country's health system.

Somaliland

Somaliland held greatly delayed parliamentary and local elections on May 31, which led to opposition control over the parliament. Not a single woman was elected to parliament. In the run-up to the May elections, a local rights organization reported that seven opposition candidates and seven journalists were arbitrarily detained.

In early October, the Somaliland authorities forcibly displaced to Puntland an estimated 1,750 people, including women, children and older people, mainly Af May speakers originating from South West State in Somalia from the contested border town of Las Anod.

Key International Actors

In January, following then-President Donald Trump's orders, the US withdrew approximately 700 ground troops from Somalia. While US airstrikes significantly decreased, AFRICOM claimed carrying out 11 strikes in Somalia at time of writing, since the start of the year. AFRICOM acknowledged responsibility for injuring three civilians during a January 1, 2021 strike. To date AFRICOM has not provided compensation to any civilian victims or their families.

International and regional actors were by and large focused on political stalemates around the electoral process and security concerns, often at the detriment of continuing to push for key rights reforms. International partners, including the European Union, suspended their budgetary support to Somalia in response to the electoral stalemate. The suspension was still in place at time of writing.

During Somalia's Universal Periodic Review in May, international donors pressed Somalia to introduce policies and legislation to tackle sexual violence and pass child rights legislation in line with the Convention on the Rights of the Child. Many international partners called for improved media freedoms, including a review of the new media law. EU member states also called for a moratorium on the death penalty. The US called for an end to military court trials of civilians.

South Africa

South Africa failed to take meaningful measures to improve protection of social and economic rights, which has been undermined by widespread unemployment, inequality, poverty, the government's response to the Covid-19 pandemic, and corruption. The authorities struggled to ensure law enforcement responded effectively to some of the worst riots and looting in the country since the end of apartheid. The violent riots triggered by the imprisonment of former President Jacob Zuma for contempt of court claimed more than 330 lives and caused an estimated 50.4 billion rands (US$3.4 billion) in damage. Other human rights concerns include violence against women, failure to ensure justice and accountability for past xenophobic violence, and violence against environmental activists.

The government's Covid-19 aid programs, including food parcels during national lockdown, overlooked people with disabilities, refugees and asylum seekers, and many lesbian, gay, bisexual, and transgender (LGBT) people.

Attacks on Environmental Rights Defenders

The killing of environmental rights activist, Mama Fikile Ntshangase, in her house in KwaZulu-Natal province, on October 22, 2020, highlighted the plight of rights defenders in mining-affected communities across the country. Activists have experienced threats, physical attacks, and damage to their property because of their activism—which police failed to investigate. There was no progress in identifying or arresting the killers of Sikhosiphi Rhadebe, a Xolobeni community activist killed in 2016 in the Eastern Cape province.

Ntshangase was a vice-chair of a subcommittee of the Mfolozi Community Environmental Justice Organization, a community-based organization that publicly denounced the impacts of the coal mine on their health and livelihoods and legally challenged the displacement of 19 families from their ancestral land to make way for expansion of a coal mine. As of November 2021, no arrests had been made in connection with Ntshangase's killing.

On March 3, the United Nations expert on human rights defenders highlighted Ntshangase's story in a report to the Human Rights Council on the risks faced by environmental defenders. On July 23, the UN special rapporteur on the rights to freedom of peaceful assembly and to freedom of association highlighted the killing of Ntshangase in his report as an example of the dangers women environmental human rights defenders are facing.

Rule of Law

On June 29, South Africa's Constitutional Court convicted and sentenced former president Zuma to 15 months' imprisonment for contempt of court. Zuma refused to obey the court's order to appear before a judicial commission of Inquiry into allegations of state capture, corruption, and fraud in the public sector. In compliance, Zuma reported to a prison in KwaZulu Natal province on July 8, the first time a former president has been jailed in South Africa. Holding Zuma accountable has been celebrated as a victory for the rule of law and has confirmed South Africa's robust democracy and independent judiciary.

On September 5, just over two months after his incarceration, the Ministry of Justice and Correctional Services announced that Zuma had been released on medical parole and would serve the remainder of his 15-month sentence under supervision in the community corrections system. On September 17, the Constitutional Court dismissed Zuma's application to rescind his conviction.

During 2021, the authorities failed to ensure justice for xenophobic violence. While the 2019 National Action Plan to combat xenophobia, racism, and discrimination marked a key step toward recognizing and addressing these abuses, it has not significantly improved accountability for xenophobic crimes.

Police Conduct

Serious concerns remain about the conduct and capacity of the South African Police Services (SAPS), particularly its compliance with lawful use of force and its ability to deal with riots in a rights-respecting manner. Authorities have yet to end the rampant impunity that encourages abusive behavior by the police. They have not devoted adequate resources to improving police training, including training on the use of non-lethal weapons, legal and appropriate interrogation techniques and on human rights.

The SAPS used excessive and disproportionate force to disperse student protesters at the University of the Witwatersrand (Wits) on March 10, 2021, killing a bystander. The police initially failed to quell violent riots and massive looting that occurred following Zuma's contempt of court conviction. The authorities later deployed 25,000 military troops to support the police to restore order. The riots, which President Cyril Ramaphosa labelled an attempted "insurrection," were the worst since the end of apartheid in 1994.

Women's Rights

Among countries that collect gender-based violence (GBV) statistics, South Africa has one of the highest rates of GBV in the world. Police statistics show that between 2019 and 2020, the rate of reported sexual offences in South Africa increased by an average of 146 incidences a day, 116 of which were cases of rape. In May, the Committee on the Elimination of Discrimination gainst Women (CEDAW), reported that South Africa's low levels of prosecution and conviction in domestic violence cases and the frequent failures by the police to serve and enforce protection orders, exposed survivors to repeated abuses and resulted in the violation of women's rights.

Covid 19 put the spotlight back on GBV as many experts worried about victims being locked down with perpetrators and unable to reach help. Some frontline health workers reported increases in cases of GBV.

In August, a 23-year-old University of Fort Hare law student Nosicelo Mtebeni was killed allegedly by her boyfriend. Parts of her dismembered body were found in the house she shared with her boyfriend, who was in custody facing murder charges at time of writing. On August 22, 28-year-old Ndivhuwo Munyai was shot, allegedly by her husband, a police sergeant in Thohoyandou, Limpopo Province, who then apparently turned the gun on himself in a murder suicide.

South Africa continues to criminalize sex work and prohibit other aspects of sex work, including running or owning a brothel, living off the earnings of "prostitution," and enticing a woman into "prostitution." Criminalization has undermined sex workers' access to justice for crimes committed against them and exposed them to abuse and exploitation by law enforcement officials, including police officers.

Sexual Orientation and Gender Identity

The National Action Plan to combat Racism, Racial Discrimination, Xenophobia and Related Intolerance (NAP), launched in 2019 recognizes LGBT individuals as a priority group given the constitutional goals of equality and non-discrimination and the need for protection against racism, racial discrimination, xenophobia, and related intolerance.

In March, Human Rights Watch filed a submission with the South African Department of Home Affairs on the Draft Official Identity Management Policy to address the inadequacies in the current system which do not cater for changes in the gender/sex attribute of the identity system. In July, Human Rights Watch filed a submission with the Department of Justice and Constitutional Development on their Draft National Intervention Strategy (NIS) 2021-2025, that provides the framework to counter violence and discrimination based on sexual orientation, gender identity, gender expression and sex characteristics.

At least 19 LGBT persons were murdered in South Africa in 2021.

Children's Rights

Across South Africa, more than 13 million children were affected by nationwide school closures (both full and partial) which lasted most of 2021, due to the Covid-19 pandemic. Children with disabilities, already most at risk of being excluded from accessing quality, were most impacted. Covid-19 remote learning response exacerbated existing inequalities as children from poor communities had limited access to online resources, leading to further exclusion.

Some 500,000 learners reportedly dropped out of school permanently during the pandemic, according to the United Nations International Children's Emergency Fund (UNICEF).

South Africa has a high rate of teenage pregnancies. Adolescent girls and women face many barriers to their rights to education and sexual and reproductive rights, and tens of thousands experience unwanted pregnancies. Between 2017 and the first quarter of 2021, over 512,000 girls and young women ages 10 to 19 delivered children in health facilities and close to 57,000 terminated their pregnancies, according to government data.

Covid-19-Related Abuses

As of October 3, 2021, South Africa had 2,906,422 confirmed Covid-19 cases with 87,780 deaths, the highest documented figure across Africa. The government's Covid-19 aid programs, including food parcels, overlooked refugees and asylum seekers, including many LGBT people, and undocumented migrants, some of whom also faced barriers accessing shelters, either because there were unaware of these services, or they feel unwelcome at the shelters. Sex worker rights groups also noted that they had also been left out of relief planning.

At the end of September, more than 8.6 million people, that is over one-fifth of South Africa's adult population, had been fully vaccinated. While the government committed to include refugees and asylum seekers with documentation in the country's vaccination rollout, undocumented migrants faced barriers to vaccine access.

Climate Change Impacts and Policy

South Africa is among the top 20 emitters of greenhouse gases—and the top emitter in Africa. It is also among the world's top 10 coal producers and fourth biggest exporter, contributing to the climate crisis that is taking a growing toll on human rights around the globe. Although South Africa has included renewable energy in its energy mix, it continues to heavily rely on coal for 70 percent of energy demand, and government has declared that this will be the case for the foreseeable future.

In March, the government proposed its Nationally Determined Contribution (NDC), a Paris Agreement-mandated five-year national climate change action plan. In June 2021, the Presidential Climate Commissions recommended that the plan be strengthened to prevent warming greater than 1.5°C compared to pre-industrial levels, with the hope of averting some of the most dramatic impacts of climate change on at-risk populations.

As a water-scarce country, South Africa is particularly vulnerable to the impacts of climate change. Droughts and storms have become more intense because of climate change. On 24 January 2021, Cyclone Eloise made landfall in South Africa's northern provinces, resulting in extreme flooding and the displacement of 3,200 people.

Foreign Policy

In July, the ruling African National Congress party called on the government of Eswatini to implement political reforms and address the legitimate concerns of protestors. In the same month, South Africa, as a member state of the Southern African Development Community, approved the deployment of 1,495 troops to help Mozambique fight an Islamic State-linked insurgency. President Cyril Ramaphosa's special envoys appointed in August 2020 to mediate in the Zimbabwe political crisis, remained, for the most part, inactive during 2021.

In his address to the 76th UN General Assembly on September 23, President Ramaphosa reiterated the call for fair and equitable distribution of Covid-19 vaccines across the world.

South Korea

The Republic of Korea (South Korea) is an established democracy that largely respects civil, political, economic, social, and cultural rights, although significant human rights concerns remain.

Discrimination against women is pervasive, as well as discrimination against lesbian, gay, bisexual, and transgender (LGBT) people, racial and ethnic minorities, and foreign migrants and refugees. The government also retains draconian criminal defamation laws and sweeping intelligence and national security laws that chill speech critical of the government and corporations.

In 2021, the South Korean government implemented public health measures to limit the spread of Covid-19, but some of its policy responses and implementation raised privacy rights concerns. While schools remained partially or fully open for much of the year, closures due to Covid-19 still affected over 10 million children.

Women and Girls' Rights

Discrimination against women and girls is widespread in South Korea. The gender pay gap, at 31 percent, is the widest among countries that belong to the Organisation for Economic Co-operation and Development (OECD). South Korea has been consistently ranked by *The Economist* as having the worst working environment for women among the 29 advanced economies it analyzes.

South Korea's #MeToo movement gained some ground in the past two years, although it also faced backlash. In May, "men's rights" groups targeted several South Korean retailers for using "pinching hand" signs in their ads, which the men claimed was similar to the logo of Megalia, a controversial online feminist community known for ridiculing men that was shut down in 2017. Following threats of boycotts, the GS25 convenience store chain apologized for hurting men's feelings, disciplined employees, and took down an ad campaign. In June, Lee Jun-seok, a politician who advocates for "men's rights" and claims that men in South Korea are targets of reverse discrimination, was elected leader of the main opposition conservative People Power Party.

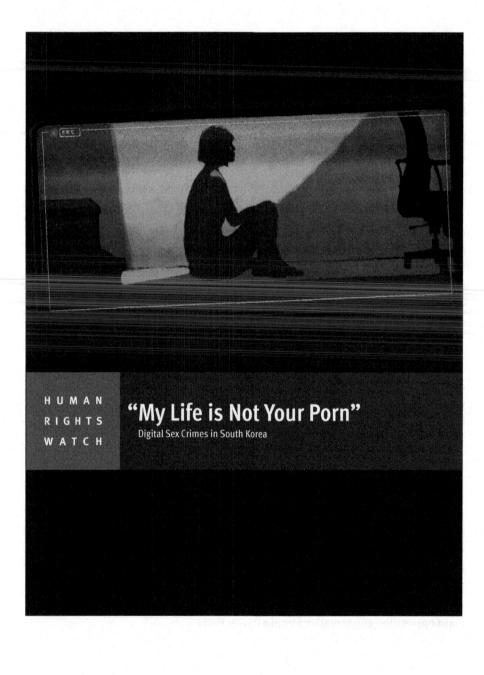

The government continues to struggle to address rampant problems with online gender-based crimes, including widespread internet posting of sexual images of women and girls without their consent. In November 2020, Cho Joo-bin, one of the operators of an infamous network of chat rooms on the Telegram messaging app—where users were viewing, sharing, and trading non-consensual images of dozens of women and girls, including of acts of sexual violence obtained through coercion and blackmail—was sentenced to 40 years in prison in the so-called "Nth Room" case. On April 8, Moon Hyeong-wook, who opened the first chat rooms of the network in 2015, was sentenced to 34 years in prison for forcing 21 young women, including girls, into making sexually explicit videos and sharing them. The police identified approximately 1,100 women and girls who were victims of this network.

Sexual Orientation and Gender Identity

The LGBT rights movement in South Korea is growing but continues to face hostility and severe discrimination, especially in the armed forces. In October, a South Korean court ruled that the military unlawfully discriminated against Byun Hee-su, the country's first openly transgender soldier, when it discharged her after she underwent a gender affirming surgery in 2019. The court ordered her reinstatement, but Byun died by suicide in March. The Constitutional Court is also currently reviewing the 1962 Military Criminal Act, which punishes sexual acts between soldiers with up to two years in prison under a "disgraceful conduct" clause, regardless of consent.

In schools, LGBT children and young people experience severe isolation and mistreatment including bullying and harassment, a lack of confidential mental health support, exclusion from school curricula, and gender identity discrimination.

Activists and progressive legislators have actively advocated for the National Assembly to develop and pass a broad-based national anti-discrimination law protecting LGBT persons as well as women, children, people with disabilities, older people, and foreigners. But the government did not make meaningful progress on such a law, citing a vocal Christian conservative group's anti-LGBT opposition.

HUMAN
RIGHTS
WATCH

"I Thought of Myself as Defective"
Neglecting the Rights of LGBT Youth in South Korean Schools

Freedom of Expression

Although South Korea has a relatively free press and lively civil society, the South Korean government continues to use draconian criminal defamation laws and sweeping intelligence and national security laws to restrict speech. Implementation of these laws creates a chilling effect that limits critical scrutiny of the government as well as corporations.

In December 2020, the South Korean government amended the National Intelligence Service Act using broad, vague language and authorizing the authorities to continue collecting information under the abusive and outdated National Security Law. The law criminalizes dissemination of anything that the government classifies as North Korean "propaganda," as well as creating, joining, praising, or inducing others to join any political association considered an "anti-government organization," a term not clearly defined in law.

In the same month, it adopted an amendment to the development of the Inter-Korean Relations Act, widely known as the anti-leaflet law, which imposes strict limitations on North Korean escapees and civil society organizations that work to send information and ideas from South Korea to the North Korean people. The law bans sending "leaflets, articles (including advertisements, printed matters, auxiliary storage devices, etc.), money or other financial benefits" through the country's northern border and includes sentences of up to three years in prison or fines of up to 30 million won (US$25,000), which violate the principle of proportionality in punishments.

The special rapporteurs on freedom of expression, peaceful assembly, human rights defenders, and on the situation of human rights in North Korea, raised concerns regarding its vague wording, its possible disproportionate penalization of some forms of political expression and legitimate activities of some civil society members, and the effects it may have on access to information inside North Korea.

In September, the South Korean government backed down in the face of serious criticism and shelved amendments to a law tackling "false reporting" that prompted concerns about repression of media freedom. As the special rapporteur on the right of freedom of expression raised, the proposed amendments to the Press Arbitration Law would have imposed disproportionate sanctions for vaguely defined "false and manipulated" reporting. Criminal defamation laws already have a chilling effect on media reporting in South Korea, as they allow for up to seven years' imprisonment and a fine, and truth is not a defense if the court finds what was said or written was not in the public interest.

Workers' Rights

South Korea joined the International Labour Organization (ILO) in 1991 but has only ratified four of the ILO's eight core conventions. On July 7, the cabinet approved the Labor Ministry's motion for parliamentary ratification of three ILO conventions on freedom of association, the right to organize and collectively bargain, and the prohibition of forced labor.

On September 2, the South Korean government raided the Korean Confederation of Trade Unions (KCTU) headquarters and arrested its president, Yang Kyung-soo, for organizing rallies between May and July calling on the government to adopt policies and programs to address economic inequalities deepened by the pandemic. The government had banned the rallies, citing Covid-19 public health measures. Police accused Yang of breaking the Assembly and Demonstration Act and the Infectious Disease Control and Prevention Act, as well as disrupting traffic. The union claimed that a major rally on July 3 drew about 8,000 participants, but all wore masks and followed government guidelines for social distancing.

Policy on Human Rights in North Korea

President Moon Jae-in's administration weakened its criticism of North Korea's human rights record. South Korea had previously co-sponsored annual resolutions at the United Nations condemning North Korea's human rights abuses since 2008 but starting in 2019 it changed policy and declined to do so at both the UN Human Rights Council and the General Assembly.

South Korea has yet to fully implement the North Korean Human Rights Law that came into effect in September 2016 and failed to establish the North Korea Human Rights Foundation, designed to support research on North Korea's rights situation and fund groups working on North Korean rights issues. The foundation is also supposed to help the government develop a strategy to promote human rights in the North. Since 2017, the government has left vacant the legislatively created position of ambassador at large on North Korean human rights.

South Sudan

Intercommunal conflict, abuses by security forces and armed groups, and entrenched impunity continued to take a heavy toll on civilians. Covid-19 and severe weather conditions also contributed to a dire humanitarian situation, with the United Nations declaring that the country faced the worst levels of food insecurity since independence.

In May, President Salva Kiir appointed members of the reconstituted Transitional National Legislative Assembly as stipulated in the 2018 peace deal. In August, following months of delays, the president swore in members of National Legislative Assembly with a first-ever female speaker.

The parties to the peace deal failed to implement major provisions of the agreement, including security arrangements and the establishment of accountability mechanisms. While the government approved the establishment of these accountability mechanisms in January, including a hybrid court, at time of writing the government had taken no concrete steps to operationalize the court.

While the government, the Sudan People's Liberation Movement/Army in Opposition (SPLA/IO), the National Democratic Front and non-signatory groups to the 2018 peace deal, recommitted themselves to a ceasefire in March, there were multiple violent incidents between the main signatories.

The government failed to rein in its abusive national security agency, including by reforming the agency's legal mandate. Authorities continued to arbitrarily detain critics, including members of civil society and journalists, often holding them for extended periods without charge or trial.

School closures due to the Covid-19 pandemic affected 1.5 million children. After the pandemic's start in 2020, schools were closed or partially closed for 378 days, including from January to early May 2021.

Intercommunal Violence, Violence against Civilians

The United Nations Mission in South Sudan (UNMISS) documented hundreds of cases of civilian killings and injuries, the majority by community based "civil defense groups." UNMISS also documented cases of arbitrary killings, abductions, conflict-related sexual violence, arbitrary arrests and detention, torture and ill-treatment, forced military recruitment and the looting and destruction of civilian property by civil defense groups, government forces, and rebel forces.

In June, the UN reported that more than 80 percent of civilian casualties in the country were attributed to intercommunal violence and community-based militias. Intercommunal fighting, cattle raiding, and revenge attacks between armed youth groups in Central Equatoria, the Greater Pibor Administrative Area (GPAA) in Jonglei, Lakes, Unity, Western Bahr el-Ghazal and Warrap states resulted in hundreds of deaths and injuries, displaced hundreds of thousands, and led to the suspension of humanitarian services in some areas.

In Upper Nile, tensions over the status of Malakal town persisted. On March 27, members of the internally displaced community, many residents of the town's protection of civilian site, were attacked by suspected Dinka Padang militia in Malakal town as they travelled to meet the newly appointed Shilluk governor. Four civilians died and 7 were injured in the attack.

In Jonglei, intercommunal violence displaced about 20,000 people in the Greater Pibor Administrative Area with an estimated 68 people killed and 27 injured in early May when allied Gawaar Nuer and Dinka from Ayod, Uror and Duk marched into the GPAA to retrieve cattle raided by the Murle.

In Greater Equatoria, there was violence over land rights, cattle migration and fighting took place between the government forces and the National Salvation Front (NAS) .

In Tambura, Western Equatoria state, violence broke out in June between government forces, SPLA/IO forces and community militias, resulting in killings of civilians. The violence displaced approximately 80,000 civilians, including into neighbouring countries, and hampered humanitarian assistance.

Violence against Women and Girls

Sexual violence, including conflict-related sexual violence, against women and girls has been widespread and an ongoing problem in South Sudan. Between late 2020 and late July 2021, UNMISS documented 48 incidents of conflict-related sexual violence, primarily by community militias and government forces, including rape, gang rape, forced nudity, and attempted rape, of victims as young as 2.

Impunity remained widespread, with only a handful of cases of security forces being tried for sexual violence related crimes in front of military court or in civilian trials.

Child marriage remains widespread. In late 2020, United Nations Children's Fund (UNICEF) reported that more than half (52 percent) of South Sudanese girls between the ages of 15 and 18 are married, with some marrying as young as age 12.

South Sudan's Penal Code Act of 2008 criminalizes consensual same-sex conduct, for both women and for men. Article 248 entitled "Unnatural Offences," outlaws "carnal intercourse against the order of nature" with up to 10 years' imprisonment and stipulates that such "may also be liable to a fine." The code also criminalizes sex work.

Attacks on Aid Workers

Aid workers continued to be attacked, hampering greatly needed aid efforts, with the UN warning that South Sudan was becoming one of the most dangerous places for humanitarian workers to operate.

In January, a humanitarian worker was shot dead while returning from his work supporting vulnerable families near Bentiu. In February, a group of unknown gunmen attacked a humanitarian vehicle carrying polio vaccines between Rumbek Centre to Rumbek North in Lake state killing three health workers and injuring four others.

In April, staff from a UN agency and a national nongovernmental organization (NGO) were physically assaulted by youth in separate incidents in Torit town, Eastern Equatoria. In Jamjang in Ruweng Administrative Area, youth entered an International Rescue Committee (IRC) compound and physically attacked staff, resulting in multiple injuries.

In May, a female aid worker from Cordaid was shot dead in Budi County, Eastern Equatoria state. On May 21, Dr. Louis Edward, an IRC health worker died inside a health facility in Ganyliel Payam, Panyijiar County, in "unclear circumstances."

Arbitrary Detentions, Freedom of Media

Security forces, notably the National Security Service (NSS), continued to repress dissent. In response to calls for peaceful protests by the People's Coalition for Civic Action, a civic action group, the authorities detained political activists throughout August, shut down the SUDD institute—a think tank linked to the coalition—harassed the press and threatened to use live ammunition against protesters. The authorities detained Kuel Aguer, a leader of the People's Coalition for Civic Action, on August 2 and he remained in detention in Juba at time of writing. On August 27, NSS shut down Radio Jonglei FM, and briefly detained three media workers on accusations of supporting the People's Coalition for Civil Action activities.

On the eve of the planned protest, the government shut down internet across Juba and its suburbs for a day.

On August 30, the NSS detained three activists in Wau, Western Bahr el-Ghazal, for allegedly meeting and planning demonstrations.

In February, Amnesty International reported on the government's abusive physical and communications' surveillance capacity and how it is being deployed without safeguards, creating a pervasive climate of fear and self-censorship among citizens.

Impunity

In late January, the cabinet approved the implementation of the Chapter V accountability mechanisms provided for in the 2018 peace agreement, including the establishment of the Hybrid Court for South Sudan, a Commission for Truth, Reconciliation and Healing, and a Compensation and Reparations Authority. While in May the government established a committee to conduct consultations around the enabling legislation for the truth commission, at time of writing, the government had taken no concrete steps to operationalize the hybrid court.

Between April and June, on the orders of the Warrap state governor, security forces executed at least 21 people accused of murder, theft, and other offenses, including in the towns of Kuajok, Romic, Alabek, Twic, Aliek, and Warrap. This included the summary execution of at least eight suspected criminals, including two children, in Kuajok and Nyang Akoch. UNMISS also documented the executions of 29 males in the state, including boys and elderly men.

In September, the UN Commission on Human Rights in South Sudan reported that South Sudanese political elites had diverted US$73 million since 2018, undermining the promotion of key rights and directly contributing to ongoing conflict. The Commission noted that the government deliberately limited independent oversight of oil revenues to facilitate the misappropriation of public funds.

On April 10 President Kiir, with apparent disregard for the many crimes committed by the NSS, promoted one of its top officials, Akol Koor Kuc, to the rank of First Lieutenant General. In the same reshuffle, Kiir appointed Santino Deng Wol, a man sanctioned by the UN for his role in a May 2015 offensive in Unity State, during which government forces killed dozens of women, children, and older people, and looted civilian property, as the new army chief of staff.

Key International Actors

In March, the UN Security Council renewed the mandate of UNMISS for another year with demands that parties to conflict immediately end fighting, launch a political dialogue, implement permanent ceasefire. That same month, the UN Human Rights Council, following a close vote, renewed the mandate of the Commission on Human Rights in South Sudan, for another year.

In May, the UN Security Council renewed the arms embargo, travel ban and assets freeze imposed on South Sudan for another year and extended for 13 months the mandate of the panel of experts, despite government lobbying against the renewal. The resolution requires South Sudan to achieve progress on five key benchmarks including: progress on disarmament, demobilization and reintegration; progress on properly managing existing arms and ammunition stockpiles; and the implementation of the Joint Action Plan for the Armed Forces on addressing conflict-related sexual violence.

UNMISS continued to handover protection of civilian sites to the government, with the handover of Bentiu in March. Malakal retained its status as a result of "a volatile security situation."

In March, the European Union sanctioned South Sudan Army Gen. Gabriel Moses Lokujo over human rights violations, including extrajudicial executions and killings, in connection with his defection from the SPLA/IO to the government forces. The United States extended its recognition of a state of emergency for South Sudan, thereby extending related sanctions.

The African Union Commission (AUC) has a responsibility under the 2018 peace agreement to establish the Hybrid Court for South Sudan, but it failed to move ahead with the court's creation or press for greater action by South Sudanese authorities to establish the court together with the AUC.

Spain

Spain pushed migrants and asylum seekers back at its borders while hundreds died at sea attempting to reach the Canary Islands. As poverty increased with the Covid-19 pandemic, people faced obstacles applying for a new social security support scheme. The government announced legislative reforms to counter gender-based violence and allow for gender self-recognition for trans people. The government granted partial pardons for nine politicians and activists convicted for their actions during the disputed 2017 referendum on Catalan independence.

Covid-19

The World Health Organization estimated that a further 32,902 people had died from Covid-19 by November 4, bringing the total death toll to 87,462. A nationwide vaccination program had ensured that 88.7 percent of the population had received a full dose of Covid-19 vaccine by November 4.

In July, the Supreme Court ruled that the government's March 2020 decree imposing a "state of alarm" to deal with the Covid-19 pandemic had unconstitutionally restricted fundamental rights and that the government should have sought parliamentary approval to declare a state of emergency instead. The "state of alarm" expired in May.

Migrants and Asylum Seekers

According to the UN refugee agency, UNHCR, by October 31, at least 33,706 people had arrived irregularly by sea to Spain's mainland, the Canary Islands, in the Atlantic Ocean, and Ceuta and Melilla, the country's enclaves in north Africa, while 1,068 arrived by land. These figures did not include data regarding the arrivals from May 17 onwards into Ceuta (see below). As of mid-September, an estimated 1,025 people had died or gone missing at sea during the year en route to Spain, most of them in the Atlantic, according to the International Organization for Migration.

In April, four UN special rapporteurs wrote to the Spanish government about abusive pushbacks from its enclaves to Morocco, following fresh allegations of ill-treatment by Spanish border guards in January. Nonetheless, there were reports of summary returns throughout the year, and the governing coalition did not endorse reforming existing law allowing for this practice.

Between May 17 and 19, an estimated 10,000 people entered Ceuta, swimming or wading across a beach frontier, after Moroccan authorities reportedly stopped enforcing border controls following a diplomatic dispute with Spain. The group, of whom between 1,500 and 3,000 were estimated to be children, faced summary returns and pushbacks upon arrival as well as mass "voluntary" returns within days, giving rise to concerns that Spanish authorities blocked access to asylum, returned third country nationals to Morocco, and failed to determine children's best interests before sending them back. Ceuta's already overcrowded reception facilities were overwhelmed by those whom the Spanish authorities did not immediately expel, with local authorities setting up makeshift shelters, including for the more than 700 children who remained. Thousands of other migrants were left sleeping rough in substandard conditions.

On August 13, the Spanish government began returning some of the children to Morocco under a readmission agreement; the national human rights ombudsperson immediately told the government to stop what it called an unlawful practice. Media documented that more children were returned despite the ombudsperson's ruling, during the following two days, until a local court ordered a stop to further returns on August 16.

In September, Spanish armed forces stationed on another military outpost in North Africa, Peñón de Vélez de la Gomera, summarily returned approximately 125 people, including eight children, who had walked across a small strip of sand connecting it to Moroccan territory.

The UN Committee on the Rights of the Child set out concerns in two cases, made public in February and August, about the inappropriateness of processes used by Spanish authorities to determine the age of unaccompanied migrant and asylum-seeking children and young people.

In June, the national human rights ombudsperson called on the government to improve access to residence permits for young people who had been given temporary authorization to work in the agricultural sector during the pandemic. In October, the government approved a decree tabled by the Ministry of Inclusion,

Social Security and Migration setting out a clear legal pathway for approximately 15,000 young migrants to obtain residence permits after turning 18.

Spanish forces airlifted 2,206 Afghans to Spain in August following the Taliban takeover in Afghanistan and set up a reception hub through which approximately 3,000 more evacuees passed to other EU and NATO member states. Despite these efforts, at least a few dozen Afghan interpreters and other staff who had assisted Spanish forces remained stranded after formal evacuation efforts ended.

Poverty and Inequality

A leading anti-poverty NGO calculated that 620,000 people joined the 12.5 million people already "at risk of poverty or social exclusion" in the country, with the first annual increase after five years of steady decline, and found that by the end of 2020, 4.5 million people in Spain were living in extreme poverty (defined as below 40 per cent of median national income, or less than €6,417.30 (US$7,423) per household per year).

Although the country's Minimum Vital Income scheme (IMV), established in May 2020 to provide financial support to people living in poverty helped mitigate the increase, people making applications faced bureaucratic delays and exclusionary criteria. Some welfare advisers estimated in February that two out of three applications for IMV support were rejected. Spain's main food bank network estimated in February that it was providing up to 60 percent more aid than in 2020.

Right to Housing

Despite a government decree allowing tenants with documented "economic vulnerability" to apply for temporary relief from evictions and utility cut-offs, official data showed that 22,532 evictions were carried out during the first eight months of the year, the majority for non-payment of rent.

In two separate cases communicated in March, the UN Committee on Economic, Social and Cultural Rights found that Spain had violated the housing rights of families living in poverty, with a child or children with disabilities, and facing eviction.

In July, a Barcelona court acquitted three housing rights activists of charges related to protests against an eviction in 2018. The prosecution had sought three-year jail sentences, which were widely criticized as a punitive response to lawful protest, including in a joint letter by four UN special rapporteurs.

At time of writing, an estimated 4,000 people, including more than 1,500 children, living in parts of Cañada Real, an informal settlement in greater Madrid, had been without electricity after authorities and energy providers cut off the supply in October 2020, citing illegal use. They faced a second successive winter without heat or electricity.

Gender-Based Violence

Draft legislation introduced by the government in July providing a clearer definition of consent and a right to reparation for victims of gender-based violence, among other measures, was before parliament at time of writing.

In September, the Supreme Court issued important guidance, with 27 clear rules for courts, on domestic abuse and threatening behavior, based on a case that came before it from Galicia.

Abortion

According to official statistics, 6 of Spain's 19 autonomous communities and cities had no public health facilities providing abortion. Serious concerns remained about conscientious objection by health workers acting as an obstacle to women who needed abortion care.

Right to Education

By April, Spain had managed to ensure greater access to in-person education during the Covid-19 pandemic than any comparable OECD country.

In September, local authorities in Melilla allowed some 160 children from families without regular migration status, or unable to provide documentary evidence of residence, to enroll for school. The step came following years of campaigning by local children's rights activists about the difficulties children from families with Moroccan nationality or of Moroccan origin faced in enrolling children for school, repeated recommendations from the national human rights ombudsperson, and a ruling by the UN Committee on the Rights of the Child in June.

Disability Rights

In June, parliament adopted a legal capacity reform law, providing for mechanisms to support people with disabilities to make decisions for themselves, such as whether to marry or to sign a contract. However, the law did not completely abolish substitute decision making and courts can continue to appoint another person to make decisions on behalf of a person with a disability.

Discrimination and Intolerance

In February, European Commission Against Racism and Intolerance (ECRI), the Council of Europe's anti-racism monitoring body, called on the Spanish government to take concrete steps to end the segregation of Roma children in schools.

In March, the Ministry for Equality published Spain's first official report on the experience of African and Afro-descendant people, which showed strong evidence of structural discrimination against Black people in the country.

In May, the lower house of parliament rejected a bill that would have allowed for legal gender recognition based on self-identification for transgender and non-binary people, including children. At the time of writing, the government was preparing a new draft law to address Spain's current pathologizing gender recognition procedure and expand protections for lesbian, gay, bisexual and transgender (LGBT) people.

Disputed 2017 Catalan Independence Referendum

In June, the government granted conditional pardons to nine pro-independence Catalan politicians and activists jailed for their role in relation to the region's disputed 2017 referendum.

Freedom of Expression

The European Court of Human Rights ruled in unrelated cases, in March and June respectively, that Spain had violated the right to free expression of three activists. The first case involved two environmental activists in Aragon convicted of insulting a judge in a 2010 letter to a newspaper editor, and the second a Basque activist convicted of glorification of terrorism and incitement to hatred and violence during a 2008 speech.

Law Enforcement and Police Abuse

In November, the Council of Europe's Committee for the Prevention of Torture published a report documenting physical ill-treatment, including slaps, punches, and baton blows, and a systemic failure to document, report and investigate allegations of ill-treatment in police custody and prisons. The Committee also found that falaka, a torture method involving baton blows to the soles of the feet, continued to be used in prisons, and called on Spain to abolish the use of incommunicado detention.

The same month, media reports indicated that the governing coalition had reached an agreement to amend a problematic 2015 public security law, lifting or mitigating restrictions on freedom of expression and assembly and curtailing police powers relating to detention and the use of rubber bullets.

Sri Lanka

In March 2021, the UN Human Rights Council, responding to continuing abuses and the failure of accountability in Sri Lanka, mandated the Office of the UN High Commissioner for Human Rights to collect and prepare evidence of grave crimes for use in future prosecutions.

Under the administration of President Gotabaya Rajapaksa, Sri Lankan security forces harassed and threatened human rights defenders, journalists, lawyers and the families of victims of past abuses, while suppressing peaceful protests. The government continued to target members of the Tamil and Muslim minority communities using the country's overbroad counterterrorism law, and policies that threaten religious freedom and minority land rights.

In June, President Rajapaksa pardoned 16 people convicted under the draconian Prevention of Terrorism Act. However, all those pardoned were either nearing the end of their sentences or had already exceeded their term. The president also pardoned political ally Duminda Silva, who had been convicted for the 2011 murder of a rival politician.

The country struggled to cope with surging Covid-19 cases, which contributed to widespread economic distress, but a response to the pandemic under military control led to further serious rights violations.

Accountability and Justice

UN Human Rights Council Resolution 46/1, adopted on March 23, strengthens the capacity of the Office of the UN High Commissioner for Human Rights to collect, consolidate, analyze, and preserve evidence of international crimes committed in Sri Lanka, and to develop strategies for future accountability processes. Numerous grave abuses were committed by both sides during the 26-year civil war, which ended in 2009, and by the government in its aftermath.

After Rajapaksa's election in November 2019, he withdrew Sri Lanka from a 2015 council resolution agreed by the previous government to promote truth, justice, and reconciliation. Rajapaksa said he would not tolerate any action against "war heroes" and instead appointed several officials implicated in war crimes to his

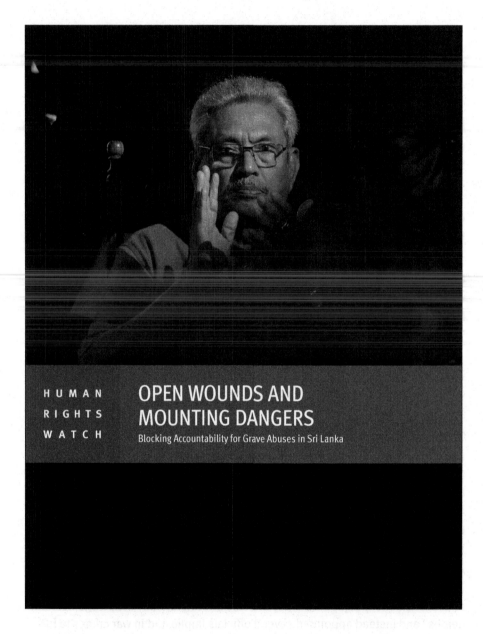

HUMAN
RIGHTS
WATCH

OPEN WOUNDS AND
MOUNTING DANGERS
Blocking Accountability for Grave Abuses in Sri Lanka

administration. The UN human rights chief, Michelle Bachelet, noted that "Sri Lanka remains in a state of denial about the past, with truth-seeking efforts aborted."

In January, the cabinet approved the recommendations of the Commission of Inquiry to Investigate Allegations of Political Victimization, which President Rajapaksa set up to derail criminal investigations into abuses. These included cases in which evidence implicates the president himself. A resolution to implement the commission's recommendations is before parliament.

Presidential appointments severely undermined the independence of human rights institutions, including the Office of Missing Persons, which is responsible for investigating thousands of enforced disappearances. The Global Alliance of National Human Rights Institutions is reviewing the status of the Human Rights Commission of Sri Lanka after its independence was removed by a constitutional amendment in 2020.

Attacks on Human Rights Defenders

The government continued to harass, threaten and surveil victims' families, as well as lawyers and groups representing them. Intelligence agencies and the military interfere in the work of civil society organizations, particularly in the north and east, and suppress perceived dissent. Human rights organizations reported regular visits to their offices by security agencies including the police Terrorism Investigation Division. The government attempted to disrupt foreign funding of rights groups on the pretext of countering "terrorist financing."

Counterterrorism Laws

The Prevention of Terrorism Act (PTA) has for decades been used to enable prolonged arbitrary detention and torture. In 2021, President Rajapaksa issued two ordinances that would make the law more abusive.

An order issued in March, which has been challenged in the Supreme Court, would allow two years of "rehabilitation" detention without trial for anyone accused by the authorities of causing "religious, racial, or communal disharmony." In June, the president announced that a police facility in Colombo would become an additional site for holding PTA prisoners.

Many prisoners, especially from minority communities, remain in pretrial detention lasting many years under the PTA, or are serving lengthy terms following convictions based on confessions obtained using torture. In August, Inspector General of Police C.D. Wickramaratne said that 311 people were in custody, under investigation, or awaiting trial for the deadly 2019 Easter bombings that killed over 250 people.

Freedom of Expression and Association

The government suppressed freedom of expression, including by detaining and interrogating journalists. The government introduced regulations to prevent sharing information related to the pandemic. The Bar Association of Sri Lanka said police orders to combat "fake news" "could be misused by police officers in order to stifle the freedom of speech and expression."

In February, authorities attempted to ban a protest march by Tamil conflict victims, activists, and others. Numerous participants were arrested or harassed by police or intelligence agencies.

In July, trade unionists, activists, and teachers were arrested during a protest in Colombo against legislation they said would militarize higher education and were detained at quarantine facilities after being granted bail by a magistrate. In August, police arrested trade unionists and students are protesting the bill.

Deaths in Custody

The police were implicated in several unlawful deaths, including three men whose deaths in May and June were linked to disproportionate and abusive enforcement of measures to control Covid-19. Other cases were linked to an abusive anti-drugs policy. After two suspects were shot dead in police custody in May, the Bar Association of Sri Lanka said the cases "have all the hallmarks of extra-judicial killings."

Sexual Orientation and Gender Identity

Same-sex relations are criminalized in Sri Lanka, and a law banning "imperson-ation" is used to target transgender people. Authorities use these powers to ha-rass, detain, and extort gay, lesbian and transgender people, who also face societal discrimination.

Labor Rights

The government ordered garment factories, which employ one in seven Sri Lankan women, to remain open when most other parts of the economy were shut down to control the spread of Covid-19. Outbreaks were reported at numerous factories, as well as in the congested boarding houses where many workers live. Labor rights activists alleged that employers were under-testing and under-re-porting cases to maintain production levels. Garment workers reported lost pay and benefits when they fell sick or needed to quarantine, and that the police or military personnel intimidated them to stop them from speaking out.

Women's Rights

The cabinet approved reforms to the Muslim Marriage and Divorce Act (MMDA) to make 18 the minimum age for marriage, ensure women sign their marriage regis-tration certificates, ban polygamy, and end the Quazi system of male-only judges in Islamic family courts. However, the proposed reforms were not published, nor presented to parliament.

Key International Actors

UN High Commissioner for Human Rights Michelle Bachelet warned of "clear early warning signs of a deteriorating human rights situation," and called upon UN member countries to consider imposing targeted sanctions against alleged perpetrators, and to pursue prosecutions in national courts under universal juris-diction. A group of nine UN rights experts wrote to urge "the Sri Lankan authori-ties to stop rolling back hard fought progress made in recent years."

The core group on Sri Lanka (the UK, Canada, Germany, Montenegro, North Macedonia, Malawi) at the Human Rights Council successfully led the adoption of Resolution 46/1, which established an international evidence-gathering mechanism, which has now been established as the OHCHR Sri Lanka Accountability Project. Among Sri Lanka's key trading partners, India and Japan abstained, while China opposed the resolution.

In June, the European Parliament passed a resolution calling upon the European Union to ensure Sri Lanka abides by its human rights commitments under the GSP+ program. However, the EU, like other foreign partners including the United States, Australia, and the United Kingdom, was reluctant to publicly call upon the Sri Lankan government to end abuses.

Sudan

The second year of Sudan's democratic transition has been marred by political instability that slowed the pace of rights and rule of law reforms, and a dire economic situation that compounded public discontent. The government failed to implement key institutional and law reforms stipulated in the August 2019 constitutional charter, including the establishment of a transitional legislative council and commissions with mandates to address peace, transitional justice, and corruption. In June, in response to growing criticism, Prime Minister Abdalla Hamdok outlined plans to tackle the "national political crisis," with an emphasis on the need for security sector reform. On September 21, authorities announced that a coup attempt had been quashed in Khartoum, and the prime minister said officers affiliated with former President Omar al-Bashir's regime were involved.

Notwithstanding progress in eight cases implicating government forces in killings of protesters, justice for serious government abuses has been largely lacking due to broad immunities, an apparent lack of commitment to pursue these cases, limited resources, and the absence of clear prosecution strategies. Government officials reaffirmed their previously expressed commitment to cooperate with the International Criminal Court (ICC) and the Cabinet of Ministers agreed in June to hand over suspects to the court. However, the cabinet and Sovereign Council, which includes military leaders, has to consider the decision at a joint meeting which has yet to be scheduled. It was unclear whether the Sovereign Council would approve the transfers despite the government's international obligation to do so.

Despite the government's commitment to protect civilians in Darfur after the departure of the United Nations-African Union hybrid peacekeeping operation (UNAMID) in December 2020, violence in Darfur continued, with a notable increase in West Darfur. There have been killings and widespread displacement of civilians, as well as destruction of civilian property. In 2020, the United Nations Security Council established the UN Integrated Transition Assistance Mission (UNITAMS), a nationwide mission tasked to support Sudan's political transition and has no mandate to provide physical protection.

Security sector reforms, such as vetting and removal of suspected perpetrators from security apparatuses, failed to move forward. Progress in the implementa-

625

tion of the Juba Peace Agreement, signed in October 2020, between the government and multiple rebel groups, notably the integration of rebel forces into the government forces and the formation of joint forces for Darfur, has been slow.

As a result of conflict in Ethiopia's Tigray and Amhara regions, over 55,000 Ethiopians fled to eastern Sudan as of August 2021.

On October 25, the military leaders of the transitional government carried out a coup, arresting civilian officials and dissolving the transitional government. Protesters took to the streets rejecting the coup, and security forces responded violently with lethal force, detaining protesters and political leaders, as well cutting off internet for almost 3 weeks.

On November 21, a deal was signed between now reinstated prime minister and the military, allowing the first to be released from his house arrest and to form a new technocratic government, The deal was rejected by protesters and other political groups.

Conflict, Abuses in Darfur and Eastern Sudan

In January, armed Arab militias launched attacks against internally displaced people from the Massalit and other African ethnic groups, in al-Genaina, the capital of west Darfur, killing around 150 people.

Between April 4-8, another cycle of attacks in al-Genaina killed over 120 civilians according to local doctors, displaced thousands, and left thousands of civilian homes destroyed. Some government forces sided with armed assailants while others failed to intervene. According to the UN, 65,000 people were displaced by the fighting, with around 2,000 fleeing into neighboring Chad.

In May, the Red Sea state in Eastern Sudan witnessed another bout of intercommunal violence which left around five dead and 13 wounded according to state media.

Ongoing Crackdowns on Protesters

Groups organized protests in Khartoum and other towns against the poor economic situation and delayed reforms. On June 30, police used tear gas to disperse protests against economic reforms that led to high prices.

On May 11, 2021, Sudan armed forces used excessive and lethal force against peaceful protesters gathered in Khartoum leading to 2 deaths. The protests were to commemorate the victims of the deadly crackdown against the June 3 sit-in in Khartoum in 2019. After the reported arrest of 99 army soldiers, at least 7 of whom were charged, the army handed over investigation findings to the then attorney-general. If any further steps have been taken, they have not been made public.

Security forces killed a student in Zalingei, South Darfur, on September 1, during student protests against security forces' refusal to hand over a vacated UNAMID facility, promised to the university.

In response to anti-coup protests, Security forces have repeatedly used excessive force, including lethal force, against demonstrators. Forty-two people were killed in Khartoum between October 25 and November 21 including five children and one woman. Sixteen people were shot dead on November 17, 2021, alone, including a woman and a child, the deadliest response to date.

Accountability

Despite ongoing calls for justice for serious crimes, accountability for atrocities was limited.

According to the office of the attorney-general, eight cases involving protester killings have been recommended to move to courts this year. At time of writing, there were two ongoing criminal trials in Khartoum and three in Atbara, Northern Sudan state, in which members of the security forces are facing charges of murder and crimes against humanity.

In July, a court in White Nile state sentenced a police officer to death for killing a child during December 2018 protests. Another court in August in the same state sentenced a police officer for killing a protester on December 21, 2018. On May 24, a court in Khartoum sentenced a Rapid Support Forces (RSF) officer to death for the June 3, 2019 killing of a 22-year old protester. A court in El-Obeid, South Kordofan sentenced six RSF soldiers to death over the killing of four students during a protest in 2019.

The committee to investigate the violent dispersal of protests in Khartoum on June 3, in which more than 120 were killed, has not released its findings. Victims' families and activists have criticized this delay. The head of the committee said he requested technical support from the African Union (AU) to analyze video footage, but that the AU said it lacked the necessary resources and expertise to assist.

Media reported that over 150 bodies were discovered in April in a morgue outside Khartoum, prompting activists and families of missing persons to raise concerns over authorities' attempt to obstruct justice and tamper with evidence.

On May 24, ICC judges confirmed charges against Ali Mohamed Ali (known as Ali Kosheib, also spelled Kushayb), a former Janjaweed leader who surrendered in 2020. The court announced that his trial would begin on April 5, 2022.

Four suspects sought by the ICC on charges of genocide, war crimes and crimes against humanity committed in Darfur, including ex-President al-Bashir, remain fugitives from the court, although three are currently in Sudanese custody.

In June, then ICC prosecutor Fatou Bensouda visited Darfur for the first time. In an August visit, the new prosecutor, Karim A.A. Khan, signed a new memorandum of understanding with the authorities to facilitate the prosecutor's access to Sudan and ensure cooperation on all cases in which arrest warrants have been issued, following a memorandum that was signed specifically for cooperation in the Kosheib case. That same month, the Cabinet of Ministers agreed to handover the ICC suspects in custody, including ex-President al-Bashir, to the Hague.

Al-Bashir also is currently standing trial in Sudan, alongside other 27 former officials, on charges of undermining the constitutional order during the 1989 coup against Sudan's last elected government.

There has been no progress on the establishment of the Darfur special criminal court, which was provided for in the Juba Agreement, signed in October 2020.

Other Reforms

On January 11, the former attorney-general issued an instruction limiting the power to arrest and detain civilians to police and prosecution and declaring that arrests made by intelligence or military forces would be considered unlawful.

This came after a detainee was killed in RSF custody in December 2020, and activists took to the streets to call for an end to RSF abuses.

On February 23, at a joint meeting of the cabinet and Sovereign Council (serving as the legislative body in the absence of a transitional legislature) ratification of both the International Convention for the Protection of All Persons from Enforced Disappearance and the United Nations Convention against Torture was approved.

On April 24, the joint meeting approved laws on formation of peace, transitional justice, and anti-corruption commissions.

The cabinet of ministers approved a law to ratify the Rome Statute of the ICC on August 3. Ratification requires approval by the joint meeting to take effect.

Unlawful Detention

As the military moved with the coup, security forced rounded up dozens in and out of Khartoum, including at least 30 civilian officials, who were detained in undisclosed locations and with no access to family or lawyers. As part of the November 21 deal, number of detainees were released. At least seven detainees, including a former minister, were charged with sedition and kept in detention, according to their families.

Sexual Orientation, Gender Identity

Sudan's Criminal Act of 1991 in Article 148 continues to criminalize sodomy with punishment of up to life in prison, while Article 151 provides for up to a year in prison for "indecent acts," including between women.

Key International Actors

On January 6, Sudan and the United States signed an agreement normalizing relations with Israel. This follows the decision by the US to lift sanctions against Sudan in 2020.

On May 17, France hosted a donors conference to support Sudan's transition, attended by heads of governments from the European Union, Gulf and African states, as well international and regional financial institutions. Focused on the country's economic crisis, Sudan secured international contributions for debt relief and for plans of future investments.

In June, the International Monetary Fund (IMF) granted Sudan a $2.5 billion loan. In March, the IMF and World Bank approved Sudan's request for debt relief under the Heavily Indebted Poor Countries (HIPC) initiative, which required the government to adopt hard-hitting IMF-supervised economic reforms, including eliminating fuel subsidies and introducing exchange rate reform.

AU-mediated talks on the filling and operation of the Grand Ethiopian Renaissance Dam (GERD) between Egypt, Sudan, and Ethiopia in Kinshasa continued with no results. Sudan said the country would not join any new AU-led negotiations unless experts and observers were given a greater role. The UN Security Council issued a statement in September encouraging Sudan and others to resume talks.

Syria

2021 marked a decade since the peaceful uprising in Syria turned into a brutal conflict. Since the start, parties to the conflict have flagrantly disregarded human rights and humanitarian law protections. Human Rights Watch has determined that some attacks by the Russia-Syria alliance are war crimes and may amount to crimes against humanity.

In May 2021, Bashar al-Assad secured a fourth term as president for seven more years in elections that did not occur under the auspices of the United Nations-led political process and failed to adhere to standards for free and fair elections. His renewed term as president came as his security services continued to subject hundreds, including returning refugees, to arbitrarily arrest and torture, while millions go hungry due to his government's diversion of aid and failure to equitably address a debilitating economic crisis brought on primarily by the destruction of infrastructure and crises in neighboring countries.

Routine shortages in basic goods, including bread and fuel, have become commonplace and the number of people in need of humanitarian assistance increased by 21 percent in 2021—reaching a total of 13.4 million people, with 1.48 million in "catastrophic" need, according to the UN Office for the Coordination of Humanitarian Affairs (UNOCHA). A little over 1 percent of the country's total population was fully vaccinated against Covid-19 at time of writing, and there were concerns about the government's ability to distribute vaccines equitably, even within areas under its control.

According to World Vision, by 2021 the economic toll of the war was US$1.2 trillion. The costs incurred are largely due to the destruction of infrastructure and massive displacement caused by a decade of war using prohibited tactics, primarily by the Syrian-Russian military alliance. Human Rights Watch has determined that some attacks by the alliance are war crimes and may amount to crimes against humanity. The US-led anti-ISIS coalition have also violated international humanitarian law, by conducting indiscriminate strikes in northeast Syria that resulted in civilian death and destruction

Prohibited attacks by the Syrian-Russian military alliance continue to be used in Idlib where, despite a tenuous ceasefire, the alliance still poses a threat to over

HUMAN
RIGHTS
WATCH

"Our Lives Are Like Death"
Syrian Refugee Returns from Lebanon and Jordan

three million civilians trapped there. Meanwhile the dominant anti-government armed group, Hay'et Tahrir al-Sham, restricts civilians' freedoms.

In Turkish-occupied territories, Turkey and local Syrian factions are abusing civilians' rights and restricting their freedoms with impunity.

Following the territorial defeat of the Islamic State (ISIS) in northeast Syria, Kurdish-led authorities and the US-led coalition have yet to provide compensation for civilian casualties, offer support for identifying the fate of those kidnapped by ISIS, and adequately address the plight of more than 60,000 Syrian and foreign men, women, and children indefinitely held in dire conditions in closed camps and prisons as ISIS suspects and family members.

The UN Security Council failed to renew the full cross-border aid mechanism, leaving only one border crossing open and exacerbating humanitarian crises in non-government areas. Meanwhile, the UN-led peace process continued to stagnate.

Despite the government's record of human rights abuses against its own citizens, this year also saw several countries normalize with the Syrian government, including the United Arab Emirates and Jordan, and make commitments to cooperate, leading to concerns about premature return of refugees and potential facilitation of rights abuse.

Abuses by the Syrian-Russian Military Alliance

While all sides to the conflict have committed heinous laws-of-war violations, the Syrian-Russian military alliance has conducted indiscriminate aerial bombing of schools, hospitals, and markets—the civilian infrastructure essential to a society's survival. According to Airwars, a UK-based monitoring group, the Russian air force alone has carried out around 39,000 airstrikes in Syria since 2015.

Tensions between government loyalists and anti-government forces in Daraa governorate intensified in June 2021, following a popular rejection of the results of the Syrian presidential elections in May 2021. Between June and September 2021, Syrian armed forces, and affiliated militias launched dozens of indiscriminate attacks on populated areas in Daraa, while anti-government fighters also attacked government-held areas leading to civilian casualties.

An estimated 55,000 civilians in Dara al-Balad, an area affiliated with anti-government sentiment, were besieged and restricted from accessing bread, fuel, electricity, and healthcare services. As a result of the siege and clashes, at least 38,000 were displaced to nearby areas. In September, a Russian-brokered reconciliation agreement was announced which mandated the entry of the Syrian government to these areas, and that civilians and opposition fighters sign so-called reconciliation agreements to be allowed to stay. Dozens of Syrians who refused were transferred to Idlib. Human Rights Watch has previously documented how the guarantees provided within reconciliation agreements fall short of providing necessary protections for Syrians. Following the agreement, a Syrian Arab Red Crescent (SARC) food truck was allowed to enter the area for the first time in months.

Economic Crisis and Rights Implications

By 2021, Syria's economic output shrunk by 60 percent, the national currency depreciated by 99 percent and more than 90 percent of the population live below the poverty line according to the UN Office for the Coordination of Humanitarian Affairs (OCHA). At least 12.4 million Syrians—out of an estimated population of around 16 million—are food insecure, according to the World Food Programme (WFP), an alarming increase of 3.1 million in one year. More than 600,000 children are chronically malnourished. The Syrian government has exacerbated the economic crisis' impact by failing to fairly and adequately address bread and fuel shortages, instead allowing discriminatory and inequitable distribution.

Residents also report severe electricity cuts and shortages. In areas re-taken by the government, the majority of those interviewed by Human Rights Watch still had their houses completely or partially destroyed and could not afford to rebuild or renovate. The Syrian government provides no reconstruction assistance even years after the territory has been re-taken. As such, many residents are living in makeshift tents, and boiling water for drinking. They are unable to afford rent elsewhere.

In reclaimed parts of Idlib and Hama, Syrian authorities, through pro-government militias and the government-controlled "Peasants' Unions," unlawfully confiscated the homes and lands of Syrians who fled Syrian-Russian military attacks and are selling them through auctions.

In February 2021, Col. Elias al-Bitar, head of the army's Exemptions and Reserves Branch, reminded the country of a late 2019 amendment to the conscription law that allows authorities to seize property of "military evaders" who fail to pay absurdly high fines.

Obstacles to Humanitarian Aid and Reconstruction

At least 13.1 million Syrians need humanitarian aid across Syria.

Millions in northeast and northwest Syria rely on the cross-border flow of food, medicine, and other lifesaving assistance—including the Covid-19 vaccine. Aid workers told Human Rights Watch that non-UN agencies have nowhere near the UN's capacity to buy supplies and transport them into the northwest. They said that shutting down UN aid supplies and ending UN funding would deny aid to millions of people.

Non-UN aid groups in northeast Syria, which is mostly under the control of the Kurdish-led Autonomous Administration, a quasi-autonomous authority, say they have been unable to bring in enough aid, particularly for health care, since the UN was forced to stop its cross-border operations between Iraq and Syria in January 2020.

In July 2021, the UN Security Council renewed its authorization for cross-border humanitarian aid through the Bab al-Hawa crossing from Turkey to northwest Syria, the only remaining cross-border aid corridor which has not yet been barred by Russia's UNSC veto power.

As of September 2021, 610,257 Covid-19 vaccine doses had been administered in Syria including 119,158 doses in the northwest and 19,354 in the northeast. Around 3 percent of Syria's total population were able to receive the vaccine.

The Syrian government continued to impose severe restrictions on the delivery of humanitarian aid in government-held areas of Syria and elsewhere in the country, and to divert aid to punish those who express dissent.

In 2021, it imposed a siege on the city of Daraa al-Balad, preventing humanitarian agencies from accessing the area and severely restricting food, aid and medical supplies. The Syrian government continues to bar access to al-Rukban camp near the Jordanian border where the last UN humanitarian aid delivery took place in September 2019.

Arbitrary Detentions, Torture, Extrajudicial Executions, Enforced Disappearances

Syrian security forces and government-affiliated militias continue to arbitrarily detain, disappear, and mistreat people across the country, including children, people with disabilities and older people, and returnees and individuals in re-taken areas who have signed so-called reconciliation agreements.

Human Rights Watch has documented 21 cases of arrest and arbitrary detention including 13 cases of torture, 3 kidnappings, 5 extrajudicial killings, and 17 enforced disappearances between 2017 and 2021 among refugees who had returned to Syria from Jordan and Lebanon.

On November 4, 2020, the Syrian government released 60 individuals from detention facilities in southern Syria and Damascus. However, thousands remain locked away in Syria's secretive detention system, many held from as far back as 2011, and with no clue as to their whereabouts.

According to the Syrian Network for Human Rights (SNHR), nearly 15,000 have died due to torture since March 2011, the majority at the hands of Syrian government forces.

The network also estimates that at least 100,000 Syrians remain forcibly disappeared, with nearly 85 percent at the hands of Syrian government forces. The UN Commission of Inquiry (COI) was also able to document cases of sexual violence inflicted during detention in government facilities, including rape, assault, and sexual humiliation against women, men, and girls and boys as young as 11 years old.

On October 21, the Syrian Ministry of Justice announced the execution of 24 individuals, and gave five minors sentences between 10-12 years, for involvement in setting wild fires in Syria last year. The government justified the decision under its overbroad and abusive Counterterrorism Law of 2019.

Women's Rights

Women continue to face discrimination in relation to marriage, divorce, child custody and inheritance under the Personal Status Law. A woman loses her right to financial maintenance from her husband if she refuses to live with her husband in the marital home without a legitimate excuse or if she works outside the marital home without her husband's permission." While authorities amended the law twice in 2019 removing the language of "disobedience", the law still punishes women for some acts of disobedience relating to mobility.

While the authorities in 2020 repealed Article 548 of the penal code which allowed men to receive reduced sentences if they injured or killed their wives or immediate female relatives on finding them engaging in an "illegitimate" sexual act, other articles remain that could allow men to receive reduced sentences for violence against women. The Penal Code also criminalizes adultery in a manner that discriminates against women and provides a longer prison sentence for adultery for women than men.

Sexual Orientation, Gender Identity

Syrian state and non-state actors have subjected men, boys, transgender women, and nonbinary people to sexual violence during the Syrian conflict, resulting in severe physical and mental health consequences. Under Article 520 of the Syrian penal code, "unnatural sexual intercourse" is punishable by three years in prison.

Violations by Turkey and Turkish-Backed Forces

Turkey invaded and occupied parts of northeastern Syria in October 2019, where it remains in control. In the immediate aftermath, many homes and private properties held by the local Kurdish population were looted and seized. By December 2019, Turkish authorities and an armed group affiliated with the Turkish-backed anti-government group—the Syrian National Army (SNA)—arrested and illegally transferred at least 63 Syrian nationals from northeast Syria to Turkey to face trial on serious charges that could lead to life in prison. Five of the 63 Syrians were sentenced to life in prison in October 2020.

In the first half of 2021, the SNA arbitrarily detained 162 individuals, according to the Syrian Network for Human Rights.

SNA factions continue to recruit children; a 2021 Syrians for Truth and Justice report found at least 20 cases of child recruitment.

Violations by Hay'et Tahrir al-Sham, and Other Anti-Government Groups

Anti-government groups in Syria continue to resort to abusive detention practices in areas under their control. In Idlib, Hay'et Tahrir al-Sham (HTS), an Al-Qaeda affiliate, continues to raid and arbitrarily detain activists, humanitarian workers, and civilians voicing critical opinions.

According to the Syrian Network for Human Rights, during the first half of 2021, HTS arbitrarily arrested at least 57 individuals. According to local sources, in some cases. HTS imposes the death penalty on detainees.

The group is increasingly interfering in every aspect of civilian life, limiting women's movements, imposing dress codes and even hair styles, and levying taxes and fines haphazardly. It has also seized many homes and properties held by Christians.

The number of child soldiers recruited by HTS increased from 61 cases to 187 cases in the first half of 2020, according to a 2021 UN report.

On October 20, a bomb exploded on a military bus at a highly populated area in Damascus, killing 14 and wounding others. An insurgent group called Saraya Qasioun claimed responsibility for the attack.

Violations by the Syrian Democratic Forces and US-Led Coalition

The Syrian Democratic Forces, a Kurdish-led armed group, has carried out mass arrest campaigns against civilians including activists, journalists, and teachers. In the first half of 2021, the SDF arbitrarily detained 369 individuals, according to the Syrian Network for Human Rights.

More than 60,000 men, women and children remain detained in degrading, arbitrary, and often inhuman and life-threatening conditions by regional authorities in northeast Syria. They include nearly 43,000 foreigners—27,000 of them children—from nearly 60 countries who have been held for more than two years without ever being brought before a court. Only 25 countries are known to have repatriated or helped bring home any of their nationals and most of these have allowed only a limited number to return.

Virtually no progress has been made by the Kurdish-led authorities or the US-led coalition to determine the fate of thousands disappeared by the Islamic State (also known as ISIS).

Displacement Crisis

The Syrian displacement crisis remains one of the most dire and protracted consequences of the war. Since 2011, 12.3 million were forced to flee since the onset of the war, according to UNOCHA, with 6.7 million currently internally displaced across the country.

In 2021, efforts to force refugees to return have taken on new dimensions. In March, Denmark became the first European country to inform 94 Syrian refugees that their "temporary protection" status will not be renewed after a flawed report by Danish immigration services claiming that Damascus, and Damascus countryside are safe for returns, notwithstanding ample evidence that the risk of persecution remains pervasive.

Despite a decrease in active hostilities in Syria, returnees faced a host of human rights violations, including arbitrary detention, torture, forced disappearances, and abuse by Syrian authorities, providing additional evidence that Syria is not safe. Returning refugees also faced extreme economic hardship, unable to afford basic food items. Most also found their homes either totally or partially destroyed and were unable to afford the costs of renovation. The Syrian government provided no assistance in repairing homes.

Schooling of refugee children, including children with disabilities, in refugee-hosting countries was severely impacted by the Covid-19 pandemic, particularly in Lebanon, where the problems posed by the pandemic are additionally compounded by a severe political, financial, and economic crisis. There, hundreds of thousands of Syrian refugees faced heightened risks of dropouts, child labor, and child marriage.

International Accountability Efforts

In February 2021, a German court sentenced Eyad A., a former Syrian intelligence official, to four and a half years in prison for aiding and abetting crimes against humanity. This was the first verdict in a historic trial of two former Syrian intelligence officials, on charges related to state-sponsored torture in Syria.

In March, the UN International, Independent, Impartial Mechanism for Syria reported that it has provided information and evidence of atrocity crimes to 12 national jurisdictions. That month, Canada joined the Netherlands in efforts to hold the Syrian government accountable for torture under the United Nations Convention against Torture. The Dutch correspondence is an important step that could eventually lead to proceedings against Syria at the International Court of Justice (ICJ).

In September, France's highest court, the Cour de cassation, ruled that an indictment against the company Lafarge for complicity in crimes against humanity was wrongly canceled by the Paris Appeals Court.

Key International Actors

The UN-led peace process, including the constitutional committee, made virtually no progress this year, following a fifth round of talks held in January 2021. Russia, Turkey, and Iran, continue to provide military and financial support to warring factions and to shield them from accountability.

In July 2021, the UN Security Council failed to reauthorize full cross-border operations into the region and authorize a resumption of aid flows from Iraq to northeast Syria, due to the threat of a Russian veto. Instead, the Security Council was able to extend the opening of one border crossing to Northwest Syria.

In April 2021, states parties to the Chemical Weapons Convention voted to suspend Syrian rights and privileges at the Organisation for the Prohibition of Chemical Weapons (OPCW). Syria's government forces have repeatedly used chlorine and the nerve agent sarin against men, women, and children over the course of the war. ISIS militants have on several occasions used sulfur mustard, according to the UN and OPCW.

Individuals responsible for atrocity crimes, entities within or affiliated to the Syrian government, and ISIS continue to be under robust sanctions by the United States, European Union, and the UK, in addition to a few sector-wide sanctions.

In July 2021, the US sanctioned financial facilitators who supported Hay'et Tahrir al-Sham as well.

Israel has increasingly and frequently conducted aerial strikes on Iranian or Hezbollah-manned targets in Syria. The United States and other members of the anti-ISIS coalition continue to support ISIS counteroperations, through their support of the Syrian Democratic Forces.

Tajikistan

Tajikistan's human rights record continued to deteriorate amid an ongoing crackdown on freedom of expression and the political opposition, as well as targeting of independent lawyers, journalists, and family members of opposition activists abroad. The government blocked access to websites that post information critical of the government and harassed human rights groups.

Freedom of religion and belief is severely limited. Lesbian, gay, bisexual, and transgender (LGBT) people are subjected to wide-ranging discrimination and societal antipathy. Domestic violence continued to be a serious problem. Significant legislative gaps, lack of accountability for family violence, and authorities' inadequate response deter women from seeking help and support. Following the Taliban takeover in Afghanistan, Tajikistan received thousands of refugees, with many more gathering at the border. In January, President Emomali Rahmon declared the country coronavirus-free, allowing re-opening of schools and mosques, However, as the number of cases soared in June, authorities re-introduced some social distancing measures.

Civil Society

Many civil society groups conducting community and humanitarian work experienced a renewed sense of purpose helping people through the Covid-19 pandemic, in response to what they saw as poor government response. Although the government initially opposed such activism, it eventually accepted and even supported this work.

Working on political rights, torture, electoral issues, corruption, freedom of religion, or LGBT rights/issues, however, remained sensitive and often led to harassment of activists. Human rights defenders complained of the work of state-supported "troll factories" that aim to discredit critical voices online.

Prison Conditions and Torture

Tajik prisons remain ill-equipped and overcrowded, with prisoners routinely facing ill-treatment. In February, the Ministry of Justice approved plans to implement a strategy for penal system reform. In July, some 1,700 prisoners, including

Rakhmatullo Radjab, member of the banned Islamic Renaissance Party of Tajikistan, were transferred from the Dushanbe prison to a newly constructed prison in Vakhdat, with reportedly better conditions.

In September, more than 650 prisoners were released under the country-wide amnesty granted mostly to women, people under the age of 18 or over 55, and people with disabilities. Some 10,000 additional prisoners will be released in 2021. However, the amnesty will not affect political prisoners.

In June, three police officers were sentenced to lengthy jail terms for using torture to extract a false confession in a murder case in 2017. They beat and used electricity on Hasan Yodgorov, who served six months before being released after the real murderer was caught.

In April, 80-year-old Doniyor Nabiev, sentenced in December 2020 to seven years on charges of "organizing activities of an extremist organization" was released on amnesty due to his old age and poor health. Prior to his detention and imprisonment, Nabiev helped families of imprisoned members of the banned Islamic Renaissance Party of Tajikistan.

Physical and sexual violence against women by police officers in detention centers is also widespread. In 2019, Tajikistan's Civil Society Coalition Against Torture documented that while N.B., a 24-year-old woman, was in detention for two days accused of theft, Vakhsh district police officers physically and verbally abused her, injected her with a shot that paralyzed her limbs, and raped her. To date, none of the police officers have been charged, as N.B.'s official complaint remains under consideration.

Harassment of Critics and Dissidents

In 2021, Tajikistan continued to harass and imprison government critics, opposition, and foreign-based dissidents and their family members within the country.

In June, the Khujand city court sentenced former member of the banned Islamic Renaissance Party of Tajikistan, Mirzo Hojimuhammad, also known as Mirzoqul Hojimatov, to five years in prison for "membership in a banned extremist organization." Hojimuhammad had lived in Russia since 2019, having quit IRPT in 2015, and upon his return to Tajikistan in February was banned from leaving the country. He was arrested in May.

In March, migrant workers' rights defender, Izzat Amon, who has been critical of the Tajik government on social media, was abducted in Moscow and forcibly returned to Tajikistan. Amon worked for Tojikon, the Moscow-based legal center for Tajik migrants. Amon's whereabouts were unknown for two days until the Tajikistan Ministry of Interior said that he was in pretrial detention on alleged fraud charges. In a September court hearing the state prosecutor requested nine years' imprisonment.

In August, Tajik authorities opened a criminal investigation against Khuseyn Ishankulov, one of Amon's now former colleagues at the Tojikon, on charges of "public calls for extremist activities," allegedly for urging Amon's supporters to call for his release on social media.

Freedom of Expression

Under the pretext of protecting national security, Tajikistan's state telecommunications agency regularly blocks websites that carry information potentially critical of the government, including Facebook, Radio Ozodi, the website of Radio Free Europe's Tajik service, and opposition websites. Journalists and bloggers are prosecuted for their critical opinions posted on social media, based on 2017 legal amendments allowing security services to monitor individuals' online activities, including by keeping records of mobile messages and comments.

In June, lawyer Abdulmajid Rizoev was sentenced to five years and six months' imprisonment for "public calls for extremist activities using mass media or Internet" under Article 307 of the criminal code. Rizoev was detained in November 2020 and the first hearing on his case was in February 2021, when the state prosecution declared his posts and reposts on Facebook to be of "extremist" nature. The publications questioned participation rates in the 2020 parliamentary elections and quoted classics of Tajik literature about wise and unwise governments.

In September, journalist and activist of the banned Islamic Renaissance Party of Tajikistan, Hikmatullo Sayfullzoda, sentenced to 16 years in prison in 2015, was attacked in the prison hospital. Earlier this year, Reporters Without Borders had called on Tajik authorities to release Sayfullzoda under the amnesty, due to fears for his safety in prison.

As of October, Radio Ozodi reported that eight longstanding accreditation requests for its journalists were still awaiting a decision by the Foreign Ministry, and several staff members received accreditation only for several months, contrary to the terms of Tajik legislation on media accreditation. Tajik security officers continue to intimidate Ozodi journalists at their workplaces and in their homes with threats of severe consequences should they continue working at the service.

Freedom of Religion and Belief

The Tajik government severely curtails freedom of religion or belief, proscribing certain forms of dress, including the hijab for women and long beards for men. Salafism, a fundamentalist strand of Islam, has been officially banned in Tajikistan since 2011 and authorities regularly arrest individuals for alleged membership in Salafi groups.

In June, a closed-door trial of 18 suspected members of the Salafi movement began, with scant information made public about the defendants or the charges they faced. The suspects—all residents of the Bobojon Ghafurov district in northern Tajikistan—were arrested in a police raid in February. The defendants deny having links with the Salafi movement or any other religious extremist group, their relatives said. They accused police of torturing the detainees to obtain confessions. In July, 14 of the 18 defendants were sentenced to five and five-and-a-half years in prison. The remaining four were convicted of not reporting a crime and sentenced to one year in prison.

In October, the Tajik parliament started consideration of amendments to the criminal code on tightening penalties for illegal religious education, including online education, with imprisonment of up to three years. Previously this was punishable with an administrative fine of up to 72,000 somoni (approximately US$6,000) or a prison term of up to three years for a repeat offence.

Conflict at the Kyrgyzstan-Tajikistan Border

A two-day border conflict between Kyrgyzstan and Tajikistan in late April—the worst in Central Asia in decades—killed over 40 people, most of them civilians, and injured hundreds. The conflict began over control of a crucial water-intake facility that diverts to Kyrgyzstan a small part of a river that flows naturally into Tajikistan, in line with a water-sharing protocol.

About 58,000 people in Kyrgyzstan and Tajikistan fled their homes or were evacuated. Dozens of houses and at least three schools were damaged or destroyed. The two countries quickly called a ceasefire and committed to rebuilding houses damaged during the conflict in their respective territories. As of September, three nationals of Kyrgyzstan, ethnic Tajiks, and two nationals of Tajikistan were on trial in Kyrgyzstan for looting private property during the conflict.

There were no reports of an impartial investigation by Tajikistan into whether its military violated the laws of war during the conflict. However, the Tajik prosecutor general has initiated a criminal investigation into the Kyrgyz military attack on the Chorkukh community in Sughd region that borders Kyrgyzstan. Some small-scale conflicts between villagers in the border areas have been reported since the conflict.

Domestic Violence

Domestic violence in Tajikistan is prevalent. The 2013 law on the prevention of violence in the family, while offering some protection to survivors, does not criminalize domestic violence or marital rape, and remains poorly implemented. Survivors lack adequate support and protection and have little recourse to justice. Social stigma, economic dependencies, impunity for perpetrators, lack of accessibility in protection measures for women with disabilities, including shelters, and insufficient number of shelters pose serious barriers for survivors' access to help, especially in rural areas.

Service providers lack specialized victim-focused training and regularly face lack of funding. Police fail to pursue investigations, to enforce protection orders, or to arrest people who commit domestic violence. In the first eight months of the year, one of the only three shelters for victims of domestic violence conducted as many consultations as it had during all of 2020.

Crisis in Afghanistan and Refugees

Following the Taliban takeover of Afghanistan in August 2021, the Tajik government announced it would seek to protect the rights of ethnic Tajiks, the second largest ethnic group, in Afghanistan.

An estimated 10,000 Afghans have fled in recent years to Tajikistan, which shares more than 1,400 kilometers of border with Afghanistan. Refugee camps have been established in the Khatlon region of Tajikistan with a capacity to accommodate 5,000 refugees. The camps are supported with funding from the European Union. According to the United Nations Refugee Agency, up to 50,000 refugees could be registered in Tajikistan after the total withdrawal of allied troops from Afghanistan by the end of 2021.

Key International Actors

In February, during its Cooperation Council with Tajikistan, the EU pressed Tajikistan to improve its track record on human rights and fundamental freedoms. However, EU High Representative Josep Borrell, following his meeting with President Rahmon in Brussels in October, did not raise any human rights issues.

In May, after the escalation of border conflict between Kyrgyzstan and Tajikistan, the European Union, Organization for Security and Co-operation in Europe (OSCE), and the UN all offered their assistance in resolving the conflict and responding to the immediate consequences for the livelihoods of people on both sides of the border.

Following the Taliban takeover of Kabul in August, Tajikistan's international partners have stepped up engagement on security cooperation and refugee management with the government. In September, the EU provided Tajikistan €160,000 (around $180,000) in humanitarian aid to assist most vulnerable Afghan refugees. In September, members of the Collective Security Treaty Organization (CSTO) signed an agreement at a summit in Tajikistan to strengthen the Tajik-Afghan border.

At the UN Universal Periodic Review of Tajikistan in November several states made recommendations for Tajikistan to allow political opposition groups to operate, release political prisoners, end the use of torture, respect freedom of expression and take steps to end domestic violence against women and girls, as well as adopt comprehensive anti-discrimination legislation that would protect LGBT people, among others.

Tanzania

President Samia Suluhu Hassan became Tanzania's first female president on March 19, following the death of President John Magufuli on March 17, 2021. Magufuli died five months into his second term as president.

President Hassan took measures to respond to some rights concerns, but the government continued to restrict media and civic space, arbitrarily arrest journalists and critics of the government, enforce a discriminatory ban on pregnant students in schools, and undermine the rights of women and children. The authorities have not conducted meaningful investigations into serious abuses that marred the 2020 elections. Tanzania's Sexual Offenses Special Provisions Act of 1998 continues to punish consensual adult same-sex conduct by up to life imprisonment.

Freedom of Expression and Media

Although President Hassan pledged to remove existing restrictions on the media on April 6, authorities continued the Magufuli administration's crackdown on the media.

The media and human rights groups reported that on April 12, police arrested journalists Dickson Billikwija and Christopher James, detaining them for three hours within the premises of Temeke municipal government on the orders of the Temeke district executive director.

On April 21, 2021, three security officers with the Kikosi cha Valantia Zanzibar (KVZ), an armed paramilitary group controlled by Zanzibar's government, assaulted Jesse Mikofu, a reporter with the privately owned *Mwananchi* newspaper, after he photographed them forcibly evicting market traders from the Darajani area of Stone Town.

On August 11, 2021, the government suspended *Uhuru*, a newspaper owned by the ruling party, Chama Cha Mapinduzi (CCM), for publishing a story suggesting that President Hassan may not contest the 2025 presidential elections, the first newspaper suspension under President Hassan.

On September 5, 2021, the Ministry of Information, Culture, Arts and Sports suspended the privately owned *Raia Mwema* newspaper for 30 days for "repeatedly publishing false information and deliberate incitement." The paper had published an article linking a gunman who had shot and killed four people outside the French Embassy to the CCM party.

Legislative Reform

On April 21, Justice and Constitutional Affairs Minister Palamagamba Kabudi told Parliament that the Law Reform Commission was doing the groundwork for review of the Economic and Organized Crime (Control) Act, which provides for non-bailable offenses, including money-laundering, which the government has in the past used to detain government critics and journalists.

The authorities have started the process of amending the online content and the radio and television broadcasting content regulations of the Electronic and Postal Communications Act. The current regulations give the Tanzania Communications Regulatory Authority (TCRA) wide discretionary powers to license blogs, websites, and other online content, and prohibit radio and television broadcasters from working with foreign broadcasters unless staff from the communications authority or other government department are physically present.

Government Opponents and Other Critics

On January 5, a court in Dar es Salaam ordered the release of human rights activist Tito Magoti and information technology professional Theodory Gyan from prison after paying a fine of Sh17.3 million (US$7,500). Magoti and Gyan had spent two years in detention on economic crimes charges, including money laundering and leading organized crime. On December 20, 2019, police arrested Magoti after luring him to "a meeting" through text messages from Giyani, his acquaintance.

On June 22, the High Court overturned the September 2020 decision of the Tanganyika Law Society to suspend human rights lawyer and government critic Fatma Karume from practicing law on mainland Tanzania. Karume's suspension was in response to allegations of misconduct after she challenged President Magufuli's appointment of the attorney general of Tanzania.

On July 21, police in Mwanza, northern Tanzania, surrounded the hotel occupied by members of the country's main opposition party, Chadema, and arrested 11 party members, including the party chairman, Freeman Mbowe, ahead of a conference to discuss reforms to the country's constitution. The day before the scheduled meeting, authorities in Mwanza announced a ban on "unnecessary gatherings," ostensibly to prevent the spread of Covid-19. The authorities later charged Mbowe with economic sabotage, conspiracy, and financing terrorist activities and placed him in pretrial custody.

In 2012, the government embarked on a review of the constitution, but the process stalled in 2015 after President Magufuli took office and made it clear the review was not a priority for his administration, saying his government would instead pursue development projects. On June 29, President Hassan continued this policy, informing the media that before the country embarks on a constitutional reform process, she should first be allowed to fix the economy.

On September 22, the director of public prosecutions withdrew sedition charges against opposition politician Tundu Lissu, newspaper editor Simon Mkina, newspaper publisher Ismail Mehbood, and journalist Jabir Idrissa Yunus, over a 2016 *Mawio* newspaper headline "Machafuko yaja Zanzibar" ("Chaos is coming to Zanzibar").

Refugee Rights

In 2021, Human Rights Watch received credible reports of threats, harassment, and arrests of Burundian refugees by Tanzanian security forces. Tanzanian authorities also forcibly returned or "pushed back" thousands of Mozambicans fleeing violence in the country's northern Cabo Delgado province during 2020 and 2021.

In July, the United Nations refugee agency (UNHCR) and the African Commission on Human and Peoples' Rights expressed concern with Tanzania's forced returns of over 9,700 Mozambican asylum seekers at the Negomano border point between January and June, without an assessment of their international protection needs. Many were fleeing armed conflict and insecurity in the coastal city of Palma, following a brutal attack by non-state armed groups in March 2021. The pushbacks violated the principle of non-refoulement under international standards and regional refugee law.

Women's Rights

On August 23, at a ceremony hosting the Tanzania men's football team, the president made remarks that cast aspersions on the "femininity" and gender of Tanzanian women footballers, which was widely condemned by activists.

Children's Rights

The Tanzanian government continues to discriminate against girls by subjecting them to mandatory pregnancy tests and explicitly barring students who are pregnant or are mothers from attending public schools.

In June 2017, Magufuli officially declared a ban on pregnant students and adolescent mothers attending school. Pursuant to its agreement with the World Bank, tied to a $500 million loan for the government's Secondary Education Quality Improvement Program, the Tanzanian government announced that it would allow students who were pregnant or were mothers to enroll in a parallel accelerated education program, described as "alternative education pathways." However, these centers are often not accessible because of the long distances students must travel to reach them and because they charge fees, unlike public primary and secondary schools that are tuition-free.

At time of writing, the government had not outlawed child marriage, meaning the authorities had not complied with a 2016 High Court decision to amend the Marriage Act to raise the legal age of marriage to 18 years for girls and boys.

"People Can't Be Fit into Boxes"

Thailand's Need for Legal Gender Recognition

HUMAN
RIGHTS
WATCH

มูลนิธิเครือข่ายเพื่อนกะเทยเพื่อสิทธิมนุษยชน
The Foundation of Transgender Alliance for Human Rights

Thailand

The government of Prime Minister Gen. Prayut Chan-ocha, in 2021, restricted fundamental rights, particularly free expression and assembly, arbitrarily arrested democracy activists and critics of the monarchy, and enforced a nationwide state of emergency using the Covid-19 pandemic as a pretext. The authorities suppressed youth-led democracy protests, sometimes violently. The government introduced a draft law to tightly control all civil society organizations, restrict foreign funding for nongovernmental organizations (NGOs), and imposed compulsory registration.

Youth-Led Democracy Protests

There were thousands of democracy protests across Thailand in 2020 and 2021. Rather than engaging with them on the issues, the authorities seemed intent on preventing protests from gaining support and spreading across the country.

The youth-led uprising became widely known for its iconic three-finger salute displayed by tens of thousands in the streets demanding a new democratic constitution be introduced with reforms to the monarchy. The momentum of the protests was seriously disrupted by the pandemic and subsequent lockdown measures, as well as criminal prosecution, violent crackdowns, and harassment of protesters.

Since August, the street protests have become increasingly leaderless and represented by the largely underprivileged, heavily impacted, urban poor. These protesters, some as young as 12, are demanding Prime Minister Prayut step down as a first step toward ending authoritarian rule, cronyism, corruption, and government inefficiency.

The front line of increasingly violent confrontations was in Bangkok's Din Daeng district. Protesters vandalized and burned traffic police booths, police vehicles, and royal portraits. Riot police used water cannons mixed with dye and teargas chemicals, as well as teargas grenades and rubber bullets to disperse the crowds. While the authorities claimed to follow international standards for crowd control, in practice riot police routinely used excessive force against protesters, in some cases causing serious injuries. Protesters, widely referred to by the media as *Taluh Gas* (shattering teargas), used slingshots, fireworks, and Molotov cocktails to attack the police.

Covid-19 State of Emergency, Restrictions on Freedom of Expression

In September, the government ordered the extension of its nationwide enforcement of the draconian Emergency Decree on Public Administration in Emergency Situation to November, continuing the authorities' broad powers to restrict fundamental freedoms with impunity. It was the fourteenth extension since March 2020. At least 1,100 people who took part in democracy protests have been charged with violating social distancing measures, curfew restrictions, and other emergency measures. Some of them have also been charged with sedition.

The government used the emergency measures to clamp down on freedom of expression and media freedom. In July, Prime Minister Prayut issued emergency regulation number 29, empowering the authorities to censor online expression and prosecute individuals responsible for communications that may "instigate fear" or distort information about the pandemic. The government revoked this regulation in August, after the Bangkok Civil Court ruled that it violated the constitutionally recognized right to freedom of expression.

In November 2020, Prime Minister Prayut ordered Thai authorities to use "all laws and all articles" against democracy protesters, bringing back *lèse-majesté* (insulting the monarchy) prosecutions after a three-year hiatus. The authorities have since charged at least 151 people, including 12 children, under Article 112 of the penal code in relation to various activities at democracy protests or comments on social media. Making critical or offensive comments about the monarchy is also a serious criminal offense under the Computer-Related Crime Act.

Prominent democracy activists, including Arnon Nampha, Parit Chiwarak, Jatupat Boonpattararaksa, and Panupong Jadnok, have been put in pretrial detention in lèse-majesté cases that could take years to be concluded in the courts.

In January 2021, former opposition leader Thanathorn Juangroongruangkit was charged with lèse-majesté and cybercrimes for criticizing Siam Bioscience, a company owned by the king that produces Covid-19 vaccines.

In January, the Bangkok Criminal Court sentenced Anchan Preelert to 87 years in prison (later halved after she pleaded guilty), setting a new record for length of imprisonment meted out in a lèse-majesté conviction.

Torture and Enforced Disappearance

On September 16, the parliament approved the first reading of the Prevention and Suppression of Torture and Enforced Disappearance Bill.

Torture and enforced disappearance have long been problems in Thailand. Most of the reported cases have not been resolved, and hardly anyone has been punished.

Human Rights Watch has documented numerous cases related to counterinsurgency operations in Thailand's southern border provinces in which police and military personnel tortured ethnic Malay Muslims in custody. There are also credible reports of torture being used as a form of punishment of military conscripts. During the five years of military rule after the 2014 coup, many people taken into incommunicado military custody alleged they were tortured or otherwise illtreated while being detained and interrogated by soldiers. In addition, police and military units have often carried out anti-drug operations without effective safeguards against torture and other abuses. In August, police officers tortured to death a suspected drug trafficker in Nakhon Sawan province.

Since 1980, the United Nations Working Group on Enforced or Involuntary Disappearances has recorded 91 cases of enforced disappearance in Thailand, including of the prominent Muslim lawyer Somchai Neelapaijit in March 2004. In recent years, at least nine dissidents who fled persecution in Thailand have been forcibly disappeared in neighboring countries. In September, the working group raised concerns in its annual report about enforced disappearances in the context of transnational transfers between Thailand and neighboring countries.

Thailand is a state party to the Convention against Torture and Other Cruel, Inhuman or Degrading Treatment or Punishment and also signed, but did not ratify, the International Convention for the Protection of All Persons from Enforced Disappearance.

Lack of Accountability for State-Sponsored Abuses

Despite evidence showing that soldiers were responsible for most of the casualties during the 2010 political confrontations with the United Front for Democracy Against Dictatorship (the "Red Shirts") that left at least 99 dead and more than 2,000 injured, no military personnel or officials from the government of then-Prime Minister Abhisit Vejjajiva have been charged.

The government also has failed to pursue criminal investigations of extrajudicial killings related to anti-drug operations, especially the more than 2,800 killings that accompanied then-Prime Minister Thaksin Shinawatra's "war on drugs" in 2003.

Human Rights Defenders, NGO Law

The government has failed to fulfill its obligation to ensure human rights defenders can carry out their work in a safe and enabling environment.

On May 4, a gunman fatally shot Somsak Onchuenjit, a lawyer and land rights activist, in Trang province.

The police has made no progress in investigating violent attacks in 2019 targeting prominent democracy activists Sirawith Seritiwat, Anurak Jeantawanich, and Ekachai Hongkangwan.

Cover-up actions and shoddy police work continue to hamper the efforts to prosecute soldiers who shot dead ethnic Lahu activist Chaiyaphum Pasae in March 2017 in Chiang Mai province and park officials involved in the murder of ethnic Karen activist Porlajee "Billy" Rakchongcharoen in April 2014 in Phetchaburi province.

Despite the adoption of Thailand's National Action Plan on Business and Human Rights in 2019, Thai authorities have failed to protect human rights defenders from reprisals and end the abusive use of strategic lawsuits against public participation (SLAPP). Former National Human Rights Commissioner and Magsaysay Award winner Angkhana Neelapaijit is one of the many activists hit with such retaliatory lawsuits.

The government took no steps to reform the National Human Rights Commission of Thailand, which was downgraded by the Global Alliance of National Human Rights Institutions in 2016 because of its substandard selection process for commissioners and its lack of political independence.

In February 2021, the government approved in principle the Operations of Not-for-Profit Organizations Bill. The authorities would have broad discretion under the proposed law to arbitrarily deny registration of nongovernmental organizations (NGOs) and make them subject to criminal charges that include up to five years' imprisonment and a fine of THB100,000 (US$3,225).

In addition, NGOs will be required to seek prior approval from the minister of interior for activities supported with foreign funding. The bill also permits the authorities to enter NGO offices for inspection and to obtain electronic communications. After massive international criticism and a growing national campaign against the draft law, the government sent it for revisions by the Council of State, the government's legal arm.

Violence and Abuses in the Southern Border Provinces

The armed conflict in Thailand's Pattani, Yala, Narathiwat, and Songkhla provinces, which has resulted in more than 7,000 deaths since January 2004, subsided in the first half of 2021, partly due to the unilateral ceasefire announcement by Barisan Revolusi Nasional (BRN) to facilitate humanitarian assistance for people affected by the Covid-19 pandemic. The ceasefire ended when BRN issued a statement on July 20, criticizing the government for taking advantage of the situation to raid their strongholds. Insurgent attacks on military targets and civilians have since increased.

The government has not prosecuted members of its security forces responsible for torture, unlawful killings, and other abuses of ethnic Malay Muslims. In many cases, the authorities provided financial compensation to the victims or their families in exchange for their agreement not to speak out against the security forces or file criminal cases against officials. Thailand has not endorsed the Safe Schools Declaration.

Refugees, Asylum Seekers, and Migrant Workers

Thailand is not a party to the 1951 Refugee Convention or its 1967 protocol. The authorities continue to treat asylum seekers as illegal migrants subject to arrest, detention, and deportation.

In September, the Bangkok Criminal Court released Malaysian transgender activist Nur Sajat, who was recognized as a refugee by the UN High Commissioner for Refugees, on bail after she was arrested on illegal entry charges. The Malaysian authorities unsuccessfully attempted to extradite her from Thailand to face charges of insulting Islam for having dressed as a woman.

The authorities have made no progress in investigating the apparent enforced disappearance of exiled dissidents from Vietnam and Laos in Bangkok.

The government refused to let the UN refugee agency conduct status determinations for Lao Hmong, ethnic Rohingya, and Uighurs, and people from Myanmar and North Korea held in immigration detention. More than 50 Uighurs and several hundred Rohingya remain in indefinite detention in squalid conditions in immigration lockups.

Despite government-instituted reforms in the fishing industry, many migrant workers face forced labor, remain in debt bondage to recruiters, cannot change employers, and receive sub-minimum wages that are paid months late.

The government has failed to adequately provide migrant workers with internationally recognized worker rights, such as protection for freedom of association and collective bargaining. Migrant workers are barred in law from organizing and establishing labor unions, or serving as a government recognized labor union leader.

The government ordered factories, construction sites, markets, and worker dormitories to be temporarily sealed off during the pandemic, locking tens of thousands of migrant workers inside with limited access to essential supplies and health care.

Thammakaset Company Limited continues to retaliate against migrant workers, rights activists, and journalists who report on abusive labor conditions at its chicken farm in Lopburi province.

In July, Thailand was downgraded in the US Trafficking in Persons (TIP) Report from Tier 2 to the Tier 2 Watchlist for the first time in four years.

Gender Inequality

In February 2021, Thailand passed a law permitting abortion during the first 12 weeks of pregnancy. This reform is an important advance, but falls short of fully protecting pregnant people's reproductive rights. The criminal code continues to impose up to six months in jail and fines on those who seek abortions after 12 weeks of pregnancy if they cannot meet criteria set by the Medical Council of Thailand.

While Thailand enacted the Gender Equality Act in 2015, implementation remains problematic. There has been little progress in the parliamentary review of the Life Partnership Bill. If enacted, this law will be an important step towards recognizing the fundamental dignity of same-sex couples and providing them with important legal protections. The current draft, however, still needs improvements to comply with international standards on equality and non-discrimination. On September 28, the Constitutional Court postponed its ruling on whether the Civil and Commercial Code, which currently only recognizes marriage between a man and a woman, contravenes the constitution.

Despite being a popular destination for gender-affirming health care, Thailand continues to lack a procedure by which transgender people can change their legal gender.

Key International Actors

The US and like-minded countries raised concerns in 2021 about the government's proposed rights-violating NGO law and other major human rights issues, but did not publicly speak out. The United States, European Union, United Kingdom, Australia, and Canada have been instrumental in providing protection for refugees and asylum-seekers arrested by the authorities and at risk of refoulement.

The EU continued to take steps towards the resumption of negotiations for a bilateral free trade agreement with Thailand, which have been frozen since the 2014 coup.

In November, the UN Human Rights Council held the third cycle Universal Periodic Review (UPR) of Thailand. Key issues raised by member states and rights groups included torture, enforced disappearance, freedom of expression, association and peaceful assembly, refugees, the rights of older people, the death penalty, impunity for state-sponsored rights abuses, emergency powers, and national rights mechanisms.

Tunisia

In 2021, security forces continued to use violence to curb socio-economic protests in several parts of the country. In January, police in several cities beat demonstrators, detaining hundreds, many of them minors. Clashes with police in the city of Sbeitla led to the death of a young man. At least two more men died in Sfax and Sidi Hassine during clashes with the police.

On July 25, President Kais Saied announced that he was assuming exceptional powers, following months of political deadlock and a severe economic crisis exacerbated by Covid-19 pandemic.

Saied's measures encompassed suspending parliament, removing the immunity of parliamentarians, dismissing the prime minister, removing other high-level officials from their positions and assuming oversight of the office of the public prosecutor. On August 24, Saied expanded on the exceptional measures and announced their indefinite extension. On September 29, Saied appointed a prime minister and on October 11 swore in a cabinet of ministers that he had approved.

On July 24, President Saied extended until early 2022 the state of emergency that has been in effect almost continuously since it was first put in place in 2015 following a series of terrorist attacks.

Implementation of the Constitution

Successive parliaments have failed, since the adoption of the constitution in 2014, to put in place the Constitutional Court, a key independent judicial body tasked with ensuring respect of the constitution. Parliament could not reach the two-thirds majority needed to select its allotted share of judges. President Saied refused in April to sign a law that would have lowered the two-thirds threshold.

Freedom of Expression, Association and Assembly, and Conscience

Members of Tunisian security forces allegedly used excessive violence to suppress protesters denouncing economic hardship and demanding social justice and an end to police repression during nationwide protests that erupted on January 15. Police officers allegedly beat up protesters, arrested hundreds of them, including many minors, fired excessive teargas to break up protests, and attacked journalists. Haykel Rachdi, 21, from Sbeitla, died on January 18 after sustaining a head injury following police intervention during a protest.

On January 17, police in the Mourouj district near Tunis arrested 25-year-old student Ahmed Ghram at his home for Facebook posts criticizing police repression, impunity, and corrupt governance. Authorities accused Ghram of "inciting actions of chaos and disorder." Ghram spent 11 days in pretrial detention before he was acquitted and released.

Transitional Justice

More than one year after the publication on June 24, 2020, of the final report of the Truth and Dignity Commission, a state body established in 2013 to expose and investigate systematic human rights abuses that occurred in Tunisia over a five-decade period, the commission's recommendations to implement major institutional reforms remain unfulfilled. The commission's recommendations include establishing rehabilitation centers and support services for victims, ensuring effective judicial monitoring of places of detention, and allowing monitoring bodies regular and timely access to places of detention and direct interactions with the prisoners. The government has yet to fulfill its obligations under article 70 of 2013 transitional justice law, which requires it to put in place a plan to implement the recommendations of the commission.

Counterterrorism and Detention

At least 10 women with ties to suspected members of Islamic State (ISIS), released from Libyan prisons and handed over to authorities in Tunisia in March, remain in detention. Some have reported abuse in prison. Fourteen children were also repatriated, 12 of whom have been released to the care of relatives.

At least 16 more women and 19 children suspected of links to ISIS members remain detained in Tripoli's Mitiga prison, according to the Tunisian Observatory for Human Rights.

Women's Rights

Tunisian law discriminates against women in inheritance rights. At time of writing parliament had still not approved a bill supported by the late President Beji Caid Essebsi in 2018, while he was in office, to set equality in inheritance rights as the default. The bill would allow persons to opt out of the equality framework and choose instead to have their wealth distributed according to the previous legal framework.

During a parliamentary plenary session on June 30, 2021, two male MPs physically assaulted Abir Moussi, an opposition MP. She had been the target of a series of verbal and physical attacks in and outside parliament, including gender-specific epithets. The National Associative Coalition for the Elimination of Violence, the Tunisian Association of Democratic Women, and the Tunisian Human Rights League condemned the attacks as gender based.

In July, the Ministry of Women, Family, Children, and Seniors launched the website Toutes et tous Uni.e.s (Together against Violence), a platform providing information and support available in relation to gender equality, violence against women, protection of women, as well as violence against children. The website provides tools to help prevent violence against women and raise awareness of these issues.

Despite the 2017 violence against women law, which set out new protection mechanisms for survivors, reports show gaps in implementation of the law particularly in the way police deal with complaints by women of domestic violence. On May 9, 2021, Refka Cherni, a 26-year-old mother, was allegedly shot dead by her husband, an officer in the National Guard, two days after she went to her local police station to file a complaint against him for allegedly trying to strangle her. According to a spokesperson of Kef First Instance court the police neither arrested nor issued a restraining order against him, after Cherni had decided to drop her complaint.

Refugees and Migrants

Maritime operations to intercept or rescue migrants off the coast of Tunisia increased by 90 percent in the first six months of 2021, according to the International Organization for Migration. On September 26, Tunisian authorities intercepted at sea and expelled to the desert at the border with Libya around 100 sub-Saharan African migrants, including children, in violation of prohibitions of non-refoulement and collective expulsions under international and regional law. Due to the continued absence of a national legal framework on asylum, refugees and asylum seekers in Tunisia did not have formal legal status, limiting their ability to access certain services. However, refugees, asylum seekers and migrants were included in the national Covid-19 vaccination campaign that began in March 2021.

Sexual Orientation and Gender Identity

Tunisian police officers repeatedly targeted lesbian, gay, bisexual, transgender, and intersex (LGBTI) activists at general protests that took place in January in Tunis against deteriorating economic conditions and the government's handling of the pandemic and singled them out for mistreatment. Officers arbitrarily arrested LGBTI activists, assaulted them, and threatened several of them with violence including rape and murder. Some used social media to harass and "out" the identity of the activists by revealing private information such as their home addresses and phone numbers, and incited individuals to ridicule and harass them.

Authorities continued to prosecute and imprison presumed gay men under Article 230 of the penal code, which provides up to three years in prison for "sodomy." Damj Association for Justice and Equality, a Tunis-based LGBT group, said there were 1,458 convictions based on Article 230, ranging between four months to three years in prison, between 2011 and 2020.

On March 4, a Tunis court sentenced Rania Amdouni, a queer and feminist activist, to six months in prison and a fine for "insulting a public officer during the performance of his duty, "causing embarrassment and disruption," and "apparent drunkenness." Police arrested Amdouni on February 27 for shouting outside a police station, after officers had refused to register her complaint relating to repeated harassment to which she said police officers had subjected her on the street and online. On March 17, the Court of Appeal in Tunis upheld her conviction and suspended her prison sentence. After her release, Amdouni obtained asylum in France.

Turkey

The authoritarian and highly centralized presidential government of Recep Tayyip Erdoğan has set back Turkey's human rights record by decades, targeting perceived government critics and political opponents, profoundly undermining the independence of the judiciary, and hollowing out democratic institutions. Turkey withdrew from the Council of Europe Convention on Preventing and Combating Violence against Women and Domestic Violence, known as the Istanbul Convention, a major reversal for women's rights.

Freedom of Expression, Association, and Assembly

While most news outlets are owned by companies with close government links, independent media in Turkey mainly operate via online platforms but are subject to regular removal of content or prosecution for news coverage critical of senior government figures and members of President Erdoğan's family or deemed to constitute an offense under Turkey's highly restrictive Anti-Terror Law. At time of writing, 58 journalists and media workers were in prison or serving sentences for terrorism offenses because of their journalistic work or association with media.

In November, on the grounds that it restricted reporting and media freedom, Turkey's top administrative court halted the implementation of an Interior Ministry April circular banning citizens or journalists from recording videos or taking photos of police officers on duty.

After strong criticism on social media of the authorities' response to wildfires in Turkey's forested Mediterranean region, the government signaled plans to further tighten restrictions on social media by making "disinformation" via social media an offence punishable with a prison sentence of between two to five years. No legal amendment had been made at time of writing. Thousands of people every year already face arrest and prosecution for their social media posts, typically charged with defamation, insulting the president, or spreading terrorist propaganda.

Major social media platforms such as YouTube, Facebook, and Twitter complied with a 2020 legal amendment requiring them to set up offices in Turkey, raising concerns that they may in future be forced to increase their compliance with government censorship in order to avoid heavy fines and other penalties.

Provincial authorities selectively used Covid-19 as a pretext to ban peaceful protests by students, workers, political opposition parties, and women's and lesbian, gay, bisexual and transgender (LGBT) people's rights activists. President Erdoğan's appointment of an unelected rector to the prestigious Boğaziçi University sparked protests, which were met with violent police crackdown and prosecutions against dozens of student protesters.

Rollbacks on Women's and LGBT Rights

Turkey is the first country to have withdrawn from the Istanbul Convention. The move in March drew widespread criticism internationally, and saw protests by women's rights groups. It spells a major reversal for efforts to combat gender-based violence and promote women's rights in Turkey. Government officials justified the withdrawal and attempted to appeal to conservative voters with the specious claim that the Convention "normalizes homosexuality." Hundreds of women are murdered annually in Turkey and reported incidents of domestic violence remain high.

The government banned the annual LGBT Pride march in Istanbul for the seventh successive year and police violently dispersed and detained protesters. Senior government officials have on several occasions attacked and encouraged discrimination against LGBT people in their political speeches.

Human Rights Defenders

The four-year detention and ongoing trial of Osman Kavala, a leading figure in civil society, exemplified the enormous pressure on human rights groups and other nongovernmental groups (NGOs) critical of the government. Kavala is on trial on baseless charges in connection with the 2013 Gezi Park protests and the July 2016 failed coup. Turkey has flouted a European Court of Human Rights' judgment ordering his immediate release on grounds of insufficient evidence. The judgment found that Kavala's detention sought to silence him as a human rights defender.

Authorities continued to use terrorism and defamation charges to harass rights defenders, and to violate their right to assembly. The Court of Cassation has yet to review the 2020 convictions for membership of a terrorist organization and aiding and abetting terrorism of Taner Kılıç, the former chair of Amnesty International Turkey, and three others for their participation in a human rights education workshop.

On 15 February, an Istanbul court convicted Eren Keskin, co-chair of the Human Rights Association, on charges of "membership of a terrorist organization" on the basis of her role as co-editor-in-chief of the pro-Kurdish *Özgür Gündem* newspaper. She has appealed. On March 19, Keskin's co-chair, Öztürk Türk-doğan, was briefly detained and remains under investigation for "membership of a terrorist organization" with a travel ban. Two activists running the Diyarbakır-based Rosa Women's Association have appealed convictions on the same charge and others in the association face continuing prosecution.

In January, the Law on Preventing Financing of Proliferation of Weapons of Mass Destruction came into force. Although Turkey has justified the law as an effort to bring the country into compliance with binding United Nations Security Council resolutions to prevent financing of terrorism and weapons proliferation, the law instead furnishes the Interior Ministry with greater powers to target NGOs' legitimate and lawful activities and the right to association of their members.

Torture and Ill-Treatment in Custody, Enforced Disappearances

There was little evidence to suggest prosecutors made progress in investigating the rising allegations of torture and ill-treatment in police custody and prison reported over the past five years. Few such allegations result in prosecution of the security forces, and a pervasive culture of impunity persists.

In two May 2021 rulings, the Constitutional Court found violations of the prohibition on ill-treatment and ordered new investigations into complaints that prosecutors had dismissed at the time they were lodged in 2016. One concerned the complaint of torture and rape in police custody lodged by a male teacher A. A. in the town of Afyon, the second a complaint by a male teacher E. B. in Antalya alleging police tortured him in custody requiring him to undergo emergency surgery.

No progress was reported in the prosecutor's investigation of the case of Osman Şiban and Servet Turgut, two Kurdish men detained by military personnel in their southeast village in September 2020, taken away in a helicopter, and later found by their families seriously injured in hospital. Turgut died of his injuries.

In the case of the June 5 death in police custody in Istanbul of private security officer Birol Yıldırım, weeks after media aired camera footage of police beating him, a deputy superintendent was detained and is on trial with 11 other police officers.

An investigation into the full circumstances behind the death on February 19 of Kadir Aktar,17, at Maltepe Children's Prison, continues. Reported by the media as a suicide, medical records present substantial evidence that Aktar was ill-treated in police custody.

Abductions and enforced disappearances continue to be reported and are not investigated properly. Those disappeared for the longest periods have been individuals the authorities allege have links with the movement run by US-based cleric Fethullah Gülen, which Turkey deems a terrorist organization responsible for the July 2016 military coup attempt. Hüseyin Galip Küçüközyiğit, a former civil servant, disappeared in Ankara on December 29, 2020. On July 14, authorities informed his family that he was held in pretrial detention. There had been no information about his whereabouts for over seven months. Yusuf Bilge Tunç, another former civil servant, remained missing after he disappeared in August 2019.

Turkish authorities continued to seek the extradition of alleged Gülen movement supporters, many of them teachers, from countries around the world. Some countries that complied with Turkey's requests bypassed legal procedures and judicial review and colluded in abductions, enforced disappearances, and the illegal transfer of individuals. Two such cases in 2021 were the abduction on May 31 and rendition to Turkey from Kyrgyzstan of Orhan İnandı, a director of schools in Kyrgyzstan; and Turkey's announcement on May 31 that it had "captured" and transferred to Turkey Selahaddin Gülen, a Turkish national and registered asylum seeker in Kenya.

Some individuals active in leftist or Kurdish politics reported that plain-clothed security personnel abducted and detained them in undisclosed sites for shorter periods. One such case was that of Gökhan Güneş, whose complaint to the prosecutor of being abducted in Istanbul on January 20, interrogated, tortured, and released on January 26 resulted in a September decision that there was no case to pursue. His lawyers have appealed.

Kurdish Conflict and Crackdown on Opposition

Occasional armed clashes between the military and the armed Kurdistan Workers' Party (PKK) continued in rural areas of Turkey's eastern and southeastern regions although Turkey has concentrated its military campaign including drone strikes in the Kurdistan Region of Iraq, where the PKK bases are located. In February, the Turkish military reported that an operation to rescue 13 soldiers and police officers held hostage by the PKK in northern Iraq had resulted in the PKK killing the 13.

In 2021, the Erdogan ruling coalition intensified its ongoing campaign to criminalize the legitimate political activities of the opposition Peoples' Democratic Party (HDP), which won 11.7 percent of the national vote in 2018 parliamentary elections. The government refuses to distinguish between the HDP and the PKK. There were physical attacks on HDP offices, most notably in June in the western province of Izmir where a gunman shot dead party member Deniz Poyraz.

Scores of former HDP politicians including mayors are held as remand prisoners or are serving sentences after being convicted of terrorism offenses on the basis of their legitimate non-violent political activities, speeches, and social media postings. In one such case beginning in May, dozens of current and former HDP politicians, including the jailed former co-chairs Selahattin Demirtaş and Figen Yüksekdağ, stood trial in a new proceeding for their alleged role in violent protests on October 6-8, 2014, that led to 37 deaths. The earlier ongoing case files against Demirtaş and Yüksekdağ have been combined with this case. The trial was ongoing at time of writing.

In June, the Constitutional Court accepted an indictment filed by the Court of Cassation chief prosecutor to permanently shut down the HDP and impose a five-year ban from political activity on 451 politicians and party officials. The case was ongoing at time of writing.

HDP MP Ömer Faruk Gergerlioğlu was released from prison and reinstated to his parliamentary seat in July after the Constitutional Court found that a conviction for a social media post resulting in his expulsion from parliament in March and imprisonment in April violated his rights.

Justifying its January 2018 and October 2019 military incursions into areas of northeast Syria as part of an effort to combat PKK affiliates, Turkey continues to occupy territory and has illegally transferred Syrian nationals to Turkey to face trial on terrorism charges that could lead to life imprisonment.

Refugees, Asylum Seekers, and Migrants

Turkey continues to host the world's largest number of refugees, around 3.7 million from Syria granted temporary protection status, and over 400,000 from Afghanistan, Iraq, and other non-European countries, who under Turkish law cannot be fully recognized as refugees.

Continuing its policy of securing its borders against the entry of more asylum seekers and migrants, Turkey continued building a wall in 2021 along its eastern border with Iran, and summarily pushing back Afghans and others apprehended attempting to cross the border.

There have been signs of a rise in racist and xenophobic attacks against foreigners. On August 10, groups of youths attacked workplaces and homes of Syrians in a neighborhood in Ankara a day after a fight during which a Syrian youth allegedly stabbed two Turkish youths, killing one. Two Syrian youths are on trial for murder. The prosecutor's investigation into dozens of youths for damaging property, theft, and other crimes continues. Opposition politicians have made speeches that fuel anti-refugee sentiment and suggest that Syrians should be returned to war-torn Syria.

There were reports, including by the Turkish coast guard, that migrants attempting to cross into Greece from Turkey through sea and land borders were summarily and violently pushed back by Greek security forces.

Key International Actors

Turkey has a troubled political relationship with the EU, mitigated by a transactional relationship on issues such as migration. Turkey's accession process to the EU is at a standstill. The EU provides financial support to Turkey in return for restrictions on entry of refugees and migrants to the bloc. The European Council in June reiterated its concerns regarding rule of law and fundamental rights in Turkey, without making human rights a priority in the relationship.

Turkey's failure to implement binding European Court of Human Rights judgments calling for the release of rights defender Osman Kavala and Kurdish politician Selahattin Demirtaş has set back its relationship with the Council of Europe. In its September session, the Council of Europe's Committee of Ministers reiterated its call for the immediate release of both men and decided that a failure to release Osman Kavala by the December session would spell notification of infringement proceedings against Turkey, a sanction method involving further application to the European Court only used against a Council of Europe member state once before.

The Council of Europe's commissioner for human rights, the UN Committee on the Elimination of Discrimination against Women, UN human rights special rapporteurs and the UN Human Rights Office have criticized Turkey for withdrawing from the Istanbul Convention.

The deep crisis in Turkish-US relations continued under the Biden administration. Multiple reasons include Turkey's purchase of Russian S-400 missiles, the presence on US soil of Fethullah Gülen, and US support for Kurdish-led forces in northeast Syria. For the first time, the US State Department added Turkey to its 2021 Trafficking in Persons list of countries implicated in using child soldiers in connection with its backing for a Syrian armed opposition group. The Biden administration also formally recognized the Armenian genocide committed by the Ottoman government 100 years ago.

In October, Turkey ratified the Paris Agreement, the international treaty on climate change adopted in Paris in December 2015, while also committing to a goal to reach net zero emissions by 2053. As one of the world's top 20 greenhouse gas emitters, Turkey is contributing to the climate crisis that is taking a mounting toll on human rights around the globe.

Turkmenistan

Turkmenistan continued to be one of the world's most oppressive and closed countries, ruled by authoritarian President Gurbanguly Berdymukhamedov, his relatives, and associates. Authorities failed to address the impact of the country's multi-year economic crisis on people's food security and other basic needs.

The country remained among the few countries without a single registered Covid-19 case, despite credible reports clearly indicating otherwise. Authorities tightly control access to information, severely restrict media and religious freedoms, and allow no independent monitoring groups. Independent activists, including in exile, and their relatives were subject to government reprisals. Dozens of people remained victims of enforced disappearance. The government continued to interfere with people's right to freedom of movement.

Covid-19 Response

Despite authorities' refusal to acknowledge Covid-19 cases in Turkmenistan, media outlets reported that hospitals are overwhelmed with patients with Covid-19 symptoms and there is a serious shortage of drugs to treat them. The number of Covid-19 deaths is unknown. Turkmen.news, a Netherlands-based outlet, created an online memorial to 55 people who died of Covid-19 like symptoms. The government-imposed lockdowns in some districts in August, expanded them in September throughout the country, and

continued to threaten and jail people for openly demanding access to information about the spread of Covid-19. The authorities continued to require the burning of harmala plants in such public spaces as hospitals, shops, and the like, alleging, with no evidence, that the smoke has disinfecting properties.

Meanwhile, the government has taken measures to prevent Covid-19. Since July, vaccination is mandatory for all citizens above 18, except those who have specified medical contraindications, such as a history of anaphylaxis, or are pregnant.

Although no formal punishment was introduced for refusing vaccination, authorities have threatened people who refuse vaccination with criminal charges for malicious refusal of treatment for an infectious disease, which is punishable by a maximum two-year prison term, higher if there are aggravating circumstances. In August, Radio Azatlyk, the Turkmen-language service of the US government-funded Radio Liberty, reported that authorities in Lebap region fined people and threatened to withhold pensions for refusing to be vaccinated. Police fined people for not wearing masks, and unvaccinated civil servants were threatened with dismissal. Authorities occasionally imposed internal travel bans on people above 50 and restrictions on prison visits, parcels and correspondence, citing Covid-19 related quarantine measures. As of August 29, 52 percent of the population has been fully vaccinated. No data has been reported since then.

Food Insecurity

Turkmen authorities did not acknowledge a rise in poverty due to the pandemic and the shrinking availability of affordable food in the country and failed to ensure an adequate standard of living and the right to food to economically vulnerable groups.

In some parts of the country, state-subsidized food staples were unavailable for months at a time. Meanwhile, the demand for state-subsidized food has increased. Authorities threatened and detained shoppers who vented their frustration in long lines outside supermarkets.

The Turkmen Initiative for Human Rights, a Vienna-based group, found the authorities' policy of delivering subsidized foods to households, introduced in spring 2021, proved inefficient, leaving some households with no subsidized food. In-store purchases of subsidized food were subject to heavily staggered schedules.

Civil Society

The government does not allow any vestige of independent civil society expression. Nongovernmental organizations (NGOs) are prohibited unless registered, and the registration procedure is burdensome. International human rights NGOs are denied access. Activists face a constant threat of government reprisal. Turkmen authorities force dissidents and activists in exile into silence, including by targeting their relatives.

In September 2020, Nurgeldy Halykov, 26, a freelance correspondent with the independent Turkmen.news, was sentenced to a four-year prison term on fabricated fraud charges. Police arrested Halykov in July 2020, shortly after Turkmen.news published a photo it received from him of the World Health Organization's (WHO) delegation during its 2020 Covid-19-related visit to Turkmenistan.

Activist Murad Dushemov was fined and jailed in two separate incidents after publicly questioning the authorities' claim about the absence of Covid-19 in Turkmenistan and refusing to comply with Covid-19 related rules. He received a four-year prison term on trumped up extortion and battery charges stemming from an alleged fight with a cellmate during his 15-day jail sentence, which activists said was a provocation.

Turkmen authorities repeatedly retaliated against the Turkmenistan-based relatives of Turkmens living abroad who criticize the government. In May, security officials questioned and threatened a 14-year-old boy in retaliation for the outspoken views of his uncle, Rozybai Jumamuradov, a Turkmen activist in exile. In March, unidentified people called the boy's family and threatened to kill them unless they ceased communicating with Jumamuradov. The Turkmenistan Helsinki Foundation (THF), a human rights organization in exile, and the Memorial Human Rights Center, an independent Russian group, reported in July that Turkmen authorities repeatedly harassed and intimidated Aziza Khemraeva in retaliation for the activities of her brother based in Turkey, who actively criticizes the Turkmen government online. In October, the two organizations reported more incidents of such harassment, including Turkmen security services pressuring Tazegul Ovezova to convince her son, a blogger living in Turkey, to end his activism.

On August 1 in Istanbul, Turkey, unknown individuals attacked a group of Turkmen migrant workers, preventing them from holding a rally at the Turkmen consulate there. Turkish police briefly detained about 10 Turkmen nationals who attempted to participate in the protest. Unidentified men beat and stabbed Aziz Mammedov, after he posted online a video of the attack. Three men lured blogger Farhad Durdyev into the consulate, where several people, including diplomats, beat and threatened him for several hours. Durdyev was released several hours later, after Turkish police intervened.

Pygambergeldy Allaberdyev, a lawyer, sentenced in September 2020 on trumped up charges to a six-year prison term for alleged connections with activists of the protest movement abroad remained imprisoned. Mansur Mengelov, an activist for Baloch minority rights, continued to serve his 22-year prison term, handed down in 2012, on bogus narcotics charges.

The fate and whereabouts of Omriuazk Omarkulyev, who had created an informal Turkmen students' club in Turkey, remain unclear. In 2018 Omarkulyev went missing after authorities had lured him into into returning to Turkmenistan and then banned him from returning to Turkey. The authorities claimed he was performing his obligatory military service, but independent sources reported that he was sentenced to 20 years in prison on unknown charges. In October, a government spokesperson publicly stated that Omarkulyev finished his military service and was living with his family. However, this could not be independently confirmed.

Freedom of Media and Information

Turkmenistan has one of the world's worst media freedom records. All print and electronic media are tightly controlled or owned by the state. Authorities routinely suppress independent voices and severely retaliate against Turkmen nationals who report for foreign outlets.

Internet access in Turkmenistan is highly censored. Many websites and applications are blocked. Authorities closely monitor all means of communication. Although Turkmen law does not explicitly ban Virtual Private Networks (VPNs), it bans "uncertified" encryption programs and criminalizes "deliberately providing illegal services that provide technical programs" online, for which the maximum penalty is seven years in prison. The authorities systematically block VPNs and intimidate and penalize people who allegedly use them. Azatlyk reported in April that police in eastern Turkmenistan issued warnings to and fined at least two high school teachers because about a dozen of their students were allegedly suspected to have been using VPNs on their mobile phones.

In January police confiscated mobiles of 10th and 11th graders in one of Ashgabat's schools, reportedly following security services' orders to check their photo and video content, and websites accessed. Azatlyk reported that at least one parent was able to obtain the return of his child's smartphone after paying an administrative fine.

In May, the Turkmen Initiative for Human Rights (TIHR), an exiled group, and the International Partnership for Human Rights (IPHR) reported that between December 2020 and March 2021 internet users were summoned, questioned, and intimidated by security services for using VPNs and in March authorities ramped up efforts to block VPN access.

In May, TIHR reported that its website was subject to distributed denial-of-service (DDOS) attack.

Freedom of Movement

Turkmen authorities impose arbitrary travel bans on various groups of people and violate people's right to freedom of movement.

In July, Radio Azatlyk reported that authorities in one region orally ordered public sector workers to turn their passports over to migration authorities and stated they would not issue or renew passports for these workers.

The Turkmen government has not responded to a 2019 United Nations Human Rights Committee (UNHRC) request for information regarding the case of the Ruzimatov family, relatives of a former official who has emigrated. Authorities have banned the family from traveling abroad since 2003.

The government's continued refusal to renew expiring passports continued to deprive many Turkmen citizens living abroad of their right to freedom of movement and interfered with their ability to obtain legal status in host countries, exposing them to the risk of a range of human rights violations. Following June amendments to the migration law, authorities began extending the validity of passports with an expiration date of January 1, 2020, through December 30, 2022. The extension applies mainly to people stranded due to the Covid-19 pandemic and does not address the needs of many Turkmen emigrants whose passports have expired and who have no plans to return to Turkmenistan.

Freedom of Religion

Turkmenistan bans unregistered congregations or religious groups, and registration requirements are cumbersome. Unregistered activity is forbidden and punishable by administrative penalties and authorities often use pretexts to criminally prosecute people for their presumed religious affiliations or practices. The government censors all religious literature.

Forum 18, an independent religious freedom group, reported in May that 16 men, all Jehovah's Witnesses, jailed for conscientious objection, had been amnestied. Dozens of Muslims, including Bahrom Saparov, continue to serve long prison terms on politically motivated religious "extremism" charges related to their religious practice and affiliations.

In January 2021 police in Lebap region detained about 10 Muslims allegedly for "following their [Muslim] faith too closely," forcibly shaved off one man's beard, forced him to drink alcohol, and fined him on unknown grounds. In a separate incident also in January, 10 other Muslims who had gathered to pray, were detained by police allegedly for violation of lockdown restrictions, although no lockdown restrictions were in place at the time.

Political Prisoners, Enforced Disappearances, Torture, Rule of Law

Authorities continued to conceal the fate and whereabouts of dozens of people, who disappeared in Turkmen prisons following convictions on what appear to be politically motivated charges. The exact number of political prisoners remains unknown due to the lack of transparency in the justice system and closed nature of trials in sensitive cases. The government imprisons people who expose injustices, incompetence and corruption. Torture and ill-treatment in custody persist.

Dozens of prisoners who have been denied access to family and lawyers, remained victims of enforced disappearance or held incommunicado, following convictions in the late 1990s and early 2000s. The international Prove They Are Alive campaign, which seeks to end enforced disappearances in Turkmenistan, estimates that at least 120 people have been forcibly disappeared. The fate and whereabouts of at least nine disappeared persons whose terms expired or were scheduled to expire in 2021, remain unknown.

Azat Isakov went missing in Turkmenistan after Russian authorities returned him to Turkmenistan in October. Isakov, who had been living in Russia, actively criticized the Turkmen government and was presumed to have been taken into custody upon arrival in Turkmenistan. At time of writing, there was no information about his fate or whereabouts.

In July, police arrested Khursanai Ismatullaeva, a doctor, one day after a human rights defender participating in a European Parliament (EP) panel discussed her unsuccessful efforts to get reinstated after being unfairly fired from her job. In August, a court sentenced her to nine years in prison on presumably bogus fraud charges.

Political dissident Gulgeldy Annaniazov, who should have been released in March 2019 after serving his full 11-year sentence on politically motivated charges, remains on a five-year term of forced internal exile. His health has significantly deteriorated.

Sexual Orientation and Gender Identity

Consensual same-sex conduct between men is a criminal offense under Turkmen law, punishable by a maximum two-year prison sentence. In September, according to Turkmen News, police in Turkmenabat detained approximately 20 men suspected of having sex with other men. In August, police in Turkmenabat detained a well-known barber and stylist in a similar raid and allegedly tried to compel him to name other men believed to be gay. As of end of October 2021 they remained in custody.

Key International Actors

In July, the World Bank approved a US$20 million loan to the Turkmen government for "preparedness against the health and social risks of the COVID-19 pandemic." The loan is intended to, among other things, "provid[e] COVID-19-related care to all citizens, including vulnerable population groups." There is no information available about how the bank will ensure people get Covid-19-related care while the authorities deny any Covid-19 infections in the country.

During its annual human rights dialogue with Turkmenistan in June, the European Union stressed the need for concrete improvements in human rights and the importance of the full independence of the Ombudsperson's office and called for strengthened cooperation with the United Nations to tackle enforced disappearances. Ratification of a bilateral partnership and cooperation agreement between the EU and Turkmenistan remains pending since 2010 due to Turkmenistan's poor human rights record.

The US State Department redesignated Turkmenistan as "a country of particular concern" for religious freedom. In June, the US State Department's Trafficking in Persons Report re-designated Turkmenistan a Tier 3 country, for its insufficient efforts to eliminate human trafficking. A June statement by the US mission to the Organization for Security and Co-operation in Europe (OSCE) expressed concerns about 'the severe restrictions of human rights and fundamental freedoms...' and about enforced disappearances.

Despite a standing invitation of the Turkmen government since 2018 to all UN special procedures to visit the country, 15 United Nations special procedures have requested, but have not been granted, access to the country.

Uganda

There was a marked deterioration in Uganda's human rights environment over the past year. President Yoweri Museveni was re-elected in January 2021 in a general election marred by widespread abuses. Security forces arbitrarily arrested and beat opposition supporters and journalists, killed protesters, and disrupted opposition rallies.

Shortly before the elections, the government shut down the internet for five days, and restricted access to social media sites including Twitter and YouTube for a month. The authorities indefinitely blocked access to Facebook after the network announced it had taken down a network of accounts and pages linked to the government.

The authorities in Uganda restricted right to freedom of movement and assembly, in particular for political opposition leaders, and violated rights to freedoms of association and expression, as security forces beat and at times arbitrarily detained journalists and opposition members.

Freedom of Expression and Assembly

Two days before the January 14, 2021, elections, the Uganda Communications Commission ordered internet service providers to block social media access. The next day, the government shut down internet access across the country for five days. The authorities restored partial access to social media websites, excluding Facebook, in February. During election campaigns, the authorities restricted media coverage of opposition party candidates, in some instances beating and shooting at journalists with rubber bullets.

In February 2021, military police beat at least 10 journalists covering opposition presidential candidate, Robert Kyagulanyi, as he delivered a petition to the United Nations Office of the High Commissioner for Human Rights in Kampala over the abuses against his supporters. The next day, the army announced that a military court had sentenced seven members of the military police to two months detention in a military facility but provided no details on its investigations or the military trial.

Security forces conducted a spate of abductions and arrests of opposition supporters, government critics, and other people for allegedly participating in protests over the November 18, 2020 arrest of Kyagulanyi in Luuka, Eastern Uganda. On March 4, 2021, Internal Affairs Minister Jeje Odongo presented a list to parliament of 177 people in military detention who had been arrested between November 18, 2020, and February 8, 2021, allegedly for participating in the protests as well as for being in "possession of military stores," and "meetings planning post-election violence." On March 8, in a public letter to the media, President Yoweri Museveni said that 50 people were being held by the Special Forces Command, a unit of the Ugandan army, for "treasonable acts of elements of the opposition."

In May 2021, police detained 24-year-old law student Michael Muhima for a tweet parodying the police spokesperson, charged him with "offensive communication," and denied him access to lawyers or family for five days before he was released on bail.

The government in June cancelled a social media tax requiring users of WhatsApp, Twitter, and Facebook, among other sites, to pay a daily fee of 200 Ugandan Shillings (US$0.05) that had been in force since 2018, and replaced it with a general 12 per cent tax on the purchase of internet data, further restricting access to many Ugandans.

Sexual Orientation and Gender Identity

Uganda's penal code punishes "carnal knowledge" between people of the same gender with up to life in prison. On May 3, Parliament approved the 2021 Sexual Offenses Bill which proposed to criminalize all sexual relations between people of the same gender, anal sex between people of any gender, and sex work. President Museveni later declined to sign the Bill and returned it to Parliament on August 17 for reconsideration.

In May 2021, police raided a private celebration at the Happy Family Youth shelter in Wakiso District and arrested 44 people, initially accusing them of holding a same-sex wedding, then charged them with "negligent acts likely to spread infection of disease." Police subjected 17 of the accused to forced anal examinations. A court dismissed the charges against them on September 23 following the prosecution's failure to present witnesses.

Women's Rights

In August 2021, following a petition from women's rights organizations, lawyers and activists, the Constitutional Court annulled the 2014 Anti-Pornography Act. The Act criminalized the sharing of nude photos and in some instances, was used to arrest women whose intimate photos were leaked online. The Court also disbanded the nine-member Pornography Control Committee, set up in 2017 to enforce the law.

Arrest and Harassment of Opposition Members and Supporters

In the leadup to Uganda's January 2021 elections, security forces beat and arrested scores of opposition supporters and journalists, killed dozens, and disrupted opposition rallies. Presidential candidates, Patrick Amuriat, of the Forum for Democratic Change and, Robert Kyagulanyi of the National Unity Platform were among those arrested.

On January 8, police charged 49 National Unity Platform supporters with alleged possession of ammunition belonging to the Ugandan army. On January 9, security officials surrounded Kyagulanyi's home and prevented people from entering or exiting for days, including the United States Ambassador to Uganda, Natalie E. Brown. Media reported that soldiers beat Francis Zaake, an opposition member of parliament, when he attempted to visit Kyagulanyi. On January 18, security forces blocked access to Kyagulanyi's party's head office in Kampala, allegedly to "counter any plans to violent demonstrations and mass riots."

Attacks on Civil Society

The authorities restricted the work of activists and civil society groups. On election day, January 14, police arrested over 20 people working with Citizen Watch-IT and the Women's Democracy Network, election monitoring groups, for allegedly operating a "parallel tallying center."

On February 17, 2021, the government indefinitely suspended the Democratic Governance Facility (DGF) in Uganda, a European Union donor fund for non-governmental groups, saying the government lacked oversight over the fund.

Ugandan authorities on August 20, 2021, announced, without prior notification, that they had halted the activities of 54 civil society groups, including human rights and election monitoring organizations. The National Bureau for Non-governmental Organizations, a state regulatory body, only started notifying the groups hours or even days after the announcement.

Forced Evictions

Following years of forced evictions carried out by security forces in Apaa, Northern Uganda, thousands of eligible voters were unable to participate in the 2021 elections because Uganda's Electoral Commission updated the national voters' register, but excluded Apaa.

On August 12, President Museveni met with nine leaders from Acholi sub-region to discuss Apaa. During the meeting the leaders agreed to establish a commission of inquiry into the evictions, the land dispute, how long people have lived in the area, and review the process of the government's 2002 decision to turn Apaa into forestry and wildlife reserves. In the same meeting, Museveni directed the environment minister to evict people from Zoka forest, in the north of Apaa, claiming it is a forestry reserve.

Prosecutions for Serious Crimes

On February 4, 2021, International Criminal Court (ICC) judges convicted Dominic Ongwen, a former leader of the Lord's Resistance Army, on 61 counts of war crimes and crimes against humanity. The crimes include attacks on the civilian population, murder, torture, persecution, forced marriage, forced pregnancy, sexual slavery, enslavement, rape, pillage, destruction of property, and recruitment and use of children under the age of 15 to participate in the hostilities. On May 6, ICC judges imposed a 25-year-sentence on Ongwen, the first conviction and sentencing of an LRA leader.

Jospeh Kony, the LRA's founding leader and the only living remaining ICC suspect of LRA crimes, remains a fugitive.

Wider accountability for crimes committed during the 25-year conflict in northern Uganda remains limited. Abuses by the Ugandan armed forces during the conflict, including torture, rape, arbitrary detention, unlawful killings, and forced displacement of citizens, have rarely been prosecuted. The Ugandan army has said that soldiers who committed these abuses have been prosecuted and convicted but has not provided details of such cases.

Uganda's International Crimes Division, which was established in 2008, has pursued only one case involving crimes committed in northern Uganda, against LRA commander Thomas Kwoyelo. The trial has proceeded in fits and starts, suffering many delays. Some former LRA fighters, including senior commanders, were integrated into the Ugandan military without investigation into crimes they may have committed in the LRA.

In December 2020, the ICC prosecutor's office concluded an assessment of a 2016 police and military operation in western Uganda in which about 150 people were killed. The prosecutor's office found Ugandan security forces committed murder and used indiscriminate and disproportionate force but was unable to conclude that the acts took place as part of a policy, a necessary element for the ICC's jurisdiction. There has been no domestic accountability for the crimes.

Children's Rights

To stop the spread of Covid-19, President Museveni ordered the closure of all schools on March 18, 2020, affecting more than 15 million students. Schools were partially open for university, secondary and primary candidate classes in 2021, but largely remained closed since the pandemic's start in 2020. On September 22, President Museveni announced the reopening of post-secondary institutions in November 2021, and other schools at the beginning of January 2022.

Uganda adopted universal primary education in 1997 and universal secondary education in 2007, abolishing tuition fees and prohibiting schools from introducing other costs that could create barriers for students from low-income households and those living in poverty. In practice, many public schools still levy fees.

Prohibitive school fees and the under-resourcing of public primary and secondary schools are significant barriers for many children.

Child labor rates rose in 2020 as the economic impact of the Covid-19 pandemic, together with school closures and inadequate government assistance, pushed children into exploitative and dangerous work. Working children told Human Rights Watch that in addition to helping their family during the Covid-19 pandemic, they also hoped to save money to cover school fees once schools reopened.

Ukraine

The armed conflict in the Donbas region of eastern Ukraine continued to pose a grave threat to civilian safety and impede access to food, adequate housing, and schools. Covid-19 pandemic-related travel restrictions, introduced by Russia-backed armed groups and the government, blocked access to health care and pensions and worsened hardships for the already impoverished population of the conflict-affected Donbas.

Armed groups forcibly disappeared, tortured, and arbitrarily detained civilians and repeatedly denied some of them access to urgent medical care.

A bill reforming Ukraine's notoriously abusive security service advanced in parliament despite human rights concerns.

Members of groups advocating hate and discrimination continued putting ethnic minorities, lesbian, gay, bisexual, and transgender (LGBT) people and rights activists at risk, subjecting them to physical attacks and hate speech.

Armed Conflict

A spike in hostilities, despite the ceasefire, led to civilian casualties. According to United Nations human rights monitoring mission reports, in the first six months of 2021, 56 civilians were killed or injured by shelling, small arms weapons fire, mine-related incidents, and unmanned aerial vehicles (UAV) strikes.

Russia-backed armed groups in Donetska and Luhanska regions continued to torture, arbitrarily detain, and forcibly disappear civilians and to deny them access to medical care. As of July, an estimated 300-400 conflict-related detainees were being held by these armed groups.

There were no reports of prolonged arbitrary detention by the Ukrainian authorities in 2021. The investigation into alleged grave abuses in unofficial detention facilities by Ukraine's secret services in 2016 remained open and has borne no results.

Excessive and arbitrary restrictions imposed by armed groups in Donestska and Luhanska regions continue to unduly burden civilians. The Ukrainian government ended most Covid-19-related restrictions in June. In welcome moves, in August the authorities temporarily suspended the requirement for pensioners residing in nongovernment- controlled areas to regularly confirm displaced person registration and in September, announced plans to introduce remote identity verification. If enacted, the latter step would help address discrimination against pensioners residing in nongovernment-controlled areas, in particular helping to eliminate barriers that pensioners who cannot travel due to limited mobility have faced accessing their pensions since 2014.

Lack of access to quality health care remained a key concern for conflict-affected parts of eastern Ukraine, where approximately 1.3 million people continued to face difficulties in accessing essential health services. Women have been disproportionately impacted, due in part to limited options for maternal and other sexual and reproductive healthcare in these regions, the poor quality of these services, and traditional gender roles that leave women with little time and few resources to prioritize and address their own health.

Rule of Law, Administration of Justice

In October 2020, the Constitutional Court of Ukraine stripped the national anti-corruption agency of its essential powers, effectively dismantling the system of publicly accessible asset declarations. The ruling was followed by President Zelensky's bill to terminate the Constitutional Court's powers. Zelensky withdrew the bill in January.

The trial of four defendants over the 2014 downing of Malaysia Airlines flight MH17 advanced to evidentiary hearings.

An October 2020 draft law meant to reform the Security Service of Ukraine progressed in parliament, despite granting the agency overly broad powers without sufficient human rights safeguards.

The criminal case involving the 2014 abduction and torture of two Maidan protestors, which resulted in the death of one of them progressed in April, with two men arrested and charged. Also in April, a district court sentenced a leader of the responsible group to nine years in prison. The group, known as "titushky" consisted of anti-Maidan activists recruited by law enforcement to attack protesters during Maidan protests. In December 2020, the State Bureau of Investigations indicted a Maidan activist on homicide charges in connection with the February 2014 arson of the Party of Regions office.

There has been no further progress in investigations and trials related to the 2014 Odesa clashes.

A January European Court of Human Rights decision found that the Ukrainian government committed multiple breaches of the European Convention on Human Rights in the course of public order operations during the Maidan protests, including the right to life, the prohibition of torture, and the right to liberty and security.

In May, parliament adopted a long overdue law aligning Ukraine's national legislation with international law to allow for effective domestic prosecutions of grave international crimes, including those committed in Donbas and Crimea. At time of writing, because Zelensky has not signed the law, it has not gone into effect. Additional changes are likely to be needed to the Criminal Procedural Code to support effective investigations and prosecutions.

In late June, Ukraine's prosecutor general removed Gyunduz Mamedov as director of the government's specialized war crimes department. Human rights and watchdog groups criticized the decision as groundless and politically motivated.

Freedom of Expression, Attacks on Journalists

Physical attacks and online threats against human rights defenders, anti-corruption activists, environmental activists, and independent journalists have been numerous while investigations into the incidents have been slow, and at times ineffective. As of September, the Institute of Mass information, a watchdog group, recorded 73 cases of obstruction of journalists' professional activities, 17 beatings, 12 threats, and 11 restrictions on access to information.

A suspect in the 2016 killing of journalist Pavel Sheremet was released from detention and placed under house arrest in April, pending trial. One other suspect remains under house arrest, and the third one was released on bail in May 2020.

The investigation into the 2018 killing of activist Kateryna Handziuk has led to prison sentences for five men. However, progress in efforts to charge those allegedly responsible for ordering the attack has been slow.

A February decree by Zelensky led to the extrajudicial banning of three pro-Russia television channels and threatened media pluralism in Ukraine. The decree was based on a law that grants the government authority to sanction foreign individuals and entities that it deems have engaged in activities which could threaten Ukraine's national interests, national security, sovereignty, and territorial integrity.

Hate Crimes

In the first half of 2021, civil society groups reported a sharp increase in attacks against LGBT, anti-corruption, and women's rights activists, including by far-right groups and individuals.

In May, parliamentary committees began discussing a bill that would increase liability for discrimination and intolerance. In April, the Health Ministry lifted restrictions against gay people on donating blood.

In May, LGBT activists held a pride march in Kyiv in support of transgender people, under police protection. Far-right activists organized a counter protest but did not attack the march.

The police prevented attempted attacks on pride marches in Odesa and Kharkiv, held in August and September. In Odesa, the police arrested over 50 people who tried to attack the pride participants. Twenty-nine officers were injured during the clashes.

In March, members of a far-right group assaulted six participants of the Women's Rights march in Kyiv. Four men have been arrested.

On May 29, far-right groups disrupted outdoor events in Kyiv and Odessa, held by LGBT rights group Insight.

Also in May, far-right radicals in Kyiv sprayed teargas at the screening of a film about Ukraine's LGBT community. Twenty people received minor eye burns.

The LGBT Association LIGA faced threats, online bullying, and attacks in Odesa and Mykolaiv. In May, masked men threw stones at the building of the LIGA's office in Odesa, damaging it.

Roma people remained a target of online hate speech and occasional physical violence. In April, local media published a video from the meeting of the Ivano-Frankivsk mayor with local police, where he ordered them to "move Roma people back to Zakarpattya."

No progress has been made in ensuring accountability for the 2017 murder of Mykola Kaspitsky, the leader of Roma community in Kharkiv region. In January the case was closed for the fourth time. Throughout the year, activists raised concerns over the police allegedly sabotaging the case.

In January. police broke up two protests against far-right groups, under the pretext of Covid-19 restrictions, while other protests were allowed to go on unrestricted.

In June, Ukraine repatriated a mother and her seven children held in dire conditions in a camp for Islamic State (ISIS) suspects and family members in northeast Syria. The authorities had repatriated two other Ukrainian women and seven children in 2020.

Crimea

Russian authorities in Crimea continued to persecute Crimean Tatars, including by conflating religious or political beliefs as affiliation with Hizb ut-Tahrir, banned in Russia as a "terrorist" organization but legal in Ukraine. Dozens of Crimean Tatars continued to serve prison sentences on arbitrary charges for real or perceived affiliation with the organization—many of them members of the Crimean Solidarity, a group that supports Crimean Tatars arrested on politically motivated grounds. In February and August, a total of 11 men were arrested on similarly spurious claims.

In September, authorities arrested Nariman Dzhelyal, one of the few Crimean Tatar leaders remaining in Crimea, on trumped-up charges of "aiding sabotage." Authorities detained four other Crimean Tatars in connection with the case.

A new wave of house searches in March led to the detention of four men and one woman who are Jehovah's Witnesses, which is banned as "extremist" in Russia. In March, a court sentenced Viktor Stashivskyi to 6.5 years in prison for "organizing the activities of an extremist organization," the longest sentence yet given to a Jehovah's Witness.

Russian authorities continued to conscript males in occupied Crimea to serve in Russia's armed forces, in violation of international humanitarian law. Conscription was carried out in tandem with enlistment advertising campaigns in Crimea and military propaganda for schoolchildren.

Key International Actors

In January, the European Court of Human Rights found a Ukrainian inter-state complaint against Russia to be partially admissible. The court recognized that Russia had "exercised effective control" over Crimea since 2014, paving the way for accountability for violations of the European Convention on Human Rights by Russia during its occupation of the peninsula.

In April, the European Union issued a statement formally accusing Russian authorities in Crimea of conducting a conscription campaign, labelling it a "violation of international humanitarian law." The EU also condemned in September the detention of Crimean Tatar leaders and called for the release of Ukrainian citizens detained in Crimea.

In May, during their annual human rights dialogue, the European Union welcomed the adoption of Ukraine's recent National Strategy for Human Rights and the Action Plan, while also calling for further progress in reform of multiple sectors and successful resolution of the Maidan and Odesa investigations. During the EU-Ukraine Summit in October, both parties reaffirmed their commitment to strengthening the political and economic integration of Ukraine with the EU without a particular emphasis on human rights and the rule of law issues.

During their first meeting at the White House in August, US President Joseph Biden and President Zelensky committed to upholding human rights in Ukraine, including in such areas as reforming the judiciary, combatting corruption and fighting discrimination against the LGBT community. The presidents committed to holding Russia accountable for abuses in the territories of Ukraine controlled or occupied by Russia and to seeking the release of political prisoners held there.

A July report from the UN Human Rights Monitoring Mission in Ukraine condemned arbitrary detention and torture by both the Ukrainian government and non-government armed groups throughout the conflict in eastern Ukraine.

The government failed to submit the Council of Europe Convention on the Prevention of Violence against Women and Domestic Violence (the Istanbul Convention) to parliament for ratification. Ukraine signed the convention in 2011 and has repeatedly committed to ratification.

No public steps were taken to move toward a formal investigation following the December 2020 announcement by the Office of the Prosecutor at the International Criminal Court that the situation in Ukraine merited ICC action.

United Arab Emirates

In 2021, United Arab Emirates (UAE) authorities continued to invest in a "soft power" strategy aimed at painting the country as a progressive, tolerant, and rights-respecting nation, yet the UAE's intolerance of criticism was reflected in the continued unjust imprisonment of leading human rights activist Ahmed Mansoor and others.

The UAE continued to develop its surveillance capabilities, both online and through mass facial recognition surveillance in public spaces. New reports emerged of UAE authorities misusing Israeli spyware to gain access to the private and encrypted communications of journalists, activists, and world leaders.

In 2021, a UAE Interior Ministry official ran as a candidate for president of Interpol and won, an appointment that jeopardizes the global police organization's commitment to its human rights obligations given the UAE state security apparatus' long record of multiple abuses.

The UAE blocked representatives of international human rights organizations and UN experts from conducting in-country research and visiting prisons and detention facilities.

Freedom of Expression

Scores of activists, academics, and lawyers are serving lengthy sentences in UAE prisons following unfair trials on vague and broad charges that violate their rights to free expression and association.

Ahmed Mansoor, a leading Emirati human rights defender, remained imprisoned in an isolation cell for a fourth year. New details regarding UAE authorities' persecution of Mansoor emerged in 2021 revealing grave violations of his rights and demonstrated the State Security Agency's unchecked powers to commit abuses. In July, a private letter he wrote detailing his mistreatment in detention leaked to regional media, sparking renewed concern over his well-being and possible retaliation.

Prominent academic Nasser bin-Ghaith, serving 10 years on charges stemming from criticism of UAE and Egyptian authorities, and university professor and

THE PERSECUTION OF AHMED MANSOOR

How the United Arab Emirates Silenced its Most Famous Human Rights Activist

HUMAN
RIGHTS
WATCH

GCHR
مركز الخليج لحقوق الإنسان

human rights lawyer Mohammed al-Roken, serving 10 years following his conviction alongside 68 other people in the grossly unfair "UAE 94" trial, also remained in prison.

As of September 2021, UAE authorities continued to hold Khalifa al-Rabea, an Emirati who completed his sentence on state security charges July 2018. Al-Rabea was convicted in 2014 based on his ties to al-Islah, which was a legally registered Islamist political movement that the UAE later banned in 2014 as a "terrorist entity." Authorities arbitrarily kept him behind bars for "counselling," according to Emirati activists. Authorities also held past their sentences four Emirati dissidents convicted in the UAE 94 trial and who completed their sentences in 2019 and 2020 and two women prisoners who completed their sentences in 2020.

In October 2020, a UAE court sentenced a Jordanian resident of the UAE to 10 years in prison based entirely on peaceful Facebook posts criticizing Jordan's government.

Arbitrary Arrests, Detainee Abuse, and Forcible Deportations

UAE authorities arbitrarily targeted Pakistani Shia residents by subjecting them to enforced disappearance, incommunicado detention, and eventually groundless deportations. Reports of UAE authorities' arbitrarily targeting Shia residents, whether Lebanese, Iraqi, Afghan, Pakistani or otherwise, often emerge at times of increased regional tensions.

In late June, UAE authorities reportedly arrested hundreds of African migrant workers from Cameroon, Nigeria, and Uganda, arbitrarily detained them for weeks, and illegally deported them en masse without allowing them to challenge their deportations. Thomson Reuters Foundation reported in September that UAE authorities deported Cameroonians despite their stated concerns about ongoing violence back home.

Especially in cases purportedly related to state security, detainees were at serious risk of arbitrary and incommunicado detention, torture and ill-treatment, prolonged solitary confinement, and denial of access to legal assistance. Forced confessions were used as evidence in trial proceedings, and prisoners complained of overcrowded and unhygienic conditions and inadequate medical care.

Throughout 2021, UAE prison authorities denied detainees living with HIV uninterrupted access to lifesaving antiretroviral treatment, in flagrant violation of their right to health and essential medicines. In at least two UAE prisons, detainees living with HIV were segregated from the rest of the prison population and faced stigma and systemic discrimination. Prisoners living with HIV in the UAE who have been denied adequate medical care are at risk of experiencing serious complications if infected with the Covid-19 virus.

Despite international calls to do so, the UAE refused to allow independent international monitors to enter the country and visit prison and detention facilities.

Unlawful Attacks and Detainee Abuse Abroad

Despite announcing the withdrawal of most of its ground troops from Yemen in 2019, the UAE continued to play a leading role in a coalition conducting military operations, and continued to provide support for certain Yemeni forces who have committed grave abuses over the past several years. In February, Human Rights Watch reported on the detention of a Yemeni journalist who was first threatened by an official from the UAE and detained and mistreated by UAE-backed forces.

In Libya, the UAE conducted air and drone strikes, some of which killed and wounded civilians. The strikes were in support of the Libyan Arab Armed Forces (LAAF), the eastern-based armed group under the command of General Khalifa Hiftar and one of two major Libyan parties to the armed conflict that began in April 2019 .

Migrant Workers

Foreign nationals accounted for more than 80 percent of the UAE's population, according to 2015 International Labour Organization figures.

The *kafala* (sponsorship) system tied migrant workers' visas to their employers, preventing them from changing or leaving employers without permission. Those who left their employers without permission faced punishment for "absconding," including fines, arrest, detention, and deportation, all without any due process guarantees. Many low-paid migrant workers were acutely vulnerable to forced labor.

The UAE's labor law excluded from its protections domestic workers, who faced a range of abuses, from unpaid wages, confinement to the house, and workdays up to 21 hours to physical and sexual assault by employers. Domestic workers faced legal and practical obstacles to redress. While a 2017 law on domestic workers guarantees some labor rights, it is weaker than the labor law and falls short of international standards.

The Covid-19 pandemic has further exposed and amplified the ways in which migrant workers' rights are violated. Tens of thousands of migrant workers lost their jobs and were trapped in the country in dire conditions. Many lived through strict lockdowns in crowded and unhygienic housing. While thousands left the UAE after facing summary dismissals, many struggled to return to their home countries because of travel restrictions and expensive plane tickets, and many were left unable to pay rent or buy food. Many migrant workers also faced unpaid wages for work they had done before being dismissed.

Authorities imposed stricter Covid-19 lockdown conditions on domestic workers than other migrant workers, advising employers not to allow their domestic workers to meet anyone outside. Given that many employers already confine domestic workers to the household and overwork them, such conditions left them even more at risk of abuse, including increased working hours, no rest days, and physical and verbal abuse.

In September, Euro-Med Human Rights Monitor and ImpACT International documented that on June 24 and 25 authorities arrested, detained, and tortured over 800 African migrant workers before the mass deportation of many. The organizations report that the majority were deported despite valid residence visas and/or work permits, and that an unknown number remain in detention.

Climate Change Policies and Impacts

As one of the world's top 10 crude oil producers—and a top five per capita emitter of greenhouse gases—UAE is contributing to the climate crisis that is taking a mounting toll on human rights around the globe. The UAE has taken some positive steps to reduce emissions, including increased renewable energy capacity and removing some fossil fuel subsidies. Yet it maintains plans for significant fossil fuel use and production, both for export and domestic purposes. Its 2020 update to its national climate action plan—which pledges to reduce emissions by 23.5 percent by 2030—is "insufficient" to meet the Paris Agreement's goal to limit global warming to 1.5°C above pre-industrial levels, according to the Climate Action Tracker.

The UAE is particularly vulnerable to the impacts of climate change including from extreme heat, increased droughts, and sea level rise, requiring the UAE to take steps to protect at-risk populations from their foreseeable harms. Eighty-five percent of its population lives along coastlines that are just several meters above sea level.

Women's Rights

The UN Committee on the Elimination of Discrimination against Women commenced its process to review the UAE's five-year women's rights record. While the UAE has made a few reforms, it continues to discriminate against women in law and practice.

Some provisions of the law regulating personal status matters discriminate against women. For a woman to marry, her male guardian must conclude her marriage contract. Men can unilaterally divorce their wives, whereas a woman must apply for a court order to obtain a divorce. A woman can lose her right to maintenance if, for example, she refuses to have sexual relations with her husband without a lawful excuse.

Although changes to the law in 2020 repealed provisions that criminalized extramarital sex, the authorities still make it difficult for unmarried pregnant women to access prenatal healthcare and register their children. Official government websites still require marriage certificate to obtain birth certificates of their children, and health policy directives state that unmarried females should not be offered maternity insurance cover, as well as hospitals that still require marriage certificates for women to access some forms of sexual and reproductive healthcare.

In November 2020, the UAE also repealed an article in the penal code that allowed men to receive lighter sentences for killing a female relative if they found them in the act of extramarital sex. However, the law still allows families of the murder victim to waive their right to see the person punished in return for compensation (blood money) or choose to freely pardon them. In such cases, the accused can be subject to a minimum sentence of seven years in prison instead of life. When family members kill a woman, including in so-called "honor" killings, the victim's family is also the family of the murderer and is likely to allow men to receive lighter sentences.

The UAE's nationality law provides that children of Emirati men are automatically entitled to UAE citizenship; however, children born to Emirati mothers and foreign fathers are not.

The government did not take steps to fulfil its commitment, at its UN Universal Periodic Review in 2018, to ban corporal punishment of children in all settings.

In February, the BBC revealed secret videos of Sheikha Latifa, daughter of the Dubai ruler, detailing her alleged forced confinement in a Dubai villa following her abduction and forcible return in 2018. Since May, Latifa was pictured in malls in Dubai and then abroad with friends on Instagram. It is unclear under what conditions she has been granted such freedoms, nor the status of her sister Shamsa who was also subject to abduction and forcible return from the UK in 2000.

Sexual Orientation and Gender Identity

Article 358 of the penal code criminalizes a "flagrant indecent act" and any saying or act that offends public morals. A 2020 decree amending the penal code changed the punishment from a minimum of six months to a fine of Dh1,000 to Dh50,000 (US$270-$13,000). If it is a repeated offense, the punishment is up to three months' imprisonment or Dh100,000 ($27,000). In 2020, the UAE also amended article 356 of the penal code to remove language that had previously criminalized the vague offense of consensual indecency or debasement and was used to punish individuals who engaged in consensual sexual relations outside marriage, or *zina*, with a minimum one-year prison sentence.

The UAE's federal penal code punishes "any male disguised in female apparel and enters in this disguise a place reserved for women or where entry is forbidden, at that time, for other than women" with one year's imprisonment, a fine of up to 10,000 dirhams ($2,723), or both. In practice, transgender women have been arrested under this law even in mixed-gender spaces.

Key International Actors

As a party to the armed conflict in Yemen, the US provided logistical and intelligence support to Saudi and UAE-led coalition forces. Human Rights Watch called on the Biden administration in December to end arms sales to the UAE until it takes meaningful steps to end abuses in Yemen and act to hold those responsible for war crimes to account. In February, the Biden administration announced that it would end support for "offensive operations" in Yemen, but in April the administration greenlighted a Trump-era $23 billion arms sale to the UAE that includes highly advanced aerial weaponry.

In September, the European Parliament passed a resolution calling on its member states not to participate in the Expo 2020 taking place in Dubai between October and March 2022, and for international companies to withdraw their sponsorship due to the UAE's human rights record.

United Kingdom

The UK government pursues laws and policies with little regard for their impact on human rights. The government cut social security affecting millions despite clear warnings it would increase food insecurity, debt, and homelessness. The response to increased migrant boat crossings across the English Channel was draft legislation and proposed pushbacks at odds with refugee and human rights law. A landmark parliamentary oversight report found that existing social, economic, and health inequalities and failures in the UK government's Covid-19 pandemic response led to disproportionately high death rates among people in institutions such as care homes, people with learning disabilities and autism, and Black and ethnic minority people. The government again failed to take meaningful steps to tackle institutional racism. Although the UK government worked in coalition with partners to call out human rights abuses on key issues, when weighed against other interests, it did not always prioritize human rights in its foreign policy agenda.

The Rule of Law and Human Rights

In March, the government published an independent review of the power of courts to hold the executive to account. It recommended only modest changes to judicial review and while the legal profession remains cautious about the government's intentions, its proposals for legislative change are more limited than initially feared.

A separate review into the Human Rights Act was expected to publish its findings in late 2021. Although the government says it intends to remain party to the European Convention on Human Rights, the ruling Conservative party's track record of hostility to the act and comments from the justice minister raised concerns that the review could be used to water down rights and other legal protections.

Asylum and Migration

The UK ratcheted up rhetoric and efforts to restrict arrivals of migrants and people seeking asylum crossing the English Channel from France in small boats, raising concerns for the rights and safety of people making the dangerous journey. By the end of September, an estimated 17,085 people had crossed the Channel in this way during 2021. After announcing plans to push back such boats into French territorial waters in September, UK border enforcement guards were filmed conducting drills in which they appeared to practice potentially dangerous techniques such as pushing and ramming boats with jet-skis.

Measures proposed in a draft migration law in July would undermine international refugee and human rights obligations, including further criminalizing people seeking asylum (increasing the sentence for "illegal entry," penalizing people based on their mode of arrival, and broadening the definition of "assisting unlawful immigration"); allowing offshore processing and detention of asylum-seekers; creating a discriminatory, two-tier system of protection based on how a person sought safety in the UK; increasing maritime pushback powers; and providing immunity to border guards from civil or criminal proceedings arising from engaging in maritime pushbacks.

The Nationality and Borders Bill was widely criticized by the UN refugee agency and domestic civil society groups. At time of writing, the bill was being examined by the parliamentary human rights committee.

UK authorities pledged to resettle 5,000 Afghan refugees in 2021 and a further 15,000 within five years following the Taliban's seizure of power and the NATO troop withdrawal, in addition to facilitating the evacuation of nationals and Afghans who are eligible under the UK's Afghan Relocations and Assistance Policy.

A Home Office scheme, set up in 2019 to compensate a group of Black British citizens, known as the "Windrush generation," wrongly threatened with deportation or deported from the UK, continued its work, but faced criticism from victims and a parliamentary oversight committee for being too slow. Two men, aged 55 and 67, from the Windrush generation began litigation in September seeking greater transparency on the process for expediting urgent claims.

Rights to Social Security, Adequate Standard of Living

In October, the government cut up to £1,040 (US$1,439) per year from social security support to people on the Universal Credit system, despite widespread warnings that doing so would further exacerbate poverty. The government argued it was ending a temporary Covid-19 relief measure, but failed to disclose its impact assessment of the cut on approximately 6 million people. Domestic civil society groups and frontline professionals predicted the step would increase food insecurity, debt, and homelessness and harm physical and mental health. The UN special rapporteur on extreme poverty warned that the cut did not comply with the UK's socioeconomic rights obligations.

Rights groups raised concerns about people with disabilities receiving inadequate social security support, including an estimated 2 million people, many of them people with disabilities or long-term health conditions, on "legacy" benefits which predated the Universal Credit system, who never received the additional £1,040 per year.

Right to Food

Official data published in March, but collected prior to the pandemic, showed 43 percent of households receiving Universal Credit were experiencing food insecurity. The data showed the disproportionate impact of food insecurity on families headed by a single adult (predominantly women) or a Black person, families living on less than £200 ($276) per week, and people with disabilities.

Demand for food banks grew as the number of Universal Credit claimants increased to 6 million by March, doubling since the onset of the pandemic.

The country's largest food bank network reported that it had given out 2.5 million emergency food aid packages between April 2020 and March 2021, up 33 percent compared to the prior year, and its data showed lack of income and inadequate social security support as the main drivers.

In July, the National Food Strategy, an independent review into the country's food systems, recommended removing obstacles for families seeking free school meals for children; ensuring long-term food provision for children during school vacations; and extending an existing food subsidy program for pregnant people and families with young children.

Children's Rights

In March, Scotland's parliament passed a law incorporating the UN Convention on the Rights of the Child into Scottish law. In October, the UK Supreme Court ruled, following a constitutional challenge by the UK government, that the Scottish legislature had acted beyond its powers and asked for the legislation to be revised.

In July, the Supreme Court rejected a human rights challenge to the "two child limit" welfare policy, which caps payments to families with more than two children born after April 2017. Although the court accepted that the policy disproportionately affected women and children, it found it objectively justifiable. Official statistics published later that month estimated that the policy affected 1.1 million children in Great Britain.

In an important case about access to health care for trans young people, the Court of Appeal affirmed in September that children under 16 are capable of consent to treatment, and that clinicians rather than courts can determine if they have exercised it.

The number of people living in "temporary accommodation" or housing or hostel places provided by local government for homeless families increased by 75 percent over the prior decade. Official data published in September estimated that 30,700 households with children were living in temporary accommodation in London alone and growing up in substandard conditions, due to a lack of suitable affordable permanent alternatives. Children faced severe impact on their rights to an adequate standard of living and education.

Abortion

In July, the UK government, using new powers, directed Northern Ireland authorities to fund and make available abortion services by March 2022. Access to abortion in Northern Ireland limited, with one medical trust unwilling to perform abortions and others underfunded. In October, the Northern Ireland High Court ruled that the UK government had failed to act "expeditiously" to ensure access to abortion services.

Gender-Based Violence

The Domestic Abuse Act, which entered into force in April, introduced positive changes, including a statutory definition of "domestic abuse," new offences, better protection in family courts, and enhanced duties for local authorities to support survivors. However, women's rights organizations criticized the bill's failure to protect migrant women adequately. The UK has not ratified the Council of Europe Convention on Preventing Violence Against Women and Domestic Violence (known as the Istanbul Convention), which requires states to ensure such protection. At time of writing, the UK had also not ratified the Violence and Harassment at Work Convention of the International Labour Organization (ILO).

Following the government-commissioned Rape Review's report in June, ministers apologized for failing rape victims and committed to reversing a downward trend in rape prosecutions and convictions despite increased reports to police. In July, official criminal justice statistics showed a further drop in proportions of suspects charged with rape or domestic abuse during 2020-21, despite a documented increase in domestic violence during the Covid-19 lockdowns.

At time of writing, 112 women had been killed in the UK in 2021, according to Counting Dead Women. They include men killing women walking in public such as Sabina Nessa killed by a man five minutes from her home in September, and Sarah Everard, who was kidnapped, raped, and killed by a serving police officer in March. Everard's killing prompted protests and widespread concern that police are not serious about tackling violence against women, including by police officers. Revelations during the prosecution of Everard's killer in addition to reports from former and serving female police officers raised alarms about ongoing sexism and misogyny within the police force.

In October, an employment tribunal in Scotland found that a female firearms officer had been victimized by a sexist workplace culture. Women's rights activists oppose a policing bill that would not address police failures to tackle violence against women and would curb other freedoms, including the freedom to protest.

In September, the Investigatory Powers Tribunal ruled that police had violated multiple human rights of an environmental activist, when a male police officer formed an intimate relationship with her between 2003 and 2005 as part of undercover policing practice. The activist, Kate Wilson, is one of several women who have come forward to report institutionally sexist practices in covert policing. A broader public inquiry into undercover policing remains ongoing and is expected to report back in 2023.

Racial and Ethnic Discrimination

A government-appointed commission to review racial disparities received widespread criticism for finding in April that "institutional racism" had largely disappeared. The Windrush scandal, multiple government-commissioned reports and official data indicated that, to the contrary, racial and ethnic disparities continue, including in employment, criminal justice, and health.

A draft policing law proposed in July drew widespread criticism, including for planned curbs to protest rights, and the likely impacts of wider police search powers on people from ethnic minorities, especially Black people, and wider anti-trespass powers on Gypsy, Roma, and Traveller people living in informal settlements. The government's equalities impact assessment acknowledged the disproportionate discriminatory impact of the search and trespass powers but argued that such discrimination was indirect and justifiable.

Impunity for Conflict-Related Abuses

In April, the Overseas Operations Act became law, creating a presumption against prosecution for some crimes committed by UK forces overseas. Following widespread criticism, the government removed the worst provisions of the law, which would have effectively created immunity for genocide, crimes against humanity, and war crimes.

In July, the government proposed a statute of limitations on prosecutions relating to over three decades of political violence in Northern Ireland. Family members of people killed by security forces, and the region's lawyers' association, opposed the plan, seeing it as a de facto amnesty. In September, the Council of Europe's human rights commissioner criticized the proposals.

Grenfell Tower Fire and Right to Safe Housing

An inquiry into the June 2017 Grenfell Tower fire that killed 71 people continued, hearing evidence of a catalogue of failures, including to listen to the concerns of residents, many of migrant or ethnic minority background, whose warnings of fire risk were ignored. In February, the government announced a £3.5 billion ($4.85 billion) fund for low-interest loans to apartment owners in private high-rise buildings needing to replace dangerous cladding similar to that in Grenfell. Fire safety legislation passed in April began translating some of the inquiry's first recommendations into law.

Terrorism and Counterterrorism

In February, in a case relating to withdrawing citizenship from UK nationals who travel to join armed groups abroad, the Supreme Court ruled that Shamima Begum did not have the right to return to the UK from northeast Syria to partici-pate in court proceedings to challenge the UK's revocation of her citizenship after she joined the extremist armed group Islamic State (also known as ISIS) in Syria. The citizenship revocation left Begum, who joined ISIS when she was a child, effectively stateless. More than 50 UK women and children previously linked to armed groups remain in camps in northeast Syria.

Climate Policy and Impacts

The United Kingdom is among the top 20 emitters of the greenhouse gases re-sponsible for the climate crisis taking a growing toll on human rights around the globe. Prior to hosting the 2021 UN climate conference in October, it embraced ambitious emissions reduction targets—first through its national climate plan commitment to reduce emissions by 68 percent by 2030 compared to 1990 lev-els, and in June 2021 through a legislated target to reach a 78 percent reduction by 2035 compared to 1990 levels. According to the Climate Action Tracker, the UK's 2030 target is aligned with the country's aim to reach net-zero emissions by 2050, and with the Paris Agreement goal to limit global warming to 1.5°C above pre-industrial levels. However, the UK is not on track to fulfill these commit-ments. Indeed, the UK continues to expand fossil fuel production and channels billions in domestic support to fossil fuels despite its commitment to phase out fossil fuel subsidies.

According to the UK's climate advisory body, the UK's climate adaptation efforts have not kept pace with the country's increasing climate risks, including risks of heat-related health impacts, and climate impacts on infrastructure and food security.

In November, a regulation was adopted to restrict imports of agricultural commodities linked to illegal deforestation or the violations of laws pertaining to the ownership or use of land, as defined by the commodity's country of origin laws. Many of the essential aspects of the legislation, including the enforcement mechanisms and the commodities that are covered, are to be defined by the secretary of state. The government should have shown greater ambition by defining land rights along international human rights standards.

Foreign Policy

Since its departure from the European Union, the UK has proven its commitment to some key issues related to working closely with partners to call out and pressure certain states that fail to comply with their human rights obligations. However, when weighed against other interests, the UK did not always prioritize human rights in its foreign policy agenda.

The Foreign, Commonwealth and Development Office continued to work to develop an Open Societies Strategy. The strategy, part of the work of a new Open Societies and Human Rights Directorate, represents an important potential opportunity to mainstream and prioritize human rights in UK foreign policy.

However, during 2021, the government significantly cut its foreign aid budget, which supports human rights and civil society globally. There were also signs that the UK would prioritize trade over human rights, including reinstating trade preferences for Cambodia that had been withdrawn by the EU for human rights violations, while at the same time opposing effective parliamentary oversight over any new trade deals.

The UK refused to impose mandatory human rights due diligence on UK businesses and continued to license the export of billions of pounds of arms sales to countries such as Saudi Arabia where they are used in the war in Yemen.

The UK took more concrete steps in response to China's ongoing human rights violations in Xinjiang, Hong Kong, and Tibet. The UK imposed human rights sanctions on Chinese officials (to date only in relation to Xinjiang), supported a joint statement at the United Nations Human Rights Council (HRC), and made a further statement that called for a HRC resolution on China—the first time a state has publicly called for this.

The UK took robust action in response to the military coup and related human rights violations in Myanmar. It imposed sanctions on number of key individuals and entities and suspended all support involving the government directly or indirectly other than for exceptional humanitarian reasons. However, as pen holder on Myanmar at the UN Security Council, the UK failed to push for any meaningful action. The UK co-led a Special Session of the HRC in February in response to the coup, and while the text was weakened to maintain consensus, it supported a relatively strong resolution at the ensuing March HRC session. As president of the G7, the UK led three strongly worded G7 statements on Myanmar.

The UK played a largely positive role at the HRC with some stark exceptions. The UK sponsored and successfully advocated for the renewal and strengthening of a resolution to advance accountability in Sri Lanka, supported the creation of a special rapporteur on climate change and Afghanistan, and joined statements denouncing widespread human rights violations by Egypt, Russia, and China.

The UK also voted in favor of the resolution, which recognizes the right to a safe, clean, healthy and sustainable environment. However, it voted against a commission of inquiry into the root causes of recurrent tensions, instability, and protraction of conflict in the Occupied Palestinian Territories and Israel, despite unanimously supporting every HRC resolution creating a UN inquiry over the past decade (except those on Israel/Palestine).

This was coupled with the publication in April of a letter by the prime minister to an internal party group, which asserted that the UK strongly opposed the International Criminal Court's Palestine Investigation and suggested that the UK would seek to interfere with the independence of the court to further this end. The UK also sought to weaken an African Group resolution on systemic racism and police violence, expressing concern at references to the United Nations High Commissioner for Human Rights' (UNHCHR) transformative agenda to combat structural racism, as well as to reparations and the legacies of colonialism. Ultimately the UK supported the resolution.

The prime minister appointed a special envoy on the rights of lesbian, gay, bisexual and transgender (LGBT) people, tasked with championing LGBT equality at home and abroad.

United States

The administration of United States President Joe Biden and the US Congress took positive steps on human rights by championing the rights of women and lesbian, gay, bisexual, transgender, and intersex (LGBTI) people that had been weakened under the previous administration, committing to racial equity, and taking action to address the Covid-19 pandemic and its harmful economic impacts.

However, the United States continues to fail to fulfill its human rights commitments, most notably in the area of racial justice as reflected in the country's failure to end systemic racism linked to the legacies of slavery; abusive structures of incarceration, immigration enforcement, and social control affecting many racial and ethnic minorities; and the Black-white wealth gap that persists alongside an overall slight increase in economic inequality.

Racial Justice

Black, Latinx, and Native communities have been disproportionately burdened by the negative impacts of Covid-19, which has deepened existing racial injustices in healthcare, housing, employment, education, and wealth accumulation. While poverty fell overall due to stimulus checks and unemployment aid, the Black-white wealth gap, which is still as big as it was in 1968, persisted.

Across the country, state and local authorities launched reparations efforts seeking to repair harms that are evident in current racial disparities and connected to the legacies of slavery. In April, the US House Judiciary Committee voted H.R. 40, the Commission to Study and Develop Reparation Proposals for African Americans Act, out of subcommittee and on to consideration by the full house for the first time in the bill's 32-year history.

In May, Human Rights Watch testified alongside survivors and descendants of the 1921 Tulsa race massacre about the failure of city and state authorities in Tulsa, Oklahoma, to provide comprehensive reparations ahead of the race massacre's centennial. Following the Centennial in June, the Tulsa City Council passed an apology resolution, but failed to address the city's documented culpability in the massacre or provide full and effective reparations.

Hate crime incidents targeting people of Asian descent and Black people spiked significantly in 2021 compared to 2019 levels.

Poverty and Inequality

Economic inequality remains high and has slightly increased in the United States, with wealth disparities rising faster than inequality in income. The total combined wealth of US billionaires increased from $2.9 trillion in March 2020 to $4.7 trillion in July 2021. According to US government sources, poverty dropped and hardship indicators improved since December 2020, aided primarily by government benefits.

The American Rescue Plan, enacted on March 11, which built on earlier direct payments by the administration of former President Donald Trump, included $1,400 payments for most adults in the US alongside other assistance to struggling households. Food hardship among adults with children also fell after the federal government began monthly payments under the expanded Child Tax Credit on July 15, along with improved food assistance. Federal and state eviction moratoriums protected millions of tenants during the pandemic.

Still, Census Bureau data show that in September 2021 some 19 million adults were living in households with insufficient food, 11.9 million adults were behind on rent, and some of the progress from late March had stalled as relief measures were reduced in legislative negotiations. The impacts of the pandemic and the economic fallout have been widespread, but remain particularly prevalent among Black adults, Latino adults, and other people of color.

Criminal Legal System

The US continues to report the world's highest criminal incarceration rates, with nearly 2 million people held in state and federal jails and prisons on any given day and millions more on parole and probation. Despite some reductions in incarceration rates for Black people, they remain vastly overrepresented in jails and prisons. Following a trend starting in 2009, prison populations have decreased steadily, without substantially dismantling the mass incarceration system.

Prisons have often failed to provide sufficient protections against Covid-19 infection. One-third of all people in US prisons have contracted the virus and over 2,700 have died from it. Many jurisdictions reduced incarceration in response to the pandemic, but detained populations began returning to their pre-pandemic numbers in 2021 even as Delta variant cases surged.

Despite widespread calls for systemic reform during the summer of 2020, especially to reduce overreliance on policing and address societal problems with investment in supportive services, few jurisdictions have enacted meaningful measures. Some localities have made efforts to deploy mental health care professionals instead of police in appropriate circumstances; some have funded non-law enforcement violence interrupters. However, police budgets overall have not shrunk. Congress has not passed even the weak reforms proposed in the federal Justice in Policing Act.

Most US police departments refuse to report data on their use of force, necessitating nongovernmental data collection and analysis. As of November 3, police had killed over 900 people in 2021, similar to numbers in years past. On a per capita basis, police kill Black people at three times the rate they kill white people.

Children in the Criminal and Juvenile Justice Systems

Despite declines in the number of youth incarcerated, racial and ethnic disparities continue. The Sentencing Project reports that Black youth are more than four times, Latinx youth 1.3 times, and tribal youth more than three times as likely to be incarcerated as white youth.

Nearly two in three youth ordered into residential placement were placed in the most restrictive facilities.

Slow progress is being made to end the sentence of life without parole for children. According to the Campaign for the Fair Sentencing of Youth, 30 states have no one serving the sentence or have banned it for people under age 18.

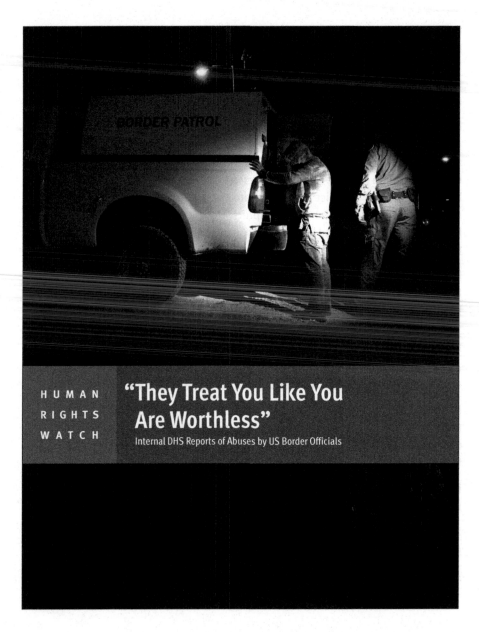

HUMAN
RIGHTS
WATCH

"They Treat You Like You
Are Worthless"

Internal DHS Reports of Abuses by US Border Officials

Drug Policy

Drug overdose deaths reached the highest number ever recorded during the Covid-19 pandemic according to data from the Centers for Disease Control and Prevention (CDC), over 93,000 people died in 2020 from a drug overdose death—a 30 percent increase compared to 2019.

These overdose deaths are part of an increase in mortality associated with unemployment, alcohol poisoning, and suicide, circumstances related to economic insecurity and mental health challenges. A Rhode Island study found increased overdose deaths among people experiencing job loss and in subgroups with mental health diagnoses in 2020 during the Covid-19 pandemic compared to 2019.

US drug laws prioritizing criminalization do not address the root causes of overdoses and have had devastating impacts in Black and brown communities. This continued focus on criminalization in such laws continues to be an obstacle to life-saving harm reduction services in many states, and gaps remain in accessible, affordable evidence-based treatment for substance use disorders.

Rights of Non-Citizens

Despite promises made during the presidential campaign, the Biden administration kept in place Trump-era policies denying access to asylum at US borders. At time of writing, the administration had carried out 753,038 expulsions under Title 42, an illegal policy to expel migrants arriving at land borders based on specious public health grounds.

Title 42 expulsions single out migrants arriving at land borders—who are disproportionately Black, Indigenous, and Latino, particularly from Central America, Africa, and Haiti—for discriminatory treatment, while thousands of other travelers are able to cross the border without any health screening. Expulsions under Title 42 put migrants in harm's way with thousands suffering kidnapping, rape, assault, extortion, and other abuse after expulsion to Mexico alone. In September, the government showed total disregard for the right to seek asylum when immigration agents on horseback used long reins as whips to control and deter a group of about 15,000 largely Black Haitian migrants in Del Rio, Texas.

Throughout 2021, the Biden administration sent a series of expulsion flights to Haiti, exposing approximately 10,000 migrants to conditions the US government currently recognizes as being too dangerous for safe returns of Haitians already present inside the US.

In October, Human Rights Watch reported on Department of Homeland Security documents cataloguing over 160 internal reports of US border officials physically or otherwise abusing asylum seekers and subjecting them to due process violations.

Before a federal court blocked the Biden administration's termination of the Trump-era Migration Protection Protocols, commonly known as "Remain in Mexico," about 13,000 of the 70,000 people returned to Mexico had been allowed to enter the United States to pursue their asylum claims. The administration's diplomatic pressure on Mexico, Guatemala, El Salvador, and Honduras to stop migrant flows resulted in serious abuses against migrants due to US policies, but far from US borders.

After detention levels reached historic lows due to releases prompted by the Covid-19 pandemic, the Biden administration dramatically increased the number of people detained for immigration reasons and also increased the number placed on electronic monitors, which facilitates invasive surveillance.

According to data current through August 2021, the United States decided over 18,000 asylum cases in fiscal year 2021 (which ended on September 30), of which 63 percent were denied asylum, 36 percent were granted asylum, and 1 percent were granted a different legal status. Despite the administration's decision to raise the limit to 62,500, only 11,445 refugees were admitted to the US during fiscal year 2021.

Health and Human Rights

The US government failed to curb the spread of the virus that causes Covid-19 and by September 2021, the pandemic had become the deadliest infectious disease event in the country's history, tallying 676,000 deaths, 94 percent of which were of people over the age of 50 and including at least 3,600 healthcare workers, most of whom were people of color. Structural racism impacted people's experiences of the pandemic, with Black and brown people more likely to suffer severe illness and die from Covid-19, as well as face additional barriers to vaccines. In April, the Centers for Disease Control and Prevention declared racism a serious threat to public health.

Schools in some areas were closed for an entire school year, if not longer, impacting nearly 78 million students. Students of color were particularly adversely impacted as they tend to attend less well-resourced schools and have more limited access to the internet for remote schooling. Meanwhile, unregulated drug prices in the US have contributed to a crisis of affordability for essential medicines. And despite positive court rulings, Indigenous communities in the United States continue to face significant barriers to accessing adequate health services.

Voting Rights

The country grappled with baseless accusations of mass election fraud, ongoing suppression, and disenfranchisement of voters of color, and efforts to undermine election procedures set up to ensure everyone eligible can easily vote in US elections. After comprehensive voting rights legislation failed to pass the US Senate in June, a compromise bill, the Freedom to Vote Act, was introduced in September. Also pending was the John Lewis Voting Rights Advancement Act, intended to update and restore the landmark Voting Rights Act of 1965.

Climate Change Policy and Impacts

Historically, the United States is by far the country that has most contributed to the climate crisis that is taking a mounting toll on human rights around the globe and remains amongst the world's top emitters.

President Biden announced he would prioritize addressing climate change, and rejoined the Paris Agreement on his first day in office. However, the United States' emissions reduction target in its national climate plan, is not sufficient to meet the Paris Agreement goal to limit global warming to 1.5°C above pre-industrial levels, according to the Climate Action Tracker. If all countries' commitments were in the same range, warming would reach just under 2°C, risking catastrophic human rights harms. Further, although the Biden administration has taken significant steps to reduce emissions, the United States is not on track to reach its target.

Heatwaves, hurricanes, and other extreme weather events linked to climate disproportionately impact marginalized populations in the United States. Authorities have not adequately protected at-risk populations—including pregnant people, people with disabilities, and older people—from such foreseeable impacts.

Women's and Girls' Health and Rights

Lack of access to health insurance and care contributed to higher rates of maternal and cervical cancer deaths than in comparable countries, with Black women dying at higher rates. President Biden issued a presidential memorandum on protecting women's health on January 28, rescinding actions by the Trump administration that created difficulties for women to speak freely with doctors, access health services, and get health information.

On March 8, Biden issued an executive order establishing the White House Gender Policy Council tasked with increasing access to comprehensive health care, addressing health disparities, and promoting sexual and reproductive health and rights, among other goals. On October 22, 2021, it issued a national strategy on gender equity and equality.

States continue to pass increasingly extreme abortion restrictions. Harmful laws in the majority of US states force young people under 18 to involve a parent in their abortion decision, or go to court to receive a judicial bypass. These laws can delay or prevent access to care. access to care.

In September, a new law in Texas effectively prohibited nearly all abortions after six weeks of pregnancy, before most people know they are pregnant, with no exception for rape or incest. At time of writing, the law remained in place after the Supreme Court declined to block the law in response to an emergency application; a second challenge was pending before the court.

At time of writing, the Supreme Court was scheduled to hear oral arguments in *Dobbs v. Jackson Women's Health Organization*, a case concerning a Mississippi abortion restriction that could have significant implications for abortion rights in

"The Only People It Really
Affects Are the People It Hurts"
The Human Rights Consequences of Parental Notice of Abortion in Illinois

HUMAN
RIGHTS
WATCH

ACLU
Illinois

HUMAN
RIGHTS
WATCH

"I Just Try to Make It Home Safe"
Violence and the Human Rights of Transgender People in the United States

the United States. A decision is expected in 2022.

As abortion access in some states became more restrictive, the Food and Drug Administration issued permission in April for mifepristone, a drug used in medical abortions, to be prescribed and administered by mail through the duration of the pandemic.

Disability Rights

Police violence against Black and Latinx people with disabilities (especially people with mental health conditions, but not exclusively) continued in 2021, partly due to lack of community-based support services for mental health crises. Illinois and California passed legislation to address the growing concern.

Older People's Rights

As of September, approximately one-third of Covid-19 deaths were in long-term residential facilities. There were also serious concerns about abuse and neglect in nursing homes during the pandemic. Staffing shortages, a longstanding issue, and limits on family visitors, who often assisted staff, may have contributed to neglect and decline. In June, the Centers for Medicare and Medicaid Services undid a Trump administration rule that restricted monetary fines for certain nursing home violations. Congress considered bills to enhance nursing home accountability, address elder abuse, expand home and community-based services, and improve direct care workers' wages and benefits.

Sexual Orientation and Gender Identity

The Biden administration took swift steps to restore rights limited by the Trump administration, instructing federal agencies to combat discrimination based on sexual orientation and gender identity.

The administration also issued a memorandum to advance the human rights of LGBTI people in US foreign policy, and reversed the discriminatory transgender military ban.

Lawmakers in US states introduced more than 110 bills targeting transgender people, particularly transgender children, threatening their health and rights. Alabama, Arkansas, Florida, Mississippi, Montana, Tennessee, Texas, and West

Virginia enacted laws prohibiting trans children from participating in sports consistent with their gender identity. Arkansas and Tennessee enacted laws preventing children and adolescents from obtaining gender-affirming healthcare.

The Senate did not pass the Equality Act, which would expressly prohibit discrimination based on sexual orientation and gender identity under various federal civil rights laws.

National Security

On January 6, armed rioters encouraged by then-President Trump broke into the US Capitol in an attempt to disrupt the certification of vote counts for the presidential election. Five people died and more than 600 people have been charged in the attack. The rioters included white supremacists and anti-government militia members, and demonstrated that the extreme-right remains a major domestic security threat.

The Biden administration announced it would review the legal and policy frameworks governing lethal targeting of terrorism suspects abroad, but that review has not been made public. On August 29, two days after the Kabul airport suicide bombing claimed by the Islamic State of Khorasan Province (ISIS-K or ISKP) that killed at least 170 Afghans and 13 US servicemembers, the US launched a drone strike on a car it claimed was filled with explosives headed to the airport. On September 17, the Defense Department admitted the strike was a "tragic mistake," killing 10 civilians including seven children. Following an investigation, the US concluded that there was no "criminal negligence among military personnel" involved in the operation. The US announced it would provide "ex gratia condolence payments" to the victims' families.

President Biden pledged to end detention at Guantanamo Bay but the US released only one detainee in 2021. Thirty-nine men remain detained at time of writing: 10 were being prosecuted by military commission and two were serving sentences. While some pretrial hearings before Guantanamo's flawed military commissions resumed in September after extensive delays, no trials are expected until 2022, including for the five alleged September 11 plotters.

Foreign Policy

Upon taking office, the Biden administration announced that it was committed to a foreign policy "that is centered on the defense of democracy and the protection of human rights," as well as to increasing multilateral cooperation. The United States was reelected to the UN Human Rights Council, and rejoined the World Health Organization (WHO) and the Paris Climate Accord.

In April 2021, President Biden lifted sanctions against senior International Criminal Court (ICC) officials but opposed ICC investigations that could include scrutiny of the conduct of US and Israeli nationals. The US hosted a Summit for Democracy intended to spur commitments by invited countries on human rights, anti-corruption, and anti-authoritarianism.

The Biden administration revoked the Protecting Life in Global Health Policy, also known as the "Global Gag Rule," which damaged sexual and reproductive health and rights globally. It also committed to restoring consideration of reproductive health and rights to its annual global human rights report.

A US Special Envoy to Advance the Human Rights of LGBTQI+ Persons was appointed, a vacant position since 2017. Secretary of State Antony Blinken rejected the findings of the State Department's Commission on Unalienable Rights—a Trump administration initiative advocating for a hierarchical approach to human rights—noting that human rights are "interdependent" and cannot be ranked.

While the Biden administration adopted the Trump administration's determination of genocide and crimes against humanity by China's government for its treatment of Uyghurs, it did not announce a legal determination on military abuses against the Rohingya in Myanmar or on abuses committed in Ethiopia's Tigray region. The United States urged the UN Security Council to discuss the humanitarian and rights crises in Myanmar and Tigray, but at time of writing had not called on the council to impose an arms embargo or individual UN sanctions on those responsible for abuses.

The United States pursued sanctions on a range of human rights violations. In response to China's use of forced labor and other abuses of Uyghurs in Xinjiang, the Biden administration issued an advisory warning that US companies conducting business in the region run a "high risk of violating US law." The administration imposed sanctions on Chinese and Hong Kong officials and companies over the crackdown on democracy in Hong Kong. On Myanmar, the administration imposed sanctions on the junta following the February coup. The US took similar action against Belarus, Cuba, and Nicaragua in response to increasingly authoritarian governance and rights violations. President Biden also issued an executive order allowing for US sanctions against individuals committing abuses in the Ethiopia conflict and terminated Ethiopia's trade status under the African Growth and Opportunity Act (AGOA) due to human rights violations.

The Biden administration did not impose sanctions on Saudi Crown Prince Mohammed bin Salman following the release of a US intelligence report that concluded that he approved the 2018 murder of journalist Jamal Khashoggi.

In July, President Biden launched a US strategy to address the root causes of migration in Central America, including promoting respect for human rights. The impact of this strategy has been limited.

President Biden announced a full US troop withdrawal from Afghanistan without ensuring that Afghans accepted under the Special Immigrant Visa (SIV) program and others at risk would be evacuated and resettled. On August 15, the Taliban completed a rapid takeover of Afghanistan and the US-backed government, creating chaotic and dangerous conditions for Afghans fearing Taliban retribution. The US evacuated over 60,000 Afghans, many of whom had worked directly with the US government or US organizations, but thousands of human rights defenders, journalists, and others left behind remained at risk. The legal status abroad of many other evacuated Afghans remained unclear. The US also evacuated thousands of Afghans who had worked for CIA-backed strike forces, including some accused of summary executions and other abuses.

The Biden administration pursued arms sales and security assistance to countries with poor human rights records. Though the United States pledged to end offensive weapons sales to Saudi Arabia and the UAE due to their role in the war in Yemen, it pursued arms deals with both governments. The Biden administration authorized over $2.5 billion in arms sales to the Philippines and requested $1.3 billion in security assistance to Egypt despite deteriorating human rights in both countries. President Biden also skirted congressional legislation that requires $300 million of US security assistance to Egypt to be conditioned on human rights, withholding only $130 million despite ongoing abuses.

The United States funded an additional $735 million in arms sales to Israel over the annual $3.8 billion commitment, even as Israeli forces used US-made weapons in May airstrikes in Gaza that violated the laws of war and apparently amount to war crimes.

The Biden administration stated its willingness to return to compliance with the 2015 Joint Comprehensive Plan of Action if Iran does the same. At time of writing, the US and Iran had agreed to resume multilateral talks at the end of November. Broad US sanctions on Iran remain in place.

Uzbekistan

The pace of human rights reforms in Uzbekistan stalled and backtracked on some aspects in 2021, especially in the months leading up to presidential elections in late October, which the incumbent president Shavkat Mirziyoyev won. Uzbekistan's political system remains deeply authoritarian.

Freedom of speech and the media experienced clear setbacks, with authorities targeting outspoken and critical bloggers, including Otabek Sattoriy, who was sentenced to six-and-a-half years in prison in May. Authorities continued to deny registration to independent human rights groups and to criminalize consensual same-sex relations. Authorities used anal exams, a form of torture, in prosecutions of gay men. Impunity for ill-treatment and torture remained the norm.

The government's promised legislative reforms, including a new criminal code, stalled. A new law on religion fell far short of international standards. On June 7, Uzbekistan ratified the Convention on the Rights of Persons with Disabilities.

Presidential Elections

Uzbekistan's electorate re-elected President Mirziyoyev with 80.1 percent of the vote on October 24. No opposition candidates, including Khidirnazar Allakulov, whose Truth and Progress Party was denied registration by the Justice Ministry, or Jahongir Otajanov, nominated by the unregistered Erk Democratic Party, were allowed to participate. Authorities harassed Allakulov and others who supported him in the lead up to elections. In July, Otajanov announced he was dropping out of politics completely.

The Organization for Security and Co-operation in Europe's (OSCE) Office for Democratic Institutions and Human Rights (ODIHR) election monitoring mission found "significant procedural irregularities" and that the election lacked genuine competition. Monitors also expressed concern about the overall restrictive legal framework for media.

Freedom of Speech

Although media activity in Uzbekistan has increased considerably since 2016, there was a notable decline in respect for speech and media freedoms in 2021. Journalists faced harassment, prosecution, and assault. Defamation and insult remain criminal offenses, despite President Mirziyoyev's decriminalization pledge in 2020. In March, Uzbekistan adopted legislative changes criminalizing online criticism of the president. Radio Ozodlik, the Uzbekistan branch of Radio Free Europe/Radio Liberty, remains blocked. In June the Foreign Affairs Ministry denied accreditation to Agnieszka Pikulicka, a Tashkent-based foreign correspondent.

Authorities have targeted multiple bloggers with criminal or administrative charges. In May, a Surkhandaryo court sentenced the outspoken blogger Otabek Sattoriy to six-and-a-half years in prison following a dubious conviction on slander and extortion charges. Despite significant public outcry, his sentence was upheld on appeal in July. A Tashkent-based blogger, Miraziz Bazarov, was attacked by a mob after he expressed support for lesbian, gay, bisexual, and transgender (LGBT) rights, and had to be hospitalized.

Members of Tashkent's diplomatic community expressed concern about the attack. Upon being discharged from hospital, authorities placed Bazarov under house arrest on politically motivated charges of slander. In August, the blogger Valijon Kalonov was placed under arrest on charges of insulting the president online after he criticized the president and called for a boycott of presidential elections.

Civil Society

Uzbek authorities severely hinder the work of independent nongovernmental organizations (NGOs) with excessive and burdensome registration requirements. The Justice Ministry continued to deny registration to independent groups. In April, the Humanitarian Legal Centre in Bukhara was denied registration for the ninth time. In September, after being denied registration for the eighth time, the founders of the rights group Human Rights House filed a lawsuit against the Justice Ministry.

Uzbek authorities continue to refuse to restore full legal status and rights to more than 50 people, including human rights defenders, who, since 2016, had been released from prison after having served politically motivated sentences. In January, a Kashkardarya court ruled that Elyor Tursunov, who served nearly seven years of a 17-year sentence and who was acquitted and released in March 2018, should receive approximately US$8,650 in compensation from the government for his wrongful imprisonment.

Criminal Justice, Torture

A draft criminal code, published by the Prosecutor General's office in February, retained many problematic articles, including overbroad and vague offences of extremism and incitement that would violate international human rights standards, if adopted. Following its publication, review of the draft criminal code stalled.

On May 25, the United Nations Working Group on Arbitrary Detention (WGAD) issued its opinion on the case of Kadyr Yusupov, a former diplomat who, in January 2020, was sentenced to five-and-a-half years in prison for treason. WGAD found that Yusupov was arbitrarily deprived of his liberty and said the Uzbek government should "take urgent action to ensure [Yusupov's] immediate release." Yusupov alleged he had been tortured in detention.

Torture and ill-treatment remain common in places of detention, with human rights groups and the media reporting on credible allegations of torture. Although Uzbek authorities said in 2019 that they had shuttered the notoriously abusive Jaslyk prison, the local human rights group Ezgulik reported in April that up to 100 people could still be imprisoned there.

On June 26, President Mirziyoyev signed a decree on "improving [Uzbekistan's] system for detecting and preventing cases of torture," which includes a provision establishing prevention monitoring groups under the office of the ombudsman tasked with carrying out prison visits.

Freedom of Religion

Uzbekistan adopted a new law on religion in early July. Officials did not make public the bill before it was adopted. In a joint July 29 communication to President Mirziyoyev, five UN special rapporteurs expressed serious concern about provisions in the law, such as the prohibition of all forms of peaceful missionary activity and the banning of non-state-approved religious education and of the manufacture, import, and distribution of non-state-approved religious material.

Muslims who practice their faith outside state controls continued to be targeted by authorities with spurious religious extremism-related criminal charges. In January, seven Muslims who in November 2020 were sentenced to between four and 11 years in prison on extremism related charges after meeting together to discuss Islam, began serving their prison sentences. In June, police brought extremism-related charges against Fazilkhoja Arifkhojaev, an outspoken Muslim government critic, and he was sent to pre-trial detention for three months.

Freedom of Assembly

Review of a draft law on public assemblies, published in August 2020, continued to stall in 2021. Amendments to Uzbekistan's Informatization Law adopted in March prohibited bloggers and others calling online for participation in protests "in violation of the established order." Spontaneous small-scale protests over social and economic issues occurred intermittently throughout 2021.

Sexual Orientation and Gender Identity

Men in Uzbekistan who engage in consensual same-sex sexual conduct face arbitrary detention, prosecution, and imprisonment under art. 120 of the criminal code, which carries a maximum sentence of three years in prison. Gay men also face threats and extortion by both police and non-state actors. Uzbekistan's draft criminal code, pending further review, retains the offense under article 154, with the wording unchanged.

Uzbek police and courts have relied on the conclusions of forced anal examinations conducted between 2017 and 2021 to prosecute men for consensual same-sex relations. Such exams are a form of violence and torture, according to the World Health Organization (WHO).

Women's Rights

Deep inequality between men and women persists in Uzbekistan. Domestic violence remains a serious problem. Neither domestic violence nor marital rape are explicitly criminalized, and the draft Criminal Code, published in February, did not include a standalone offence of domestic violence. Between January and March, the Internal Affairs Ministry registered 11,070 complaints of harassment and violence against women. While the State Commission on Gender Equality reported in 2019 that it had opened 197 rehabilitation and adaptation centers for women who experience violence, a June media report found that many such centers "did not exist" or "did not function" as intended.

Forced Labor

Uzbekistan continued to make significant efforts to reduce forced labor in its cotton sector. Although the International Labour Organization (ILO) concluded in January that there was no systemic forced or child labor in the 2020 cotton harvest, it noted that "about four percent [of pickers] were subject to direct or perceived forms of coercion," that is, approximately 80 thousand people. The ILO reported that "there were only isolated cases of minors below the legal working age picking cotton." The lack of independent trade unions and civil society organizations in Uzbekistan undermines sustainability of progress made so far.

Refugees

After the Taliban seized control of neighboring Afghanistan, Uzbekistan contributed to the evacuation effort by allowing planes to refuel and passengers to transit to safe, third countries, but closed its land border to Afghan refugees, and to date, continues to refuse to offer international protection to at-risk Afghans fleeing the country. Uzbekistan is not a signatory to the 1951 United Nations Refugee Convention.

Key International Actors

In January, Uzbekistan assumed a seat on the UN Human Rights Council (HRC). The Uzbek government signed a new members' pledge to promote international human rights standards during its term.

The European Union in April granted Uzbekistan Generalised Scheme of Preferences (GSP+) unilateral trade preferences, a schemed conditioned on the ratification and implementation of core human rights treaties, despite acknowledging persistent concerns about Uzbekistan's compliance. In June the EU's Subcommittee on Justice and Home Affairs, Human Rights and related Issues "registered its concerns" relating to freedom of expression and assembly, registration of NGOs, and anti-discrimination, and called on Uzbekistan to investigate attacks against bloggers or protesters. In October, the EU expressed "regret" at the lack of genuine competition in Uzbekistan's presidential elections.

During a trip to the US in July, Foreign Minister Abdulaziz Kamilov met with Secretary Antony Blinken, who called the US-Uzbek relationship "vital," with the US offering "support for Uzbekistan's continuing reforms, including strengthening human rights and democracy." In early October, the US Deputy Secretary of State visited Tashkent and met with the Uzbek president and foreign minister where she "stressed the importance of continued progress on democratic reforms and promoting respect for human rights."

Venezuela

The Nicolás Maduro government and its security forces are responsible for extra-judicial executions and short-term forced disappearances and have jailed opponents, prosecuted civilians in military courts, tortured detainees, and cracked down on protesters. They used a state of emergency implemented in response to Covid-19 as a pretext to intensify their control over the population. The lack of judicial independence contributed to impunity for these crimes. Judicial authorities have participated or been complicit in the abuses.

A United Nations Fact-Finding Mission (FFM) identified patterns of violations and crimes that were part of a widespread and systematic course of conduct that it concluded amounted to crimes against humanity. In November 2021, International Criminal Court (ICC) prosecutor Karim Khan announced his decision to open an investigation into possible crimes against humanity committed in Venezuela.

Venezuela is facing a severe humanitarian emergency, with millions unable to access basic healthcare and adequate nutrition. Limited access to safe water in homes and healthcare centers and a vaccination plan marred by opacity may have contributed to the spread of Covid-19.

Starting in August 2021, government and opposition representatives held meetings in Mexico to negotiate issues including electoral guarantees, the lifting of sanctions, respect for rule of law, humanitarian aid, and political rights. The government withdrew from negotiations in October, following the extradition to the United States of Colombian businessman Alex Saab, a close government ally. The negotiations had not resumed at time of writing.

Prior to the negotiations, the government had made limited concessions, largely due to increased international pressure, including naming new National Electoral Council members and allowing the World Food Program (WFP) to deploy.

An independent EU electoral mission that monitored the November regional elections reported that political opponents remained arbitrarily disqualified from running for office, there had been unequal access to the media, and the lack of judicial independence and of respect for the rule of law had undermined the election's impartiality and transparency.

Persistent concerns include brutal policing practices, abject prison conditions, impunity for human rights violations, and harassment of human rights defenders and independent media.

The exodus of Venezuelans fleeing repression and the humanitarian emergency represents the largest migration crisis in recent Latin American history.

Persecution of Political Opponents, Arrests, and Torture

The government has jailed political opponents and disqualified them from running for office. As of October 25, there were 254 political prisoners, the Penal Forum, a network of pro-bono defense lawyers, reported. While some detainees were released or transferred from intelligence installations to common prisons, a revolving door persists, with new critics being subject to arbitrary prosecutions.

Security agents arbitrarily detained Freddy Guevara, of the Popular Will party, on July 12. Officials accused him of working with gangs that had engaged in a deadly standoff with police in Caracas, and charged him with terrorism, attacking the constitutional order, conspiracy to commit a crime, and treason. He was held incommunicado at the Bolivarian National Intelligence Service (SEBIN) headquarters until August 15 and released following the first round of negotiations in Mexico on the condition that he appear in court every 30 days.

Intelligence and security forces have tortured various detainees and their family members. In 2020, the UN Office of the High Commissioner for Human Rights (OHCHR) reported cases of alleged torture and ill-treatment including severe beatings with boards, suffocation with plastic bags and chemicals, submersion in water, electric shocks to eyelids and genitals, exposure to cold temperatures, and handcuffing for extended periods.

During several crackdowns since 2014, security forces and pro-government armed groups known as colectivos have attacked demonstrations. Security forces have severely injured and occasionally killed demonstrators they had deliberately shot at point-blank range with riot-control munitions, brutally beaten others who offered no resistance, and staged violent raids on apartment buildings.

Of the 15,756 people arbitrarily arrested since 2014, 9,406 had been conditionally released as of July 2021, but remained subject to prosecution, and 872 had been prosecuted in military courts, according to the Penal Forum.

In June 2021, OHCHR reported continuing torture, ill-treatment, enforced disappearances, and arbitrary detentions.

Alleged Extrajudicial Killings

Between 2016 and 2019, police and other security forces killed more than 19,000 people, alleging "resistance to authority." In June 2021, OHCHR reported that killings by security forces had slightly declined but continued. Many of these were consistent with previous patterns of extrajudicial executions, OHCHR said.

Agents of FAES, a special police force, and others have killed and tortured with impunity in low-income communities, instilling fear and maintaining social control. Previously, military and police raids in low-income communities, called "Operations to Liberate the People" by authorities, resulted in widespread allegations of extrajudicial killings, arbitrary detentions, mistreatment of detainees, and forced evictions.

Armed Groups

Armed groups—including the National Liberation Army (ELN), Patriotic Forces of National Liberation (FPLN), and groups that emerged from the Revolutionary Armed Forces of Colombia (FARC)—operate mostly in border states. In Apure, they establish and brutally enforce curfews; prohibitions on rape, theft, and murder; and regulations governing everyday activities. Impunity is the norm, and residents say security forces and local authorities often collude with armed groups.

Starting in March 2021, Venezuelan security forces committed egregious abuses against Apure residents during a weeks-long operation against a FARC dissident group known as the Martin Villa 10th Front. The operation led to the execution of at least four peasants, arbitrary arrests, the prosecution of civilians in military courts, and the torture of residents accused of collaborating with armed groups.

Hundreds were forcibly displaced within Venezuela and at least 5,800 people fled to Colombia, according to the Office of the United Nations High Commissioner for Refugees (UNHCR). Most had returned to Venezuela by August, but confrontations continued.

Environment and Human Rights

Mining is the leading driver of deforestation in the Venezuelan Amazon, after agriculture. After President Maduro illegally declared the creation in 2016 of a special mining zone in the north of Bolívar state that covers 24 percent of the country's Amazon rainforest, the area has lost more than 230,000 hectares of forest cover, according to a study by the non-governmental organization SOS Orinoco. Analysis of satellite imagery suggests mining operations currently occupy at least 20,000 hectares of the special zone.

The special mining zone encompasses 14 Indigenous territories, whose residents were reportedly not consulted before its creation. People in multiple riverside Indigenous communities within and downstream from the mining zone are reportedly experiencing severe mercury poisoning, a toxic substance used to separate gold from impurities.

Bolívar state is the epicenter of malaria in Venezuela, accounting for 55 percent of all cases, and there is a high prevalence of malaria among gold miners, whose high mobility represents an important vector of contagion. Pools of stagnant and polluted water resulting from mining activity have also become malaria breeding grounds, OHCHR reported.

Illegal gold mining in Bolívar state is largely controlled by criminal groups—"syndicates"— and Colombian armed groups which police citizens, impose abusive working conditions, and viciously treat those accused of theft and other offenses, sometimes dismembering and killing them in front of others. The syndicates operate with government acquiescence and sometimes involvement. In September, the Organisation for Economic Co-operation and Development (OECD) reported that the Venezuelan military and political elites, Colombian armed groups, and domestic gangs continued to be key actors in the gold trade.

Judicial Independence and Impunity for Abuses

The judiciary stopped functioning as an independent branch of government when former President Hugo Chávez and supporters in the National Assembly took over the Supreme Court in 2004. Supreme Court justices have openly rejected the separation of powers and consistently upheld abusive policies and practices.

There has been no meaningful justice in Venezuela for the victims of extrajudicial killings, arbitrary arrests, and torture committed by security forces with the knowledge or acquiescence of Venezuelan high-level authorities. Judicial authorities have been complicit in the abuses, the UN Fact-Finding Mission reported in September 2021, including by issuing retrospective arrest warrants for illegal arrests, routinely ordering pre-trial detention, upholding detentions based on flimsy evidence, and failing to protect victims of torture. Judges allowed significant procedural delays and interfered with the right to choose one's own lawyer.

The Attorney General's Office reported that between August 2017 and May 2021, 716 officials were charged with crimes connected with human rights violations, 1,064 were indicted, 540 arrested and 153 convicted. The Fact-Finding Mission noted some discrepancies in the numbers provided by Venezuelan authorities and found that there was no evidence that authorities were carrying out investigations into responsibility for violations further up the chains of command.

In June, Maduro announced a legal reform of the judicial system, creating a special commission headed by his wife and National Assembly deputy Diosdado Cabello. The focus of the reform so far has been on reducing overcrowding in pretrial detention centers, which held 38,736 people in June 2021, up from 22,759 in May 2016.

Right to Vote

In December 2020, government supporters gained control of the National Assembly in elections of widely disputed legitimacy. The government disbanded a National Constituent Assembly established in 2017 to rewrite the constitution, which had effectively replaced the National Assembly.

In 2020, the Supreme Court orchestrated the takeover of several opposition political parties, replacing their leadership with government supporters ahead of the December elections. In 2021, the new National Electoral Council announced that some opposition political parties would be able to participate in November 2021 elections. The opposition confirmed its participation as the Unitary Platform. The European Union, a delegation of members of the European Parliament, the Carter Center, and the United Nations monitored elections.

Humanitarian Emergency and Covid-19

The WFP estimates that one in three Venezuelans is food insecure and in need of assistance. In 2019, 9.3 million Venezuelans suffered from food insecurity, which was projected to increase significantly. UNICEF reported 5.8 percent of children screened between January and June 2021 with acute malnutrition, including 1.5 percent with severe acute malnutrition.

Venezuela's collapsed health system has led to the resurgence of vaccine-preventable and infectious diseases, and hundreds of people allegedly dying due to barriers to performing transplants. Shortages of medications and supplies, interruptions of utilities at healthcare centers, and the emigration of healthcare workers have led to a decline in operational capacity.

OHCHR expressed concern over the absence of public data to monitor and adequately inform public health policies. The government has not published epidemiological data since 2017.

School attendance, already low due to the humanitarian emergency, has declined further because of Covid-19 and related restrictions. UNICEF reported that 6.9 million students in Venezuela missed almost all classroom instruction between March 2020 and February 2021. In-person classes resumed in October 2021, but with limited attendance.

As of October 28, Venezuela had confirmed 403,318 cases of Covid-19 and 4,848 deaths. Given limited availability of reliable testing, lack of government transparency, and persecution of medical professionals and journalists who report on the pandemic, the actual numbers are probably much higher. Access to maternal health and sexual and reproductive services, already dire, has further deteriorated with the pandemic as the government failed to ensure access to services.

Monitor Salud, a nongovernmental organization (NGO), reported 83 percent of hospitals have insufficient or no access to personal protective equipment such as masks and gloves, and 95 percent similarly lack sufficient cleaning supplies, including soap and disinfectant. As of October 28, 779 doctors and nurses had reportedly died from Covid-19.

Venezuela's Covid-19 vaccination has been marred by corruption allegations and opacity regarding the acquisition and distribution of vaccines and other medical supplies. The government scheduled vaccinations using the "Fatherland ID," a document provided to Venezuelans since 2017 to access public benefits, which has been used to exercise social and political control, especially during elections.

On October 27, the government reported that 61.6 percent of Venezuelans had received at least one dose of the Covid-19 vaccines. Yet only 21.6 percent of Venezuelans were fully vaccinated as of that date, according to the Pan American Health Organization, and 25 to 28 percent of health professionals were still waiting for their second vaccine shot in August.

Refugee Crisis

Some 5.9 million Venezuelans, approximately 20 percent of the country's estimated total population, have fled their country since 2014, the Inter-Agency Coordination Platform for Refugees and Migrants from Venezuela reports.

While many neighboring governments welcomed Venezuelans, lack of a coordinated regional strategy left many stranded in inadequate conditions or unable to receive refugee status or other legal protections. In some countries, Venezuelans are being deported or facing xenophobia and difficulties obtaining affordable health care, education, or legal status that would allow them to work.

The economic impact of the pandemic and host government lockdowns led an estimated 151,000 Venezuelans to return home between March 2020 and March 2021, the United Nations System reported. Returnees were held in overcrowded, unsanitary quarantine centers, suffering threats, harassment, and abuse by Venezuelan authorities and colectivos.

Freedom of Expression

The government has expanded and abused its power to regulate media and close dissenting outlets and carried out campaigns of stigmatization, harassment, and repression against the media. While a few newspapers, websites, and radio stations criticize authorities, fear of reprisals has made self-censorship a serious problem.

In May, authorities seized the headquarters of newspaper *El Nacional*, after the Supreme Court ordered it to pay more than US$13 million in damages for alleged defamation of Diosdado Cabello. The move appears intended to silence one of the few remaining independent outlets in Venezuela.

In 2017, the Constituent Assembly passed a vague Law Against Hatred, forbidding political parties that "promote fascism, hatred, and intolerance," and establishing prison sentences of up to 20 years for publishing "messages of intolerance and hatred." During the Covid-19 state of emergency, many people sharing or publishing information on social media questioning officials or policies have been charged with incitement to hatred and other crimes.

Human Rights Defenders

In 2010, the Supreme Court ruled that individuals or organizations receiving foreign funding can be prosecuted for treason, and the National Assembly prohibited international assistance to organizations that "defend political rights" or "monitor the performance of public bodies."

Starting in November 2020, Venezuelan authorities and security forces have conducted a systematic campaign against human rights and humanitarian groups, freezing bank accounts, issuing arrest warrants, and raiding offices, as well as detaining members for questioning. They have adopted new measures to restrict international funding and require NGOs to provide sensitive information regarding their activities and contributions.

In July, police detained three members of FundaRedes after they reported harassment by intelligence services and unidentified armed men to the prosecutor's office in Falcon state. The group had recently accused Venezuelan authorities of links to armed groups in Apure state. The activists were charged with treason, terrorism, and incitement to hatred, based on publications on social media and the organization's website. Two of them were released on October 26 on the condition that they appear in court every eight days; the organization's director was still being held incommunicado at the SEBIN headquarters at time of writing.

Prison Conditions

Corruption, weak security, deteriorating infrastructure, overcrowding, insufficient staffing, and improperly trained guards allow armed gangs effectively to control detainees. Excessive use of pretrial detention contributes to overcrowding.

Lack of access to clean water and sufficient, nutritious food, as well as low quality hygiene and medical services, have contributed to a high incidence of hunger and disease in prisons. The Venezuelan Observatory of Prisons (OVP) reported that 73 percent of detainee deaths due to health conditions in the first half of 2021 were from malnutrition or tuberculosis, both of which are preventable. Inadequate conditions may have also contributed to the spread of the virus that causes Covid-19. Based on official statements, the OVP reported 135 cases of Covid-19 in prisons and detention centers in 2020, and two deaths. Given insufficient testing, the real numbers are likely much higher.

Key International Actors

During a visit to Venezuela in November 2021, ICC Prosecutor Karim Khan announced that his office would open an investigation into possible crimes against humanity committed in the country. The situation in the Venezuela had been under preliminary examination by the Office of the Prosecutor since February 2018. A June 2021 prosecution filing before the ICC, made public in August, reported the office's conclusion that Venezuelan authorities were unwilling to genuinely investigate and prosecute relevant cases.

In September, the United Nations Fact-Finding Mission on Venezuela found that the justice system has played a significant role in the repression of opponents. Procedural irregularities and interference in the judiciary, including by high-ranking authorities such as Maduro and Diosdado Cabello, have ensured impunity for human rights violations. A previous report concluded there were reasonable grounds to believe that pro-government groups and high-level authorities had committed violations amounting to crimes against humanity.

OHCHR maintains an in-country presence, which increased to 12 officers in 2021. The office updated the UN Human Rights Council in 2021 on continuing abuses. In June, it found Venezuela had made limited progress towards the implementation of its recommendations from previous reports. Both OHCHR and the UN special rapporteur on unilateral coercive measures highlighted in September that unilateral sectorial sanctions have exacerbated Venezuela's pre-existing economic and social crises, although OHCHR also pointed to other problems, including lack of official information and the need to investigate allegations of discrimination in food and health care access.

In April, after more than a year of negotiations, the WFP announced an agreement with the Maduro government, allowing it to supply food to young children. The agency started delivering aid in July and planned to reach 185,000 children by the end of 2021.

In March 2021, the US government granted temporary protected status for 18 months to Venezuelans already in the US. The decision followed the Colombian government's landmark announcement, in February, granting 10 years of legal status to the estimated 1.7 million Venezuelans there, and to those who enter Colombia legally during the next two years.

Several governments and institutions have imposed targeted sanctions on Venezuelan officials implicated in human rights abuses and corruption by canceling their visas and freezing their funds abroad. Others imposed financial sanctions, including the US, which during the administration of then-President Donald Trump imposed a ban on dealings in new stocks and bonds issued by the Venezuelan government and its state oil company. They remained in effect at time of writing. Despite a humanitarian exception, these sanctions could exacerbate the humanitarian emergency which predates them, due to overcompliance.

The administration of US President Joe Biden has publicly criticized human rights abuses by the Maduro government and expressed willingness to lift sanctions in exchange for concrete progress during the Mexico negotiations.

In addition to adopting targeted sanctions, the European Union has consistently condemned abuses by the Venezuelan government, including at the UN Human Rights Council, and plays a leading role in the International Contact Group, which seeks a political solution to the Venezuelan crisis and works to lay the groundwork for credible elections. Norway facilitated the Mexico talks, in which the Netherlands and Russia participated as guarantors.

An estimated 7 million people needed humanitarian assistance in 2020, the UN Humanitarian Response Plan for Venezuela noted. The plan, updated in 2021, calls for $708.1 million to assist 4.5 million of the most vulnerable Venezuelans. As of October 28, more than $210 million had been disbursed, and from January through July, 2.5 million people had received assistance. International organizations continued to face limitations importing humanitarian supplies, obtaining visas for personnel, acquiring movement permits, and accessing gasoline. This often led to delay or suspension of activities.

As a member of the UN Human Rights Council, Venezuela votes regularly to prevent scrutiny of human rights violations, including in Syria, Yemen, Belarus, Burundi, Eritrea, and Iran.

The Inter-American Commission on Human Rights continues to monitor Venezuela, applying the American Declaration of the Rights and Duties of Man, after Venezuela withdrew from the American Convention on Human Rights in 2013.

Vietnam

Vietnam systematically suppresses basic civil and political rights. The government, under the one-party rule of the Communist Party of Vietnam (CPV), severely restricts freedom of expression, association, peaceful assembly, movement, and religion.

Prohibitions continued in 2021 on the formation or operation of independent unions and any other organizations or groups considered a threat to the Communist Party's monopoly on power. Authorities blocked access to sensitive political websites and social media pages, and pressured social media and telecommunications companies to remove or restrict content critical of the government or the ruling party.

Critics of the government or party face police intimidation, harassment, restricted movement, arbitrary arrest and detention, and imprisonment after unfair trials. Police hold political detainees for months without access to legal counsel and subject them to abusive interrogations. Party-controlled courts sentence bloggers and activists on bogus national security charges.

In January 2021, the CPV held its 13th congress, during which it selected the country's new politburo. Of the 18 members, at least seven, including Vietnam's new prime minister, Pham Minh Chinh, have affiliation with the Ministry of Public Security. In May, Vietnam held a tightly controlled and scripted national election in which all candidates had to be approved by the CPV. Several dozen independent candidates were intimidated and disqualified, and two were arrested.

Vietnam boasted successes in 2020 and the first five months of 2021 in combating Covid-19. But as the Delta variant swept through the region, by early November there were more than 939,000 positive cases and more than 22,000 deaths. Law enforcement violated rights by using excessive force to make people undergo compulsory Covid-19 tests and quarantine, and to enforce compliance with the lockdown.

Authorities in Ho Chi Minh City, Hanoi, and other places put up blockades and locked gates to restrict movement during the lockdown without measures in place to ensure people could evacuate in case of emergency, access urgent medical care, or procure food and other necessities. Authorities provided inadequate pandemic relief. Many people, especially migrant and freelance workers, relied heavily on help from community networks, both for food and medical services. Hundreds of thousand people fled Ho Chi Minh City for their hometowns as soon as the strict lockdown was eased.

Freedom of Expression, Opinion, and Speech

Dissidents and rights activists face routine harassment, intimidation, arbitrary arrest and imprisonment. In 2021, the courts convicted at least 32 people for posting critical opinions about the government and sentenced them to many years in prison. Police arrested at least 26 other people on fabricated political charges.

The government regularly uses penal code Article 117, criminalizing the act of "making, storing, disseminating, or propagandizing information, materials and products that aim to oppose the State," against civil society activists. In January, a Ho Chi Minh City court put prominent members of the Independent Journalists Association on trial. Pham Chi Dung, Nguyen Tuong Thuy, and Le Huu Minh Tuan were convicted and sentenced to between 11 and 15 years in prison.

In May, a court in Hoa Binh province sentenced land rights activist Can Thi Theu and her son Trinh Ba Tu each to eight years in prison. In July, a Hanoi court convicted writer Pham Chi Thanh and sentenced him to five years and six months in prison. The authorities sent at least 12 other people to prison for violating Article 117, including Dinh Thi Thu Thuy in Hau Giang (seven years); Vu Tien Chi in Lam Dong (10 years); Le Viet Hoa, Ngo Thi Ha Phuong and Nguyen Thi Cam Thuy in Khanh Hoa (five, seven, and nine years respectively); Tran Thi Tuyet Dieu in Phu Yen province (eight years); Dang Hoang Minh in Hau Giang (seven years); Cao Van Dung in Quang Ngai (nine years); N.L.D. Khanh in Da Nang (four years); Nguyen Van Lam in Nghe An (nine years); Tran Quoc Khanh in Ninh Binh (six years and six months); and Nguyen Tri Gioan in Khanh Hoa (seven years).

Police arrested rights defender Nguyen Thuy Hanh in April, blogger Le Van Dung (known as Le Dung Vova) in June, and former political prisoner Do Nam Trung in July, also for allegedly conducting propaganda against the state. Others arrested and held under the same charge include Le Trong Hung, Nguyen Duy Huong, Nguyen Bao Tien, Tran Hoang Huan, Bui Van Thuan, Nguyen Duy Linh, Dinh Van

Hai, and Le Van Quan. Prominent dissident Pham Doan Trang was held for more than a year without access to legal counsel and family visits.

In 2021, the courts convicted and sentenced at least 11 people including Le Thi Binh, sister of former political prisoner Le Minh The, for "abusing the rights to freedom and democracy to infringe upon the interests of the state" under Article 331 of the penal code. Police also arrested at least 12 other people on the same charge, including members of Bao Sach (Clean Newspaper), a group of independent journalists fighting against corruption and rights abuses. In October, a court in Can Tho province sentenced members of Bao Sach to between two and four-and-a half-years in prison.

Freedom of Media, Access to Information

The government prohibits independent or privately owned media outlets, and imposes strict control over radio and television stations, and print publications. Authorities block access to websites, frequently shut down blogs, and require internet service providers to remove content or social media accounts deemed politically unacceptable.

In July 2021, state media in Vietnam reported that the Ministry of Information and Communications praised Facebook and Google for responding to requests from the Vietnamese government. They said that during the first six months of 2021, Facebook removed 702 posts and accounts, and Google removed 2,544 videos and channels on YouTube that "distorted leaders of the Party, the State, and the 13th Party Congress." The government also claimed Facebook responded affirmatively to 97 percent, and Google to 98 percent, of the government's requests, and usually acted within 24 hours.

Reuters reported that Facebook also removed a number of pro-government groups and accounts for "coordinating attempts to mass report content."

Facebook did not comment on the statement from the Vietnam government, but in a communication to Human Rights Watch in November 2021, acknowledged that "we do restrict some content in Vietnam to help ensure our services remain available for millions of people who rely on them every day." Google did not respond to Human Rights Watch's request for comment at time of writing.

During the year, authorities also imposed monetary fines on hundreds of people for spreading what the government claimed was misinformation relating to Covid-19 and the government's handling of the pandemic. Several people were arrested for posting allegedly distorted, fabricated, or fake news.

Freedom of Association, Assembly, and Movement

Government prohibitions remain in place on independent labor unions, human rights organizations, and political parties. People trying to establish unions or workers' groups outside approved government structures face harassment, intimidation, and retaliation from the authorities. Authorities require approval for public gatherings, and systematically refuse permission for meetings, marches, or public gatherings they deem to be politically unacceptable.

The Vietnamese government routinely violates the right to freedom of movement by subjecting dissidents, environmental activists, human rights defenders, and others to arbitrary periods of house arrest, intimidation, and even kidnapping to stop them from attending protests, criminal trials, meetings with diplomats, and other events. In January, a number of dissidents and activists including Huynh Ngoc Chenh, Nguyen Thuy Hanh, Dinh Duc Long, Truong Thi Ha, Tran Bang, Mac Van Trang, and Nguyen Thi Kim Chi reported that they were placed under house arrest during the Communist Party Congress. In August, during the visit of United States Vice President Kamala Harris to Hanoi, security agents also put Huynh Ngoc Chenh under house arrest.

Authorities blocked critics from domestic and international travel, including by stopping them at airports and denying passports or other documents that allow them to leave or enter the country.

Freedom of Religion

The government restricts religious practice through legislation, registration requirements, and surveillance. Religious groups must get approval from, and register with, the government and operate under government-controlled management boards. While authorities allow government-affiliated churches and pagodas to hold worship services, they ban religious activities that they arbitrarily deem to be contrary to the "national interest," "public order," or "national unity," including many ordinary types of religious functions.

Police monitor, harass, and sometimes violently crack down on religious groups operating outside government-controlled institutions. Unrecognized religious groups—including Cao Dai, Hoa Hao, Christian, and Buddhist groups—face constant surveillance, harassment, and intimidation. Followers of independent religious groups are subject to public criticism, forced renunciation of faith, detention, interrogation, torture, and imprisonment.

In August, a court in Gia Lai put Rah Lan Rah, Siu Chon, and Ro Mah Them on trial for being associated with an independent religious group disapproved by the government, sentencing them to between five and six years in prison.

Rights of Women and Children

Violence against children, including sexual abuse, is pervasive in Vietnam, including at home and in schools. Numerous media reports have described cases of guardians, teachers, or government caregivers engaging in sexual abuse, beating children, or hitting them with sticks. During the first six months of 2021, amid the pandemic lockdown, there were reports of increasing physical and sexual abuses of children in Vietnam.

The pandemic was also linked, including in 2021, to rising incidence of violence against women, while organizations assisting survivors of gender-based violence struggled to adapt and continue their services during the pandemic.

Sexual Orientation and Gender Identity

In recent years, the Vietnamese government has taken modest strides to recognize the rights of lesbian, gay, bisexual, and transgender (LGBT) people, including by removing prohibitions on same-sex relationships and legal gender change. However, the government has not added explicit protections for LGBT people. Vietnamese LGBT youth face widespread discrimination and violence at home and at school. Pervasive myths about sexual orientation and gender identity, including the false belief that same-sex attraction is a diagnosable and curable mental health condition, is common among Vietnamese school officials and the population at large.

Key International Actors

Vietnam continues to balance its relationships with China, its largest trade partner, and the United States, its second largest trade partner.

Maritime disputes continue to complicate the relationship with China, which carried out military drills on the disputed seas in 2021, while Vietnam raised repeated protests. However, during high-ranking visits, the two communist parties formally applauded their friendship and solidarity.

The relationship between the United States and Vietnam stayed strong. Vietnam received Vice President Kamala Harris in August. During her visit, Harris mentioned human rights in passing. Hanoi released two Vietnamese-American prisoners convicted for being affiliated with political groups outlawed by the Vietnamese government and deported them to the US before Harris' arrival.

Amid intensifying repression in Vietnam, the European Union Commission has yet to provide any display of the stronger leverage to address human rights abuses with Hanoi ostensibly provided by the EU-Vietnam Free Trade Agreement (EVFTA), which entered into force in August 2020.

In January, the EU's diplomatic branch and the European Parliament deplored the harsh sentencing of journalist Pham Chi Dung, who has been jailed since 2019 for his outreach to the European Parliament in the context of the EVFTA ratification process, and of his colleagues Nguyen Tuong Thuy and Le Huu Minh Tuan. In July, the EU did not react publicly to the arrest by Vietnamese authorities of journalist Mai Phan Loi and lawyer Dang Dinh Bach on trumped-up charges as they were working to promote the participation of independent civil society in the Domestic Advisory Group (DAG) as stipulated in the EVFTA.

Australia's bilateral relationship with Vietnam continues to grow even as an Australian citizen, Chau Van Kham, remains in prison in Vietnam for his alleged involvement in an overseas political party declared unlawful by the Vietnamese government.

Japan remains the most important bilateral donor to Vietnam. As in previous years, Japan has declined to use its economic leverage to publicly urge Vietnam to improve its human rights record.

Zimbabwe

The administration of President Emmerson Mnangagwa failed to take meaningful steps to uphold human rights and ensure justice for serious abuses primarily committed by security forces in 2021. There has been no accountability for abuses by security forces, including the August 2018 post-election violence, and killings and rape during the January 2019 protests. Abductions, torture, arbitrary arrests, and other abuses against opposition politicians and activists have not been meaningfully investigated. The government has yet to establish an independent complaint system—as provided for in Zimbabwe's Constitution—to receive and investigate public complaints against the security services. Other human rights concerns include a severe water and sanitation crisis, including during the Covid-19 pandemic, forced evictions, and child marriages.

The United States, United Kingdom, and European Union all renewed targeted sanctions against Zimbabwe for serious human rights abuses by security forces, corruption, and failure to ensure justice for past abuses.

Restrictive legislation, section 73 of the Criminal Law (Codification and Reform) Act, 2004, which punishes consensual same-sex conduct between men with up to one year in prison or a fine or both, contributes to stigma and discrimination against lesbian, gay, bisexual, and transgender (LGBT) people.

Confronting Past Abuses

During 2021, authorities did not take concrete steps to ensure justice and accountability for serious abuses, most of which were committed by the security forces. President Mnangagwa appointed the Motlanthe Commission of Inquiry to investigate the August 2018 post-election violence, which found that six people had died and 35 others were injured because of actions by state security forces. Yet, three years later, the authorities have not implemented the commission's recommendations, including to hold to account members of the security forces responsible for abuses and for compensating the families of those killed or who lost property.

There was no attempt to investigate and prosecute other serious violations that the state security forces have committed: including violent attacks, abductions, torture, and other abuses against members of the political opposition and civil society activists. Human Rights Watch investigations found that security forces used excessive and lethal force to crush nationwide protests in January 2019. Local groups reported that security forces fired live ammunition that killed 17 people, and uniformed soldiers raped at least 17 women during and after these protests. No security personnel have been arrested or prosecuted.

Unresolved cases in which there has been no accountability include the abduction and torture of rural teachers' union president Obert Masaraure, comedian Samantha Kureya (known as "Gonyeti"), activist Tatenda Mombeyarara, and students Tawanda Muchehiwa and Takudzwa Ngadziore.

In May 2020, three Movement for Democratic Change (MDC) Alliance politicians, Cecilia Chimbiri, Netsai Marova, and member of parliament Joanna Mamombe, were abducted from police custody by suspected state agents for taking part in a protest in Harare. They were assaulted and sexually abused by their abductors, then dumped in Bindura, 80 kilometers from Harare. While receiving treatment for their injuries, the trio were rearrested at the hospital and charged with making false reports about their abduction. At time of writing their trial was ongoing.

Right to Water and Sanitation

During 2021, hundreds of thousands of residents of Zimbabwe's capital, Harare, including nearby municipalities of Chitungwiza and Epworth, continued to face a potable water crisis three years after a deadly cholera outbreak. The authorities in central and Harare city have failed to ensure clean water. Several factors have contributed to the city's severe water problems, including economic decay; perennial droughts affecting Lake Chivero, which is dammed to supply Harare with water; the lack of maintenance of the old water infrastructure; the inability to procure the necessary chemicals to treat water sources; political struggles between the central government under the ruling party and the opposition-controlled city council; and corruption.

The water crisis has affected Harare residents' rights to water and sanitation as well as other related rights, including the rights to life, food, and health. Many common water sources, namely shallow wells, taps, and boreholes—deep, narrow wells—are often contaminated. However, despite the known risk of contaminated water, there is no specific official information on which water sources are safe, leaving residents to take their chances.

Zimbabwe's long-standing severe water and sanitation crisis has been worsened by the Covid-19 pandemic which increased demand for access to clean water for hygiene and the government's imposition, since March 30, 2020, of a nation-wide lockdown that continues to be in force at the time of writing. The provision of safe water is an important measure to combat the spread of the virus that causes Covid-19.

Forced Evictions

On February 26, 2021, the local government, urban and rural development minister, July Moyo, published a legal notice ordering thousands of people to either acquire fresh rights of use or occupation or immediately vacate approximately 12,940 hectares of Chilonga communal land in Chiredzi, southeastern Zimbabwe. The legal notice, Statutory Instrument 50 of 2021, which the government later repealed and replaced, said the land was being set aside for lucerne grass production—farming grass for stockfeed. Chilonga community members went to court, which ordered the arbitrary evictions to be stopped until the government provides alternative land, compensation, and shelter.

Other Indigenous communities also faced evictions to make way for mining and commercial farming projects in 2021. This included the Dinde community in Hwange as well as communities in Mutoko, Chipinge and Chivhu. Hundreds of Dinde villagers are fighting against threats of eviction from their ancestral land to pave way for a planned coal-mining project by a Chinese company. In Mutoko, hundreds of villagers have been living in fear of imminent eviction from their ancestral land to make way for granite rock mining operations by another Chinese company. In Chivhu, hundreds of villager's face eviction from their ancestral land to pave way for a 12,000-hectare iron and steel mining project by a third Chinese company.

Children's Rights

During 2021, the authorities failed to fully enforce the ban on child marriages, exposing millions of underage girls to abuse. A landmark 2016 Constitutional

Court decision declared child marriages unconstitutional and set 18 as the minimum marriage age for girls and boys, without exceptions.

A 14-year-old girl who had been forced into marriage died during childbirth in July, at a Marange Apostolic church, in Manicaland province, highlighting the high price girls pay for the practice of child marriage, which remains rampant in Zimbabwe. The practice is prevalent among Indigenous apostolic churches, an evangelical group that mixes Christian religious beliefs with traditional cultures and has millions of followers across the country.

Key International Actors

In February, the UK's Office of Financial Sanctions Implementation (OFSI) placed four top Zimbabwe security officials—Owen Ncube, Anselem Sanyatwe, Godwin Matanga, and Isaac Moyo—on targeted sanctions for being responsible for serious human rights violations. In July, the UK imposed sanctions on President Mnangagwa's economic advisor, Kudakwashe Regimond Tagwirei, "for profiting from misappropriation of property when his company, Sakunda Holdings, redeemed Government of Zimbabwe Treasury Bills at up to ten times their official value. His actions accelerated the deflation of Zimbabwe's currency, increasing the price of essentials, such as food, for Zimbabwean citizens." Tagwirei was placed under US sanctions in 2020.

The European Union on February 19 renewed its arms embargo and targeted asset freeze against Zimbabwe Defense Industries, a state-owned military company. The EU said the restrictive measures were in light of the continued need to investigate the role of security force actors in human rights abuses as well as concern about "a proliferation of arrests and prosecutions of journalists, opposition actors and individuals expressing dissenting views." It said that these measures would not affect the Zimbabwean economy, foreign direct investment, or trade, but "to encourage a demonstrable, genuine and long-term commitment by the Zimbabwean authorities to respect and uphold human rights and the rule of law."

In March, US President Joe Biden extended for another year the targeted sanctions against designated Zimbabwean government officials and other private individuals. Biden told Congress that "President Emmerson Mnangagwa has not made the necessary political and economic reforms that would warrant terminating the existing targeted sanctions program."